Sociology of
North American Sport

Eighth Edition

Sociology of North American Sport

D. Stanley Eitzen and
George H. Sage

Paradigm Publishers
Boulder • London

All rights reserved. No part of this publication may be transmitted or reproduced in any media or form, including electronic, mechanical, photocopy, recording, or informational storage and retrieval systems, without the express written consent of the publisher.

Copyright © 2009 Paradigm Publishers

Published in the United States by Paradigm Publishers, 3360 Mitchell Lane Suite E, Boulder, CO 80301 USA.
Paradigm Publishers is the trade name of Birkenkamp & Company, LLC,
Dean Birkenkamp, President and Publisher.

Library of Congress Cataloging-in-Publication Data
Eitzen, D. Stanley.
  Sociology of North American sport / D. Stanley Eitzen and George H. Sage.—8th ed.
    p. cm.
  Includes bibliographical references and index.
  ISBN 978-1-59451-575-0 (pbk. : alk. paper)
   1. Sports—Social aspects—United States. 2. Sports—Social aspects—Canada. 3. Sports—United States—Sociological aspects. 4. Sports—Canada—Sociological aspects. I. Sage, George Harvey. II. Title.
GV706.5.E57 2008
306.4'83—dc22
                      2007052282

Printed and bound in the United States of America on acid-free paper that meets the standards of the American National Standard for Permanence of Paper for Printed Library Materials.

Designed and typeset by Mulberry Tree Enterprises.

13 12 11 10 09   1 2 3 4 5

Eighth Edition

Sociology of North American Sport

D. Stanley Eitzen and
George H. Sage

Paradigm Publishers
Boulder • London

All rights reserved. No part of this publication may be transmitted or reproduced in any media or form, including electronic, mechanical, photocopy, recording, or informational storage and retrieval systems, without the express written consent of the publisher.

Copyright © 2009 Paradigm Publishers

Published in the United States by Paradigm Publishers, 3360 Mitchell Lane Suite E, Boulder, CO 80301 USA.
Paradigm Publishers is the trade name of Birkenkamp & Company, LLC,
Dean Birkenkamp, President and Publisher.

Library of Congress Cataloging-in-Publication Data
Eitzen, D. Stanley.
　Sociology of North American sport / D. Stanley Eitzen and George H. Sage.—8th ed.
　　p. cm.
　Includes bibliographical references and index.
　ISBN 978-1-59451-575-0 (pbk. : alk. paper)
　1. Sports—Social aspects—United States.　2. Sports—Social aspects—Canada.　3. Sports—United States—Sociological aspects.　4. Sports—Canada—Sociological aspects.　I. Sage, George Harvey.　II. Title.
GV706.5.E57 2008
306.4'83—dc22
　　　　　　　　　　　　　　2007052282

Printed and bound in the United States of America on acid-free paper that meets the standards of the American National Standard for Permanence of Paper for Printed Library Materials.

Designed and typeset by Mulberry Tree Enterprises.

13　12　11　10　09　　1　2　3　4　5

Contents

Preface xi

Chapter 1 The Sociological Analysis of Sport in Society 1

The Pervasiveness of Sport 2
The Discipline of Sociology 3
   Assumptions of the Sociological Perspective 3
   The Sociological Imagination 5
   Problems with the Sociological Perspective 6
   Units of Sociological Analysis 6
   Sociological Theories: Contrasting Ways to See and Understand Social Life 10
Sport as a Microcosm of Society 14
   Common Characteristics of Sport and Society 14
Levels of Sport 16
   Informal Sport 16
   Organized Sport 16
   Corporate Sport 17
Summary 17
Web Resources 18
Notes 19

Chapter 2 Social and Cultural Sources for the Rise of Sport in North America 21

Pre-Columbian and Colonial Traditions in North America 22
   The Colonists Restrict Physical Activities 23
The Early Nineteenth Century: Takeoff of Industrialization and Technology 24
   Building a Framework for Modern Sport 24
   The Technological Revolution and Sport 25
The Latter Nineteenth Century: The Beginnings of Modern Sport 27
   Urbanization and the Rise of Modern Sport Forms 27
   The Cult of Manliness and Sport 31
   Technological Innovation and Sport: Transportation 32
   Technological Innovation and Sport: Communication 34
   Other Technological Breakthroughs and Sport 35
   Equipment to Play Modern Sports 35
   Social Philosophy and Modern Sport 36
The Twentieth Century: The Modern World 37
   The Maturing of Modern Sport 37
   Twentieth-Century Technology and Sport: Transportation 40
   The Technological Revolution and Sport: Communication 42
   Other Technological Innovations and Sport 43
   Sport in Education 43
Summary 44
Web Resources 44
Notes 44

Chapter 3 Sport and Societal Values 47

The American Value System 48
   Success 48
   Competition 49
   The Valued Means to Achieve 50
   Progress 51
   Materialism 51
   External Conformity 51
Societal Values and Sport 52
   Competition and Success in Sport 53
   The Valued Means to Achievement in Sport 56
   Progress in Sport 57
   Materialism in Sport 57
   External Conformity in Sport 58
Summary 58
Web Resources 58
Notes 59

Chapter 4 Youth and Sport 60

Youth Sports Programs: Something for Everyone 61
The Rise of Youth Sports Programs: The Takeoff and Expansion of a New Form of Sport 62
Objectives of Youth Sports Programs: What Do Young Athletes Want? What Do Their Parents and Coaches Want? 63
Socialization and Sport: Involvement in Sport and Its Consequences 64
Socialization into Sport: Why Do Children Get Involved in Organized Sports? 65
   Families 65
   Parents 65
   Siblings 66
   Peers 67
   Coaches 67
   Schools 67
   Mass Media 67
   Participants 68
Socialization via Sport 69
   Two Forms of Play 69
Development of Personal-Social Attributes through Sport 71
   Youth Orientation toward Sport 72
   Sportsmanship in Youth Sport 72
   Character Development in Youth Sports 73
Potential Psychosocial Problems of Youth Sports 75
   Adult Intrusion in Youth Sports 75
   Disruption of Education 80
   Risk of Injury 81
   The "Winning Is the Only Thing" Ethic and Youth Sports 81
Sports Alternatives for the Young Athlete 82
   Emphasizing Personal Growth and Self-Actualization 83
   Alternative Sports 83
   Cooperative Games 84
   Youth Sports Coaches 84
   Bill of Rights for Young Athletes 84
Summary 86
Web Resources 86
Notes 87

Chapter 5 Interscholastic Sport 90

The Status of Sport in Secondary Schools 91
The Consequences of Sport for Schools, Communities, and Individuals 92
   The Consequences of Sport for the School 93
   The Consequences of Sport for the Community 94
   The Consequences of Sport for the Participant 95
Problems, Dilemmas, and Controversies 97
   The Subversion of Educational Goals 98
   The Reinforcement of Gender Roles 98
   Cheating 98
   Unsportsmanlike Behavior of Fans 100
   Autocratic Coaches 100
   Excessive Pressures to Win 100
   Elitism 101
   Sport Specialization 101
   Budget Shortfalls 102
   Corporate High School Sport for Boys' Programs 102
Efforts to Reform High School Sports 104
Summary 107

Web Resources 108
Notes 108

Chapter 6 Intercollegiate Sport 111

College Sport as Big Business 112
The Consequences of a Money Orientation in College Sports 114
A Contradiction: Athletes as Amateurs in a Big Business Environment 116
The NCAA and Student-Athletes 117
The Enforcement of "Amateurism" 117
The Restriction of Athletes' Rights 119
The Educational Performance of Student-Athletes 121
Intellectual Performance of Student-Athletes for College 121
Academic Performance 121
Graduation Rates 121
The Impediments to Scholarly Achievement by College Athletes 122
Reform 124
The Administration of College Sports 124
Emphasizing the Education of Student-Athletes 125
Commitment to Athletes' Rights 125
Summary 126
Web Resources 126
Notes 126

Chapter 7 Social Problems and North American Sport: Violence, Substance Abuse, Eating Disorders, and Gambling 129

Violence in Sport: Is It Violence or Aggression? Confusion in the Literature 130
Theories about the Connection between Violent Behavior and Sport 131
Aggression Theories and Research on Sports 132
Violence in North America 134
Violence in Historical Context 134
Violence in Contemporary Society 135
Violence in North American Sport 135
Violent Behavior by Athletes as Part of the Game 136
Borderline Violence 138

Fostering and Supporting Player Violence 139
Television 139
Fans 139
Pressures on Athletes to Be Violent 140
Coaches, Owners, Commissioners 140
Violence against Athletes 140
Social Problems and Athletes off the Field of Play 141
Sources for Violence by Male Athletes in Their Private Lives 142
Athletes' Violence against Teammates: Hazing 144
Sports Fans: Violent and Abusive Actions 145
Factors Associated with Fan Violence and Abusive Behaviors 146
Game and Postgame Sports Violence 147
Abusive Behavior by Fans 148
Reducing Fan Violence and Abusive Behavior 148
Substance Abuse and Sport 148
The Scope of Substance Abuse in Sport 149
Substance Abuse Not New to Sports 150
Reasons for Substance Abuse among Athletes 152
Reducing and Preventing Substance Abuse in Sports 154
Eating Disorders in Sport 155
Gambling and Sports 156
Summary 160
Web Resources 161
Notes 161

Chapter 8 Sport and Religion 165

Religion and Society 166
Personal and Social Role of Religion 167
The Relationship between Religion and Sport 168
Pre-Columbian Societies 168
Ancient Greece 168
The Early Christian Church 169
Reformation and Protestantism in the North American Colonies 169
Religious Objections to Sport Declined in the Nineteenth Century 170

Religion and Sport Conciliation 170
Sport as Religion 171
Religion Uses Sport 173
   Churches 173
   Religious Leaders 174
   Church Colleges and Universities 174
Religious Organizations and Sports 175
   The Fellowship of Christian Athletes 175
   Religion and Professional Sports Organizations 175
   Sport and Religion Publications 176
   Missionary Work of Churches and Sport 176
   Religious Evangelizing by Athletes and Coaches 176
   The Promise Keepers: Sportianity, Gender, and Sexuality 177
   Sportianity Confronting Social Issues 178
Value Orientations of Religion and Sport 179
   The Protestant Ethic and Sports 179
   Protestantism and Contemporary Sport 182
Sport Uses Religion 182
   The Use of Prayer and Divine Intervention 182
   The Use of Magic 188
   Magic and Its Uses in Sports 189
Summary 192
Web Resources 192
Notes 193

Chapter 9 Sport and Politics 195

The Political Uses of Sport 198
   Sport as a Propaganda Vehicle 198
   Sport and Nationalism 200
   Sport as an Opiate of the Masses 202
   The Exploitation of Sport by Politicians 203
   Sport as a Vehicle of Change in Society 203
The Globalization of Sport 205
The Political Olympics 206
   Political Problems 206
   A Proposal for Change 210
Summary 211
Web Resources 212
Notes 212

Chapter 10 Sport and the Economy 214

Who Benefits Economically from Sports? 215
Professional Sport as a Business 220
   Professional Sport as a Monopoly 220
   Public Subsidization of Professional Team Franchises 221
   Ownership for Profit 224
The Relationship between Owner and Athlete 226
   The Draft and the Reserve Clause 227
   Free Agency 227
   Salaries 231
   A Radical Question: Are Owners Necessary? 233
Amateur Sport as a Business 234
   The Economics of Collegiate Sport 234
Summary 237
Web Resources 237
Notes 238

Chapter 11 Sport and the Mass Media 240

Social Roles of the Mass Media 241
   Prominent and Subtle Roles of the Media 241
The Symbiosis of Mass Media and Sport 242
   Linkages between the Mass Media and Sport 242
Television: The Monster of the Sports World 244
   Increasing TV Sports Coverage 245
   Economic Aspects of Televised Sports 245
Television's Influence on Sport 247
   Increases in Sport Revenue 247
   Indirect Business Linkages between Media and Sport 248
   Popularity Shifts 249
   Professional Sports Franchise Locations and the Media 249
   Intercollegiate Sport 249
   High School Sport 251
   Modifying Sports to Accommodate TV 252
   Television's Own Sports 253
   Televised Sport as a Mediated Event 254
The Impact of Sport on the Mass Media 256
   Increased Sport in the Media 256

    Sport's Privileged Treatment by the Media   257
    Sports Consumers and the Mass Media   257
    The Internet: The Newest Form of Mass Communications for Sports   258
    Reproduction of Hegemonic Masculinity in Media Sport   259
    Media Sport and Gender Inequities   260
    Media Sport and Racial and Ethnic Inequities   262
Sports Journalism and the Mass Media   263
    Sportscasters: Narrators of Mediated Sport   264
    Wrapping Up   265
    Minority Sport Journalists and Broadcasters   266
    Women Sport Journalists and Broadcasters   267
Summary   267
Web Resources   268
Notes   269

Chapter 12   Sport, Social Stratification, and Social Mobility   271

Major Concepts   272
Dimensions of Inequality   273
Social Class and Sport   273
    Adult Participation Preferences for Sports by Socioeconomic Status   273
    Youth Sport Participation by Socioeconomic Status   275
    Spectator Preferences for Sports by Socioeconomic Status   276
    Segregation in Sports by Social Class   279
Social Mobility and Sport   280
    Sport as a Mobility Escalator   280
    Demythologizing the Social-Mobility-through-Sport Hypothesis   282
Summary   286
Web Resources   287
Notes   287

Chapter 13   Racial-Ethnic Minorities and Sport   290

Racial-Ethnic Minorities: Some Definitions   291

Sports Participation among Racial-Ethnic Minorities   293
    The History of African American Involvement in U.S. Sport   293
    Latino Involvement in U.S. Sport   295
    Asian American Involvement in U.S. Sport   298
    Native American Involvement in U.S. Sport   300
    The Effects of Globalization on Ethnic Diversity in U.S. Sport Participation   301
Black Dominance in Sport   303
    Race-Linked Physical Differences   303
    Race-Linked Cultural Differences   304
    Social Structure Constraints   305
Racial Discrimination in Sport   307
    Stacking   307
    Rewards and Authority   310
Summary   312
Web Resources   312
Notes   313

Chapter 14   Gender in North American Sport: Continuity and Change   315

The Heritage of Gender Inequality in Sport   316
Social Sources of Gender Inequality in Sport   318
    Parental Child-Rearing Practices and Gender Construction   318
    The School and Gender Construction   319
    The Mass Media and Gender Construction   319
    Nicknames, Mascots, and Heroines   320
Females Surmount Social Barriers to Participation in Sport   321
    Negative Myths   321
    Attitudes toward Female Athletes   325
The Opportunity and Reward Structure for Females in Sport   326
    From Boys-Only Youth Sports to Opportunities for Both Sexes   326
    Toward Gender Equity in High School Sports   326

    Toward Gender Equity in Intercollegiate Sports 328
    Title IX and Subsequent Legislative and Legal Incidents 328
    Governance and Control Issues 330
    Gender Equity and Men's Intercollegiate Sports 331
Men Rule in the Coaching and Administration of Women's Sports 333
    High School and College Women's Coaching and Administration 333
Ownership, Management, and Coaching in Professional Sports 335
    Coaching and Administration in U.S. Olympic Organizations 336
    Why Have Men Been Hired to Coach and Administer Women's Sports? 336
    Gender and Careers at the Top Levels of Sport 336
    Female Olympic Athletes 338
Sport and Gender Identity for Males 339
Summary 342
Web Resources 342
Notes 343

Chapter 15 Contemporary Trends and the Future of Sport in North America 346

Demographic Trends in North America 347
    Population Composition 348
    Location of Population 349
    Population Trends and Sport 349
Dominating Forces in Our Lives: Work, Technology, and Sporting Activities 351
    An Information/Service North American Society 352
    The Information/Service Workplace and Sporting Activities 352
A Future Society and Sport 354
    Cerebral Sports of the Future 354
    Violent Sports of the Future 355
    Technology and Future Sport 356
    A Counterpoint to Technosports: Ecosports 358
Trends in the Economy and Future Sports 361
    The Future of Professional Sports 361
    The Future of Televised Sports 362
    Internet Technology and Sports Viewing 363
    Video Technology and Sports Video Games 364
    Intercollegiate Athletics and the Future 364
    Secondary School Sports and the Future 365
Trends in Social Values and Future Sport 366
    The Quest for Democracy and Equality 366
    Trends in Sports Values 366
Summary 372
Web Resources 373
Notes 373

Index 377

Preface

Sport is sometimes trivialized as a playground off to the side of the real world. To the contrary, sport is a microcosm of society as well as a site for changing society. Moreover, it has a profound influence on the social life of large numbers of people of all ages.

PURPOSE OF THIS TEXT

Three goals guide our efforts in writing this book. In the analysis of the sport structure in societies, our first goal is to analyze sport critically and in so doing demythologize sport. Thus, the reader will understand sport in a new way. The student will also incorporate implicitly the sociological perspective in his or her repertoire for understanding other parts of the social world.

Our second goal is to impress on our readers in physical education and sociology the importance of including the sociology of sport as a legitimate subfield in each of the two disciplines. Although the mechanical and physiological factors of sport are important, the social milieu in which participation is embedded is crucial with respect to who participates, when, where, and the consequences of such participation. Sport involvement is more than making use of the levers of the body and using strength and endurance to achieve objectives. To sociology students, our message is that sport is a social activity worthy of serious inquiry. It is a substantive topic as deserving of sociologists' attention as are the standard specialties: family, religion, and politics. Not only is sport a microcosm of the larger society, but sports phenomena also offer a fertile field in which to test sociological theories.

Our final goal is to make the reader aware of the positive and negative consequences of the way sport is organized in society. We are concerned about some of the trends in sport, especially the movement away from athlete-oriented activities toward the impersonality of what we term "corporate sport." We are committed to moving sport and society in a more humane direction, and this requires, as a first step, a thorough understanding of the principles that underlie the social structures and processes that create, sustain, and transform the social organizations within the institution of sport.

All of the chapters in this edition have been thoroughly revised, and the content has been updated. We have tried to incorporate the salient research and relevant events that have occurred since the publication of the preceding edition of this book.

The focus of the first two editions was on sport in American society. Although that emphasis remains, the focus in all subsequent editions, including this one, has been broadened to include sport in Canadian society. There are many parallels with sport and society in the United States and Canada, as well as important differences. Finally, we have made a special effort in this edition to incorporate issues of social class, race/ethnicity, and gender throughout the text.

ORGANIZATION

In chapter 1, we describe the focus of sociology as a discipline and identify the different analytic levels employed by sociologists. We identify four major sociological theories that provide different and important ways to understand sport. Next, we show how sport provides an ideal environment for utilizing certain sociological instruments and methodologies and affords a setting for the testing of sociological theories.

The phenomenon of sport represents one of the most pervasive social institutions in North America. In chapter 2, we discuss the relationships between technological, industrial, and urban developments and the rise of organized sport.

The major theme of this book is that sport is a microcosm of society. Salient social values are identified in chapter 3, and we discuss how sport reflects and reinforces the core values, beliefs, and ideologies of North American society.

For millions of people, involvement in sport begins in youth sports programs. In chapter 4, we describe how children are socialized into sport, and we discuss some of the consequences of these sports experiences.

Sport and education are inexorably intertwined in society. Chapter 5 examines interscholastic sport, focusing on the social sources responsible for the promotion of sports programs, the consequences of school sports programs, and the problems surrounding school sport.

Chapter 6 is devoted to big-time intercollegiate sport. Although this level of sport is extremely popular, we focus here on the many problems that compromise the integrity of the educational mission of universities.

Chapter 7 analyzes two major social problems in sport—violence (participant and fan) and substance abuse by athletes. Included here are topics such as athletes' abuse of women, violence against athletes, sports gambling, and athletes with eating disorders.

In chapter 8, we explore the relationship between one of the oldest universal social institutions—religion—and one of the newest—sport. We trace the changing relations between the two institutions and show how contemporary sport has many of the characteristics of a religion. We also describe how religious agents and agencies use sport to promote religion and how athletes employ magico-religious rituals, taboos, and fetishes in the hope of enhancing their performances.

Although the sport establishment publicly disavows any relationship between politics and sport, the two are closely related. In chapter 9, we discuss the close ties between the two and show that there are several characteristics inherent in both institutions that serve to guarantee this strong relationship.

Economic factors play an overriding role in much of contemporary sport. Not only have the growth of the economy and the emergence of unprecedented affluence, especially in the past two decades, influenced sports, but the enormous increase of interest in sport has had a dramatic economic impact. Chapter 10 describes the multidimensional aspects of economic considerations in sport, including the ongoing problems between owners and players.

There is a symbiotic relationship between sport and the mass media. In chapter 11, we review the social purposes of the mass media and their relation to sport, the influence of the mass media on sport and the impact of sport on the mass media, and the role of the sports journalist.

Sport is typically assumed to be an egalitarian and meritocratic institution. In chapter 12, we examine these two assumptions as they relate to social class and social mobility. The analysis shows that these beliefs are largely myths.

Systematic and pervasive discrimination against racial and ethnic minorities has been a historical feature of American society, but many Americans believe that sport has been and is free of racism. Chapter 13 documents the historical and contemporary facts illustrating that sport has had and still has many of the same racial problems as the larger society. Although the focus of this chapter is on African Americans and sport, also included are Latinos, Asian Americans, and Native Americans and their connections to the sports world in the United States.

The theme of chapter 14 is that the world of sport has been the exclusive domain of males and that sociocultural forces have combined to virtually exclude female sport involvement. We discuss how the opportunity structure is changing, yet problems of equity remain. Also included in this chapter are issues of sexuality as they relate to women and men athletes.

The final chapter speculates on the future of sport in North America. The basic theme is that since sport reflects society, as society changes, sport will also undoubtedly undergo some transformation. We discuss several current trends and possible future changes in society and discuss how each is likely to be manifested in sport changes.

Each chapter in this edition has a notes section that provides readers with relevant references to the various topics found in the chapter. These, along with the websites at the end of each chapter, can be quite useful to students and researchers who seek additional information on a given topic.

NEW TO THIS EDITION

Updated content and references. This edition focuses on current issues, such as the changing role of parents and coaches in youth sports, sports academies, and youth sports as "traveling leagues." Featuring the most up-to-date analysis in the field, the book has many references that reflect this new content.

Expanded focus on diversity. Although this text has always recognized the importance of diversity in sport and society, this edition includes more information on Native Americans, Latinos, Asians, and other minority groups in relation to sport.

Thinking about Sport boxes. These boxes feature thought-provoking essays on sport issues, such as the "glamour" of playing in college sports, violence and sport, and negative symbols used in sports.

Web Resources boxes. These boxes highlight sports organizations and resources and include annotated website information.

ABOUT THE AUTHORS

We believe that our sports backgrounds and academic interests harmonize in such a way that we form a unique team for writing a book on sport sociology. Both of us are former high school and collegiate athletes. Eitzen has coached on the high school level and has been involved in various capacities in youth sports programs. He also was a referee of high school sports. Sage has coached at the youth, high school, and college levels. We have conducted considerable research and published widely in sport sociology. Eitzen is known for his studies of racism in sport and his critiques of various aspects of the social organization of sport, and he has two other books on sport: *Sport in Contemporary Society,* an anthology now in its seventh edition, and *Fair and Foul: Beyond the Myths and Paradoxes of Sport,* currently in its third edition. Sage is known for his studies of coaches, analysis of professional teams, and corporations tied to sport; Sage's books on sport are *Power and Ideology in American Sport,* second edition, and his anthology, *Sport and American Society.* Although our backgrounds are in kinesiology (Sage) and sociology (Eitzen), our approaches to the sociology of sport are remarkably similar.

CHAPTER 1

The Sociological Analysis of Sport in Society

"Sport is a window on a changing society."
—David Halberstam

Fans at a football game in a packed stadium. Sport is an institution that provides scientific observers with a convenient laboratory within which to examine values, socialization, stratification, and bureaucracy to name a few structures and processes that also exist at the societal level. (iStockphoto)

The subject of this book is sport—an extraordinarily pervasive social phenomenon in North America. The sociological perspective is the analytical approach we will use to examine this very important human activity. We begin with a brief description of the importance of sport in society, followed by an introduction to the discipline of sociology, and how the sociological approach aids in our understanding of sport.

THE PERVASIVENESS OF SPORT

Social scientists are especially interested in sport because this phenomenon is so pervasive in the United States and Canada. Although seemingly a trivial aspect of life, sport is important, particularly as society becomes increasingly leisure-oriented. Many millions of Americans and Canadians are vitally interested in sport. It constitutes much of their conversation, reading material, leisure activity, and discretionary spending. More than one-tenth of the *World Almanac* is annually devoted to sports. In fact, sports receive more coverage in the almanac than politics, business, or science. *USA Today*, the most widely read newspaper in the United States, devotes one-fourth of its space to sports. The sports section is, for many, the most closely examined part of the daily newspaper. Newspapers, in turn, devote more space to sports than to a variety of other topics, including business news, which should be of central importance in a capitalist economy. Evidence of sportsmania is also seen in the amount of television time devoted to sport—almost one-fifth of major network time is devoted to sport, and some cable networks provide twenty-four-hour sports coverage. Historically, the most-watched television events are sports spectacles such as the Super Bowl.

Moreover, sport is big business: the total revenue of the U.S. sports industry in 2006 was $390 billion, up from $213 billion in 2000. Television networks bid billions of dollars for multiyear rights to televise college basketball tournaments, professional sports, and the Olympic Games. A thirty-second advertisement at the 2007 Super Bowl on CBS cost $2.6 million. Approximately $8 billion was bet illegally with bookies, offshore, and on the Internet on that Super Bowl outcome. According to an estimate by *Forbes* magazine, the New York Yankees were worth $1.2 billion in 2007. Soccer star David Beckham signed a five-year contract in 2006 with the Los Angeles Galaxy that could be worth $50 million a year, but that is only half of what golfer Tiger Woods makes annually from endorsements, exhibitions, and earnings from tournaments. Each team in a Bowl Championship Series (BCS) bowl game in 2007 received $17 million. In 2006, Ohio State had an athletic budget of $101.8 million. Table 1.1 shows the very large scale of sports spectatorship in the United States. When these numbers are multiplied by the average cost of tickets, parking, and refreshments, the amount generated by sports attendance is huge. Similarly, with about half of the U.S. population regularly participating in sports, the amount spent on sports-related equipment is enormous (about $104 billion in 2006 just for recreational users).

Sport is an important component of society worthy of serious sociological analysis, but all too often it has been relegated to popular commentators because academics have tended to ignore it as a frivolous activity. Traditionally, the leading sociological journals have published few articles on sport. Our goal is to demonstrate throughout this book that sport merits scientific and critical analysis. We will use the tools of modern sociology to analyze sport in society.

Table 1.1   Number of Spectators at Major Sports Events for 2006

Sport	Number of Spectators
Major League Baseball	75,997,622
National Basketball Association	21,595,804
National Football League	17,340,879
National Hockey League	20,854,169
College Basketball	
Men's	25,808,346
Women's	7,093,642

Source: U.S. Bureau of the Census, *Statistical Abstract of the United States: 2007.* (Washington, D.C.: U.S. Government Printing Office, 2007).

THE DISCIPLINE OF SOCIOLOGY

Sociology is the scientific discipline that describes and explains human social organization. The size of a human group under study can range from a couple to a church, from a family business to a corporation, from a community to a society. The sociologist is interested in the patterns that emerge whenever people interact over periods of time. Although groups may differ in size and purpose, similarities exist in their structures and in the processes that create, sustain, and transform their structures. In other words, a group that forms to make quilts for charity will be similar in important ways to a group that forms with the goal of winning football games. We know, for example, that through recurrent interaction certain characteristics emerge: (1) a division of labor; (2) a hierarchical structure of ranks (i.e., differences in power, prestige, and rewards); (3) rules; (4) punishment for the violation of rules; (5) criteria for the evaluation of things, people, ideas, and behavior; (6) a shared understanding of symbols with special meanings (specialized language such as nicknames, gestures, or objects); and (7) member cooperation to achieve group goals.[1]

Sociologists are interested not only in the underlying order of social life but also in the principles that explain human behavior. Sociology is joined in this quest by other disciplines, especially biology and psychology. Biological explanations of human behavior focus on the structure (potentials and limitations) of the human body and the innate drives (hunger, thirst, sex, and comfort) that constrain humans. The book *Sociobiology*, by Edward Wilson, for example, presents the controversial but forceful argument that human genetic heritage explains much human behavior, from the way human life is ordered in groups to the prevalence of violence.[2]

Psychological explanations of human behavior focus on mental processes and human behavioral characteristics. Psychology is helpful, for example, in explaining why particular individuals may be violent, self-destructive, criminal, humanitarian, saintly, prejudiced, alcoholic, or failure-prone.

Biological and psychological explanations are only partially useful, however, because they focus exclusively on the individual. The sociological approach, in contrast, stresses those factors external to the individual. These might be social conditions in the community or society such as varying degrees of unemployment, inflation, leisure time, urban blight, or restricted opportunities for minority groups. An extremely important external influence on human behavior is the understanding of meanings that the members of a social organization share. These shared meanings constitute culture. Under the rubric of culture are the standards used to evaluate behavior, ideology, customs, expectations for persons occupying various positions, and rules—all of which limit the choices of individuals, regardless of their biological heritage or their psychological proclivities. A final external source of control is an individual's social location. Each individual in society is—because of his or her wealth, occupation, education, religion, racial and ethnic heritage, gender, and family background—ranked by others and by himself or herself. Placement in this complex hierarchy exerts pressures, subtle and blatant, on people to behave in prescribed ways.

Although sociology is typically superseded by psychological explanations, the goal of this book is to provide a purely sociological analysis and explanation of sport in North America. Such an inquiry, we hope, not only will be interesting and insightful but also will introduce the reader to a new and meaningful way to understand the social world in general and the phenomenon of sport in particular.

Assumptions of the Sociological Perspective

We have seen that human behavior is examined through different disciplinary lenses and that each field of inquiry makes important contributions to knowledge. Of the disciplines focusing on human behavior, sociology is commonly the least understood. The implicit goal of this book is to introduce you to the sociological ways of perceiving and interpreting the role of sport in society. We begin by enumerating the assumptions of the sociological approach that provide the foundation for this unique way of viewing the world.[3]

1. Individuals Are, by Their Nature, Social Beings

There are two fundamental reasons for the assumption that humans are naturally social beings. First, children enter the world totally dependent on others for their survival. This initial period of dependence means, in effect, that each individual is immersed in social groups from birth. Second, throughout history individuals have found it advantageous to cooperate with others (for defense, for material comforts, to overcome the perils of nature, and to improve technology).

2. Individuals Are, for the Most Part, Socially Determined

The assumption that individuals are socially determined stems from the first assumption of the sociological approach, that people are social beings. Individuals are products of their social environments for several reasons. During infancy, children are at the mercy of others, especially parents. These persons can shape the potential behaviors of infants in an infinite variety of ways, depending on their proclivities and those of the society. Parents will have a profound impact on their children's ways of thinking about themselves and about others; they will transmit religious views, attitudes, and prejudices about how other groups are to be rated. Children will be punished for certain behaviors and rewarded for others. Whether children become bigots or integrationists, traditionalists or innovators, saints or sinners, athletes or nonathletes depends in large measure on parents, siblings, peers, and others with whom they interact.

Parents may transmit to their offspring some idiosyncratic beliefs and behaviors, but most significantly they act as cultural agents, transferring the ways of the society to their children. As a consequence, a child is born not only into a family but also into a society, both of which shape the personality characteristics and perceptions of each individual. Sociologist Peter L. Berger summarized the impact of society on individual development, "Society not only controls our movements, but shapes our identity, our thoughts and our emotions. The structures of society become the structures of our own consciousness. Society does not stop at the surface of our skins. Society penetrates us as much as it envelops us."[4]

The individual's identity is socially bestowed and is shaped by the way he or she is accepted, rejected, and defined by others. Whether an individual is attractive or plain, witty or dull, worthy or unworthy depends on the values of the society and the groups in which the individual is immersed. Although genes determine an individual's physical characteristics, the social environment, especially an individual's social class location, determines how those characteristics will be evaluated. Suggesting that people are socially determined is another way of saying that we are, in many ways, puppets dependent upon and manipulated by social forces. A major function of sociology is to identify the social forces that affect us so greatly. Freedom, as Reece McGee pointed out, can come only from a recognition of these unseen forces:

> Freedom consists in knowing what these forces are and how they work so that we have the option of saying no to the impact of their operation. For example, if we grow up in a racist society, we will be racist unless we learn what racism is and how it works and then choose to refuse its impact. In order to do so, however, we must recognize that it is there in the first place. People often are puppets, blindly danced by strings of which they are unaware and over which they are not free to exercise control. A major function of sociology is that it permits us to recognize the forces operative on us and to untie the puppet strings which bind us, thereby giving us the option to be free.[5]

Accordingly, one task of sociology is to learn, among other things, what racism, sexism, and homophobia are and to determine how they work. This is often difficult, though, because we typically do not recognize their existence. Social forces may have prompted us to believe and to behave in racist, sexist, and homophobic ways.

To say that people are puppets is too strong, however. The assumption that individuals are shaped by their society is not meant to imply a total social determinism. The puppet metaphor is used to convey the idea that much of who we are and what we do is a product of our social environment. However, society is not a rigid, static entity composed of robots; there are nonconformists, deviants, and innovators as well. Although the members of society are shaped by their social environment, they also change that environment. Human beings are the shapers of society. This is the third assumption of the sociological approach.

3. Individuals Create, Sustain, and Change the Social Forms within Which They Conduct Their Lives

Although humans are often puppets of their society, they are also puppeteers. In brief, the argument is that social groups of all sizes and types (families, peer groups, work groups, athletic teams, corporations, communities, and societies) are formed by their members. The group that interacting persons create becomes a source of control over them (i.e., they become puppets of their own creation), but the continuous interaction of the group's members also changes the group.

Three important implications stem from this assumption that groups are created by persons in interaction. First, these social forms that are created and changed by people have a certain momentum of their own that defies change. The ways of doing and thinking that are common to the group are accepted as natural and right. Although human-made, the group's expectations and structures take on a sacred quality—a sanctity of tradition—that constrains behavior in socially prescribed ways.

The second implication is that social arrangements, because they are a result of social activity, are imperfect. Slavery benefits some segments of society by taking advantage of others. A competitive free-enterprise system creates winners and losers. The wonders of technology make worldwide transportation and communication easy and relatively inexpensive, but they also create pollution and waste natural resources. These examples show that both positive and negative consequences emanate from human organization.

The third implication is that through collective action individuals are capable of changing the structure of society and even the course of history. Individuals are not passive. Rather, they actively shape social life by adapting to, negotiating with, and changing social structures. This process is called *human agency*.

The Sociological Imagination

C. Wright Mills (1916–1962), in his classic *The Sociological Imagination* (1959), wrote that the task of sociology was to realize that individual circumstances are inextricably linked to the structure of society. The *sociological imagination* involves several related components:[6]

- The sociological imagination is stimulated by a willingness to view the social world from the perspective of others.
- It involves moving away from thinking in terms of the individual and her or his problem, focusing rather on the social, economic, and historical circumstances that produce the problem. Put another way, the sociological imagination is the ability to see the societal patterns that influence individuals, families, groups, and organizations.
- Possessing a sociological imagination, one can shift from the examination of a single unemployed person to the societal shift from manufacturing to a service/knowledge economy, from a homeless family to the lack of affordable housing, and from a racist coach to institutional racism.
- To develop a sociological imagination requires a detachment from the taken-for-granted assumptions about social life and the establishment of a critical distance. In other words, one must be willing to question the structural arrangements that shape social behavior.
- When we have this imagination, we begin to see the solutions to social problems not in terms of changing problem people but of changing the structure of society.

Problems with the Sociological Perspective

Sociology is not a comfortable discipline, and therefore it will not appeal to everyone. Looking behind the "closed doors" of social life is dangerous. The astute observer of society must ask such questions as these: How does society really work? Who really has the power? Who benefits under the existing social arrangements, and who does not? To ask such questions means that the inquirer is interested in looking beyond the commonly accepted explanations. Berger put it, "The sociological perspective involves a process of 'seeing through' the facades of social structures."[7] The underlying assumption of the sociologist is that things are not as they seem. Do school sports serve educational goals? Are athletes in big-time college programs exploited? Does participation in sport build character? Are sports free of racism? Are school sports sexist? Is sport a realistic mechanism of upward mobility for lower-class youth? Is success or failure the most common experience of athletes? To make such queries is to question existing myths, stereotypes, and official dogma. The critical examination of society tends to demystify and to demythologize. It sensitizes the inquirer to the inconsistencies present in society.

The sociological assumption providing the basis for this critical stance is that the social world is made by people and therefore is not sacred. A society's economic system, its law, its ideology, its distribution of power, and its sports institutions are all created and sustained by people. They can be changed by people as a consequence. If we wish to correct imperfections in our society, then we must truly understand how social phenomena work and learn what changes will help achieve our goals. The central task of this book is to aid in such an understanding of sport in society.

The sociological perspective is also discomforting to many because understanding the constraints of society is liberating (traditional gender roles, for example, are no longer "sacred" for many persons). However, liberation from the constraints of tradition also means freedom from the protection that custom provides. The robotlike acceptance of tradition is comfortable because it frees us from choice (and therefore blame) and from ambiguity. The understanding of society is a two-edged sword, freeing us but also increasing the probability of our frustration, anger, and alienation.

A final source of discomfort is that the behavior of people is not always certain. Prediction is not always accurate because people can choose between options and because they can be persuaded by rational and irrational factors. The result is that even when sociologists know the social conditions, they can predict the consequences only in terms of probabilities. On the other hand, chemists know exactly what will occur if a certain measure of one chemical element is mixed with a precise amount of another in a test tube. Civil engineers, armed with the knowledge of rock formations, types of soils, wind currents, and temperature extremes, know exactly what specifications are needed to build a dam in a certain place. They could not determine these, however, if the foundation and the building materials kept shifting. That is the problem, and the source of excitement, for the sociologist. Social life is highly complex, and its study is beset by changes and uncertainties. Although the goal of the sociologist is to reduce the margin of error, its complete elimination is impossible as long as humans are not robots.

Units of Sociological Analysis

We have seen that sociologists are interested in social organizations and in how social forces operate to channel human behavior. The scope of sociology ranges from individuals sharing common social characteristics to small groups to society.

The Micro Level

At the micro level, the emphasis is on the structure of relatively small groups (e.g., families, friendship groups, and such organizations as the Friday Night Poker Club, the local Nazarene Church, the African Violet Society, and the Pretty Prairie High School football team). Some of the research questions of interest at this level are these: What are the principles underlying group formation, stability, and change? What are the

American high school football competition. Sports teams are especially useful research settings in which to test theories about social organization. (iStockphoto)

most effective forms of organization to accomplish group goals? Under what conditions is member cooperation maximized? Under what conditions is member behavior least predictable?

Sports teams are especially useful research settings in which to test theories about social organization. Sociologists of sport have researched, for example, the organizational characteristics correlated with success (leadership style, leadership change, homogeneity of members). They have examined where in sports organizations racial discrimination is most likely to occur.

As a final example of the micro level, sport sociologists have researched sports teams to examine the important social processes of competition and cooperation. Sport provides innumerable instances in which competition and cooperation occur separately and simultaneously. On the one hand, sports contests are instances of institutionalized conflict. Therefore, they may serve to control undesirable aggression and violence in socially acceptable channels. On the other hand, sports teams require cooperation to be effective. An important question (some would say the central question) in sociology is this: What facilitates group cohesion? (Under what conditions do members pull together, and when do they pull apart?) The leaders of sports teams (coaches, managers, and athletic directors) spend a good deal of their time working to build group unity. Some are successful; others are not. Is it a matter of charisma, authoritarianism, homogeneity of personnel, winning, social control, or what?

The Macro Level
Small groups such as families, friendship groups, and sports teams illustrate nicely the process and components of social organization. Each of these groups, however, exists in a larger social setting—a context that is also structured—with its own

norms, statuses, roles, and mechanisms of social control. These components of social structure constrain social groups and the attitudes and behaviors of individuals, regardless of their group memberships.

Societal Norms. There are societal prescriptions (*norms*) for how one should act and dress in given situations—for example, at a football game, concert, restaurant, church, park, or classroom. In other words, norms are situational. Why is the national anthem always played at sports events but not at concerts? Clearly, behavior considered appropriate for spectators at a football game (e.g., spontaneous screams of exuberance or despair, the open criticism of authority figures, and even the ritual destruction of goalposts) would be inexcusable behavior at a poetry reading. We know what is expected of us in these different situations. We also know how to act with members of the opposite sex, with elders, with social inferiors, and with equals. Thus, behavior in society is patterned. We know how to behave, and we can anticipate how others will behave. This allows interaction to occur smoothly.

Values. As bases for the norms, values are also part of society's culture. *Values* are the criteria used in assessing the relative desirability, merit, or correctness of objects, ideas, acts, feelings, or events. This is the topic of chapter 3, so we will only state here that the members of society are taught explicitly and implicitly how to judge whether someone or something is good or bad, moral or immoral, appropriate or inappropriate. North Americans, for example, believe that winning (in school, in sports, in business, and in life) is the highest goal. They not only value success; they know precisely how to evaluate others and themselves by this critical dimension.

Status and Role at the Societal Level. Societies, like other social organizations, have social positions (*statuses*) and behavioral expectations (*roles*) for the occupants of these positions. There are family statuses (daughter, son, sibling, parent, husband, wife); age statuses (child, adolescent, adult, elder); gender statuses (male, female); racial statuses (African American, Hispanic, Native American, white); and socioeconomic statuses (poor, middle-class, wealthy). For each of these statuses, there are societal constraints on behavior. To be a male or a female in U.S. society, for example, is to be constrained in a relatively rigid set of expectations. Similarly, African Americans and others of minority status have been expected to "know their place." Historically, their "place" in sport was segregated as they were denied equal access to sports participation with whites. Since racial integration, the "place" of racial minorities often remains unequal (at certain playing positions, head coaching, management).

Societal Institutions. One distinguishing characteristic of societies is the existence of a set of institutions. The popular usages of this term are imprecise and omit some important sociological considerations. An institution is not merely something established and traditional (e.g., a janitor who has worked at the same school for forty-five years). An institution is also not limited to a specific organization such as a school, a prison, or a hospital. An institution is much broader in scope and in importance than a person, a custom, or a social organization. *Institutions* are social arrangements that channel behavior in prescribed ways in the important areas of societal life. They are interrelated sets of normative elements, such as norms, values, and role expectations, devised by the persons making up the society and passed on to succeeding generations to provide "permanent" solutions for crucial societal problems.

Institutions are cultural imperatives. They serve as regulatory agencies that channel behavior in culturally prescribed ways. As Peter Berger has written: "Institutions provide procedures through which human conduct is patterned, compelled to go in grooves deemed desirable by society. And this trick is performed by making the grooves appear to the individual as the only possible ones."[8] For example, a society instills in its members predetermined channels for marriage. Instead of being allowed a whole host of options (e.g., polygyny, polyandry, or group marriage), sexual partners in the United States and Canada are expected to marry and to set up a conjugal household. Although the actual options are many, the partners tend to choose what society demands. In fact, they do not consider the other options valid. The result is a patterned arrangement that regulates sexual behavior and ensures a stable environment for the care of dependent children.

Institutions arise from the uncoordinated actions of multitudes of individuals over time. These actions, procedures, and rules evolve into a seemingly designed set of expectations because the consequences of these expectations provide solutions that help maintain social stability. The design is not accidental, however; it is a product of cultural evolution.

All societies face problems in common and are continually seeking solutions. Although the variety of solutions is almost infinite, there is a functional similarity in their consequences; that is, stability and maintenance of the system. All societies, for instance, have some form of family, education, polity, economy, and religion. The variations on each of these themes found in societies are almost beyond imagination.[9] See Table 1.2 for a list of common societal problems and the resulting institutions.

Sport, too, is an institution. What societal needs are served by sport? (1) Sport serves as a safety valve for both spectators and participants, dissipating excess energies, tensions, and hostile feelings in a socially acceptable way; (2) athletes serve as role models, possessing the proper mental and physical traits to be emulated by other members of society; and (3) sport is a secular, quasi-religious institution that uses ritual and ceremony to reinforce the values of society, thereby restricting behavior to the channels prescribed by custom.[10]

Institutions are, by definition, conservative. They provide the answers of custom and tradition to questions of societal survival. For this reason, any attack on an institution is met by violent opposition. This is surely true for sport, as Harry Edwards has noted: "If this characterization is correct, one would expect that any attack upon the institution of sport in a particular society would be widely interpreted (intuitively, if not explicitly) as an attack upon the fundamental way of life of that society as manifest by the value orientations it emphasizes through sport. Hence, an attack upon sport constitutes an attack upon the society itself."[11]

Institutions provide the unity and stability crucial for the survival of society. Although they are absolutely necessary, institutions in contemporary society are often outmoded, inefficient, and unresponsive to the incredibly swift changes brought about by technological advances, population shifts, changing attitudes, and increasing global interdependence. Institutions are made by women and men, and therefore they can be changed by these same people. We should be guided by the insight that although institutions appear to have the quality of being sacred, they are not. They can be changed. Critical examination is imperative, however. Social scientists must look behind the facades. They must not accept the patterned ways as the only correct ways. Questioning patterned ways is part of the democratic heritage as defended in the U.S. Declaration of Independence, for example. Jerome H. Skolnick and Elliott Currie have noted:

> Democratic conceptions of society have always held that institutions exist to serve man [sic], and that, therefore, they must be accountable to men [sic]. Where they fail to meet the tests imposed on them,

Table 1.2 Common Societal Problems and Resulting Institutions

Societal Problems	Institution
Sexual regulation; maintenance of stable units that ensure continued births and care of dependent children	Family
Socialization of newcomers to the society	Education
Maintenance of order; distribution of power	Polity
Production and distribution of goods and services; ownership of property	Economy
Understanding the transcendental; searching for the meaning of life, death, and humankind's place in the world	Religion
Understanding the physical and social realms of nature	Science
Providing for physical and emotional health care	Medicine

democratic theory holds that they ought to be changed. Authoritarian governments, religious regimes, and reformatories, among other social systems, hold the opposite: in case of misalignment between individuals or groups and the "system," the individuals and groups are to be changed or otherwise made unproblematic.[12]

This book will focus on sport at the societal level. We will describe how sport reinforces societal values. We will analyze the reciprocal linkages with other institutions—sport and education, sport and religion, sport and politics, sport and the economy. And, we will ask: Who benefits, and who does not, from the way sport is organized? Although the level of analysis is macro, the research findings from social-psychological and micro studies will be included whenever appropriate.

Sociological Theories: Contrasting Ways to See and Understand Social Life

Each sociologist is guided by a theoretical perspective. The focus of attention, the questions asked, the relationships sought, the interpretations rendered, and the insights unraveled are rooted in a theoretical base. Michael Harrington put it this way:

> Truths about society can be discovered only if one takes sides.... You must stand somewhere in order to see social reality, and where you stand will determine much of what you see and how you see it. The data of society are, for all practical purposes, infinite. You need criteria that will provisionally permit you to bring some order into that chaos of data and to distinguish between relevant and irrelevant factors or, for that matter, to establish that there are facts in the first place. These criteria cannot be based on the data for they are the precondition of the data. They represent—and the connotations of the phrase should be savored—a "point of view." That involves intuitive choices, a value-laden sense of what is meaningful and what is not.[13]

Harrington suggests that there are various vantage points from which to view social life. Each of these vantage points (theoretical perspectives) guides our thinking, narrows our perceptions to certain relevant phenomena, and, in doing so, helps us understand. We present here four major theoretical perspectives that are used to understand the social world and—for our purposes—the world of sport. Each is useful because each focuses on a different aspect of social life, giving us insight missing from the others.

Functionalism

The functionalist perspective attributes to societies the characteristics of cohesion, consensus, cooperation, reciprocity, stability, and persistence.[14] Societies are viewed as social systems, composed of interdependent parts that are linked together into a boundary-maintaining whole. The parts of the system are basically in harmony with each other. The high degree of cooperation (and societal integration) is accomplished because there is a high degree of consensus on societal goals and on cultural values. This consensus is achieved through socialization. Moreover, the different parts of the system are assumed to need each other because of complementary interests. Even though there are differences in resources by various groups in society, there are countervailing pressures that prevent abuse and domination by one group. The disadvantaged do not rebel because they accept the values of society and they believe the system is inherently just. All social change is gradual, adjustive, and reforming because the primary social process is cooperation and the system is highly integrated. Societies are therefore basically stable units.

For functionalists the central issue is this: What is the nature of the social bond? What holds groups together? One way to focus on integration is to determine the manifest (intended) and latent (unintended) consequences of social structures, norms, and social activities. Do these consequences contribute to the integration (cohesion) and, therefore, the maintenance of the social system?

Functionalists focusing on sport look, for example, for the ways in which sport unifies and preserves the status quo. They assess how sport contributes to the socialization of youth. They show how sport serves as a model for the striving and achievement of excellence. Finally, they determine the ways sport serves as an inspiration.

Conflict Theory

The assumptions of conflict theory are opposite from those of functionalist theory. Conflict theory focuses on the social processes leading to disharmony, disruption, instability, and conflict. From this perspective, the basic form of interaction is not cooperation but competition, which often leads to conflict.[15] Conflict is endemic in social organizations because of social structure, especially class differences. The things that people desire, such as property, prestige, and power, are not distributed equally, resulting in a fundamental cleavage between the advantaged and the disadvantaged. Moreover, the powerful use their power to maintain their power and economic advantage. This is done sometimes through force but more often through control of the decision-making apparatus. More subtly, the powerful maintain their power by achieving ideological conformity through the media, schools, churches, and other institutions. This is a most effective means of social control because it results even in individuals defining conditions that are against their interests as being appropriate, a condition that Karl Marx called *false consciousness*.

A prominent assumption of the conflict perspective is that the understanding of society or any of its institutions requires the analysis of the political economy. Power and wealth are inextricably intertwined, and they dominate the rest of society. Therefore, the conflict theorist must consider the type of economy, the ways that members are organized for production and consumption, the distribution of material goods, the way decisions are made, and the distribution of power.

Conflict theorists focusing on sport would, for example, examine intercollegiate athletics by focusing on the power of the National Collegiate Athletic Association (NCAA) over athletes, the cozy relationship between that organization and the television networks, the resistance of the NCAA and university administrators to implement Title IX (which requires equal treatment for women), big-time college sport as big business, illegal tactics by coaches in recruiting athletes, and the exploitation of the athletes. Functionalist theorists, on the other hand, would focus on the integrating effects of intercollegiate sport for students, faculty, alumni, and community members. They would also look for the positive consequences for participants such as grades, self-esteem, character traits, career aspirations, and the career mobility patterns of former athletes.

Sport from the Functionalist and Conflict Perspectives: Different Views of Social Order

Functionalists examining any aspect of society emphasize the contribution that part makes to the stability of society. Sport, from this perspective, preserves the existing social order in several ways. To begin, sport symbolizes the American way of life—competition, individualism, achievement, and fair play. Not only is sport compatible with basic American values, but it also is a powerful mechanism for socializing youth to adopt desirable character traits, to accept authority, and to strive for excellence. Sport also supports the status quo by promoting the unity of society's members through patriotism (e.g., national anthem, militaristic displays, and other nationalistic rituals that accompany sports events). Can you imagine, for example, a team that espouses antiestablishment values in its name, logo, mascot, and pageantry? Would we tolerate a major league team called the Atlanta Atheists? the Boston Bigamists? the Pasadena Pacifists? or the Sacramento Socialists? Finally, sport inspires us through the excellent and heroic achievements of athletes, the magical moments in sport when the seemingly impossible happens, and the feelings of unity in purpose and loyalty of fans.

Clearly, then, sport from the functional perspective is good. Sport socializes youth into proper channels, sport unites, and sport inspires. Thus, to challenge or criticize sport is to challenge the very foundation of society's social order.

Conflict theorists argue that the social order reflects the interests of the powerful. Sport is organized at whatever level, whether youth, high school, college, or professional, to exploit athletes and meet the goals of the powerful (e.g., public relations, prestige, and profits).

Sport inhibits the potential for revolution by society's "have-nots" in three ways. First, sport validates the prevailing myths of capitalism, such as anyone can succeed if he or she works hard enough. If a person fails, it is his or her fault and not that of the system. Second, sport serves as an "opiate of the masses" by diverting attention away from the harsh realities of poverty, job insecurity, rising debt, and dismal life chances by giving them a "high." Third, sport gives false hope to blacks and other oppressed members of society as they see sport as a realistic avenue of upward social mobility. The high visibility of wealthy athletes provides "proof" that athletic ability translates into monetary success. The reality, of course, is that only an extremely small percentage of aspiring athletes ever achieves professional status.

Conflict theorists agree with functionalists on many of the facts but differ significantly in interpretation. Both agree that sport socializes youth, but conflict theorists view this negatively because they see sport as a mechanism to get youth to follow orders, work hard, and fit into a system that is not necessarily beneficial to them. Both agree that sport maintains the status quo. Instead of this being interpreted as good, as the functionalists maintain, conflict theorists view this as bad because it reflects and reinforces the unequal distribution of power and resources in society.

Critical Theories

Critical theories (there are several variations) seek to understand the sources of power, how power works, and how individuals and groups exert human agency as they cope with, adapt to, and change existing power relationships. These theories are a reaction to the grand theories of functionalism and conflict theory. Instead of seeing society as dominating the individual completely, critical theories emphasize human agency. While recognizing that sport is a microcosm of society, critical theorists go beyond that insight to emphasize that the conditions of sport can change from the top down (from power structures) or from the bottom up (from the interaction of the participants themselves). Social life is complex. Whereas functionalism and conflict theory explain social life as deriving from a single source (value consensus for functionalists and the economy for conflict theorists), critical theorists emphasize the diversity of social life. Understanding of social phenomena requires looking at a number of forces (e.g., historical, cultural, economic, political, and the media). Let's take a brief look at two variations of critical theory—hegemony theory and feminist theory.

Hegemony Theory. This approach focuses on the political, economic, and cultural patterns of dominance and influence in society. George H. Sage describes this perspective:

> [Hegemony theory sensitizes us to] the role dominant groups play in American government, economic system, mass media, education, and sport in maintaining and promoting their interests. By dominant groups, I mean the powerful and wealthy who own most of the land, capital, and technology and who employ most of the nation's labor. They also translate their enormous economic resources into social and political power by occupying the top elective and appointed governmental positions, regardless of the political party to which they belong. The social structure of dominance in American society also privileges men over women, rich over poor, and whites over people of color.[16]

Hegemony theory stems from conflict theory, but it adds ideology and culture to the importance of the economy. Again, George Sage says, applying hegemony theory to sport:

> A critical social perspective invites us to step back from thinking about sport merely as a place of personal achievement and entertainment and study sport as a cultural practice embedded in political, economic, and ideological formations. Relevant issues involve how sport is related to social class, race, gender, and the control, production, and distribution of economic and cultural power in the commodified sport industry.[17]

Feminist Theory. Feminist theories began as critiques of the dominant social theories that did not include women or did not take women's issues seriously.[18] Feminist theory rests on two fundamental assumptions. First, human experiences are gendered. Second, "All feminists share an assumption that women are oppressed within patriarchy and a commitment to change those conditions."[19] Sport, then, is seen as a gendered activity where males have the power. Some examples of feminist research topics focusing on sport are the ideological control of women through the underrepresentation of women athletes in media images, the trivialization of women athlete's accomplishments, the hidden discourse of homophobia, and "the construction of women as unnatural athletes and of female athletes as unnatural women."[20]

Interactionist Theory

The preceding theories are all in one way or another structural theories. That is, they key on the components of society: institutions, the economy, culture, the media, social classes, and gender. Although critical theories pay attention to how people give meaning to their lives, interactionist theory focuses exclusively on this aspect of human activity.

Individuals and groups interpret and understand their social worlds by attaching meaning to symbols. This is an ongoing process, as the social world is continually constructed and reinvented by the participants.[21] The important sociological insight is that meaning is not inherent in an object. Rather, people learn how to define reality from other people in interaction and by learning the culture. This process is called the "*social construction of reality.*" Race, for example, is socially constructed as people attach social meanings to physical differences (see chapter 13).

Sociologists of sport using interactionist perspectives have conducted various kinds of research by interviewing subjects, watching them, and listening to them. The goal is to determine how participants (players, coaches, officials, administrators, and spectators) understand their world. Some of these focus on topics such as socialization into sport, the retirement process from sport, male bonding in locker rooms, sport rituals, and the characteristics of sport subcultures (e.g., rock climbers, skateboarders, boxers, pool hustlers, playground basketball, high school football teams, and professional women golfers). (We will discuss these in more detail in various chapters.)

Theory Revisited

A sociological theory offers an explanation of social life by making assumptions about the general patterns found. It is a way of making sense out of the complex social world, but as such it is always tentative, subject to new research findings and changing social conditions. As Susan Birrell states: "A theory is a framework for understanding, but it always develops within a particular cultural context and is always provisional. Theory is never perfect, never complete, never proven. Instead, theory provides us with a starting point for our understanding but it begs to be expanded, contradicted, refined, replaced."[22]

We have presented four major theoretical approaches and two theories subsumed under one of them. Not one of them is the answer. Each has its faults, usually because it is limited in scope. Each focuses on an aspect of social life, asking its unique set of questions stemming from its view of the social world, and presenting valuable insights—but none is complete. We will incorporate each of these theories as it is appropriate, describing the research and insights that flow from each. Overall, though, we have our own view of the social world, one that takes the best from the conflict and critical theories. Our perspective assumes a basic skepticism about current cultural and social patterns. We distrust existing power arrangements because they are, by definition, oppressive to the powerless segments of the population. We question dominant ideologies because they support the status quo. We measure myths against reality. This critical examination of social structure demystifies, demythologizes, and, sometimes, emancipates. This, we feel, is the core of the sociological perspective.

Second, our perspective directs attention toward social problems emanating from current structural arrangements. We ask: Under these social arrangements, who gets what and why? Who benefits from and bears the social costs of change and stability? Sport, just like the core institutions of the economy, religion, and family, is an area where these kinds of questions typically are not asked.

Third, our critical perspective seeks to determine how social arrangements might be changed to enhance the human condition. We have two goals in writing this book: (1) to report what is known about sport and society from social science research[23] and (2) to make the case for reform. As social scientists, we are obliged to be as scientific as possible (using rigorous techniques and reporting all relevant findings whether they support our values or not). At the same time, however, we are committed to moving sport and society in a more humane direction.

To accomplish these goals, we will question established orthodoxies, demythologize sport, and point out the gaps between values and actual practices. We intend, then, to combine a scientific stance with a muckraking role. The latter is important because it forces us to examine such social problems as drug usage in sports, the prevalence of racism and sexism in sports, illegal recruiting, the inhumane treatment of players by bureaucratic organizations and authoritarian coaches, and the perversion of the original goal of sport. Only by a thorough examination of such problems, along with the traditional areas of attention, will we realistically understand the world of sport and its reciprocal relationship with the larger society.

SPORT AS A MICROCOSM OF SOCIETY

The analyst of society is inundated with data. She or he is faced with the problems of sorting out the important from the less important and with discerning patterns of behavior and their meanings. He or she needs shortcuts to ease the task. To focus on sport is just such a technique for understanding the complexities of the larger society.

Sport is an institution that provides scientific observers with a convenient laboratory within which to examine values, socialization, stratification, and bureaucracy, to name a few structures and processes that also exist at the societal level. The types of games people choose to play, the degree of competitiveness, the types of rules, the constraints on the participants, the groups that do and do not benefit under the existing arrangements, the rate and type of change, and the reward system in sport provide us with a microcosm of the society in which sport is embedded.

Common Characteristics of Sport and Society

Suppose an astute sociologist from another society were to visit the United States and Canada with the intent to understand North American values, the system of social control, the division of labor, and the system of stratification. Although she or he could find the answers by careful study and observation of any single institution (i.e., religion, education, polity, economy, or family), an attention to sport would also provide answers. In the United States, it would not take that sociologist long to discern the following qualities in sport that are also present in the larger society.

The High Degree of Competitiveness
Competition is ubiquitous in North American society. North Americans demand winners. In sports (for children and adults), winning, not pleasure in the activity, is the ultimate goal. The adulation given winners is fantastic while losers are relatively forgotten. Consider, for example, the difference in how the winner and the loser in the Super Bowl are evaluated. Clearly, to be second best is not good enough. The goal of victory is so important for many that it is laudable even if attained by questionable methods.

The Emphasis on Materialism
Examples of the value North Americans place on materialism are blatant in sport (e.g., players signing multimillion-dollar contracts, golfers playing weekly for first-place awards of more than a million dollars, professional teams being moved to more economically fertile climates, and stadiums being built at public expense for hundreds of millions of dollars).

The Pervasiveness of Racism
Racist attitudes and actions affect the play, positions, numbers of starters, and futures of minority group members in North American sport. Just as

in the larger society, racial minorities in sport are rarely found in positions of authority.

The Pervasiveness of Male Dominance

Sport contributes to the perpetuation of male dominance through four minimalizing processes: (1) defining—by defining sport as a male activity; (2) directly controlling—men control sport, even women's sport; (3) ignoring—by giving most attention to male sports in the media and through community and school budgets, facilities, and the like; and (4) trivializing—women's sports and women athletes are belittled and diminished.[24]

Mariah Burton Nelson reminds us that sport provides many subtle and not-so-subtle messages about the relative importance of men and the relative unimportance of women. She says:

> We live in a country in which the manly sports culture is so pervasive we may fail to recognize the symbolic messages we all receive about men, women, love, sex, and power. We need to take sports seriously—not the scores or the statistics, but the process. Not to focus on who wins, but on who's losing. Who loses when a community spends millions of dollars in tax revenue to construct a new stadium and only men get to play in it, and only men get to work there?
>
> Who loses when football and baseball so dominate the public discourse that they eclipse all mention of female volleyball players, gymnasts, basketball players, swimmers?
>
> Who loses when coaches teach boys that the worst possible insult is to be called "pussy" or "cunt"?
>
> Who loses when rape jokes comprise an accepted part of the game?[25]

The Domination of Individuals by Bureaucracies

Conservative bureaucratic organizations, through their desire to perpetuate themselves, curtail innovations and deflect activities away from the wishes of individuals and from the original intent of these organizations.

The Unequal Distribution of Power in Organizations

The structure of sport in the United States is such that power is in the hands of the wealthy (e.g., boards of regents, corporate boards of directors, the media, wealthy entrepreneurs, the United States Olympic Committee [USOC], and the National Collegiate Athletic Association). Evidence of the power of these individuals and organizations is seen in the antitrust exemption allowed them by Congress in dealing with athletes, in tax breaks, and in the concessions that communities make to entice professional sports franchises to relocate or to remain, and, incidentally, to benefit the wealthy of that community.

The Use of Conflict to Change Unequal Power Relationships

Conflict (in the forms of lawsuits, strikes, boycotts, and demonstrations) is used by the less powerful (e.g., African Americans, women, and athletes) to gain advantage in sport and in society.

Sport Is Not a Sanctuary; Deviance Is Found throughout Sport

Because sport reflects society, bad actors and bad actions will be found in sport as they are in society. Both fairness and unfairness are found. There are ethical and unethical athletes, coaches, and athletic administrators. Focusing on the negative, sportswriter Bernie Lincicome has argued:

> Sports is not a sanctuary from life. It is simply another room in the same troubled house.... Cynicism has become an endangered sentiment. It is impossible to imagine the worst about sports anymore. It's all true. Games are rigged. Drugs are common. Cheating works.... Nothing is beyond belief, not pushers in the clubhouse or rapists in the locker room or point-shavers on the court or illiterates in the yearbook.... Seven, count 'em, seven Nebraska football players have been arrested this summer for one thing or another, and four players at Georgia are out of the team's opener this weekend for, in no particular order, domestic abuse, battery, stalking, harassing phone calls and criminal trespass.... How about this? Women's swimming at Southern Cal has been put on probation for academic cheating.... Against all this, how insignificant does it seem that Danny Almonte, the Dominican kid who pitched a perfect game for the Bronx team in the Little League World Series, is 2 years older than he is supposed to be? Except this

is where it starts. It starts with adults—parents, coaches, hustlers—and it starts with the kid, too.[26]

LEVELS OF SPORT

One final task remains for this first chapter. We need to establish at the outset the subject matter of this book. Our object of study is *sport, which we define as any competitive physical activity that is guided by established rules.* Competition, the first of the three characteristics of sport, involves the attempt to defeat an opponent. This opponent may be a mountain, a record, an individual, or a team. The second characteristic involves physical activity. One attempts to defeat an opponent through physical abilities such as strength, speed, stamina, and accuracy. (Of course, the outcome is also determined by the employment of strategy, not to mention chance.) Rules, the final characteristic of sport, distinguish it from more playful and spontaneous activities. The scope, rigidity, and enforcement of the rules, however, vary by type and level of sport, as we shall see.

Our definition of sport is too broad to be entirely adequate. A pickup game of basketball and a game in the National Basketball Association (NBA) are examples of two related but at the same time very different activities that fall under our definition.[27] In the same way, an improvised game of one-on-one is sport; so is professional football—although it has been argued that professional football is not sport because of its big-business aspects or because it is more like work than play for the participants. Clearly, there is a need to differentiate several levels: informal sport, organized sport, and corporate sport. The first and last of these distinctions were first made by Bil Gilbert, and many of the ideas that follow stem from his insights.[28]

Informal Sport

Informal sport involves playful physical activity engaged in primarily for the enjoyment of the participants. A touch football game, a neighborhood basketball game, and a game of workup (baseball)

Informal sport, such as a neighborhood game of basketball, involves playful physical activity engaged in primarily for the enjoyment of the participants. (iStockphoto)

are examples of this type of sport. In each of these examples, some rules guide the competition, but these rules are determined by the participants and not by a regulatory body.

Organized Sport

The presence of a rudimentary organization distinguishes *organized sport* from informal sport. There are formal teams, leagues, codified rules, and related organizations. These exist primarily for the benefit of the players by working for fair competition, providing equipment and officials, scheduling, ruling in disputed cases, and offering opportunities for persons to participate. Young Men's Christian Association (YMCA) leagues, city leagues, Little League programs, interscholastic teams and leagues, and low-pressure college team leagues are examples of organized sport that have not lost the original purposes of the activity.[29] A strong case can be made, however, that many Little League programs have become too organized to maintain the goal of fun through the participation of youth. If so, they belong in the "corporate" category.[30] The same is true for high school sport in some situations,[31] as we will see in chapter 5.

Corporate Sport

Corporate sport has elements of informal sport and organized sport, but it has been modified by economics and politics. In Bil Gilbert's words, corporate sport is "a corrupted, institutionalized version of sport."[32] Here, we have sport as spectacle, sport as big business, sport as an extension of power politics. The pleasure in the activity for the participants has been lost in favor of extrinsic rewards for them and pleasure for fans, owners, alumni, and other powerful groups.

Whereas sports organizations at the organized sport level devote their energies to preserving the activities in the participants' interest, organizations at the corporate sport level have enormous power (often a monopoly). As their power increases, they devote less and less of their energy to satisfying the needs for which they were created. They become more interested in perpetuating the organization through public relations, making profits, monopolizing the media, crushing opposing organizations, or merging leagues to limit opposition and to control player salaries. They also reduce their own risk by being inflexible and noninnovative. Professional sports leagues, big-time college athletics governed by the NCAA, and the International Olympic Committee (IOC) are examples of the bureaucracies that characterize corporate sport and subvert the pleasure of participating for the sake of the activity itself.

These three levels of sport can be placed on a continuum from play to work. As one moves from informal to corporate sport, the activities become more organized with a subsequent loss of autonomy and pleasure for athletes. Corporate sport dominates sport in North America; therefore, we will focus on that level in this book. That level is but an extension of the organized sport level, however, so we will at times direct our attention toward noncorporate organized sport as well.

Pseudosport is another activity often included in the sports pages of newspapers, but one that we claim falls outside even our broad definition. Professional wrestling and activities involving teams such as the Harlem Globetrotters are examples of pseudosport. Although athletes are involved in these activities and the activities involve physical prowess, they are not sport because they are not competitive. They may be packaged as competition, but these activities exist solely for spectator amusement.

SUMMARY

The perspective, concepts, and procedures of sociology are used in this book to describe and explain the institution of sport in society. The subject matter of sociology is social organization. Sport involves different types of social organizations, such as teams and leagues. These, in turn, are part of larger social organizations, such as schools, communities, international associations, and society. The task of this book is to understand the principles that underlie the structures and processes that create, sustain, and transform these social organizations. Most importantly, this undertaking requires that the observer examine the social arrangements of sport from a critical stance.

Some sample questions that must direct the serious investigator are these: How does the organization really work? Who really has the power? Who benefits, and who does not?

The two fundamental themes of this book have been introduced in this chapter. The first is that sport is a microcosm of society. Perceiving the way sport is organized, the types of games people play, the degree of emphasis on competition, the compensation of the participants, and the enforcement of the rules is a shorthand way of understanding the complexities of the larger society in which sport is embedded. The converse is true also. The understanding of the values of society, of its types of economy, and of its treatment of minority groups, to name a few elements, provides important bases for the perception or understanding of the organization of sport in society.

The second theme is that the prevailing form of sport—the corporate level—has corrupted the original intentions of sport. Instead of player-oriented physical competition, sport has become a spectacle, a big business, and an extension of power politics. Play has become work. Spontaneity has been superseded by bureaucracy. The goal of pleasure in the physical activity has been replaced by extrinsic rewards, especially money.

WEB RESOURCES

Sport

www.sportsjones.com
An alternative to some of the mainstream sports newsmagazines, including essays on issues central to the sociology of sport.

www.bus.ucf.edu/sport
The Institute for Diversity and Ethics in Sport provides useful information, especially on race and gender.

www.sportinsociety.org
The site for the Center for the Study of Sport in Society.

www.nassslistserv.bc.edu
The list service for the North American Society for the Sociology of Sport and its members, with daily offerings on current issues, bibliographic information, job openings, and notices of upcoming conferences.

http://www.naslin.org
Nasline is the newsletter of the North American Sport Library Network.

http://u2.u-strasbg.fr/issa
The official site of the International Sociology of Sport Association.

www.cnnsi.com
The website for CNN and *Sports Illustrated,* with data and features. Also, link to Frank Deford's Insider Archive for copies of his thoughtful essays on sport given weekly on National Public Radio.

www.sportdiscus.com
An international database of sports information.

Sociological Theories

www.csf.colorado.edu/psn/marxist-sociology/index.html
Resources from the American Sociological Association Section on Marxist Sociology.

www.asanet.org/theory.htm
Resources from the American Sociology Association Section on Theory.

www.sun.soci.niu.edu/~sssi
Resources from the Society for the Study of Symbolic Interaction.

www.2.uchicago.edu/jnl-crit-inq
Resources on critical theory from the University of Chicago.

www.feminist.org/research/sports2.html
This site highlights the issues important in a feminist analysis of sports.

www.eddie.cso.uiuc.edu/Durkheim
Resources on the classic functionalist Emile Durkheim.

www.utc.edu/~kswitala/feminism
A feminist theory website.

www.feminist.org/research/sports2.html
Reports on the issues that are important to feminists studying sport.

www.ualberta.ca/~jrnorris/qual.html
Resources for qualitative sociologists.

General Sources

www.census.gov/statab/www
Summary information on economic, demographic, social, and other characteristics of the U.S. population as found in the latest edition of the *Statistical Abstract of the United States*.

www.infoplease.com
All the data that make almanacs useful, retrievable by key word or category.

Search Engines

www.altavista.digital.com
www.excite.com
www.google.com
www.lycos.com
www.yahoo.com/search.html

NOTES

1. See Muzafer Sherif and Carolyn W. Sherif, *Groups in Harmony and Tension* (New York: Octagon Books, 1966); William F. Whyte, *Street Corner Society* (Chicago: University of Chicago Press, 1943); and Elliot Liebow, *Tally's Corner: A Study of Negro Street Corner Men* (Boston: Little, Brown, 1967).

2. Edward O. Wilson, *Sociobiology: The New Synthesis* (Cambridge, Mass.: Belknap Press, 1975).

3. For an elaboration of the discipline of sociology and the sociological perspective, see D. Stanley Eitzen and Maxine Baca Zinn, *In Conflict and Order: Understanding Society*, 11th ed. (Boston: Allyn & Bacon, 2007), chaps. 1–2; Joe R. Feagin and Hernan Vera, *Liberation Sociology* (Boulder, Colo.: Westview, 2001); Charles Lemert, *Social Things: An Introduction to Sociological Life* (Lanham, Md.: Rowman & Littlefield, 1997); John Walton, *Sociology and Critical Inquiry: The Work, Tradition, and Purpose*, 2nd ed. (Belmont, Calif.: Wadsworth, 1990); Randall Collins, *Sociological Insight: An Introduction to Non-Obvious Sociology*, 2nd ed. (New York: Oxford University Press, 1992); Peter L. Berger, *Invitation to Sociology: A Humanistic Perspective* (Garden City, N.Y.: Doubleday Anchor Books, 1963); and C. Wright Mills, *The Sociological Imagination* (New York: Oxford University Press, 1959).

4. Berger, *Invitation to Sociology*, 121.

5. Reece McGee, *Points of Departure: Basic Concepts in Sociology* (Hinsdale, Ill.: Dryden Press, 1975), x–xi.

6. D. Stanley Eitzen and Kelly Eitzen Smith, *Experiencing Poverty: Voices from the Bottom* (Belmont, Calif.: Wadsworth, 2003), 8.

7. Berger, *Invitation to Sociology*, 31.

8. Ibid., 87.

9. The discussion on institutions is taken from Eitzen and Baca Zinn, *In Conflict and Order*, 42–44.

10. See Harry Edwards, *Sociology of Sport* (Homewood, Ill.: Dorsey, 1973), 84–130.

11. Ibid., 90.

12. Jerome H. Skolnick and Elliott Currie, "Approaches to Social Problems," in *Crisis in American Institutions*, ed. Jerome H. Skolnick and Elliott Currie (Boston: Little, Brown, 1970), 15.

13. Michael Harrington, *Taking Sides* (New York: Holt, Rinehart & Winston, 1985), 1.

14. For a full description of functionalism, see John W. Loy and Douglas Booth, "Functionalism, Sport and Society," in *Handbook of Sport Studies*, ed. Jay Coakley and Eric Dunning (London: Sage, 2000), 8–27.

15. For a discussion of the conflict perspective, see Bero Rigauer, "Marxist Theories," in *Handbook of Sport Studies*, ed. Coakley and Dunning, 28–47.

16. George H. Sage, *Power and Ideology in American Sport: A Critical Perspective*, 2nd ed. (Champaign, Ill.: Human Kinetics, 1998), 10.

17. Ibid., 11.

18. The following is from Susan Birrell, "Feminist Theories for Sport," in *Handbook of Sport Studies*, ed. Coakley and Dunning, 61–76.

19. Birrell, "Feminist Theories for Sport," 62.

20. Ibid., 68.

21. Peter Donnelly, "Interpretive Approaches to the Sociology of Sport," in *Handbook of Sport Studies*, ed. Coakley and Dunning, 77–92. For an insightful example of interpretative sociology, see Joseph R. Gusfield, "Sport as Story: Form and Content in Athletics," *Society* 37 (May/June 2000): 63–70.

22. Birrell, "Feminist Theories for Sport," 62.

23. For summaries of what is known and bibliographies for the study of the sociology of sport, see especially *Handbook of Sport Studies*, ed. Coakley and Dunning; and Robert E. Washington and David Karen,

"Sport and Society," *Annual Review of Sociology* 27 (2001): 187–212.

24. Lois Bryson, "Sport and the Maintenance of Masculine Hegemony," *Women's Studies International Forum* 10 (1987): 349–360.

25. Mariah Burton Nelson, *The Stronger Women Get, the More Men Love Football: Sexism and the American Culture of Sports* (New York: Harcourt Brace, 1994), 8.

26. Bernie Lincicome, "Little League Lie Doesn't Even Cause Us to Bat an Eye," *Rocky Mountain News*, 1 September 2001, p. 20.

27. For elaborate discussions on the differences between play, game, and sport, see Johan Huizinga, *Homo Ludens: A Study of the Play Element in Culture* (Boston: Beacon Press, 1955); Roger Caillois, *Man, Play and Games* (London: Thames & Hudson, 1962); John W. Loy, Jr., "The Nature of Sport: A Definitional Effort," in *Sport in the Socio-Cultural Process*, ed. M. Marie Hart (Dubuque, Iowa: Wm. C. Brown, 1972), 50–66; Edwards, *Sociology of Sport*, 43–61; John W. Loy, Jr., Barry D. McPherson, and Gerald S. Kenyon, *Sport and Social Systems* (Reading, Mass.: Addison-Wesley, 1978), 3–26; and Allen Guttmann, *From Ritual to Record* (New York: Columbia University Press, 1978), 1–14.

28. Bil Gilbert, "Gleanings from a Troubled Time," *Sports Illustrated,* 25 December 1972, 34–46.

29. For examples of people who compete for the sheer joy of the competition, see Robin Chotzinoff, *People Who Sweat: Ordinary People, Extraordinary Pursuits* (New York: Harcourt Brace, 1999).

30. John Underwood, *Spoiled Sport* (Boston: Little, Brown, 1984), 151–173.

31. See H. G. Bissinger, *Friday Night Lights: A Town, a Team, and a Dream* (Reading, Mass.: Addison-Wesley, 1990).

32. Gilbert, "Gleanings from a Troubled Time," 34.

CHAPTER 2
Social and Cultural Sources for the Rise of Sport in North America

Women's college basketball team, 1901. In the first thirty years of the twentieth century the athletic spirit became a prominent part of the social life of large numbers of people. Between 1900 and World War II, sport became the most pervasive popular cultural practice in North America. (Photo courtesy of the University of Northern Colorado)

The forms, functions, and practices of sport in any given society are rooted in historical, social, and cultural traditions, and it is our contention that a study of sport based solely on the present will result in an incomplete picture of sport as a social and cultural practice. Thus one who studies the sociology of sport without studying sport's history will never truly understand the social and cultural forces that underpin contemporary sport. In this chapter we examine the changing sociocultural conditions of Canadian and American societies over the past four hundred years and attempt to demonstrate how these conditions have affected and influenced the rise and current state of North American sport.

The United States and Canada have experienced similar stages of historical development. Each went through a period of British control; each had a period of westward expansion; each experienced a massive influx of immigrants from Europe; and each underwent urbanization and industrialization during the late nineteenth century. The two countries share a common language; they share a border for more than three thousand miles, and about 85 percent of the Canadian population lives within one hundred miles of the American-Canadian border. It is hard to imagine any two countries in the world having closer social and cultural ties than Canadians and Americans.[1]

Over the past four centuries, the United States and Canada have grown from a few widely scattered and disunited settlements located along the eastern seaboard of part of North America into two of the most modern and industrially advanced nations in the world. They have also become two of the leading nations in sports. Fostered by a variety of historical, political, social, and economic conditions, sports have become a major national pastime for the people of both countries. From agrarian societies whose inhabitants had little time for games and sports, except on special occasions, North Americans have become two nations of citizens who watch ten to twenty hours of sports on television each weekend and consider it almost a duty to participate in some form of exercise or sport for recreation.

PRE-COLUMBIAN AND COLONIAL TRADITIONS IN NORTH AMERICA

For many centuries before European colonization began in what is now Canada and the United States, Native American settlements were scattered throughout North America. It is estimated

Sheet music cover showing Native Americans and white men playing lacrosse. Lithograph, ca. 1830–1910. (Library of Congress)

that some six to eight million native peoples were dispersed across the continent at the time of Columbus's voyages. What is quite clear is that although there was great diversity among the cultures of Native Americans, they all enjoyed a variety of physical play and game activities. In his book *American Indian Sports Heritage,* Joseph Oxendine asserts that "games among traditional American Indians ranged from the seemingly trivial activities primarily for the amusement of children to major sporting events of significance for persons of all ages."[2] Typically, there was a close linkage between the games and sports and the world of spiritual belief and magic. Lacrosse was quite popular with Native Americans long before European settlement in North America. It is perhaps the best-known Native American game because it is currently played in clubs, secondary schools, and universities throughout North America. In 1994 the Canadian Parliament recognized lacrosse as Canada's "national summer sport."[3]

The Colonists Restrict Physical Activities

During the two centuries following Columbus—the sixteenth and seventeenth centuries—Spain, France, and England explored and colonized most of North America. But by the late eighteenth century, Great Britain had triumphed over the other two countries and controlled the entire eastern half of what is now the United States and the eastern two-thirds of what is now Canada (except for two small fishing islands off the coast of Newfoundland, which remained under the control of France).

We are accustomed to thinking that the wide array of formalized participant and spectator sport that we enjoy has always existed. But, unimaginable as it seems, there were no formally organized participant or spectator sports during the colonial period in North America. In the first place, people had very little leisure time or opportunity to engage in games and sports. The harsh circumstances of wresting a living from the environment necessitated arduous daily work. Colonists had to devote most of their efforts to basic survival tasks. A second factor restricting sports involvement was the church. Religion was the most powerful social institution in the North American colonies. Puritanism was prominent in the New England colonies, and other Christian religions dominated social life in the middle and southern colonies.[4] (The subject of sport and religion is examined more fully in chapter 8.)

All of these religious groups placed severe restrictions on play and games, with the Puritans being the most extreme. They directed attacks at almost every form of amusement: dancing for its carnality, boxing for its violence, maypoles for their paganism, and play and games in general because they were often performed on the Sabbath. Moreover, religious sanctions were closely bound to the dislike for playful activities of any kind. Honest labor was the greatest service to God, and a moral duty. Any form of play or amusement signaled time-wasting and idleness and was therefore defined as wicked. That everyone has a calling to work hard was a first premise of Puritanism. Followers believed that it was not leisure and amusement but diligent work that symbolized the glorification of God.

Laws prohibiting a form of social behavior and the actual social customs and actions of a people rarely coincide. In the case of the colonies, religious and legal strictures failed to eliminate the urge to play among the early North Americans. Although frequently done in defiance of local laws, sports such as horse racing, shooting matches, cockfights, footraces, and wrestling matches were engaged in throughout the colonies to break the monotony of life. Moreover, farm festivals in which barn raisings, quilting bees, and cornhusking activities took place also provided occasional amusement and entertainment. The most popular sports of the gentry were cockfighting, hunting, dancing, and—most popular of all—horse racing. Other recreational activities were popular for those who frequented the taverns. The tavern was a social center, primarily for drinking but also for all manner of popular pastimes, such as cards, billiards, bowling, and rifle and pistol target shooting.[5]

As colonial settlement moved west into the hinterland in the eighteenth century, religious restrictions against sport became less and less effective. Men and women in the backcountry enjoyed a variety of competitive events when they met at barbecues and camp meetings. They gambled on these contests, especially horse races, cockfights, and bearbaiting. The physical activities that marked these infrequent social gatherings were typically rough and brutal. Two popular activities were fistfights, which ended when one man could not continue, and wrestling, in which eye gouging and bone-breaking holds were permitted.[6] Horse racing was the universal sport on the frontier, for every owner of a horse was confident of its prowess and eager to match it against others. Both men and women were skillful riders. The other constant companion of the frontiersman—the rifle—engendered a pride in marksmanship, and shooting matches were a common form of competition.[7]

THE EARLY NINETEENTH CENTURY: TAKEOFF OF INDUSTRIALIZATION AND TECHNOLOGY

Play, games, and sports in every society are always closely tied to the political, economic, religious, and social institutions as well as the cultural traditions and customs. The major catalyst for the transformation of North American sport was a series of inventions in England in the late eighteenth century that completely changed the means by which goods were produced. These inventions made possible technological advances that ushered in two of the most important developments in human history—the industrial revolution and the technological revolution.

The major characteristic and social consequence of the industrial revolution was the factory system. The initial impact was seen in the textile industry. The spinning of thread and the weaving of cloth had traditionally been done at home on spinning wheels and handlooms, but new methods for performing these tasks enabled them to be done in factories by power-driven machinery.

Other industries emerged. The successful smelting of iron with the aid of anthracite coal was perfected around 1830. By 1850 improved methods of making steel had been developed. Steel production was the backbone of industrial development because the machinery for factories was primarily made from steel. Artisans and craftspersons were transformed into an industrial workforce. As Figure 2.1 shows, the proportion of the workers engaged in agriculture steadily decreased—from approximately 90 percent in 1800, to 40 percent in 1900, to less than 10 percent in 2000. Industry needed a plentiful supply of labor located near plants and factories, so population shifts from rural to urban areas began to change population characteristics and needs. Urbanization created a need for new forms of recreational activities, and industrialization gradually supplied the standard of living and the leisure time necessary to support broad-based forms of recreation and organized sport.[8]

Building a Framework for Modern Sport

In the first few decades of the nineteenth century, North Americans enjoyed essentially the same recreations and sports as they had during the colonial period. Those turbulent, expansive years

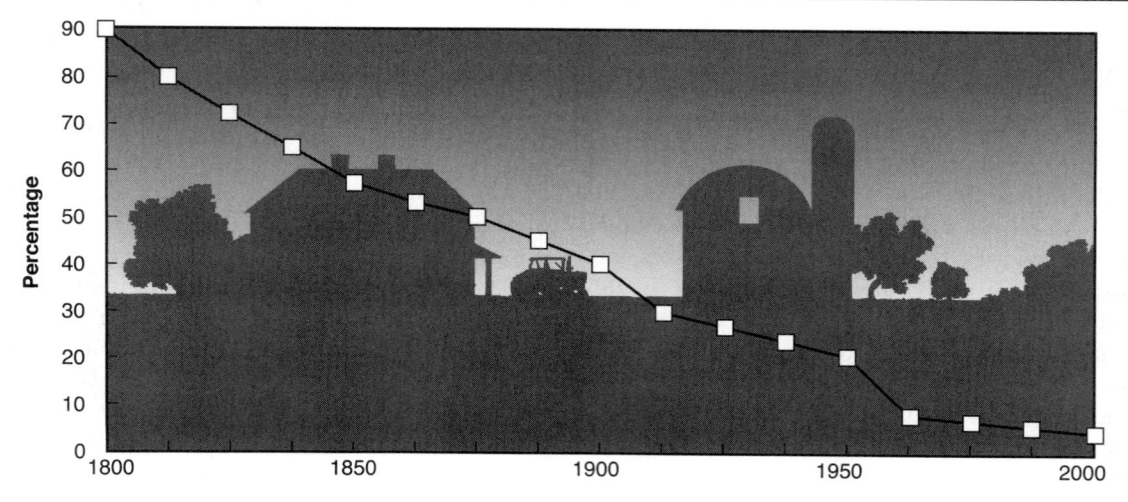

Figure 2.1 Percentage of Labor Force in Agriculture

Sources: U.S. Bureau of the Census, *Historical Statistics of the United States, Colonial Times to 1970,* Bicentennial ed., Parts I and II. Washington, D.C., 1975 and U.S. Bureau of the Census, *Statistical Abstract of the United States: 2001.* (Washington, D.C., 2001.)

brought important changes, and an increasing number of early-nineteenth-century North Americans found time for recreational activities, including sport.

As conditions changed from a rural to an urban population and from home trades and individualized occupations to large-scale industrial production, a growing interest emerged in spectator sports. Rowing, prizefighting, footracing (the runners were called pedestrians), and similar activities were especially popular, but the sport that excited the most interest was horse racing, with its traditions going back to early colonial days.

In May of 1823 a horse race between Eclipse and Sir Henry attracted one of the largest crowds ever to witness a nineteenth-century sporting event in North America. A crowd estimated at seventy-five thousand overwhelmed the racecourse. Thoroughbred racing was not the only popular form of horse racing. It has been claimed that harness racing was the first modern sport in North America.[9]

Horse racing was much in demand in Canada. In *Canada's Sporting Heroes*, S. F. Wise and Douglas Fisher described its popularity in Quebec. "Almost from the outset of British rule in 1763 French Canadians took readily to . . . horse racing. . . . By 1829, interest was so great that special boat trips were laid on to bring Montrealers to Quebec for the races, and the Montreal newspaper *La Minerve* held its presses in order to bring its readers the latest results. . . . By the 1850s . . . regular race meetings were held in forty towns and villages throughout the province."[10]

Native American, French, and British traditions contributed to Canada's other sporting interests in the early nineteenth century. Native American games of lacrosse, snowshoeing, and canoe activities were adopted by the settlers. British and French settlers also took enthusiastically to physical activities that could be played in the cold northern climate, so sleighing, ice-skating, and curling were popular in the winter, while hunting, fishing, fox hunting, and horse racing were popular in the short Canadian summers.[11]

The transformation from occasional and informal sport to highly organized commercial spectator sport began for both the United States and Canada during the period before the American Civil War. Thus, the framework of modern sport was established during the first half of the nineteenth century, setting the stage for the remarkable expansion of mass popular sport and professional sport that followed in the last half of the nineteenth century.

The Technological Revolution and Sport

One of the most significant forces transforming sport from informal village festivals to highly organized sports was the technological revolution. Beginning in the early nineteenth century, technological advances made possible the large-scale manufacturing that is characteristic of industrialization. Through technology, which is the practical application of science to industry, many kinds of machines, labor-saving devices, and scientific processes were invented or perfected. Of course, the technological revolution was only one of the determining factors in the rise of modern sport, but ignoring its influence would result in an incomplete understanding of contemporary sport forms.

New Forms of Transportation Broaden Sport Opportunities

One area of technological innovation that had an enormous impact on the rise of sport was transportation. Travel of any kind was difficult and slow in the pre-1800 period. A distance that today takes hours to travel took more than the same number of days in those times. Modes of transportation were limited to foot, horse, and boat. Roads, when they existed, were primitive, dangerous, and often blocked by almost impassable rivers.

The first notable technological breakthrough in transportation came in the early nineteenth century with the development of the steam engine. This invention and its use on boats made it possible to fully develop river traffic. The first successful steamboat in North America, the *Clermont,* was built by Robert Fulton, and in 1807 it chugged 150 miles up the Hudson River from New York to

Albany in about thirty hours. In time, steamboats stimulated the building of canals and the enlarging of rivers, thus opening new areas that had previously been isolated and cut off from commerce and trade.

The steamboat did not solve all the transportation problems; river travel was of no help to people who did not happen to live near large rivers. Furthermore, it was not a particularly fast mode of transportation because the large steamers sometimes had to thread their way carefully through very narrow or shallow water. A new form of transportation began to compete with river transportation about the time that canal building reached its peak. This was the railroad. A fourteen-mile stretch of the Baltimore and Ohio Railroad was opened in 1830. Railroad construction expanded rapidly—mostly short lines connecting principal cities—and by 1840 nearly three thousand miles of track were in use in the United States.

It was the steamboats and railroads of the first half of the nineteenth century that had the first significant impact on sport. As one of the first products of the age of steam, steamboats served as carriers of thoroughbred horses to such horse racing centers as Vicksburg, Natchez, and New Orleans, all located along the Mississippi River. Crowds attending horse races or prizefights were frequently conveyed to the site of the events via steamboats. The riverboats on the Mississippi and the St. Lawrence also served as carriers of racing or prizefight news up and down the river valleys.

More important to the development of organized sport was the railroad. In the years preceding the American Civil War, the widespread interest in thoroughbred and harness races was in great part nurtured by railroad expansion, as horses and crowds were transported from one locality to another. Similarly, participants and spectators for prizefights and footraces were commonly carried to the sites of competition by rail. Scheduling the fights where they would not be disrupted by the authorities frequently became necessary because prizefighting was outlawed in many cities. This meant that spectators often had to use the railroad to get to the site of the bout.

New Forms of Communication Enable Dissemination of Sport Information

As important as transportation was to the rise of North American sport, the new forms of communications over the past century and a half have been equally significant. The invention and development of the telegraph was the most important advance in communication during the first half of the nineteenth century. Samuel F. B. Morse perfected an electrical instrument by which combinations of dots and dashes could be transmitted along a wire, and the first telegraph line was built between Baltimore and Washington, D.C., in 1844. Soon telegraph lines stretched between all the principal cities, and by 1860 some fifty thousand miles of line existed east of the Rockies. Meanwhile, Western Union was extending its lines to the Pacific coast, putting the Pony Express out of business a little more than a year after it was founded.

From its invention in 1844, the telegraph rapidly assumed a significant role in the dissemination of sport news because newspapers and periodicals installed telegraphic apparatuses in their offices. Only two years after its invention, the *New York Herald* and the *New York Tribune* had telegraphic equipment. By 1850, horse races, prizefights, and yachting events were being reported over the wires.

Simultaneously with the development of the telegraph, a revolution in the dissemination of news occurred with improvements in printing presses and in other processes of newspaper and journal production. The telegraph and the improved press opened the gates to a rising tide of sports journalism, but the journalistic exploitation of sports did not actually take off until the last two decades of the nineteenth century.

While advances in electrical forms of communication were instrumental in the rise of sport, other communications media supplemented and extended sport publicity. In the early years of the nineteenth century, sports were more directly aided by magazine and book publishers than they were by newspapers. However, the rise of sports journalism was closely tied to new inventions in printing processes as well as to the telegraph network that spanned the continent in the mid-1800s. As early as the 1830s, several of the largest newspapers were giving extensive coverage to prizefights, footraces, horse races, and other sports. What was perhaps the most notable newspaper concerned with sports in the United States—*The Spirit of the Times*—appeared in 1831 and survived until 1901.[12]

THE LATTER NINETEENTH CENTURY: THE BEGINNINGS OF MODERN SPORT

Entering the second half of the nineteenth century, North America was predominantly a land of small farms, small towns, and small business enterprises. But over the next fifty years economic, technological, and social changes transformed the lives of Americans and Canadians. Both countries evolved from rural and traditional societies into modern, industrialized nations. By the beginning of the twentieth century, citizens and immigrants in both nations were laboring in factories owned by large corporations.

Before 1850, U.S. industry had been largely concentrated in New England and the mid-Atlantic states, but by 1900 industrialization and manufacturing spread out to all parts of the country. As the factory system took root, however, a capitalistic class began to emerge, and a new form of business ownership, the corporation, became the dominant form of organization. By the 1890s, corporations produced nearly three-fourths of the total value of manufactured products in the United States. The large corporations developed mass-production methods and mass sales, the bases of big business, because of the huge amounts of money they controlled.

Meanwhile, the conflict over control of the vast Canadian expanse of the continent, which had remained unresolved throughout the sixteenth, seventeenth, and eighteenth centuries, was finally settled with the Confederation of Canadian Provinces in 1867. Canada became the first federal union in the British Empire, and the second half of the nineteenth century was a period of consolidation of provinces within the union. Canadian industrialization was proceeding along a similar trajectory.

At the time of confederation, manufacturing in Canada was still primarily of a local handicraft nature requiring very little capital, and much of the trade was based on farming, fishing, and timber products. Beginning in the 1870s, Canadian manufacturing received an impetus from the new industrial revolution of steel and railroads, and advanced technology and corporate organization fostered a unified market and a factory system of specialized mass production to serve it.

As technology increased the means of industrial production in North America, more and more people gave up farming and came to the cities to work in the factories and offices. They were joined by a seemingly endless stream of immigrants who sought a better life in North America. Factories multiplied, and towns and cities grew rapidly. The first U.S. census, completed in 1790, recorded a population of nearly 4 million, about 6 percent of whom were classified as urban; by 1900 the population had risen to 76 million, with some 40 percent living in urban areas.

Figure 2.2 shows the general pattern of growth in urban population. From 1860 to 1910 the number of U.S. cities with populations over 100,000 increased from 9 to 50. The 1871 census of Canada reported that there were only 20 communities with more than 5,000 residents; by 1901 there were 62, and 24 of those had a population of more than 10,000.

Urbanization and the Rise of Modern Sport Forms

Urban influences in both the United States and Canada made their marks by the mid-nineteenth century, and the increasing concentration of city populations and the monotonous and wearisome repetition of industrial work created a demand for more recreational outlets. Urbanization created favorable conditions for commercialized spectator sports, while industrialization gradually provided the leisure time and standard of living so crucial

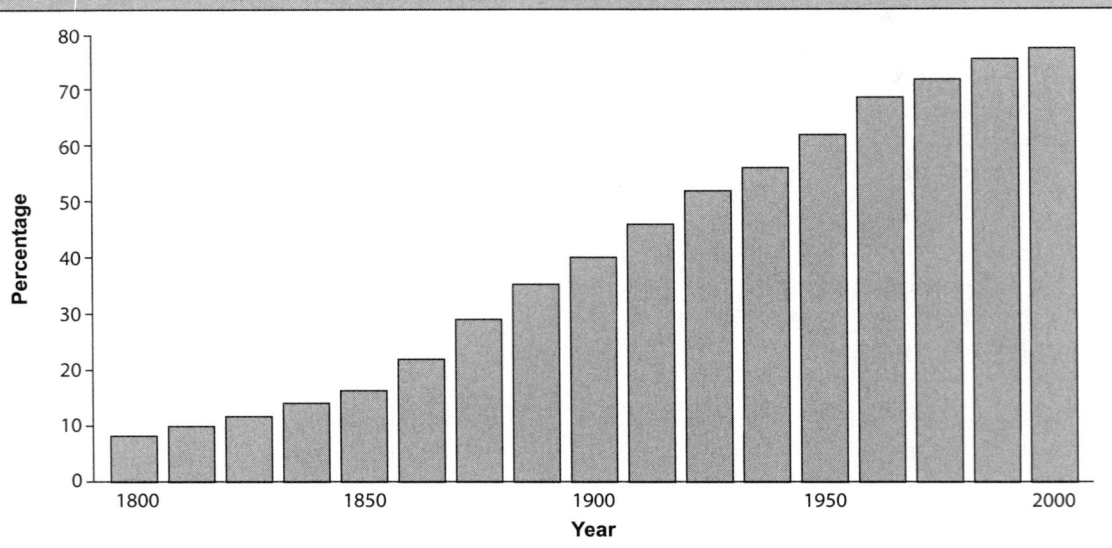

Figure 2.2 Percentage of U.S. Population in Urban Areas

Sources: U.S. Bureau of the Census, *Historical Statistics of the United States, Colonial Times to 1970,* Bicentennial ed., Parts I and II. Washington, D.C., 1975; and U.S. Bureau of the Census, *Statistical Abstract of the United States: 2001.* (Washington, D.C., 2001.)

to the growth and development of all forms of recreation.

Towns and cities were natural centers for organizing sports. The popular sport of horse racing centered in New York, Boston, Charleston, Louisville, and New Orleans, and the first organized baseball clubs were founded in such communities as New York, Boston, Chicago, St. Louis, and Toronto. Yachting and rowing regattas, footraces, billiard matches, and even the main agricultural fairs were held in or near the larger cities.

Diffusion of Sport from the Upper to the Lower Classes

Nothing in the recreational and sport scene was more startling than the sudden spread of sporting activities from the wealthy class into the upper-middle, the middle, and even the working class. Millionaires pursued horse racing, yachting, lawn tennis, and golf. Working women and young ladies of the middle class turned to rowing and cycling, and the working class played pool, fished, hunted, backed their favorite boxers, and gradually tried their hands at the sports of the affluent classes. The long winters in Canada provided plenty of opportunity for both affluent and working people to participate in skiing, ice-skating, curling, and other cold weather sports.

During the second half of the nineteenth century, people tried to adapt to the new urban-industrial society by forming subcommunities based on status. One type of status community was the athletic club, formed by younger, wealthy men who shared a common interest in sports. The private clubs were a major stimulus to the growth of yachting, baseball, lawn tennis, golf, track and field, and country clubs. Essentially the same pattern of upper-class promotion of organized sport through social elite sports clubs existed in Canada. Thus, members of the social elite in both the United States and Canada deserve much credit for early sporting promotion and patronage.[13]

New sports introduced by the wealthy were often adopted by the working class. Baseball is a classic example of this pattern. From an informal children's game played throughout the eighteenth century, baseball developed codified rules in the 1840s, and groups of upper-social-class men orga-

Portraits of the original Cincinnati Red Stockings team members, ca. 1869. This was the first professional baseball team in the United States. The Red Stockings played games from coast to coast and chalked up a fabulous winning streak of sixty-five games without a defeat. (Library of Congress)

nized clubs, taking care to keep out lower-social-class persons. The first of these baseball clubs, the Knickerbockers of New York, was primarily a social club with a distinctly upper-class flavor; it was similar to the country clubs of the 1920s and 1930s before they became popular with the middle class. A baseball game for members of the Knickerbockers was a genteel amateur recreational pursuit, with an emphasis on polite social interactions rather than an all-out quest for victory.[14]

In the United States the Civil War wiped out this upper-class patronage of the game, and a broad base of popularity existed in 1869 when the first professional baseball team, the Cincinnati Red Stockings, was formed. This was followed in 1876 by the organization of the first major league, and baseball became firmly entrenched as the American national pastime by the end of the century.

Baseball attracted the interest of Canadians as well, and by 1859, Torontonians had begun playing the game, spurring an expansion of play to other cities. In the mid-1880s, clubs from Toronto, Hamilton, London, and Guelph had formed Canada's first professional baseball league. By the end of the nineteenth century, baseball play in Canada was solidly embedded in Canada's sporting culture. At about the same time, ice hockey, which was to become Canada's national pastime, was making its own early history. It seems to have been played in its earliest unorganized form in the mid-1850s, but the first public showing of the game took place in 1875. Ice hockey quickly became a favorite sport of Canadians.[15]

As cities grew, an element of the population that journalists referred to as "rabble" and "rowdies" stimulated interest in organized sports. Wherever sports events were held, this group could be found gambling on the outcome and generally raising the emotional atmosphere of the event by wildly cheering their favorites and booing or attempting to disconcert those whom they had bet against. Although sports organizers publicly condemned the actions of this unruly element, they secretly spurred them on because this group often helped ensure the financial success of sporting events.

The Role of African Americans in Sports

Despite living under conditions of slavery in the southern colonies, African Americans engaged in a wide variety of games and sport (see Box 2.1, *Thinking about Sport*). Some were even trained by their plantation owners as boxers and jockeys. Emancipation in the mid-1860s gave African Americans hopes of participating in sports along with whites, but the post–Civil War years saw a mass social disenfranchisement of African Americans. Although a few African Americans played on professional baseball teams in the second half of

> **Box 2.1 Thinking about Sport Horse Racing and the Great African American Jockeys**
>
> Baseball was not America's first "national pastime." Before the Civil War it was horse racing that captured the sporting interest and enthusiasm of Americans, and 150 years before Jackie Robinson, African American jockeys competed alongside whites in horse races throughout the country. In spite of the slavery system, racehorse owners and trainers recognized the skill, courage, and determination of African American jockeys and didn't hesitate to use them to win horse races. But most people are unaware of the excellence of the African American jockeys during this period because, as one historian said, "The black jockeys were ridden out of history."
>
> The status and deeds of black jockeys remained high in the years immediately following the Civil War. Indeed, in the first Kentucky Derby, held in 1875, the jockey on the winning horse was an African American, Oliver Lewis. More impressive, of the fifteen jockeys in that race, thirteen were African Americans. This was not unusual: until Jim Crows laws set in, segregating blacks and whites near the end of the nineteenth century, African Americans dominated the sport of horse racing—the way they do NBA basketball today. Most horse racing historians regard Isaac Murphy as the greatest jockey in the decade and a half between 1884 and 1900. Murphy won his first Kentucky Derby in 1884. He became the first jockey to win two consecutive Kentucky Derbys, and Murphy's record of riding three Kentucky Derby winners was not equaled until 1930.
>
> By the end of the 1890s, African American jockeys were the subjects of virulent racism sweeping the country in the form of a landmark U.S. Supreme Court decision, *Plessy v. Ferguson,* which upheld the constitutionality of racial segregation in public venues, under the doctrine of "separate but equal." In his book *The Great Black Jockeys,* historian Edward Hotaling laments, "By the early 1900s, the great black jockeys had gone from winning the Kentucky Derby to not being able to get a mount. . . . For all intents and purposes they had vanished from the American racetrack." And their records of excellence, courage, and achievements have all but vanished from sports history and the admiration that should be theirs.
>
> *Source*: Edward Hotaling, *The Great Black Jockeys* (Rocklin, Calif.: Forum, 1999).

the nineteenth century, many white players refused to play with the black players, so team owners stopped hiring blacks. As other professional and amateur sports developed during the latter nineteenth century, African Americans were barred from participation in most of them. This issue is discussed in more detail in chapter 13.

The Role of Immigrants

Between 1870 and 1900, some twelve million persons immigrated to the United States. At the beginning of this period, one-third of all U.S. industrial workers were immigrants; by 1900, more than half were foreign-born. Immigrants also contributed to the rise of sport in a variety of ways. First, many immigrants settled in the cities and became a part of that urban population who sought excitement through sport and recreation as an antidote to the typically dull and monotonous jobs they held. Second, because a great many of these mid-nineteenth-century immigrants did not possess the strict religious attitudes toward play and sport of the fundamental Protestant sects, they freely enjoyed and participated in sports of all kinds. Third, the immigrants brought their games and sports with them to North America. Cricket, horse racing, and rowing were widely popular with the British immigrants. The Germans brought their love for lawn bowling and gymnastics. German *turnverein* (gymnastic clubs) were opened wherever Germans settled; by the time of the Civil War, there were approximately 150 American *turnverein* with some ten thousand members.[16]

In Canada in 1859, German migrants had organized a *turnverein* in what is now Kitchener, and a Turner Association with forty members was active in Toronto in 1861. The Scots pioneered in introducing track-and-field sports to North America with their annual Caledonian games. In a definitive study, sport historian Gerald Redmond quite convincingly showed that the "emigrant Scots" were a dominant force in the development of Canadian sport in the nineteenth century.[17]

The Irish seemed to have a particular affinity for the prize ring, and some of the most famous nineteenth-century boxers in North America were immigrants from Ireland. Two Irish American boxing champions, John L. Sullivan and James J. Corbett, were among the most popular sports heroes of the century.

Muscular Christianity and Intellectuals

The grasp of religion on the early-nineteenth-century mind was so strong and conservative that sport could penetrate only the periphery of social life. But reaction to the Puritan belief that pleasure was the companion of sin emerged when liberal and humanitarian reform became a major concern. One aspect of the social reform movement was the effort to improve the physical health of the population. The crusaders noted that a great deal of human misery was the result of poor health, and they believed that people would be happier and more productive if they engaged in sport to promote physical fitness and enhance leisure.

Leaders in what became known as the "Muscular Christianity Movement" were highly respected persons, willing to risk their positions and reputations on behalf of exercise and sport. The Beecher families, famous for their Christian reform positions, were among the active crusaders for exercise and sport. Catharine Beecher wrote a book in 1832 entitled *Course of Calisthenics for Young Ladies*, but her most influential book was *A Manual of Physiology and Calisthenics for Schools and Families*, published in 1856. This book not only advocated physical exercise for girls as well as for boys but also promoted the introduction of physical education into American schools.[18]

Throughout the second half of the nineteenth century, physical activity continued to be supported by many respected persons. Noted author Oliver Wendell Holmes was "convinced that greater participation in sport would improve everything in American life from sermons of the clergy to the physical well-being of individuals." Equally vigorous in his advocacy of sport was the renowned Ralph Waldo Emerson, and his status in the intellectual community served to increase the impact of his support. The combined attention of the clergy, social reformers, and intellectuals to the need for physical fitness and wholesome leisure had a favorable effect upon public attitudes because sport suddenly became important to many people, especially the young, who had previously shunned it.[19]

The Cult of Manliness and Sport

The social and occupational changes of the nineteenth century brought a concern about the impact of modernization on male roles and behavior. Modernization was altering institutions of socialization and drastically changing traditional male roles and responsibilities. Writers, educators, and influential national leaders expressed fear that men were losing "masculine" traits—like toughness, courage, ruggedness, and hardiness—to effeminacy. There were even worries about the future of the nation, if men lost their masculine traits. Various organizations—the Boy Scouts, YMCA, and athletic clubs—arose to promote a broadly based devotion to manly ideals to toughen up boys for life's challenges.

Within this perceived threat to masculinity, sport, with its demands for individual competition and physical challenge, was advocated as an important preparation for manhood. In towns and cities throughout the United States and Canada, sport rose as a counterforce to what many men saw as the "feminization" of North American civilization. Sport was seen as a sanctuary from the world of female gentility; it catered to men who felt a need to demonstrate their manhood. Sport participation became a prominent source for male identity and a primary basis for gender division.

The cult of manliness became pervasive in the upper and middle classes and rapidly trickled down to working-class social life. One sport historian asserted: "The frequency with which writers began to assert that sport could serve as a means of promoting manliness was in direct response to both the impact of modernization on urban society and the role of modernization in redefining the masculine role and creating a new middle-class view of proper sexual behavior."[20]

Defining sport as an inculcator of manliness had the obvious effect of discouraging women from all but a few sports—and women could participate in those only in moderation. Indeed, women who wished to participate in competitive sports and remain "feminine" faced almost certain social isolation and censure.

Of course, it was not just the cult of manliness that discouraged female involvement in sport. Responsibility for domestic labor and child rearing weighed heavily against women's engaging in sport as either participants or spectators. Victorian attitudes and religious moral codes also militated against sport for women. In spite of these obstacles, many upper-class and college women were ardent participants in croquet, archery, lawn tennis, rowing, and bicycling.[21]

The Beginnings of Intercollegiate Athletics

The first North American colleges were established during the colonial period. They were small, widely scattered, and religiously oriented, and in what became the United States, most were less than thirty years old when the colonial period ended. During the latter half of the nineteenth century, colleges became the source for one of the most popular forms of sport: intercollegiate athletics.

Intercollegiate athletics began in the United States in 1852 with a rowing match between Harvard and Yale. But it was not until the 1870s and 1880s that intercollegiate sports became an established part of higher education and contributed to the enthusiasm for athletic and sporting diversions. Football became an extremely popular spectator sport during this era. Football was a sport for the affluent classes rather than for the masses because it largely reflected the interests of the college students and alumni; the pigskin game, nevertheless, did develop into a national sport by 1900.

After students organized teams, collegiate sports revolutionized campus life, serving as a major source of physical activity for many students and a significant source of entertainment for other students, alumni, and the general public. In the United States, intercollegiate athletics gradually became more than merely a demonstration of physical skills between rival institutions. The students, alumni, and public began to regard victory as the measure of a college's prestige. Campus and commercial editors increased their coverage, and sports events became featured items in newspapers and magazines. As a result, this increased coverage focused attention on winning and made contest results appear to be an index of an institution's merit.[22]

Thus, a belief emerged throughout American colleges that winning teams favorably advertised the school, attracted prospective students, enhanced alumni contributions, and—in the case of state-supported universities—increased appropriations from the state legislature. The notion that successful teams brought renown to the college (and to its president) must surely have been in the mind of University of Chicago president William Rainey Harper when he hired Yale All-American Amos Alonzo Stagg in 1890. He asked Stagg to "develop teams which we can send around the country and knock out all the other colleges. We will give them," wrote Harper, "a palace car and a vacation too."[23]

Technological Innovation and Sport: Transportation

Technological innovation continued to serve as a dominant force for shaping social change throughout the last half of the nineteenth century. Transportation was one of the most prominent areas of its influence, as the growth of the railroad industry continued throughout the latter nineteenth century. Shortly after the Civil War, the Central Pacific and Union Pacific workers laid the final rail to complete the first transcontinental line in North America. Other lines followed in the last three decades of the 1800s. Similar events were occurring in Canada. In November 1885 the transcontinental Canadian Pacific Railway was completed.

The railroad played an instrumental role in staging the first intercollegiate athletic event, a rowing race between Harvard and Yale. According to sport historian Ronald A. Smith, "the offer by a railroad superintendent to transport and house the crews of the two most prestigious colleges [Harvard and Yale] at a vacation spot over a hundred miles from the Cambridge campus and nearly twice that distance from New Haven was the beginning of . . . college sport in America."²⁴ The offer was accepted, and the Boston, Concord, and Montreal Railroad transported the participants and fans to New Hampshire's Lake Winnipesaukee for the event.

In 1869 the first intercollegiate football game between Rutgers and Princeton was attended by students riding a train pulled by a "jerky little engine [that] . . . steamed out of Princeton, New Jersey, on the memorable morning of November 6, 1869."²⁵ The historic McGill-Harvard football match of 1870, which pitted a Canadian university against a North American university, would not have been played without the convenience of railway transportation. Throughout the final decades of the nineteenth century, intercollegiate athletic teams depended upon the railroad to transport teams and supporters to football, baseball, and rowing events as well as to other collegiate athletic contests.

The fledgling professional baseball clubs made use of the rapidly expanding railroad network in the 1870s, and the organization of the National League in 1876 became possible primarily because of the continued development of connecting lines. As Major League Baseball developed, the formation of teams followed the network of rail lines, a pattern that remained basically undisturbed until the late 1950s, when teams began to travel by air.

Many other sporting pursuits were fostered by railroad development after 1865. Widespread interest in thoroughbred and trotting racing was in large part sustained by the expansion of the railway

The start of the race, Kelowna, British Columbia, 1909. Thoroughbred and trotting racing were among the sporting pursuits fostered by railroad development. (G. H. E. Hudson/Library and Archives Canada)

system. Interregional races became possible, and horses and spectators were carried from all over the country to track races. Realizing the financial advantage of encouraging horse racing, many railroads transported horses at reduced prices. The rail lines capitalized on public interest in prizefighting, too, despite its illegality, and frequently scheduled excursion trains for important bouts. America's first heavyweight champion, John L. Sullivan, acquired his popularity largely through his train tours to various parts of the country.

The role played by the railroads in the promotion of sport in the United States was being duplicated in Canada. According to one sport historian, the Canadian Pacific Railway Company had a special interest in the Montreal Baseball Club and offered full exemption for team managers, and special half-fare rates to teams willing to play the club. Rowing was also popularized by the railroads as there were many generous concessions granted to rowing enthusiasts.[26]

Technological Innovation and Sport: Communication

The Atlantic cable, successfully laid in 1866 by Cyrus Field, did for intercontinental news what the telegraph had done for national communication. The cable reduced the time necessary to send a message between Europe and North America from ten days (by steamship) to a moment or so. This advance in communication was a boon to sports enthusiasts, for it overcame the frustration of having to wait two or three weeks to get sports results from England and Europe. In 1869, when the Harvard crew traveled to England to row against Oxford on the Thames, enormous national interest centered on the match. Along the sidewalks in New York, the Harvard-Oxford race was the main topic of conversation. The results of the race were "flashed through the Atlantic cable as to reach New York about a quarter past one, while the news reached the Pacific Coast about nine o'clock, enabling many of the San Franciscans to discuss the subject at their breakfast tables, and swallow the defeat with their coffee."[27] All this was the culmination of a campaign in transatlantic news coverage that had begun months earlier and served as the first real test of the Atlantic cable. The combination of telegraph and Atlantic cable aroused great interest in international sport.

The major communications breakthrough in the latter part of the nineteenth century was the telephone, which was first exhibited at the Centennial Exposition in Philadelphia in 1876. There, Alexander Graham Bell demonstrated that an electrical instrument could transmit the human voice. Although at first most people thought of the telephone as a plaything, business and industrial leaders saw its possibilities for maintaining communication with their far-flung interests.

Newspapers were one of the first businesses to make extensive use of telephone service, and the sports departments founded by many of the newspapers in the last two decades of the nineteenth century depended on the telephone to obtain the results of sports events. By the end of the century, the telephone was an indispensable part of sports journalism.

The expansion of sports journalism in the latter three decades of the nineteenth century related not only to the universal use of telegraphy by publishers, which made possible instantaneous reporting of sports events, but also to the realization by editors of the popular interest in sports. Indeed, sport emerged as such a standard topic of conversation that newspapers and magazines extended their coverage of it in the 1880s and 1890s. At the same time, the number of newspapers in the United States increased sixfold between 1870 and 1900 (from 387 to 2,326), and their combined circulation rose from 3.5 million to 15 million. Publishers and editors recognized the growing interest in sport and began to cater to it to win large circulations. New York papers such as the *Herald*, the *Sun*, and the *World* devoted enough attention to sports that a new form of reporter, the sports journalist, emerged. It remained, however, for William Randolph Hearst to develop the first sports section for his paper, the *New York Journal*.[28]

The publication of various kinds of books about sports increased in the mid-nineteenth century, too. Athletic almanacs and dime novels extolling the exploits of athletes and sportsmen grew in popularity. Two books by Thomas Hughes, *Tom Brown at Rugby* and *Tom Brown at Oxford*, were responsible for a rising desire for sports fiction. In 1896 Gilbert Patten began pouring out a story a week of the heroic achievements of a fictional athlete by the name of Frank Merriwell to meet the demand for boys' sports stories. At the height of Frank Merriwell's popularity, circulation reached an estimated two hundred thousand copies per week. Before he was through, Patten had produced 208 titles, which sold an estimated 25 million copies.[29]

Other Technological Breakthroughs and Sport

Other technological advances had a marked, though perhaps less obvious, influence on the transformation of sport. Improvements in photography developed rapidly in the years following the Civil War, as cumbersome equipment was replaced by the more mobile Eastman Kodak, which also produced clearer pictures. Indeed, sport played an important role in the early development and popularization of the camera. In 1872 Eadweard Muybridge, with the prodding of Leland Stanford, made the first successful attempt to record the illusion of motion by photography. He was interested in discovering whether a trotting horse left the ground entirely at some point in its gait (it does). By setting up a battery of cameras that went off sequentially, he successfully photographed the movements of the horse. The clarity of these pictures led Muybridge to realize that his technique could be extended to analyze the movements of all kinds of species. He subsequently photographed a host of walking and running animals. His monumental eleven-volume study, titled *Animal Locomotion* (1887), included thousands of pictures of horses, birds, and even human athletes. Other experimenters gradually perfected the techniques that gave birth to the true motion picture.

We have already described how advances in the use of electricity led to important developments in communication, but the use of electricity to produce light had an equally significant impact on sport. When Thomas A. Edison invented the incandescent bulb in 1879, he inaugurated a new era in the social life of North Americans. With the invention of the lightbulb, sports events for the first time could be held at night. Within a few years, electric lighting and more comfortable accommodations helped lure athletes and spectators into school and college gymnasiums and into public arenas and stadiums. Prizefights, walking contests, horse shows, wrestling matches, basketball games, ice hockey games, curling matches, and other sports began to be held indoors in lighted facilities. Madison Square Garden in New York City had electric lights by the mid-1880s (the current Madison Square Garden is its fourth incarnation), where they were used for a variety of sports events. Much of the appeal of indoor sporting events was directly attributed to the transformation that electric lighting made in the nightlife of the cities.

One final example of the part an invention has played in sport is the vulcanization of rubber by Charles Goodyear in the 1830s. It eventually influenced equipment and apparel in every sport. Elastic and resilient rubber balls changed the nature of every sport in which they were used; equipment made with rubber altered many tactics and techniques. The pneumatic tire developed in the 1880s revolutionized cycling and harness racing in the following decade, and it played a vital role in the rise and spectacular appeal of auto racing.

Equipment to Play Modern Sports

Modern sports are dependent upon inexpensive and dependable equipment for their popularity. Mass production of goods and corporate organization developed in sport just as they did in other industries. Although the manufacturing and merchandising of sporting goods were still in the pioneer stage of development in the late nineteenth century, much of the growing popularity of sport and outdoor recreation was due to the standardized manufacture of bicycles, billiard tables, baseball equipment, sporting rifles, fishing rods, and numerous other items.

The first major sporting goods corporation was formed in 1876 by Albert G. Spalding, a former pitcher for the Boston and Chicago baseb clubs. Beginning with baseball equipment, he branched out into various other sports. By the end of the century, A. G. Spalding and Brothers Company had a virtual monopoly in athletic goods. Department stores, led by Macy's of New York City, began carrying sporting goods on a large scale around the early 1880s. Sears, Roebuck devoted eighty pages of its 1895 catalog to sporting equipment.[30]

With the rising popularity of numerous sports in the twentieth century, with advances in technology making possible the introduction of newer and better equipment, and finally with improved manufacturing and distribution methods, the sporting goods industry has become a multimillion-dollar-a-year industry. Several large corporations control a major portion of the business, but with the proliferation of sports, many small companies as well produce a variety of sports equipment.

Social Philosophy and Modern Sport

The profound changes in interpersonal relations created by the technological and industrial revolutions required that moral and social justifications be sought for the role of capitalism, the economic system in which trade and industry are controlled by private owners for profit. Leading capitalists found their chief justification in two related ideas, the gospel of wealth and social Darwinism. According to the gospel of wealth, money and success are the just rewards for hard work, thrift, and sobriety; the mass of humanity remains poor because of their own laziness and natural inferiority. Government, according to this notion, should merely preserve order and protect property; it should leave control over the economy to the natural aristocracy, who have won and hold their leadership in the competitive struggle of the marketplace.

Social Darwinism, probably the most important social philosophy in the latter third of the nineteenth century, supplied a biological explanation for the gospel of wealth. As an integrated philosophy, it was largely the product of the fertile mind of the British sociologist Herbert Spencer.

Spencer was profoundly impressed by Charles Darwin's findings in the field of biology, and he constructed his system on Darwin's principles of the survival of the fittest. Darwin had reported that in the animal world an ongoing, fierce struggle for survival destroys the weak, rewards the strong, and produces evolutionary change. Struggle, destruction, and the survival of the fit, Spencer argued, were essential to progress in human societies as well. The weak threaten the road to progress and deserve to perish. The strong survive because they are superior.

Spencer's theories had great popularity and markedly penetrated North American thought. American historian Richard Hofstadter claimed that "American society saw its own image in the tooth-and-claw version of natural selection and . . . its dominant groups were therefore able to dramatize this vision of competition as a thing good in itself." This was the case for several reasons but perhaps chiefly because social Darwinism was made to order to suit the needs of the ruling business interests. It justified the "success ethic" in the name of progress; it justified economic warfare, poverty, exploitation, and suffering as the survival of the fittest.[31]

The chief North American expositor of social Darwinism was William Graham Sumner, who in 1875 at Yale taught one of the first sociology courses in North America. Sumner based his sociology on the notion that human life encounters formidable obstacles and threats to its survival. There is a fundamental struggle to "win" (a favorite word of Sumner's) under the conditions imposed by nature. In this process humans always compete with others. Sumner argued, "Every man who stands on the earth's surface excludes every one else from so much of it as he covers; everyone who eats a loaf of bread appropriates to himself for the time being the exclusive use and enjoyment of so many square feet of the earth's surface as were required to raise the wheat."[32]

Sumner linked competition to the emergence of virtues, such as those of perseverance and hard work, that were presumed to be answers to the struggle against nature. Winning was seen as the just reward of the superior individual; losing was viewed as the overt manifestation of inferiority.

A number of observers have noted that the rise of highly organized sport coincided with the emergent popularity of social Darwinism and that the high degree of emphasis on winning games demonstrated in North American sport is an orientation congruent with this social philosophy. American football players often remark that success in their sport is like "the law of the jungle" or "the survival of the fittest." Similar opinions about ice hockey are sometimes expressed by Canadian hockey players.

THE TWENTIETH CENTURY: THE MODERN WORLD

The United States witnessed a population explosion in the twentieth century; it began the century with 76 million and ended it with a population in excess of 281 million and an urban population of around 85 percent of the total. Canada experienced a similar trend. In 1900 its population was approximately 4 million, with less than 20 percent living in towns and cities; in 2000 Canada had a population of more than 30 million, more than 77 percent of whom were urbanites.

The concentration of large groups of people in towns that soon would become thriving cities made it possible for sport to be transformed from informal and spontaneous events to organized, highly competitive activities. In other words, industrialization and urbanization were major contributors to the rise of sport, greatly enhanced, of course, by the revolutionary transformations in communication, transportation, and other technological advances.

The Maturing of Modern Sport

The final three decades of the nineteenth century saw the rising tide of sports begin to take a place in the lives of North Americans, but it was in the first thirty years of the twentieth century that the athletic spirit became a prominent part of the social life of large numbers of people. Between 1900 and World War II, sport became the most pervasive popular cultural practice in North America.

Urban areas fostered sport through better transportation facilities, a growing affluent class, a higher standard of living, more discretionary funds for purchasing sporting equipment, and the ease with which leagues and teams could be organized. The wealthy were no longer the only people with the leisure and the means to enjoy recreational pursuits. Working-class persons gradually won shorter working hours and higher wages, enabling them to spend larger sums of money on entertainment, one form of which was sport. Thus, sport discarded its aristocratic trappings and rapidly emerged as a popular form of entertainment and recreation. James Bryce, a British observer of American life in 1905, wrote, "[Sport] occupies the minds not only of the youth at the universities, but also of their parents and of the general public. Baseball matches and football matches excite an interest greater than any other public events except the Presidential election, and that comes only once in four years. . . . The American love of excitement and love of competition has seized upon these games."[33]

No single event heralded the beginning of what has been designated as the era of modern sports, but the Roaring Twenties acted as a bridge connecting the old pastimes to contemporary sport. Sport seemed to be the most engrossing of all social interests in the 1920s; it became a bandwagon around which students and alumni, business and transportation interests, advertising and amusement industries, cartoonists and artists, novelists and sports columnists rallied. Indeed, the 1920s are still looked upon by some sport historians as sport's golden age. Some of America's most famous athletes rose to prominence during those years: Babe Ruth, the "Sultan of Swat"; Knute Rockne and the "Four Horsemen of Notre Dame"; Jack Dempsey, heavyweight boxing champion; Bill Tilden and Helen Willis Moody in tennis; and Bobby Jones and Glenna Collett in golf. In Canada, Howie Morenz, James Ball, Ethel Catherwood, Bobbie Rosenfeld, and Myrtle Cook thrilled the masses with their sports achievements. These are only a few of the coaches and athletes who contributed to the growing popularity of sports.[34]

From the 1920s onward, sport became a pervasive part of North American life, penetrating into every level of the educational systems and into the programs of social agencies and private clubs. This became especially true of the business world; sport affected such areas of the economic system as finance, fashion, mass media, transportation, communication, advertising, the sporting goods industry, and a variety of marginal enterprises that profit from sport.

North American business and labor organizations contributed to the rise of sport through organized industrial recreation programs for millions of workers. During the nineteenth century most industrial leaders showed little interest in the health and welfare of their employees; by the beginning of the twentieth century, however, voices inside and outside industry were pleading for consideration of the worker as a human being, with special focus on the worker's physical and mental health. Business and labor leaders began to realize that perhaps opportunities for diversion, whether in intellectual or recreational directions, might enhance employee health and morale and increase productivity.

The idea of providing company-sponsored recreation as a phase of business management caught on, and programs of all sorts came into existence. By the 1950s some twenty thousand companies were sponsoring various forms of industrial recreation with more than 20 million employees participating. From the 1930s to the 1950s, the best amateur teams in basketball, baseball, and softball were company-sponsored teams. The National Industrial Basketball League included the Phillips 66ers, the Goodyear Wingfoots, and the Peoria Caterpillars. Championships in the National Baseball Congress and Amateur Softball Association were dominated by company-backed teams.

Industrial employee recreation programs have grown enormously over the past fifty years, and today industry spends more on sports equipment than all schools and colleges combined. Industry is probably the biggest user of bowling lanes, table tennis tables, and volleyball, basketball, and softball equipment in the country. Three-fourths of all firms employing more than one thousand people have some form of exercise and athletic program, and more than ten thousand companies now have full- or part-time recreation managers.[35]

Labor unions, originally formed to acquire better pay and working conditions for industrial employees, gradually broadened their interests to include the health and mental welfare of their members. The United Automobile Workers (UAW) established a recreation department in 1937 based on a strong policy of organized recreation for all ages. Other unions have programs that include almost everything in the way of leisure-time activities: Among these are team and individual sports, social functions, dancing instruction, handicrafts, orchestras, and hobby clubs. Some unions have acquired large tracts of land on which they have built elaborate recreational facilities for the use of their members.

Two major developments in sport characterize the past thirty years: the colossal expansion of amateur and professional sports and the boom in participant sports. Amateur sports, from youth to intercollegiate athletic programs, have multiplied at a bewildering pace. Baseball and football in the United States and ice hockey in Canada were once about the only sports sponsored for youngsters, but now there are organized youth programs in more than twenty-five sports—from swimming to motor bicycling—and it is possible for children as young as six years of age to win a national championship. High school and collegiate programs, which used to be limited to three or four sports for males, have now been expanded to include twelve to fifteen sports for both males and females.

Professional sports teams are corporate organizations that function similarly in many respects to corporations of any other kind, albeit with certain tax and monopolistic advantages not given to other businesses. In 1922 the United States Supreme Court exempted baseball from antitrust legislation. Since that time owners of baseball and other professional sports teams have used that decision, and more recent ones, to define their special legal and economic position. (The legal and economic position of corporate sport is more fully discussed in chapter 10.)

The first professional baseball team was player-owned and player-controlled, but major league teams were organized into business corporations in the latter part of the nineteenth century and continue as business enterprises made up of separate corporations under a cartel. The National Football League (NFL) began in 1920, and industry had a hand in its development. The Acme Packing Company in Green Bay, Wisconsin, sponsored a local team, which was fittingly called the Packers; and in Decatur, Illinois, the A. E. Staley Manufacturing Company started the team that became known as the Chicago Bears. From these humble beginnings, professional football is now a $1 billion–a–year business, and each franchise in the NFL is worth more than $550 million.[36]

Ice hockey is another team sport that first became popular in the late 1800s, but its early development took place in Canada rather than the United States. The first professional hockey team was formed in 1903, and the first professional league was established a year later. In 1917 the National Hockey League (NHL) was organized. The first rules for basketball were written up in 1891 by James Naismith, a physical training instructor at what is now Springfield College. Basketball quickly became popular in secondary schools and colleges, especially women's colleges; by the 1920s, teams of paid players were touring North America. But it was not until after World War II that a stable professional league was established; in 1949 the National Basketball Association organized.

Men's college football team of the late nineteenth century. Football had become the most popular college sport by the beginning of the twentieth century. (Photo courtesy of the University of Northern Colorado)

Over the course of the twentieth century more than a dozen professional team sport leagues were formed, but the Big Four—consisting of baseball, ice hockey, football, and basketball—retained an enduring dominance in spectator attendance and general popularity. Table 2.1 outlines the origins of the Big Four.

On-site spectator sports in the United States have gross paid admissions of an estimated $1 billion per year. Some 45 million admissions are paid to horse racing, 76 million to professional baseball, 21 million to professional basketball, 22 million to the NHL, 43 million to college football, 39 million to college (men's and women's) basketball, and about 21 million to professional football.[37] These figures are, of course, dwarfed by the number of people who watch televised sports events.

Participant sports, the second main development of the past generation, have been products of increased leisure and income. The construction of facilities and the manufacture of equipment inexpensive enough for the large mass of working-class people have had an important impact on participant sports. Moreover, a concerned awareness of the increasingly sedentary lifestyle of persons in all socioeconomic strata and of the rise in diseases related to this lifestyle has stimulated mass participation in sport and exercise. Perhaps most remarkable is the running boom that has swept North America, where there are more than twenty-five million runners/joggers. Virtually every major city has a marathon that draws thousands of runners (e.g., Boston, New York, Toronto, Atlanta, Montreal). Even allowing for a considerable margin of error in the participation reports, sport involves an enormous number of people. Increased leisure and income are undoubtedly the main causes for the extraordinary development of participant sport in the current generation. See Table 2.2 for an example of Canadian sport participation.

Twentieth-Century Technology and Sport: Transportation

By the beginning of the twentieth century, almost every realm of American and Canadian social life,

Table 2.1 Origins of the Four Major Professional Team Sport Leagues

League	Founding Year
Baseball	
National League	1876
American League	1901
Hockey	
National Hockey League	1917
Football	
National Football League	1920
Basketball	
National Basketball Association	1949

Table 2.2 Canadian Sport Involvement

	Both Sexes Thousands	%	Males Thousands	%	Females Thousands	%
Population aged 15 years	24,260	—	11,937	—	12,323	—
Regularly participate in sport	8,309	34.2	5,140	43.1	3,169	25.7
Through a club organization	4,599	19.0	2,338	19.6	2,261	18.3
Competition and/or tournament	2,992	12.3	2,076	17.4	916	7.4
Involved in amateur sport as a:						
Coach	1,729	7.1	962	8.1	766	6.2
Referee	937	3.9	537	4.5	399	3.2
Administrator/helper	1,706	7.0	842	7.1	864	7.0
Spectator at amateur sport Competitions	7,651	31.5	4,040	33.8	3,611	29.3

Source: Statistics Canada, *General Social Survey,* last modified 2004, http://www40.statcan.ca/l01/cst01/arts18.htm?sdi=sport%20involvement.

including sport, shared in the powerful impact of the railroad, and in the years up to World War II this influence continued unabated. Perhaps one of the most significant contributions of the railroad to sport in the twentieth century was the opening of new areas for recreation. For example, the initial stimulus for the popularization of skiing was the "snow train." The first snow train left Boston's North Station in 1931. Four years later such trains were leaving New York's Grand Central Station; on board were thousands of ski enthusiasts intent on spending a weekend on the slopes of New England. Railroads were responsible for the development and promotion of a number of North America's most popular winter sports resorts in the western states and provinces.

As important as the railroads were to improving transportation and stimulating industrialization, their impact on the social life and transportation habits of North Americans was minuscule in comparison to that of the development of the automobile. This invention, and subsequently that of the airplane, were two modes of transportation that completely revolutionized travel and numerous other aspects of life. In addition to their contributions to transportation, the automobile and airplane created very new industries involving billions of dollars in capital and employing millions of workers. They stimulated the construction of millions of miles of highways, and they spawned many industries and occupations related to auto and aircraft production and use. The growth of metropolitan areas, especially suburban and satellite towns outside large cities, was also stimulated by the automobile.

Inventors in Europe and the United States had successfully developed an internal combustion engine powered by gasoline by the last decade of the nineteenth century. Initially, however, there was little general interest in the converted bicycles that were the first automobiles because they were used either for racing or as a toy for the rich. Then a young man by the name of Henry Ford saw the potential of the automobile as a means of popular transportation. Realizing that he would have to gain financial backing for the auto through racing, he built a huge-engined racing car, the "999," and hired a professional bicycle rider by the name of Barney Oldfield to race it. After the "999" easily won against its challengers, Ford wrote: "The '999' did what it was intended to do: It advertised the fact that I could build a fast motorcar. A week after the race I formed the Ford Motor Company."[38]

Racing was the first and foremost attraction of the automobile in the days when its usefulness for any other purpose was questioned. In 1895 H. H. Kohlsaat, publisher of the *Chicago Times-Herald*, sponsored the first automobile race in America; automobile races had already become the fad in Europe. Early automobile manufacturers recognized the commercial value of races and used them as a major marketing technique to win public interest. This particular aspect of automobile racing continues. Throughout the twentieth century, automobile racing grew in popularity and included a bewildering array of forms—midget autos, stock cars, hot rods, drag racing, and so forth.

The automobile contributed to the rise of sport in many ways beyond racing. For countless millions, the auto progressively opened up broader horizons of spectator and participant sport. It provided an easy means of transportation from city to city and from the country to the town or city. Thus, large stadiums and other sports facilities could be conveniently reached by large groups of people. Also, for the first time, golf courses, ski resorts, tennis courts, bathing beaches, and areas for such field sports as fishing, camping, and hunting were within practical reach of large masses of the population. All this would have been impossible without the transportation provided by the automobile.

In 1903 Orville and Wilbur Wright successfully flew an airplane, but it was not until World War I that airplanes were used on any large scale, first for scouting enemy movements and later in actual combat. During the 1920–1940 era, aircraft design was improved, airports were constructed, and regular passenger, mail, and express lines were established. World War II provided for further development, and soon airplanes became the prominent mode of long-distance public transportation. Airplanes have in effect shrunk the continent by reducing traveling time.

Airplane races have never held the spectator appeal of auto racing, but air transportation has had a significant impact on sport in other ways. Until about the mid-1950s, most professional and collegiate athletic teams traveled by rail. With improvements in all phases of air transportation, the airplane became the common carrier of teams. The expansion of professional sports franchises from the East and Midwest into the West and the South and the increased number of pro sports teams could only have been achieved with air travel. Interregional collegiate football and basketball games were rare until air travel made it possible to take long trips in a short period of time. Interregional contests then became a part of the weekly schedule of collegiate sports.

The Technological Revolution and Sport: Communication

Mass communication is the glue that serves to integrate people into their society, and it has helped shape and mold the development and popularity of sport. In 1896 an Italian scientist, Marchese Guglielmo Marconi, patented the wireless technology and showed the possibility of telegraphy without the use of wires. Within a few years, wireless telegraphy was carrying messages to all parts of the world. One of the first stories to be covered by wireless was a sports event. Marconi was hired by the Associated Press in 1899 to report on the international yacht race involving Sir Thomas Lipton's *Shamrock* and America's *Columbia*. Thus, wireless communication took its place along with the telegraph and the telephone in intensifying public interest in sport and stimulating the rise of sport.

The next important step in electrical communication was the radio, which until 1920 was mainly a toy for amateur scientists. However, in 1920 a radio station in Pittsburgh began broadcasting, and a new communication medium and industry was under way. Radio's dominance in broadcasting was during the 1930s and 1940s; it was not until the early 1950s that television began to overshadow radio in providing information and home entertainment.

Radio broadcasting of sports events actually preceded the beginning of public broadcasting. On 20 August 1920 the radio station of the *Detroit News* went on the air to announce the results of the World Series baseball games. This was before the first public radio station in Pittsburgh made its initial broadcast in November of that year. Also in 1920, the first college football game was broadcast from a station in Texas.[39]

Radio came of age in the hectic 1920s, and while music and news broadcasts were the standard programs, sports events were rapidly absorbed into the entertainment schedule. One early historian of radio noted: "Sportscasting had no crawling or creeping stages. Broadcasters, with no experience or training and some with little knowledge of sports, just jumped right in and started doing a job." Radio and sports were natural partners. Broadcasting, for the first time, brought all the drama of the diamond, ringside, gridiron, and racetrack into homes from coast to coast.

Persons under the age of forty have grown up watching television; it is just taken for granted. Indeed, TV is on for an average of eight hours per day in U.S. and Canadian homes. Some media experts claim that college students today spend more waking hours watching television than doing any other single thing.

Although television had been experimentally developed prior to World War II, it was not until the late 1940s that technology and marketing combined to produce models for home use. The major television boom occurred in the early 1950s; the number of sets rose from ten million to sixty million in a single decade, and the number of broadcasting stations rose from one hundred to seven hundred. By 1957 television was a fixture of most households and no longer a novelty. As television sets became available to the public and the broadcasting of programs expanded, it quickly became evident that televised sports events would be immensely popular, and television continually expanded its coverage of sports. More will be said about the television-sport nexus in chapter 11.

During the twentieth century the sports page became an indispensable part of every newspaper.

From a concentration on a few sports, such as baseball, college football, horse racing, and boxing, attention was gradually given to an enormously wide range of sports. Currently, many newspaper publishers believe that the sports section is the most important factor in a newspaper's circulation.

Along with the newspaper, magazines and books have done much to attract attention to sports in the past century and a half. Even before the American Civil War, a host of turf journals appeared; many periodicals were also devoted to field sports and outdoor life. Sports journals proliferated greatly in the late nineteenth century, so that almost every sport had at least one periodical devoted to it. This trend has continued, and a substantial portion of shelf space in newsstands is occupied by magazines about sports (more will be said about this in chapter 11).

In its early years the motion picture industry concentrated primarily on boxing. The first commercial motion picture was a six-round bout between Young Griffo and Battling Barnett in 1895. Motion pictures of boxing championships were one of the most popular forms of spectator sport in the first three decades of the twentieth century and served to stimulate the public appetite for organized sports. In recent years the videotape, computers, and compact discs (CDs) have become indispensable instruments—for coaches for scouting opponents and for reviewing the performances of their own athletes. Collegiate and professional coaches of some sports spend as much time electronically viewing as they spend on almost any other coaching task. Undoubtedly, the motion picture has contributed to the remarkable advances in the technical aspects of sport.

The impact of the still camera cannot be overlooked either. Beginning in the early years of the twentieth century, newspapers and magazines made extensive use of pictures to show the performance of athletes in the heat of competition or to illustrate the correct (or incorrect) method of performing a skill. The popularity of sports magazines, especially *Sports Illustrated*, is largely due to the superb photographs that are part of each issue. This has had the effect of further nurturing sports by keeping them in the public eye.

Other Technological Innovations and Sport

Although indoor sports were greatly stimulated by electric lighting, baseball, America's national pastime, did not discover the value of this invention until the 1930s. Social historians record 1930 as the year of the emergence of night baseball. The first such ventures took place in Des Moines and Wichita in the summer of 1930. Several minor leagues quickly adopted night baseball, but it was not until 1935 that Cincinnati played the first night major league game. Only in the 1940s did night baseball gain general acceptance in the major leagues; the first World Series night game was not played until 1975. The owner of the Chicago Cubs for many years, Phillip K. Wrigley, never accepted night baseball, and lights were not installed at Wrigley Field until the summer of 1988.

Sport in Education

As stated previously, intercollegiate sport began as a form of student recreation but rapidly grew in popularity among the general public. Indeed, during the past fifty years it has become a form of big business. The practice of using sport as the right arm of the public relations department of a college, which began in the late nineteenth century, continues to the present. This system of intercollegiate sport is unique to the United States, and it has been one of the most significant forces in the development of American organized sports. High school sports are modeled on this system, and many nonschool youth sports programs have been organized as feeder systems to the high school and college programs. Finally, the intercollegiate programs serve as a farm system for many of the professional sports. (Chapters 5 and 6 will discuss the topic of sport in education in depth.)

Until the 1970s, Canadian universities tended to model athletic programs after the British tradition, meaning that programs were primarily sponsored and administered by students, and little emphasis was given to their commercial exploitation. In recent years an "American model" in intercollegiate sports has been increasingly adopted, causing some observers to claim that this is another example of the homogenization of American and Canadian cultures.

SUMMARY

In this chapter we have reviewed the rise of sport in North America. Contemporary sports are grounded in political, economic, technological, and social conditions and events of the past. Sports today are possible only because of what has happened in the past, and sports of the future will depend on what happens in today's societies.

Despite overwhelming natural and social barriers that made involvement in games and sporting activities difficult for European colonists in North America, colonists still engaged in a wide variety of playful physical activities. But it was not until the beginning of the nineteenth century that conditions became favorable for organized sports to become a popular cultural practice for large numbers of citizens. Technological innovations and the accompanying industrial revolution were instrumental in stimulating a transformation in social conditions that gave rise to modern sport. Urbanization was also a significant factor, because the evolution of modern sports in North America became possible only with large urban populations scattered across the continent. During the nineteenth century, influential persons among the clergy and the intelligentsia, as well as social reformers, helped develop the attitudes, values, and beliefs that are the foundation of modern sport.

During the first half of the twentieth century, sport became a pervasive part of North American life, penetrating into every level of the educational systems and into the economic and cultural systems in the form of professional sports. The two major trends in sport that characterize the past thirty years are the enormous expansion of amateur and professional sports and the burst of growth in participant sports.

WEB RESOURCES

www.nassh.org
Official website of the North American Society for Sport History. This site lists sport history publications and sport history scholars. One of the links of this website is to the *Journal of Sport History*. This site seeks to support and promote the study of all aspects of sport history.

www.nascsports.org
The website of the Native American Sports Council. Its mission is to promote and preserve traditional Native American sports and games.

www.northnet.org/stlawrenceaauw/sports.htm
The website of Women's Sport History Resources. It is a clearinghouse for many women's sports websites that focus on the history of women in sport.

www.baseball-almanac.com/
The online baseball almanac. A reference source for individual and team records and statistics.

NOTES

1. David M. Thomas, ed., *Canada and the United States,* 2nd ed. (Peterborough, Ont.: Broadview Press, 2000).

2. Joseph B. Oxendine, *American Indian Sports Heritage* (Champaign, Ill.: Human Kinetics, 1988), 3; see also C. Richard King, ed., *Native Athletes in Sport and Society: A Reader* (Lincoln, Neb.: Bison Books, 2006).

3. Thomas Vennum, Jr., *American Indian Lacrosse: Little Brother of War* (Washington, D.C.: Smithsonian Institution Press, 1994); see also *Lacrosse* magazine—Mike Keegan, John Jiloty, and Matthew F. Sacco (contributors), *Lacrosse: North America's Game* (Carpenter Publishing, 2004).

4. Richard Middleton, *Colonial America: A History, 1565–1776* (New York: Blackwell Publishers, 2002); Alan Taylor, *American Colonies: The Settling of North America* (New York: Penguin, 2002).

5. Herbert Manchester and Paula Welch, *Four Centuries of Sport in America, 1490–1890* (Lanham, Md.: Derrydale Press, 2001); see also Elliott J. Gorn, *A Brief History of American Sport* (Urbana: University of Illinois Press, 2004).

6. Elliott J. Gorn, "'Gouge and Bite, Pull Hair and Scratch': The Social Significance of Fighting in the Southern Backcountry," in *Sport in America*, ed. David K. Wiggins (Champaign, Ill.: Human Kinetics, 1995), 35–50.

7. Nancy L. Struna, *People of Prowess: Sport, Leisure, and Labor in Early Anglo-America* (Urbana: University of Illinois Press, 1996). For an excellent discussion of Canadian sports and other physical activity during this period, see Don Morrow and Kevin B. Wamsley, *Sport in Canada: A History* (New York: Oxford University Press, 2005).

8. Paul Le Blanc, *A Short History of the U.S. Working Class: From Colonial Times to the Twenty-first Century* (Amherst, N.Y.: Humanity Books, 1999).

9. Edward L. Bowen, *The Jockey Club's Illustrated History of Thoroughbred Racing in America* (Boston: Little, Brown, 1994); Nancy L. Struna, "The North-South Races: American Thoroughbred Racing in Transition, 1823–1850," *Journal of Sport History* (Summer 1981): 28–57; Melvin L. Adelman, "The First Modern Sport in America: Harness Racing in New York City, 1825–1870," in *Sport in America*, ed. Wiggins, 5–32.

10. S. F. Wise and Douglas Fisher, *Canada's Sporting Heroes* (Don Mills, Ont.: General Publishing, 1974), 7.

11. Alan Metcalfe, *Canada Learns to Play: The Emergence of Organized Sport, 1807–1914* (Toronto: McClelland & Stewart, 1987).

12. W. D. Sloan and J. D. Startt, *The Media in America: A History*, 4th ed. (Northport, Ala.: Vision Press 1999).

13. Benjamin G. Rader, *American Sports: From the Age of Folk Games to the Age of Televised Sports*, 5th ed. (Upper Saddle River, N.J.: Prentice Hall, 2004), 67–83; Rader, *American Sports*, 85–95. In 1897 one of these clubs, the Boston Athletic Association, sponsored the first Boston Marathon, now one of the world's premier sports events.

14. George Vecsey, *Baseball: A History of America's Favorite Game* (New York: Modern Library, 2006).

15. William Humber, *Diamonds of the North: A Concise History of Baseball in Canada* (New York: Oxford University Press, 1995).

16. Robert K. Barney, "Forty-Eighters and the Rise of the Turnverein Movement in America," in *Ethnicity and Sport in North American History and Culture*, ed. George Eisen and David K. Wiggins (Westport, Conn.: Greenwood Press, 1994), 19–42; see also Annette R. Hofmann, "Lady *Turners* in the United States: German American Identity, Gender Concerns, and *Turner*ism," *Journal of Sport History* 27 (Fall 2000): 383–404.

17. Gerald Redmond, *The Sporting Scots of Nineteenth-Century Canada* (East Brunswick, N.J.: Fairleigh Dickinson University Press, 1982); see also Ann Donaldson, *The Scottish Highland Games in the United States* (Gretna, La.: Pelican, 1986).

18. Tony Ladd and James A. Mathisen, *Muscular Christianity: Evangelical Protestants and the Development of American Sport* (Grand Rapids, Mich.: Baker Books, 1999).

19. Harvey Green, *Fit for America: Health, Fitness, Sport, and American Society,* reprint ed. (Baltimore: Johns Hopkins University Press, 1988); J. C. Whorton, *Crusaders for Fitness: The History of American Health Reformers*, reprint ed. (Princeton: Princeton University Press, 1984).

20. Michael Kimmel, *Manhood in America: A Cultural History,* 2nd ed. (New York: Oxford University Press, 2005).

21. Patricia A. Vertinsky, *Eternally Wounded Woman: Women, Doctors, and Exercise in the Later Nineteenth Century* (Urbana: University of Illinois Press, 1994).

22. Ronald A. Smith, *Sports and Freedom: The Rise of Big-Time College Athletics* (New York: Oxford University Press, 1988); John S. Watterson, *College Football: History, Spectacle, Controversy* (Baltimore: Johns Hopkins University Press, 2000).

23. Amos Alonzo Stagg, quoting William Rainey Harper, in a letter to his family, 20 January 1891, quoted in Richard J. Storr, *Harper's University: The Beginnings* (Chicago: University of Chicago Press, 1966), 179.

24. Smith, *Sports and Freedom*, 27–28.

25. Parke H. Davis, *Football, the American Intercollegiate Game* (New York: Scribner's, 1911), 45.

26. Trevor Williams, "Cheap Rates, Special Trains and Canadian Sport in the 1850s," *Canadian Journal of History of Sport* 12 (December 1981): 84–93.

27. *Frank Leslie's Illustrated Newspaper* 29 (New York), 28 September 1869, p. 2.

28. Sloan and Startt, *The Media in America: A History.*

29. Rader, *American Sports,* 106; see also Don Morrow, Mary Keyes, Frank Cosentino, Ron Lappage, and Wayne Simpson, *A Concise History of Sport in Canada* (Toronto: Oxford University Press, 1989): 274–281.

30. George H. Sage, "The Sporting Goods Industry: From Struggling Entrepreneurs to National Businesses to Transnational Corporations," in *The Commercialization of Sport,* ed. Trevor Slack (New York: Routledge, 2004), 29–51.

31. Richard Hofstadter, *Social Darwinism in American Thought* (New York: G. Braziller Publisher, 1959), 201; see also Mike Hawkins, *Social Darwinism in European and American Thought, 1860–1945: Nature as Model and Nature as Threat* (New York: Cambridge University Press,

1997); Alexander Rosenberg, *Darwinism in Philosophy, Social Science, and Policy* (New York: Cambridge University Press, 2000).

32. Albert Galloway Keller, ed., *Essays of William Graham Sumner*, vol. 1 (New Haven, Conn.: Yale University Press, 1934), 386.

33. James Bryce, "America Revisited: The Changes of a Quarter-Century," *Outlook* 25 (March 1905): 738–739.

34. Mark Dyreson, "The Emergence of Consumer Culture and the Transformation of Physical Culture: American Sport in the 1920s," in *Sport in America*, ed. Wiggins, 207–223.

35. John R. Kelly and Rodney B. Warnick, *Recreation Trends and Markets: The 21st Century* (Champaign, Ill.: Sagamore Publishing, 1999); Mark S. Searle and Russell E. Brayley, *Leisure Services in Canada*, 2nd ed. (State College, Pa.: Venture, 2000).

36. Jerry Gorman and Kirk Calhoun, *The Name of the Game: The Business of Sports* (New York: Wiley, 2004); see also "Forbes Franchise Values," 8 January 2007, available at http://espn.go.com/sportsbusiness/s/forbes.html.

37. U.S. Bureau of the Census, *Statistical Abstract of the United States: 2007*, 126th ed. (Washington, D.C.: 2007), 765–766.

38. Henry Ford in collaboration with Samuel Crowther, *My Life and Work* (Garden City, N.Y.: Doubleday, 1922), 51.

39. Sloan and Startt, *The Media in America: A History*.

CHAPTER 3
Sport and Societal Values

New York Giants quarterback Eli Manning (10) and Madison Hedgecock celebrate after their team scored the winning fourth-quarter touchdown during the Super Bowl XLII football game against the New England Patriots at University of Phoenix Stadium, 3 February 2008 in Glendale, Arizona. (AP Photo/Elaine Thompson)

If sport is a microcosm of society, then the types of sports, the way in which sport is organized, who participates and who does not all offer clues about the nature of the society. The study of sport, like the study of any institution, should provide important indicators about (1) a society's values, (2) a society's social structure (social stratification and social organization), and (3) a society's problems.

This chapter examines the reciprocal relationship between sport and societal values. The relationship is interdependent because societal values affect the kinds of sports that are played, the way they are organized, the way they are played, and the motivations for participation in them. However, the converse is also true in that sport affects values. Sport, like all institutions, is conservative primarily because it reinforces certain values.

Our description is limited to American values, but these resemble, albeit somewhat imperfectly, the predominant values of Canadians as well. The factors that work to differentiate Canadian values from American values are, first, that Canada has a long history of having accepted English rule after the Americans rebelled against it; second, that Canadians have two dominant religions, the Anglican religious heritage from the British and the Catholic heritage from the French, while Americans are more pluralistic; and third, that Canada wants to be different from its neighbor to the south. Strong factors also work toward a congruence of values: (1) Many Canadians have received their higher education in the United States, (2) Canadians typically watch U.S.-made television and movies and read American newspapers and magazines, and (3) American corporations have a strong presence in Canada.[1]

THE AMERICAN VALUE SYSTEM

People are valuing creatures.[2] That is, human beings live in an affectively charged world where some things are preferred over others. Some objects, people, or ideas are considered wrong, bad, or immoral; others are believed correct, good, or moral. Some goals are deemed worthy; others are not.

Values are the bases for making decisions. Values are the culturally prescribed criteria by which individuals evaluate persons, behaviors, objects, and ideas as to their relative morality, desirability, merit, or correctness. The phrase *culturally prescribed* is an important qualifier in this definition because it implies that human beings are *socialized*—that is, taught the criteria by which to make such judgments. Children learn from their parents, peers, churches, schools, and the media what is right or wrong, moral or immoral, correct or incorrect.

Although individuals may have their own idiosyncratic criteria for evaluation, we will examine those values widely held in U.S. society. Several caveats should be mentioned at the outset, however. First, diversity in the United States precludes any universal holding of values. Some individuals and groups reject the dominant values, and members of certain ethnic and religious groups have very different values. Moreover, differences in emphasis of the dominant values exist because of region, social class, age, and size of community.

Second, the system of American values is not always consistent with behavior. For example, Americans have always valued hard work as the means to success, yet rich persons who may have inherited their wealth are highly esteemed in American society. Moreover, the value of equality of opportunity that Americans verbally embrace is inconsistent with the injustices suffered by people on the margins, most notably the poor and minority groups.

Third, the values themselves are not always consistent. How does one reconcile the coexistence of individualism with conformity or of competition with cooperation? To minimize the problem of inconsistencies, we will present only the most dominant of U.S. values in this section.[3]

Success

The highly valued individual in American society is the self-made person—the person who has achieved money and status through his or her own efforts in a highly competitive system. Our cultural heroes are persons like Warren Buffett, Bill

Gates, Oprah Winfrey, and Samuel Walton, each of whom rose from humble origins to the top of her or his profession.

Success can be achieved, of course, by outdoing all others, but to know the exact extent of an individual's success is often difficult. Hence, obvious economic success (income, personal wealth, and possessions) is the most commonly used measurement. Economic success, moreover, is often used to measure personal worth. As Robin M. Williams, Jr., has put it, "The comparatively striking feature of American culture is its tendency to identify standards of personal excellence with competitive occupational achievement."[4]

Competition

Competition is highly valued in U.S. society. It is not just competition, though; it is winning in competitive situations that is so highly valued. This winning is so highly valued that society heaps disproportionate rewards on these winners. Thus, we could be characterized as the "Winner-Take-All Society."[5] Most Americans believe it to be the one quality that has made the United States great because it motivates individuals and groups to be discontented with the status quo and with being second best. Motivated by the hope of being victorious in competition or by fear of failure, North Americans believe that the United States must not lose a war or the arms race, the Olympics, or the race to place humans on Mars. For the United States to have been the second nation to land its citizens on the moon would have been seen as a crushing defeat.

Competition pervades almost all aspects of American society. The work world, sports, organizations like the Cub Scouts, schools, and even courtship thrive on competition. The pervasiveness of competition in schools is seen in the selection process for athletic teams, cheerleading squads, debate teams, choruses, bands, and play casts. In each case, competition among classmates is the criterion for selection. Even the

Cub Scouts from Pack 143 watch model cars race in the Pinewood Derby in Great Falls, Montana, 11 March 2006. In a pinewood derby, model wood cars made by the scouts are raced down an inclined track. (AP Photo/*Great Falls Tribune,* Robin Loznak)

grading system is often based on the comparison of classmates with one another.

The Cub Scout program, because of its reliance on competition, is an all-American organization. In the first place, individual status in the den or pack is determined by the level one has achieved through the attainment of merit badges. Although all boys can theoretically attain all merit badges, the boys are pitted against one another to see who can obtain the most. Another example of how the Cub Scouts use competition is their annual event, the Pinewood Derby. Each boy in a Cub pack is given a small block of wood and four wheels, which he is then to shape into a racing car. The race is held at a pack meeting at which one boy eventually is the winner. The competition is rarely questioned, even though nearly all of the boys go home disappointed losers. Why is such a practice accepted, indeed publicized? The answer, simply, is that it is symbolic of the way things are done in virtually all aspects of American life.

An important consequence of this emphasis on the survival of the fittest is that some people take advantage of their competitors in order to compete successfully. This is done rather routinely in political campaigns with "dirty tricks," misleading advertising, and illegal contributions to win elections. In the business world, we find some people who use theft, fraud, interlocking directorates, and price fixing to get ahead dishonestly. Some examples of how this zeal to win has caused people to cheat:[6]

- About sixty major corporations have had to restate their earnings after overstating them to boost their stock value.
- The Internal Revenue Service has found consistently that three out of ten people cheat on their income taxes.
- Employees embezzle or pilfer an estimated $10 billion from their employers annually.

In the business world, theft, fraud, interlocking directorates, and price-fixing are techniques used by some individuals and corporations to get ahead. A related problem, the abuse of nature for profit (although not a form of cheating), deprives others of limited resources and degrades the general quality of life so that the profiteer can pursue economic success. The environmental crisis is caused by individuals, corporations, and communities who find pollution solutions too expensive. Thus, in looking out for themselves, they ignore the short- and long-range effects on social and biological life. In other words, competition, although a constant spur for individuals and groups to succeed, is also the source of some illegal activities and social problems in the United States.

The Valued Means to Achieve

There are three related, highly valued ways to succeed in American society. The first is through hard work. Americans, from the early Puritans to the present day, have elevated persons who are industrious and denigrated those who are not. Most Americans, therefore, assume that poor people deserve to be poor because they are allegedly unwilling to work as hard as persons in the middle and upper classes. This explanation places the blame on the victim rather than on a social system that systematically thwarts efforts by the poor. Their hopelessness, brought on by a lack of education, by one's skin color or gender, or by a lack of experience, is interpreted as their fault and not as a function of the economic system.[7] This typical interpretation, moreover, is buttressed by the success of some athletes who were raised in poor circumstances, such as Venus and Serena Williams. They are presented as dramatic evidence that a meteoric rise in fame and fortune is possible through the blending of hard work and talent. One could argue that these persons succeed in the sports world because sport has become relatively immune to the racism present in the larger society. One could also argue, however, that these persons succeed not because of the openness of the system but because they managed somehow to overcome its roadblocks.

The two remaining valued means to success are continual striving and deferred gratification. *Continual striving* has meaning for both the successful and the not-so-successful. For the former, it means that a person should never be content with what she or he has; there will always be more land to own, more money to make, or more books to write. For the latter, continual striving means a never-give-up attitude, a belief that economic success is always possible, if not for oneself, at least for one's children.

Deferred gratification refers to the willingness to deny immediate pleasure for the sake of later rewards. The hallmark of the successful person in the United States has such a willingness, whether to stay in school or to work at two jobs or to go to night school. One observer has asserted, for example, that the difference between the poor and the nonpoor in this society is whether they are future- or present-time oriented.[8]

Superficially, this assessment appears accurate, but we argue that the lack of a future-time orientation among the poor is not a subcultural trait but basically a consequence of their hopeless situation due to structural constraints. Moreover, there is a question whether this value still prevails among the children of the nonpoor.

Progress

Societies differ in their emphasis on the past, on the present, and on the future. American society, while giving some attention to each time dimension, stresses the future. Americans neither make the past sacred nor remain content with the present. They place a central value on progress—on a brighter tomorrow, a better job, a bigger home, a move to the suburbs, a college education for their children, and self-improvement.

Americans are not satisfied with the status quo; they want growth (bigger buildings, faster planes, bigger airports, more business moving into the community, bigger profits, and new world records). Many want to change and conquer nature (dam rivers, clear forests, rechannel rivers, seed clouds, spray parks and residential areas with insecticides, and replace grass with artificial turf), although the ecological crises are leading more and more to question this value.

Although the belief in progress implies that change is good, some things are not to be changed, for they have a sacred quality: the political system, the economic system, American values, and the nation-state. Thus, Americans, even while valuing technological change, do not favor fundamental changes in the system.

Materialism

An American belief is that "hard work pays off." The payoff is success not only in one's profession but also in economic standing, in income, and in the acquisition and consumption of goods and services that go beyond adequate nutrition, medical care, shelter, and transportation. The superfluous things that we accumulate or strive to accumulate, such as country club memberships, jewelry, stylish clothes, lavish houses in prestige neighborhoods, boats, second homes, swimming pools, and season tickets to the games of our favorite teams, are symbols of success in the competitive struggle. However, these have more than symbolic value; they are elements of what North Americans consider the "good life" and, therefore, a right.

The American emphasis on materialism is reflected in the motives of college students. Recent surveys of first-year college students find that around seven out of ten say a major reason for attending college is "to be able to make more money."[9] This materialism is also seen indirectly in the most commonly chosen major—business.[10]

The emphasis on having things has long been a facet of U.S. society. This country has always been a land of opportunity and abundance. Although many persons are blocked from full participation in this abundance, the goal for most persons is to accumulate those things that bring status and that provide for a better way of life by saving labor or enhancing pleasure in their leisure time.

External Conformity

Societies cannot tolerate total freedom by individuals. Without a minimum of cooperation and of conformity to laws and customs, there is anarchy. To avoid disorder and lawlessness, society socializes individuals into acceptable beliefs and practices. For their part, individuals actually seek to be socialized. We seek the approval of our colleagues and therefore try to be successful by some shared standards of achievement or of conformity. Conformity, then, is a characteristic of all societies. The degree of conformity required, however, varies greatly from society to society.

Analytically, we can separate conformity in American society into two levels. At one level are the official expectations of behavior by the community, the state, and the nation: the customs and the laws individuals are expected to obey. Deviations from these expectations are punished by fines, imprisonment, gossip, or other negative *sanctions*. The threat of these sanctions is usually enough to ensure conformity. More than this, however, we are socialized to desire conformity.

At another more personal level, individuals tend to conform to the expectations of groups with which they closely identify: families, peers, ethnic groups, religious groups, and work groups. Thus, within the context of the society-wide expectations for behavior, there is great diversity: Suburbanites conform to other suburbanites, as do ghetto residents, teenagers, the jet set, union members, and businesspersons with their peers. David Riesman has characterized Americans as being *other-directed*.[11] By this he meant that they are oversensitive to the opinions of others. In a sense, Americans continually have their antennas out, picking up signals from those important to them. Another observer, William H. Whyte, pointed to this same phenomenon in the organizational context of social life. Whyte argued that the bureaucratic trend in American society forces many persons to conform. Rules must be followed, boats must not be rocked, if individuals are to get ahead in the bureaucracy.[12]

Bureaucratic organization is authoritarian and hierarchical. It is also rational. That is, it is based entirely on certain understood and accepted rules efficiently designed to serve the organization's goals. The interests of the organization are paramount in the development of these rules, and the formal aspects of a bureaucracy manifest these interests and rules.

The influence of bureaucracy is a source of norms regulating a large number of activities both within and beyond large-scale organization boundaries. So powerful and so pervasive are the organizations that employ bureaucratic methods that the value orientations engendered by this form of organization have attained the status of core values for American society. They so permeate the fabric of every social institution that the socialization process is largely devoted to conditioning youth to this orientation.

SOCIETAL VALUES AND SPORT

We have pointed out repeatedly that sport mirrors a society's basic structure and values. The relationship between American values and the forms of sport that prevail is the theme of this section.

Many reasons exist for the tremendous popularity of sport in the United States. The conditions of mass society constitute an important set of factors. Individuals living in an urban and bureaucratic society tend to feel alienated; in effect, they have feelings of isolation, powerlessness, self-estrangement, and meaninglessness. These persons need to identify with others in a cause that will give meaning to their existence and an escape from an otherwise humdrum world. Sports teams, each pursuing victories, representing factories, schools, neighborhoods, cities, or nations, provide an important source of identification for individuals in American society who otherwise do not feel connected with others. They provide entertainment, diversion, and great expectations.

Another reason for the popularity of sport in the United States is that the masses have been influenced by sports publicists and the media. Television, newspapers, and magazines have generated interest in sports by creating heroes and by continually bombarding the citizenry with statistics, human-interest stories, and coverage of the sporting events themselves.

A third factor that partially explains the sports mania in the United States is the increased leisure time available to most Americans. This, coupled with the relatively high standard of living that many Americans enjoy, provides much of the basis for the rise in attendance figures at sports events and the rise in sport activity by Americans.

An important underlying factor, and one emphasized in this section, is the close relationship between American sport and American values. In learning the culture (through the socialization process), most Americans have internalized values that predispose them to be interested in the outcome of competitive situations; and competition is the sine qua non of sport.

Competition and Success in Sport

As in the larger society, there is a tremendous emphasis in American sport on competitive success. Winning is glorified by all who participate. The following epigrams by various coaches exemplify this emphasis on winning:

In our society, in my profession, there is only one measure of success, and that is winning. Not just any game, not just the big game, but the last one.
—John Madden (former head coach of the Oakland Raiders)

Defeat is worse than death because you have to live with defeat.
—Bill Musselman (former head basketball coach at the University of Minnesota)

There are only two things in this league, winning and misery.
—Pat Riley (coach of the Miami Heat)

Our expectations are to play for and win the national championship every year. . . . Second, third, fourth, and fifth don't do you any good in this business.
—Dennis Erickson (when head football coach at the University of Miami)

Americans want winners, whether winning is in school or in business or in politics or in sport. In sport, we demand winners. Coaches are fired if they are not successful; teams are booed if they play for ties. Inevitably, coaches faced with the option of taking a tie or gambling on winning (with a high probability of losing) will go for the win with the comment, "We didn't come down here to tie." The thirty-one teams in the National Football League that do not win the Super Bowl in a given year are losers. Not even the members of the runner-up team consider themselves successful: They did not win the only game that really counts.

Coaches do all they can to socialize their athletes with the value of winning. They reinforce winners with praise, honor, and status. The primary goal of sports competition is to succeed (to win). Thus, coaches do all they can to instill in their athletes the character traits that they believe will bring team success (e.g., loyalty, enthusiasm, initiative, self-control, confidence, poise, hard work, and ambition). Negatively, they ridicule losers or quitters. As an example of a technique used to instill in athletes the desire to excel, one coach of a pony league football team (fourth, fifth, and sixth graders) in Lawrence, Kansas, had his young boys yell "I'm a girl!" before they could let their legs touch the ground during a leg-lift exercise. This fear of humiliation kept many boys doing the exercise beyond their normal endurance and, the coach probably assumed, increased their potential for winning.

Another coaching technique to instill in their athletes the goal of winning has been to place slogans on the dressing room walls to exhort players to value certain behaviors. Commonly, such slogans espouse the competitive spirit:

A quitter never wins, a winner never quits.
When the going gets tough, the tough get going.
It's not the size of the dog in the fight, but the size of the fight in the dog.
Never be willing to be second best.
The greatest aim in life is to succeed.
Win by as many points as possible.[13]

The demand for winners is found at all levels of sport. Even among youngsters, winning is everything, as evidenced by the pressures commonly found in adult-sponsored children's sports such as baseball, football, soccer, and swimming. Another example of the emphasis on winning among youngsters can be seen in the contests sponsored by some business corporations. Gatorade Company sponsors a "Punt, Pass, and Kick" contest for youngsters eight through thirteen; Phillips

A girls' soccer team celebrates a victory. The emphasis on winning is found at all levels of sport, as evidenced by the pressures commonly found in adult-sponsored children's sports. (iStockphoto)

Petroleum sponsors a similar "Pitch, Hit, and Throw" contest for baseball skills. In each case, winners are selected at the local level and proceed through the various state and regional tournaments until a winner is found for each age category. In one year, there were 1,112,702 entrants in the Punt, Pass, and Kick contest and only six winners. Why would an organization sponsor an event that produced six winners and 1,112,696 losers? Perhaps, the answer lies in that this, too, is a microcosm of the larger society.

The Soap Box Derby, sponsored by several major corporations, is another sport activity for youngsters. Here again, the ultimate winner is the one person who survives the tests from among the tens of thousands who initially enter the competition. This is clearly a situation of survival of the fittest. Unfortunately, the fittest is not always the winner, as attested by the scandal associated with the 1973 Soap Box Derby. In this case, victory was so important to the winning boy and his uncle that they used an illegal magnet to give the vehicle an unfair advantage at the start of each race. Moreover, a later investigation revealed that one-third of the final cars (and six of the top ten) had been altered to achieve an unfair advantage.

Such scandals are found throughout the sports world, as we shall note throughout this book. Most visible is the illegal recruiting of athletes by colleges and universities. In the quest to succeed (i.e., win), some coaches have violated NCAA regulations by arranging to have transcripts altered to ensure athletes' eligibility; by enrolling athletes in classes and obtaining for them academic credits for course work never taken; by allowing substitutes to take admissions tests for athletes of marginal educational ability; by paying athletes for nonexistent jobs; by illegally using government work-study funds for athletes; and by offering money, cars, and clothing to entice athletes to their schools.

When "winning is everything," players and coaches may turn to other forms of cheating. Many athletes take drugs to enhance their performance artificially. This practice is so commonplace, even expected, in some sports that we might call steroids that increase bulk and strength "vocational drugs." Players may try to gain an unfair advantage also by such practices as "doctoring" a pitch or "corking" a bat in baseball, curving the blades of the stick beyond the legal limits in hockey, pretending to be fouled in basketball, or "boosting" the manifold pressure to gain a horsepower advantage in automobile racing.[14] As former professional football coach Jerry Glanville has put it: "If you ain't cheatin', you ain't trying."[15]

Winning is the great North American obsession. It dominates our lives, as we have seen. One of the problems with this hyperemphasis on winning is that it tends to warp sport. Sport, in its pristine form, emphasizes the playing of the contest with thrills achieved from strategy, luck, finesse, cunning, practice, and skill. When winning is everything, however, the playing of the game becomes secondary. In effect, the destination becomes more important than the journey. When this occurs, sport is diminished. As sportswriter Bill Shirley has lamented: "Our win-at-all-costs philosophy has so distorted our sense of values that we

---

Box 3.1   Thinking about Sport The Negative Consequences of Overemphasizing Competition in Sport

When winning is the primary standard for evaluation, several negative outcomes result. Let me enumerate these, using sport for examples. First, in a competitive society there is a tendency to evaluate people by their accomplishments rather than their character, personality, and other human qualities. When "winning is everything," then losers are considered just that. One successful university basketball coach once counseled prospective coaches that if they wanted to be winners, then they should associate only with winners. Is this an appropriate guiding principle for conducting our lives?

Second, when winning is paramount, schools and communities organize sports for the already gifted. This elitist approach means that the few will be given the best equipment, the best coaching, and prime time reserved for their participating, while the less able will be denied participation altogether or given very little attention. If sports participation is a useful activity, then it should be for the many, not the few, in my view.

A third problem with the emphasis on winning is that parents may push their children beyond the normal to succeed. . . . In 1972 the national record for one-year-olds in the mile run was established by Steve Parsons of Normal, Illinois (the time was 24:16.6). [Is this an example] of child abuse or what?

A fourth problem with the primacy of winning is that coaches may push their charges too hard. Coaches may be physically or emotionally abusive. They may limit their players' civil rights. And, they may play their injured athletes by using pain killers without regard for their long-term physical well-being.

Fifth, when the desire to win is so great, the "end may justify the means." Coaches and players may use illegal tactics. Athletes may use performance enhancing drugs such as steroids and amphetamines to achieve a "competitive edge" or more subtly, but nonetheless unethical, using such means as blood doping or getting pregnant to get positive hormonal changes and then having an abortion. Both of these practices occur among endurance athletes. . . . So much, I would argue, for the myth that "sport builds character."

Sixth, when winning is all important, there may be a tendency to crush the opposition. This was the case when Riverside Poly High School girls' basketball team played Norte Vista several years ago. Riverside won by a score of 179–15 with one player, Cheryl Miller, scoring a California record of 105 points. Was the Riverside coach ethical? . . . Will the Norte Vista girls be motivated to improve their performance or will this humiliating experience crush their spirit?

Seventh, many people in a competitive society have difficulty with coming in second. . . . [For example, a few years back, a football team, composed of fifth-graders, in Florida was] undefeated going into the state finals but lost there in a close game. At a banquet following that season each player on this team was given a plaque on which was inscribed a quote from Vince Lombardi: "There is no room for second place. I have finished second twice at Green Bay and I never want to finish second again. There is a second place bowl game but it is a game for losers played by losers. It is and always will be an American zeal to be first in anything we do and to win and to win and to win." In other words, the parents and coaches of these boys wanted them to never be satisfied with being second. Second is losing. The only acceptable placement is first.

Finally, when "winning is the only thing" the joy in participation is lost. I have observed that organized sports from youth programs to the professional level is mostly devoid of playfulness. When the object is to win, then the primacy of the activity is lost. . . .

In other words, it's the process that is primary, not the outcome. White water rafters and mountain climbers understand this. So, too, do players in a pickup touch football game. Why can't the rest of us figure out this fundamental truth?

Source: Excerpts from D. Stanley Eitzen, "The Dark Side of Competition in American Society," *Vital Speeches* 56 (1 January 1990): 185–186.

have reversed the precept of Baron Pierre de Coubertin when he founded the modern Olympic Games. Today, on all levels of sports—from Little League to the National Football League—the most important thing is not merely to take part but to win; the most important thing in life is not the struggle but the triumph; the essential thing is not to have fought well but to have conquered."[16] See Box 3.1, *Thinking about Sport,* for an elaboration on the negative consequences of competition.

Such a heavy emphasis on winning is not a natural phenomenon but rather a cultural one. Games of many societies have no competitive element but reflect a different emphasis because of their cultural values. For contrast, let us examine a game from another society that would never capture the enthusiasm of North Americans.

The Tangu people of New Guinea play a popular game known as *taketak,* which involves throwing a spinning top into massed lots of stakes driven into the ground. There are two teams. Players of each team try to touch as many stakes with their tops as possible. In the end, however, the participants play not to win but to draw. The game must go on until an exact draw is reached. This requires great skill, since players sometimes must throw their tops into the massed stakes without touching a single one. *Taketak* expresses a prime value in Tangu culture, that is, the concept of moral equivalence, which is reflected in the precise sharing of foodstuffs among the people.[17]

Another example is how the Zuni Indians treat an outstanding runner, as reported by the late anthropologist Ruth Benedict.

> The ideal man in Zuni is a person of dignity and affability who has never tried to lead, and who has never called forth comment from his neighbors. Any conflict, even though all right is on his side, is held against him. Even in contests of skill like their foot races, if a man wins habitually he is debarred from running. They are interested in a game that a number can play with even chances, and an outstanding runner spoils the game: they will have none of him.[18]

These examples underscore our contention that a society's sports do mirror its basic values. Cooperative societies have sports that minimize competition, and aggressive societies have highly competitive games.

The Valued Means to Achievement in Sport

In sport, as in the larger society, the goal of individual achievement must be accomplished through continuous hard work and sacrifice. The work ethic is also the sports ethic. Someone wins with enough work and sacrifice or, conversely, someone loses without enough work. This is illustrated by the slogans that coaches use to inspire hard work in their athletes:

> *The will to win is the will to work.*
> *Practice makes perfect.*
> *Success is 99 percent perspiration and 1 percent inspiration.*
> *No one ever drowned in sweat.*
> *By failing to prepare yourself you are preparing to fail.*
> *There is no substitute for hard work.*
> *It's better to wear out than to rust out.*[19]

Americans do not like quitters in sports or in the other areas of social life. This is seen in the disdain accorded typically to school dropouts, panhandlers, people who declare bankruptcy, people who do not seek employment, and athletes who either quit the team or do not give a 100 percent effort even when the outcome of the game is no longer in doubt. Coaches, because they believe that success in sport and in life is dependent on sustained effort, do all in their power to instill in their athletes a never-give-up attitude.

Sport reinforces the success values of society for spectators as well. Susan P. Montague and Robert Morais made this point with special reference to football:

> Football validates the success model by staging a real event in which the principles of success are shown to work as promised by society. The contest actually happens before the viewer's eyes. The reality of the event is then transferred to the ideology of the success model, which is presented as accounting for the winning team's superior perfor-

mance. Of course, there is a sleight of hand going on here, because "the best team always wins." The team that wins is not necessarily best; it is best because it wins. In order to set the stage for the legitimacy of the assertion that the best team does indeed win, the teams must rigidly and publicly adhere to behaviors symbolic of the success model during their training (i.e., self-denial and hard work). It can then be argued that a team's superior performance is consonant with the expectations of the success model. The burden of proof switches to the losers: If the team that abides by the rules wins, then the team that loses must have failed to dedicate itself seriously enough.[20]

Progress in Sport

Coaches, athletes, and fans place a central value on progress. Continued improvement (in mastering new techniques, in winning more games, or in setting new records) is the aim of all athletes and teams. As an example, track-and-field stars undergo great pressures to set new records each time they compete. The demands come from the fans, from the press, from promoters, and often from the athletes themselves.

Materialism in Sport

Although the value that Americans place on success in competitive situations has the most important impact on the way sport is organized in the United States, materialism also has an important effect. Big-time college and professional teams especially are driven by money concerns. Schools, the NCAA, professional team owners, and leagues make lucrative arrangements with television networks that have a dramatic effect on sports (e.g., scheduling, timing, and number of time-outs). Professional teams that do not show a high enough profit may be moved to another city in the search for more money. Professional leagues have also secured exemptions from federal antitrust legislation to protect their investments.

Athletes, too are plainly motivated by material concerns. With free agency they move from team to team, securing ever larger contracts. Alex Rodriguez of the New York Yankees, for example, makes more than $27 million a year. That means that Rodriguez will earn two and a half times the average annual major league salary of 1975 each day of the season. Accumulating obscene amounts of money appears to be the goal of many athletes, rather than love of the game and loyalty to teammates and fans. Writing in 1972, when the money in sport was just a trickle compared to the torrent now, Tom Meschery, a former professional basketball player and coach, lamented for his sport:

> There was a time, and it was not so long ago, when things such as honor and loyalty were virtues in sport, and not objects of ridicule. It was a time when athletes drew pleasure and satisfaction from the essence of competition, not just from their paychecks. But somehow, with the introduction of big business, the concept of sports in this country has changed. The business psyche has invaded basketball and has made the players nothing but businessmen spurred by the profit motive. In some cases players make more money with their outside financial activities than they do on the court. Their sport becomes a mere showcase to keep them before the public, like an actor's guest appearance on a television talk show. The game no longer has its roots sunk into idealistic bedrock. It's just business: nine to five.[21]

Examples of the attitude Meschery described are common in all sports. Olympic athletes parlay their sports accomplishments into millions for endorsements, personal appearances, and the like. College football and basketball coaches sometimes break their contracts to coach at another school. Free agents in professional sports commonly sign with the highest bidder and often try to renegotiate contracts before they expire. In such instances, team and fan loyalty is all but forgotten. Team owners typically have no loyalty to the cities that subsidize them. They move their teams to where more money can be made or threaten to move in order to receive even greater benefits from their host cities.

Athletes hire lawyers to negotiate for the highest possible bonuses and salary arrangements. They hold out individually and even strike collectively, on occasion, for better material comforts (see chapter 10). Furthermore, athletes often engage in activities calculated to increase attendance at contests. Boxers and their promoters are well known for this. Star athletes also devote much of their energy to making money by endorsing products and projects, making personal appearances, and giving inspirational talks. Golf megastar Tiger Woods, for example, makes about $70 million or so annually just from endorsements.

Sports fans, too, are influenced by material considerations. They like plush stadiums with expensive scoreboards and other amenities. They are excited by athletes playing for large stakes (e.g., the difference between first and second place in a golf tournament may be as much as five hundred thousand dollars).

External Conformity in Sport

Conformity is highly valued in American sport. Coaches generally demand that their athletes conform to the behavior norms of the community in hairstyles, manner of dress, and speech patterns. This is probably the result of two factors: first, coaches feel that their precarious jobs may be in further jeopardy if they permit athletes to act outside community standards; second, coaches tend to be conservative.

Coaches of team sports place a high value on team unity, emphasizing subordination of self to team success. Athletes are expected to subordinate their wills to achieve team success, as the following coaching cliches indicate:

> There is no "I" in team.
> There is no "U" in team.
> A player doesn't make the team, the team makes the player.
> United we stand, divided we fall.
> Cooperate—remember the banana; every time it leaves the bunch, it gets skinned.[22]

Another aspect of external conformity, found in both sport and in the larger society, is the acceptance of authority. The system, the rules, and the structure of power are not challenged. Coaches typically structure coach-athlete relationships along authoritarian lines. They analyze and structure team positions for the precise specialization of the athletes, and they endeavor to control player behavior not only throughout practice and contest periods but also on an around-the-clock basis. Under this form of management, the athletes are the instruments of organizational goals. In most cases they are not consulted about team membership, practice methods, strategy, team rules, or any of the other dynamic functions of a team. In a biting critique of modern sport, Jean-Marie Brohm stated: "Sport is basically a mechanization of the body, treated as an automaton, governed by the principle of maximizing output. The organism is trained to sustain prolonged effort and maintain the necessary regularity of pace. . . . In the guise of a game which is supposed to freely develop the strengths of the individual, sport in fact reproduces the world of work."[23] Thus, play has been transformed into work. The playfulness, fun, and creativity of sport are controlled by the absolute control of coaches over their teams and players; if players wish to participate, they must conform to the coach's system. The typical coach's philosophy is "It's my way or the highway."

SUMMARY

American values clearly affect American sport. Just as important is the insight that sport in society, through its organization and the demands and the emphases of those in power, reinforces societal values. This mutual reinforcement places sport squarely in the middle of society's "way of life." It is precisely because sport is so intertwined with the fundamental values of society that any attack on sport is usually interpreted as unpatriotic. Hence, criticism of sport is rarely taken seriously. We should keep this in mind as we examine the positive and negative consequences of sport in society. Any proposed changes in sport must be related to the values of society.

WEB RESOURCES

www.siu.edu/-hawkes/methods
Resources for qualitative research.

www.asanet.org/sections/culture.html
The American Sociological Association's sociology of culture website.

www.demographics.com
American Demographics magazine, which supplies demographic information and behavior patterns for various U.S. population groups.

www.sportsethicsinstitute.org
This site focuses on ethical issues in sport.

NOTES

1. Craig Crawford and James Curtis, "English-Canadian-American Differences in Value Orientations: Survey Comparisons Bearing on Lipset's Thesis," *Studies in Comparative International Development* 14, nos. 3–4 (1979): 23–44.

2. Much of this discussion on values is taken from D. Stanley Eitzen and Maxine Baca Zinn, *In Conflict and Order: Understanding Society*, 11th ed. (Boston: Allyn and Bacon, 2007), 93–102.

3. We have relied on three sources that were especially helpful for the delineation of North American values: Robin M. Williams, Jr., *American Society: A Sociological Interpretation*, 3rd ed. (New York: Knopf, 1970), 438–504; Cora Dubois, "The Dominant Value Profile of American Culture," *American Anthropologist* 57 (December 1955): 1232–1239; and Phillip Slater, *The Pursuit of Loneliness: American Culture at the Breaking Point* (Boston: Beacon Press, 1970).

4. Williams, *American Society*, 454–455.

5. Robert H. Frank and Philip J. Cook, *The Winner-Take-All Society* (New York: Free Press, 1995).

6. Mortimer B. Zuckerman, "Our Cheating Hearts," *U.S. News & World Report*, 6 November 2006, 88. See also David Callahan, *The Cheating Culture* (New York: Harcourt, 2004).

7. See William Ryan, *Blaming the Victim*, rev. ed. (New York: Pantheon Books, 1976).

8. Edward C. Banfield, *The Unheavenly City: The Nature and Future of Our Urban Crisis* (Boston: Little, Brown, 1970). For a critique of Banfield's position, see William Ryan, "Is Banfield Serious?" *Social Policy* 1 (November–December 1970): 74–76.

9. Alex P. Kellogg, "Looking Inward, Freshmen Care Less about Politics and More about Money," *Chronicle of Higher Education*, 26 January 2001, A47–A49.

10. Ibid.

11. David Riesman et al., *The Lonely Crowd* (New Haven, Conn.: Yale University Press, 1950).

12. William H. Whyte, Jr., *The Organization Man* (New York: Simon & Schuster, 1956).

13. Eldon E. Snyder, "Athletic Dressing Room Slogans as Folklore: A Means of Socialization," *International Review of Sport Sociology* 7 (1972): 89–102.

14. For many other examples, see D. Stanley Eitzen, *Fair and Foul: Beyond the Myths and Paradoxes of Sport*, 3rd ed. (Lanham, Md.: Rowman & Littlefield, 2006), chap. 4.

15. Quoted in Tim Green, "Cheating to Win Is Rule of Thumb for Teams' Survival," *USA Today*, 6 November 1997, p. 4C.

16. Bill Shirley, "Is It Really a Sin to Lose?" *Denver Post*, 11 November 1983, sec. D, p. 1.

17. George B. Leonard, "Winning Isn't Everything: It's Nothing," *Intellectual Digest* 4 (October 1973): 45. See also Alfie Kohn, "Sports Create Unhealthy Competition," in *Sports in America: Opposing Viewpoints*, ed. William Dudley (San Diego: Greenhaven Press, 1994), 17–20.

18. Ruth Benedict, *Patterns of Culture* (New York: Mentor Books, 1934), 95; see also John Garrity, "A Clash of Cultures on the Hopi Reservation," *Sports Illustrated*, 20 November 1989.

19. Snyder, "Athletic Dressing Room Slogans as Folklore," 89–102.

20. Susan P. Montague and Robert Morais, "Football Games and Rock Concerts: The Ritual Enactment of American Success Models," in *The American Dimension: Cultural Myths and Realities*, ed. W. Arens and Susan P. Montague (Port Washington, N.Y.: Alfred, 1976), 42.

21. Tom Meschery, "There Is a Disease in Sports Now," *Sports Illustrated*, 2 October 1972, 56.

22. Snyder, "Athletic Dressing Room Slogans as Folklore," 89–102. See also Mariah Burton Nelson, "Learning What 'Team' Really Means," *Newsweek*, 19 July 1999, 55.

23. Jean-Marie Brohm, *Sport: A Prison of Measured Time* (London: Ink Links, 1978), 55.

CHAPTER 4

Youth and Sport

"If I can't win I don't want to play"
—slogan on a T-shirt of a fourteen-year-old girl training at the
International Performance Institute at IMG Academies in Bradenton, Florida

The first- and second-place runners in the young men's class of the New Mexico Junior Olympics 800-meter race, 23 June 2007, Las Cruces, New Mexico. The Junior Olympics Sports Program sponsors more than 2,000 local, state, regional, and national events in twenty-one different sports. (AP Photo/*Las Cruces Sun-News*, Norm Dettlaff)

More people participate in sport during their youth than at any other time in their lives. Although for many young boys and girls sports involvement is limited to informal, neighborhood play, an increasing number of North American youth participate in highly organized athletic competition. Youth sports programs have grown to include greater numbers of participants, and new programs have been created to include a bewildering variety of sports. Thus, a great deal of the social life of youngsters is spent playing sports.

YOUTH SPORTS PROGRAMS: SOMETHING FOR EVERYONE

Nonschool youth sports programs in North America are organized by more than twenty-five agencies and by thousands of local and regional sports organizations. The National Council of Youth Sports estimates that more than fifty-two million boys and girls participate in organized youth sports throughout the United States, while some four million Canadian youth participate. Thus, about 65 percent of all American and Canadian youth under the age of seventeen participate in at least one organized sport as they pass through childhood and adolescence.

Little League baseball is the largest of the youth sports organizations, with leagues in every U.S. state and in eighty countries (200,000 leagues at present) and with more than 2.5 million youngsters engaged in Little League annually. Pop Warner football celebrated its seventy-ninth year in 2008 and has 400,000 kids in its program. However, in terms of participants, soccer has been growing faster than any other youth team sport during the past decade and now has some 10,000 teams and 4.8 million young boys and girls playing the sport. More than three thousand YMCAs in the United States and Canada provide some 8 million boys and girls the opportunity to participate in organized sports. The Junior Olympics Sports Program sponsors more than 2,000 local, state, regional, and national events in twenty-one different sports.

The popularity of ESPN's X Games has stimulated the rise of several new youth-oriented extreme sports; in-line skating, freestyle bicycling, snowboarding and skateboarding have had explosive growth. There is even a National Hot Rod Association Jr. Drag Racing League and go-kart racing with more than 55,000 youngsters ages eight to seventeen competing at more than 150 racetracks. Girls' participation in organized sports in the United States and Canada has experienced dramatic increases over the past twenty years and represents about 40 percent of the participants.[1]

The programs are becoming more elaborate and are enlisting younger participants each year. There is a well-organized outlet for almost every child who has an interest in being involved in sports. Parents can enroll their children in age-group gymnastics and swimming programs at three years of age; ice hockey, soccer, football, T-baseball, and a half dozen other sports begin at age four. Indeed, an early start is considered essential, when parents or children have professional or Olympic-level aspirations. Starting at ten or eleven years of age is considered too old in this case.

The major promotional forces behind these youth sports programs have been parents and interested laypersons, while educators, physicians, and psychologists have tended to be less enthusiastic. Indeed, educators have rather effectively prohibited interscholastic sports in the elementary schools and have severely restricted school sports in the junior high schools. They have, however, been ineffectual in controlling nonschool programs.

As sports for children and adolescents have expanded and diversified, a wide variety of sponsors have emerged. The types of agencies that sponsor youth sport in the United States are quite varied, and an example of each is shown in Table 4.1. Canadian youth sport funding comes from various sources. The major sources are the government, community fund-raising, private sponsorships, and registration fees. Virtually all of the national associations receive over half of their money from the federal government. At the local level, fund-raising and registration fees account for more than half of the total money.

Such a bewildering number of youth sports programs with varying structural arrangements exist that it is somewhat foolish to talk about them

Table 4.1 Categories of Agencies Who Organize Youth Sports

Type of Agency	Example of Type
National youth sport organization	Little League Baseball
National youth agency	Boys and Girls Clubs of America
National governing body	U.S. Wrestling
National service organization	American Legion Baseball
National religious organization	Catholic Youth Organization
Regional youth sport organization	Soccer Association for Youth
State school activity association	Ohio High School Activities Association
Local school district	Norton, Kansas, Public School
Local service club	Greeley Lions Club
Municipal recreation department	Fort Collins Recreation Department
Private sports club	Front Range Volleyball Club

as though they were all alike. There are programs that emphasize participation and carefully regulate the type and extent of stress placed on the players. On the other hand, there are programs in which adults intrude enormously on the play of the youngsters; in many of these the purpose is simply to train children to become champions. An example of the former is the IMS Sports Academies in Florida, which are quite clearly devoted to producing champions in several sports. Accounts of the lives of the prodigies at these academies clearly demonstrate that their only goal in sports, or at least the goal of their parents and coaches, is to become an intercollegiate, professional, or Olympic-level athlete. There are many academies and clubs in a variety of sports scattered across North America training athletes to become pros or Olympic-level competitors. Indeed, the U.S. Soccer Federation established Project 2010, a program to recruit and train young soccer players with the aim of winning the World Cup by 2010.[2]

Despite variations in youth sports forms and functions, advocates of youth sports programs claim that they provide a means for the development of such personal-social attributes as self-discipline, cooperativeness, achievement motivation, courage, persistence, and so forth. Proponents of organized youth sports typically view them as good preparation for the realities of adult life. Additionally, advocates contend that the physical activity involved in playing sports promotes health and fitness.

On the other hand, critics of youth sports claim that excessive psychological and physical demands are frequently placed on participants. They also contend that the encroachment of adults into the world of young persons reduces the value of play as a spontaneous, expressive experience. Finally, critics observe that youth sports frequently seem to be conducted for the self-serving needs of parents and youth sports leaders. Pressure from parents and coaches forces many elite child athletes to strive for perfection, and that pressure is responsible for dropping out, burnout, overuse injuries, and a host of other physical and psychological ailments.[3]

THE RISE OF YOUTH SPORTS PROGRAMS: THE TAKEOFF AND EXPANSION OF A NEW FORM OF SPORT

Two independent but interrelated developments in the sociocultural milieu of North American society in the past two generations were primarily responsible for the rise and expansion of youth sports programs. The first was the rise of organized and corporate sport in all parts of both the U.S. and Canada. The first half of the twentieth century witnessed an enormous growth in popular spectator sports, such as Major League Baseball, collegiate football, professional ice hockey, boxing, and others. High school athletics became an integral part of North American education, and the overall obsession with these forms of organized sport eventually trickled down to preadolescent youth.

The second development promoting the growth of youth sports programs was that North Americans began to realize the need and importance of protecting and providing varied opportunities for children. Increasingly, childhood was seen as a particularly opportune time for nurturing attitudes and habits that would prepare youth for adulthood. Youth leaders urged the use of sports for the development of desirable personal-social skills. When the schools refused to sponsor sports for preadolescent youth, the task was left to voluntary agencies, and responsibility for sport competition for the preadolescent group was assumed by child-oriented organizations outside of the educational framework.[4]

Girls playing soccer. Until the 1970s most organized youth sports programs were for boys only, but with a growing awareness of gender discrimination raised by the women's movement, exclusion of girls became unacceptable. (iStockphoto)

Until the 1970s most organized youth sports programs were for boys only, but growing out of the attack on gender discrimination in all aspects of social life by the women's movement, exclusion of girls from organized sport became unacceptable. The Little League's ban against participation by girls was challenged in 1973, and after several lawsuits girls legally won the right to participate in Little League baseball. Over the past twenty years organized youth sport has become available in almost every sport in which girls have wished to participate. The initial reservations, and even objections, to girls' sports participation have gradually declined and have been replaced by enthusiastic endorsement by almost everyone. However, there are those who question the wisdom of merely incorporating females into the prevailing youth sport system. They argue that the structure of traditional youth sports programs allows little creative development and little chance to invent new ways of organizing sporting activities.

OBJECTIVES OF YOUTH SPORTS PROGRAMS: WHAT DO YOUNG ATHLETES WANT? WHAT DO THEIR PARENTS AND COACHES WANT?

Regardless of the sponsoring organization, the objectives of most youth sports programs are quite similar. They are intended to provide young boys and girls with opportunities to learn culturally relevant sports skills. Inasmuch as sport is such a pervasive activity in North American culture, developing sports skills becomes almost a public duty. Equally important in the objectives of these programs, however, is the transmission of attitudes and values through interpersonal associations with teammates and opponents and through deliberate actions on the part of coaches, officials, and parents.

Thus, youth sports are viewed as an environment for promoting attitudes and values about such things as competition, sportsmanship, discipline, authority, and social relationships. The original certificate of the federal charter granted to Little League baseball illustrates the objectives of most youth sports programs: "To help and voluntarily assist boys in developing qualities of citizenship, sportsmanship, and manhood. Using the disciplines of the native American game of baseball, to teach spirit and competitive will to win, physical fitness through individual sacrifice, the values of team play, and wholesome well-being through healthful and social association with other youngsters under proper leadership."[5] Girls are now participants in Little League baseball, but otherwise its objectives are still the same. A Girls Softball program was introduced in 1974. Today more than fifty-two hundred charters and more than 350,000 youngsters participate in this phase of the Little League program.

Many books and articles for parents, coaches, and athletes about youth sports have enumerated lists of the values of sports for young athletes. The most commonly listed values are:

1. Helps a child's overall physical development.
2. Gives the child the opportunity to become familiar with his/her body and to learn the body's needs and limitations.
3. Is social as well as physical and thus teaches young athletes how to interact with his/her peers.
4. Teaches cooperation, teamwork, and how to follow rules.
5. Helps the child learn for him/herself if winning or losing is important.
6. Gives parents the opportunity of offering the child unqualified support.
7. Helps the child gain acceptance and credibility among his/her peers.

Beyond the benefits that youth sports are believed to provide for participants, community-based programs may function to satisfy a community need by contributing what appears to be a link with symbols of stability, order, tradition, and a communal focus. The extent to which youth sports actually serve these functions is hard to quantify, but there is little doubt that substantial community financial and human resources are poured into the programs. Local merchants sponsor teams; coaches volunteer their time; groundskeepers, concession-stand operators, scorekeepers, and so forth facilitate the ongoing operations of the programs; and parents turn out in large numbers to cheer their children. In addition, playing fields are built and maintained, and equipment is largely furnished, with taxpayers' money. Youth sports are indeed a significant community activity in towns and cities throughout Canada and the United States.

SOCIALIZATION AND SPORT: INVOLVEMENT IN SPORT AND ITS CONSEQUENCES

With youth sports as pervasive as they are in North America, questions about the social sources for the promotion of youth sports involvement are important for understanding how youngsters get into organized sports and what the consequences are of these experiences. In the broadest sense the process of becoming a young athlete is part of a socialization process.

Socialization is the process of learning and adapting to a given social system. In the context of society, the activity of socialization is called cultural transmission and is the means by which a society preserves its norms and perpetuates itself. At birth, infants are certainly living organisms, but they are not social beings. Humans raised in isolation develop only their animal nature, but those raised in human society demonstrate the human aspects that derive from social living. They also demonstrate the impact of their culture upon them, and this is called socialization.

Socialization begins at birth and continues throughout an individual's life cycle, but the years from birth to adolescence are considered critical, for in these years the basic cultural transmission takes place. Numerous people are involved in the socialization of an individual, but because of their frequency of contact, their primacy, and their control over rewards and punishments, the primary agents and agencies for socialization are families, peer groups, schools, churches, and mass media.

The outcomes of the socialization process are attitudes, values, knowledge, and behaviors that are related to the culture of which individuals are a part and to the roles that they will play in it. Thus, as children in a society interact with others through language, gestures, rewards, and punishments, they learn the attitudes, the values, and the expectations of various individuals in that society as well as the behaviors considered appropriate to the various situations of their social life. The process of socialization is, however, not merely a one-way process from socializers (parents, peers, and so forth) to the children; instead a reciprocal interaction process is also at work, and youngsters actually influence the attitudes, values, and behaviors of adults. Often-heard comments among parents include "I've certainly learned some things from my kids" and "My kids have made me change my mind about _____." There is little doubt that young athletes continually influence the attitudes and behaviors toward sport of various socializing agents, including parents, coaches, teachers, and peers.

The topic of socialization and sport may be divided into two subtopics for analysis: (1) socialization into sports and (2) socialization via sports. In the first the focus is on the agents and agencies that attract, or draw, children into sports. That is, an analysis of the ways in which children become involved in sports. An analysis of socialization via sports concentrates on the consequences, or outcomes, of sports involvement. In the next section, we direct our attention to socialization into sport; socialization via sport is addressed later in this chapter.

SOCIALIZATION INTO SPORT: WHY DO CHILDREN GET INVOLVED IN ORGANIZED SPORTS?

An analysis of socialization into sports is concerned with who gets involved in sport, which social agents and agencies are responsible for guiding young people into such involvement, how persons learn sports roles, and what the social processes for becoming involved are. One thing is quite clear: There is an enormous diversity in the process of becoming involved in sport. Canadian sport sociologist Chris Stevenson has conducted several research projects on the life histories of athletes in an attempt to discover how they became involved in sport. He found that "here were fathers involved, mothers involved, friends, teachers, sisters and brothers, coaches, and friends of the family."[6]

Families

The family is the first and perhaps the most important social environment in a young person's life, and there is overwhelming evidence that the family—its social status, its structure, and its patterning of activities—is a significant influence in socializing boys and girls into sport.

One important factor on the sport involvement of youngsters is the structure of the family. Families vary in size from a single child to sometimes more than a dozen offspring; following divorce or the death of one parent, some families become single-parent families. According to the U.S. Bureau of the Census, traditional families, meaning married couples with or without children, are at the lowest rate, 52 percent, in at least two hundred years. Almost half of all children are growing up without both natural parents in the household.[7]

Participation in youth sports programs cuts across all socioeconomic strata; however, children from working-class families are overrepresented in some youth sports, and children from upper-middle-class families in others. Parents socialize their children into sports that are deemed most appropriate for their socioeconomic status. For example, age-group tennis players, skiers, gymnasts, golfers, and swimmers tend to come from upper-middle-class families. On the other hand, youth baseball, boxing, wrestling, and football programs tend to attract youngsters from middle- and working-class families. (Chapter 12 deals with the social stratification aspects of sports in more detail.)

Parents

Children tend to adopt the attitudes and values of their parents. Parents who reward the acquisition of motor skills and who themselves engage in sporting activities tend to socialize their children to an interest in physical activity. Indeed, several investigators have found that parents are important agents of sport socialization for both their sons and their daughters.

Parental influence appears to occur through their own participation (the modeling influence) and through their interest in and encouragement of their offspring's involvement in sport. Surveys of North American families have found that around 75 percent of parents engage in some kind of sports activity with their children. Thus, research suggests that parental encouragement and actual participation are primary sources of sport socialization. A high percentage of fathers and mothers of young female athletes actually engaged in sport themselves, and overall, parents are the most salient social agents in encouraging female athletes to participate.[8]

Although parents have received considerable attention as a factor in influencing the sport involvement of their offspring, very little is known about the specific contributions that each parent makes. Some investigators have reported that the father was frequently the most significant socializing agent in the family and the most important predictor of sport participation for both boys and girls. Others have reported a tendency for the same-sex parent to have greater influence on sport involvement than the opposite-sex parent. More specifically, they have found that fathers' sports interests were more strongly related than mothers' interests to direct primary participation for both males and females. Christine Brennan, sports columnist for *USA Today*, recounts how her father nurtured her interest in sports. "I got my first inkling something was up with this man [her father] when his 5-year-old daughter [Christine] told him what she wanted for her birthday and he went right out and bought it for her. It was a baseball mitt." She continues: "Immediately, this man became the only guy in town who was playing catch in the backyard with a girl." Later, "he went back to the store and bought the girl a baseball bat. . . . In the years that followed, this man would attend almost every high school game his children ever played."[9]

Parents who have been asked about their children's involvement in organized sports programs have usually expressed rather strong support, and parents of youth sport athletes have rated the coaches as excellent or good. They generally view sports as having had a positive effect on family life and view sports as helping parents in socializing their children, in that they teach youngsters useful personal and social skills. Overall, parents were pleased with their community's sports programs and with their children's involvement.

For those parents whose children are training for elite status, for instance to be an Olympic-level athlete or a professional athlete, there are fears, sacrifices, and constant pressures. Is the child being robbed of his or her childhood in the tightly structured training environment? Are the sacrifices of the child living away from home year-round worth it? Are the costs for coaching worth it? There is also the constant realization that unless the child continues to improve against the competition, he or she will be dropped by the coach or the program or both.[10] When parents set for their child the goal of achieving professional standing, pressures are inevitably applied to the child's performance.

In the literature on socialization into sport, little attention has been given to the ways in which youths influence their parents to become involved. Instead, most research has presented a unidimensional socialization process in which the offspring are the learners and the parents are the socializers. Some sociologists have called for greater attention to the symbolic interactionist perspective, which sees social interacting as reciprocal and negotiable. In this view, analysis of parent effects needs to be balanced by analysis of child effects and of the two-way "reciprocal-effects synthesis." With respect to sport, in addition to parental encouragement of offspring, some family adjustments may produce reverse socialization, with parents being socialized into sport through their children's participation. Indeed, many parents learn about sport and become involved in sport from their children. Therefore, the socialization between parents and their children is frequently bidirectional. Thus, although parents may initially steer their children into sport, the child's involvement often has behavioral and attitudinal consequences for the parents.

Siblings

A rather consistent association has been shown between parents' sports involvement, their support, and their encouragement and the involvement of their children in sport, but the influence of siblings is not so clear. Still, a number of studies examining factors that affect the sport and physical activity participation of youngsters have identified siblings as a positive social influence. It is probable that the example of an older brother or sister participating in organized sport spurs younger children to become involved. One of the athletes Chris Stevenson was interviewing about becoming involved in sport said: "I have two brothers and we used to play hockey and we used to play football. . . . When I was little I used to do everything they would do."[11] A broad base of familial support is probably present in most cases when children become involved in sport. The ability of siblings to influence the social environment apart from parents is certainly a positive factor.

Peers

As important as the family is, the neighborhood and the peer group also serve as powerful socializing agents for sport involvement, especially as youngsters move into adolescence. Typically, during adolescence less time is spent with the family, and more time is spent with peers. Interactions with peers in the neighborhood and at school almost force compliance with their interests and activities. When peers are involved in sports, young people frequently experience a great deal of pressure to become involved also or to give up cherished social relationships. Several studies examining the influence of socializing agents on the process of socialization of boys and girls into sports have found that peers are a major influence throughout childhood and adolescence.[12]

Coaches

Coaches are not often the persons responsible for initiating young boys and girls into sports, but for many youngsters an extremely close, emotional bond develops between athlete and coach, a bond that frequently becomes the main reason for continuing involvement. From the huge number of volunteer coaches to those who make their living coaching, coaches exert a tremendous influence on young athletes. Most young athletes perceive that the role of "coach" is socially admired. Also, young athletes' abilities, an important source of self-esteem, have been developed by their coach. The coach is, therefore, seen as someone who has helped the athlete acquire some of his/her most important possessions. Many ex–youth athletes, years after they have stopped competing, still consider their former coaches to be the most significant adults in their lives.[13]

Schools

Of course, the school, with its physical education classes, is a significant socializing agent for North American children. Thanks to universal education and a physical education curriculum that typically puts a great deal of emphasis on learning sports skills, most children are taught the rudiments of a variety of sports in school. (Chapter 5 deals further with sport in high school.)

Mass Media

The mass media is a powerful force for the sport role socialization of young boys and girls. Youngsters are virtually inundated with sports via newspapers, magazines, the Internet, and especially television. It is obvious that the mass media brings sports to the attention of the young. Few youngsters do not know the names of the NFL, NHL, NBA, and Major League Baseball teams. A great many boys and girls have heroes among professional and Olympic athletes, and many of them have plastered their bedroom walls with sports posters.

During the past decade, television programming has expanded to include a number of youth sports events. Perhaps the most prominent of these is the Little League World Series. Several days of the series are shown on TV. Several other youth championship events also are now televised. *USA Today,* which is sold worldwide, has a prominent place in its sports section for high school sports—including state-by-state results of high school championship events and a national ranking of the top twenty high school teams in several sports. Many young television viewers and readers of *USA Today* are undoubtedly influenced to become involved in sports because of the media coverage of high school sports. After all, the most immediate role models and heroes of younger athletes are the high school athletes.

Parents, siblings, peers, coaches, schools, and the media, then, are the sport socializing agents and agencies that act on youth. They are so influential that it is a rare youngster who is not affected in some way by sport as he or she passes through childhood and adolescence.

Participants

Studies of participants in youth sports programs usually find that they have positive attitudes toward their experiences. When asked what they like most about their sports experiences, participants typically list the fun of being on an organized team, the chance to meet others and to make friends, and the opportunity to improve their skills. Comprehensive analyses of youth sports have found there is a common cluster of the most important reasons kids play organized sport (see Table 4.2). In a study of nearly fifteen hundred girls and boys for the United States, New Zealand, and Australia, sport psychologists had findings that generally corroborated those that are listed in Table 4.2. Young athletes in their study reported that their motivation to play sport was based primarily on competition—with social, fitness/fun, and teamwork reasons also contributing. There were few cultural differences in the motivations to play sports between the participants in the three countries.[14]

Although millions of youngsters enthusiastically participate in organized youth sports each year and many continue for as long as they are eligible, a surprisingly large number do not continue to take part in sport; they become dropouts. Indeed, as many as one-third of youth sports participants voluntarily drop out of sport each year. Seventy percent of kids by the age of thirteen drop out of youth sports programs. Researchers have tried to ascertain the motives for sports withdrawal. They have found that the disappointment of not getting to play, poor umpiring, and being scolded for mistakes by coaches, parents, or both are the things that young participants dislike most.[15] In studies that asked participants why they discontinued youth sports involvement, the ten most often cited reasons for both boys and girls were these:

1. I lost interest.
2. I was not having fun.
3. It took too much time.
4. Coach played favorites.
5. Coach was a poor teacher.
6. I was tired of playing.
7. Too much emphasis on winning.
8. Wanted a nonsport activity.
9. I needed more time to study.
10. Too much pressure.[16]

Table 4.2 Ten Most Important Reasons Why Youth Play Sports

Boys	Girls
1. To have fun	1. To have fun
2. To improve skills	2. To stay in shape
3. For the excitement of competition	3. To get exercise
4. To do something I'm good at	4. To improve skills
5. To stay in shape	5. To do something I'm good at
6. For the challenge of competition	6. To be part of a team
7. To be part of a team	7. For the excitement of competition
8. To win	8. To learn new skills
9. To go to a higher level of competition	9. For the team spirit
10. To get exercise	10. For the challenge of competition

Source: "The State of Amateur Sport," *The Sporting Goods Dealer.*

The picture that emerges from studying young athletes and their views of participation in youth sports is that they want to have fun and learn skills, but since many of them encounter pressures to train and win, some simply drop out of organized sport programs. For them, the promise of fun, sociability, and skill acquisition through sports is lost.

SOCIALIZATION VIA SPORT

The extent to which the attitudes, values, beliefs, and behaviors of North American young people are actually influenced by participation in organized youth sports programs is largely unknown because few investigations have been undertaken on this topic. Thus, little empirical evidence exists to substantiate the many claims that have been made for the contributions of sport to psychological and social attributes of participants. The major reason is that sport constitutes only one of many forces operating on young people. Every child is subjected to a multitude of social experiences that are not sport-related. Thus, much of what we think we know about the effects, or consequences, of sport participation is impressionistic, and this fact needs to be remembered in any discussion of the topic.

There are several principles of socialization theory, however, that likely hold true with regard to youth sports. In general, the influence of sports experiences will be stronger (1) when the degree of involvement is frequent, intense, and prolonged; (2) when the participation is voluntary rather than involuntary; (3) when the socializer (e.g., the coach) is perceived as powerful and prestigious; and (4) when the quality of relationships is high in expressiveness.

Two Forms of Play

Several social scientists have suggested that the social context in which a sport activity takes place determines its social outcomes. The observational studies of several social scientists who have studied children and adolescents and their sports involvement indicate that there are two distinct social contexts in which sports activities take place: "peer-group" and "adult-organized." They have characterized and contrasted the potential socialization outcomes for these two forms of play in terms of their organization, process, impetus, and social implications.

Organization

In organized team sports the most salient characteristic is that both action and involvement are under adult control and the actions of the players are strictly regulated by specialized rules and roles. For example, Little League games are organized as performances rather than play. They are modeled after professional sports. Young athletes on organized sports teams learn to stand still—with mouth closed—and listen to the coach's instructions or weather the coach's sometimes blistering criticism.

Youth sport coaches are remarkably similar in the way they organize practice sessions. Activities during practice tend to be very rule-bound. Coaches allow little flexibility in the executing of skills or in the performing of other tasks associated with practice. The youngsters tend to wait to be told what to do, often waiting for directions on how to do things that are routine. Spontaneous behavior, when it occurs, consists of "horsing around" while waiting to practice some given task. Very few decisions on any aspect of the practice are made by the youngsters. Most decisions are made by the coaches, and the participants are expected to carry them out obediently. The emphasis in the organized setting tends to be on the development of sport skills, not on the development of interpersonal skills.

With respect to play, before the age of seven children rarely play games spontaneously; if they play them at all, it is usually on the initiative of adults or older children. Thus, organized sports programs for youngsters under the age of seven are not organized extensions of what children of that age would be doing anyway; they are simply testaments to the power and influence adults have on young children.

When peer play is found, usually among youngsters over the age of seven, it is player-controlled. Players rely on informal norms of conduct and informal rules to regulate the game. The youngsters make consensual decisions on groupings and game rules. Teams are usually organized informally; this is done quickly and typically with little friction. The games children choose in free play generally have fewer rules and fewer specialized roles than the games organized by adults, and children vary the rules in the process of play to suit the situation. In informal peer "sandlot" games the authority structure operates uniquely. There is an authority structure, but the structure works through moral suasion rather than through role occupancy.

Process

The process of play in peer-group sport and adult-organized sport is also quite different. In the former, teams are chosen, and the game usually begins quickly. Field researchers of children's informal sports frequently note the efficiency with which the youngsters go about getting the teams chosen and the game under way. Arguments about rule interpretations or a "call," such as whether a player is "safe" or "out," when they do occur, usually cause only minimal delays. Shouts of "Let him have it" or "Play it over" usually settle the debate, and play is resumed.

In the informal peer-group games the primary focus tends to be on a combination of action, personal involvement, keeping the game close, and the reaffirming of friendships. The quest for victory, or a "win," is not one of the salient outcomes; instead of a narrow focus on winning there is often a search for self-mastery; that is, attempting to create situations that require performing up to a personal standard of satisfaction.

By contrast, in the play process of organized youth sports, there tends to be an emphasis on order, punctuality, respect for authority, obedience to adult directions, and a strict division of labor. Coaches typically insist on order, sometimes prohibiting participants from talking unless the coach speaks to them. The coach's concern for order and discipline often reduces the amount of playing time. Organizing the practice session or stopping practice to discuss mistakes or to punish misbehavior sometimes takes up significant portions of the practice session. The participants become so accustomed to following orders in an organized sport setting that they frequently will cease to play altogether if the coach is absent or not directly supervising. Close observation by the coach is required to keep them playing.[17]

In organized youth sports the participants have no say in the rules; adults make the rules. In the programs of national sports agencies (such as Little League baseball), a national rulebook is published to which all participants must conform. Thus, in this form of sport, participants are merely followers, not makers or interpreters, of the rules.

Winning is frequently the overriding goal in formal youth sports programs. By striving for league standings, by awarding championships, by choosing all-star teams, such programs send the not-so-subtle message to youngsters that the most important goal of sports is winning.

Impetus

The impetus of peer play comes entirely from the youngsters; they play because they enjoy it. They are free to commence and terminate a game based on player interest. Conversely, the impetus of play in organized sports programs comes from the coaches; they schedule the practices for a given time and end practices when they see fit. Games are scheduled by a league authority and are played in a very rigid time frame. The youngsters have no choice but to play in the way the adults wish them to play. Their own enjoyment appears to be of little concern to the adults. In her book about elite gymnasts and figure skaters, Joan Ryan recounts that one "skater says her coach resorted to physical abuse to motivate her skaters: 'We'd practice our figure eights in strips on the ice and the girl next to me had terrible figure eights and she'd get screamed at, hit and her hair pulled. The behavior wasn't considered abusive; it was considered discipline.'"[18] Coaches and many players expect participants to adhere to a Puritan work ethic, and the word *work* is ever-present in practices and games. "Come on, work hard" and "Take pride in your work!" are proddings frequently used by coaches and parents.

Social Implications

Adult-sponsored youth sport is basically an organized structuring of groupings, activities, and rules that are imposed upon the participants. Peer play, on the other hand, is a voluntary activity with a flexible process of social exchange based on consensus. Youngsters are therefore exposed to quite different experiences in what appear to be similar sport activities.

What are the social implications of these two different forms of organization of play activities for the socialization of youngsters? The application of arbitrary, adult-imposed rules in organized youth sport markedly contrasts with the spontaneous group-derived rules in peer-group play. This contrast is a function of the different roles of the peer group and of adults in the socialization process. The role of the peer group serves to bridge the gap between the individualistic world of children and the orientations of the wider society. The role of the organized team serves to emphasize the adult, universalistic-achievement orientations deemed appropriate by the society.

The differences between the goals of peer-group play and organized team effort become apparent in their emphasis on means and ends. In the peer context, play is not overly concerned with ends; the essence of the play is the play—its fun, decisions, ritual, and personal interactions. In contrast, in organized sports, play tends to be incidental.

For the adults who organize sport programs, play is identified with ends. That is, to win, to teach youngsters to play soccer, baseball, and so forth in the short run, and to develop certain attitudes and values toward social relationships and activities that in the long run tend to reproduce the requirements of occupational life by emphasizing punctuality, periodicity, and performance. Indeed, it has been argued that organized sport socializes young athletes to accept authoritarian leadership and carry out coaches' directions without question, thus suppressing their own creative initiatives and personal growth.[19]

In peer play, there tends to be an elaboration of means either through varying the rules, particularizing relationships, or encouraging novelty. The games chosen in free play (in which less specialization of roles tends to occur) permit more elaboration of means. For example, the youngsters find many ways to use the same ball in their games. In organized sports the codified rules (enforced by coaches and officials) permit only one way to use a ball, a one-size field, a certain number of players to a side, and so forth. In organized sports programs, disputes about "calls" or about rules do not occur between players because they are made and applied by referees and coaches. Therefore, the experience in peer-play emphasizes interpersonal skills (negotiations and compromise), while the experience in organized sport is dominated by a knowledge and dependence on strict rules and with the acceptance of the decisions of adults, who are in positions of legitimate authority.

Applying a model of enjoyment of social experience, the Flow Model, to formal and informal sport settings, two noted researchers and authors of *Flow in Sport* report a high positive correlation between challenges and skills in informal sports settings but not in adult-supervised settings. They suggest that the flow experience is easier to achieve when adolescents are in control of the activity, probably because they can manipulate the balance between challenges and skills more easily in an informal setting.[20]

What is implied by an analysis of these two play forms is that play behavior in the peer group is quite different from play behavior in the youth sports program. We are not arguing that one of these forms of play is good and the other bad. What we are emphasizing is that the variations in the social organization of children's play undoubtedly have different social consequences for them.

DEVELOPMENT OF PERSONAL-SOCIAL ATTRIBUTES THROUGH SPORT

As noted earlier in this chapter, the primary justifications of youth sports programs are the opportunities they provide for young boys and girls to learn culturally relevant sport skills and to develop desirable personal-social characteristics. "Sport builds character" is one of the most frequently recited slogans for the supposed outcomes of sport for youth. It inevitably is used by community leaders, school officials, parents, coaches—virtually everyone—when a discussion turns to the purpose of organized sports for children and adolescents. Although the learning of attitudes, values, and moral behavior is a core aim of youth sports, there is very little definitive research on the outcomes of sports participation—that is, the effects of sport involvement on the personal and social development of children.

Youth Orientation toward Sport

There has been a sustained interest in the effects of sports experiences on the orientations youth have toward sport. One of the orientations sport sociologists have focused on is whether participation in organized sport influences what participants think is most important about playing. Specifically, they have studied orientations that emphasize the process (playing fair, playing for fun) and orientations that emphasize the product (playing to win); the latter is called a "professional" attitude.

Researchers found, overall, that there is a strong tendency for both males and females who have been involved in organized sports to have more professionalized orientations than peers who have not been involved in organized sports. Elite athletes, both males and females, display a strong professional orientation toward sport. These findings are probably not surprising, given the structural conditions of organized sport, which socializes youngsters into accepting and internalizing values of success-striving, of competitive achievement, of personal worth based upon sports outcomes, and of subjection of self to external control. Although it is difficult to credit (or discredit) sports participation entirely for greater professionalized attitudes toward sport, it does seem that sport for fun, enjoyment, fairness, and equity is often sacrificed at the altar of skill and victory as children continue their involvement in organized sports.[21]

Sportsmanship in Youth Sport

Sportsmanlike behavior—striving to succeed but committed to playing by the rules and observing ethical standards that take precedence over strategic gain when the two conflict—is universally admired, but it sometimes conflicts with the quest for victory. In the sport culture at all levels, good sportsmanship and fair play are the accepted standards and are overwhelmingly practiced by those involved in organized sports. But the multitude of good sportsmanship throughout sports is rarely noted in the public discourse or in the media. This is true because it is the expected, the normative, behavior. On the other hand, poor sportsmanship, like deviant behavior in most social settings, gets noted, gets attention, gets reactions, and therefore often seems to overshadow good sportsmanship in personal conversations and in media stories. In the following paragraphs on this topic, we will describe some findings about poor sportsmanship, but the reader should keep in mind what we have said here about good sportsmanship.

Competition is inextricably connected to sportsmanship. Sportsmanship and fairness underlie the social convention of virtually all youth sports programs, but on the other hand, victory in organized sports competition often carries more salient rewards. The slogan "It's not whether you win or lose but how you play the game," while never universally embraced in the culture of organized sport, was acknowledged by many coaches, athletes, and parents as an appropriate attitude for playing well, playing within the rules, and playing in a sportsmanlike manner rather than for the mere winning of a sporting event. That standard has become challenged by the slogan "Winning isn't everything, it's the only thing." When taken seriously, this latter slogan suggests that any means or methods are legitimate in the pursuit of victory. It has been accompanied with practices like trash talking, intimidating opponents, taunting and ridiculing opponents, and deliberately violating the rules of the sport—all in the interest of "getting the edge" and winning the sporting event. For example, a study of youth sports conducted by researchers at the University of Missouri–St. Louis, the University of Minnesota, and Notre Dame involving 803 young athletes ages nine to fifteen, along with 189 parents and 61 coaches, found, according to the athletes:

- two in ten admitted to cheating often.
- nineteen percent had tried to hurt an opponent often.
- twenty-seven percent had acted like "bad sports" after a loss.
- seven percent of their coaches had encouraged the athletes to cheat.
- eight percent of their coaches had encouraged the athletes to hurt an opponent.[22]

These percentages may seem low, but they are made up of hundreds of individual respondents, so the sum of the incidents is actually quite large, and thus disturbing. See Box 4.1, *Thinking about Sport*, for further discussion on this topic.

There are a number of sources of a trend toward increasingly unsportsmanlike attitudes and behaviors in youth sports. Professional and college athletes have always profoundly influenced young athletes. Professional and college players are the role models and heroes of youth sport athletes, and young athletes adopt the attitudes, manner, and behavior of their heroes. It is those heroes that often display the trash talking, intimidating, ridiculing, and rule breaking that have sifted down to youth athletes.

Coaches and parents are other powerful sources for socializing young athletes about sportsmanship attitudes and behaviors. Many coaches and parents are aware of their influence on their children and make a valiant effort to make sport a positive experience, emphasizing fun, fair play, and good sportsmanship. Unfortunately, it appears that a growing number of other coaches and parents are out of control. Many of them have become models of bad sportsmanship for the young athletes. More about this can be found in the "Adult Intrusion in Youth Sports" section of this chapter.

There is also an ominous societal trend that might be contributing to the growing unsportsmanlike behavior of young athletes. There is widespread acknowledgment that acts of "incivility" between people have become more common in North American culture (more about this in chapter 15). Such actions undoubtedly influence the culture of sport and become translated into poor sportsmanship at all levels.

Efforts are being made to counteract the prevailing trend toward unsportsmanlike conduct. The Institute for International Sport at the University of Rhode Island has been sponsoring an annual National Sportsmanship Day for more than fifteen years. Also, the National Alliance for Youth Sport and a number of professional and amateur sports organizations like the Institute have publicly affirmed "good sportsmanship" and committed to developing policies to reward sportsmanlike behaviors and punish unsportsmanlike actions in events under their jurisdiction. Even though these efforts are against the prevailing trend, there are encouraging signs that they are having some positive effects on sports at all levels.[23]

Character Development in Youth Sports

From the beginning of organized youth sports forms there has been a prevailing impression that the sporting environment is particularly useful for young athletes to learn moral values and principles.

Box 4.1 *Thinking about Sport* Which Is It, Poor Sportsmanship or Just Being a Great Competitor?

As the emphasis on winning and "doing whatever it takes" to win has become more prevalent in youth sports, the line between good and poor sportsmanship has become blurred for many youth sport coaches, athletes, and parents. Here is an example: Referring to one of his young pitchers, a coach explained, "He's just a fierce competitor. Nobody competes better." The coach went on to recount how once when this pitcher lost his bid for a perfect game in the sixth inning, "he didn't get upset. He didn't say anything. You couldn't tell by his demeanor, but he wound up and hit the next batter right between the shoulder blades." The coach proudly exclaimed: "I love to have pitchers who are great competitors like that." The young pitcher was praised for deliberately hitting a batsman for something he had nothing to do with—spoiling the pitcher's perfect game. What did the young pitcher learn from his coach about sportsmanship in this episode?

The often-used slogan to affirm this is "sport builds character." Like most slogans, this one is not grounded in empirical findings, and when research has been conducted to ascertain the effects of sport involvement on character development, the findings have provided little in the way of specific or consistent answers.

Because the word *character* is so ambiguous, and therefore has so many meanings to people, researchers have turned to assessing moral development and moral reasoning as a means of measuring the "character" outcomes of sports involvement. At the Center for Ethics at the University of Idaho, Sharon Kay Stoll and her colleagues Angela Lumpkin and Jennifer M. Beller conduct research about competitive ethics, moral development, and moral reasoning. Moral development, for Stoll and her colleagues, refers to "the evolving growth process by which one learns to take the welfare of others into consideration when making moral decisions," and moral reasoning is "the ability to systematically think through a moral problem, taking into consideration one's own values and beliefs while weighing them against what others value and believe."[24] Moral development and moral reasoning are primarily acquired through an individual's social learning experiences. Political leaders, business leaders, sport administrators, coaches, parents, and virtually all sectors of public life see organized youth sports as a perfect classroom for improving moral development and moral reasoning.

Several researchers have used moral development and reasoning theories to study the effects of sport involvement on athletes. Because these terms involve the decision processes whereby the rightness or wrongness of behaviors is determined, the focus is on how one decides whether a particular course of action is right or wrong.

A substantial body of research findings on moral development and reasoning among athletes and their nonathlete peers suggests that young athletes who have been involved in organized sports programs have significantly less mature levels of moral development and reasoning than nonathletes. On the other hand, there are some researchers who have found no significant differences between athletes and nonathletes.[25]

Critics of the findings of differences between athletes and nonathletes point to both theoretical and methodological limitations of this research. Others argue that the reasons for such differences may or may not be related to sports experiences of the athletes—that is, the differences may have existed prior to the sports involvement of the athletes. Unfortunately, the research design of these studies makes it impossible to determine whether the differences found between sports participants and nonparticipants are the result of participation or whether persons with certain personal-social characteristics are initially attracted to and remain involved in sports. Therefore, differences that exist between young athletes and nonathletes are not necessarily a consequence of sport involvement.

The effects of sports involvement on young athletes' moral development are still a topic for future researchers to unravel. However, the findings of the empirical research at this time do suggest that slogans implying that youth sporting experiences universally develop positive personal-social characteristics—and thus "build character"—are too simplistic.

Are there experiences during sports participation that *might* hamper moral development? If we accept the notion that children learn normative behavior from sports and if we agree that social-norm deviance is present in sport, clearly youth sports programs may be providing patterned reinforcement of attitudes, values, and behaviors that are at variance with the development of moral reasoning. Deviation from the ideal norms occurs frequently in sports (e.g., incidents of athletes physically attacking one another during games, the booing of officials, and even the incorporation of deviance as part of the strategy of the game, such as spearing in football, illegal body checking in hockey, and so forth). There are well-planned, deliberate violations of the rules to make winning difficult for the opponent in most sports. Acceptance of such behavior is likely associated with internalization of lower levels of reasoning.

Although one may question the extent to which moral learning in sports generalizes to larger social relations, one certainly must consider the possible social effects on athletes who play under coaches who encourage unethical behavior. Convincing evidence from social learning experiments demonstrates that youngsters do model the attitudes and behaviors of people they respect and admire, and young athletes almost universally have high regard for their coaches.

Besides moral development, there are other social outcomes to which sports involvement during youth may contribute. Competence in sports skills apparently does influence self-evaluation and social esteem with peers. Sports provide innumerable opportunities for the individual to perceive the feelings of others and their judgments. Thus, experiences in sports may be instrumental in development of a self-image or self-concept. Several investigations have shown that sports abilities and interests are related to a positive self-concept, and research has consistently shown that young sports participants score higher in a variety of tests that measure mental health. But, again, most of the research here is designed to measure relationships between the variables, not causal outcomes.

POTENTIAL PSYCHOSOCIAL PROBLEMS OF YOUTH SPORTS

A variety of social problems have arisen with the growth and expansion of organized youth sports, and there is increasing apprehension about potential harm to youngsters in these sports programs. Although youth sport literature is rich with critics who have axes to grind or converts to proselytize, the fact is they often make some very telling points. There is little doubt that some very abusive practices are taking place in the world of youth sports. Having said this, we wish to reemphasize the point we made in the previous section, namely that many young people experience positive personal-social growth experiences through youth sports. The kinds of outcomes experienced by youngsters are primarily contingent upon parents and coaches, for they are the most powerful "significant others" in the lives of young boys and girls.

In this section we discuss some of the most common problems of youth sports. It is not our intent to make specific accusations or to condemn all youth sports. We merely suggest that the social experiences of some youth sports athletes may have social consequences that are perhaps unintended and unwanted.

Adult Intrusion in Youth Sports

The rationale behind the organization of youth sports programs is admirable: to provide young boys and girls with structure for their sports, opportunities for wide participation, proper equipment for their safety, and adult coaching to help them learn the fundamental skills and strategies. But there is overwhelming agreement that one of the major problems of youth sports is the intrusion of adults into the sports life of youngsters. The communications director for the National Alliance for Youth Sport recently noted: "Physical and verbal abuse involving parents, coaches, and officials is widespread. Parents assault coaches, coaches assault officials, and parents and coaches demean children."[26]

Many parents and coaches live vicariously through the youngsters, living out their unfulfilled sports dreams through the children, making considerable emotional and, sometimes, financial investments in the young athletes. Therefore, they expect a payoff and that payoff is athletic achievement by way of victories and championships. When a youngster achieves, parents and coaches see that success as, in a way, their own personal achievement. If the young athlete fails to live up to performance expectations, he or she may feel like a personal failure, as well as feeling he or she didn't fulfill the expectations of others.

These pressures on a young athlete are described quite articulately by Christopher Andersonn in his book titled *Will You Still Love Me If I Don't Win?* He is a consultant on emotional stress in sports to coaches, parents, and athletes. Andersonn recounts a conversation he had with a young age-group swimmer who had been throwing up before each meet in which he competed. He began by asking the young swimmer: "Are you a pretty good swimmer?" The boy shyly replied, "I guess so . . . I don't know." Andersonn continued: "Are your parents very interested in your swimming?" "My dad is," replied the boy. Andersonn continues: "I asked if his dad attended all his practices. Yes, he did, the boy answered. I asked him if he was concerned that his dad might be disappointed in him if he didn't do well. He thought so. Then I asked if he thought his dad might stop loving him if he didn't continue to improve. He looked at me for the longest time, then finally lowered his eyes and said in a very soft voice, 'I don't know.'"[27]

For parents and coaches whose aspirations are national rankings and a professional sports career for the youngsters involved, youth sports are not play and games; they are a way of life. Sports psychologist Rick Wolff asserted: "Excelling in sports has become as much a part of the American dream for parents as getting their kids into the best school and living in the best neighborhoods."[28] The parents of Venus and Serena Williams and Tiger Woods have become the poster models for thousands of parents throughout North America. The parents of these athletes have devoted most of their adult lives, and the childhood lives of these athletes, to the pursuit of their children's professional sports careers. Their success in achieving professional sports careers for their offspring, and the celebratory status accompanying it, have set a course that countless parents now follow for their children. "If the Williamses and Woodses can do it, we can too" seems to be the attitude of parents who adopt this course. In addition to professional careers, some parents aspire for their child to receive a college athletic scholarship, while others aspire to their child winning an Olympic berth.

Because such aspirations have become so commonplace, they have changed the structure of youth sports and some families' lives. In stories detailing the changing structure of youth sports, two *USA Today* columnists assert: "Kids used to play year-round alternating the sport with the season. That's not the case anymore as parents let unrealistic dreams shoehorn their children into one-sport misery." "The day of the three-sport high school athlete is rapidly disappearing as coaches tell even 10-year-olds who show some promise in a particular sport to stick to that sport year-round."[29]

Now it is "traveling teams" or "club teams" that have become a popular form of youth sport organization. They are composed of kids who have risen through local teams to be selected for the more competitive travel teams. These young athletes are drawn from mostly suburban neighborhoods and towns in a given region. They have two- to three-hour practices three or four times per week, and they make single-day or weekend-long pilgrimages to play other similarly skilled teams in distant towns—often in other states or provinces. The extremes to which this goes are illustrated in an article titled "Baseball or Bust," describing the saga of a boy who played 127 baseball games in one year in the ten-and-under leagues. The founder of the National Alliance for Youth Sports says, "we have reached the point of saturation—a vicious revolving door of never-ending seasons."[30]

For both the young athletes and their families the commitment to traveling teams is almost total. The young athletes must abandon other organized sports to concentrate on the travel team. They must commit to specializing in one sport, and often must compete with their team year-round. Family lives must be recentered around the sports world of the traveling teams. The new breed of sports parents are road warriors who drive thousands of miles every season and spend weekends and evenings watching their kids' practice and play. And they write many checks because it is very expensive to support a traveling or club team athlete.[31]

The trends of parental intrusion into youth sports, traveling teams, hyperorganization, and hypercompetitive youth sports has spawned a commercial industry devoted to coaching and training young athletes for the lofty sports goals they and their parents often have. This new industry goes way beyond the traditional sports camps that have been held by college coaches and professional athletes for the past twenty-five years. Although the daily or weekly sports camps are still popular throughout North America, sports academies have become the ultimate in coaching and preparing young athletes whose parents strive for

NCAA Division I college scholarships, professional careers, and Olympic berths for their children.

International Management Group (IMG), headquartered on a sprawling 180-acre campus in Bradenton, Florida, is the elite model of the academies. According to its website, "IMG Academies is the largest, most successful multi-sport training and education institution in the world. More than 12,000 junior, collegiate, adult and professional athletes from over 75 countries attend each year. IMG has five different sports academies—for tennis, golf, soccer, baseball, and basketball." A basic one-year term will have a tuition starting at over twenty-five thousand dollars. With the addition of special private lessons, some parents pay up to one hundred thousand dollars per term. Some children remain at IMG academies for several years.[32]

Similar high-tech sports performance training centers are popping up, mostly in suburbs, across the country. Some cater to young athletes who want to become "the best" in specific sports; others focus on arcane skills designed to improve agility, strength, speed, and power—the fundamentals of all sports. Overwhelmingly the athletes come from affluent families. Sports academy and sports performance training center athletes tend to be members of middle- and upper-middle-class families. Parents of these athletes report annual expenses for their athlete-son or -daughter ranging from twelve thousand dollars to one hundred thousand dollars.

IMG Sports Academies officials admit that the real basis for admission is parents' ability to pay, not physical prowess. Golf's renowned teaching pro, David Leadbetter, says of his IMG Leadbetter Academy, "We don't want only rich kids to come here." But he acknowledges, "there's certainly a class factor. It's expensive to play golf." Obviously, poor families cannot afford such expenses for their children's sports programs. In recent years public money for recreation centers and after-school sports programs has declined, and for children growing up in poor families in poor communities, youth sports opportunities are severely limited.

Commenting on how the academy system/training centers system disadvantages youth from poor families and the schools sports teams they belong to, the former commissioner of the Colorado High School Activities Association said: "They bust their butt at [inner-city schools] and once in a while put together good teams. But mostly, they get kicked; they have no chance. It's totally a case of haves and have-nots. You can almost name the sport. Even volleyball and basketball. These are inner-city games, but it's the well-heeled suburban schools who have the best teams."[33]

One infamous exception to this system of social class privilege is youth basketball. Basketball shoe corporations Nike and Adidas, working with the Amateur Athletic Union (AAU) and sport-shoe-sponsored coaches, seduce young, mostly poor inner-city kids to play in tournaments all over North America. The youngsters and their parents are showered with merchandise, flown to tournaments, fawned over, and then subtly steered toward high schools whose teams happen to have lucrative shoe deals with the companies. Even one of the driving forces behind this system admits he is one of the people who keeps this cesspool of amateur basketball bubbling.

Like Mount Everest climbers, a few youth sport athletes do make it to the top and become professional athletes or Olympians. They become celebrities, and newspaper and magazine stories about them frequently report their odyssey through youth sports programs. But they are the very few out of millions of youth who play sports each year, and whose parents fantasize that their son or daughter will become the next Tiger Woods, Venus Williams, Derrick Jeter, or Annika Sorenstam. Unfortunately, despite thousands of dollars spent by parents and untold hours of practicing and playing games by young athletes, fewer than 1 percent of them will even receive a college athletic scholarship. And less than 1 percent of those who play college sports will become professional or Olympic athletes. Occasionally the stories of athletes who did not fulfill their, or their parents', dreams of sporting fame come to light. There are even the sad stories of successful professionals and Olympians who publicly share their experiences of pressure, abuse, depression, and the loss of childhood through the years of struggling to achieve sporting prominence.

Certainly, children who are sent to train in sports academies in another part of the country are coached by well-known coaches, compete in national and international sports events, or turn professional during their adolescence are under immense pressures for they are competing to live up to their parents, coaches, media, and their own expectations, and it is a heavy burden.

As one young golfer enrolled in the IMG Leadbetter Golf Academy said, "My father has paid hundreds of thousands of dollars for me to be here. I want to pay him back and get a scholarship for college so he doesn't have to pay for college."[34]

Many former youth sports athletes remember their years in youth sports programs as being fun, exciting, and even, for some, the best years of their lives with their family. However, several writers have documented these years as being filled with stress, fear, abuse, and torment for some young athletes. Fred Engh's book *Why Johnny Hates Sports* details the impact of parents who lose perspective and, driven by their own aspirations and goals for their children, subject the kids to unrelenting pressure and anxiety. Engh offers many excellent suggestions that will lead to better sports for youth.

Christopher Andersonn's book *Will You Still Love Me If I Don't Win?* describes some of the sad stories of parental insensitivity to their children's developmental needs in their maniacal mission to raise a professional athlete or an Olympian. Andersonn also shows how to improve parenting skills so that sports can be fun and rewarding for both young athletes and their parents.[35]

Adult intrusion into the world of youth sports can rob the young participants of some of the greatest potential of sports, and that is the opportunity to have fun and to develop self-discipline and responsibility for one's own actions. Many youth sports programs are dominated by the coaches, who make all the decisions; they decide who plays, where they play, what tactics to employ, and what plays to run. In effect, the youngsters are the "hired help," who carry out the orders and do not ask questions, if they do not want to be labeled "problem athletes." Thus, the imposition of adult dominance and decision making in youth programs appears to do little to develop self-discipline and self-responsibility in children.

We want to make clear that we do not condemn all youth sports programs, but dominance by some parents and coaches tends to conflict with the true spirit of play by exaggerating the importance of technique, efficiency, and winning—such programs can deprive youngsters of the fun and play elements of sport. (See Box 4.2, *Thinking about Sport*.)

Box 4.2 *Thinking about Sport* **A Teachable Moment or Reaction by the Coach?**

Behind by one run in the fifth inning of the Colorado state-qualifying American Legion B District Tournament baseball game against an arch rival, the coach yanked his centerfielder from the game after the player threw his glove twice in a fit of anger when he failed to make a play that allowed a run to score.

The coach's action may not seem too unusual, but in this case the coach showed the extent of his priorities because he did not have another player to replace the one that was yanked. The team had no substitutes on the bench.

With only eight players to finish the game, the disciplinary action put the coach's team at a huge disadvantage because the team would have to finish the game with only two outfielders and accept an automatic out every time the yanked player's place in the lineup came up.

The coach said he did what he did because he thought it was important to show [the disciplined player] the value of "trusting your teammates and not being an individual. If we didn't care about him or we didn't think he was a player then you just let that kind of stuff go. When you know he's a player and he's a good kid you can't let it go."

Postscript: After prolonged discussion by the umpires, and over the vigorous objection of the coach, the umpires ruled—incorrectly it turns out—that a coach cannot remove a player from a game if it does not have another player to replace the removed one.

Source: Coach quoted in Tom Wright, "Coach Calls It Right in Defeat," *Greeley Tribune*, 21 July 2007, p. B5.

Perhaps the most objectionable forms of adult intrusion into children's sports involve violent behavior: physical assaults by parents and coaches, and sexual abuse of young athletes by youth sport coaches. With regard to physical assaults, youth sport administrators admit they are dealing with what many call "sideline rage" and they say it is at epidemic levels. Recent reports from over two thousand chapters of the National Alliance for Youth Sports have indicated that about 15 percent of youth games involve some sort of verbal or physical abuse from parents or coaches.[36] The specific incidents vary, but they are widespread throughout North America and they all involve assaultive actions. In a recent reader survey by *Sports Illustrated for Kids,* 74 percent of more than three thousand respondents reported they had witnessed out-of-control adults at their games. A similar survey by *Sporting Kids Magazine,* with 3,300 coaches, parents, youth sports administrators, and youth athletes responding, found that 84 percent said they had seen parents acting violently, such as shouting, berating, and using abusive language. Here are two accounts of recent incidents:

- After a basketball game between ten- and eleven-year-olds in Iowa, a mother of one of the players attacked a pregnant referee. According to police reports, the attacker grabbed the referee by the hair, threw her to the ground, and kicked her.
- At a girls' rugby tournament game in California, a coach and several parents beat the opposing coach unconscious with kicks to the head and face, according to witnesses.[37]

Social scientists who have tried to explain these violent incidents point to the culture of violence in the wider society. Richard Lapchick's Institute for Diversity and Ethics in Sport at the University of Central Florida studies the interrelationships between society and sport. Lapchick blames the increase in parental violence on the rise of violence in other sectors of society. Indeed, one of the most hotly discussed current social issues is the rise in interpersonal incivility today. Other social analysts suggest that the excesses, aggression, and "in your face" actions that characterize contemporary cultural behavior are at work in professional sports for all to see: NFL players spitting in the face of opponents; NBA Indiana Pacers' players charging into the stands to punch fans; NHL's Todd Bertuzzi of the Vancouver Canucks sucker-punching Steve Moore of the Colorado Avalanche, knocking Moore unconscious, and then driving Moore headfirst into the ice.

Parents and coaches are part of a social system that is larger than just sport; they are not immune to happenings in the broader society and in professional sports. There is also an additional factor for them. Many parents and coaches have become so ego- and emotionally involved with their children's sports or with the kids they are coaching that they have lost control over their own behavior.

Social problems typically produce collective actions aimed at remedying them. Various efforts are being made to stem the tide of escalating parental and coaches' "sideline rage." The goal is to educate parents and coaches and hold them accountable for their actions. For the past decade the Positive Coaching Alliance (PCA) has been holding workshops for youth sport coaches. According to its website, the PCA is a nonprofit organization based at Stanford University with the mission to transform youth sports so sports can transform youth. PCA was created to transform the culture of youth sports to give all young athletes the opportunity for a positive, character-building experience. It has three national goals:

1. To replace the "win-at-all-cost" model of coaching with the "Double-Goal Coach" who wants to win but has a second, more important, goal of using sports to teach life lessons;
2. To teach youth sports organization leaders how to create an organizational culture in which Honoring the Game is the norm; and
3. To spark and fuel a "social epidemic" of Positive Coaching that will sweep this country.

Since 1998, PCA has conducted thousands of workshops nationwide for roughly two hundred thousand youth sports leaders, coaches, parents, and athletes that have helped create a positive sports environment for more than one million youth athletes.[38]

The National Alliance for Youth Sports is another organization that advocates for positive and safe youth sports. It created the Parents Association for Youth Sports (PAYS) to give parents a clear understanding of their roles and responsibilities for youth sport. It does that through a thirty-minute program that teaches parents sportsmanlike behaviors they can then pass on to their children. Parents access the program through a participating sports organization or online. Over five hundred organizations are currently using PAYS in an effort to prevent parent behavior problems in their programs.[39]

Some communities have begun hiring paid, trained supervisors to oversee all youth sports in the community. Other communities now require parents and coaches to sign an agreement spelling out a code of conduct. Without the signatures, parents' children cannot play in the programs and coaches cannot coach.

As serious as the physical assaultive behavior of some parents and coaches is, surely the most distressing and odiously violent adult in youth sports is the child molester, the pedophile (a Greek word literally meaning "lover of children"). Until a few years ago, molestation was a nonissue in youth sports. The few scattered reports of sexual abuse of young athletes had been so rare that the media had largely ignored them. But in the fall of 1999, a *Sports Illustrated* special report entitled "Every Parent's Nightmare" shocked people in both the United States and Canada. The report began: "The child molester has found a home in the world of youth sports, where as a coach he can gain the trust and loyalty of kids—and then prey on them." The report identified a half-dozen or so youth sport child molesters and described their molestation tactics. One of the perpetrators confessed that he had molested "a couple of hundred children over three decades."[40]

The fact that sexual molesters are found in youth sport is just another example of the linkages between the sports world and the broader society. Pedophiles pose a major social problem for society because of the devastating consequences for their victims, the difficulty of apprehending molesters, and the issue of what is the most appropriate punishment for them. As for youth sport, the recent revelations and frightening truth about child molestation in youth sports have made everyone connected to youth sports more vigilant in the selection and monitoring of coaches.

Disruption of Education

Another major social problem for young boys and girls who are being groomed for professional careers and Olympic status is that normal school attendance becomes impossible. At first the sports career and school may coexist peacefully, but when young athletes must practice six to eight hours per day, travel to distant cities and even foreign countries to participate in competition, and perhaps move from one region of the country to another to receive the desired coaching, normal educational routines must be disrupted. One example of this situation is sports academies, where more and more of the young athletes are being groomed for pro sport careers, Olympic berths, and a shot at fame and fortune.

Tennis, golf, swimming, figure skating, speed skating, skiing, soccer, and gymnastics require most of those who hope to become national- and international-level performers to train with the best coaches. There are so few of them in each sport that most athletes have to leave their home and take up residence sometimes thousands of miles away to be near the best coaches and facilities.

Several solutions have emerged to meet the needs of young athletes who are in full-time training. One solution is the employment of tutors for the youngsters. Increasingly, however, such informal arrangements are giving way to more formal academies where children live, train, and go to school in one complex.

Most of the sports academies point with some pride to the academic records of their students. Of course, these students are almost uniformly from upper-middle-class families, and they receive tutorial instruction or are in classes with a low student-to-teacher ratio. While these alternatives may result in a good education for such youngsters, a question can be raised about the disruptive effects of going to school in an environment dominated by sport practices and competition, and about the restricted interpersonal relationships present in such an environment.[41]

This leads to a fundamental question: Is sport involvement so important during the growing-up years that children must be robbed of the normal experiences of childhood? Undoubtedly, some parents and coaches answer yes, and for those very, very few who become Olympic champions or successful professionals, this assessment may be justified. For the vast majority of young athletes who endure this lifestyle and do not achieve the desired goal, however, a childhood may be lost. Examples of this abound in the stories of former athletes who spent their youth in sports academies and never became college, professional, or Olympic athletes.

Risk of Injury

Daily living has risks and the potential for injury. Going through childhood and adolescence without risk and injury would be like missing a part of one's life. Given this, there are nevertheless some activities in which the chance of injury is greater than normal, and when these activities are forced on youngsters by adults, the issue of abuse is present. Medical concern for the young athlete has a long history, and most persons associated with youth sports have heard the arguments about "Little League elbow" and about the dangers of tackle football and ice hockey for preadolescent youngsters.

There is, however, a growing concern that goes beyond Little League elbow and broken bones in football or hockey to "swimmer's shoulder" and "gymnast's back." According to Safe Kids USA, more than 3.5 million children ages fourteen and under receive medical treatment for sports injuries each year. Thirty percent of parents report that their child has been injured while playing a team sport; half of these say the child has been injured more than once. Nearly a quarter of these parents report that the injury was serious. Those injuries, in some cases, can lead to arthritis or require extensive surgery to repair.[42]

The accelerated training regimens of many current youth athletes that extend up to eight hours per day, six—even seven, in some cases—days a week, throughout the year, raise serious questions about physical injury. Physicians are seeing a dramatic increase in overuse injuries among children in organized sports. Several years ago, the Committee on Sports Medicine and Fitness (CSMF) published this statement in *Pediatrics* journal: "The necessary commitment and intensity of training [in some youth sports programs] raise concerns about the sensibility and safety of high-level athletics for any young person. . . . It is important to make efforts to assist young athletes in avoiding potential risks from early excessive training and competition."[43] In the ensuing years the CSMF has not changed its position on this issue.

The "Winning Is the Only Thing" Ethic and Youth Sports

The final topic we discuss in this section, one that lurks throughout youth sports, is what we call the "winning is the only thing" ethic. To understand this ethic in youth sport, it is helpful to understand its linkages to the broader American culture. Social analysts of American culture have noted what many have referred to as a hypercompetitive feature that is not as salient in other modern societies. Most of our social institutions are grounded in a rather domineering form of competition.

Our form of capitalist economy came into prominence with the robber barons of the latter nineteenth century and continues today with most industries dominated by huge corporations that have driven other enterprises out of business. The major form of testing in America's educational system is based on competition against other students or against standardized norms for good grades and educational advancement. America's media compete vigorously against each other for readers, listeners, and viewers. The political system is democratic and citizens have an opportunity to vote for the candidates of their choice, but the candidates compete fiercely to win the election.

It is perhaps not surprising, then, that hyper-competitiveness has permeated American sports since the rise of organized sports forms. At every level of organized sports, winning has been richly rewarded, either in monetary form or in social status. Some of the most admired sports celebrities have exuded a win-at-all-costs attitude—Pete Rose in baseball, Bill Romanowski in football, and similar models in other sports. The slogans of sports culture have emphasized an uncompromising attitude about winning: "Winning isn't everything, it's the only thing"; "Show me a good loser, and I'll show you a loser"; "*Lose* is a four-letter word"; "Feel no sympathy for the loser."

As we have previously noted, coaches and athletes at the professional, college, and high school levels are the role models and heroes of youth sport athletes, who tend to internalize the attitudes, values, and behaviors of older athletes. Their other role models and heroes are parents and coaches who are in daily contact with them and are powerful and direct in their socializing influence. Young athletes form fundamental attitudes, values, and beliefs from these interactions.

Although "winning is the only thing" is widely accepted for child athletes thrown into the big business of elite sports, such an ethic can become a terrible burden for young athletes. Win-loss records define them, and the records become the basis for assigning worthiness to individuals. Winners are accorded prestige and honor; losers suffer disdain and ridicule. Because being labeled a loser is the epitome of criticism in our society, many young athletes experience stress and develop anxiety and other forms of psychological trauma.

With more and more professional athletes making huge salaries, and top amateur athletes earning money and getting considerable media attention, more and more junior and age-group athletes are in training to become professional or Olympic-level athletes, and the pressures have become even more intense on these youngsters. What for most boys and girls is play becomes a job for some young athletes. In spite of the hours, even years, of hard work put in by these ambitious young athletes (and their parents), the issue of child labor has rarely come up, and the laws prohibiting child labor have never been applied to elite youth athletes. This point is forcefully made by Joan Ryan, author of a book about young elite gymnasts and figure skaters. She argues: "There simply is no safety net protecting these children. Not the parents, the coaches, or the federations. Child labor laws prohibit a thirteen-year-old from punching a cash register for forty hours a week, but that same child can labor for forty hours or more inside a gym or an ice skating rink without drawing the slightest glance from the government."[44]

The extent parents, coaches, and young athletes will go to, when winning becomes the only thing, has been well documented. The types of behaviors, with the attitudes toward sports to which they have been conditioned, do little to promote personal growth and the "character traits" that are universally endorsed as outcomes of sports involvement.

We wish to reemphasize that we are not denying the quest for victory has its place in youth sports. Striving for victory in a competitive situation is a perfectly legitimate goal. We do think, however, given the organizational nature of many youth sports programs and the emphasis on winning for elite-level young athletes, that there is a tendency to allow winning to become the only goal. When this happens in youth sports, the enormous potential benefit of sport involvement for a healthy self-concept development is jeopardized.

SPORTS ALTERNATIVES FOR THE YOUNG ATHLETE

Although youth sports programs have many problems, the alternatives that many children and adolescents have adopted have a variety of problems in terms of promoting their physical, mental, and social development. According to the Centers for Disease Control and Prevention (CDC), "the fundamental nature of American childhood has changed. . . . Today, childhood is spent mostly indoors, watching television, playing video games and working the Internet." Studies by the National Sporting Goods Association found that "the shift to an indoor childhood has accelerated in the past decade, with huge declines in spontaneous outdoor activities such as bike riding, swimming and touch football." The enticement of video games and television is not the only thing keeping young boys and girls indoors. Frequent news reports of pedophiles and missing children have made parents fearful of allowing their kids to play on their own in the neighborhood and parks. Richard Louv, author of *Last Child in the Woods,* claims "parents think their kids are safer in front of the X Box in the next room."[45]

One of the major consequences of childhoods spent mostly indoors playing video games and watching television is the increase in obesity among the young population. Two surveys by the CDC, one from 1976 to 1980 and one from 2003 to 2004, show that the prevalence of overweight is increasing. For children aged 2–5 years, prevalence increased from 5.0 to 13.9 percent; for those aged 6–11 years, prevalence increased from 6.5 to 18.8 percent; and for those aged 12–19 years, prevalence increased from 5.0 to 17.4 percent. CDC defines overweight as being at or above the 95th percentile of the CDC Body Mass Index. Thus, the percentage of youth overweight has more than tripled over the past thirty years. Overweight and obesity are major risk factors for chronic diseases, including type 2 diabetes, cardiovascular disease, hypertension, osteoporosis, and some cancers. Some children may develop sleep apnea, mature early, have increased low-density lipoprotein (LDL, the so-called bad cholesterol), and run the risk of liver and gall bladder diseases.[46]

Emphasizing Personal Growth and Self-Actualization

Our major contention in this book is that sports for youth have virtually unlimited potential for promoting personal growth and self-actualization. Therefore the goal of youth sports should be nothing less than self-fulfillment of the individuals engaged in and influenced by them. The emphasis of such programs should be upon personal expression and the value of participation, upon offering everyone the opportunity to engage in sports in a way that youngsters experience no feeling of humiliation if the contest is lost. Why must sport be justified on the basis that it does things other than providing a lot of joy and self-fulfillment for the participants?

An increasing number of attempts have been made to improve youth sports by designing programs based on principles that place the personal-social needs of the participants first and the ambitions of adults far behind. There is a growing literature describing these programs and discussing ways and means by which parents and coaches can improve the quality of the sporting experience for young boys and girls. Several of the best books on this subject are *Whose Game Is It, Anyway?: A Guide to Helping Your Child Get the Most from Sports, Organized by Age and Stage; Home Team Advantage: The Critical Role of Mothers in Youth Sport; So, You Want Your Kid to Be a Sports Superstar; Surviving Youth Sports;* and *101 Ways to Be a Terrific Sports Parent: Making Athletics a Positive Experience for Your Child.*[47]

Alternative Sports

Baseball, football, basketball, and ice hockey were the dominant sports when organized youth sports programs were first getting started in North America. Although these are still quite popular youth sports, there is now much more variety in the sports available for kids. The newest trends in youth sports are coming from what are called "alternative sports" and "extreme sports"—sports that youngsters are developing largely themselves. The term *alternative sports* is used because many youngsters have become involved in them as a rejection of the norms and values of traditional youth sports.

One of the problems alternative sports have all experienced is corporate takeover: Advertisers and television executives discovered they could package these sports to make them attractive to young television audiences, and that they could sell TV commercial time to advertisers with products appealing to teenage and young adult male audiences. The X Games were created by ESPN to capture the growing popularity of alternative and extreme sports among the young for the purpose of generating profits for ESPN and the advertising corporations. This ESPN-X Games nexus will be discussed in more detail in chapter 11.

Cooperative Games

Cooperative games have been advocated by many youth sports leaders who believe that one of the objectives of sports and physical activity programs for youth should emphasize the learning of cooperative behavior. A number of educators and coaches have experimented with play and games as a means of developing positive cooperative behavior among children. They have found that cooperatively structured games are effective in producing cooperative social interaction among children.[48]

Youth Sports Coaches

It is estimated that there are some 7.5 million volunteer youth sports coaches in North America, most of whom have had no formal instruction in the developmental or educational aspects of teaching/coaching. Thus, there is agreement by almost everyone associated with youth sports that the vast majority of youth sports coaches are ill equipped for their role. Without them, though,

A coach reviewing strategies with his team. There are an estimated 7.5 million volunteer youth sports coaches in North America. (iStockphoto)

millions of boys and girls would not have the opportunity to participate in organized sports.

In an effort to help volunteer coaches become more knowledgeable, some youth sports programs have instituted mandatory clinics, workshops, and certification programs for all of their coaches. The American Sport Education Program (ASEP) is a complete education package that has been adopted by many youth sports organizations throughout the United States and Canada. Since its founding in 1976, ASEP has been a valuable education training tool for youth sports coaches. ASEP coaches learn to teach skills and strategies, plan effectively for their season, prepare athletes for competition, and understand the developmental needs of young athletes. Its curriculum is built on the philosophical foundation of "Athletes First, Winning Second."[49] (See Box 4.3, *Thinking about Sport*.)

The National Youth Sport Coaches Association (NYSCA) has been a pioneer in the development of a national training system for volunteer coaches. More than 1.2 million coaches have attended NYSCA clinics since the program began in 1981. At the end of each NYSCA clinic, coaches must (1) pass an exam that tests their understanding of the information conveyed in the clinic and (2) sign a pledge committing them to uphold the association's code of ethics. The NYSCA Coaches' Code of Ethics is shown in Box 4.4.

In Canada, the 3M National Coaching Certification Program (NCCP) is a collaborative program of the government of Canada, the provincial/territorial governments, the national and provincial/territorial sport organizations, and the Coaching Association of Canada. Many youth sports organizations encourage, and some even require, formal training for their coaches. The NCCP attempts to ensure that youth coaches have the necessary knowledge, skill, and values that are prerequisite to effective youth sport coaching.[50]

Bill of Rights for Young Athletes

Guarantees of personal liberty for all U.S. citizens are found in the Bill of Rights, which are the first ten amendments to the Constitution of the

> **Box 4.3 Thinking about Sport Top Five Steps to Being a Good Sports Parent**
>
> 1. Do not pressure your child into participating in sport; ask if she or he is interested.
> 2. If your child plays youth sports, continue to inquire whether he or she is enjoying it.
> 3. Don't criticize your child's coaches or referees on the field or in front of your child.
> 4. Make fun and skill development top priorities in your child athlete's participation—not just winning and losing.
> 5. Be supportive of your child's sport participation. Frequently tell your child how much you enjoy watching her or him play.

> **Box 4.4 NYSCA Coaches' Code of Ethics**
>
> I hereby pledge to live up to my certification as an NYSCA Coach by following the NYSCA Coaches' Code of Ethics.
>
> - I will place the emotional and physical well-being of my players ahead of a personal desire to win.
> - I will treat each player as an individual, remembering the large range of emotional and physical development for the same age group.
> - I will do my best to provide a safe playing situation for my players.
> - I will promise to review and practice the basic first aid principles needed to treat injuries of my players.
> - I will do my best to organize practices that are fun and challenging for all my players.
> - I will lead by example in demonstrating fair play and sportsmanship to all my players.
> - I will provide a sports environment for my team that is free of drugs, tobacco, and alcohol, and I will refrain from their use at all youth sports events.
> - I will be knowledgeable in the rules of each sport that I coach, and I will teach these rules to my players.
> - I will use those coaching techniques appropriate for each of the skills that I teach.
> - I will remember that I am a youth sports coach, and that the game is for children and not adults.
>
> *Source:* National Alliance for Youth Sports, http://www.nays.org/.

United States. Similar safeguards have also been written into most state constitutions. In Canada the Charter of Rights and Freedoms guarantees Canadians with a broad range of personal liberties. Many business organizations have also developed a bill of rights for their employees as a commitment to employees that they will be treated with dignity and respect, and that their needs and interests will be protected.

In an attempt to protect youth from adult exploitation in sports, a group of medical, physical education, and recreation leaders formulated a Bill of Rights for Young Athletes several years ago. The ten rights are targeted to coaches, leaders of recreation programs, officials, and parents in the hope that their implementation will promote the beneficial effects of athletic participation for all who are involved. These rights are:

1. The right to participate in sports.
2. The right to participate at a level commensurate with each child's maturity and ability.
3. The right to have qualified adult leadership.
4. The right to play as a child and not as an adult.
5. The right to share in the leadership and decision making of their sport participation.
6. The right to participate in safe and healthy environments.
7. The right to proper preparation in sports.
8. The right to an equal opportunity to strive for success.
9. The right to be treated with dignity.
10. The right to have fun in sports.

Many youth sport organizations have adopted the Bill of Rights for Young Athletes as a guarantee to the young athletes and their parents that the athletes' development and welfare will be protected. Typically, the bill of rights is included in materials given to the athletes and their parents when they sign up to play in a particular sports program.[51]

In Canada, a National Task Force on Children's Play, created by the Canadian Council on Children and Youth, has formulated Fair Play Codes that emphasize sport's potential for promoting desirable values among youthful participants.

SUMMARY

There has been an enormous increase in community-sponsored youth sports programs. There has also been a growth in elite youth sport in which the youngsters train and compete with aspirations of becoming professional or Olympic-caliber athletes. An estimated fifty-two million North American and some four million Canadian boys and girls participate in these programs each year. Two of the most salient factors contributing to the growth of these programs are (1) the rise of organized and corporate sport, followed by the desire to participate and to spectate on the part of large numbers of people, and (2) the realization by Canadians and Americans of the importance of providing varied opportunities for their children.

The objectives of most youth sports programs are to provide participants with an opportunity to learn culturally relevant sport skills and to develop attitudes and values about such things as competition, cooperation, sportsmanship, discipline, authority, and social relationships. There are, however, programs that are blatantly career-training programs.

The extent to which the attitudes, values, beliefs, and behaviors of participants are actually influenced by organized youth programs is largely unknown. Most studies of attitudes toward youth sports suggest that parents and participants believe that they are more beneficial than detrimental to the development of young boys and girls. Participants in these programs are socialized into them by a variety of social agents and agencies, parents, siblings, peers, coaches, the mass media, and so forth.

The social context of the informal, peer-organized sports activities is vastly different from that of the adult-organized youth sports programs. Thus, the play behavior in the two social contexts is likely to lead to quite different learning.

There are a number of problems in organized youth sports. One is that the intrusion of adults into the play of youngsters may rob the young participants of many of the values of play. A second is that the norm learning involved may actually be at variance with North American social norms. A third is that normal educational experiences may become impossible. A fourth is that intense training and competition for prolonged periods of time may cause both acute and chronic injury. Finally, the overemphasis on winning in some youth programs threatens to overshadow the expressive, self-fulfilling potential of sports participation.

A number of interesting efforts have been made to develop alternative youth sports programs; in most cases the emphasis of these programs is on fun, participation, and skill learning. One group of researchers has developed a system for helping coaches improve their coaching behavior, and in both the United States and Canada, courses have been developed to help coaches become more effective. In an attempt to protect young athletes from adult exploitation in sports, a Bill of Rights for Young Athletes and Fair Play Codes have been formulated.

WEB RESOURCES

www.nyssf.org
Home page of the National Youth Sports Safety Foundation (NYSSF). The NYSSF is a national nonprofit, educational organization dedicated to reducing the number and severity of injuries youth sustain in sports and fitness activities.

www.asep.com
The American Sport Education Program. When it was founded, ASEP was called the American Coaching Effectiveness Program (ACEP). ASEP's goal is to provide quality education for coaches, officials, administrators, parents, and athletes in

order to make the sport experience the best it can be for all involved. Volunteer Education Program courses and resources are for adults who work with community-based youth sport programs where coaches and officials are most often volunteers. Professional Education Program courses and resources are for adults who are involved in school, college, and competitive club sports programs.

www.nays.org/
As part of the National Alliance for Youth Sports (NAYS), the National Youth Sport Coaches Association provides training, support, and continuing education to adults who volunteer to coach out-of-school youth sports teams. The NYSCA program works to "sensitize" coaches to their responsibilities when working with children in sports and hold them accountable to a Code of Ethics.

www.coach.ca
The 3M National Coaching Certification Program in Canada is designed to improve the sport experience for coaches working with developing athletes involved in school, club, or community sport and to improve the success of high-performance athletes competing at the provincial, national, or international level.

www.sportsparenting.org
The Center for Sports Parenting provides parents with answers to questions and issues that surface with children in sport.

www.littleleague.org
The official site of Little League baseball.

www.youthsportsusa.com
A good overall site for a broad range of information about youth sports.

www.safekids.org
This site is dedicated to providing information and educational resources to protect kids from their number one killer—unintentional injury. The "In the News" link provides information about sport injuries to youth.

NOTES

1. Little League Baseball, http://www.littleleague.org; Pop Warner Little Scholars, Inc. (PWLS), http://www.popwarner.com; Jr. Drag Racing League, http://jrdragster.nhra.com/#; Dan Steinberg, "Children, Start Your Engines," *Washington Post,* National Weekly Edition, 15–21 August 2005, pp. 30–31.

2. Jerry Langdon, "A First Look at Project 2010," *SoccerTimes.com,* www.soccertimes.com/langdon/1999/aug31a.htm.

3. Bobby Fernandez, "When It Comes to Young Athletes, How Much Is Too Much Control?" *Greeley Tribune,* 24 September 2006, pp. B1–B9; David Oliver Relin, "Who's Killing Kids' Sports?" *Parade,* 7 August 2005, 4–5; C. John McCoglin, *Surviving Youth Sports* (Victoria, B.C.: Trafford Publishing, 2006).

4. Jack W. Berryman, "The Rise of Boys' Sports in the United States, 1900–1970," in *Children and Youth in Sport: A Biopsychosocial Perspective,* ed. Frank L. Smoll and Ronald E. Smith (Madison, Wis.: Brown & Benchmark, 1996), 4–14; see also Fred Engh, *Why Johnny Hates Sports* (Garden City Park, N.Y.: Avery, 1999), 29–38; Lance Van Auken and Robin Van Auken, *Play Ball!: The Story of Little League Baseball* (University Park: Pennsylvania State University Press, 2001).

5. Public Law 88-378, 88th Congress, 16 July 1964.

6. Christopher Stevenson, "Becoming an International Athlete: Making Decisions about Identity," in *Inside Sports,* ed. Jay Coakley and Peter Donnelly (New York: Routledge, 1999), 89.

7. U.S. Bureau of the Census, *Statistical Abstracts of the United States: 2007,* 126th ed. (Washington, D.C.: U.S. Government Printing Office, 2007), 52.

8. Brooke de Lench, *Home Team Advantage: The Critical Role of Mothers in Youth Sport* (New York: Collins, 2006); Sohaila Shakib and Michele D. Dunbar, "How High School Athletes Talk about Maternal and Paternal Sporting Experiences," *International Review for the Sociology of Sport* 39, no. 3 (2004): 275–299; Joel Fish and Susan Magee, *101 Ways to Be a Terrific Sports Parent: Making Athletics a Positive Experience for Your Child* (New York: Fireside, 2003).

9. Christine Brennan, "Old Sportsman Saw Way before Title IX," *USA Today,* 17 May 2001, p. 3C; for an excellent review on this topic, see Thelma S. Horn and Jocelyn L. Horn, "Family Influences of Children's Sport and Physical Activity Participation, Behavior, and Psychosocial Responses," in *Handbook of Sport Psychology,* 3rd ed., ed. Gershon Tennenbaum and Robert C. Eklund (New York: John Wiley, 2007), 685–711.

10. Donald W. Albertson, *Catch a Rising Star: The Adult Game of Youth Sports* (Austin, Tex.: Turnkey Press, 2006); see also Clay Latimer, "Giving the Young a Sporting Chance," *Rocky Mountain News*, 17 December 2005, pp. 1B, 12B–13B.

11. Stevenson, "Becoming an International Athlete," 89; see also Horn and Horn, "Family Influences of Children's Sport and Physical Activity Participation, Behavior, and Psychosocial Responses," 702–706.

12. Stevenson, "Becoming an International Athlete," 89–92.

13. The American Sport Education Program (ASEP), a department of Human Kinetics Publishers, has published more than twelve books on coaching youth sports.

14. Robert Weinberg et al., "Motivation for Youth Participation in Sport and Physical Activity: Relationships to Culture, Self-Reported Activity Levels, and Gender," *International Journal of Sport Psychology* 31 (2000): 321–346.

15. Engh, *Why Johnny Hates Sports*, 3–4, 128–131; Robert S. Weinberg and Daniel Gould, *Foundations of Sport Psychology and Exercise Psychology*, 4th ed. (Champaign, Ill.: Human Kinetics, 2007).

16. For a good discussion of this topic, see Angela Lumpkin, Sharon K. Stoll, and Jennifer M. Beller, *Sport Ethics: Applications for Fair Play*, 3rd ed. (New York: McGraw-Hill, 2003), 111–118; see also Engh, *Why Johnny Hates Sports*, 132–133.

17. Bob Bigelow and Tom Moroney, *Just Let the Kids Play: How to Stop Other Adults from Ruining Your Child's Fun and Success in Sports* (Deerfield Beach, Fla.: HCI, 2001); Patricia A. Adler and Peter Adler, *Peer Power: Preadolescent Culture and Identity* (New Brunswick, N.J.: Rutgers University Press, 1998).

18. Joan Ryan, *Little Girls in Pretty Boxes: The Making and Breaking of Elite Gymnasts and Figure Skaters*, rev. ed. (New York: Warner Books, 2000).

19. Albertson, *Catch a Rising Star*.

20. Susan A. Jackson and Mihaly Csikszentmihalyi, *Flow in Sports: The Keys to Optimal Experiences and Performances* (Champaign, Ill.: Human Kinetics, 1999); see also Bigelow and Moroney, *Just Let the Kids Play*; Kenneth R. Ginsburg, "The Importance of Play in Promoting Healthy Child Development and Maintaining Strong Parent-Child Bonds," *American Academy of Pediatrics* 119, no. 1 (2007): 182–191.

21. For a review of the professionalization research, see David Light Shields and Brenda Light Bredemeier, "Advances in Sport Morality Research," in *Handbook of Sport Psychology*, ed. Tennenbaum and Eklund, 663–664.

22. David Light Shields, Brenda Light Bredemeier, Nicole M. LaVoi, and F. Clark Power, "The Sport Behavior of Youth, Parents, and Coaches: The Good, the Bad, and the Ugly," *Journal of Research in Character Education* 3, no. 1 (2005): 43–59. See also Greg Toppo, "Image of Youth Sports Takes Another Hit," *USA Today*, 6 September 2006, p. 7D; Update, "Youth Coach Convicted in Beanball Incident," *USA Today*, 15 September 2006, p. 19C.

23. See, for example, National Alliance for Youth Sports, http://www.nays.org/; Bruce B. Svare, *Reforming Sports before the Clock Runs Out* (Delmar, N.Y.: Bordalice Publishing, 2004); Elaine Raakman, "Just Play," *Journal of Physical Education, Recreation, and Dance* 77, no. 6 (2006): 20–24; Mary Sara Wells, Edward Ruddell, and Karen Paisley, "Creating an Environment for Sportsmanship Outcomes," *Journal of Physical Education, Recreation, and Dance* 77, no. 7 (2006): 13–17.

24. Lumpkin, Stoll, and Beller, *Sport Ethics*, 267–268; see also David Shields and Brenda Jo Bredemeier, *Character Development and Physical Activity* (Champaign, Ill.: Human Kinetics, 1995); Sigmund Loland, ed., *Fair Play in Sport: A Moral Norm System* (New York: Routledge, 2002).

25. For the most recent thorough review of this topic, see Shields and Bredemeier, "Advances in Sport Morality Research," 662–684; see also President's Council on Physical Fitness and Sports, "Sports and Character Development," *Research Digest*, March 2006.

26. Quoted in Greg Bach, "The Parents Association for Youth Sports," *Journal of Physical Education, Recreation, and Dance* 77, no. 6 (2006): 19; McCoglin, *Surviving Youth Sports*.

27. Christopher Andersonn, *Will You Still Love Me If I Don't Win?* (Dallas, Tex.: Taylor, 2000), 10–11; see also Svare, *Reforming Sports before the Clock Runs Out*; Albertson, *Catch a Rising Star*.

28. Quoted in Tim Wendel, "The Specialists," *USA WEEKEND.com*, 27 August 2000, p. 3, http://www.usaweekend.com/00_issues/000827/000827kidsports.html.

29. Quoted in Tim Wendel, "When Smiles Leave the Game," *USA Today*, 23 August 2005, p. 13A; Patrick Welsh, "One-Sport Athletes: A Losing Proposition for Kids," *USA Today*, 23 August 2004, p. 11A. See also Tim Wendel, "The Specialists," *USA WEEKEND.com*, 27 August 2000, p. 3, http://www.usaweekend.com/00_issues/000827/000827kidsports.html.

30. Quoted in Wendel, "When Smiles Leave the Game," p. 13A; "Baseball or Bust," *Sports Illustrated*, 6 October 2003, 63.

31. Rick Wolff, *The Sports Parenting Edge* (Philadelphia: Running Press, 2003), 87–99; Bruce Weber, "A Fierce Investment, in Skates and Family Time," *New York Times*, 16 January 2005, pp. 1, 23.

32. IMG Academies, http://www.imgacademies.com; see also Clay Latimer, "Studies in Determination," *Rocky Mountain News*, 20 December 2005, pp. 1C, 11C–13C.

33. Quoted in Clay Latimer, "Under a Nonstop Watch," *Rocky Mountain News*, 19 December 2005, p. 8C.

34. Mark Hyman, "Reading, Writing—and Winning," *Business Week*, 2 April 2001, 60; see also Douglas Robson, "Could This 5-Year-Old Be the Future of Tennis?" *USA Today*, 30 July 2007, pp. 1A–2A.

35. Engh, *Why Johnny Hates Sports;* Andersonn, *Will You Still Love Me If I Don't Win?;* see also Ken Paul Mink, *So, You Want Your Kid to Be a Sports Superstar* (Victoria, B.C.: Trafford Press, 2006); McCoglin, *Surviving Youth Sports*.

36. Reported in Matt Schuman, "Parents Need Self Control," *Greeley Tribune*, 24 September 2006, p. B9.

37. Incidents reported in Bach, "The Parents Association for Youth Sports," 16.

38. Positive Coaching Alliance, http://www.positivecoach.org/default.aspx.

39. Parents Association for Youth Sports, http://paysonline.nays.org; see also Bach, "The Parents Association for Youth Sports"; Center for Sport Parenting, http://www.sportsparenting.org/.

40. William Nack and Don Yaeger, "Every Parent's Nightmare," *Sports Illustrated*, 13 September 1999, 40, 42.

41. Clay Latimer, "Change Is in the Heir," *Rocky Mountain News*, 22 December 2005, pp. 1C, 12C.

42. Safe Kids USA, http://www.usa.safekids.org/; see also Mike Chambers, "Protecting Young Arms," *Denver Post*, 24 June 2007, pp. 1B, 5B; Christine Gorman, "To an Athlete Aching Young," *Time*, 18 September 2006, 60–62.

43. Committee on Sports Medicine and Fitness, "Intensive Training and Sports Specialization in Young Athletes," *Pediatrics* 106, no. 1 (July 2000): 154, 156.

44. Ryan, *Little Girls in Pretty Boxes*, 11; see also Peter Donnelly and Leanne Petherick, "Workers' Playtime? Child Labour at the Extremes of the Sporting Spectrum," *Sport in Society* 7, no. 3 (Autumn 2004): 301–321.

45. All quotations from Dennis Cauchon, "Childhood Pastimes Are Increasingly Moving Indoors," *USA Today*, 12 July 2005, pp. 1A–2A; for an excellent review of the research literature on physical activity of children, see President's Council on Physical Fitness and Sports, "Physical Activity for Children: Current Patterns and Guidelines," *Research Digest*, June 2004; see also Richard Louv, *Last Child in the Woods: Saving Our Children from Nature-Deficit Disorder* (Chapel Hill, N.C.: Algonquin Books, 2006).

46. Centers for Disease Control and Prevention, "Childhood Overweight," http://www.cdc.gov/nccdphp/dnpa/obesity/childhood/index.htm.

47. Richard D. Ginsburg, Stephen Durant, and Amy Baltzell, *Whose Game Is It, Anyway?: A Guide to Helping Your Child Get the Most from Sports, Organized by Age and Stage* (Boston: Houghton Mifflin, 2006); de Lench, *Home Team Advantage;* Mink, *So, You Want Your Kid to Be a Sports Superstar;* McCoglin, *Surviving Youth Sports;* Fish and Magee, *101 Ways to Be a Terrific Sports Parent*.

48. Terry Orlick, *Cooperative Games and Sports: Joyful Activities for Everyone* (Champaign, Ill.: Human Kinetics, 2006); Josette Luvmour and Sambhava Luvmour, *Everyone Wins: Cooperative Games and Activities* (Stony Creek, Conn.: New Society Publishers, 2007); Bobbi Conner, *Unplugged Play: No Batteries. No Plugs. Pure Fun* (New York: Workman Publishing, 2007).

49. American Sport Education Program, http://www.asep.com/.

50. 3M National Coaching Certification Program, http://www.asep.com/.

51. David Paulo, *Human Rights in Youth Sports: A Critical Review of Children's Rights in Competitive Sport* (New York: Routledge, 2005).

CHAPTER 5

Interscholastic Sport

Interschool high school sports in the United States have become vitally important as a means of unifying the entire school in a common cause—the defeat of an enemy outside the group. (AP Photo/Michael Thomas)

Sport and education are inexorably intertwined in American society; virtually every secondary school is engaged in some interschool sport competition. To ascertain the degree to which sport contributes to the educational process, however, is difficult. The conventional view is that participation in sport has educational benefits. High school athletes benefit, it is commonly believed, from adult supervision, by ego enhancement, by learning to play by the rules, by working together with teammates toward a common goal, by being achievement oriented, and by working at schoolwork to stay eligible.

A contrary view, less widely held, is critical of sport as now constituted in our schools. From this perspective, sport is believed to detract from educational goals. Moreover, the critics assert that although athletic participation may lead some individuals to be good sports, it may lead others to be bad sports; although some play by the rules, others circumvent them; and although there is integrity in some sports programs, there is hypocrisy in others. In short, these critics believe that sport and education are incompatible.

The subjects included in this chapter are directly or indirectly related to this controversy. We describe first the status of sport in American education; next, we explore the positive and negative consequences of sport for the school, the community, the individual, and the society; finally, we assess the relationship between sport and education by examining inherent problems and dilemmas.

THE STATUS OF SPORT IN SECONDARY SCHOOLS

Although the main thrust of this book is corporate sport in society, much of the material in this chapter is devoted to organized sport—that is, sport at the high school level. We shall see, however, that sport in American education varies from organized to corporate.

High school sports are central in U.S. schools. In the 2005–2006 school year, about 7.2 million boys and girls in the United States were involved in thirty different sports at the high school level (41.2 percent of this total were girls and 58.8 percent boys).[1] This high level of involvement, however, is not the case in many other countries. In most countries, sports programs for high-school-age youth are organized through community-based athletic clubs, *not through the schools*. England, on the other hand, has school sports.[2] Canada is somewhat unusual because it has both school sports and community sports clubs for adolescents. Hockey, the most popular sport for male participation in Canada, is organized only as a community sport in most areas. The less popular male sports and all of the female sports are organized primarily through the schools but are no more important than other extracurricular school activities.

Interschool high school sports in the United States have become so vitally important that contemporary schools might appear to an outsider to be more concerned with athletics than with scholarly endeavors. Writing in 1961, James Coleman describes what was typical of high schools then and now:

> A visitor entering a school would likely be confronted, first of all, with a trophy case. His examination of the trophies would reveal a curious fact: the gold and silver cups, with rare exception, symbolize victory in athletic contests, not scholastic ones. The figures adorning these trophies represent men passing footballs, shooting basketballs, holding out batons; they are not replicas of "The Thinker." The concrete symbols of victory are old footballs, basketballs, and baseballs, not works of art or first editions of books won as literary prizes. Altogether, the trophy case would suggest to the innocent visitor that he was entering an athletic club, not an educational institution.
>
> Walking further, this visitor would encounter teenagers bursting from classrooms. Listening to their conversations, he would hear both casual and serious discussions of the Friday football game, confirming his initial impression. Attending a school assembly that morning, he would probably find a large segment of the program devoted to a practice of school cheers for the athletic game and the announcement of a pep rally before the game. At lunch hour, he would be likely to find more boys shooting baskets in the gymnasium than reading in the library. Browsing through a school yearbook,

he would be impressed, in his innocence, with the number of pages devoted to athletics.

Altogether, this visitor would find, wherever he turned, a great deal of attention devoted to athletics. As an impressionable stranger, he might well suppose that more attention is paid to athletics by teenagers, both as athletes and as spectators, than to scholastic matters. He might even conclude, with good reason, that the school was essentially organized around athletic contests and that scholastic matters were of lesser importance to all involved.[3]

A consequence of the extraordinary popularity of sport in United States secondary schools is its generation of status for males and, increasingly, for females as well. Foremost, for males the athlete, regardless of other attributes, is favored over the nonathlete, with the highest preference being "scholar-athlete." For young women, popularity is judged more by their being in the "in-group" than by their scholarship. Membership in the "in-group" is crucial and being an athlete is not sufficient for inclusion. This is especially true for women in "gender-inappropriate" sports (i.e., sports generally considered not "feminine").[4] Second, the importance of athletics for the male status system acts as a deterrent to academic achievement, a most important implication for the goals of schools. It does so because persons are encouraged to divert their energies away from scholarship to athletics and social activities. Thus, groups and individuals in the school (with the aid of the administration and the community) actually work against the academic objectives of the school.

A third generalization is that achievement in athletics, not social background, is for the most part the basis for status among male peers. For females, social background and physical appearance are more important for social status than athletic achievement. This may be changing for high school women as female participation in sports in high schools is becoming more and more acceptable and their participation has increased so rapidly since Title IX. The conclusion by Jay Coakley seems appropriate:

> because males and females in North America are still treated and evaluated in different ways, adolescents use different strategies for seeking acceptance, autonomy, and sexual development, and recognition as young adults. As things are now, sport participation for young men is an important basis for popularity, as long as they don't completely neglect their academic lives.[5]

A high school varsity basketball point guard playing in the state tournament at the Tacoma Dome in Tacoma, Washington. Participation by girls in high school sports has increased dramatically since Title IX was enacted. (Big Stock Photo)

THE CONSEQUENCES OF SPORT FOR SCHOOLS, COMMUNITIES, AND INDIVIDUALS

Clearly, high school athletes receive substantial rewards for their activities. They receive fame and acclaim from peers, neighbors, teachers, and even strangers. A high school star (especially a male) can become a legend, a deity canonized in newspapers and immortalized through countless retold exploits. Even nonstar athletes have celebrity status. They enjoy praise and honor, special favors from businesses and the community, and popularity with the opposite sex. Moreover, schools and communities are usually much more willing to spend great sums of money for athletic equipment and arenas than they are for academic equipment and buildings. They are also willing to allow a disproportionate amount of time to be spent on athletics and related activities.

Why are athletes and athletics given such extraordinary importance? The answer is because sport has positive consequences for the participants, the schools, and the communities.

The Consequences of Sport for the School

All organizations must have a minimal amount of unity; members must give an organization some allegiance for it to survive. Allegiance can stem from pay, ideology, chances for promotion, or the cooperative need to accomplish a collective goal. Schools, however, do not have the usual means to motivate their members. Grades, the equivalent of pay, do not always work because part of the school population is indifferent to them, and because they are so often dependent on defeating one's peers. Moreover, students are forced by custom and by law to attend school; this ensures their physical presence but not their involvement in the school's academic objectives. Aside from athletic contests, schools do not have collective goals, only individual ones. Therefore, any activity that promotes loyalty to the school serves a useful and necessary purpose. James Coleman showed how athletics provides a unifying function for the school:

> Athletic contests with other schools provide, for these otherwise lifeless institutions, the collective goals that they lack. The common goals shared by all make the institution part of its members and them part of it, rather than an organization outside them and superimposed upon them. The results are evident to any observer: the adolescent social system is centered at the school, not at the drugstore; the name by which the teenagers identify themselves is that of the school ("Those are East High kids; I'm from Tech."); the teenagers think of the school, the team, and the student body as one and use the pronoun "we" in referring to this entity ("We're playing Parkville Friday.").

Thus, the importance of athletic contests in both high schools and colleges lies, at least in part, in the way the contests solve a difficult problem for the institution—the problem of generating enthusiasm for and identification with the school and of drawing the energies of adolescents into the school.[6]

Interschool sports competition, then, is a means of unifying the entire school. Different races, social classes, fraternities, teachers, school staff, and students unite in a common cause—the defeat of a common enemy outside the group. An athletic program sometimes keeps potentially hostile segments from fragmenting the school. The collective following of an athletic team can also lift morale, thereby serving to unify the school (although we should remember that unity is usually accomplished when teams win; losing teams may actually increase the possibility of division).

Athletics serves not only to unify student bodies but also to minimize conflict between students and teachers. Sociologist Willard Waller, writing in 1932, writes of the unifying force of school sports, which is just as true today.

> There is a tendency for the school population to split up into hostile segments of teachers and students and to be fragmented by cliques among both groups. The division of students into groups prevents a collective morale from arising and thereby complicates administration; the split between students and teachers is even more serious, for these two groups tend to become definite conflict groups, and conflict group tensions are the very antithesis of discipline. This condition athletics alleviates. Athletic games furnish a dramatic spectacle of the struggle of picked men against a common enemy, and this is a powerful factor in building up a group spirit which includes students of all kinds and degrees and unifies the teachers and the taught.[7]

In addition to the unifying function of athletics, it serves a social control function. Waller gave the following advice to school administrators:

> The organization of the student body for the support of athletics, though it is certainly not without its ultimate disadvantages, may bring with it certain benefits for those who are interested in the immediate problems of the administration. It is a powerful machine which is organized to whip all students into line for the support of athletic teams, and adroit school administrators learn to use it for the dissemination of other attitudes favorable to the faculty and the faculty policy.[8]

Assuming that school administrators can manipulate students through sport, what social control functions may be performed? First, athletic activity may make students more tractable because it drains their surplus energies. For athletes and nonathletes alike, sport furnishes a diversion of attention from undesirable to desirable channels. It gives students something to think about and something to do with their time, thereby keeping them from mischief and from questioning the system. Second, athletes, because they must obey school rules and training rules if they want to compete, serve as examples of good behavior. Athletes have high status in the school system, and by virtue of their favored position, they tend to have the conservatism of the privileged classes. If this assumption is correct and nonathletes tend to admire them, then athletes serve to preserve the system as it is.

The school advocates sports participation for self-serving reasons (school and community cohesion, financial support, and social control). Administrators and school boards encourage participation not only because they want to encourage physical fitness but, more importantly, because they believe that sports participation inculcates the values of society into individuals. Schools want individuals to follow rules, to be disciplined, to work hard, to fit in. Athletics accomplishes these aims. Thus, athletics is believed by those in authority to be justified.

A final social control function of athletics is its dampening of violent rivalries between towns, neighborhoods, and schools. Athletic contests are often symbolic contests between rivals. The official goal of civil order (minimizing real violence) is believed to be accomplished because the contests are routinized and institutionalized (by the rules of the game and the sanctions that can be applied for violations). The problem is that ritualized violence may erupt into actual violence between players, spectators, or both at any time. It has been generally assumed by school authorities that the benefits outweigh the potential for actual conflict. However, especially in urban areas, sporting events between schools have actually intensified the probability of violence. As a consequence, some contests have been either canceled or held without spectators.

Sports can also be used by the school to encourage intellectual activities among the students. A contingency for participation in sports is the maintenance of a certain grade point average, so athletes must at least meet this minimum. The existence of sports may also keep some youngsters from dropping out of school because of their desire to participate.

The Consequences of Sport for the Community

We have already noted that school athletics appears to be an effective means for channeling the interest and loyalty of the community. Clearly, this enthusiasm generated by sports is a unifying agent for the community. Regardless of occupation, education, race, or religion, residents can and do unite in backing a school's teams against the common enemy.

Sports provide action in an otherwise humdrum world. They offer not only excitement but also fantasy and escape. Thus, they entertain.

Communities vary in their attachment to high school athletic teams. Most often, individual sports are ignored by communities. The girls' games are often minimized, too. Typically, the community members concentrate their interests around boys' football and basketball. Small communities are generally more involved in high school sports than are large urban communities. The focus on a sport may also vary by geographical location, with high school basketball the rage in Indiana, hockey in Minnesota, and football in Texas. H. G. Bissinger, for example, has written of the importance of high school football in Odessa, Texas. Bissinger, a Philadelphia reporter, lived in Odessa for a year chronicling life in that town as it centered on high school football. One excerpt from Bissinger's book *Friday Night Lights* illustrates the importance of football to the town and its inhabitants: "Bob Rutherford, an affable realtor in town, might as well have been speaking for thousands when he casually said one day as if talking about the need for a rainstorm to settle the dust, 'Life really wouldn't be worth livin' if you didn't have a high school football team to support.'"[9]

The Consequences of Sport for the Participant

Individuals participate in sports for a variety of reasons. Perhaps most important is the desire for high status and the approval of fans, press, peers, parents, teachers, and others. H. G. Bissinger has described just how important it was to be a football player at Permian High School in Odessa, Texas: "[They were] gladiators, the ones who were envied by everyone else, the ones who knew about the best parties and got the best girls and laughed the loudest and strutted so proudly through the halls of school as if it was their own wonderful, private kingdom."[10] They may also participate because they enjoy the activity and being physically fit and because they derive great pleasure from being part of a cohesive unit striving for a common goal. Sometimes forgotten, however, is that many persons participate because all of the normative influences pull them in that direction. There are many pressures to participate, whether an individual wants to or not. Of course, if youngsters are socialized to desire participation, they may not feel the constraints.

Regardless of the motivation for participation in sport, there are some important consequences of participation. Several are considered here: academic benefits, character development, and adjustment to failure and life after sport.

Academic Benefits

The empirical evidence is that high school athletes as a group receive better grades than nonathletes, and they have higher academic aspirations. This consistent finding validates, seemingly, the conventional wisdom that athletic participation builds discipline, the work ethic, and other achievement-oriented qualities that translate into better students.

Some problems of interpretation exist, however, whenever athletes are compared with nonathletes.[11] The two categories differ not only in physical characteristics but in other significant dimensions as well. First, when grades are compared, athletes may have a higher grade point average (GPA) because they must meet a minimum level to be eligible for sports. This grade barrier keeps some students who are poor in academic performance from ever attempting to participate in athletics. Second, either rebellious youth may choose not to participate in sport or coaches may dismiss them because they do not fit in. Third, we cannot determine whether the relationship between athletic involvement and academic achievement is a causal one. The relationship between high school participation and grades may be the result of other factors, such as receiving extra help from tutors and teachers, taking easier courses in order to handle the rigors of being an athlete, or outright gifts of good grades from sympathetic teachers. The result may be good grades for being an athlete but not because being an athlete makes one a good student.

Most important, athletes may be different from nonathletes, but not because of sport. Elmer Spreitzer analyzed data from a national probability sample of twelve thousand high school students. The information was collected from high school sophomores and seniors and then from these same students over a six-year period after they left high school. Spreitzer summarizes the results:

> In this article, we corroborated the widely shared perception among sport scientists that selectivity factors prevent us from making straightforward conclusions concerning the effects of sports participation during one's youth. We identified two sources of selectivity that prevent such simple conclusions: a

filtering process in terms of who enters high school athletics and a filtering process in terms of who drops out of high school athletics between the sophomore and senior years. The data from this national probability sample of American youths clearly show that those who begin and continue with high school athletics tend to be from more advantaged social backgrounds in terms of parental social class, level of cognitive ability, academic achievement, and level of self-esteem.[12]

In short, high school athletes are more advantaged academically before they participate in high school sports than their nonathlete peers. Thus, we should not infer that athletic participation makes one perform better in the classroom.

Building Character

We noted in our earlier discussion that there is a negative side to the conventional assumption that sport builds character, a position that Charles Banham summarized. Such an assumption, he said,

> is not sound because it assumes that everyone will benefit from sport in the complacently prescribed manner. A minority does so benefit. A few have the temperament that responds healthily to all the demands. These are the ones able to develop an attractively active character. Sport can put fresh air in the mind, if it's the right mind; it can give muscle to the personality, if it's the right personality. But for the rest, it encourages selfishness, envy, conceit, hostility and bad temper. Far from ventilating the mind, it stifles it. Good sportsmanship may be a product of sport, but so is bad sportsmanship.[13]

The results of research on whether sport builds character are contradictory.[14] The problem is that sport produces positive outcomes for some individuals and negative ones for others. Terry D. Orlick summed up this dualism:

> For every positive psychological or social outcome in sports, there are possible negative outcomes. For example, sports can offer a child group membership or group exclusion, acceptance or rejection, positive feedback or negative feedback, a sense of accomplishment or a sense of failure, evidence of self-worth or a lack of evidence of self-worth. Likewise, sports can develop cooperation and a concern for others, but they can also develop intense rivalry and a complete lack of concern for others.[15]

An important study examined the larger issue of whether or not participation in high school sports builds character. Frank M. Howell, C. Roger Rees, and Andrew W. Miracle analyzed data collected from a national sample, beginning with twenty-five male sophomores in each of eighty-seven high schools. These students were interviewed at the beginning of the sophomore year and again at the conclusion of the senior year. The data showed that participation in varsity sports tended to increase self-esteem but also increased the negative traits of aggression and irritability and reduced the importance of being honest, of self-control, and of independence. In general, though, the researchers concluded that high school sports do not do much to "build character" in adolescent boys—in either prosocial or antisocial ways.[16]

A longitudinal study surveyed 5,669 female students during their sophomore and senior years to ascertain the effects of sports participation on their development. The results were mixed. The researchers found that athletic participation was modestly related to perceived popularity and slightly related to educational aspiration. Participation was not related to psychological well-being, self-esteem, sociability, academic achievement, or sex-role attitudes.[17]

On the other hand, studies by Marsh[18] and Fejgin[19] found that participation in sport in high school had no negative effects and several positive effects, such as higher educational aspirations and disciplined behavior. These mildly positive results are offset, however, by the research of Beller and Stoll, who analyzed high school student-athletes' cognitive moral reasoning compared with that of their nonathlete peers. Their findings included these: (1) Athletes scored lower on moral development than did their nonathlete peers, and (2) moral reasoning scores for athletes steadily declined from the ninth grade through twelfth grade, whereas scores for nonathletes tended to increase.[20] We suggest that these findings from Beller and Stoll will be stronger the more the particular school team fits the characteristics of corporate sport—where winning is overemphasized, high school athletes are used as public entertainers, and sport is an all-consuming activity for the participants.[21]

The overarching question is this: Does sports participation make a difference? As we have shown, the data are contradictory. It is difficult to make the causal link. We believe that sports participation does not build character, discipline, and other achievement-related qualities in young men and women. Instead, researchers find the consequence of rigorous selection processes where young boys and girls are weeded out by coaches or drop out voluntarily because they do not possess the traits needed, while those who are already imbued with the positive traits of hard work, discipline, goal orientation, and willingness to obey orders remain in sport.

Adjustment to Failure and Life after School Sport

Two problems for individual high school athletes are often overlooked. First, for many, sport leads to a series of failures. Either they fail to make the team, or if they make the team, they sit on the bench, or their team loses many more times than it wins. In a success-oriented society, what are the effects of all the failures that sport generates? At the individual level, failure can be devastating for some. They may be defined by others and by themselves as losers, which is a strong negative label in a society that places such high value on winning. This may negatively impact their self-esteem, confidence, and assertiveness. It may lead to mental health problems.

Another problem is one of adjustment after a career in sport is finished. The odds of making a team at the next level are remote: Only 4 percent of high school football players and 2 percent of male high school basketball players will participate in college; the odds of making it from college into the pros are even lower. Clearly, these long odds mean that most high school athletes will terminate their careers at the conclusion of high school. After the glory years, what happens to former athletes when they are considered has-beens? Does participation in sport have carryover value to other endeavors where there is no hero worship, no excitement, and no fame? What happens to the athlete who finds himself or herself suddenly outside the world that has until now been at the center of his or her life and the principal source of identity and social status? Do former athletes become embittered and turn away from sport, or do they fill their time reliving the past, attending games, Monday-morning quarterbacking, and watching sports on television? How does the athlete, when compared to the nonathlete, adjust to job, marriage, and upward or downward mobility? An ex-athlete from Permian High School in Odessa, Texas, was interviewed by H. G. Bissinger:

> He saw the irresistible allure of high school sports, but he also saw an inevitable danger in adults' living vicariously through their young. And he knew of no candle that burned out more quickly than that of the high school athlete.
>
> "Athletics lasts for such a short time. It ends for people. But while it lasts, it creates this make-believe world where normal rules don't apply. We build this false atmosphere. When it's over and the harsh reality sets in, that's the real joke we play on people."[22]

Little research has been done on the effects of this shift away from the athletic limelight.[23]

PROBLEMS, DILEMMAS, AND CONTROVERSIES

Although, as we have noted, sport in secondary schools has positive consequences for the schools, the participants, and the spectators, critics wonder about the educational benefits of sport activities. This section focuses on the fundamental problem of interscholastic sport as it is presently organized: that it is not designed to maximize its educational potential. Implicit in this criticism is the assumption that sport participation is a worthwhile school-related activity if it is congruent with educational goals.

The Subversion of Educational Goals

The subversion of education by sports in high school occurs in several ways.[24] First, as we have seen, the amount of time in the school day and the amount of money from the budget devoted to sports are heavily skewed. Second, there is the tendency to give star athletes a pass in their schooling. Athletes may be passed even though they have not mastered the work. Third, one estimate is that 50 percent of high school coaches are not high school teachers.[25] They have never taught in the classroom and have little training or certification in coaching. In short, the coach in many schools has no connection with the academic institution. Fourth, as we will emphasize shortly, high school sports are becoming less about education and more about entertainment. And, finally, the emphasis is on sports that have no connection with lifelong health and fitness-for-life concepts. The skills emphasized in football and basketball, objects of most public attention, are irrelevant beyond the school years. Moreover, at a time when obesity is becoming more and more of a problem, athletes in some sports are encouraged to gain weight. For example, the offensive line of Santa Ana Mater Dei High School (California) in 2006 averaged 282 pounds (that's 24 pounds more per man than the five linemen who started for the 1972 Miami Dolphins).[26]

The Reinforcement of Gender Roles

Sport in American schools has historically been almost exclusively a male preserve. This is clearly evident as one compares by gender the number of participants and facilities. We will examine sexism in sport in greater detail in chapter 14; therefore, the discussion here is limited to the unintended ways in which school sport works to maintain the conventional expectations for masculine and feminine roles.

What is the impact of a society that encourages its boys and young men to participate in sports while expecting its girls and young women to be spectators and cheerleaders? (See Box 5.1, *Thinking about Sport,* for further discussion on this topic.) The answer is that the society thereby uses sport to reinforce societal expectations for males and females. Males are to be dominant and aggressive, the doers, while females are expected to be passive supporters of men, attaining status through the efforts of their menfolk.

With the implementation of Title IX (see chapter 14) and the efforts to bring gender equity to school athletic programs, the number of female sport participants increased dramatically—from three hundred thousand girls involved in high school sports in 1971 to more than 2.95 million in 2006. Put another way, the growth in girls playing high school sports rose from 1 in 27 in 1971 to 1 in 2.5 in 2006. Also, about 1 in 50 high school wrestlers in 2006 were girls, a sport traditionally male.[27]

Although attempts have been made to equalize female and male programs in facilities, equipment, coaching, and transportation, inequities remain. Football, with its high cost and large number of participants, continues to skew budgets in favor of males. The scheduling of games and media attention also stress male sports.

Finally, a major trend in women's sports is that as women's sports have gained in popularity, money, and respect, men have gained more and more control over them. Men are more likely than women to be athletic directors and coaches of women's sports at the high school and college levels. Male athletes see male role models exclusively as coaches and administrators, but female athletes in their formative years are usually denied female role models in positions requiring decisiveness, confidence, and self-assurance. Thus, females once again receive the unambiguous message that the more responsible a position in an organization is, the more likely men are to occupy it.

Cheating

Cheating involves a violation of the rules to gain an unfair advantage over an opponent. It occurs at all levels of sport and may be done by individual players, teams, or coaches. The types of cheating

Box 5.1 *Thinking about Sport* The Pepettes

At Permian High School in Odessa, Texas, there is an organization called the Pepettes. H. G. Bissinger describes this group and the ways they support the school's football team.

> [The Pepettes were] a select group of senior girls who made up the school spirit squad. The Pepettes supported all teams, but it was the football team they supported most. The number on the white jersey each girl wore corresponded to that of the player she had been assigned for the football season. With that assignment came various time-honored responsibilities.
>
> As part of the tradition, each Pepette brought some type of sweet for her player every week before the game. She didn't necessarily have to make something from scratch, but there was indirect pressure to because of not-so-private grousing from players who tired quickly of bags of candy and not so discreetly let it be known that they much preferred something fresh-baked....
>
> In addition, each Pepette also had to make a large sign for her player that went in his front yard and stayed there the entire season as a notice to the community that he played football for Permian. Previously the making of these yard signs, which looked like miniature Broadway marquees, had become quite competitive. Some of the Pepettes spent as much as $100 of their own money to make an individual sign, decorating it with twinkling lights and other attention-getting devices. It became a rather serious game of can-you-top-this, and finally a dictum was handed down that all signs must be made the same way, without any neon.
>
> A Pepette also had responsibility for making smaller posters, which went up in the school halls at the beginning of each week and were transferred to the gym for the mandatory Friday morning pep rally. The making of these signs could be quite laborious as well, and one Pepette during the season broke down in tears because she had to stay up until the wee hours of the morning trying to keep up with the other Pepettes and make a fancy hall sign that her player never even thanked her for.
>
> These were the basic Pepette requirements, but some girls went beyond in their show of spirit. They might embroider the map of Texas on towels and then spell out MOJO [the school nickname] on pillowcases that the players could take with them during road trips. Or they might place their fresh-baked cookies in tins elaborately decorated in the Permian colors of black and white. In previous years Pepettes had made scrapbooks for their players, including one with the cover made of lacquered wood and modeled on Disney's *Jungle Book*. The book had clippings, cut out in ninety-degree angles as square and true as in an architectural rendering, of every story written about the Permian team that year. It also had beautiful illustrations and captions that tried to capture what it meant to be a Pepette.
>
> "The countryside was filled with loyal and happy subjects serving their chosen panther," said a caption in a chapter entitled "Joy," and next to it was a picture of a little girl with flowers in her hand going up to a panther, the Permian mascot, roaring under a tree....
>
> "It's very revered to be a Pepette or a cheerleader," said Julie Gardner, who had come to Odessa from a small college town in Montana as a sophomore. "It's the closest they can get to being a football player."

Source: Excerpts from H. G. Bissinger, *Friday Night Lights: A Town, a Team, and a Dream* (Reading, Mass.: Addison-Wesley, 1990), 45–46, 138.

depend on the sport and the ingenuity of the participants.[28] Clearly, cheating is antithetical to educational values and should have no place in educational programs.

Some high school players are coached to use illegal but difficult-to-detect techniques. One example is holding or tripping by offensive linemen in football. In basketball it is often advantageous to touch the lower half of the shooter's body because the referee usually watches the action around the ball. A form of cheating often taught basketball players is to fake being fouled. The intent is to fool an official who is out of position and to receive an undeserved free throw. Similar faking of an injury to get an advantage occurs commonly in soccer when a player is bumped during play and then acts as if he or she has been fouled, writhing in pseudopain in the hope that the referee will award him or her a penalty kick for the phony injury. So, too, in football when kickers act as if they had been hit by an onrushing lineman.

Coaches sometimes break the spirit of a rule if not the rule itself. For example, teams may not have organized practices before a certain date, yet coaches insist on players practicing, with captains in charge or coaches at a distance yelling orders.

The Narbonne High School girls' basketball team in Los Angeles had to forfeit its state title in 1998 because three players had supplied false addresses to make it appear that they lived within the school's attendance area. Similarly, the Miami Senior High School boys' basketball team forfeited its

1998 state championship because five of its players had lived with coaches or team boosters in violation of state rules.[29] The Colorado High School Activities Association has reduced the likelihood of this kind of cheating by allowing students to transfer before the start of the school year even if their only reason for transferring is sports. Such a rule invites recruiting and various inducements to athletes and their parents to change schools.

In 2007 the U.S. Supreme Court heard arguments in a case in Tennessee where the coach of a private school sent a letter to eighth-grade boys admitted to the school, inviting them to spring football practice (i.e., to practice with the high school players while they were still eighth graders). The Court will decide if this was in violation of the recruiting policy of the Tennessee Secondary School Athletic Association (TSSAA), as claimed by the TSSAA, which fined the school three thousand dollars, or whether the TSSAA was wrong because it denied the coach and his school freedom of expression.[30]

A different form of cheating involves the use of drugs so that an athlete may compete at a higher-than-normal level of ability (see chapter 7). This is sometimes done at the insistence of trainers and coaches, sometimes by an athlete's own decision. A 2004 survey by the University of Michigan found that for high school seniors, 4.4 percent of boys and 2.3 percent of girls had taken anabolic steroids to increase weight and muscle.[31]

Unsportsmanlike Behavior of Fans

The intensity of the competition sometimes leads some fans to cross the line. This may involve fighting, insulting opposing teams' players and fans, yelling obscenities, and other obnoxious behaviors. Several unhealthy examples from the Phoenix area illustrate this point:[32]

- When a football player was injured, fans from the opposing team shouted "broken neck."
- Students shouted vulgar comments about the sexuality of the players from the all-boys' school they were playing.
- Students wore green T-shirts implying that the players on the largely Latino team they were playing had green cards.

"Personal attacks, jeers and politically incorrect clothing can detract from the sportsmanship and camaraderie that high school athletics are supposed to promote. They can also lead to violence, stereotyping, loss of self-esteem and distractions for players trying to focus on the game."[33]

Autocratic Coaches

Another criticism of high school sports is the almost total control that coaches exercise over their players' lives. Many coaches, for example, dictate hairstyles, clothing, dating, whom the players associate with, church attendance, and the like. Many also monitor their players' behavior off the field (bed checks) and restrict freedom of choice (what position to play, mandatory off-season weight lifting). Most coaches impose their will on their teams concerning team rules, discipline, play calling, and personnel decisions.

Whether coaches have the right to infringe upon the civil liberties of their charges is certainly a legal question. Beyond that, there is the question of the educational value of controlling these youngsters on and off the field. A system that denies personal autonomy apparently fosters dependence and immaturity rather than the presumed virtues of participation, which are leadership, independence, and self-motivation. Moreover, does subservience to a dictator prepare one for life in a democracy?[34]

Excessive Pressures to Win

Many of the problems found in school sports result from the excessive emphasis on winning. The sociological explanation for the tendency of coaches to be authoritarian, or to cheat, or to be hypocritical lies not in their individual psyches but in the intensely competitive system in which they operate.

In American society the success or failure of a team is believed by most persons to rest with the coach. This pressure to win brings some coaches to use illegal inducements to attract athletes to their schools, or to teach their linemen to hold without getting caught, or to look the other way when athletes (who face the same pressures to succeed) use drugs to enhance performance. The absolute necessity to win also explains why some coaches drive their players too hard. Thus, what some persons might label brutality has been explained by some coaches as a necessity to get the maximum effort from players. Finally, authoritarianism can be explained by the constraints on the coaching role. Democracy is unthinkable to most in the coaching profession because coaches are liable for the outcome in an extremely uncertain situation. They cannot control injuries, officiating, mental lapses by athletes, or the bounce of the ball, so most coaches are convinced that they must seek to control as much else as possible. As Willard Waller has said:

> A more serious indictment of the social system which allows the livelihood of a man and his family to depend upon the athletic achievements of boys is that the coach is so pressed that he uses his human material recklessly. He trains his "men" (aged sixteen) a bit too hard, or he uses his star athletes in too many events, or he schedules too many hard games; all this he does from a blameless desire to gain a better position or a rise in salary for himself, but he often fails to consider the possible effects upon the physical well-being of the rising generation.[35]

Another consequence of the excessive stress on winning is that sports participation becomes work rather than play. The emphasis is on the outcome rather than on enjoyment of the process. Fun has become equated with winning rather than with pleasure in participating.

Elitism

Interscholastic sport programs are elitist. That is, they are for the few, not the many. If sports participation is believed to have educational benefits, how can schools justify limiting teams to the most gifted athletes? Why should participation be restricted almost exclusively to the fast, the strong, or the tall? As a *Los Angeles Times* article said: "High school athletes are fitter, more skilled and better trained than ever before. But these top-notch athletes, say many health and fitness experts, have become the singular focus of the youth sports system—while teenagers of average or low ability no longer warrant attention."[36]

There are two reasons for fewer sports opportunities for high school students. One is that school boards and administrators funnel most of their limited funds toward those sports that entertain the public (football and basketball). Second, because of limited financial resources, many schools have eliminated freshman/sophomore teams, some sports programs such as golf and tennis, and intramural sports programs. Even physical education classes have been cut from many schools.

The result is that sports and the use of sports facilities are limited more and more to the physically gifted who exhibit their prowess publicly. In effect, then, the goal of high school physical activities has shifted from an educational endeavor to public entertainment.

School sports have typically been for the physically gifted. This has meant that schools have overlooked sports programs for students with disabilities. In the 2005–2006 school year, only 426 schools out of more than 17,000 U.S. high schools provided sports for students with disabilities, with 3,423 participants.[37] The most popular "*adapted sport*" was floor hockey.

Sport Specialization

A growing trend in high school sports is specialization, that is, athletes limiting their participation to one sport that is trained for on a year-round basis. This has tended to be the case in individual sports (running, swimming, gymnastics, tennis), but it is increasingly found in team sports as well, especially in large schools. The arguments for this practice are that refined skill levels lead to optimal individual and team performance, it encourages excellence, and it increases the chances for obtaining a college athletic scholarship. The possible negative consequences of this practice include physical and psychological burnout, injuries from overuse, creation of a professional atmosphere for athletes that is inappropriate for adolescents, friction among coaches who compete for athletes, and the use of athletic facilities limited to the few.

Budget Shortfalls

School districts fund sports in their districts, supplemented by ticket sales. Many districts have experienced a fiscal crisis with declining appropriations from the federal and state governments. This has especially affected urban school districts, as wealth has left the city for the suburbs. The trend appears to be for more budget tightening as the federal government shifts more programs to the states and the mode of the electorate is to reduce taxes.

Three strategies to overcome these declining revenues have been employed to continue the financing of sports (and other extracurricular activities), each having negative consequences. First, schools have reacted to budget shortfalls by reducing or eliminating some sports (almost always individual sports with no potential for producing revenue) or the number of teams (eliminating sophomore or junior varsity teams). This solution, of course, reduces the number of participants and makes the sports all the more elitist. Football, by the way, is typically not subject to removal (although the number of players might be reduced). This is ironic because it is the most expensive sport in the number of coaches required, the cost of equipment (about four hundred dollars per player), and the cost of insurance. The sacredness of football poses another problem—because it is almost exclusively for males (in 2006 there were 3,423 females playing on high school football teams out of the slightly more than one million football players),[38] and lots of them, as other sports are reduced or eliminated, the proportion of the athletic budget going for males becomes all the more unbalanced.

A second solution to meager budgets is to charge a fee for all participants. Pay-for-play has been tried throughout the country, with the fees varying from fifty dollars per sport to as much as six hundred dollars. The institution of this practice usually has resulted in reduced numbers of participants. Most important, this has created difficulty for students from lower-income families, especially reducing their participation. Thus, sport becomes not only elitist in skill level but also elitist in terms of social class.[39]

The third strategy employed by some districts has been to encourage corporate sponsorship. Corporations have been solicited to promote certain events, purchase advertising, and buy scoreboards, artificial turf, a track, or a team bus (a few schools in Texas have sold the naming rights of their stadiums for $1 million). Two questions arise when this practice occurs. Is the commercialization of high school sport compatible with educational goals? Will those who control the resources of a program ultimately control it? In other words, will companies that donate thousands of dollars to a high school program have an influence on schedules, coach selection, and use of the facilities? Will they encourage a win-at-any-cost philosophy, since they do not want to have their products associated with a loser?

Corporate High School Sport for Boys' Programs

There are five indicators that sport is already at the corporate level in some schools and moving generally in that direction across the United States.

First, some schools are closely resembling sports programs in big-time universities (see chapter 6) by selling naming rights to stadiums and arenas, hiring coaches for salaries far exceeding those of teachers, selling personal seat licenses (e.g., reserving seats for as much as $1,000 a season), spending vast sums on football and basketball budgets (Valdosta, Georgia, budgeted $419,000 on its high school football program in 2003), and spending in an "arms race" on facilities. On this last point, consider the following examples.[40] In 2004, fifteen new or pending high school stadiums in the Dallas area had a combined price tag of $179.2 million (an average of $11.95 million each). Lafayette, Indiana, spent $8 million on a stadium with synthetic turf, video scoreboard with instant replay, and a 22,000-square-foot athletic complex with locker, weight, and training rooms, coaches' offices, and classroom space. Although these are extreme examples, there are other schools in Texas, Ohio, Pennsylvania, Louisiana, Georgia, Florida, and elsewhere with similar outlays for their male programs, revealing the priority of sport in these schools and making it clear that sport has taken on the characteristics of corporate sport.

A second indicator of corporate sport at the high school level is the existence of fraudulent "prep schools" that exist basically to inflate transcripts of those who are marginal students but excellent athletes. These schools play the best schools around the country, providing their athletes exposure but also making their transcripts acceptable to big-time college sports programs. The NCAA in 2007 beefed up its transcript screening operation and inspection of these schools, disqualifying some. The *New York Times* editorialized that the problems may go deeper: "The storefront prep schools have been easy enough to identify. But the N.C.A.A. must now take a closer look at schools one level down that look legitimate but that may be just as willing to shortchange athletes' education as their fly-by-night counterparts. State departments of education also have a major role to play in curbing these abuses."[41]

A third indicator that sport in high school is becoming corporate is the combined effect of increased exposure and commercialization, which is moving high school sport to more closely resemble big-time college programs. High schools used to play games against league rivals and participate in tournaments at the state level. For many schools this continues to be the case, but some now participate in national tournaments in Hawaii, Florida, Las Vegas, and elsewhere. These events are sponsored by corporations (for example, the McDonald's Classic in Honolulu, the Dr. Pepper Classic in Dallas, and the Arby's Classic in Bristol, Tennessee). For example, in 2006, Oak Hill Academy, of Mouth of Wilson, Virginia, traveled 13,600 miles for basketball games (the University of North Carolina, in contrast, playing more games than Oak Hill, covered just 9,100 miles in that basketball season).[42] In the past, media attention tended to be local. *USA Today*, however, lists the twenty-five top-ranked high schools for the sport in season (separate lists for boys' and girls' teams) in the nation. *USA Today, Parade,* and other national publications select high school All-American teams and coaches of the year. SportsChannel, Madison Square Garden, Fox Sports Net, and ESPN now produce weekly "magazine" shows on high school sports. Moreover, the National Federation of State High School Associations receives money from cable stations to televise football and basketball games nationally on cable. Nike, Reebok, and Adidas pay some of the coaches of the nationally ranked teams thousands of dollars to outfit their teams in their products and to help steer them to play in colleges that are "Nike schools" or "Adidas schools" or "Reebok schools."

The fourth indicator of high school sports becoming corporate is the channeling of elite athletes into "professionals." It starts with some promising elementary and junior high school athletes being "redshirted" (held back a year) to give them an extra year before college to increase their skills, size, speed, strength, coordination, and maturity. Many young athletes are recruited to attend certain high schools. While in high school, many accept gratuities that technically make them professionals. "Elite schoolboy ballplayers in Southern California are, by any honest measure, professionals. They are routinely paid—by coaches or agents—with cash, cars and other considerations."[43] Many athletes are recruited to attend certain high schools. Take, for example, the case of Dominguez High School in Compton, California. By all accounts, this school is insufficiently financed, the education is below par, and the neighborhood is dangerous.

> Still, ballplayers come to Dominguez from points all over California and beyond. They transfer because the Dons win; the Dons win because, year after year, the finest players transfer in, partly because of the imprimatur of Nike, which plies the school with traveling money, shoes, and gear. The Compton schools place at or near the bottom of rankings using almost any criteria.[44]

These children specialize. They play and train at their sport year-round. During the summers they play in high-level leagues and attend camps run by college coaches or shoe companies to hone skills and become recognized by agents, scouts, and coaches. This continues throughout the high school years, with increased pressure to succeed. What was once play has become work.

Finally, the fifth indicator is that the elite high school athletes are the objects of intense recruitment by colleges throughout high school. The experience is flattering to the athletes, but it has a tendency to inflate their egos and get in the way of their education. It also tends to make them cynical about education because of the often sleazy aspects of recruiting. A more important consequence is that these athletes are on the market. As such, they ultimately will be purchased by a university athletic department. For high school athletes to be treated as commodities is the essence of corporate sport.

EFFORTS TO REFORM HIGH SCHOOL SPORTS

Many educators and others are concerned with the path that high school sports have taken. As we have seen, there are school districts with twenty-thousand-seat stadiums, there are high school coaches who do not teach in the classroom, some high school coaches make thousands from shoe companies, and there are nationally televised games. Under these conditions, the pressure on coaches and athletes becomes heavier. As a result some coaches have become even more demanding.

The potential for abuse and exploitation of athletes has increased. There have been more and more scandals involving payments and other gifts to high school players, recruiting, altered transcripts, and pressures on teachers to "give" athletes grades. Clearly, the education of the players tends to become secondary. In short, high school sport is moving in the same direction as sport at the college level, that is, toward commercialization, overemphasis, exploitation, and elitism and away from the educational mission of schools.

What follow are suggestions for reforming high school sports. The principle guiding these suggestions is that high school sports should be organized to maximize educational goals.

1. *Resist all efforts to "corporatize" high school sports.* High school sports should not be in the entertainment business. Nor should they allow the encroachment of corporations into their world. Moreover, high school sports should be kept in perspective; that is, they should not put undue pressure on coaches and players. In effect, to counter high school sport becoming corporate, several reforms must be instituted:

- Ban the national televising of high school sports. John Eisenberg has argued that such televising is wrong:

    High school should be a time to build an academic foundation; sports, no matter how talented the athlete, should be an extracurricular activity, not a televised, overemphasized spectacle. Now, I am not naive. I know sports is much more than an extracurricular activity to many top high school athletes. But shouldn't we be trying to correct the problem, not worsen it? Isn't it part of the reason college sports is such a cesspool? These kids need to concentrate more, not less, on classwork. They don't need distractions. And the lure of television would, assuredly, be distracting.[45]

- Schedule teams only within your area. As George Vecsey of the *New York Times* has suggested: "Let's pass a bus rule. If a team can get there comfortably in a bus, it's tolerable. But sending high school teams winging around the country is an abuse."[46]
- Eliminate postseason all-star games.
- Do not permit the involvement of athletic shoe companies and other corporations to intrude in high school sports. This means that these corporations must not be allowed to have high school coaches on their payrolls or to sponsor summer camps.

2. *Enforce an educationally defensible standard for school performance for athletes to be eligible to participate in sports.* Many school districts and states have low academic requirements for athletes. Many districts

accept a D average for sport eligibility. Low eligibility standards do not prepare athletes for college, and they proclaim the message that academics are not important.

Some states have instituted a "No Pass No Play" rule, requiring at least a C in all subjects to be eligible to participate in extracurricular activities.

Another example of efforts intended to help reform school athletics through academic standards was instituted by the NCAA at the behest of the American Council on Education. These rules have changed since their beginning in 1986, but essentially they require a minimum GPA in core high school courses and a minimum Scholastic Achievement Test (SAT) score.

The evidence is that the NCAA eligibility rules are working; that is, high school athletes are apparently better academically prepared for college than they were a generation ago. The number of new college recruits who are ineligible is diminishing. Again, caution should guide the interpretation of this apparent good news. This lower rate may not be a consequence of better preparation for students. The colleges may be less willing than in earlier years to offer scholarships to marginal students because their scholastic failures are embarrassing to the academic community. Another possibility is that marginal students opted to play in community colleges where the rules do not apply. Despite these cautions, it appears that the new academic demands are working. High school athletes and their coaches are taking academics more seriously.

3. *Bring coaches back into the teaching profession.* High school coaches should be part of the faculty, teaching courses and being responsible for nonsport duties just as are other faculty members. Coaches should be certified coaches, trained in first aid, the technical aspects of their sport, and the physiological and psychological aspects of adolescence. Coaches must be certified teachers, subject to the same rights and responsibilities as other teachers, including tenure. This will enhance the job security of coaches, thereby lessening somewhat the fanatical "win-at-all-costs" attitude.

4. *Minimize the elitism of sports.* Must sports only be for the unusually tall, large, and quick? (See Box 5.2, *Thinking about Sport.*) Schools should provide more school teams in more sports.

Why not have two football teams, one for those weighing more than 150 pounds and one for those under that weight? Basketball could be divided into teams over and under a certain height. As Jay Coakley has said:

> Why not give higher priority to sports involving active participation rather than just being a spectator? For example, there could be more combined male/female teams in sports such as long-distance running, doubles tennis and badminton, bowling, golf, cycling and tandem cycling, soccer, hacky sack, wall climbing, archery and shooting, volleyball swimming, racquetball, and billiards. If a person's high school years were a time for social development, playing these sports would be more valuable than watching spectator sports based on entertainment models.[47]

5. *Increase student involvement in sports programs.* One of the great ironies of school sports programs is that they are thought to enhance responsibility, autonomy, and leadership qualities in participants. However, as presently organized with autocratic coaches, imposed rules, and all decisions made by adults, these goals are not being achieved.

Could sports be organized so that the athletes are involved in the rule-making? Could they be organized so that elected player representatives could apply punishments for rule violations? Could team captains work with coaches on game strategies and make decisions during games?

Although rare, there have been some experiments promoting athlete involvement in decision-making. One radical experiment with democracy in football was used by George Davis, a football coach at several California high schools and a junior college. At St. Helena High School, his teams won forty-five consecutive games. The Davis system of coaching was unique. His players voted on who should be in the starting lineup; they decided what positions they wanted to play; and they established the guidelines for discipline. In other words, Davis's revolutionary system was democratic. Some critics in Willits, a community where Davis wanted to establish this system, were upset

Box 5.2 Thinking about Sport Should Everyone Make the Team?

Jerry Goldsberry was cut from his college baseball team. Two decades later, he still remembers: "I was practicing base-running, and the coach called me over and said, 'I don't think you have the talent for baseball.' I don't know why he had to put it that way."

Venetia Faulkenberg was cut from her junior high school cheerleading squad. "It had an impact on the whole family," she says. "Parents feel the rejection almost as much as their kids do."

Geoff Bradley played two years of college basketball but was dropped from the team his junior year. "They said, 'We don't believe you can help our program'" he recalls. "That's a blow to your ego."

As far as I could tell, Goldsberry, Faulkenberg and Bradley have grown up into happy, well-adjusted adults. But I was struck by the fact that each of them still remembers vividly an incident from youth that—at least for a time—wounded them emotionally. Being cut, for most kids, is a hurtful experience; for some, it can even leave lingering feelings of insecurity and worthlessness.

I went to Plainfield, Ind., recently to find out how one school has helped to put an end to this unnecessary trauma of growing up—Plainfield Community Middle School, where Geoff Bradley is the athletic director, Venetia Faulkenberg is a teacher and cheerleader sponsor and Jerry Goldsberry is the principal.

Plainfield's middle school separated from the high school and moved into its own building last year. Before that, however, for both academics and extracurricular activities, faculty committees recommended something called "widespread participation"—the idea that schools

need to involve more kids in more activities. Their proposal for this town just nine miles from the sports capital of Indianapolis? "They said, 'We want to come up with a no-cut policy,'" recalled Goldsberry.

What this meant is that every child would have an equal chance at feeling like an important part of a team or activity. If a child wanted to sing in the choir, he could; if a student wanted to belong to the swim team or run track, she could. With a little thought and planning, administrators discovered that they could apply the no-cut principle to all except two school activities—volleyball and basketball, where the limited space would allow for teams that were large but still finite.

"We felt, 'How is a student going to know what his strengths or weaknesses, likes and dislikes are, unless he tries?'" says Goldsberry. And under the no-cut system, a child would have the chance to improve or blossom.

The students came out in droves. The last year in the old building, only 13 kids showed up for cross-country; under the first year of the no-cut system, the number went to 78. Instead of 67 students on the track team, there were 120; the swim team grew from 50 to 64. Overnight, more than half of the 800 children at the middle school were taking part in activities. "The biggest problem was that we needed two school buses for everybody on the team," recalls the cross-country coach, Bruce Baker. Parent volunteers help out.

In track and field events, a school can enter an unlimited number of students—but only the times of the top

continues

---

with it. They accused Davis of shirking responsibility, promoting disunity, and aiding Communist agitators. The irony is that these evils were the presumed consequences of a democratic system.

Davis believed that his system would:

1. Increase confidence between players and coaches.
2. Promote team cohesion.
3. Teach responsibility, leadership, and decisionmaking, thereby fostering maturity rather than immaturity and independence rather than dependence.
4. Increase player motivation—instead of being driven by fear, harassment, and physical abuse by the coach, the players would have to impress their peers.
5. Free the coach to teach skills, techniques, and strategies.
6. Allow the players to experience the benefits of democracy.

Davis summed up his system this way:

> What does the vote achieve? It takes the problems of discipline and responsibility and puts them where they belong, with the players. The coach becomes a teacher, what he is being paid to do, a resource unit. My job is to teach, to help athletes reach a level of independence. At any level this is how democracy works and why it succeeds.[48]

> **Box 5.2 Continued**
>
> finishers count toward the final result. In other sports, of course, team sizes are limited. With its 66-member football squad, Plainfield has to be inventive to make all the kids feel included. "We still try to field our best team and, at the same time, balance that with getting more kids to participate," says Geoff Bradley.
>
> When a limited number of students can take part in a meet—as in some track and all wrestling events—the school will hold intramural contests beforehand to select the kids who compete in that week's contest. A student who does not compete early in the season might be a regular starter by the end.
>
> I stopped in as Mike Cummings was conducting a sixth-grade band rehearsal. The students were playing with all their hearts and sounded much like any junior high band. "If someone says, 'I have this trumpet, but I'm not quite sure what to do with it,' we say, 'You're in the band,'" Cummings told me. When the choir began this year, a number of students couldn't match the tune that the others were singing. "We surrounded them with stronger voices," said the co-director, Jonelle Heaton. "Now most of them are matching perfectly. One young man even was given a solo in our Christmas concert."
>
> Surely, I thought, no-cut must have a devastating effect on the success of the athletic teams. Not so. "Last year, we had eight championships," Bradley told me. "And we were county-wide champions in wrestling, boys' cross-country and boys' swimming."
>
> A sampling of parents I spoke with offered nothing but support. "I think it's great that all the kids in the school get to have the experience of participating," said Jim Horstman, summing up the general attitude.
>
> Some people might argue that a no-cut policy is no preparation for the real world, where competition and disappointment happen to everybody. Bruce Baker, who is a counselor as well as a coach, responds, "These are still kids here. They're 11, 12, 13, 14, years old. I've had to cut kids that age from teams in the past, and it's devastating to them, no matter how you explain it. So we decided we wanted to make this a safe place for kids to be. They know it will be different in high school and college, but here they can still be kids."
>
> But the last, and best, argument for no-cut is one I got from an eighth-grader on the school's cheerleading squad—one of the 73 cheerleaders at the school. No, they don't all perform at once; they're broken into three squads, which alternate games. And, no, they're not yet ready for the Rose Bowl, though virtually nobody else is at that age, either. They have lots of spirit, they're proud of what they do—and they're having fun.
>
> Just before she was to perform at a basketball game, this girl told me, "I'm going to high school next year, and I know I won't make the cheerleading squad there. I know there are a lot of girls who are better at it than I am. But at least I got to have the experience. And that's something I can remember all my life."
>
> *Source:* Michael Ryan, "Here, Everybody Gets to Play," *Parade,* 15 March 1992, 10.

SUMMARY

The theme of this chapter has been the relationship between school sport and educational goals. Our conclusion is that for sport to be compatible with educational goals, it should be structured as organized sport, not corporate sport. The data presented in this chapter, however, suggest that school sport is moving in the direction of corporate sport.

Sport at the elementary school level tends to accomplish educational goals (e.g., fostering good health practices, teaching skills, demonstrating the value of teamwork, and providing the experience of striving for a goal) in a playful, enjoyable atmosphere. At each successive educational level, however, the nature of sport changes; it becomes more serious, bureaucratized, and elitist, and its outcome becomes more crucial. Figure 5.1, provided by sociologists Eldon E. Snyder and Elmer A. Spreitzer, shows the progression in school sports from informal sport to corporate sport.

The serious question for educators is whether there is a place for corporate sport in education. This does reflect the corporate domination of American institutions, but is it appropriate for sport in high schools? To resist this trend is a form of emancipation with sport as the tool. As Harry Edwards said: "What's 'wrong' with sport and sport in education in America reflects America itself—particularly the relationships between

Figure 5.1 Attributes of Sports at Different Education Levels

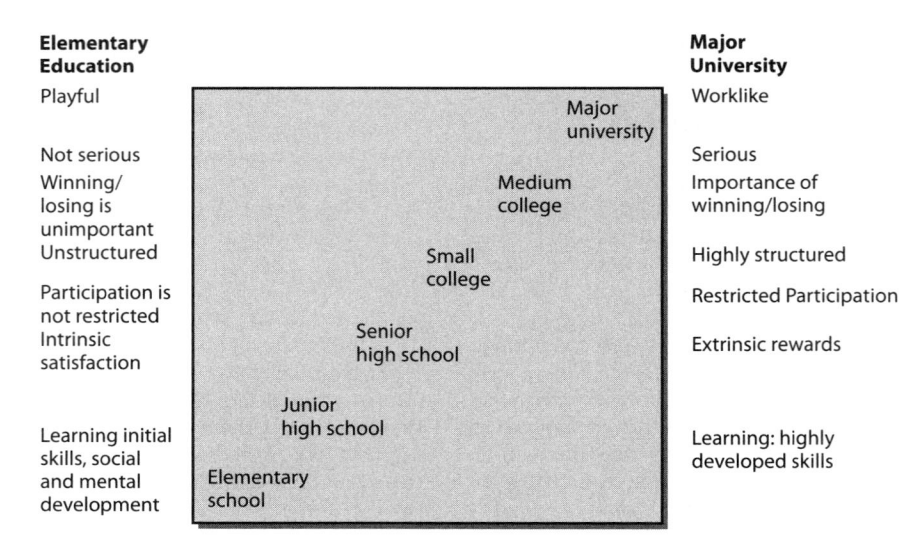

Elementary Education		Major University
Playful	Major university (top right)	Worklike
Not serious	Medium college	Serious
Winning/losing is unimportant		Importance of winning/losing
Unstructured	Small college	Highly structured
Participation is not restricted	Senior high school	Restricted Participation
Intrinsic satisfaction		Extrinsic rewards
	Junior high school	
Learning initial skills, social and mental development	Elementary school	Learning: highly developed skills

Source: Reprinted from Eldon E. Snyder and Elmer A. Spreitzer, "Sport, Education, and Schools," in *Handbook of the Social Science of Sport,* ed. Gunther R. F. Luschen and George H. Sage (Champaign, Ill.: Stripes, 1981), 138.

contemporary social, political, and economic realities and this nation's value priorities, its attitudes, and its perspectives."[49]

WEB RESOURCES

www.nfhs.org
The website for the National Federation of State High School Associations supplies data on a variety of topics, including participation by gender.

www.ed.gov/pubs/TitleIX/index.html
The U.S. Department of Education's assessment of progress toward gender equity in the thirty-five years since Title IX was instituted.

www.aahperd.org
The website of the American Alliance for Health, Physical Education, Recreation and Dance includes general information of high school under the National Association for Sport and Physical Education.

NOTES

1. National Federation of State High School Associations, 2006, http://www.nfhs.org/sports.aspx.
2. C. Roger Rees and Andrew W. Miracle, "Education and Sports," in *Handbook of Sport Studies,* ed. Jay Coakley and Eric Dunning (London: Sage, 2000), 277–290.
3. James S. Coleman, *The Adolescent Society* (New York: Free Press, 1961), 309.
4. T. J. L. Chandler and A. D. Goldberg, "The Academic All-American as Vaunted Adolescent Role-Identity," *Sociology of Sport Journal* 7, no. 3 (1990): 287–293; Alyce Holland and Thomas Andre, "Athletic Participation and the Social Status of Adolescent Males and Females," *Youth and Society* 25 (March 1994): 388–407.
5. Jay J. Coakley, *Sport in Society: Issues and Controversies,* 9th ed. (New York: McGraw-Hill, 2007), 489.
6. James S. Coleman, *Adolescents and the Schools* (New York: Basic Books, 1965), 49.
7. Willard Waller, *The Sociology of Teaching* (New York: Wiley, 1965), 115–116. This was first published in 1932.
8. Ibid., 116. For a general discussion of social control and sport, see D. Stanley Eitzen, "Social Control

and Sport," in *Handbook of Sport Studies,* ed. Coakley and Dunning, 370–381.

9. H. G. Bissinger, *Friday Night Lights: A Town, a Team, and a Dream* (Reading, Mass.: Addison-Wesley, 1990), 20. For another, more scholarly, ethnography of sport in a Texas community, see Douglas E. Foley, *Learning Capitalist Culture: Deep in the Heart of Tejas* (Philadelphia: University of Pennsylvania, 1990), especially 28–62.

10. Bissinger, *Friday Night Lights,* 127.

11. See the excellent summary of the methodological problems found in such studies in Christopher L. Stevenson, "Socialization Effects of Participation in Sport: A Critical Review of the Research," *Research Quarterly* 46 (October 1975): 287–301; and Christopher L. Stevenson, "College Athletics and Character: The Decline and Fall of Socialization Research," in *Sport and Higher Education,* ed. Donald Chu, J. O. Segrave, and B. J. Becker (Champaign, Ill.: Human Kinetics, 1985).

12. Elmer Spreitzer, "Does Participation in Interscholastic Athletics Affect Adult Development?: A Longitudinal Analysis of an 18–24 Cohort," *Youth and Society* 25 (March 1994): 384.

13. Charles Banham, "Man at Play," *Contemporary Review* 207 (August 1965): 62.

14. For a comprehensive survey of the literature, see Robert K. Fullenwider, "Sports, Youth, and Character: A Critical Survey" (Circle Working Paper 44, The Center for Information and Research in Civic Learning and Engagement, February 2006).

15. Terry D. Orlick, "The Sports Environment: A Capacity to Enhance—A Capacity to Destroy" (paper presented at the Canadian Symposium of PsychoMotor Learning and Sports Psychology, 1974), 2. For two examples of this complex relationship between sport and good/bad behaviors, see Jan Sokol-Katz, Margaret S. Kelley, Lorrie Basinger-Fleischman, and Jomills Henry Braddock II, "Re-examining the Relationship between Interscholastic Sport Participation and Delinquency: Type of Sport Matters," *Sociological Focus* 39 (August 2006): 173–192; and John P. Hoffman, "Extracurricular Activities, Athletic Participation and Adolescent Alcohol Use: Gender-Differentiated and School-Contextual Effects," *Journal of Health and Social Behavior* 47 (2006): 275–290.

16. See C. Roger Rees, Frank M. Howell, and Andrew W. Miracle, "Do High School Sports Build Character? A Quasi-Experiment on a National Sample," *Social Science Journal* 27 (1990): 303–315; and Andrew W. Miracle and C. Roger Rees, *Lessons of the Locker Room: The Myth of School Sports* (Buffalo, N.Y.: Prometheus Books, 1994).

17. Merrill J. Melnick, Beth E. Vanfossen, and Donald F. Sabo, "Developmental Effects of Athletic Participation among High School Girls," *Sociology of Sport Journal* 5 (March 1988): 22–36.

18. Herbert W. Marsh, "The Effects of Participation in Sport during the Last Two Years of High School," *Sociology of Sport Journal* 10 (March 1993): 18–43.

19. Naomi Fejgin, "Participation in High School Competitive Sports: A Subversion of School Mission or Contribution to Academic Goals?" *Sociology of Sport Journal* 11 no. 3 (1994): 21–30.

20. Jennifer M. Beller and Sharon K. Stoll, "Sport Participation and Its Effect on Moral Reasoning of High School Athletes and General Students," *Research Quarterly for Exercise and Sport* 65 (Supplement) (March 1994); "Do Sports Build Character?" in *Sports in School,* ed. John R. Gerdy (New York: Teachers College Press, 2000), 20–24.

21. George H. Sage, *Power and Ideology in American Sport,* 2nd ed. (Champaign, Ill.: Human Kinetics, 1998), 266–267.

22. Bissinger, *Friday Night Lights,* xiv.

23. See Donald W. Ball, "Failure in Sport," *American Sociological Review* 41 (August 1976): 726–739; Donald S. Harris and D. Stanley Eitzen, "The Consequences of Failure in Sport," *Urban Life* 7 (July 1978): 275–280; Jay J. Coakley, "Leaving Competitive Sport: Retirement or Rebirth?" *Quest* 35, no. 1 (1983): 1–11; JoAnn T. Drahota and D. Stanley Eitzen, "The Role Exit of Professional Athletes," *Sociology of Sport Journal* 15, no. 3 (1998): 263–278.

24. The following is from John R. Gerdy, *Air Ball: American Education's Failed Experiment with Elite Athletics* (Jackson: University Press of Mississippi, 2006), 34–45. See also Etta Kralovec, *Schools That Do Too Much: Wasting Time and Money in Schools and What We Can All Do about It* (Boston: Beacon Press, 2003).

25. Tim Flannery, National Federation of State High School Associations, quoted in Gerdy, *Air Ball,* 41.

26. Martin Henderson, "Carrying a Hefty Amount of Risk: Large Young Athletes Face Obesity Problems after Playing Days End," *Los Angeles Times,* 14 December 2006, http://www.latimes.com/sports/higghschool/la-sp-biglinemen14dec14,0,51145509,print.stor.

27. Joshua Cooley, "Gender Bender," *Sports Illustrated,* 22 January 2007, 35; and Tamar Lewis, "In Twist for High School Wrestlers, Girl Beats Boy," *New York Times,* 17 February 2007, p. 1A.

28. D. Stanley Eitzen, *Fair and Foul: Beyond the Myths and Paradoxes of Sport*, 3rd ed. (Lanham, Md.: Rowman and Littlefield, 2006), 51–71.

29. Grant Wahl, "Traveling Violations," *Sports Illustrated*, 21 September 1998, 27.

30. Joan Biskupic, "Case Could Have Lasting Effect on School Sports," *USA Today*, 17 April 2007, p. 4A.

31. "The Monitoring the Future Study," University of Michigan, National Institute on Drug Abuse (2006).

32. Colleen Sparks, "Intense Rivalries Pose Concerns," *Arizona Republic*, 9 February 2007, pp. A1, A16–A17.

33. Ibid, p. A16.

34. Eitzen, *Fair and Foul*.

35. Waller, *The Sociology of Teaching*, 114–115.

36. Shari Roan, "Narrowing the Field," *Los Angeles Times*, 2 October 2006, http://www.latimes.com/features/health/la-he-sports2oct02,1,3222033,print.story?coll=la-h.

37. National Federation of State School Associations.

38. Ibid.

39. Deven Carlson, Leslie Scott, Michael Planty, and Jennifer Thompson, *Statistics in Brief: What Is the Status of High School Athletes Eight Years after Their Senior Year?* NCES 2005-303 (Washington, D.C.: U.S. Department of Education, 2005).

40. Steve Wieberg, "Football 'Arms Race' Reaches Down a Level," *USA Today*, 6 October 2004, pp. 1A, 5A.

41. "Shutting Down Fake 'Prep Schools,'" *New York Times*, 10 March 2007, http://www.nytimes.com/2007/03/10/opinion/10sat3.html?_oref=slogin&pagewanted.

42. L. Jon Wertheim and George Dohrmann, "Going Big-Time," *Sports Illustrated*, 13 March 2006, 62–69.

43. Alexander Wolff and George Dohrmann, "A School for Scandal," *Sports Illustrated*, 26 February 2001, 75.

44. Ibid.

45. John Eisenberg, "Is Prep TV, 'Final Four' Going Too Far?" *Denver Post*, 4 March 1989, p. F6.

46. George Vecsey, "Young Athletes Deserve Good Old School Days," *New York Times*, 10 March 1989, p. B11.

47. Jay J. Coakley, *Sport in Society: Issues and Controversies*, 7th ed. (New York: McGraw-Hill, 2001), 441.

48. Neil Amdur, *The Fifth Down: Democracy and the Football Revolution* (New York: Delta Books, 1972).

49. Harry Edwards, *Sociology of Sport* (Homewood, Ill.: Dorsey Press, 1973), 361.

CHAPTER 6
Intercollegiate Sport

*"The business of college sports is not a necessary evil.
Rather it is a proper part of the overall enterprise."*
—Myles Brand, president of the NCAA

Festivities at Texas Memorial Stadium before a game between the home Texas Longhorns and the Texas A&M Aggies on 24 November 2006. (Wikipedia)

The first intercollegiate sports contest in the United States was a rowing race between Harvard and Yale in 1852. In 1869 the first intercollegiate football contest took place between Princeton and Rutgers. These early collegiate sports were run by students. The faculties, administrators, and alumni were not involved. According to George H. Sage, "The original form of governance was modeled after the well-established sports in the private secondary schools of England. In the British model the sports were for the students, and as student recreations they were expected to be organized, administered, and coached through student initiative, not adult intervention."[1] Students soon began losing control over their sports. The first college faculty athletic committee was formed by Princeton in 1881 and by Harvard a year later. As early as 1883, faculty representatives from several colleges met to discuss common problems surrounding sports. In 1895 the first league (later known as the Big Ten) was formed. By 1905 there was a need for a national organization to standardize rules and address problems associated with college sport. The Intercollegiate Athletic Association was formed in that year. Its name was changed in 1910 to the National Collegiate Athletic Association (NCAA). That organization has controlled college sport ever since, except for small colleges, which later came to be controlled by the National Association of Intercollegiate Athletics (NAIA), and for women's college sport, which it did not control until 1981. All of this is to say that what was once a student-run activity has been transformed so that now students have virtually no voice in athletic policies, control being vested in coaches, school administrations, athletic corporations, booster organizations, leagues, national organizations, and television. Moreover, college sport has been transformed from an activity for the participants to large-scale commercial entertainment, at least at the NCAA Division I level—the focus of this chapter.[2]

Along with this transformation of intercollegiate sport have come many abuses, such as illegal recruiting practices, altered transcripts, phantom courses, the physical and psychological abuse of athletes, and the exploitation of athletes.[3] These abuses occur for two related reasons, which are pressure to win on the field and pressure to succeed financially. William F. Reed of *Sports Illustrated* wrote a characterization of college basketball almost two decades ago, which is just as relevant for big-time college football and basketball today, that suggests the magnitude of the problem:

> Every fan knows that underneath its shiny veneer of color, fun and excitement, college basketball is a sewer full of rats. Lift the manhole cover on the street of gold, and the odor will knock you down. . . .
>
> The misdeeds allegedly committed by college basketball programs today are the same stuff that has plagued the game for decades—buying players, cheating in academics, shaving points, etc. And the NCAA is powerless to stop it. Make a statement by coming down hard on a Kentucky or a Maryland, and what happens? Nothing, really. The filth merely oozes from another crack.[4]

If these harsh words are true, and we believe from the evidence that they are irrefutable, then big-time intercollegiate athletics has severely corrupted the goals and ideals of higher education.

This chapter on big-time college sport is divided into four parts: (1) college sport as big business, (2) the NCAA and student-athletes, (3) the education and noneducation of student-athletes, and (4) efforts to reform big-time college sports.

COLLEGE SPORT AS BIG BUSINESS

College sports involve money, more than $5 billion annually. A disproportionate amount of that is for a few schools—those with big-time sports programs. The intrusion of money into collegiate sport at that level is evident in the following representative examples:

- The NCAA will receive an average of $545 million annually through 2013 from CBS for the rights to televise the Final Four men's basketball tournament. Advertisers pay CBS $1 million for a thirty-second television ad during the title game.

- Coca-Cola Company has an eleven-year, $500 million contract with the NCAA giving it the exclusive right to advertise and promote its beverages at the eighty-six championships in twenty-two sports sponsored by the NCAA.
- Each team playing in a BCS game (Sugar, Orange, Fiesta, and Rose Bowls) received $17 million in the 2006–2007 bowl schedule.
- The Division I-A schools spent $4 billion in the 2004–2005 school year on their athletic programs.
- The University of Minnesota sold the naming rights to its football stadium to TCF Bank for $35 million.
- The nation's largest athletic department, Ohio State, had a budget in 2006–2007 of $104.7 million and employed more than 300 full-time workers and nearly 1,600 part-time employees. It oversees 377 acres, 16.9 million square feet of buildings, 926 varsity athletes, and 36 varsity sports.[5]
- A season ticket to the seven home games at Ohio State in 2006 cost $413 ($59 a game).
- There is a wide disparity in budgets among the 121 Division I-A athletic programs. In 2006–2007, five schools had athletic revenues above $80 million. At the bottom end, five schools had revenues of $10.1 million or less, with Virginia Military Institute (VMI) having the least revenue at $5.5 million.
- The University of North Carolina at Chapel Hill has an agreement with Nike worth $3.54 million annually in equipment and cash. Ohio State has a seven-year deal worth $11.9 million from Nike. Nike has similar, but less lucrative, arrangements with about two hundred other college and university athletic departments. Other sports outfitters are also involved. Under Armour, for example, signed Auburn to a five-year deal for $10.6 million beginning in the summer of 2006.
- Notre Dame has a $45 million contract with NBC to televise its football games over several years. The sale of Notre Dame merchandise brings the school another $2 million in royalties, and the appearance in a bowl game raises more millions.
- In 2005, T. Boone Pickens donated $165 million to the Oklahoma State athletic department.
- Schools sell licensing rights for the right to use their logos on clothes, beer mugs, and other items. In the year following winning the football national championship, the University of Texas received licensing royalties of $8.2 million.
- Beginning in 2006 the schools of the Big 12 had committed slightly less than $500 million on improving and expanding football stadiums and other football-related facilities. Among those purchases is a new football stadium high-definition video display scoreboard at the University of Texas, called "Godzillatron," that is 55 feet tall and 134 feet wide, costing $8 million.

Another set of examples shows how well the successful coaches of big-time programs are compensated:

- The salaries of the sixty-five coaches from the schools in the 2007 men's basketball tournament averaged $800,000, not including benefits, perks, and incentives. Twenty of the coaches exceeded $1 million a year, with lavish bonuses for winning for various achievements. The highest-paid men's basketball coach—Rick Pitino of Louisville—makes about $4 million. The highest-paid women's basketball coach—Pat Summitt of Tennessee—is guaranteed $1.125 million annually.
- The 2007 salaries for the University of Florida head coaches in football (Urban Meyer) and basketball (Billy Donovan) were $3.25 million and $3.5 million, respectively. The salary of athletic director Jeremy Foley was $1.2 million. The president of the university, Bernie Machen, had a relatively paltry salary of $730,676 in 2006–2007.
- The salary of the 121 football coaches in Division I-A averaged $950,000 in 2006, not counting extras, with 9 coaches making more than $2 million, and another 33 making between $1 million and $2 million. This salary

for football coaches is, on average, more than double that of the average salary for college presidents and almost ten times the salary of their full professor colleagues.[6] The highest-paid football coach is Nick Saban at the University of Oklahoma, who signed an eight-year, $32 million contract beginning in 2007. In addition to the $4 million a year, he can make as much as $800,000 annually in bowl game bonuses.

- Coaches in big-time programs also receive gifts of housing, paid country club memberships, use of private jets, travel allowances for family members, complimentary tickets in luxury boxes, use of vacation homes, free cars, and in some cases, million-dollar annuities. In addition, rollover contracts give coaches "golden parachutes" if they are fired prematurely. For example, when Michigan State fired John L. Smith in 2006, the university owed him $3.05 million due on his contract. Similarly, Alabama bought out Mike Shula's contract for $4 million when he was ousted.

These examples of the NCAA, the schools, and the coaches demonstrate clearly that college athletic programs are not amateur athletics. Big-time college athletic programs are big business. The athletic budgets at Division I-A schools with football at the individual schools are enormous, as high as $104 million. The money generated comes from gate receipts, student athletic fees, the educational budget of the university, booster organizations, individual contributors, advertising income, contracts with shoe and apparel companies, television, and league reimbursements for the television and bowl or tournament appearances by league members.

There is a commonly held belief that the athletic departments are doing well financially. This is a myth, for the most part. According to the U.S. Department of Education, in 2005–2006, of the 121 Division I-A schools, 57 percent reported a profit from athletics, 38 percent broke even, and 5 percent lost money.[7] These figures are misleading. The deficits would be much greater if the accounting procedures were more appropriate.

That is, the football and basketball teams play in multimillion-dollar stadiums and arenas paid for by taxpayers, contributors, and, more typically, bonds that are paid off by students' fees at no expense to the athletic departments. An analysis of the 2004–2005 athletic budgets of 164 of the nation's 215 biggest public schools found that these schools received more than $1 billion in student fees and general school funds. Without this funding, fewer than 10 percent of athletic departments would have been able to support themselves. Most would have lost more than $5 million.[8]

There are several reasons for the red ink generated by many athletic departments. First, the revenue-producing sports (football and men's basketball, and rarely women's basketball, the exceptions being Connecticut and Tennessee) are expected to pay for the entire athletic program, which may include more than thirty sports. Second, there is a constantly escalating arms race in college sport. The pay for successful coaches rises rapidly in order to keep them. When a team succeeds, the coach's salary is raised by hundreds of thousands and the assistants by tens of thousands. Typically, successful programs constantly upgrade their facilities, including expanding the seating, adding luxury boxes, and improving weight rooms, locker rooms, and practice fields, which will either bring in more revenue or help in recruiting.

Third, the athletic departments spare no expense to fund the revenue-producing sports. Employees in these athletic departments tend to be paid better than employees elsewhere in their universities. Travel budgets for the teams and for recruiters are generous. A common practice, for example, is for the football team and for some basketball teams to stay in a local hotel the night before home games. Fourth, universities sponsor pregame and postgame parties for influential alumni, boosters, and legislators that can exceed two hundred thousand dollars a year in costs.

The Consequences of a Money Orientation in College Sports

What are the consequences of college sports programs being so focused on money? First, the lack of adequate monies leads to a reduction in the number of sports offered by these institutions. Football and men's basketball produce revenue; therefore they are exempt from budget cuts. When the cuts are severe, some programs may be eliminated, and these casualties are in the so-called minor sports such as wrestling, lacrosse, gymnastics, swimming, water polo, tennis, and golf. Women's sports are less vulnerable than the men's minor sports because of Title IX (see chapter 14), but their programs are also subject to cuts. The point is that the necessity of raising money through sports programs tends to make college sport more elitist (fewer and fewer participants) and limited to certain skills and physical types (the tall or the large or both). It ensures the dominance of male sports, at least football and basketball.

Second, money has prostituted the university and the purpose of sport. The necessity of making more and more money is a major source for the many abuses found in big-time college sport. Teams and coaches do not make millions without winning. This necessity of winning is a primary reason why some coaches cheat and dehumanize their players. The pressures to win may be responsible for the use of drugs to enhance performance beyond normal limits. As Maurice Mitchell, former chancellor of the University of Denver, characterized the situation:

> The curse of big-time athletics still plagues the American university. Athletics has nothing to do with the primary purpose of the university. It is an embarrassment and in many cases a demonstration of immorality, of hypocrisy, a reallocation of scarce university resources, and an involvement with a group of people who, in most cases, should not be on a university campus. Big-time athletics demonstrate—to students and faculty alike—that the university is willing to operate under a double standard. Big-time athletics on university campuses may be a symbol of our willingness to use our institutions of higher learning, which were established for sacred purposes, for the least sacred of purposes. Like prostitution, it is accepted but not honored.[9]

Another consequence of an athletic department's search for money is that decision making tends to leave the university and flow toward the sources of revenue. The money chase has meant that teams will reschedule games to fit the demands of television, even if it inconveniences their fans or interferes with athletes' studies. Football games are now played in the heat of August, on Tuesday, Thursday, and Friday nights, and anytime on Saturdays from 11 A.M. to 9 P.M. Moreover, television has compromised the sports with scheduled time-outs. Booster organizations that supply funds may influence which coaches are hired and when they will be fired. Corporate sponsors may intrude in various ways as they give or withhold their monies. The point, as Murray Sperber says, is that these practices "undermine one of the fundamental tenets of colleges and universities—their independence."[10]

Another result of "going after the money" is that the relatively few seats available in arenas tend to go to big-spending boosters, depriving students of the chance to watch their teams play. For instance, the University of Southern California, playing football in the large Los Angeles Coliseum, allots only eight thousand seats to students. The University of Louisville provides only 10 percent of its seats for basketball games to students. Many schools with successful basketball programs such as the University of Arizona hold a lottery to choose the students who may attend games. The situation worsens during tournament time when each school is allotted relatively few tickets. These typically are given to the greatest benefactors of the athletic department rather than to students. This raises the serious question: *Should not school sports be primarily for students?*

When the pressure to win becomes too great, the result can be a sub-rosa policy of cheating, that is, a policy of offering athletes more than the legal limit to lure them to a school and keep them there or using unethical means to keep them scholastically eligible. As far back as 1929 a report by the Carnegie Foundation decried the widespread illegal recruiting practices of American colleges and universities. Since then, the problem has not only continued but intensified. The scandals involve illegal and immoral behavior of overzealous coaches, school authorities, alumni, and boosters.

These recruits are not only suspect academically, but sometimes they also go over the line in antisocial behavior.

In most instances school administrators, students, and supporters do not demand that guilty coaches be fired for their transgressions—if they win. As John Underwood has characterized the situation: "We've told them that it doesn't matter how clean they keep their programs. It doesn't matter what percentage of their athletes graduate or take a useful place in society. It doesn't even matter how well the coaches teach their sports. All that matters are the flashing scoreboard lights."[11]

The pursuit of money has prostituted the university and the purpose of sport. Education is not the goal. The physical and emotional welfare of athletes is secondary to their athletic performances. Sport as a pleasurable activity is an irrelevant consideration in the climate of big-time collegiate sport. Winning and the money generated are paramount. In this milieu the resulting evils are due not to the malevolent personalities of coaches but to a perverse system.

Perhaps the most serious result of the "winning-at-all-costs" mentality that pervades many athletic departments is that the education of the athletes is secondary. Coaches proclaim that their athletes are students first and athletes only secondarily; this is the typical recruiting speech to prospects and their parents, but in practice the reverse is often true. The relationship between coach and athlete is essentially that of employer and employee. The athlete has signed a contract and is paid for his or her athletic services (but not well). Moreover, because of such enormous demands on their time, athletes frequently must take a reduced course load and thus will not usually graduate in the normal number of years. Study halls and tutors are frequently available, even required, for college athletes, but the primary function of these adjuncts is to ensure athletic eligibility, not necessarily an education. Athletes are often counseled to take easy courses, whether or not those courses fit their educational needs. Achieving an education is incidental to the overriding objective of big-time sports. As Alabama's legendary football coach Paul "Bear" Bryant once put it: "I used to go along with the idea that football players on scholarships were student-athletes, which is what the NCAA calls them. Meaning a student first, an athlete second. We were kidding ourselves, trying to make it more palatable to the academicians. We don't have to say that and we shouldn't. At the level we play, the boy is really an athlete first and a student second."[12]

The cynicism with which some coaches regard education is seen in the revelations concerning the enrollment of athletes in "phantom" courses (correspondence or residence courses that give credit for no work or attendance). Clearly, for a coach to permit this is to admit that the athlete's eligibility supersedes his or her learning. For the athlete, the message is equally clear.

Perhaps the greatest disregard for the education of athletes occurs when those without hope of graduation are recruited. In the words of syndicated columnist George Will:

> The worst scandal does not involve cash or convertibles. It involves slipping academically unqualified young men in the back doors of academic institutions, insulating them from academic expectations, wringing them dry of their athletic-commercial usefulness, then slinging them out the back door even less suited to society than they were when they entered. They are less suited because they have spent four years acquiring the idea that they are exempt from normal standards.[13]

A Contradiction: Athletes as Amateurs in a Big Business Environment

We have seen that great sums of money are generated by big-time college sports. The university athletic departments act like corporations (indeed, many are organized separately from their universities as corporations); many businesses outside the university make considerable sums from college sports; and many individuals in the athletic departments (athletic directors, coaches, trainers, accountants, groundskeepers, equipment managers, academic advisors) make their living, some as much as $4 million annually, from their involvement in college sport. The irony is that the major labor force in producing college sport, the athletes, is not paid. Young men (and more recently young women) on athletic scholarships are limited by NCAA rules to room, board, books, and tuition to bring honor and lots of dollars to their universities. They are considered to be amateurs who participate for the love of sport untainted by money. But this is a charade, as George Sage has argued:

> In reality, the scholarship is nothing but a work contract. What colleges are really doing is hiring entertainers. The deceit of claiming that educational purposes preclude salaried compensation for athletic performances is testimony to the extensive attempts of the collegiate establishment to avoid its financial responsibilities. Athletic scholarships are actually a form of economic exploitation, the establishment of a wage below poverty level for student-athlete-entertainers who directly produce millions of dollars for athletic departments.... Paying as little as possible to operate a business is called keeping overhead low; it's what every business owner strives to do. The NCAA and major universities have mastered this principle. No other American business operates so pretentiously, making huge sums of money but insisting the enterprise be viewed as an educational service.[14]

In effect, being a scholarship athlete in a big-time program is now a year-round commitment. Football players used to arrive at school a week or so before the beginning of the fall semester and play, if they were successful, until New Year's Day, followed six weeks later by a month of spring practice. Now the season has been extended to thirteen games, and some of the games are in the last week of August, requiring that practices began three weeks earlier. In the off-season, players are expected to lift weights and spend their summers on campus with "voluntary" workouts. But despite the increased workload and the great sums generated by big-time college sports programs, the athletes continue to be limited in remuneration to room, board, tuition, and books. The huge salaries for coaches have escalated dramatically with the amounts of money generated, but this has not trickled down to the athletes, whose pay remains stagnant.

This issue raises two questions of morality: (1) Should universities use student-athletes to hustle money for the universities? and (2) if so, should the athletes be paid wages that are not commensurate with their contributions?

THE NCAA AND STUDENT-ATHLETES

The NCAA or an organization like it is necessary to administer college sports. Such an organization is needed to provide a uniform set of rules for each sport, to adjudicate disputes among members, and to organize playoffs and tournaments. Rules must be made and enforced to curb cheating, to eliminate the exploitation of athletes, to enhance the education of student-athletes, to eliminate the use of illicit drugs to enhance performance, and to maintain the integrity of the sports and athletes. What has emerged, however, is a powerful monopoly, a monopoly that controls big-time college sport *for the interests of the universities, not the student-athletes*. This occurs in two ways: the enforcement of "amateurism" and rules that limit athletes' rights.

The Enforcement of "Amateurism"

First, as we have just discussed, the NCAA rules enforce a code of amateurism on the athletes, while the NCAA and its member institutions raise millions off these athletes. By defining the athletes as amateurs, the schools keep the costs of operation low by not paying athletes what they are worth. Consider this: In 2006 North Carolina's men's basketball team had revenues of $15.2 million. If that team distributed its revenue similarly to the professional teams in the NBA, 59 percent of the revenue, or $7.6 million, would go to the players. By NCAA rules, however, the players were limited to a total of $318,097 from their scholarships.[15] The schools obviously benefit from this arrangement.

The schools also benefit when the activity is defined as amateur because it permits the monies generated from athletics to be free from taxation. Even though the scholarship appears to be a payment for services rendered, it is called a "grant-in-aid" for educational purposes. The NCAA is on shaky ground in keeping athletic monies tax-free

Seton Hall and Delaware State players during NCAA basketball, 31 December 2007, at the Prudential Center in Newark, New Jersey. NCAA rules enforce a code of amateurism on the athletes, while the NCAA and its member institutions raise millions off its athletes. (AP Photo/Bill Kostroun)

since the rules of the Internal Revenue Service stipulate that any amount received from an employer for educational expenses is taxable income.[16] Therefore, the NCAA has done all it can to retain the "amateur" status of college athletes. Specifically, the NCAA has lobbied in various state legislatures that college athletes should not be included under workers' compensation because they would then be defined as employees. Similarly, the NCAA has argued strenuously that college athletes should not be paid a stipend in addition to room, board, books, and tuition because this would lessen their case that the athletes are amateurs. Also, they do not want the athletes to be "professional" in any way. Some examples:

- Athletes are not allowed to have a financial advisor (agent) until after their final college game.
- Athletes will lose their amateur status if they allow their pictures or names to be associated with commercial enterprise, whether they are paid for it or not. For example, following the 1998 Winter Olympics, the victorious U.S. women's hockey team was invited to be pictured on the Wheaties cereal box. Missing in that photo were the five players who were college players, even though they would not have received any compensation for being in the photo.
- Athletes cannot receive payment for their athletic skills. Using this principle, the NCAA ruled that a New Mexico State University basketball player who had won a car by making a half-court shot at halftime of a professional basketball game (he was one of two spectators chosen at random for the shot) could keep either the car or his senior year of eligibility, but not both.
- Athletes cannot be used to raise money for others, even charities. For example, the Lions Club of Alachua, Florida, was not allowed to raffle off a football signed by members of the University of Florida football team to raise money for its eye bank because, the NCAA ruled, the players were being exploited by selling their autographs.
- Athletes cannot receive extra compensation from their universities. This has meant, for example, that the NCAA put Seton Hall on probation for buying a suit for a player to attend his father's funeral.

These examples show the lengths to which the NCAA will go to keep the "amateur" status of college athletes. They also demonstrate the hypocrisy of the NCAA. While keeping their athletes pure, the NCAA, the universities, and the individual coaches are engaged in a relentless pursuit of revenue estimated at well over $5 billion annually. It must be emphasized again that this revenue is generated by the athletes. Athletes literally can be walking billboards by wearing shoes, for which the coach receives thousands of dollars, but the athletes cannot receive anything other than the free shoes. Athletes cannot endorse products or otherwise use their name recognition for economic gain, but universities can use them in their publicity and can license and sell clothing, sports equipment, and souvenirs with the team logo. Athletes cannot sell their complimentary tickets (in fact, they cannot give their tickets to anyone except family members, relatives, and students), yet coaches (some with hundreds of tickets) have no restrictions on their distribution. Coaches typically receive bonuses for taking their teams to a bowl or to the NCAA men's basketball tournament but their players do not. The NCAA will not even allow schools to pay for travel expenses of players' family members to watch their sons play in the bowl or tournament, yet the schools pay the expenses for an entourage from the university to attend. Money is made, lots of it, at the expense of poorly paid workers. In the words of Mike Trope, an agent for professional athletes: "[P]eople have this perception of a benevolent NCAA that protects these poor young lads. What the NCAA protects is its own self-interest. The rules of the NCAA are created artificially to protect the profit structure of [big-time college sports]. I consider the collegiate system one of the greatest forms of labor exploitation in America."[17]

The Restriction of Athletes' Rights

The NCAA rules also work against athletes by restricting their rights. When young persons sign letters-of-intent to play for certain schools, they have made one-sided, disadvantageous agreements. Foremost, these athletes have agreed to play for four years at a given institution. Should they change their minds and switch, they must wait a year to play at a new institution. What if they selected a college because of a particular coach, and the coach leaves? Perhaps the coach may leave even before the student has enrolled in a school. Under NCAA rules, they have signed with a school, not a coach, and they must stay or lose a year of eligibility. They must also stay or lose eligibility even if they find the coach at the place they have chosen abusive, racist, or unethical. The circumstances do not matter; they are stuck. The situation is even more disadvantageous for athletes who are at odds with their coach but cannot get the coach to release them. Without the coach's release, the athlete must sit out two years instead of the customary one year.

Although the athletes sign a four-year agreement to play for a school, the schools have only a one-year commitment to the athletes. This one-year renewable commitment by the schools gives coaches extraordinary power over athletes.

Each of these rules restrains the freedom of athletes but not their schools. The athletes are bound by a contract, but the schools are not. Coaches may have contracts that allow them to leave at any time, or their schools may not hold them to their contracts; but there are no exceptions for athletes. Coaches do not have to sit out a year if they move, but players do if they leave for another school. The NCAA rules clearly protect the schools and coaches but not the players (see Box 6.1, *Thinking about Sport*).

Most interesting—and disheartening, we would add—is the tendency for the NCAA to deflect attention away from the problems resulting from the structure of sport by blaming athletes for them. The passage of rules requiring that student-athletes achieve certain minimum test scores before they can participate is a good example of this tendency. In George Sage's words:

> Of course, no rational person can really quarrel with holding athletes to academic standards. . . . But focusing on athletes' academic achievement—something around which everyone can rally—and seemingly showing how athletes are being held to academic standards, while ignoring the system of power, privilege, and exploitation, serve to suggest to the public that some social pathology with the student-athletes is the reason for the recurring scandals in collegiate athletics, not the social structure of which they are a part. Such actions deflect questions away from the more endemic social structural problems of big-time college sports, such as the appropriateness of a commercialized sport system that does not pay its main workforce a livable wage operating on college campuses.[18]

> **Box 6.1 Thinking about Sport The Big-Time College Sports Plantation**
>
> Many male youths dream of playing football or basketball for a university with a big-time college sports program. They want to be part of the pageantry, glory, excitement, shared sacrifice, bonding with teammates, and to be the object of adoring fans. Not incidentally, they would receive an all-expenses-paid college education, which if a professional sports career does not work out, will open other lucrative career opportunities. Many observers of big-time college sports accept this idealized version, but just how glamorous is participation in athletics at this level? Are the athletes as privileged as it appears?
>
> There is a dark side to big-time college sports. To show this, I will use the metaphor of big-time college sports as a plantation system. I admit that such a metaphor is overdrawn. Big-time college sports are not the same as the brutalizing, inhumane, degrading, and repressive institution of slavery found in the antebellum South. Nevertheless, there are significant parallels with slavery that highlight the serious problems plaguing collegiate athletics.
>
> There is the organization—the NCAA—that preserves the plantation system, making and enforcing the rules to protect the interests of the individual plantation owners. The plantations are the football and men's basketball factories within the universities with big-time programs. The overseers are the coaches who extract the labor from the workers. The workers are owned by the plantation and, much like the slaves of the antebellum South, produce riches for their masters while receiving a meager return on the plantation's profits.
>
> Many observers of big-time college sports, most certainly the coaches and players, would argue vehemently with this assertion that the athletes are slaves in a plantation environment. After all, they not only choose to participate, they want desperately to be part of big-time sports. Moreover, they have special privileges that separate them from other students (much like what house slaves received, when compared to field slaves of the Old South), such as more and better food, special housing, favorable handling in registering for classes, and, sometimes, generous treatment by the criminal justice system when they cross the line. Also, the athletes, unlike slaves, can leave the program if they wish.
>
> If participation is voluntary and the athletes want to be part of the system, what is the problem? My argument that these athletes are slaves in a plantation system, whether they realize it or not, involves several dimensions:
>
> - The athletes are exploited economically, making millions for their masters, but provided only with a subsistence wage of room, board, tuition, and books. This point is obvious when the television rights, coaches' salaries, revenues, and budgets of the NCAA and the participating schools are considered.
> - The athletes are controlled with restricted freedoms. Their freedom of movement (to other teams) is restricted. Their right to privacy is invaded routinely by mandatory drug testing and the monitoring of their behaviors by coaches and their representatives. Athletes do not have the right, if they want to continue playing, of speaking out against the coach, or the athletic department, or the system.
> - The athletes are subjected to physical and mental abuse by overseers. Although by no means a universal trait of coaches, physical and mental cruelty towards players does occur. They are often yelled at and humiliated in front of their peers or even the press, and they may even be hit or otherwise assaulted. Just as the owners of slaves were allowed to brutalize their chattel, so, too, are powerful and winning coaches immune from meaningful sanctions and accountability when their actions cross the line.
> - The master-slave relationship is accepted by the athletes as legitimate. Those athletes who make it to the big-time level accept the slavelike conditions. And, why not? They have been thoroughly conditioned to obey athletic authorities. They take the existing order for granted, not questioning the status quo because they are preoccupied with their own jobs or making the team and perhaps gaining national recognition. Athletes are, for the most part, willing victims whose self-worth and self-esteem are largely synonymous with their athletic prowess. Another reason for submissiveness of athletes is that they are politically disenfranchised. Those who challenge the power structure risk losing their scholarships. Athletes who have a grievance are on their own. They have no union and no arbitration board. Their sole option is to leave the plantation. If they quit, they are often viewed by others as the problem. After all, most accepted the system. Those who quit are seen not as victims, but as losers.
>
> *Source:* Excerpted from D. Stanley Eitzen, "Slaves of Big-Time College Sports," *USA Today: The Magazine of the American Social Scene* 129 (September 2000): 26–30.

THE EDUCATIONAL PERFORMANCE OF STUDENT-ATHLETES

The research indicates that college athletes in big-time football and basketball programs do not perform at the same level academically as other athletes and the general student body. Their grades are lower, and they are much more likely to take easy courses in easy majors. Most significantly, they are much less likely to graduate. Before we examine the college performance of athletes, though, let's look at their preparation for college.

Intellectual Performance of Student-Athletes for College

There are three standard predictors of college performance—the combined score on the Scholastic Assessment Test (SAT), the American College Test (ACT) composite score, and high school grade point average. Research on a number of schools shows that in most big-time programs, athletes in the revenue sports (men's football and basketball) are less prepared for college than women athletes, men in the minor sports, and the general undergraduate student population. Before Proposition 48 went into effect in 1986, requiring a minimum SAT score of 700, the revenue athletes (football and men's basketball) who entered Tulane University in 1985, for example, had an average SAT score of 648 (484 points lower than the average student).

After Proposition 48, marginal students who were good athletes continued to be recruited, despite their likely problems educationally. Football and men's basketball players in big-time sports programs are much more likely than other students to have received special treatment in the admissions process, that is, be admitted below the standard requirements for their universities. In 2004, for example, 70 percent of the football players had entered the University of Colorado with test scores below the entrance requirements for the rest of the student body. Even in schools with highly selective admission policies (e.g., Ivy League schools), athletes had a significantly better chance than nonathletes to be admitted even though their ACT/SAT scores were appreciably lower.[19] Apparently schools are willing to take marginal students because of the athletic payoff.

Academic Performance

The data on class grades are somewhat difficult to interpret. The reason is that athletes, especially those in the revenue-producing sports, are more likely than other athletes and other students to receive grades fraudulently (e.g., "shady" correspondence courses, "friendly" professors,[20] surrogate test takers or term paper writers) or to take easy courses and cluster in easy majors. Regarding "clustering," the *Chronicle of Higher Education* reported these examples:[21]

- At Texas A&M, where only 3 percent of the undergraduates majored in agricultural programs, nearly 25 percent of the Aggie football players did.
- Whereas 56 percent of Georgia Tech football players majored in management, only 11 percent of all undergraduates did.
- At Virginia Tech, less than 1 percent of undergraduates majored in residential property management, but 12 percent of the football players did.

There are several possible reasons other than a genuine interest in the major for such clustering. The favored major may have fewer courses that conflict with practices and other sport-related demands, such as afternoon labs. The major may have less stringent admission requirements. And the major may be less demanding. For these reasons the players may choose the easy route, or sometimes they are guided by academic advisors in the athletic department to keep them eligible.[22]

Graduation Rates

The most commonly used indicator of school performance is the overall graduation rate of athletes, tracking them six years after entering college. The NCAA computes graduation rates by not counting athletes who transfer in good academic standing or those who leave school early to play in professional leagues. Unfortunately, there are no comparable data for the general student body that do not count transfers. Using this measure, the NCAA provides some quite rosy statistics: Division I athletes had a graduation rate of 77 percent in 2006. This overall rate masks some important differences:[23]

- *Gender.* The graduation rate for male athletes was 70 percent, while it was 86 percent for female athletes.
- *Sport.* The lowest graduation rates for men were basketball (59 percent), baseball (65 percent), and football (65 percent). For women, the lowest graduation rates were bowling (70 percent), rifle (78 percent), and basketball (82 percent).
- *Social class.* The sports with the highest graduation rates for men were skiing, lacrosse, and fencing. For women, the highest-ranking sports were gymnastics, fencing, field hockey, and skiing. Participants in each of these sports are overrepresented among the affluent in society (see chapter 12).
- *Racial minorities.* Only 51 percent of African American male basketball players graduate compared to 76 percent of white basketball players.[24]

In 2006, *USA Today* examined the graduation rates for the top-tier schools:[25]

- Of the top twenty-five ranked football teams, sixteen were below the average for the sport. Texas, the defending champion, had a graduation rate of 40 percent.
- While three schools (Navy, Boston College, and Notre Dame) in Division I-A had rates at 95 percent or better for their football teams, three (San Jose State, Florida Atlantic, and the University of Arizona) were below 40 percent.
- For basketball, seventeen schools had 100 percent graduation rates. Three schools, however (New Mexico, Florida A&M, and the University of Georgia), had rates below 10 percent.
- Twelve Division I-A schools had sub–50 percent graduation rates in both football and basketball, including the University of Arizona, the University of California–Berkeley, the University of Georgia, Louisiana State University, University of Minnesota, and University of Texas.

The Impediments to Scholarly Achievement by College Athletes

In addition to many college athletes being ill prepared for the intellectual demands of college, they face a number of obstacles that impede their scholarly achievement. The pressures on athletes, especially those in big-time, revenue-producing sports, are well known, including physical exhaustion, mental fatigue, media attention, and demanding coaches. The time demands alone are onerous. During the season, the athletes spend many hours preparing for, participating in, recovering from, and traveling to games. Big-time college revenue sports have become a year-round occupation for the scholarship players. As Michael Goforth, Virginia Tech's head trainer, has put it: "We've got the bowl game in January, then spring practice starts, what, six weeks later? And in between that, a lot of kids have surgery. Then after spring ball, it's lifting, then summer workouts, then we're back here in the fall."[26] The NCAA permits only "voluntary" workouts in the summer, but that requirement is a sham—the athletes know they must work out or risk losing favor with their coaches, at a minimum, or even losing their scholarships.

The athletes in commercialized, professionalized college sports programs have trouble reconciling the roles associated with their dual statuses of athlete and student. Peter and Patricia Adler conducted a study of a big-time university basketball program and found that the pressures of big-time sport and the academic demands resulted in the gradual disengagement of the athletes from their academic roles.[27] Most athletes entered the university feeling idealistic about their impending academic performance; that is, they were optimistic about graduating, and they considered ambitious majors. This idealism lasted until about the end of the first year and was replaced by disappointment and a growing cynicism as they realized how difficult keeping up with their schoolwork would be. The athletic role came to dominate all facets of their existence. The athletes received greater positive reinforcement from their athletic performance than from their academic performance. They were isolated increasingly from the student body. They were segregated in an athletic dormitory. They were isolated culturally by their racial and socioeconomic differences from the rest of the students. They were even isolated from other students by their physical size, which others often found intimidating. They interacted primarily with other athletes, and these peers tended to demean academics. In their first year they were given courses with "sympathetic" professors, but this changed as athletes moved through the university curriculum. The academic expectations escalated, and the athletes were unprepared. The resulting academic failure or, at best, mediocre academic performance led to embarrassment and despair. The typical response, according to the Adlers, was role distancing: "To be safe, it was better not to try than to try and not succeed."[28] This attitude, and the resulting behaviors, were reinforced by the peer subculture.

The noneducation and miseducation of college athletes are especially acute for African Americans. Many come from economically disadvantaged backgrounds and from inadequate schools. Every study that has compared African American athletes with their white counterparts has found them less prepared for college and more likely to fulfill this prophecy in college: African Americans tend to enter college as marginal students and to leave the same way. Harry Edwards has argued that the African American "dumb jock" is a social creation: "'Dumb jocks' are not born; they are systematically created."[29] This social construction results from several factors. First, African American student-athletes must contend with two negative labels: the dumb athlete caricature and the dumb African American stereotype. This double negative tends to result in a self-fulfilling prophecy as teachers, fellow students, and the athletes themselves assume low academic performance. Moreover, as soon as an African American youngster is viewed as a potential athletic star, many teachers, administrators, and parents lower their academic demands because they assume that athletic stardom will be the athlete's ticket out of the ghetto. In junior high school and high school, little is demanded of them academically. The reduced academic expectations continue in college, or in community college if they do not qualify for college. With professors who "give" grades, occasionally altered transcripts, surrogate test takers, and phantom courses, there is "little wonder that so many black scholarship student-athletes manage to go through four years of college enrollment virtually unscathed by education."[30]

African Americans (athletes or not) on mostly white campuses (only 2 percent of the University of Colorado student body, for example, is African American) are often alienated by the actual or perceived racism they experience and by their social isolation. This compounds the problems for African American athletes.

A major unintended consequence of this situation in which African American athletes find themselves is that their individual adaptations, such as denigrating education, opting for easy courses and majors, not making progress toward a degree, emphasizing the athlete role, and eventually dropping out of education without a degree, reinforce the very racial stereotypes an integrated education is meant to negate. Thus, unwittingly, the universities with big-time programs that recruit marginal students and do not educate them offer "proof" for the argument that African Americans are genetically inferior to whites in intellectual potential.

The NCAA has attempted to remedy some of these problems. Specifically, prospective college athletes would not be permitted to participate in athletics unless they met minimum college standards. Most importantly, once athletes enrolled in a university, they must make progress toward a degree to remain eligible. Moreover, the NCAA will now penalize athletic programs that do not meet the graduation standard of 50 percent by reducing scholarships. Still, there exists a strong possibility that the gap in educational preparation and achievement between African American and white athletes and between athletes and the rest of the student body will continue. This is because athletic departments will likely be creative in finding ways for students to achieve adequate grades (easy majors and the like). Also, the composition of the general student body is becoming whiter and more affluent. The ever higher tuition costs, coupled with the drastic reduction in government loans and scholarships, are restricting access to higher education to the children of the affluent. Generally, the more affluent the student, the better he or she is prepared for academia. Thus, average SAT and ACT scores for the student body will be trending upward, increasing the gap between students and student-athletes, particularly ill-prepared African American athletes.

REFORM

Big-time college sports pose a fundamental dilemma for educators. On the positive side, the games provide entertainment, spectacle, excitement, and festival, along with excellence in athletics. On the negative side, as we have seen, big-time athletics have severely compromised academe.

Pursuit of educational goals has been superseded by the quest for big money. Winning programs realize huge revenues from television, gate receipts, bowl and tournament appearances, and even legislatures; therefore many athletic departments and coaches are guided by a win-at-any-cost philosophy.

Can this fundamental dilemma be resolved? Can the corporate and corrupt sports programs at colleges and universities be changed to redress the wrongs that are making a mockery of their educational goals? Can the abuses be eliminated without sacrificing the high level of achievement by the athletes and the excitement of college sports?

Reform must be directed at three crucial areas: the way sports are administered, the education of athletes, and the treatment of athletes. We suggest the following reforms.

The Administration of College Sports

As a beginning, athletic departments must not be separated from their institutions in self-contained corporate entities. They must be under the direct control of university presidents and boards of regents. Presidents, as chief executive officers, must be accountable for the actions of their athletic departments.[31] They must set up mechanisms to monitor athletic programs to detect illegal and unethical acts. They must determine policies to maximize the educational experiences of student-athletes.

Coaches must be part of the academic community and the tenure system, to provide them with reasonable job security and to emphasize that they, too, are teachers. As educators with special responsibilities, they should earn salaries similar to those of academic administrators. They should not receive bonuses for winning championships. Such performance incentives overemphasize winning and increase the likelihood of cheating. The outside incomes of coaches should be sharply curtailed. Money from shoe companies should go to the universities, not the coaches. If coaches fail to keep their programs ethical, they should lose their tenure and be suspended from coaching at any institution for a specified period, even, in special cases, forever. Among the important criteria for evaluating coaches' performance should be the proportion of athletes who graduate in five years.

Athletic departments must be monitored and, when warranted, sanctioned externally. The NCAA is not, however, the proper external agent, since it has a fundamental conflict of interest. The NCAA is too dependent on sports-generated television money and bowl contracts to be an impartial investigator, judge, and jury. Accrediting associations should oversee all aspects of educational institutions, including sports, to assess whether educational goals are being met. If an institution does not meet those goals because of inadequacies in the sports program, then it should lose accreditation, just as it would if the library were below standard or too few professors held doctorates. Also, because big-time sports are engaged in interstate commerce, the investigation and prosecution of wrongdoing, such as fraud, bribery, and the falsification of official records, in college sports should be pursued by federal district attorneys and the courts.

Emphasizing the Education of Student-Athletes

Academic institutions worthy of the name must make a commitment to their athletes as students. This requires, first, that only athletes who have the potential to compete as students be admitted. A few, very few, may be admitted as exceptions, but they and other academically marginal students must receive the benefits of a concerted effort by the university to improve their skills through remedial classes and tutorials so that they can earn a degree.

Second, freshmen should be ineligible for varsity sports. Such a requirement has symbolic value, because it shows athletes and the whole community that academic performance is the highest priority of the institution. More important, it allows freshman athletes time to adjust to the demanding and competitive academic environment before they also take on the pressure that comes from participating in big-time sports.

Third, colleges must insist that athletes make satisfactory progress toward a degree. There should be internal academic audits to determine whether athletes are meeting the grade point and curriculum requirements for graduation. Schools must now provide the NCAA with graduation rates based on how many athletes graduate in five years. Schools must also be required to make these rates public, including giving them to each potential recruit.

Fourth, the time demands of sports must be reduced. In-season practice time, travel, and team meetings must be kept to a reasonable minimum. Mandatory off-season workouts should be abolished. Spring football practice should be eliminated.

Commitment to Athletes' Rights

The asymmetrical situation, where schools have the power and athletes do not, must be modified. First, athletes should have the right to fair compensation from the revenues they generate. Because they receive room, board, books, and tuition, athletes are not amateurs. Neither are they well-paid professionals. They should be adequately compensated by a modest monthly stipend of, say, five hundred dollars. Also, because scholarship athletes are in effect employees of the institution, they should be eligible for workers' compensation if injured. Most assuredly, they must be fully insured by their institutions for injuries.

Second, the governing body of sports needs to establish a comprehensive athletes' bill of rights to ensure a nonexploitive context. At a minimum, it should include:

- The right to transfer to a different school after their sophomore year and be eligible to play immediately.[32]
- The right to a four-year scholarship, not the one-year renewable scholarship at the option of the coach, as is the current NCAA policy. Those athletes who compete for three years should be given an open-ended scholarship guaranteeing that they will receive aid as long as it takes them to graduate.
- The rights that other college students have, such as freedom of speech, protections from the physical and mental abuse of authorities, privacy rights, and the fair redress of grievances. There should be an impartial committee on each college campus, separate from the athletic department, that monitors the behavior of coaches and the rules imposed by them on athletes to ensure that individual rights are guaranteed.
- The right to consult with agents concerning sports career choices.

- The right to make money from endorsements, speeches, and appearances. Walter Byers, former executive director of the NCAA, under whose leadership many of the rules for these abuses were developed and enforced, has said that "the athlete may access the marketplace just as other students exploit their own talents, whether they are musicians playing at gigs on the weekends, journalism students working piecemeal for newspapers, or announcers for the college radio station filing reports for CNN radio."[33] They should also be able to pursue professionally a sport they are not playing collegiately.[34]

SUMMARY

Without designating them all as such, we have examined and demythologized several myths in this chapter. The first myth is that college athletic programs are amateur athletics. Big-time college sport is big business. The second myth is that the athletic programs in the various schools make money. Relatively few do. The rest depend on various subsidies to keep afloat. A related myth is that these programs help the universities. Almost always the surplus monies are kept within the athletic departments. So, too, are the monies that sports attract from contributors. Also, when athletic departments are put on probation or otherwise punished for transgressions, the universities are hurt by the negative publicity.

Another myth is that the NCAA protects student-athletes. As we have seen, the NCAA rules are extremely one-sided in favor of the institutions over the athletes. Clearly, we have shown that the term *student-athlete* in big-time athletic programs is an oxymoron. Scholarship athletes in the revenue-producing sports are employees of their athletic departments. Their role of student is surely secondary to the role of athlete in most big-time programs. Similarly, athletes are not amateurs. They are just poorly compensated professionals.

Finally, the notion that sport builds character is a myth at the big-time, big-business level of intercollegiate sports. Cheating in recruiting is commonplace. Payments to athletes outside the rules are widely dispensed. Athletes are sometimes pampered. Rules for admittance to schools are bent for them. They are enrolled in courses with professors friendly to the athletic department. Athletes hear the rhetoric about sport building character and that education is first, but they see a different reality. In such a climate, cynicism abounds and the possibility of positive character development is diminished.

WEB RESOURCES

www.Chronicle.com/athletics
The website for the *Chronicle of Higher Education* includes articles on college sport, including the latest data on graduation rates.

www.bus.ucf.edu/sport
This website is for the center for the Institute for Diversity and Ethics in Sport, University of Central Florida. This site provides the annual *Racial and Gender Report Card* with current data on race and gender in sport.

www.ncaa.org
The website of the National Collegiate Athletic Association.

www.ed.gov/pubs/Title IX/indes.html
The U.S. Department of Education's assessment of the progress toward gender equity in the twenty-five years since Title IX was enacted.

www.thedrakegroup.org
The Drake Group seeks to reform intercollegiate athletics. This site provides position papers and data related to college sports.

NOTES

1. George H. Sage, *Power and Ideology in American Sport: A Critical Perspective,* 2nd ed. (Champaign, Ill.: Human Kinetics, 1998), 228–231.

2. The NCAA also has Divisions II and III, schools offering fewer sports and having less emphasis on the commercial aspects of sports than Division I programs. Even less emphasis is found at NAIA schools.

3. For excellent summaries of the problems endemic to contemporary big-time college sports, see Murray Sperber, *Beer and Circus: How Big-Time College Sports Is Crippling Undergraduate Education* (New York: Henry Holt, 2000); Andrew Zimbalist, *Unpaid Professionals: Commercialism and Conflict in Big-Time College Sports* (Princeton: Princeton University Press, 1999); John Sayle Watterson, *College Football: History, Spectacle, Controversy* (Baltimore: Johns Hopkins University Press, 2000); James J. Duderstadt, *Intercollegiate Athletics: A University President's Perspective* (Ann Arbor: University of Michigan Press, 2000); William G. Bowen, Sarah A. Levin, James L. Shulman, and Colin G. Campbill, *Reclaiming the Game: College Sports and Educational Values* (Princeton: Princeton University Press, 2003); and John R. Gerdy, *Air Ball: American Education's Failed Experiment with Elite Athletics* (Jackson: University Press of Mississippi, 2006).

4. William F. Reed, "Absolutely Incredible!" *Sports Illustrated*, 26 March 1990, 66.

5. L. Jon Wertheim, "The Program," *Sports Illustrated*, 5 March 2007, 55–69.

6. Reported in Saranna Thornton, "Financial Inequality in Higher Education: The Annual Report of the Economic Status of the Profession, 2006–07" (American Association of University Professors, March/April 2007).

7. Reported in Bruce Kelly, "Let"s Fund Education, Not College Sports Machine," *Des Moines Register*, 14 March 2007, http://desmoinesregister.com/apps/pbcs.dll/article?AID=20070314/OPINION1/7031403.

8. Mark Alesia, "Colleges Play, Public Pays," *Indianapolis Star*, 30 April 2006, http://www.indystar.com/apps/pbcs.d11/article?AID=/99999999/SPORT06/399990029/.

9. Maurice Mitchell, "Higher Education in Colorado: An Act of Faith amid the Chaos," *Rocky Mountain News*, 27 August 1978, p. 58.

10. Murray Sperber, *College Sports, Inc.* (New York: Henry Holt, 1990), 65.

11. John Underwood, "A Game Plan for America," *Sports Illustrated*, 23 February 1981, 81.

12. Paul W. Bryant and John Underwood, *Bear: The Hard Life and Good Times of Alabama's Coach Bryant* (Boston: Little, Brown, 1974), 325.

13. George Will, "Our Schools for Scandal," *Newsweek*, 15 September 1986, 84.

14. Sage, *Power and Ideology in American Sport*, 179–180. See also D. Stanley Eitzen, "The Sociology of Amateur Sport: An Overview," *International Review for the Sociology of Sport* 24 (1989): 95–105.

15. Mark Alesia, "How Much Would Players Be Worth?" *Indianapolis Star*, 1 April 2006, www.indystar.com/apps.d11/article?AID=/2006041/SPORTS/60401002&theme=.

16. Robert A. McCormick and Amy Christian McCormick, "The Myth of the Student-Athlete: The College Athlete as Employee," *Washington Law Review* 81, no. 1 (2006): 71–157.

17. Mike Trope, *Necessary Roughness* (Chicago: Contemporary Books, 1987), 79.

18. Sage, *Power and Ideology in American Sport*, 246–247.

19. James L. Shulman and William G. Bowen, *The Game of Life* (Princeton, N.J.: Princeton University Press, 2001). This also occurs at elite schools in Division III, widely believed to be free of the ills of big-time college sport. See William G. Bowen and Sarah Levine, *Reclaiming the Game: College Sports and Educational Values* (Princeton: Princeton University Press, 2003).

20. See, for example, Pete Thamel, "Top Grades and No Class Time for Auburn Players," *New York Times*, 14 July 2006, http://www.nytimes.com/2006/07/14/sports/ncaafootball/14auburn.html?ei=5094&en=817.

21. Welch Suggs, "Jock Majors," *Chronicle of Higher Education*, 17 January 2003, A33–A34.

22. For how this has been done at Texas A&M, see Tim Griffin, "Getting a Push in the Right Direction," *San Antonio Express-News*, 14 September 2003, pp. 1C, 7C.

23. Erik Christianson, "Division I Graduation Success Rate Climbs to 77 Percent," *NCAA*, 27 September 2006, http://www2.ncaa.org/portal/mediaandevents/pressroom/2006/september/20060927.

24. Institute for Diversity and Ethics in Sport, "Academic Progress/Graduation Rate Study on Division I NCAA Men's Basketball Tournament Teams" (University of Central Florida, 12 March 2007).

25. Steve Wieberg, "Grad Rates Show Improvement in Most Sports," *USA Today*, 28 September 2006, p. 8C.

26. Quoted in Welch Suggs, "Players' Deaths Prompt Questions about 'Balance' in Athletes' Lives," *Chronicle of Higher Education*, 7 September 2001, A55, A57–A58.

27. Peter Adler and Patricia A. Adler, "From Idealism to Pragmatic Detachment: The Academic Performance of College Athletes," *Sociology of Education* 58 (October 1985): 241–250. See also Patricia A. Adler and

Peter Adler, *Backboards and Blackboards: College Athletes and Role Engulfment* (New York: Columbia University Press, 1991); and Krystal Beamon and Patricia A. Bell, "Academics versus Athletics: An Examination of the Effects of Background and Socialization on African American Male Student Athletes," *Social Science Journal* 43, no. 3 (2006): 393–403.

28. Adler and Adler, "From Idealism to Pragmatic Detachment," 247. The conclusions of the Adlers for men's basketball have not been found for women. See Barbara Bedker Meyer, "From Idealism to Actualization: The Academic Performance of Female College Athletes," *Sociology of Sport Journal* 7 (March 1990): 44–57.

29. Harry Edwards, "The Black 'Dumb Jock': An American Sports Tragedy," *College Review Board,* no. 131 (Spring 1984): 8.

30. Ibid., 9. See also D. Stanley Eitzen, "Racism in College Sports: Prospects for the Year 2020 and Proposals for Change," in *Racism in College Athletics: The African-American Athlete's Experience,* 2nd ed., ed. Dana D. Brooks and Ronald C. Althouse (Morgantown, W.Va.: Fitness Information Technology, 2000), 293–306; and Timothy Davis, "The Myth of the Superspade: The Persistence of Racism in College Athletics," *Fordham Urban Law Journal* 22 (1995): 615–698.

31. Scott S. Cowen, "College Presidents Must Take Charge of College Sports," *Chronicle of Higher Education,* 7 January 2005, B20.

32. Alexander Wolff and Dick Friedman, "The Athlete's Bill of Rights," *Sports Illustrated,* 5 March 2007, 69.

33. Walter Byers, *Unsportsmanlike Conduct: Exploiting College Athletes* (Ann Arbor: University of Michigan Press, 1999), 374.

34. Wolff and Friedman, "The Athlete's Bill of Rights."

CHAPTER 7

Social Problems and North American Sport

Violence, Substance Abuse, Eating Disorders, and Gambling

Indiana Pacers' Ron Artest is restrained by Austin Croshere before being escorted off the court following their fight with the Detroit Pistons and fans on 19 November 2004, Auburn Hills, Michigan. NBA commissioner David Stern suspended Artest for the remainder of the season and disciplined eight other members of the Pacers and Pistons, sending a strong message that the league won't tolerate the type of unprecedented violence displayed by the team members. (AP Photo/Duane Burleson)

Throughout this book we have emphasized the close relationship between sports and the broader North American society. It is not an exaggeration to say that the United States and Canada are plagued by a number of common major social problems—poverty, racism, sexism, health care, environmental destruction, and crime, to name just a few. Given the close connections between sport and society, it should come as no surprise that there are also pervasive social problems in North American sports.

In the past decade, there have been a variety of social problems at every level of the sports world. For example, the summer of 2007 was rocked by a perfect storm of malfeasance in the Big Three of professional team sports—the NBA, NFL, and Major League Baseball (MLB)—and the Tour de France, one of the marquee international sports events in which many North American cyclists participate. NBA referee Tim Donaghy admitted gambling on games he officiated and supplying inside information to gamblers. One of the NFL's marquee quarterbacks, Atlanta Falcon Michael Vick, admitted that he was involved in a multistate dogfighting operation headquartered in a house Vick owned. Dogfighting is illegal in all fifty states, and in connection with the dogfighting, there is always the specter of illegal gambling. Vick was sentenced to twenty-three months in prison, and faced additional jail time from State of Virginia dogfighting charges. Accompanying Barry Bonds's quest to break the major league all-time record for home runs—which he did on 14 August 2007—was the subject of an ongoing federal investigation into his alleged use of steroids. Internationally, once again the Tour de France was laced with positive drug tests and doping charges, and the leader of the race in the final week was dismissed by his team for not complying with drug-testing rules prior to the race.[1]

On almost everyone's list of social problems, violence, substance abuse, eating disorders, and gambling have a prominent place. Literally hundreds of violent sports incidents occur each year. Many of these involve groups of athletes, as in bench-clearing brawls; many other incidents are between spectators and athletes or just among spectators. A 2004 NBA game between the Detroit Pistons and Indiana Pacers, in which players went into the stands to fight fans throwing objects at them, was perhaps the most shocking example of sports violence in recent years. Substance abuse and eating disorders are also prevalent in sports. Steroids have been a staple among male athletes for decades, but researchers have recently found that steroid use has increased at an alarming rate among females. When the widespread use of Sudafed, a medication with pseudophedrine, was revealed, it was referred to as the "NHL's dirty little secret" because of the on-ice "boost" it gave the players. Eating disorders are common among females in so-called lean build sports and among male athletes in sports that use weight classifications, such as wrestling, weight lifting, and boxing. Deaths of both male and female athletes have been linked to eating disorders.

Gambling has been one of the most popular forms of excitement and entertainment in human history. It is common in all cultures, all social strata, most periods of the life cycle, and in both men and women. One by-product of gambling is addiction, and the behavior of addicted gamblers often becomes a social problem. Gambling on sports events has many ominous social ramifications. Gamblers can become addicted, they can attempt to influence the outcome of sporting events, gambling athletes might accept money from gamblers to fix an event, athletes themselves might bet on games in which they play, and so forth.

These are the sports social problems that will be examined in this chapter. They all are pervasive in North American sports, and they all have troubling consequences for the participants, fans, and others associated with sports.

VIOLENCE IN SPORT: IS IT VIOLENCE OR AGGRESSION? CONFUSION IN THE LITERATURE

It is necessary to begin with a brief excursion into the meaning of two key concepts that will be used in the first part of this chapter. The words *violence* and *aggression* are often found together, and some writers use them as synonyms. On the other hand, some behavioral and social scientists differentiate sharply between these two words. Still others believe that the concepts have come to have so many meanings that they do not have any meaning at all anymore.

In spite of the variety of definitions and meanings assigned to the two concepts, we believe that a definition of aggression and violence in sport proposed by sport psychologist John Kerr is worth using as an operational framework for the purposes of this chapter. Kerr states:

> Aggression can be seen as unprovoked hostility or attacks on another person which are not sanctioned by society. However, in the sports context, the aggression is provoked in the sense that two opposing [athletes] or teams have willingly agreed to compete against each other. Aggression [and violence] in . . . [some] sports is intrinsic and sanctioned, provided the [behavior] remains permissible within the boundaries of certain rules, which act as a kind of contract in the pursuit of aggression (and violence) between consenting [athletes].[2]

We would add this qualifying statement: Illegal, unacceptable, and unsanctioned aggression and violence is any action in violation of the written and unwritten rules or norms of a sport.

In this chapter we shall use these two words in the way we just described, but when referring to other theorists' and researchers' works, it will be necessary to employ their terminology.

THEORIES ABOUT THE CONNECTION BETWEEN VIOLENT BEHAVIOR AND SPORT

Two theories of human aggression dominated the scientific literature during the first three-quarters of the twentieth century: instinct theory and frustration-aggression theory. The first postulated that aggressive behavior is based in human instincts; indeed, this notion was so popular it has been called the folk theory of aggression. The instinct theory of aggression owed its popularity to two major proponents: Sigmund Freud, the founder of psychoanalysis, and Konrad Lorenz, a world-renowned ethologist. Both claimed that aggression is instinctive in humans and that humans can do very little to change or control this aggressive impulse. See Box 7.1 *Thinking about Sport*, for additional descriptions of these theories.

Basing his theory of aggression on his studies of various animal species, Lorenz concurred with the outlines of Freud's notion that humans possess an aggressive impulse that requires periodic release and that by venting aggressive energy we become less aggressive, an effect known as "catharsis." Aggressive releases of energy can take benign forms or destructive forms, and Lorenz believed that sports can help channel aggressive behavior into benign forms. This model of aggression has been roundly attacked by both social and biological scientists.

A second theory of aggression that generated much interest and research is called frustration-

---

Box 7.1 *Thinking about Sport* **Theories about Aggression/Violence**

INSTINCT AGGRESSION THEORY

Aggressive behavior is based in human instincts; humans cannot change or control this aggressive impulse. Aggressive impulse requires periodic release; sports can help channel aggressive behavior into benign forms.

FRUSTRATION-AGGRESSION THEORY

When an individual is frustrated, he or she will aggress in order to purge the pent-up frustration; the aggression then produces a catharsis, a reduction to further aggression.

AGGRESSION SOCIALLY LEARNED THEORY

Emphasis is on the learning of aggression via vicarious or observational learning and reinforcement through the interaction-socialization process; focus on learning, thinking, and interacting with peers, family, community, social institutions, and cultural practices in shaping aggressive behavior.

aggression theory (F-A). This theory proposed a specific process by which the underlying instinct to aggression is triggered: When an individual is frustrated by someone or something, he or she will aggress in order to purge the pent-up frustration. In other words, the existence of frustration leads to some form of aggression, although not necessarily an overt act of violence, which then produces a catharsis, a reduction in the instigation to further aggression.

When examined by the methods of empirical research, the F-A hypothesis, like the Freud-Lorenz theory, has not stood up. Most studies show that aggression does not always occur when a person has been frustrated and that there is no cathartic effect after aggression is employed. One of the most telling arguments against the F-A hypothesis is research that has persuasively shown that not all aggressive behavior stems from prior frustrations and that the linkage between frustration and aggression is not as close as the theory claimed.[3]

The most recent theorizing about aggressive behavior has come from scholars who postulate that aggression is a learned social behavior (e.g., social learning theory, social cognitive theory, and social interaction theory). These theories emphasize the learning of aggression via vicarious or observational learning and reinforcement and through the interaction-socialization process. A major assumption of these models is that individuals who observe esteemed others (parents, teachers, peers, coaches) exhibiting aggressive behavior and being rewarded for it will experience a vicarious reinforcement that has the same effect as personally receiving the positive reinforcement. Moreover, individuals who exhibit aggressive behavior and receive approval for it will tend to employ aggressive behavior in future situations that are similar.

In both cases, the prediction is that continued rewards for aggressive acts will eventually form a tendency to respond to various situations with aggressive actions. In sum, according to these socially grounded theories, the conditions most conducive to the learning of aggression seem to be those in which the individual is rewarded for his or her own aggression, has many opportunities to observe aggression, or is the object of aggression. Individuals who mature under such conditions learn to assume that violent behavior is natural and, thus, an appropriate interpersonal response in many situations. These individuals will continue to rehearse violent actions in both actual situations and in fantasy. They will dismiss alternative actions as inappropriate or inadequate. They will also come across situations in which such responses are readily elicited because of the similarity of cues to former situations in which a violent response was learned.

The converse is also true. That is, if an individual receives, or observes esteemed others receiving, some form of negative sanction or punishment, that aggressive behavior will be inhibited. Thus, negative reinforcement will eventually form a habit or tendency to respond to various situations nonaggressively.

It may be seen, then, that social learning, social cognition, and social interactionist theories depart drastically from the older models for explaining aggression. Whereas the instinct and F-A models ground aggression in biological explanations, the socially grounded theories focus on learning, thinking, and interacting with peers, family, community, social institutions, and cultural practices in the environment as shaping aggressive behavior.[4]

Socially based theories and cultural explanations have much more research support than the other aggression models, and we will describe some of that research in the next section. This is not to say, however, that the issue of the roots of aggression has been settled once and for all. Scientists of several disciplines continue to probe for answers to the mysteries surrounding the pervasiveness of human aggression.

AGGRESSION THEORIES AND RESEARCH ON SPORTS

Advocates of the instinct and F-A theories have often claimed that participation in and observation of aggressive activities have a cathartic effect by allowing one to discharge pent-up aggressive energy, and sporting activities have often been suggested as a means of dispelling aggression in a socially healthy way. William James, considered by many as America's first psychologist, suggested that sport is the moral equivalent of war. One disciple of Freud called sports "a salutary purgation of combative instincts," and he claimed that if those instincts are dammed up within, they will break out in disastrous ways. Konrad Lorenz said: "The most important function of sport lies in furnishing a healthy safety valve for that most indispensable and, at the same time, most dangerous form of aggression that I have described as collective militant enthusiasm."[5] He even suggested that if nation-states would devote more energy to sporting activities, the chances for war between countries would be reduced.

The basic problem with the notion that sports provide an outlet for the aggressive instinct is that it doesn't have a sound empirical basis. James, Freud, Lorenz, and anyone else can make claims about the connections among instinct, aggression, and sport, but in order for the claims to be credible they need scientific confirmation. No empirical findings, from James, Freud, Lorenz, or any others, have provided compelling research evidence in support of their claims.

Applying the F-A theory to sport, it has been suggested that sports provide a setting for expressing aggression, thus producing a catharsis—a reduction in aggressive inclinations. On the other hand, it has been noted that frustrations that often accompany sporting contests can trigger aggressive and violent behaviors. In what has become a classic test of the prediction of instinct and F-A theories about sport having cathartic effects, researchers assessed the hostility of male spectators before and after a football game and a gymnastics meet. They found that, contrary to the predictions of these theories, hostility actually increased significantly after observing the football game (a violent event), regardless of the preferred outcome of the game. However, there was no increase in hostility from spectators after observing the gymnastics meet (a nonviolent event). In a follow-up to that study, the researchers studied men and women who were exposed to a professional wrestling match, an ice hockey game, or a swimming event. General support was found for the previous finding of increased spectator hostility as a result of observing violence. Hostility among subjects increased at wrestling and hockey events, but such increases did not occur at the swimming competition.[6] One researcher found that homicide rates in the United States increased immediately after televised broadcasts of highly publicized boxing matches; another found that domestic violence by men against women increases dramatically during the Super Bowl. These findings are exactly the opposite of what should happen according to the cathartic effect of aggression. Overwhelmingly, the findings suggest that, contrary to the predictions of instinct and F-A theories, aggression tends to produce more aggressive predispositions and actions rather than serve as a catharsis.

Several studies seem to support the view of socially oriented scientists that learned cultural behavior patterns explain aggressive behavior rather than aggressive behavior being the result of an innate drive in humans. A unique and interesting study by an anthropologist focused on the relationship between war and sport forms in different types of cultures. He assessed the correlation between types of societies, warlike and nonwar-like, and the existence of combative sports. Using cross-cultural data on ten warlike and ten nonwar-like cultures, the researcher found that warlike societies and combative sports were positively correlated—90 percent of warlike societies had combative sports, but only 20 percent of nonwar-like societies had combative sports.

This same anthropologist did a time-series case study of the United States to see if the popularity of combative sports (e.g., boxing, hockey, and football) rose or fell during times of war. He found that during wartime, combative sports indeed rose in popularity and noncombative sports declined. Both investigations lead to the conclusion that war and combative sports are found together in societies. Combative sports are not channels for the discharge of aggressive tensions but rather seem to promote aggression.[7]

Directly and indirectly, sports research studies have found no support for the instinct and F-A theories of aggression. At the same time, support for the socially oriented theories has accumulated from a variety of sources.

VIOLENCE IN NORTH AMERICA

Given the state of theories of aggression and the research findings about these theories, we take a socially oriented perspective as the most viable. Therefore, an assumption underlying the following sections is that violent behavior in sport must be understood within a historical, social, and cultural framework. Understanding how the ways and means by which violence has come to play such a salient role in sports requires historically situating and culturally locating it within the larger culture in which sports are embedded.

Violence in Historical Context

In this section we emphasize the prominent role violence has played in North American history, but we want to acknowledge that we do not know nor understand why violence has been an integral part of much of human history. Our focus in this section is limited to North America because North America is the focal point of this book.

Canada and the United States were literally born through violence. Early colonists in North America encountered a native population that the colonists systematically imprisoned, killed, or placed in reserved lands. Thus, mostly through violent means, European settlers acquired almost all of the land in the North American continent.

Both nations began in a climate of warfare. In the case of the American colonists, the Declaration of Independence literally furnished the rationale for the legitimate use of violence by the colonists. In Canada, settlers from France and England, principally, contended over the vast northern expanse of landmass for more than two hundred years, fighting many bloody battles until the Peace of Paris in 1763 finally ceded Canada to Great Britain.

Over the past two centuries, oppressed groups in North America have been subject to the violence of their oppressors and have used violence to struggle against their oppressors. Many Africans brought to North America throughout the colonial period and up to the U.S. Civil War were the subjects of daily violence by the slave owners. Violence against African Americans continues, as examples of police brutality recorded by citizens with camcorders have vividly shown. At the same time, African Americans have resorted to violence in every era of North American history to redress their grievances; as one African American civil rights activist said in justifying the use of violence: "Violence is as American as apple pie."

Actually, every ethnic minority group in North America has encountered hostility and violence and has also resorted to violent means to protect themselves or to gain a measure of revenge. Asians, Chicanos, Hispanics, Irish—you name it—every newly immigrated ethnic and racial group has been subject to violence in some form.

Throughout the nineteenth century, capitalism brought wage labor, horrible working conditions, and autocratic, sometimes brutal, bosses. By the latter nineteenth century, workers had begun to organize into unions for collective action against the policies and practices of the industrialists. Such organizations were often met with force, which then turned to violence by both capitalists and workers. During the past hundred years, strikes and labor disputes have been more prevalent and violent in the United States than in almost any other country of the world.[8]

The expansion of the U.S. territories, which began in the early nineteenth century, has been mostly accomplished through violent military actions. Native Americans had most of their land taken away by violent means. Mexicans were driven out of what is now the southwest United States. Cuba and the Philippines were invaded and subjected to U.S. control. Within the past three decades the U.S. military invaded three countries—Grenada, Panama, and Iraq—without having been attacked. In summarizing the history of violence in American society, sociologists D. Stanley Eitzen and Maxine Baca Zinn say:

Violence was necessary to give birth to the United States. Violence was used both to keep the blacks in servitude and to free them. Violence was used to defeat rebellious Indians and to keep them on reservations. Additionally, violence has been a necessary means for many groups in American society to achieve equality or something approaching parity in power and in the rights that all Americans are supposed to enjoy.[9]

This heritage of violence is learned in informal and formal ways by each new generation of young people, and it becomes embedded in their understandings about the culture of which they are a part.

Violence in Contemporary Society

Violence in North America seems like an unpleasant fact, perhaps even an inevitable feature of modern society. All anyone has to do is read today's newspaper or watch today's television news to get the latest stories of gruesome violence. The phrase "If it bleeds, it leads" captures television news directors' preference for opening newscasts with the most violent stories they can find. For the past century the United States has had the highest homicide rate of all of the "developed" countries—from four to twenty times the rates in other industrial nations. Although the Canadian homicide rate is less than one-half the U.S. rate, it ranks fairly high among English-speaking developed countries. Although the annual number of homicides in the United States has declined over the past decade, in 2005 there were still more than sixteen thousand per year.[10]

Other serious crimes of violence are prevalent as well, even though these have declined in the past decade. The United States has three to six times more rapes and robberies than other industrialized countries. Americans living in cities report an alarmingly high rate of fear of being involved in a violent confrontation; that is, robbed, burglarized, or raped.

Many popular films, TV programs, and video games are violent: for example, the movies *300*, *Kill Bill*, and *Saw*. No other nation comes close to the United States with respect to TV violence; children's daytime programs average 24.1 violent acts per hour, and evening prime-time programs average 7.5. The TV series *The Sopranos* and *CSI* are prime examples; a content analysis of the widely popular video games found that 89 percent of them contain content based on violent actions—*Halo* and *Grand Theft Auto*, for example—and the video player controls the weapons of murder and destruction. The bullets, missiles, and other lethal objects produce spectacular explosions and bloody images as they hit their targets. The overall ambiance is one of extreme, violent imagery. People do not have to leave their living rooms to witness massive doses of violence.

Several media studies over the past decade estimated that by the time the typical American reaches the age of eighteen, she or he has witnessed 200,000 dramatized acts of violence and 40,000 dramatized murders—not counting video games. A number of noted scholars from a variety of fields of study have reported a connection between movie-TV-video viewing and pro-violence attitudes and aggression in childhood and later aggressive behavior in adulthood for both males and females.[11] More than any other Western nation, the culture of the United States promotes and glorifies violence, and people in other countries are baffled by the salience of violent behavior and imagery in our culture. Added to a heritage of violence, then, is a contemporary culture of violence that many people throughout the world find astounding.

To return to the basic theme of this chapter—the connections between sport and North American society—sporting practices would be an anomaly if violent behaviors did not play a prominent role.

VIOLENCE IN NORTH AMERICAN SPORT

Violent actions have been a part of sporting practices for as long as we have records of organized sports. Any doubt about that can be quickly dispelled by a perusal of the book *Combat Sports in the Ancient World: Competition, Violence, and Culture*,

A tester works on a *Halo* game at the company's headquarters in Kirkland, Washington, 2007. A content analysis of widely popular video games such as *Halo* found that 89 percent of them contain content based on violent actions. (AP Photo/Elaine Thompson)

which is a compendium of sports with varying degrees of violence that were popular in ancient societies. In the ancient Olympic Games, the Greeks had boxing and pancration as a regular part of the program of events. In the former, there were no rounds and no weight classifications. The boxers continued to pummel each other until one boxer was hurt so badly that he could not continue or he acknowledged defeat. The pancration was a brutal all-out combination of wrestling and what we would call street fighting. The rules permitted almost anything, including kicking, choking, hitting, and twisting of limbs. Gouging of eyes and biting were illegal. The object was to maim the opponent so badly he could not continue or to force him to admit defeat, as in boxing.[12] Physical tests of strength, endurance, and skill were popular in the Roman civilization and the Middle Ages, and many, such as gladiator spectacles, chariot races, jousts, and tournaments, were quite violent; indeed, deaths were common in these events. The irrepressible bare-knuckle boxing and the precursors to team sports, such as soccer and football, were popular in England and Europe during the eighteenth and nineteenth centuries; all were extremely violent.[13]

Violent Behavior by Athletes as Part of the Game

Just bring along the ambulance
And call the Red Cross nurse,
Then ring the undertaker up,
And make him bring a hearse;
Have all the surgeons ready there,
For they'll have work today,
Oh, can't you see the football teams
Are lining up to play.
—A popular jingle in the 1890s

Violent actions in sports have always had a special meaning separate from violence in the wider social context. Violent behavior in the larger society, except for a few situations, such as war, typically carries with it negative sanctions in the form of norms or laws; violent behavior is punished. On the other hand, violent actions are actually encoded into the rules of some sports, and there are sport-specific techniques, tactics, and strategies that are quite violent but considered perfectly appropriate in playing the sport. In a book titled *Making Violence Part of the Game*, the author describes the nature of violence in professional sports:

> Sport as an economic institution, is sometimes separated from social reality by the courts who view its violence as a "special case." As a commercial enterprise, its reliance on "controlled rage," "reckless abandon," and its description by some courts as involving "no duty of care between participants," and as having left the "restraints of civilization on the sidelines," leads one to conclude that sport, in its Corporate form, is the most violent and dangerous of all.[14]

One major justification for the legitimate use of violence in sport is that participants play knowing the rules and therefore understanding that they will be subject to violent actions against them. Just the opposite is typically true in the larger society: People expect they will not be subject to violence and that there are laws that protect them from violent actions. Of course, as we have previously described, this has not always been the case. If, as some analysts have suggested, violence is as American as apple pie, violence in North American sport is as natural as the knockout punch or the "bell-ringing" tackle. Sports and violence are almost inseparable. One example can suffice to illustrate this point. In a recent *Sports Illustrated* article titled "The Big Hit," the writer states:

> Everything in [NFL] football begins with the big hit and flows from there, like blood pumping from a beating heart, feeding limbs and organs. . . . And big hits are big business. They not only fuel the core audience but also spawn cottage industries such as ESPN's Monday-night "Jacked Up" segment highlighting the weekends' five biggest legal, non-injury hits, and EA Sports's fabulously popular *Madden NFL* video games, in which crushing hits are enabled by movements on the controllers.[15]

Philadelphia Eagles player Sheldon Brown claims "people want to see violence, and every collision in the NFL is violent."[16] The nature of some sports, the skills required to achieve victory, the strategy and tactics, and the rules literally demand violent actions. Boxing is perhaps the most obvious example. The entire object of a boxing match is for the two contestants to try to injure the other so severely that one cannot continue. A knockout, in which one's opponent is rendered unconscious (or at least semiconscious), is what every fighter strives for. In the sixty-year period between the end of World War II and 2005, over 550 boxers died from injuries sustained in the ring, mostly from cerebral blood clots. Ultimate Fighting Championship (UFC)—which combines the striking techniques of boxing and kickboxing with the ground techniques of jujitsu and wrestling—has recently become the most popular hand-to-hand combat sport. In 2007, UFC broke the pay-per-view industry's records for a single year, surpassing World Wrestling Entertainment (WWE) and boxing.

Other "body contact" sports include football, ice hockey, and lacrosse (some would include basketball). Tackling, body checking, collisions, and legal "hits" of various kinds are inherent to the action of these sports. Indeed, it is taken for granted that when athletes engage in these activities they automatically accept the inevitability of contact, the probability of some bodily injury, and even the prospect of serious injury.

Still, few people understand the relationship between the violence of a sport and the frequency of injuries, and how serious some of them are. But they are the markers of the violence in a sport. Injuries are so common in the National Football League that during the season, newspapers publish a weekly "casualty" list of each team in the league. In some seasons, up to five hundred NFL players, or 21 percent of the total players, are hurt seriously enough to miss at least one game a year because of injury. In a survey of 870 former NFL players, 65 percent reported they had suffered a "major injury," one that forced them to miss at least eight games. Seventy-eight percent reported some kind of physical disability from their pro football injuries. One retired player has had 30 knee surgeries, dating back to his college days. Another retired player suffered at least 15 concussions while playing in the NFL. One Denver Broncos guard had 28 surgeries and was still an active player. After 13 surgeries on the ankle of another former NFL player, the physicians cut off the leg eight inches below the knee.[17]

College and high school football violence takes its toll too. According to the National Athletic Trainers' Association, about 37 percent of U.S. high school football players are injured badly enough each year to be sidelined for at least the remainder of the day. About eight high school football players die each year from football-related injuries.

Casualty rates in the Canadian Football League are comparable. But in Canada it is ice hockey where playing with pain and injuries has always been an essential part of the sport culture. As one NHL general manager noted, "There is a clear understanding that hockey is a physical and sometimes violent game. You are going to be injured." Playing with injuries is one of the major ways to get respect from teammates and opponents. Case in point: One NHL defenseman, when asked why he returned only one period after breaking his nose, replied, "I don't skate with my nose."[18]

A number of sports, such as baseball, basketball, soccer, National Association for Stock Car Auto Racing (NASCAR), water polo, and so forth do not have the inherent violence found in others, but the tactics increasingly employed and the way the rules are being interpreted are increasingly encouraging strategy and tactics resulting in violent actions.

Borderline Violence

What in the sports culture is called "borderline violence" is a category of violent actions that are prohibited by the official rules of a given sport but routinely occur and are more or less accepted by everyone; they have become the unofficial norms. Included here are the late hit in football, hockey fistfighting, the knockdown pitch in baseball, the high tackle in soccer, and the deliberate foul in basketball. All such actions occasionally produce serious injuries; they also occasionally trigger bench-clearing brawls among the athletes. Although penalties are often meted out for these actions, the punishments are typically not severe enough to deter their future occurrence. Often the intent behind much of this type of violence in sport is to "get the edge" over an opponent through "intimidation." The fistfight in ice hockey, the "brushback" pitch and the "break-up-the-double-play slide" in baseball, "clotheslining" and hitting wide receivers even when they are not directly involved in the play in football—all are done with the intent of breaking athletes' attention and concentration on the tasks they are trying to perform. Indeed, in NHL hockey and NBA basketball it has been a common practice of teams to carry an "enforcer" or "intimidator" on the roster. One general manager of an NHL team acknowledged that every team likes to have one or two enforcers or designated hit men so that the rest of the team feels comfortable.[19]

Although the objects of these tactics may not be physically harmed, there are cases in most sports where these "enforcer" tactics have extended beyond borderline violence and resulted in career-ending injuries: While Rudy Tomjanovich, who later coached the Houston Rockets to two consecutive NBA championships, was an NBA player, he was slugged in the face by another player, ending his playing career in basketball. In March 2004, NHL's Vancouver Canuck Todd Bertuzzi punched Colorado Avalanche's Steve Moore from behind and drove his face into the ice, causing three fractured neck vertebrae. Moore was wheeled off the ice on a gurney. In 2007, three years after the incident, Moore had not been cleared to play again by physicians.

These are, of course, some of the most well-known examples of violent actions that have led to major injuries. There are literally hundreds of other incidents where the quasi-criminal violence shortened the victim's sports career or rendered him permanently impaired for the remainder of his career. Whenever current and former pro athletes get together to talk about their playing experiences, they recount stories about the "dirty play" or the "cheap shot" that had long-term consequences for the victim.

Although comparative figures are hard to come by, there is a widely held perception that all of the types of sports violence previously described are increasing in North America. Articles deploring this trend regularly detail the latest incidents of sports violence, with pleas to everyone, from the athletes to the highest officials in government, to end the growing menace to the good health of athletes, officials, and fans.

FOSTERING AND SUPPORTING PLAYER VIOLENCE

Television

Some of the most respected researchers of television's coverage of violent play believe the mass media highlight and foster violence in sports in a number of ways. Focusing on rough play, replaying spectacular "hits" over and over, and sportscasters praising violent play are three prominent ways violent actions are promoted. Broadcast sports tend to be unrestrained odes to violent action; almost any violent behavior—the more spectacular, the better—is highlighted and given justifications. In one NFL play-off game, an instant replay showed an offensive lineman clearly and deliberately delivering a viciously illegal elbow into the face of an opponent, virtually twisting off the victim's head. This graphic illegal violence was followed by a comment from one of the sportscasters: "Nobody said this was going to be a tea party!" A similar situation in a televised college football game drew this comment from one of the sportscasters: "Anything that is not called is legal." Camera crews and sportscasters are ever vigilant to the violent collision, the late hit, the shove in the back that can be replayed over and over via instant replay to the horrified fascination of viewers.[20]

As if it weren't enough that people see violent sport actions in person and on television and hear sportscasters praise sport violence, television also helps sponsor programs whose fundamental ethos is to present gratuitous violence. The highly popular WWE events are, as one commentator put it, "celebrations of violence"—the more outrageous the better—even if not strictly real. But it is a newcomer, mixed martial arts (MMA), the most popular variation of which is UFC, that has captured the golden eighteen-to-thirty-four male demographic, and its weekly show, *The Ultimate Fighter*, on Spike TV has surpassed the TV ratings of the NBA and Major League Baseball play-offs. A match ends when one combatant cannot physically continue or gives up. UFC events attract more pay-per-view than any pro wrestling or boxing event. (More about UFC can be found in chapter 11).[21]

During the NFL season a weekly ESPN segment titled "Jacked Up" highlights the previous weekend's five most violent legal, noninjury hits. The large voyeuristic audience for shocking, even horrifying, violence is obviously ESPN's target audience for "Jacked Up."

Sports video games, TV staples for teenage and young adult males, graphically emphasize violent actions. *Madden NFL*, the most popular of these video games, selling six million units in 2007, allows gamers to make contact between players appear ultraviolent via a controller.

Fans

Organized sports are commercial endeavors, and those who produce the sporting events (professional franchise owners, university athletic departments, etc.) are dependent on fan support. Surveys of fans indicate that spectator enjoyment of games is related to the amount of violence in them. In a summary and review of research findings about viewers' enjoyment of televised sports events, communications researchers, said: "The extant evidence clearly indicates that increased player aggressiveness enhances spectators', especially male spectators', enjoyment of watching sports contests. Related evidence from studies of sports casting reveals that commentary-stressing roughness of actions can facilitate viewers' perceptions of the violence of the event, which, in turn, can lead to greater enjoyment of the sports contest. And, finally, play-by-play and color commentary that stress hostility and animosity between opponents can cause spectators to perceive play as more violent than it is and also can result in greater enjoyment for spectators."[22] Recent research corroborates this summary, thus providing support for previous findings about the relationships between viewing violent sports and fan enjoyment and mood.

Given the preferences that fans seem to have for violent action, and given that commercial sports must depend on the fans to stay in business, it should not be surprising that the sports industry is quite willing to make sure that violent play is a salient feature of the games. Professional sports executives, coaches, and players frequently exclaim: "We depend on the fans for our existence."

Pressures on Athletes to Be Violent

Pressures exist in sports to use violence, legal and illegal, in the quest for a victory. At all levels of play, coaches teach players the use of intimidating and violent tactics, and peer pressure inspires players to use violence. At all levels incentives exist for athletes to be violent. Athletes are unanimous in saying that the best way to gain coaches' recognition and praise is through aggressive play and, in "hitting" sports, to become known for violent hits.

The folklore of the sports world is that aggressive play yields positive results. Youth, high school, and college athletes often either secure a place on the team or are cut from the team, depending on the amount of aggressiveness they display. College athletic scholarships are often awarded by coaches based on the aggressive tendencies shown by recruits. Various financial incentives promote aggressive actions by professional athletes.

Coaches, Owners, Commissioners

Beginning with their first organized sports experience, athletes learn that they must please their coaches if they expect to remain a member of the team. Pleasing the coach often means doing "whatever it takes" to win. Many coaches firmly believe that the most aggressive team wins games; therefore, athletes quickly learn that being aggressive gains the coach's approval. A former NFL player said the message that coaches repeat over and over is that if you're going to make a mistake, make an aggressive one.

Welcoming violent play also applies to dealing with injuries. As one NFL lineman asserted: "If it's not bleeding and it's not completely broken, rub dirt on it and let's go." Concussions are an epidemic in the NFL, but one NFL running back had this to say about the prospect of incurring a concussion when getting hit: "I think about it, dude, I really do. But if you asked me [about running the ball], I'd do it 100 times again. I love football to death."[23]

Professional team owners refuse to condemn violence because they are convinced it attracts spectators. Among owners and general managers of professional sports franchises there is a tacit agreement that it's hard to justify making changes in the rules to reduce violence because the bottom line is that there are many fans who like it. The chairman of the International Bar Association's Sports Law Committee acknowledges that there is no economic incentive to curb violence on the playing field.

Athletes who refuse to participate in violent actions often find themselves demoted on the team roster or even dropped from the team. In professional ice hockey the expectation that players will participate in fights is so strong that in several instances when a player refused to enter a violent melee, he was sent to the minor leagues or traded.

Violence against Athletes

Violent attacks on movie stars, television personalities, musicians, and politicians have occurred with some regularity for many decades, but, except for a few very rare incidents of a fan assaulting an athlete, or athletes receiving death threats, athletes have been exempt from the kinds of attacks that other celebrities have encountered. Some exceptions are:

- Major League Baseball's Hank Aaron and Barry Bonds received death threats as they approached breaking Babe Ruth's home run record.
- Monica Seles, at that time the number-one-ranked women's tennis player in the world, was stabbed in the back during a match.
- Figure skater Nancy Kerrigan was attacked and savagely hit on the knee by a bludgeon-wielding assailant.

Given the omnipresence, adulation, and celebrity status of elite athletes, it was probably inevitable that some would become targets of fans. At the 2000 Phoenix Open Golf Tournament, a spectator who had been drinking heavily began to verbally threaten Tiger Woods. The security officers who apprehended him discovered that he was carrying a pistol. Pro tennis player Martina Hingis told a Miami court in 2001 that she had to hire bodyguards to protect herself from a man who persisted in stalking her. The stalker received a two-year jail sentence.

These attacks, threats, and stalking incidents have horrified the sports world. A different social climate now exists for athletes. Many have expressed a feeling of fear that didn't exist before these incidents. Some high-profile professional athletes now employ bodyguards to protect themselves from potential violence. A different atmosphere prevails in sporting venues, where tighter security measures have been put in place.

SOCIAL PROBLEMS AND ATHLETES OFF THE FIELD OF PLAY

Most athletes' lives are lived off the field of play. Even on days in which they practice or play sports, these activities will typically take less than 20 percent of their waking hours. Beyond their role as athletes, athletes do most of the same things that other young people do. They have friends they hang out with, they party, they drink, they develop sexual relationships, they marry and have families, and so forth. At one time, what athletes did on their "own" time was little known by the public, nor was it reported by the media. Moreover, if athletes got into trouble of any kind, coaches, owners, administrators, and the media covered it up; "taking care of the athlete" was the explanation given for this action (others have called it a "conspiracy of silence"). In effect, athletes' misbehavior, even unlawful actions, was protected from public scrutiny and the criminal justice system.

At the same time that athletes of previous eras were being protected if they ran afoul of the law, they were portrayed as honest, sober, upstanding pillars of the community and role models to be emulated. However, the accumulating literature makes quite clear that in reality many of them engaged in behavior ranging from fun-loving mischief to violent criminal behavior when they were not engaged in playing their sport.

A book by a former New York Yankees pitcher entitled *Ball Four* was the first to break down the invisible barrier between the idealized image of athletes and their real personal worlds. The author described in detail what went on in the clubhouse and what the players did in their free time. What he divulged was athletes getting drunk and going on rampages, players doing drugs just before games, married players having sexual liaisons with female "groupies" that hung around the players, and players going on voyeuristic expeditions.[24] A flood of similar books followed.

The private lives and escapades of college and professional athletes in many sports have been spelled out in detail in various mass media. In many cases, it has not been a pretty story because violent criminal behavior, especially sexual assaults and spousal abuse by the athletes, has been a rather persistent theme. These examples illustrate this point:

- During a 16-month period between 2004 and 2005, University of Tennessee football players were involved in some twenty incidents involving shoplifting, aggravated assault, gun charges, motor vehicle citations, disturbing the peace, and failing a drug test. During the same time period other Southeastern Conference (SEC) schools had their share of problems off the field: Eleven University of

South Carolina players were arrested; at the University of Georgia three players were suspended for off-field incidents and a fourth was kicked off the team.[25]
- Between spring 2005 and spring 2006, over fifty arrests were made of NFL players, including multiple arrests for several players.[26]
- Based on an investigation into the criminal histories of 177 NBA players from the 2001–2002 season, lawyer and journalist Jeff Benedict found that an alarming four out of every ten NBA players had a police record involving a serious crime, such as armed robbery, domestic violence, gun possession, and rape.[27]
- NFL player Rae Carruth was found guilty of conspiracy to commit murder, shooting into an occupied vehicle and using an instrument to destroy an unborn child. He was sentenced to eighteen to twenty-four years in prison.

There are quite different views about whether athletes as a group, especially athletes in contact sports, commit a greater share of domestic violence and sexual assaults than nonathletes. On one side, largely represented by the sports industry, is the view that the private lives of today's athletes are being scrutinized more closely by the media, and the private-life behaviors of athletes that prevailed for a long time are just now being reported. In this view, big-time college athletes and pro athletes have become celebrities, and, as with other celebrities, there is fierce competition among the media to satisfy the public's appetite for scandal. Finally, it is alleged that many of the reports of athletes' violence against women are inaccurate, charges are dropped, or athletes are not convicted of the charges.

On the other side, there is an acknowledgment that high-profile athletes in the past received special coddling by the media, and their transgressions were ignored or just not reported. Nevertheless, according to this view, athletes, especially in contact sports, are indeed overrepresented in domestic violence and sexual assaults. Empirical evidence is often cited that suggests this view, and behavioral and social theories are sometimes employed to illustrate that the norms and values of the sport culture socialize athletes into attitudes that valorize male power and control over females. One result is male athletes' propensity toward committing violence against women.[28] Obviously, athletes are not the only assailants and abusers of women. We focus on athletes because this book is about sports. According to the National Sexual Assault Online Hotline, there is an annual average of 200,780 victims of rape, attempted rape, or sexual assault; one in six American women is a victim of sexual assault. A U.S. Justice Department study titled *The Sexual Victimization of College Women* found that over the course of a four-year college career, about 12 percent of college women are raped or face attempted rape. There is little doubt that male sexual assault against women and spousal abuse are major national social problems and are not unique to the sport world.[29]

Sources for Violence by Male Athletes in Their Private Lives

What accounts for this rather alarming trail of violence by male athletes in their private lives? There is, of course, the fact that they live in a violent culture and that their lives are much more under the media's scrutiny than the average person's. These factors have been previously discussed, but are there other factors? We believe there are at least three other factors that might contribute to this subculture of violence: male bonding rituals, preconditioning to aggressive behavior, and steroid use by many athletes.

Sport Culture and Male Bonding

As part of gender development, both males and females learn culturally prescribed attitudes, rituals, symbols, and behaviors for their sex. Much of this learning, and exhibiting the effects of the learning, take place in sex-segregated activities. Sports teams provide fertile ground especially for male bonding, fostering a spirit of exclusivity, camaraderie, and solidarity among males. Given traditional masculine prescriptions of toughness, dominance, repression of empathy, and competitiveness, athletes may display the effects of this socialization by engaging in reckless and violent behavior as proof of their masculinity. One aspect of this socialization is the attitude that men have a right to dominate women. Sport studies researchers have found that the language of locker room male bonding is a language of power and control over women, of violence against women, and of taking women.

Preconditioning Males for Violence

A number of behavioral and social scientists contend that male socialization tends to be a preconditioning to aggressive behavior as an appropriate response for achieving one's goal, whether it is defending oneself in the streets, making a tackle, or satisfying one's sexual desires against a woman's wishes. Society's concept of masculinity is inextricably woven into aggressive, forceful, physical behavior. Physicality and masculinity have meant the same things for men—male dominance: force, coercion, and the ability to subdue and control the natural world, one central part of which is women.

The epitome of socially appropriate physical dominance, use of force, and violent action occurs in various sports. Pulitzer Prize–winning journalist H. G. Bissinger spent a year in a Texas community studying its high school football team. His book, *Friday Night Lights: A Town, a Team, and a Dream,* described what the players did and what they talked about, much of which was about "hitting" or "sticking" or "popping" someone. These were the things that coaches exhorted players to do. The supreme compliment was to be called a "hitter" or "headhunter." A hitter made bone-crushing tackles that knocked out or hurt his opponents. One reviewer of the book said that Bissinger chose to write about something rather small—the culture of high school football in a Texas town—but he ended up writing about something large, the core values in our society.[30] Sociologist Derek A. Kreager studied whether participation in contact sports by teenagers also promoted violence off the field and found that involvement in contact sports such as football and wrestling did indeed increase the likelihood of off-field violent behavior.[31] This suggests that a culture of violence can be nurtured on the sporting field. Behavior learned in one context, where it is appropriate, can be transferred to another, where it is not.

Steroid Use and Male Violent Behavior

There is a myriad of evidence that anabolic steroid use is widespread in many sports at the high school, collegiate, and professional levels, especially in sports involving physical contact and feats of strength. There is also convincing anecdotal as well as some empirical evidence showing that the regular use of anabolic steroids can trigger episodes of aggressive behavior in users. Researchers who have studied the effects of steroid abuse agree that athletes who are steroid users seem more inclined to extremely violent behavior than nonusers.[32] The issue of steroid use in sports is taken up again in the section "Substance Abuse and Sport" in this chapter.

Concluding Thoughts on Violence by Male Athletes in Their Private Lives

Undoubtedly, these and other factors can interact in any given situation or incident that ultimately leads to violent, even criminal, behavior by athletes. We want to emphasize, though, that we recognize that the actual percentage of athletes at any level and in any sport who are involved in violence off the field is very small. Nevertheless, there are enough incidents, and they are serious enough, for all of us to be concerned. Concerted efforts need to be made by everyone involved in sport to find ways and means to reduce, even eliminate, sexual assaultive and domestic violence by athletes that have become all too familiar.

One effort to do something about this problem has been initiated by a woman who was raped by a football player while she was a college student. She has formed the National Coalition Against Violent Athletes (NCAVA). The purpose of the NCAVA is to educate the public on various issues involving athletes and violence, while also providing support to the victims.[33] See Box 7.2,

> **Box 7.2   Thinking about Sport National Coalition Against Violent Athletes**
>
> One of the valuable roles that the Internet is increasingly playing is providing a means by which fledgling organizations can quickly communicate with large numbers of people about a social problem, educate them about that social problem, bring those who wish to do something about the problem into contact with each other, and even mobilize people into action to resolve the problem. Those are the purposes behind the founding of the National Coalition Against Violent Athletes. Contents of the home page of the NCAVA are duplicated below.
>
> > The National Coalition Against Violent Athletes was formed in 1997 in response to the growing number of violent crimes committed by athletes in all areas of the sports world. This organization is based solely on the fact that athletes should be held to the same standards and laws as the rest of society.
>
> **GAME PLAN**
>
> The purpose of the National Coalition Against Violent Athletes is to educate the public on a variety of issues regarding athletes and violent behavior, while also providing support to the victims, including, but not limited to, advocacy, referrals and research. We also strive to promote positive athlete development through education, support and accountability. In doing so, we work to curb the escalation of athlete violence and create an environment in which people are equally respected and equally held accountable. We therefore assail the entitlement given to athletes through a system in which athletes have little fear of reprisal. In doing so, we can help restore the sports world to a former level of respectability while helping its victims restore their sense of value and self-worth.
>
> *Source:* National Coalition Against Violent Athletes, http://www.ncava.org.

Thinking about Sport, for more information about the NCAVA.

Athletes' Violence against Teammates: Hazing

Rites of passage are a common feature of many cultures. They are rituals and ceremonies through which a group of people must pass in the transition from one group to another within the culture. Perhaps the most common rites of passage are those that young boys and girls must pass through to become recognized as full-fledged adult men and women of that society. The rites-of-passage principle has also been adopted by many organizations—military, business, social, sport—and specific rituals and ceremonies are established to initiate new members into these organizations. Rites of passage, in the form of initiation ceremonies and rituals, became a popular part of belonging to a team from the beginning of modern organized sports. But also from the beginning many teams employed a variation called "hazing." Hazing involves humiliating, degrading, or endangering the initiate, and hazing is illegal in more than forty U.S. states. Nevertheless, hazing has been a widespread practice, especially in high school and college sports, for more than a hundred years, and many initiates have been seriously harmed physically and/or psychologically.

Institutional officials periodically attempt to put an end to hazing, but those efforts have been largely unsuccessful. In a survey in three western Canadian cities of amateur and professional teams competing in eight contact sports and three non-contact sports, two sport sociologists found that hazing occurred routinely but in varying degrees across the sports. They concluded that despite increasing social disapproval and closer policing, hazing continues to play a significant role in both men's and women's sports teams.[34]

The most comprehensive study of hazing ever done in the United States was the National Survey of Initiation Rites and Athletics conducted at Alfred University for the NCAA. More than 325,000 athletes at more than a thousand NCAA schools participated. Following are some of the key findings:

- Two-thirds of the athletes surveyed had been subjected to humiliating hazing, such as being yelled or sworn at, forced to wear embarrassing clothing, or forced to deprive themselves of sleep, food, or personal hygiene.

- Three-fourths experienced some form of hazing to join a college athletic team.
- One-fifth were subjected to dangerous and potentially illegal hazing. They were kidnapped, beaten or tied up, and abandoned. They were forced to destroy property, harass others, and make prank phone calls.
- One-half were required to participate in drinking contests or alcohol-related hazing.
- Women were more likely to be involved in alcohol-related hazing than in other forms of hazing.
- Football players were most at risk for dangerous and potentially illegal hazing.

After reading the report, the president of Alfred University said, "I find the results of our study on hazing to be horrifying. It's pervasive. It's dangerous, and it is behavior that is forced upon student athletes as the price of admission to a team."[35]

In the past few years dozens of high schools and colleges have had hazing incidents in which school officials placed teams on probation, required that team members perform community service, or suspended team members from school. To give the reader some understanding of the kinds of hazing incidents that have occurred, excerpts of several of these follow:

- 2003, Mepham High School, Bellmore, New York: Veteran football players penetrated three junior varsity players with a broomstick, pinecones, and golf balls during several attacks. Two of the veteran players were sentenced to serve time in detention centers; two others received probation. Two coaches lost their jobs and were reassigned without teaching duties.
- 2006 (ongoing investigation in 2007), Molalla High School, Molalla, Oregon: Alleged sexual hazing and one count of alleged sodomy. At least five teenage basketball players (oldest age eighteen) and possibly more faced charges that they sexually hazed a younger player.
- 2007, University of California (UC), Berkeley: Eight Cal baseball players were cited by UC police for participating in hazing six freshman players. According to a police report, UC Police Department officers found the eight veteran baseball players with six freshman players who were wearing only G-string underwear and shoes just after 11 P.M. The six freshmen were standing outside in the thirty-four-degree weather. Hazing activities had just begun.
- 2007: The University of Maine softball team was placed on probation for three years and will delay the start of the 2008 season by one week for violating school policies that prohibit hazing.[36]

Similar incidents have occurred in virtually every corner of North America, where initiates have been showered with mixtures of urine and vomit, brutally paddled, or sodomized.

Because hazing has historically been prominent at the high school and college levels, in recent years governing bodies throughout North America have been furiously busy developing no-hazing policies. The NCAA recently mandated that each of its member institutions develop a life-skills program for athletes that includes guidelines on hazing. Individuals and organizations that develop no-hazing policies face several barriers to eliminating hazing: denial of the problem, arguments that hazing is harmless, silence among victims, fear among victims, and cultural norms that perceive hazing as normal.

SPORTS FANS: VIOLENT AND ABUSIVE ACTIONS

Spectators at a sporting event are not usually passive observers. Typically, they like to "get into it," to become part of the game, as it were. But sometimes their enthusiasm turns into violent and abusive actions. And this is not merely a contemporary phenomenon, nor is it confined to North American sports.

The word *fan* is short for *fanatic* and comes from the Latin word *fanum*. The Romans used the word to describe persons who were overly zealous while attending the chariot races. In one renowned spectator riot at the chariot races in ancient Rome, some thirty thousand fans were killed. In 1969 in a World Cup soccer series between El Salvador and Honduras, spectator violence accompanied each of the games. Finally, the riot that followed the third game resulted in the two countries severing political and economic relations and mobilizing their armies against each other; this has been called the "soccer war" between El Salvador and Honduras.

Everyone who follows North American sports is quite aware of the many incidents of spectator violence. Several years ago *Sports Illustrated* took what it called an "unscientific poll of fans" and reported that everyone who reported having ever been to a sporting event had witnessed one or more acts of violent behavior by fans. Within the past decade, major fan violence has erupted in all of the professional team sports (NFL, NHL, NBA, and MLB). It has also penetrated into high school and university campuses, where football and basketball games have been marred by riots. Indeed, due to frequent spectator riots at high school sports events, several large city school systems have imposed strict limits on the number of spectators admitted to high school basketball games in an effort to prevent fights between fans and opposing teams. Several universities have stopped scheduling games against traditional rivals because of fan violence that has accompanied the contests.[37]

Newspaper and magazine articles describing, and usually condemning, a seemingly escalating amount of fan violence are common. "Sports in USA Sick: Violence Out of Hand," "Fans Behaving Badly," and "Uncivil Disobedience" are examples of article titles found in the popular press. The theme of all of these is a contention that an excessively violent equilibrium exists in sports today at almost all levels.

Factors Associated with Fan Violence and Abusive Behaviors

Behavioral and social scientists seeking to understand and explain spectator violence and abusive actions tend to center their explanations on fans' social learning and experiences in the wider society. In support of this, there is widespread agreement—and a burgeoning list of recent books to support it—that there is an increasing lack of civility in North American society. This is manifested in growing violence and incivility in all of the major social institutions, including family, schools, business, politics, and media. Hardly a week passes without some major incidence of violence or interpersonal abuse in these social arenas. Moreover, all of the major sports themselves have become more violent, not only in the games but in the alarming lack of sportsmanship on the field and the widespread trash-talking among the athletes. Given the cultural background pervading fans' general social experiences, it is hardly a coincidence that fan violence and obnoxious actions are escalating.[38]

Actions during sporting events may play a contributing role to fans' violent and abusive behavior. Most behavioral scientists reject cathartic explanations. Instead, they contend that violence in sport contributes to violence in the crowd, as opposed to the notion that viewing violent acts results in reduced feelings of violence. A fundamental principle of social learning is that people learn what they observe, and if what they observe goes unpunished, they are likely to consider it appropriate for themselves. The sequence of witnessing violence-learning-acting might proceed in this manner: Fans watching a violent sporting event are likely to become more aggressively inclined themselves; as they witness violent behavior, they might, under just the right circumstances, act violently themselves. Of course, as we emphasized earlier in this chapter, learning the heritage and culture of violence is the lived experience of everyone in North America, so sports fans have more than their immediate experiences in the stadium or arena mediating a mindset for violence.

There are other factors as well that can precipitate spectator violence and abusive behavior that go beyond just broad enculturation and witnessing these behaviors in sports. Two forms of "perceived injustice" can trigger fan anger and abuse. The first form occurs when fans believe that officials have applied a rule unfairly or inaccurately; the second occurs when fans believe that a rule itself is unfair, regardless of how accurately employed.

Bad calls by officials, such as calling a batted baseball foul when it was fair or calling a made basket from three-point range two points are examples of the first. An example of the second might occur when a penalty kick is awarded near the end of a tie game in soccer; since it is such a high-percentage kick, it will almost always result in a victory for the kicking team. The penalty kick in soccer is uniformly condemned as unfair by soccer fans, so a situation as just described may precipitate fan violence.

One social scientist has suggested five social situational factors that can be conducive to spectator violence. They are (1) a large crowd, because of a perceived power inherent in a mass of people, and the anonymity ferments irresponsible behavior; (2) a dense crowd, because annoyance and frustration build when one's comfortable space is violated and when one is forced to be near strangers; (3) a noisy crowd, because noise is itself arousing, and arousal is a common precondition to violence; (4) a standing crowd, because standing for long periods is tiring, jostling is common, and the lack of an assigned space is frustrating; and (5) crowd composition, because drinking crowds, young male crowds, and crowds made up of people who are oppressed in the larger society are more predisposed toward violent behavior than more diverse crowds.

Game and Postgame Sports Violence

In recent years there have been several violent incidents involving athletes and fans during or immediately after a sports event. What has been called the worst brawl in NBA history took place in the Palace in Auburn Hills, Michigan, in 2004 during a game between the Detroit Pistons and Indiana Pacers. In response to objects thrown at Pacers players on the basketball court, several Pacers players went into the stands and punched several fans. During a MLB game between the Texas Rangers and Oakland Athletics, a Rangers player threw a folding chair toward fans in response to heckling by the fans. Player-fan incidents are not new to sports, but the frequency of these types of violent incidents has been on the upswing for years.[39]

There is a lengthy tradition of sports fans celebrating the winning of a championship, tournament, or contest against a bitter rival. Violence often accompanies these celebrations in stadiums and arenas, as fans storm the playing area. In football, fans tear down the goalposts; in basketball, they clip the basket nets; in hockey, they throw objects onto the ice; and so forth. Frequently these celebrations became violent because security officials attempt to thwart such actions and fans of the losing teams resent the celebrations and taunt and start fights with the celebrants. Sometimes celebratory stampedes move to city streets after an important victory. Revelers set bonfires, destroy property, turn over automobiles, and attack police and security personnel. Conversely, crucial losses by a home team have triggered similar violent street actions.

A unique form of fan celebration that has become widespread in recent years is called court or field storming. Fans pour out of the stands in celebration of an exciting victory, applauding the players, backslapping them, and sometimes lifting them into the air. With the popularity of these "stormings," injuries to fans and players have occurred. One of the most shocking and disturbing took place several years ago after a high school basketball game in Tucson, Arizona. A player dunked the ball at the end of a big home win, igniting a frenzied fan celebration. The player was grabbed, tackled, and trampled. He suffered a stroke and paralysis on his right side and has never fully recovered his physical and mental health. Dozens of court/field storming incidents like this one have resulted in injuries to players and fans.[40]

Up to this point in time, North American sport studies scholars have done little research on these forms of sports violence. Most British and

European research on sports crowd violence has centered on soccer riots and "hooliganism." Several have explained this behavior in terms of the working-class roots of soccer fans, their team loyalties, and their resentment of and alienation from the larger society. Informal analyses of postgame crowd violence at North American sports events suggest that there is little commonality between the European and British soccer fans and North American college and professional sports fans.

Abusive Behavior by Fans

The traditional, but typically good-natured, heckling of players, coaches, officials, and opponents has taken on a completely new attribute in the past decade. Fans—especially at professional and collegiate sports events—are increasingly resorting to abusive and obscene language. In addition to vocal communication, placards and wearing apparel emblazoned with obscenities are displayed. Student sections at some universities compete to be the most outrageous, vicious, obscene, and offensive, and they believe they have a constitutional right (First Amendment, free speech) to engage in such behavior.[41]

Reducing Fan Violence and Abusive Behavior

Numerous suggestions for reducing spectator violence have been proposed by researchers of violence. Common suggestions include improving the physical facilities and appearances of stadiums and arenas, making them more attractive and less foreboding places; increasing the numbers of security forces at sporting events; limiting the sale of alcohol (already done in some stadiums and arenas); changing the rules of some sports, such as soccer, to make scoring easier; keeping violence under control on the field by preventing fights, excessive displays of anger or aggression by athletes, and arm-waving displays of disapproval of officials' calls by coaches and athletes; and severely punishing offenders.

Sports administrators at all levels have been considering various options to stop court/field stormings. Professional sports and university attorneys have been asked to seek legal opinions over whether they can eject fans from games for abusive actions. University presidents, coaches, and athletic directors have been trying moral suasion, asking for civil behavior among student fans. Several university conferences have considered disbanding student sections.

All of these strategies might indeed reduce fan violence abuse to some extent. However, none of them deals with the larger, structural issue of the heritage and culture of violence and incivility that underlie much of the culture of contemporary North American society beyond the confines of sports but nevertheless affects both athletes and fans alike.[42]

SUBSTANCE ABUSE AND SPORT

Substance abuse is considered such a significant social problem that the U.S. government has pursued a "War on Drugs" for more than twenty years. But according to experts who study the importation and use of drugs, drug abuse is still widespread. The federal government estimates that 90 million Americans have used illegal drugs, and 3.6 million are dependent on an illegal drug.

Newspaper and magazine headlines tell of substance abuse in sports: "Steroids Are Just a Click Away," "Drug-Free Sports Might Be Thing of the Past," "Tour de France's Downhill Slide: Doping Scandals Sully World's Biggest Bike Race." The stories that follow these headlines poignantly tell of North America's athletes' involvement with substance abuse. As for the first headline, *USA Today* sportswriter Sal Ruibal describes how law enforcement officials are using a new tactic in the war on drugs used in sports. The article under the second headline suggests that the indifference of fans to doping by athletes makes it doubtful that sports will ever be drug-free. Moreover, elite athletes use a myriad of performance-enhancing drugs, and the laboratories and agencies that test for and regulate athletes' use of these substances find it almost impossible to detect and control all the drugs used by athletes, in spite of the advanced technologies they are able to employ. The narrative for the last headline argues that the doping scandals and organizational dysfunction of the world's biggest bike race, the Tour de France, have turned off once-rabid U.S. cycling fans.[43]

The Scope of Substance Abuse in Sport

As anyone who has followed sports in the past few years knows, any short list of drug-use issues will represent only a speck of dust in the universe of substance abuse in the sports world. Indeed, some knowledgeable authorities believe that substance use by athletes is epidemic in scope, all the way from high school to the professional level (we include Olympic athletes as professionals). Anabolic steroids have been a popular drug of choice for athletes for several decades. (See Box 7.3, *Thinking about Sport*, for a description of steroids.) For several years the U.S. Department of Health and Human Services has been surveying secondary school students who admit to using steroids. Typically some forty thousand students in more than four hundred schools are surveyed. Table 7.1 shows the trend for steroid use over the eight-year period from 1998 to 2006. These students might not all be athletes; indeed, if only athletes were surveyed, the percentages would likely be much higher.[44] However, an accurate assessment of steroid use by secondary school athletes is very difficult. Converting the percentages to numbers of steroid users, eminent steroid expert Charles Yesalis estimates that well over one million young people in the United States have used steroids at one time or another.

Studies of steroids use in intercollegiate athletics vary widely in their results. One study reported that 9.7 percent of college football players acknowledged using the drug. At the other extreme, in July 2006 the NCAA released a five-year report that indicated positive drug tests for steroids have dramatically decreased. According to the NCAA, "in year-round testing, 49 student-athletes tested positive for steroids in 2004–2005 as compared to 90 student-athletes testing positive for steroids in 1998–1999 and 92 positive tests in 1999–2000." A total of 10,094 student-athletes were tested in the 2004–2005 year-round testing program.[45]

From theses figures, the NCAA claimed that steroid use had declined dramatically, thus

---

Box 7.3 *Thinking about Sport* **Steroids: What Are They? Effects? Dangers?**

WHAT THEY ARE

Anabolic-androgenic steroids are synthetic forms of testosterone, which is a male hormone that is naturally present in the human body. They are taken either orally or by injection into the muscle.

THEIR EFFECTS

They increase lean body mass, increase strength, increase muscle definition, decrease recovery time from exercise, increase aggressiveness.

THEIR DANGERS

They cause testicular shrinkage, reduce testosterone production, cause benign and malignant liver tumors, cause bizarre and violent personality changes, cause feminized characteristics of males and masculinized characteristics of females.

Table 7.1 Tracking the Trend of Steroid Use among Secondary School Students (in percent)

Grade Level	1998	2000	2006
Eighth-Graders			
Male	1.6	2.2	1.2
Female	0.7	1.2	0.6
Tenth-Graders			
Male	1.9	3.6	1.9
Female	0.6	0.8	0.5
Twelfth-Graders			
Male	2.8	2.5	2.7
Female	0.3	1.1	0.7

Source: Monitoring the Future: National Results on Adolescent Drug Use: Overview of Key Findings, NIH Publication no. 07-6202 (Bethesda, Md.: National Institute on Drug Abuse, 2006).

displaying a complete naiveté about the sophisticated methods athletes use to avoid testing positive. Physicians who have experience with steroid users say that users have found numerous ways to beat the drug-testing systems; drug testing isn't the threat to drug-using athletes that sport organizations often portray it to be.

The situation is similar with professional and Olympic-level athletes. Use is greatest in athletes for whom power, strength, speed, and bulk are important. NFL athletes, coaches, and trainers have claimed that up to 75 percent of NFL players use or have used steroids. It has become clear in the past few years that steroid use is still present in Major League Baseball too, in spite of a stepped-up testing program now employed. It has been estimated that three to eight players per major league team are using or have used steroids. In spite of the increase in testing athletes for steroid use by sport organizations at every level of sport, Yesalis and Bahrke assert: "The level of steroid use appears to have increased significantly over the past three decades . . . and it is no longer limited to elite athletes or men."[46]

According to the website "Doping-Free Sport: Canadian Anti-Doping Program," the Canadian Anti-Doping Program (CADP) came into force in 2004 and integrates several new national and international developments, described below.

- The World Anti-Doping Code (WADC) and mandatory International Standard requirements were formally accepted by the Canadian Centre for Ethics in Sport (CCES) in March 2003. The code is expected to result in better antidoping programs for the athletes against whom Canadians compete internationally.
- The Canadian Policy Against Doping in Sport (CPADS) was approved by federal, provincial, and territorial governments in April 2004. The CPADS is committed to safeguarding the integrity and values of sport by deterring the use of banned substances and by methods to protect those who commit themselves to sport based on the principles of fair play.
- The Physical Activity and Sport Act was passed in March 2003. It sets out the federal government's new approach to physical activity and sport and establishes the Sport Dispute Resolution Centre of Canada.
- The Canadian Strategy for Ethical Conduct in Sport was approved by federal, provincial, and territorial sport ministers in April 2002. It calls for a comprehensive domestic anti-doping policy that emphasizes prevention and education and establishes clear roles and responsibilities for all stakeholders, especially governments.[47]

Substance Abuse Not New to Sports

The use of substances to enhance performance has been present throughout the history of organized sports. The ancient Greek athletes consumed mushrooms in the belief that they improved performance, and Roman gladiators used a variety of stimulants to hype them up and forestall fatigue. Athletes throughout the nineteenth century experimented with caffeine, alcohol, nitroglycerine, opium, and strychnine. Strychnine, cocaine, alcohol, and caffeine mixtures were used by boxers, cyclists, and British and European soccer players before World War II. Amphetamines and steroids began their rise to the drugs of choice among athletes in the years immediately after World War II.

The variety of substances athletes use in hope of improving their performance has become astounding: Growth-retardant hormones are used by female gymnasts to prolong their careers; archers and shooters use beta-blockers to slow the heart rate for steadier aiming; swimmers use nasal decongestants to enhance airflow through their lungs; weight lifters use amphetamines to release vast amounts of adrenalin into the blood and speed up the systems used for strength activities; endurance athletes use recombinant erythropoietin (EPO) to stimulate the production of red blood cells that transport oxygen throughout the body, thereby improving endurance; wrestlers and boxers use diuretics for weight loss to compete at lower weight classes; and drug-using athletes in many sports use diuretics to minimize detection of other drugs by diluting the urine.[48] Table 7.2 lists the performance-enhancing drugs most commonly used by athletes.

One of the newest trends in sport substance abuse is the use of nutritional supplements; creatine has become the most popular. It is touted by nutritional supplement manufacturers, and hyped by many athletes, as a muscle-building aid for increasing muscle size and strength. It is not banned by most sport governing bodies, nor is it an illegal drug. Creatine use became widespread among high school, college, and professional athletes in the last few years of the 1990s, and its popularity has continued into the early twenty-first century.

Between 8 and 12 percent of high school male athletes have said they were using creatine. As many as 60 percent of collegiate male and female athletes report having used nutritional supplements, creatine being one of them. At the same time, up to 50 percent of professional athletes in some sports have used creatine. But the use of creatine seems to have peaked in recent years, primarily because it has become associated with more dangerous performance-enhancing substances, such as anabolic steroids. Supporting this alleged association, professional athletes, such as major league home-run king Barry Bonds, have admitted to using creatine. Bonds is suspected of also using steroids.

Creatine is not the only nutritional supplement athletes are using. Sales of nutritional supplements reached more than $25 billion in North America in 2007. Other nutritional supplements that are popular in the athlete culture include cold medications, diet pills, energy pills, and sports drinks, most of which contain ephedra, or synthetic forms of ephedrine. Ephedrine stimulates the central nervous system and thus is an amphetamine-like stimulant.

In addition to the use of performance-enhancing substances, athletes, like the general population, are deeply involved in what are called "recreational" drugs. The main culprit has historically been alcohol—serious enough, to be sure, but not as deadly or debilitating a substance as cocaine, crack, heroin, or speed. Furthermore, the amount of cocaine, crack, heroin, and speed usage is minuscule compared to the use of alcohol.

Alcoholic beverages have been one of the most widely used substances by young people for a long time. In a 2006 national study of adolescent drug use, 17 percent of high school sophomores and 45 percent of seniors admitted drinking alcohol in the thirty-day period prior to the survey. A survey of almost eight hundred high school coaches asked them what they considered the greatest threat to athletes on their teams. The responses: alcohol 88 percent, cocaine/crack 6 percent, marijuana 3 percent, steroids 1 percent.[49]

College students have a well-earned reputation for frequent consumption of alcohol, and

Table 7.2   Performance-Enhancing Substances Most Commonly Used by Athletes

Substance	Expected Benefit	Users	Side Effects
Steroids	Promotes muscle growth	Speed, power, endurance athletes	Masculinization of females, feminization of males, liver and heart damage, mood changes
Testosterone	Promotes muscle growth	Speed, power, endurance athletes	Same as steroids
Human growth hormone	Promotes muscle growth	Speed, power athletes	Gigantism, joint and jaw enlargement
Erythropoietin (EPO)	Produces red blood cells	Endurance athletes	Thickened blood leading to stroke or heart problems
Androstenedione (Andro)	Promotes muscle growth	Speed, power, endurance athletes	Similar to steroids
Creatine	Energizes muscle function	Quick, power, speed athletes	Dehydration, muscle cramping, intestinal problems

several research findings indicate that male college athletes consume more alcohol and more of them binge drink than male nonathletes. Female athletes consume more alcoholic drinks than female nonathletes.[50] Although the actual incidence of alcohol consumption by professional athletes has not been studied, so many pro athletes have been arrested for drunkenness that it hardly raises eyebrows anymore when reports appear on television or in newspapers. Several high-profile pro athletes have been involved in fatal accidents in which alcohol played a role.

Although the use of cocaine, crack, heroin, and speed by athletes may be small compared to that of alcohol, this does not mean it is insignificant. In one study of intercollegiate athletes, 17 percent acknowledged using cocaine in the prior year; two years later, in a study of elite women athletes, 7 percent reported using cocaine, about half of these saying they used it before or during competition. Players representing nearly all the professional sport leagues have been involved with cocaine use in criminal cases, with some teams having several players arrested.

Reasons for Substance Abuse among Athletes

Why do athletes risk their health and their opportunity to compete by using drugs? There is, of course, no single answer to this question because athletes have different reasons. Athletes are a part of a much larger social community, and substance abuse is rampant in this larger social community. As one sport studies scholar noted, drug use among athletes "needs to be seen in the context of an increasingly pill-dependent society. It is unrealistic to expect athletes to insulate themselves from a culture which expects pharmacists and doctors to be able to supply medicines for all their ills whether physical or psychological."[51] Indeed, some experts on drug abuse refer to the United States as a "Drug Nation," and that portrayal seems accurate. If the world's countries are divided into those with high-, medium-, and low-level drug problems, the United States is the only developed country that falls into the "high-level" category.

Athletes are not immune to the societal influences under which they live. In their world, athletes see drug use all around them: aspirin, tranquilizers, amphetamines, diet pills. They see the almost universal acceptance of alcohol and tobacco. The first, considered by most health professionals to be the most abused drug in North America, is responsible for over half the traffic fatalities annually and for the estimated eighteen million alcoholics in North America. The second, tobacco, is the leading cause of lung cancer and is considered addictive by the U.S. surgeon general. Cigarettes carry a label: "Smoking is dangerous to your health."

Young athletes are especially susceptible to what they see and hear from high-profile athletes. They often hear TV sportscasters report that a given athlete was given pain suppressants, such as morphine, so that he could play in the game that day. During a Monday Night NFL football game, one of the sportscasters commented approvingly about a quarterback, "Here's a guy who probably had to take a painkiller shot in his lower back so he could play tonight." Many young athletes have seen athletic trainers' rooms, rooms that are filled with all kinds of salves, ointments, and pills, all used to help athletes perform at their best. Is it any wonder that young athletes believe that drugs are widely used in sports? The sports culture itself promotes drug usage in sports.

Another factor that motivates young athletes to turn to chemicals for performance enhancement is that there is enormous social status that goes with being an athlete; as we noted in chapter 5, being an athlete is admired by both males and females. Most people do not understand how or the extent to which the system of sport and its status-conferring and rewarding properties often lead athletes to a commitment in which they are willing to risk anything, even their life, to achieve their goal. A hypothetical scenario was posed to 198 U.S. Olympians and aspiring Olympians who were sprinters, swimmers, power lifters, and other assorted athletes:

Suppose you are offered a performance enhancing substance with two guarantees, if you choose to use it: You will win every competition you enter until you win an Olympic Gold Medal. But the substance will cause your death within a year after your achievements. Would you take it? More than 50 percent of the responding athletes said yes![52]

There are other temptations. The best high school athletes are recruited to colleges with "full ride" scholarships—a college education with all expenses paid. Although there are very few who ultimately become professional athletes or Olympic champions, there are millions of young athletes who devote themselves to years of training and personal sacrifice in attempting to attain this lofty goal. At every level the competition is keen, and athletes know that they must continue to improve if they are to move to the next rung of the ladder. Many literally devote their lives to the quest to move onward and upward, and they will try anything that will aid them in their quest. Thus, athletes striving to improve often believe that any substance that could give them even the slightest advantage over their opponents is worth trying. Rather than depending upon legitimate training methods and developing a sound psychological approach to their sport, some athletes choose to rely upon drugs to improve their performance.

It is very difficult for young athletes to do their best when they know they might be competing against athletes who are using substances that may be performance enhancing. Dr. Robert Voy, former director of drug testing for the U.S. Olympic Committee, claims: "Most of the athletes didn't want to do drugs. But they would come to me and say, 'unless you stop the drug abuse in sport, I *have* to do drugs. I'm not going to spend the next two years training . . . to be an Olympian and then be cheated out of a medal by some guy from Europe or Asia who is on drugs.'"[53]

Another factor in substance abuse among athletes is that at the high school, college, and professional levels, coaches pressure athletes to improve their performance and play when injured. Some coaches put demands on athletes to increase their strength and endurance, reduce or increase their weight, and play while injured, knowing such conditions can only be met through the use of substances that are banned. These coaches want world records and bigger-than-life athletes with tremendous physical capacities that yield medals and championships. To meet these demands, some athletes resort to drugs to enhance their performance or to play when hurt.[54]

Finally, there is the ambiguity (perhaps hypocrisy) in all of the links athletes see every day between sports and substance abuse. They see the cozy financial connection between alcohol and tobacco and big-time sports. Beer and tobacco companies are the number one sponsors and underwriters of sporting events. Beer ads dominate concession stands and scoreboards at sports venues; beer commercials dominate TV and radio advertising during sports events. It is virtually impossible to watch or listen to a sporting event in North America without feeling overwhelmed by beer ads. The St. Louis Cardinals baseball team is owned by Anheuser-Busch, which is the largest beer maker in North America, and this beer company is one of the top five media advertisers during sporting events in North America. The Colorado Rockies baseball team plays in Coors (beer) Field.

As we noted above, alcohol is "without question the most abused drug in sport," and a number of college sport officials acknowledge that alcohol is a much more pervasive problem for collegiate athletes than other substances. Still, professional leagues, Canadian and American Olympic sports organizations, and the NCAA happily accept advertising money generated by alcohol companies.[55]

Is it any wonder that athletes are confused about substance abuse? When the rules and customs governing drug use in both the larger society and the sports world itself seem arbitrary and inconsistent, it is easy to understand why athletes may view drug use as acceptable and normative behavior, in spite of the distortions they bring to the ethics of sport competition and their potentially devastating consequences to health and well-being.

Reducing and Preventing Substance Abuse in Sports

Although the evidence, incomplete as it is, strongly suggests that only a minority of athletes at any level, in terms of percentages, have a substance abuse problem, there is still the question of what is to be done with the small number who are substance abusers. There are several options, but the one that has received the most attention is the drug-testing programs of the various sports' governing bodies. But these programs have had limited success and many failures at this point. To a large extent this is because they have been implemented without fully resolving at least two important questions: (1) What are the athletes' individual rights? (2) What are the athletes' responsibilities?

With respect to athletes' rights, the Fourth Amendment to the U.S. Constitution forbids any unreasonable searches and seizures, any intrusions on human dignity and privacy, simply on the hunch that incriminating evidence might be found; this protects all U.S. citizens, including athletes. The U.S. Supreme Court has ruled that extracting bodily fluids—such as urine tests—constitutes a search within the meaning of this amendment. The U.S. Constitution, however, protects persons only from intrusion by government, and furthermore, because there can be different interpretations of "reasonableness," this has become a complicated issue involving a balancing of the invasion of personal rights and the need for the search. Determination of reasonableness requires that the court balance an individual's privacy rights against the government's legitimate interests in deterring drug use. The U.S. Supreme Court has twice made exceptions to students' privacy rights to enable schools to make random drug tests of athletes and other students who participate in extracurricular activities. Still, mandatory, random drug testing is not a fully settled issue in the U.S. court system.[56]

Although some of the major sport organizations, such as the International Olympic Committee, the NCAA, and the National Football League, have taken the lead in mandatory and random drug testing, considering it necessary and appropriate, there are many critics as well. Two Canadian health scientists argue that "the invasion of privacy caused by effective anti-doping measures cannot be justified solely by the good those measures seek to attain. . . . For drug-free sport we need effective enforcement. But the steps required for effective enforcement can be invasive of athletes' rights, particularly the personal right to privacy." They propose an alternative, a way that shares ownership of the rules of sport, and the methods for enforcing those rules, with those most affected by them: the athletes.[57]

Several unresolved issues exist where drug testing has been implemented. The validity and accuracy of the tests have been a continuing controversy, and rightly so, because the test results are not infallible. Drug-testing programs in professional sports have been frequently found to be misleading to the public and unfair to the players. Several sport organizations that now routinely test their athletes do not even have an appellate process in place; thus, an athlete who tests positive does not have a process for appealing the results of the tests.

Some authorities on drugs in sports argue that there are sports-specific reasons why teams or other sports organizations may wish to test athletes, such as preventing drug users from gaining an advantage over opponents or protecting them from drugs that might be debilitating. They claim that general reasons, including protecting athletes from long-term physical and mental disability or avoiding possible discipline problems, support testing.

Regarding athletes' responsibilities to abstain from substance abuse, various lists have been compiled that range from the personal responsibility that athletes have for keeping their bodies in excellent physical condition to their responsibilities as society's role models to their responsibilities to spectators who pay money to watch their performances. These appear to be good "common sense" reasons for athletes to abstain from drug abuse, but they ignore a number of related issues. For example, it does not take in-depth investigating into equitable treatment provisions in sports to see how blatantly athletes are victimized by the drug testing system. Although athletes often must undergo mandatory, random drug testing, there is no provision for coaches, athletic directors, sports information directors, athletic trainers, athletic secretaries, and various and sundry others who are part of the big business of sports to undergo the same testing. Instead, the public is encouraged to dwell only on drug use by athletes.

Moreover, sport organizations do not seem to understand or acknowledge that the social conditions of high-pressure sports may actually contribute to drug abuse by athletes. There is a substantial literature documenting the pressures and incredible time demands that go with being a high school, major university, or professional athlete. It does not appear to be stretching the imagination to think that some of these pressures contribute to substance abuse by athletes.

Many medical professionals, health educators, and other knowledgeable professionals who have been critical of drug-testing programs acknowledge the social structural factors that cultivate drug abuse by athletes, but they are skeptical about any immediate changes that will address the need to discourage athletes from abusing drugs. They are also scornful about random drug testing as a viable tool for behavior change. Instead, many believe that drug education programs can make a better contribution as a key component of drug abuse prevention. Not just any drug education program will do, however; certainly the "one shot" efforts of many universities and professional teams are largely a waste of time. The fundamental strength of any substance abuse prevention program for athletes should be through education, and drug education must include more than just giving information or threatening athletes with punishment for substance abuse. Such programs need to help as many athletes as possible avoid making decisions about drugs that they may regret for the rest of their lives.[58]

In the best of all possible worlds—a world for which we should all be striving—there would be no place for drug abuse among athletes. Use of performance-enhancing drugs corrupts the essence of fair sporting competition; it is cheating. As serious as this is within the bounded world of sport, performance-enhancing and recreational drug abuse is improper for a more important reason: It is dangerous to personal health; its use is an unnecessary health risk.

The structure of society, especially the political and economic institutions, is responsible for many of the problems associated with drug abuse among North Americans. At a more microsocial level, the political economy of sports has contributed to drug abuse among athletes. Thus, solutions to drug abuse among athletes must begin with structural modifications in the larger society as well as in sport culture; when this happens, serious amelioration of drug abuse among athletes will occur.

EATING DISORDERS IN SPORT

While steroid use is prevalent among male athletes who are trying to bulk up, eating disorders, mainly anorexia nervosa and bulimia, afflict mostly female athletes who want to slim down. Anorexia nervosa is a psychobiological disorder in which a person is fixated on losing weight and becoming extremely thin, either because they have a distorted perception of their body, or because they feel it is necessary for social or occupational approval. Bulimia nervosa is characterized by bingeing on food and then purging the food by vomiting, laxative abuse, and/or diuretic abuse.

These disorders are not confined to athletes. More than 8 million Americans and Canadians suffer from eating disorders, and the mortality rate for anorexia is twelve times greater than that of any other cause of death among females between the ages of fifteen and twenty-four, according to the National Association of Anorexia Nervosa and Associated Disorders. Eating disorders are widespread among women in the entertainment industry, such as actresses, musicians, and dancers. They are rampant in the fashion business among models. But thousands of adolescent girls, and some boys, are also afflicted. Most experts contend that social norms, media images of females, and advertising portrayals of the "ideal" female body as extremely thin and firmly toned are major contributing factors in the contemporary woman's obsession with thinness.[59]

An accurate assessment of anorexia and bulimia in any group of people is difficult to ascertain because of the secretiveness that surrounds these disorders, but eating disorders are a prominent health and social problem for female athletes. According to studies of college athletes within the past decade, between 20 and 33 percent of female athletes reported disordered eating. In one study 43 percent said they were terrified of being or becoming too heavy, and 55 percent reported experiencing pressure to achieve or maintain a certain weight.[60]

Female athletes are doubly at risk for developing eating disorders. They are subject to the constant social pressure to be thin that influences all females in Western countries. They are constantly bombarded with TV, movie, magazine, Internet, and fashion images of extremely thin women who are portrayed as ideally proportioned. The director of sports nutrition at the University of Pittsburgh Medical Center remarked that female athletes "look at the bodies on the cover of *Glamour* and *Shape* magazines and think those bodies are better than theirs."[61]

Female athletes not only have to contend with these forces, they have to cope with additional ones. In some women's sports, such as gymnastics, figure skating, and diving, a significant part of the judging is on "appearance," and an extremely thin silhouette is a definite advantage. Coaches and athletes know this. Many female athletes report that their coaches hammer home to them the message of "get thin and stay thin" in a variety of ways, some of which are quite abusive. Many athletes aspire to be the best, to be a national or an Olympic champion, so they are willing to sacrifice to achieve that goal. The combination of these conditions creates the social climate for the development of eating disorders.

Eating disorders also show up in male sports that have rigid weight restrictions, such as boxing, weight lifting, jockeying, and high school and college wrestling. The self-inflicted torture of drastic weight loss to "make weight" before a match has been called wrestling's dirty secret. Indeed, dangerous weight loss has long been the norm in high school and collegiate wrestling, and bulimia, laxatives, and diuretics have been some of the main methods for losing weight.

The deaths of three college wrestlers in 1997 forced the NCAA and high school sports governing organizations to adopt various policies prohibiting unsafe weight loss practices. There are, however, many high school and college wrestlers participating in international-style wrestling events, and dangerous rapid weight loss practices still existed among high school wrestlers participating in international-style wrestling seven years after the deaths of the three NCAA wrestlers. The message: Wrestling's weight loss practices still pose a problem for the athletes in that sport.[62]

GAMBLING AND SPORTS

Gambling is an economic activity with a history that dates back into antiquity. Betting on sports events was popular with the ancient Greeks five hundred years before the birth of Christ, and it was very popular in all of their Pan-Hellenic Games—one of which was the Olympic Games. Gambling reached some incredible extremes at the Roman chariot races, with rampant corruption and fixed races. Horse racing was the most popular sport in colonial North America, and one reason for its popularity was the opportunity the races provided to bet on the outcome.

Wherever gambling on sports takes place, the specter of cheating is always a companion. A colonial America historian documented a horse-racing fix scandal in 1674. One of the most stunning professional sports fixing scandals occurred in the 1919 Major League Baseball World Series and involved Chicago White Sox players. Once the fixing was discovered, that team became known as the Black Sox. Pete Rose, the record holder for the most hits in Major League Baseball, was banned from baseball when it was discovered he had bet on Major League Baseball games (more on this later in this chapter).

Gambling is a form of entertainment with excitement, risk taking, and challenge that appeals to many people, and in the United States and Canada most moral sanctions against gambling and laws outlawing gambling have largely disappeared. Over 75 percent of North American adults gamble at least once each year. They wager an estimated $500 billion legally, and legal gambling revenue (not counting most sports gambling, Internet gambling, or poker) is approximately $80 billion annually. Moreover, gambling is growing at a phenomenal rate in the United States and Canada, and one reason for this is that there are now more opportunities to gamble than ever before. Some form of gambling is now legal in forty-eight states and in each of the Canadian provinces as well as the Yukon and Northwest Territories.

Approximately 250 Native American casinos dot tribal land in thirty-two states. Every province and each of the territories of Canada has a government-run lottery. Thirty-eight states and the District of Columbia have enacted lotteries; more than eighty riverboat or dockside casinos ply the water or sit at berth in several states. The nation wagers more than $45 billion annually in state lotteries.[63]

Internet wagering is the fastest-growing new form of gambling and has become a major force in the gambling industry. It is currently a $15 billion industry, and growing each year. In 2007 there were over twenty-five hundred Internet gambling sites, and a study by the Annenberg Foundation found that 44.5 percent of young people ages fourteen to twenty-two gambled on the Internet at least once a month.[64]

With the enormous increase of interest in spectator sports over the past thirty years, there has been a corresponding explosion in gambling on sports. Although only in Nevada can a person legally bet the line at a sports book, sports betting is big business. Over $2 billion is bet annually in Nevada's 175 licensed sports books, with the books netting a profit of some $115 million. According to one sports analyst, Nevada's $2 billion handle is a "drop in the bucket" compared to the sports betting wagered illegally through offshore Internet sites, mob bookies, various casual sports pools, and fantasy sport leagues. He estimated total sports betting of $300 to $380 billion.

In the United States the most popular betting action in the Nevada sports books is with professional and college football, professional and college basketball, Major League Baseball, and NHL hockey. Betting is popular for heavyweight boxing championship events, but betting on boxing ranks low overall. The biggest legal sports gambling event is the Super Bowl, on which some $5 to $7 billion in legal and illegal wagers change hands. The most popular sports for betting by Canadians are similar to those in the United States. For ice hockey, many bettors prefer pool betting to team-versus-team betting.[65]

A study by the Annenberg Foundation reported that more than 27 percent of young people ages fourteen to twenty-two bet on sports events at least once per month. Even more troubling, sports gambling is rampant and prospering on campuses throughout the country, and the majority of bookies are students. One writer referred to this phenomenon as "the dirty little secret on college campuses"; another referred to it as a "silent addiction" for many college students. Studies of sports betting by college students have reported findings that between 35 and 50 percent of male college students and between 10 and 20 percent of female students have bet on sports events.[66]

The NCAA has been a vigorous critic of all forms of legal and illegal sports gambling, but its football and basketball games are favorites of sports bettors. The NCAA prohibits athletics department staff members and student-athletes from engaging in gambling activities as they relate to intercollegiate or professional sporting events. But that policy has not deterred some student-athletes. One study of more than 600 Division I men's football and basketball players found that 72 percent had gambled in some form, 25 percent had gambled money on other college sports events, and 4 percent had bet money on a game in which they had played. Another study assessed gambling on college and professional sports by college students classified as athletes, sports fans, and other students at colleges with students expressing differing levels of "sports interest." All groups—athletes, sports fans, and other students—had higher rates of gambling at colleges with higher sports interest. Athletes and sports fans—both male and female—reported more sports gambling compared to other students. Figure 7.1 displays the odds of frequent gambling on college sports among athletes, sports fans, and other students by the percentage of students claiming to be sports fans at the college.

Information of this kind prompted the NCAA to convince congressional leaders to introduce legislation in both chambers of Congress banning all gambling on college sporting events. This legislation would remove the "Nevada loophole," which allows Nevada to be the only state to conduct legal gambling on collegiate sports. Proponents of the multibillion-dollar Nevada sports-gambling industry have used their powerful resources to oppose the proposed legislation.

Considering the popularity of professional sports, and the huge sums of money bet on them, professional sports have been relatively free of cheating scandals—Chicago White Sox players conspiring to fix the 1919 World Series and Major League Baseball player Pete Rose being permanently banned from baseball for gambling on MLB games are the two most notorious cases. But two shocking gambling revelations that came to light in the summer of 2007 may ultimately acquire the "most notorious" tag. NBA referee Tim Donaghy

Figure 7.1 Percentage of Students Who Are Sports Fans (College-Level)

Prototypical model displaying the odds of frequent gambling on college and professional sports among male athletes, fans, and other students by the percentage of sports fans at the college (N = 10,559). Vertical scale is percentages. The scale on the horizontal axis is the percentage of college students attending colleges classified by percentage as sports fans.

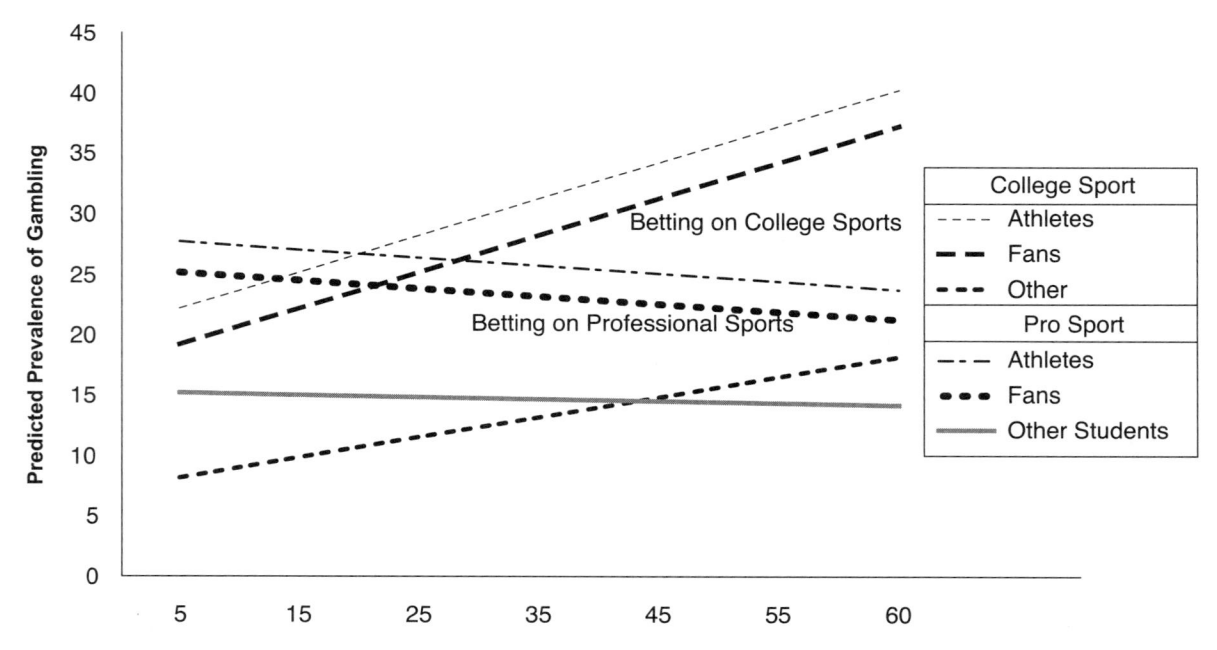

Source: Adapted from Toban F. Nelson et al., "Sports Betting and Other Gambling in Athletes, Fans, and Other College Students," *Research Quarterly for Exercise and Sport* 78, no. 4 (2007): 271–283.

admitted that he had been making bets on NBA games—including games that he refereed—for four years and, furthermore, that he had tipped off professional gamblers with inside information.[67]

NFL quarterback Michael Vick became the subject of a gambling scandal. He pleaded guilty to operating a multistate dogfighting and gambling scheme for five years, where mistreatment and killing of dogs by strangulation, drowning, or electrocution were frequent. As noted earlier in this chapter, Vick was sentenced to 23 months in prison for his involvement in this operation. The promising careers of Vick and Donaghy are likely over for both of them, and it will tarnish the sports in which they were employed.[68]

The popularity of intercollegiate football and basketball, and the naïveté and financial desperation of many college athletes, have made these sports attractive for professional gamblers. College football and basketball have gone through a series of fixing and point-shaving scandals during the past decade. Thirteen Boston College football players were suspended for betting on college and pro football. Two players bet against their team in a loss to Syracuse University. During the late 1990s two Arizona State University basketball players pleaded guilty in a point-shaving scandal, and a betting and point-shaving scandal at Northwestern University involved both football and basketball players.[69]

The legalization of gambling and the use of the profits as a source of income to help support sports organizations and state, provincial, and national governments have been proposed in a number of states and provinces in recent years, but Nevada remains the only state permitting some forms of legalized sports gambling. Given the economic crisis in sport and in government, the prospect of the enormous windfall that could be generated from legalized betting is very attractive to some sport organizations and to politicians. But there are vocal critics of legalized sport betting. First, some think that it stimulates excessive betting—betting more than the person can afford to lose. Second, there is the prospect that athletes and coaches will be corrupted. The point-shaving scandals of collegiate basketball come easily to mind. What of the heightened pressures on athletes resulting from the inevitable dropped pass, strikeout, or missed free throw? A suspicion that perhaps the action was deliberate and charges of dumping the game or shaving points would follow.

People for the Ethical Treatment of Animals (PETA) member Bill Long, of Columbus, Ohio, protests in front of the Arthur Blank Foundation offices where Atlanta Falcons owner Arthur Blank held a news conference to discuss the federal indictment of quarterback Michael Vick on charges related to involvement in dogfighting. (AP Photo/John Bazemore)

With sports gambling, just as with any other form of gambling, there is the inevitable issue of compulsive, addictive gambling. Obtaining an accurate number of compulsive gamblers is extremely difficult, but several agencies and organizations that have conducted surveys of these conditions estimate that 1.0 to 3.5 percent of the U.S. population (3 to 10.5 million) are pathological gamblers, and this disorder is more common in men than in women. Extensive research at the Center for Compulsive Gambling clearly shows that wherever there is availability and opportunity for gambling, compulsive gambling problems increase accordingly. Thus, current trends and future predictions suggest that a growing social problem for both sport and the larger society will likely be large numbers of tragic compulsive gamblers; many of these will be sports gamblers.

SUMMARY

It should come as no surprise that violent behavior, substance abuse, eating disorders, and gambling are conspicuous problems in North American sports, given the close connections between sport and society. Three theories of human aggression dominate the scientific literature: the instinct theory, the frustration-aggression (F-A) theory, and the socially grounded theory. Advocates of the instinct and F-A theories have often claimed that participation and observation of aggressive activities have a cathartic effect by allowing one to discharge pent-up aggressive energy, and sporting activities have often been suggested as a means of dispelling aggression in a socially healthy way. The research findings suggest that, contrary to the predictions of the instinct and F-A theories, aggression tends to produce more aggressive predispositions and actions rather than serve as a catharsis.

Another theory about aggressive behavior has come from scholars who advance a socially grounded perspective that postulates that aggression is learned in the social environment. This latter perspective places emphasis on the learning of aggression through the socialization process. Socially based explanations have much more research support than the other aggression models. Directly and indirectly, sports research findings have overwhelmingly supported this perspective of human aggression.

Violent behavior has been a part of sporting practices for as long as we have records of organized sports. The nature of some sports literally demands violent actions. Other sports do not have the inherent violence found in some, but the tactics employed and the way the rules are interpreted are increasingly encouraging violent actions.

Athletes feel pressure to be violent because coaches, owners, and fans all encourage player violence in their own ways. Whether there is actually more violence and criminal behavior by present-day athletes in their private lives or whether they are just scrutinized more closely than in the past is widely debated.

Violence on the playing field is often mirrored by sports fans in the stadium, arena, or the environs, and it is not merely a contemporary phenomenon, nor is it confined to North American sports. Everyone who follows North American sports is quite aware of the many incidents of spectator violence. Within the past decade, major fan violence has erupted in all levels of competition—high school, collegiate, professional.

The use of substances to enhance performance has been present throughout the history of organized sports. Some behavioral and social scientists believe that drug use by athletes is an epidemic, from the high school to the professional level. The variety of substances athletes use in the hopes of improving their performances has become astounding.

There is no single answer to the question of why some athletes risk their health and their opportunity to compete by using drugs, because athletes have different reasons. Athletes are a part of a much larger social community, and substance abuse is rampant in this larger social community. There is enormous social status that goes with being an athlete, and undoubtedly that is one factor that motivates young athletes to turn to chemicals for performance enhancement. There is also the potential of the fulfillment of young athletes' dreams of being a professional athlete or being an Olympic gold medalist.

Only a small minority of athletes at any level have a substance abuse problem. There is still, however, the question of what is to be done with those who are drug abusers. There are several options, but the one that has received the most attention is the drug-testing programs of the various sports governing bodies. Two important questions that have been raised about drug testing are what are the athletes' individual rights and what are the athlete's responsibilities? Also, several unresolved issues exist where drug testing has been implemented. The validity and accuracy of the tests have been a continuing controversy.

Use of performance-enhancing drugs corrupts the essence of fair sporting competition. As serious as this is within the world of sport, performance-enhancing and recreational drug abuse is unsuitable for another important reason: It is potentially dangerous to personal health.

Eating disorders, especially anorexia nervosa and bulimia, are common among female athletes in sports that emphasize appearance and a lean body. Female athletes are influenced by both the societal pressures that all girls and women contend with to be extremely thin and the pressures in certain sports to be thin in order to win. Although more than 90 percent of athletes with sports-related anorexia and bulimia are female, many males who compete in sports in which there are weight classifications also develop eating disorders.

Sporting events have always been a site for gambling because the events themselves are a source of great interest, the outcomes are uncertain, and sport fans often have a favorite to win. Thus, sports provide an excellent opportunity for wagering on the outcome. In North America, moral restrictions against gambling and laws prohibiting gambling have largely been swept away. Furthermore, mass communications have made sporting events more popular to the general public while also making it easier to place bets. Compulsive, addictive gambling is one of the social problems that are inevitable outcomes of gambling.

The NCAA has been trying to get legislation passed to ban college sports gambling in Nevada, the only state where it is legal. But the organization has been unsuccessful, largely because the Nevada casino industry has been successful in lobbying Congress against passing the legislation.

WEB RESOURCES

www.ncava.org
This is the home page of the National Coalition Against Violent Athletes. The purpose of the NCAVA is to educate the public on athletes' violent behavior and to provide support to the victims, including advocacy, referrals, and research.

www.ncaa.org/news
The NCAA publishes a periodical titled *The NCAA News,* which carries articles dealing with intercollegiate athletic problems, such as violence, drugs, eating disorders, and gambling. One feature of this website is an "Archives" link. You do have to have permission to access the news page on this server. Most university and public libraries computers do have this permission.

www.ahealthyme.com
Blue Cross and Blue Shield of Massachusetts makes this website available for the sole purposes of providing educational information on health-related issues and providing access to health-related resources. There are frequent articles about drug abuse and eating disorders among teenage athletes.

www.smartplay.net/moves/drugs/drugsinfo.html
This is an excellent website that is primarily intended to provide leaders with facts concerning drug use in sport. But anyone interested in having in-depth information about drugs and sport will find this website useful and informative.

www.anred.com
This is the website of Anorexia Nervosa and Related Eating Disorders. One of the specific pages in this website provides an excellent overview of athletes with eating disorders.

www.gamblersanonymous.org
This Gamblers Anonymous website indicates that the organization is a fellowship of men and women who share their experience, strength, and hope with each other so that they can solve their common problem and help others recover from a gambling problem.

NOTES

1. Jack McCallum, "Game-Fixing and Dogfighting Rock Pro Sports," *Sports Illustrated,* 30 July 2007, 34–39;

Jack McCallum, "Fed Up Yet?" *Sports Illustrated*, 6 August 2007, 41–44; Jarrett Bell, "NFL Confronts Discipline Issue," *USA Today*, 10 April 2007, pp. 1C–2C; Edward Wyatt, "Tour in Tatters: Team Ousts the Race Leader," *New York Times*, 26 July 2007, http://www.nytimes.com/2007/07/26/sports/sportsspecial1/26tour.html.

2. John H. Kerr, *Motivation and Emotion in Sport* (Hove, UK: Psychology Press, 1997), 115–116; see also John H. Kerr, *Rethinking Aggression and Violence in Sport* (New York: Routledge, 2005).

3. David Churchman, *Why We Fight: Theories of Human Aggression and Conflict* (Lanham, Md.: University Press of America, 2005).

4. Kenneth Gergen, *Social Construction in Context* (Thousand Oaks, Calif.: Sage, 2001); Ronald Akers and Gary Jensen, eds., *Social Learning Theory and the Explanation of Crime*, 3rd ed. (Piscataway, N.J.: Transaction Publishers, 2007).

5. Konrad Lorenz, *On Aggression* (New York: Harcourt, Brace & World, 1963), 281.

6. Kerr, *Rethinking Aggression and Violence in Sport*.

7. Richard G. Sipes, "Sports as a Control for Aggression," in *Sports in Contemporary Society: An Anthology*, 6th ed., ed. D. Stanley Eitzen (New York: St. Martin's Press, 1996), 154–160.

8. Paul Le Blanc, *A Short History of the U.S. Working Class: From Colonial Times to the Twenty-First Century* (Amherst, N.Y.: Humanity Books, 1999).

9. D. Stanley Eitzen and Maxine Baca Zinn, *In Conflict and Order: Understanding Society*, 10th ed. (Boston: Allyn & Bacon, 2004), 71.

10. James T. Hamilton, *Channeling Violence* (Princeton: Princeton University Press, 2000); U.S. Department of Justice, *Bureau of Justice Statistics Homicide Trends in the U.S.*, 2005, http://ww.ojp.usdoj.gov.

11. Hamilton, *Channeling Violence*; Jeanne B. Funk, Heidi Bechtoldt Baldacci, Tracie Pasold, and Jennifer Baumgardner, "Violence Exposure in Real Life, Video Games, Television, Movies, and the Internet: Is There Desensitization?" *Journal of Adolescence* 27 (2004): 23–39; L. Rowell Huesmann, Jessica Moise-Titus, Cheryl-Lynn Podolski, and Leonard D. Eron, "Longitudinal Relations between Children's Exposure to TV Violence and Their Aggressive and Violent Behavior in Young Adulthood: 1977–1992," *Developmental Psychology* 39 (2003): 201–221; Nicholas L. Carnagey, Craig A. Anderson, and Brad J. Bushman, "The Effect of Video Game Violence on Physiological Desensitization to Real-Life Violence," *Journal of Experimental Social Psychology* 43 (2007): 489–496.

12. Judith Swaddling, *The Ancient Olympic Games*, 3rd rev. ed., (London: British Museum Press, 2004); Ulrich Sinn and Thomas Thornton, *Olympia: Cult, Sport, and Ancient Festival* (Princeton: Markus Wiener, 2000).

13. Paul Plass, *The Game of Death in Ancient Rome: Arena Sport and Political Suicide* (Madison: University of Wisconsin Press, 1995); Robert Crego, *Sports and Games of the 18th and 19th Centuries* (Westport, Conn.: Greenwood Press, 2002).

14. John C. Bridges, *Making Violence Part of the Game: A Socio-Legal History of Violence in American Sport* (Commack, N.Y.: Kroshka Books, 1999), 228.

15. Tim Layden, "The Big Hit," *Sports Illustrated*, 30 July 2007, 54; see also Sigmund Loland, Berit Skirstad, and Ivan Ivan Waddington, eds., *Pain and Injury in Sport: Social and Ethical Analysis* (New York: Routledge, 2006).

16. Ibid., 54.

17. Peter King, "Painful Reality," *Sports Illustrated*, 11 October 2004; Kevin Young, ed., *Sporting Bodies, Damaged Selves: Sociological Studies of Sports-Related Injury* (Boston: Elsevier, 2004); Loland, Skirstad, and Waddington, *Pain and Injury in Sport*.

18. Michael Farber, "Stitches in Time," *Sports Illustrated*, 12 October 1998, 93; see also John H. Kerr, "Examining the Bertuzzi-Moore NHL Ice Hockey Incident: Crossing the Line between Sanctioned and Unsanctioned Violence in Sport," *Aggression and Violent Behavior* 11 (July–August 2006): 313–322.

19. Michael Farber, "It's Time to Consistently Crack Down on Enforcers," *SI.com*, http://sportsillustrated.cnn.com/2007/writers/michael_farber/03/09/simon.reaction/index.html.

20. Jennings Bryant, Dolf Zillman, and Arthur A. Raney, "Violence and the Enjoyment of Media Sports," in *MediaSport*, ed. Lawrence A. Wenner (New York: Routledge, 1998), 252–265.

21. L. Jon Wertheim, "The New Main Event," *Sports Illustrated*, 27 May 2007, 50–60.

22. Bryant, Zillman, and Raney, "Violence and the Enjoyment of Media Sports," 264; see also Arthur A. Raney and A. Depalma, "The Effect of Viewing Varying Levels of Aggressive Sports Programming on Enjoyment, Mood, and Perceived Violence," *Mass Communication and Society* 9, no. 3 (2006): 321–338; Arthur A. Raney, "Why We Watch and Enjoy Mediated Sports," in *Handbook of Sports and Media*, ed. Arthur A. Raney and Jennings Bryant (Mahwah, N.J.: Erlbaum, 2006), 313–329.

23. Briefing, "Athletes with Broken Brains," *The Week*, 9 March 2007, 15; Christopher Nowinski, *Head Games: Football's Concussion Crisis from the NFL to Youth*

Leagues (Plymouth, Mass.: Drummond Publishing Group, 2006).

24. Most recent edition, Jim Bouton, *Ball Four: The Final Pitch*, rev. ed. (New York: Bulldog Publishing, distributed by Midpoint Trade Books, 2001).

25. Ray Glier, "Is Tennessee Football Out of Bounds?" *USA Today*, 27 July 2005, p. 11C.

26. Bell, "NFL Confronts Discipline Issue."

27. Jeff Benedict, *Out of Bounds: Inside the NBA's Culture of Rape, Violence, and Crime* (New York: HarperCollins, 2004).

28. Todd W. Crosset, "Male Athletes' Violence against Women: A Critical Assessment of the Athletic Affiliation, Violence against Women Debate," *Quest* 51, no. 3 (1999): 244–257; see also Editorial, "In Handling Abuse Cases, the NFL Mirrors Society," *USA Today*, 6 September 2007, p. 12A.

29. National Sexual Assault Online Hotline, http://www.rainn.org/statistics/index.html; Bonnie S. Fisher, Francis T. Cullen, and Michael G. Turner, *The Sexual Victimization of College Women*, U.S. Department of Justice, www.ncjrs.org/txtfilesl/nij/182369.txt; Candace Kruttschnitt, Brenda L. McLaughlin, and Carol V. Petrie, eds., *Advancing the Federal Research Agenda on Violence against Women* (Washington, D.C.: National Academies Press, 2004).

30. The book by H. G. Bissinger, *Friday Night Lights: A Town, a Team, and a Dream* (Reading, Mass.: Addison-Wesley, 1990), was made into a movie, *Friday Night Lights*, in 2004; in the fall of 2006, a television serial drama by the same name began airing on NBC.

31. Derek A. Kreager, "Unnessary Roughness? School Sports, Peer Networks, and Male Adolescent Violence," *American Sociological Review* 72 (October 2007): 705–724.

32. Charles E. Yesalis and Michael S. Bahrke, "Anabolic-Androgenic Steroids: Incidence of Use and Health Implications," *Research Digest* ser. 5, no. 5 (March 2005), Washington, D.C.: President's Council on Physical Fitness and Sports; Nathan Jendrick, *Dunks, Doubles, Doping: How Steroids Are Killing American Athletes* (Guilford, Conn.: Lyons Press, 2006).

33. Home page, National Coalition Against Violent Athletes, www.ncava.org.

34. Jamie Bryshun and Kevin Young, "Sport-Related Hazing: An Inquiry into Male and Female Involvement," in *Sport and Gender in Canada*, ed. Philip White and Kevin Young (Don Mills, Ont.: Oxford University Press, 1999), 269–292; see also Jay Johnson and Margery Holman, *Making the Team: Inside the World of Sport Initiations and Hazing* (Toronto: Canadian Scholars' Press, 2004).

35. Nadine C. Hoover, "National Survey: Initiation Rites and Athletics for NCAA Sports Teams," Alfred University, 30 August 1999, http://www.alfred.edu/sports_hazing/docs/hazing.pdf; see also Tom Weir, "Hazing Issue Rears Ugly Head across USA," *USA Today*, 9 December 2003, pp. 1C–2C.

36. High School Hazing Page: Scroll Down, http://www.hanknuwer.com/hs2.html; Ryan Gorcey and Julie Strack, "Officials Investigating Baseball 'Initiation,'" *Daily Californian*, 13 April 2007, http://www.dailycal.org/printable.php?id=24177; "Maine Softball Team on Probation for Hazing," *USA Today*, 16 August 2007, p. 11C; see also Grant Wahl and L. Jon Wertheim, "A Rite Gone Terribly Wrong," *Sports Illustrated*, 22 December 2003, 68–77; Kevin L. Guynn and Frank D. Aquila, *Hazing in High Schools: Causes and Consequences* (Bloomington, Ind.: Phi Delta Kappa Educational Foundation, 2005).

37. Jodi Upton, "Violence Visits High School Football," *USA Today*, 23 November 2005, p. 1C; Jodi Upton, "Violence at Games Means Trouble for All," *USA Today*, 23 November 2005, p. 11C.

38. Jerry M. Lewis, *Sports Fan Violence in North America* (Lanham, Md.: Rowman & Littlefield, 2007); Michelle Kessler and Erik Brady, "Tension Mounts with Fans," *USA Today*, 15 September 2004, p. 3C.

39. Ibid.; see also Bill Saporito, "Why Fans and Players Are Playing So Rough," *Time*, 6 December 2004, 30–34.

40. Michael Caccamise, "Rowdy Postgame Celebrations Courting Danger," *Tucson Citizen*, 10 February 2004, http://www.tucsoncitizen.com/print/youth/021004d1_courtrushing; Scorecard, "Courting Danger," *Sports Illustrated*, 15 March 2004.

41. Erik Brady, "How Free Should Speech Be at Campus Games?" *USA Today*, 6 February 2004, pp. 1A, 5A.

42. Lewis, *Sports Fan Violence in North America*, 121–141.

43. Sal Ruibal, "Steroids Are Just a Click Away," *USA Today*, 1 March 2007, p. 3C; Tom Weir, "Drug-Free Sports Might Be Thing of the Past," *USA Today*, pp. 1A–2A; Sal Ruibal, "Tour de France's Downhill Slide: Doping Scandals Sully World's Biggest Bike Race," *USA Today*, 5 July 2007, pp. 1C–2C.

44. Lloyd D. Johnston, Patrick M. O'Malley, Jerald G. Bachman, and John E. Schulenberg, *Monitoring the Future: National Results on Adolescent Drug Use: Overview of Key Findings*, NIH Publication No. 07-6202 (Bethesda, Md.: National Institute on Drug Abuse, 2006).

45. "Report Shows Steroid Use Has Dramatically Decreased," *NCAAsports.com*, 6 July 2006, http://www.ncaasports.com/story/9543156.

46. Yesalis and Bahrke, "Anabolic-Androgenic Steroids: Incidence of Use and Health Implications," 4.

47. "Doping-Free Sport: Canadian Anti-Doping Program," http://www.cces.ca/forms/index.cfm?dsp=template&act=view3&template_id=21&lang=e.

48. Ibid.

49. Johnston, O'Malley, Bachman, and Schulenberg, *Monitoring the Future: National Results on Adolescent Drug Use: Overview of Key Findings.*

50. Ibid.

51. Barrie Houlihan, *Dying to Win: Doping in Sport and the Development of Anti-Doping Policy* (Strasbourg: Council of Europe Publishing, 1999), 30–31.

52. Michael Bamberger and Don Yaeger, "Over the Edge," *Sports Illustrated,* 14 April 1997, 60–70.

53. Quoted in ibid., 63.

54. Young, *Sporting Bodies, Damaged Selves: Sociological Studies of Sports-Related Injury.*

55. Bruce Horovitz, Theresa Howard, and Laura Petrecca, "Alcohol Makers Tread Tricky Path in Marketing to College Students," *USA Today,* 17 November 2005, pp. 1B–2B; Pamela Brogan, "Do Beer Ads, College Sports Mix?" *USA Today,* 16 March 2004, p. 4C.

56. Nathan T. Martin, "Drug Testing in Interscholastic Athletics," *Journal of Physical Education, Recreation, and Dance* 78 (March 2007): 8–9; Opinion, "Random Drug Testing Spreads, One School a Week," *USA Today,* 7 May 2007, p. 19A.

57. Angela J. Schneider and Robert B. Butcher, "An Ethical Analysis of Drug Testing," in *Doping in Elite Sport: The Politics of Drugs in the Olympic Movement,* ed. Wayne Wilson and Edward Derse (Champaign, Ill.: Human Kinetics, 2001), 129–130; see also Richard W. Pound, *Inside Dope: How Drugs Are the Biggest Threat to Sports, Why You Should Care, and What Can Be Done about Them* (New York: Wiley, 2006), 79–120.

58. Rob Beamish, *Fastest, Highest, Strongest: A Critique of High-Performance Sport* (New York: Routledge, 2006).

59. Katherine A. Beals, *Disordered Eating among Athletes: A Comprehensive Guide for Health Professionals* (Champaign, Ill.: Human Kinetics, 2004).

60. Ibid. See also Katherine A. Beals and Melinda M. Manore, "Disorders of the Female Athlete Triad among Collegiate Athletes," *International Journal of Sport Nutrition and Exercise Metabolism* 12, no. 3 (2002): 281–293; see also Tiffany C. Sanford-Martins et al., "Clinical and Subclinical Eating Disorders: An Examination of Collegiate Athletes," *Journal of Applied Sport Psychology* 17, no. 1 (2005): 79–86.

61. Quoted in Nanci Hellmich, "Athletes' Hunger to Win Fuels Eating Disorders," *USA Today,* 6 February 2006, pp. 1A, 6A; for an excellent in-depth discussion of eating disorders in sports, see Trent A. Petrie and Christy A. Greenleaf, "Eating Disorders in Sport: From Theory to Research to Intervention," in *Handbook of Sport Psychology,* 3rd ed., ed. Gershon Tenenbaum and Robert C. Eklund (New York: Wiley, 2007), 352–378.

62. Brandon L. Alderman, Daniel Landers, John Carlson, and James Scott, "Factors Related to Rapid Weight Loss Practices among International-Style Wrestlers," *Medicine and Science in Sports and Exercise* 36 (February 2004): 249–252.

63. Earl L. Grinols, *Gambling in America: Cost and Benefits* (Cambridge: Cambridge University Press, 2004).

64. Victor H. Royer, *Powerful Profits from Internet Gambling* (New York: Lyle Stuart, 2005); Angus Dunnington, *Gambling Online* (Hassocks, West Sussex, UK: D & B Publishing, 2005); Annenberg Public Policy Center, "More Than 1 Million Young People Use Internet Gambling Sites Each Month," 2 October 2006, http://www.annenbergpublicpolicycenter.org/; Annenberg Public Policy Center, "On the Path to Problem Gambling: National Survey Shows Casinos, Slots and Lotteries Attract Youth into Potentially Addictive Habit," 13 October 2003, http://www.annenbergpublicpolicycenter.org/.

65. Michael McCarthy, "Football Bettors Put Billions on the Line," *USA Today,* 8 September 2005, pp. 1C–2C.

66. Annenberg Public Policy Center, "On the Path to Problem Gambling: National Survey Shows Casinos, Slots and Lotteries Attract Youth into Potentially Addictive Habit"; McCarthy, "Football Bettors Put Billions on the Line."

67. Pat Milton, "Donaghy's Plea Could Lead to 25 Years in Jail," *Denver Post,* 16 August 2007, pp. 1D–2D; Kelly Whiteside, "Donaghy's Bets Began in 2003," *USA Today,* 16 August 2007, pp. 1C–2C.

68. George Dohrmann, "The Case against Vick," *Sports Illustrated,* 30 July 2007, 38–39.

69. Stanley H. Teitelbaum, *Sports Heroes, Fallen Idols* (Lincoln: University of Nebraska Press, 2005), 69–100.

CHAPTER 8
Sport and Religion

San Francisco Giants' Barry Bonds points skyward after hitting his 701st career home run off San Diego Padres' David Wells in the second inning, 18 September 2004, in San Francisco. (AP Photo/Ben Margot)

On the one hand, there may seem to be little in common between sport and religion; going to religious services, singing hymns, studying scripture, and worshiping God all seem quite unrelated to the activities that we associate with sport. On the other hand, like religion, contemporary sport symbolically evokes fervent commitment from millions of people. Sports fans worship their favorite athletes much as followers of various religions worship their special deities. Also, sports fans, like religious groups, consider themselves to be part of a community. Finally, the rituals and ceremonies common to religion are paralleled by rituals and ceremonies in sport. Former NFL and Major League Baseball player Deion Sanders summed up the connections between sport and religion by declaring that they go together "like peanut butter and jelly."

There are followers of a broad variety of religions in North America, but the emphasis in this chapter will be on Christian linkages to sport in these two countries. There are several reasons for this focus. First, North Americans who self-identify as Christians are the overwhelming majority; indeed about 82 percent of the citizens identify themselves as Christians. About 10 percent of North Americans say they are atheists, leaving about 8 percent who self-identify with other religions, or no religion. Second, the historical traditions of both the United States and Canada are closely tied to the United Kingdom and Western European countries, all of whom have historically been "Christian" countries. Finally, as we pointed out in chapter 2, the rise of sport in North America was closely linked to Christian leaders and organizations; therefore, Christian attitudes, values, and practices have been a dominating force in North American sport.

As sport and religion have become increasingly intertwined, each has made inroads into the traditional activities and prerogatives of the other. For example, for Christians of previous generations, Sunday was the day reserved for church and worship, but with the increase in opportunities for recreational pursuits—both for participants and for spectators—and the virtual explosion of televised sports, worship on weekends has been replaced by worship of weekends. As a result, sport has captured Sunday, and churches have had to revise their schedules to oblige sport. At most Roman Catholic churches, convenient Saturday late-afternoon and evening services are now featured in addition to traditional Sunday masses, and other denominations frequently schedule services to accommodate the viewing of professional sports events. In many respects churches have had to share Sundays with sports, and the idea that the Sabbath should be reserved for worship now seems merely a quaint idea from the past. Former *Sports Illustrated* columnist Rick Reilly noted that "priests and pastors have noticed that God is competing more and more with Sunday sports—and losing."[1]

At the same time that sport appears to be usurping religion's traditional time for worship and services, many churches and religious leaders are attempting to weld a link between the two activities by sponsoring sports events under religious auspices and by proselytizing athletes to religion and then using them as missionaries to spread the Word and to recruit new members. Thus, contemporary religion often uses sport for the promotion of its causes. Sport uses religion as well and in more ways than just seizing the traditional day of worship. People involved in sports—as participants or as spectators—employ numerous activities with religious connotations in connection with the contests. Ceremonies, rituals, taboos, fetishes, and so forth—all originating in religious practice—are standard observances in the world of sport.

In this chapter we examine the multidimensional relationship between religion and sport.

RELIGION AND SOCIETY

Religion is the belief that supernatural forces influence human lives. There are many definitions of religion, but the one by renowned French sociologist Emile Durkheim has perhaps been cited most. Durkheim said that "religion is a unified system of beliefs and practices relative to sacred things, that is to say, things set apart and forbidden—beliefs and practices which unite into one single moral community called a Church, all those who adhere to them."[2] As a social institution, religion is a system that functions to maintain and transmit beliefs about forces considered supernatural and sacred. It provides codified guides for moral conduct and prescribes symbolic practices deemed to be in harmony with beliefs about the supernatural. The world religions, including Christianity, Hinduism, Buddhism, Confucianism, Judaism, and Islam, are cores of elaborate cultural systems that have dominated world societies for centuries. For all practical purposes we may assume that religious behavior among human beings is universal in that ethnologists and anthropologists have not yet discovered a human group without traces of the behavior we call "religious"![3]

Surveys indicate that some 90 percent of Americans profess a belief in God or a universal spirit. About 82 percent identify themselves as Christians. See Table 8.1 for the self-professed identification of the adult population for the largest Christian denominations and other major religions.

Personal and Social Role of Religion

Religions exist because they perform important roles at several levels of human life, including personal, interpersonal, institutional, and societal. At the personal level, religious experience meets psychic needs by providing individuals with emotional support in this uncertain world. The unpredictable and sometimes dangerous world produces personal fears and general anxiety that revering the powers of nature or seeking cooperation through religious faith and ritual may alleviate. Fears of death, too, are made bearable by beliefs in a supernatural realm into which a believer passes. If one can believe in a God-giving scheme of things, the universal quest for ultimate meaning is validated, and human strivings and sufferings seem to make some sense.

At the interpersonal level, religion contributes to human social bonding. It unites a community of believers by bringing them together to enact various ceremonies and rituals, and it provides them with shared values and beliefs that bind them together. The need to proclaim human abilities and to achieve a sense of transcendence is met and indeed fostered by many religions through ceremonies and rituals that celebrate humans and their activities.

At the institutional level religion serves as a vehicle for social control; that is, religious tenets constrain the behavior of the community of believers to keep them in line with the norms, values, and beliefs of society. In all the major religions, morals and religion are intertwined, and schemes of otherworldly rewards or punishments for behavior, such as those found in Christianity, become powerful forces for morality. The fear of hellfire and damnation has been a powerful deterrent and control in Christian societies. The virtues of honesty, conformity to sexual codes, and all the details of acceptable, moral behavior in a society become merged with religious beliefs and practices.

One of the paramount roles of religion for society is promoting social integration. It promotes a binding together both of the members of a society and of the social obligations that help unite them because it organizes the individual's experience in terms of ultimate meanings that include but also transcend the individual. When many

Table 8.1 Self-Described Religious Identification of Adult Population in the United States, 2001 (in thousands)

Religious Group	Adult Population
Total	207,980
Christian (top eight self-described)	
Catholic	159,506
Baptist	50,873
Methodist/Wesleyan	150
Lutheran	9,580
Presbyterian	5,596
Pentecostal/Charismatic	4,407
Episcopalian/Anglican	3,451
Mormon/Latter-Day Saints	2,787
Jewish	7,740
Muslim/Islamic	2,831
Buddhist	1,104

Source: U.S. Census Bureau, *Statistical Abstract of the United States: 2007,* 126th ed. (Washington, D.C., 2007), Table 73.

people share this ordering principle, they can deal with each other in meaningful ways and can transcend themselves and their individual egoisms, sometimes even to the point of self-sacrifice.

Religious ceremonies and rituals also promote integration because they serve to reaffirm some of the basic customs and values of society. Here, the societal customs, folkways, and observances are symbolically elevated to the realm of the sacred. In expressing common beliefs about the supernatural, in engaging in collective worship activities, in recounting the lore and myths of the past, the community is brought closer together and linked with their heritage. To the extent that religious groups can reach individuals who feel isolated and abandoned and who are not being relieved of their problems elsewhere, religion is serving society.

Another social integrative role of religion is that it tends to legitimize the secular social structures within a society. There is a strong tendency for religious ideology to become united with the norms and values of secular structures, producing, as a consequence, religious support for the values and institutions of society. From its earliest existence, religion has provided rationales that serve the needs and actions of a society's leaders. It has legitimized as "God-given" such disparate ideologies as absolute monarchies and egalitarian democracies.

There are social scientists whose writings emphasize only the beneficial roles of religion for the individual and society, but there are others who, though recognizing the need that many people have for emotional support for dealing with the unknown, unpredictable, and ultimate questions about life and death, view the inclinations of people to create gods and believe in supernatural phenomena as having historically been exploited by powerful and wealthy groups to promote their privileged status and justify socially inequitable conditions. This latter approach to religion was articulated most clearly by Karl Marx, who believed that religion was primarily a tool of the rich and powerful to produce a "false consciousness" in the masses of people. One of Marx's best-known ideas was that religion is a means for legitimating the interests of the dominant class, justifying existing social injustices and inequalities, and, like a narcotic, lulling people into ready acceptance of the status quo. He argued: "Religion is the sigh of the oppressed creature, the heart of a heartless world, and the soul of soulless conditions. It is the opium of the people."[4]

THE RELATIONSHIP BETWEEN RELIGION AND SPORT

Pre-Columbian Societies

Some historians who have studied the origins of sport claim that sport began as a religious rite. The ball games of the Mayans and Aztecs are examples of pre-Columbian societies that included physical activities as part of their religious rituals and ceremonies. The purpose of many games of these societies was rooted in a desire to gain victory over foes seen and unseen, to influence the forces of nature, and to promote fertility among crops and cattle. The Zuni Indians of New Mexico played games that they believed would bring rain and thus enable their crops to grow. In southern Nigeria, wrestling matches were held to encourage the growth of crops, and various games were played in the winter to hasten the return of spring and to ensure a bountiful season. One Eskimo tribe, at the end of the harvest season, played a cup-and-ball game to "catch the sun" and thus delay its departure. In his monumental work on the Plains Indians, Stewart Culin wrote: "In general, games appear to be played ceremonially, as pleasing to the gods, with the objective of securing fertility, causing rain, giving and prolonging life, expelling demons, or curing sickness."[5]

Ancient Greece

The ancient Greeks, who worshiped beauty, entwined religious observance with their athletic demonstrations in such a way that to define where one left off and the other began is difficult. The strong anthropomorphic (humanlike) conceptions of gods held by the Greeks led to their belief that the gods took pleasure in the same things that mortals enjoyed, such as music, drama, and displays of physical excellence. The gymnasia located in every city-state for all male adults (females were not allowed in the Greek gymnasia) provided facilities and places for sports training as well as for the discussion of intellectual topics. Furthermore, facilities for religious worship, an altar and a chapel, were located in the center of each gymnasium.

The Olympic Games, the most important athletic meetings of the Greeks, were part of religious festivals. They were sacred contests, staged in a sacred location and as a sacred festival; they were a religious act in honor of Zeus, king of the gods. Athletes who took part in the Olympics did so in order to please Zeus and the prizes they won came from him. Other Pan-Hellenic games were equally religious in nature. Victorious athletes presented their gifts of thanks upon the altar of the god or gods whom they thought to be responsible for their victory. The end of the ancient Olympic Games was a result of the religious conviction of Theodosius, the Roman emperor of A.D. 392–395. He was a Christian and decreed the end of the Games as part of his suppression of paganism in favor of Christianity.[6]

The Early Christian Church

In Western societies, religious support for sport found no counterpart to that of the Greeks until the beginning of the twentieth century. The Christian religion was dominated by the Roman Catholic Church until the Reformation in the sixteenth century. Since then, Roman Catholicism has shared religious power with Protestant groups. At first Christians opposed Roman sport spectacles such as chariot racing and gladiatorial combat because of their paganism and brutality, but later Christians opposed sport because they came to regard the body as an instrument of sin.

The early Christians did not view sports as evil per se, for the Apostle Paul wrote approvingly of the benefits of physical activity. He said, for example, "Do you not know that those who run in a race, all indeed run, but one receives the prize? So run as to obtain it" (1 Cor. 9:24). In another place, Paul reminded Timothy of the importance of adhering to the rules: "One who enters a contest is not crowned unless he has competed according to the rules" (2 Tim. 2:5).

The paganism prominent in the Roman sports events, however, was abhorrent to the Christians. Moreover, early Christianity gradually built a foundation based on asceticism, which is a belief that evil exists in the body and that therefore the body should be subordinate to the pure spirit. As a result, church dogma and education sought to subordinate all desires and demands of the body in order to exalt the spiritual life. Twelfth-century Catholic abbot, Saint Bernard, argued: "Always in a robust and active body the mind lies soft and more lukewarm; and, on the other hand, the spirit flourishes more strongly and more actively in an infirm and weakly body." Nothing could have been more damning for the promotion of active recreation and sport.

Reformation and Protestantism in the North American Colonies

The Reformation of the early sixteenth century signaled the end of the viselike grip that Roman Catholicism had on the minds and habits of the people of Europe and England. But Protestantism had within it the seeds of a new asceticism, and in its Puritan form, became a greater enemy to sport than Roman Catholicism had been.

Puritans were among the earliest English immigrants to America, and they had considerable influence on the social life in the colonies. Perhaps no Christian group exercised a greater opposition to sport than the Puritans. As a means of realizing amusement and unrestrained impulses, sport was suspect for the Puritan; one historian asserted that "Puritans' opposition to sport was grounded on at least seven propositions: sport was frivolous and wasted time; sport did not refresh the body as good recreation should, but tired people instead; much sporting activity was designed deliberately to inflict pain or injury; sporting contests usually led to gambling; more sport took place on Sunday than on any other day, so sport encouraged people to defile the Sabbath; sport was noisy and disrupted others, sometimes entire communities; and many sports had either pagan or 'Popish' origins."[7] The renowned nineteenth-century English historian Thomas B. Macaulay claimed that the Puritans opposed bearbaiting (tying a bear to a stake and urging dogs to attack it) not so much because it was painful for the bear but because it gave pleasure to the spectators.

The Puritans of New England were not the only colonists who had compunctions about sports. Most of the colonies passed laws against play and sport on the Sabbath. Like the Puritans, the most prominent objection to sport by religious leaders in the other colonies was that participation would divert attention from spiritual matters. The practical matter was that survival in the New World required hard work from everyone; thus, time spent in play and games was typically considered time wasted. Finally, the associations formed and the environment in which play and sport occurred conspired to cast these activities in a bad light. The tavern was the center for gambling and table sports, dancing had obvious sexual overtones, and field sports often involved gambling and cruelty to animals.[8]

Religious Objections to Sport Declined in the Nineteenth Century

Church opposition to leisure pursuits was firmly maintained in the first few decades of the nineteenth century, and each effort to liberalize attitudes toward leisure pursuits was met with a new attack on sport as "sinful." Sports were still widely regarded by the powerful Protestant religious groups as snares of the devil himself. However, in the 1830s social problems became prominent concerns of American social reformers, many of whom were clergy and intellectual leaders. There were crusades against slavery, intemperance, and poor industrial working conditions; widespread support for the emancipation of women, for public education, and for industrial reform; and indeed, scrutiny of every facet of American life.

Social conditions had begun to change rapidly under the aegis of industrialization. The physical health of the population became a major issue leading a number of reformers to propose that people would be happier, more productive, and healthier if they engaged in vigorous sports activities. Surprisingly, some of the leading advocates of play and sport were clerics who began to soften their attitude toward play and sport. Although the development of a more liberal attitude by church leaders toward sport began to appear by the mid-nineteenth century, not all church authorities subscribed to the trend. A staid Congregationalist magazine, the *New Englander,* vigorously attacked sport:

> Let our readers, one and all, remember that we were sent into this world, not for sport and amusement, but for labor; not to enjoy and please ourselves, but to serve and glorify God, and be useful to our fellow men. That is the great object and end in life. In pursuing this end, God has indeed permitted us all needful diversion and recreation. . . . But the great end of life after all is work. . . . It is a true saying. . . . "We come into this world, not for sports." We were sent here for a higher and nobler object.[9]

Although some church leaders fought the encroaching sport and leisure mania throughout the late nineteenth century, many gradually began to reconcile play and religion in response to pressure from medical, educational, and political leaders for games and sport. Increasingly, churches broadened their commitment to play and sport endeavors as a means of drawing people together. Bowling leagues, softball leagues, and youth groups, such as the Catholic Youth Organization (CYO), were sponsored by churches for their young members. The church's prejudice against pleasure through play had broken down almost completely by the beginning of the twentieth century.

Religion and Sport Conciliation

Churches were confronted with ever-increasing changes in the twentieth century; economic pressures, political movements, and social conditions were the chief forces responsible for the drastically changed relationship between religion and sport. Increased industrialization turned the population into a nation of urban dwellers, and higher wages were responsible for an unprecedented affluence. The gospel of work (the Protestant work ethic) became less credible, and increased leisure enhanced the popularity of a new professional sports industry. However, in *Muscular Christianity: Evangelical Protestants and the Development of American Sport,* the authors—one a kinesiologist and the other a sociologist—argue that with the tumultuous social and economic transformations taking place in the first half of the twentieth century, evangelical muscular Christians began a disengagement from sport. They say, "Evangelical muscular Christians, who had earlier embraced sport to accomplish God's redemptive purposes, now found themselves trapped by the values and structures of an institution rapidly moving in a different direction."[10]

This trend gradually dissipated and the story of changes in the attitudes of religionists in the latter twentieth and early twenty-first centuries was largely one of increasing accommodation. Much of both Catholic and Protestant North America came to view sport as a positive force and even as a useful means of promoting God's work. Sports and leisure activities became an increasingly conspicuous part of the recreation programs of thousands of churches and many church colleges, a trend that one sociologist called the "basketballization" of churches. Shirl Hoffman elaborates, suggesting that sport has "captured the imagination of modern evangelical churches. No forward-looking church will overlook the value of sport as an adjunct to its social programs, and no architect will overlook the opportunity to include at least one gymnasium in first drafts for a new church."[11]

Clergy of many religions and denominations who over the centuries preached that sport is a handmaiden of the devil must be shifting uneasily in their graves at trends of the past half century. Times have certainly changed the church as well, and the conciliation between sport and organized religion has approached finality.

SPORT AS RELIGION

Sport has taken on so many of the characteristics of religion that some have argued that sport has emerged as a new religion, supplementing, and in some cases even supplanting, traditional religious expressions. A noted Catholic theologian claims that "sports are religious in the sense that they are organized institutions, disciplines, and liturgies; and also in the sense that they teach religious qualities of heart and soul. In particular, they recreate symbols of cosmic struggle, in which human survival and moral courage are not assured. To this extent, they are not mere games, diversions, pastimes. . . . Sports, in a word, are a form of godliness."[12]

A professor in the religious studies program at Pennsylvania State University is even more emphatic on this point: "For me, it is not just a parallel that is emerging between sport and religion, but rather *a complete identity. Sport is religion* for growing numbers of Americans, and this is no product of simply facile reasoning or wishful thinking. Further, for many, sport religion has become a more appropriate expression of personal religiosity than Christianity, Judaism, or any of the traditional religions. . . . It is reasonable to consider sport the newest and fastest growing religion, far outdistancing whatever is in second."[13]

For Tom Faulkner, a professor of comparative religion at Dalhousie University in Halifax, Nova Scotia, it is not sport in general that is a religion. Instead, for him it is Canadian ice hockey that is a religion. Faulkner focuses on ice hockey in Canada, and poses the question, "What if being a hockey fan or player is a way of being religious?" He uses a sociological model for religion to analyze whether it sheds light on the human phenomenon of ice hockey. He concludes his analysis by saying, "There is considerable evidence here to support the view that when one becomes a hockey fan or player, one is doing more than 'merely' taking up a game or an entertainment. There is a sense in which one is justified in speaking of hockey as a religion."[14]

Avery Brundage, an American who for twenty years was president of the International Olympic Committee, claimed that the Olympic movement itself was a religion: "The Olympic Movement is a Twentieth Century religion, a religion with universal appeal which incorporates all the basic values of other religions, a modern, exciting, virile, dynamic religion. . . . It is a religion for which Pierre de Coubertin was the prophet, for Coubertin has kindled a torch that will enlighten the world."[15]

There is no doubt that organized sport has taken on the trappings of religion. A few examples will illustrate this point:

- Every religion has its god or gods (or saints or high priests) who are venerated by its members. Likewise, sports fans have gods (superstar athletes) they worship.
- Christianity has its saints, and other religions have religious models they admire and worship. Sports fans also have their saints—those who have passed to the great beyond (such as Jim Thorpe, Knute Rockne, Tim Horton, and Babe Didrikson Zaharias).
- Religion has priests and clergy. The high priests of contemporary sport are the professional, collegiate, and national amateur team coaches who not only direct the destinies of their athletes but also control the emotions of large masses of sports fans.
- Religion has scribes who record the word of God. Sport also has its scribes, the sport journalists and sportscasters who disseminate the "word" of sports deeds and glories.
- Religion has it churches, synagogues, mosques, temples. Sport has its houses of worship, such as Yankee Stadium and Soldier Field.
- Religion has its congregations. Sport has its masses of highly vocal "true believers."
- Religion has its proverbs that express the "true" word of God. Numerous proverbs fill the world of sport: "Nice guys finish last." "When the going gets tough, the tough get going." "*Lose* is a four-letter word." And so forth. In sports, these proverbs are frequently written on posters and hung in locker rooms for athletes to memorize.
- Religious shrines are commonplace wherever religion is found. They preserve sacred symbols and memorabilia that followers can admire and honor. The achievements of athletes and teams are celebrated in numerous shrines, called halls of fame, built to commemorate and glorify sporting figures. Halls of fame have been established for virtually every sport played in North America, and some sports have several halls of fame devoted to them.[16]
- Religions demand fidelity from their followers in the form of faithfulness to obligations, duties, and observances. Symbols of fidelity abound in sport. The athletes are expected to give total commitment to the cause, including abstinence from smoking, alcohol, and in some cases even sex.
- Religions require devotion to specific beliefs, traditions, and practices. Devout followers of sports witness and invoke traditional and hallowed chants and show their devotion to the team by adding "spirit" to its cause. In cheering for the Green Bay Packers, New York Yankees, or Montreal Canadians, devoted fans can experience feelings of belonging to a "congregation." It is not unusual for these sports pilgrims to travel hundreds of miles, sometimes braving terrible weather conditions, to witness a sports event, thus displaying their devotion to their team.
- Religions sponsor a variety of holidays and festivals that function to promote communal involvement, thus nurturing a sense of belonging to the religious community. The Super Bowl functions as a major sporting festival for American culture, seeming to unite the entire nation with its pageantry and sporting extravaganza.

Two popular motion pictures, *Field of Dreams* and *Bull Durham,* used numerous religious themes and symbols suggesting baseball-as-religion. They do not claim that baseball is a religion in a traditional theological way, but they do suggest a symbiosis (an intimate association or close union) between the two. *Bull Durham* reveals how baseball exemplifies the qualities of an institutional religion. The movie opens with gospel music in the background and the female lead, Annie, delivering this prologue: "I believe in the church of baseball. I've tried all the major religions and most of the minor ones. . . . I gave Jesus a chance, but it just didn't work out between us. The Lord laid too much guilt on me. . . . There's no guilt in baseball, and it's never boring. . . . The only church that truly feeds the soul, day in and day out, is the church of baseball."

Field of Dreams makes clear its baseball-as-religion point of view. In the basic plot a supernatural voice of revelation tells a young farmer and baseball fanatic to plow up part of his cornfield and build a baseball field. The farmer does this, and soon baseball players from the past are playing on the baseball diamond, like saints from a land beyond the first rows of the cornfield. After the farmer has made a pilgrimage and faced his need for forgiveness, he is miraculously reconciled with his long-dead baseball-player father. At the end of the movie, the farmer's baseball field is a shrine that draws flocks of people seeking "the truth." The movie has many religious themes and symbols: life after death, a seeker who hears a voice and has to go on a spiritual quest, an inner healing, becoming a child in order to enter the kingdom, and losing your life to gain it.

In spite of the many seeming parallels between sport and religion, sport does not fulfill what are considered by many to be the key functions of "churchly" religion. For example, why humans are created and continue to wrestle with their purpose here on earth and life hereafter are not addressed by sports. In this regard, one social scientist noted: "In spite of the prominence and praise rendered them as forms of religion in the age of the Super Bowl, sports and play are not . . . even a natural religion but entirely different categories of human experience, beneficent in and of themselves if held in perspective. When they appear to take on the raiments of traditional religion, then heresy, we may conclude, is afoot in the land."[17]

Other critics of sport-as-religion also emphasize that many activities that humans become deeply committed to can be referred to as a religion, when speaking metaphorically, but if we include in religion all meaningful or spiritual activities, we then wind up including practically all activities into which humans pour their will, emotions, and energy. Although sport does have some religious-like symbols, rituals, legends, sacred spaces and time, and heroes, it is organized and played by humans for humans without supernatural sanction. So for James A. Mathisen, North American sport is what he calls a folk religion. He says, "Sports looks like a religion, but it is not one. It is sort of like civil religion, but not quite. The best conceptual response amid this uncertainty is to interpret American sport as a contemporary folk religion." By this he means there "is a combination of shared moral principles and behavioral customs. . . . a common set of ideas, rituals, and symbols . . . an overarching sense of unity." Joseph Price disagrees with Mathisen's comment about sport and civil religion. But for Price it is baseball, not sport in general, that is a civil religion. Price argues, "For true believers . . . the word of baseball is the gospel of an American civil religion that finds safety and wholeness—completion and salvation—where the game begins and where it ends: at home."[18] Religion from these perspectives is not the universalistic posture of the world's institutional religions.

RELIGION USES SPORT

Churches

From a position of strong opposition to recreation and sport activities, most religions have made a complete reversal within the past century and now heartily support these activities as effective tools to promote "the Lord's work." Social service is a major purpose of the religious leaders who provide play and recreation under the auspices of their churches. Church-sponsored recreation and sport programs offer services to members and sometimes the entire community that are often unavailable in acceptable forms anywhere else. Church playgrounds and recreation centers in urban areas have facilities, equipment, and instruction that municipal governments often cannot provide. The Young Men's Christian Association (YMCA), the Young Women's Christian Association (YWCA), the Catholic Youth Organization (CYO), and other church-related organizations perform a variety of social services for old and young alike, one of which is the sponsorship of sports leagues.

Promoting sport to strengthen and increase fellowship in their congregations has been beneficial to the churches as well as to their members. In a time of increasing secularization, such as that witnessed by the United States and Canada in the past fifty years, it is understandable that churches would accommodate activities that solidify and integrate church membership.

Religious Leaders

Not content merely to provide recreational and sports opportunities under the sponsorship of the church, some religious leaders outwardly avow the association between religion and sport in their preaching and use sport as a metaphor for the social enterprise of the church. Recently deceased Jerry Falwell, one of the self-styled leaders of fundamental Protestantism in the United States, told an audience: "He [Jesus] wants you to be a victor for God's glory. A champion is not an individual star but one of a team who knows how to function with others." Several of the most popular contemporary evangelists enthusiastically support the virtues of sports competition and the sanctity of Christian coaches and athletes. They have made sport a basic metaphor in their ministries. For them, the source of Christianity, the Bible, legitimates sport involvement, and they often claim that the Bible says leisure and lying around are morally dangerous for us. Sports keep us busy.

Church Colleges and Universities

Intercollegiate sports programs were originally organized and administered by the students for their own recreation and amusement. By the early years of the twentieth century, however, the programs gradually changed form and character, and one of the new features that emerged was the use of collegiate sports teams to publicize the school and to bind alumni to their alma mater. Church-supported colleges and universities began to use their athletic teams to attract students, funds, and public attention to impoverished (and sometimes academically inferior) institutions. The classic, but by no means only, example is Notre Dame; many other Roman Catholic colleges and universities also have used football and basketball for publicity. Basketball, especially, has become a popular sport for Catholic colleges; indeed, Catholic university teams have played in the NCAA basketball championship games several times.

Protestant institutions have followed the same pattern of using their athletic teams to advertise; Brigham Young University (BYU), Texas Christian University, and Southern Methodist University (SMU) are among the most visible. Of these, BYU has become a renowned athletic powerhouse. It meshes conservative religious tenets with big-time sports and produces some of the more prominent professional athletes in North America. One BYU All-American football player said that he believed the athletes bring more attention to the Mormon church than anything else, and when he enrolled at BYU, the president of the university told him: "Here's your chance to be a missionary for the church by playing football for us."[19]

Liberty University, founded by Jerry Falwell, has aggressively embraced big-time athletics to publicize the school and use the school as a means of carrying out its mission of preaching the gospel of Christ to the world. Since the founding of Liberty, Falwell stated he wanted to make Liberty University to born-again Christians what Notre Dame is to Catholics and Brigham Young University is to Mormons. "One day . . . I plan to be at the 50-yard line in South Bend when we whip Notre Dame," Falwell once asserted. To this end, he hired a former NFL coach to lead the football team. In his weekly newsletter, "Falwell Confidential," he typically included a paragraph or two about the achievements of Liberty University's sports teams. These paragraphs were headed with titles such as "A Rising Sports Power" and "A Burgeoning Athletic Powerhouse."[20] Although the Liberty University teams have not achieved the exalted status that Falwell aspired to, the university has gradually climbed to NCAA Division I status.

Ironically, it was a church college, Southern Methodist University, that was hit with the most severe penalty ever meted out by the NCAA, the so-called death penalty (abolishment of the football program for a period of time). The NCAA took this drastic action after those connected with the SMU football program continually lied, cheated, and generally violated NCAA rules.[21]

RELIGIOUS ORGANIZATIONS AND SPORTS

One of the most notable outgrowths of religion's use of sport has been the rise of nondenominational religious organizations composed of coaches and athletes. According to one estimate, some 80 organizations minister to the needs of athletes throughout the world; but it seems likely that there are many more than this, because there are more than twenty-five organizations of this type just in North America. These organizations provide a variety of programs designed to serve current members and recruit new members to religion. Several major incorporated organizations offer everything from national conferences to services before games. The best known are Fellowship of Christian Athletes (FCA), Sports Ambassadors, Athletes in Action (AIA), Pro Athletes Outreach (PAO), Motor Sports Ministries, Hockey Ministries International, and Baseball Chapel. The movement that these organizations represent has been labeled "Sportianity" or, more derisively, "Jocks for Jesus."[22]

The Fellowship of Christian Athletes

The prototypical organization for using sport as a tool for evangelism is the Fellowship of Christian Athletes, which was founded in 1954 with a focus on high school and college coaches and athletes and currently has a membership of 1.2 million athletes. Its avowed purpose, which appears on most of its publications and on the title page of each issue of the official magazine of the FCA, *Sharing the Victory*, is "to present to athletes and coaches, and all whom they influence, the challenge and adventure of receiving Jesus Christ as Savior and Lord, serving him in their relationship and in the fellowship of the Church." The FCA attempts to combat juvenile delinquency, elevate the moral and spiritual standards of sports in a secular culture, challenge athletes to stand up and be counted for or against God, and appeal to sports enthusiasts and youth through hero worship harnessed.

The FCA uses older athletes and coaches to recruit younger ones to Christianity. It has a mailing list of more than fifty-five thousand persons and a staff of over 650 nationwide. Its most important activity is the sponsorship of annual, week-long summer camps attended by more than thirteen thousand participants, where coaches and athletes mix religious and inspirational sessions with sport instruction and competition.

Another important facet of the FCA's work is the "huddle fellowship program," in which junior high, high school, and college athletes in a community or on a campus get together to talk about their faith, engage in Bible study, and pray. They also take part in projects such as becoming "big brothers" for delinquent or needy children, visiting nursing homes, and serving as playground instructors.

There are now some eight thousand high school and college huddles in North America, the bulk of which are found in the South, Southwest, and Midwest. Most of the members of the FCA are white, middle-class males; however, female athletes are admitted to the FCA, and their membership in the organization is growing. In addition to these activities, the FCA sponsors state and regional retreats and provides various informational materials such as films, records, and tapes.[23]

Religion and Professional Sports Organizations

Organizations that focus on specific athletic groups supplement the work of the FCA. The NFL and major baseball leagues sponsor chapels and Bible studies for their athletes. Baseball Chapel, an evangelical Christian ministry, provides Sunday services to teams throughout the major and minor leagues. In conjunction, many pro teams have a "God Squad," a group of teammates who pray together and make public appearances on behalf of the Christian cause.

Professional sport organizations have sponsored religious events. Several NBA teams have sponsored a God and Country Night for their fans, a mixing of basketball, church, and state that attempts to recognize the role faith and patriotism play in the lives of management, players, and fans associated with the NBA. The Cleveland Indians hosted a Catholic Family Day. "Faith Nights" began in minor league baseball parks in 2002; by 2006 over seventy Faith Nights were scheduled for minor league teams across the United States. Faith Days and Faith Nights began in MLB ballparks in 2006, and in 2007 they were held in ten MLB cities. A *New York Times* writer described these events: "Churches get discounted tickets to family-friendly evenings of music and sports with a Christian theme. And in return they mobilize their vast infrastructure of e-mail and phone lists, youth programs and chaperones, and of course their bus fleets, to help fill the stands."[24]

While these organizations and events have attracted the participation of many professional team franchises, athletes, coaches, and fans, not everyone is a fan of this practice, claiming that it signals the Christianization of pro sports. Some believe that making religion part of the spectacle of public sporting events risks trivializing God and alienating nonbelieving teammates and fans. Baseball Chapel proclaims on its website: "Our purpose is to glorify Jesus Christ." As one *USA Today* writer noted: "It is undoubtedly true that baseball, like the National Football League and National Basketball Association, has allowed itself to become a prime proselytizing vehicle for the evangelical sports ministries. No similar privilege is enjoyed by other religious movements." He continues, "major league sports do not exist for the chief purpose of promoting Christianity."[25]

Sport and Religion Publications

Several of the religious organizations identified in this chapter publish magazines or newsletters, but one publication with a focus on sport and religion but no affiliation with any specific religious organization is *Sports Spectrum*. *Sports Spectrum* is not an institutionalized evangelical organization but is, instead, a Christianized version of *Sports Illustrated*. According to its mission statement, it "seeks to highlight Christian athletes of all sports and levels to help motivate, encourage and inspire people in their faith through the exciting and challenging world of sports." Each issue covers a wide variety of sports, interviews with top athletes, and articles about top Christian athletes. Its website home page claims that *"Sports Spectrum* magazine gives you all the sports stuff you need with the values you want. . . . It is indeed the No. 1 Christian magazine for sports."[26]

Missionary Work of Churches and Sport

Religious leaders have increasingly used sport as a drawing card for attracting new members and retaining their followers. An often-used slogan of the clergy nicely sums up their view: "Many a one who comes to play remains to pray." Getting persons into church recreation and sports programs is often viewed as a first step into the church and into religious life. Playgrounds and recreation centers in or near churches, and the supervision of these facilities by clergy or laypersons with a strong religious commitment, provide a convenient setting for converting the nonchurchgoing participant. A great deal of informal but successful missionary work is done in these settings. Famous sports figures make effective missionaries because of their prominence and prestige, and virtually every religious group has used coaches and athletes as evangelists to recruit new members.

There are several dozen ministry groups within North America working with international religious groups to mobilize massive recruiting efforts at the site of each Olympic Games. They use the Olympic Games, the most prestigious sporting event in the world—and an event that attracts people from all over the world—as a venue for recruiting people. They sponsor World Congresses on Sport prior to every Olympic Games.

Religious Evangelizing by Athletes and Coaches

Of all the purposes or consequences, or both, of religion's association with sport, certainly one of the most important is the use of athletes, coaches, and the sports environment to recruit new members to the church. Evangelical athletes who have made a personal commitment to religion accept the responsibility of witnessing their faith to others. As a result, the practice of athletes and coaches serving as lay evangelists is so widespread that it has been called a modern crusade.

One of the best known of the sport missionary groups is AIA, a ministry of Campus Crusade for Christ, made up mostly of former collegiate athletes. Its mission is to build "spiritual movements everywhere through the platform of sport. . . . AIA staff reach athletic influencers for Christ and train them to talk about the Lord one-on-one, with the media, and in other public forums to help fulfill the great commission."[27] With a special dispensation from the NCAA, the AIA fields several athletic teams that compete against amateur teams throughout the world each year. As part of each appearance of an AIA team, the AIA athletes make brief evangelical speeches and testimonials to the crowds and distribute free religious materials.

One major advantage of using athletes to evangelize is access. They interact closely and for prolonged periods of time with other athletes, and because they are widely admired, they are warmly welcomed by the general public. The missionary techniques of athletes are fairly straightforward. Those who are already committed to religion convert others. Because athletes are among the most visible and prestigious persons in North America, they may be used for missionary work in spreading their religion not only to their teammates but to anyone with whom they come in contact. Religious witnessing among athletes is tolerated and has become rather common in sports in the past two decades.[28]

Combining their popular appeal as celebrities with the metaphors of the sports world, athletes are able to catch and hold the attention of large groups of people. A high-profile athlete who understands the basics of his/her faith can reach more people, and especially young people, than a typical priest or minister can ever hope to reach. As one researcher noted, "as a mode of evangelism, sport has few rivals in modern religious history. Sports fans who wouldn't dream of visiting church to hear the eloquent sermons of a seminarian will listen patiently to an athlete's stammering tribute to God, guts, and glory."[29]

The Promise Keepers: Sportianity, Gender, and Sexuality

In 1990 Bill McCartney, the University of Colorado football coach and a dedicated evangelical Christian, started the Promise Keepers as a fundamentalist Christian movement whose main goal is to evangelize men. It became one of the country's fastest-growing religious movements. The first event in Boulder, Colorado, in 1990 attracted 70 people; by 1996 over a dozen conferences were held nationwide, with between 20,000 and 75,000 in attendance at each. In the fall of 1997, an estimated 600,000 people attended a Promise Keepers "Stand in the Gap" rally on the Mall in Washington, D.C. The size, shape, and focus of Promise Keepers conferences have changed over the years. Currently, they have fewer conferences and fewer big-name speakers and are held in smaller venues.

The central philosophical message of the Promise Keepers is that God commanded that men be dominant, the head of the family, and reclaim their leadership in the family and in the community, thus becoming better men of God. The traditional patriarchical gender role, with men as the family leader, is said to be dictated by God. Its founder, Bill McCartney, said, "It's always been mandated by God that the spiritual leaders be men. It's always been God's heart that men would set the tone. . . . We are bonded. We are men of God." Tony Evans, one of the leading figures in the Promise Keepers, summarized the logic of the Promise Keepers in this way: "Don't you understand, mister, you are royalty and God has chosen you to be priest of your home."[30]

A central theme of this male-only movement is that current social problems, especially what Promise Keepers consider the moral depravity and confusion over appropriate female and male social roles in our society, are caused by a lack of appropriate male leadership. The result has been a feminization of the American male that has produced a nation of sissified men who abdicate their role as spiritually pure leaders, thus requiring women to fill the vacuum. The Promise Keepers' solution is the promotion of a traditional masculinity, with men taking the leadership roles and women accommodating to supporting roles. In line with traditional masculine/feminine role definitions, the Promise Keepers share the position of religious fundamentalist Protestants and the Catholic Church that homosexuality violates God's creative design for males and females. McCartney publicly denounced homosexuality as "an abomination of almighty God."

For women and men who have been struggling against traditional patriarchy and gender-specific social roles in contemporary society, groups like Promise Keepers seem to be a threat to the progress that has been made in recent decades. A number of women's organizations have been highly critical of the Promise Keepers, complaining that the organization preaches a subservient role for wives and, more broadly, assigns second-class citizenship to all females, a condition that women have lived with for generations. Gay and lesbian groups have expressed dismay at what they feel is a classic example of old-fashioned homophobic rhetoric.

The connections of the Promise Keepers to sport are described by two University of the Pacific professors: "Although this group does not engage in sport or directly promote sport as an important part of its movement, it has used sport symbolically to communicate the ideologies of the organization. Sport venues become religious settings, sport rituals are converted into religious ones, sport heroes are revered as saints and moral exemplars, and sport metaphors are means for communicating key truths and desirable character traits."[31]

The Promise Keepers and sports intersect in a common vision of traditional male dominance and leadership. Sports culture has long been the site of male domination and the main source for defining appropriate masculine attitudes, values, and behaviors. As sport sociologist Becky Beal explains, "The Promise Keepers' use of sport examples, images, and metaphors provides powerful cultural symbols to rally men's support, under the assumption of males' rightful place as leader in society."[32]

Sportianity Confronting Social Issues

There is little inclination on the part of religious leaders and the various organizations that make up Sportianity to confront the pressing social issues of sport or of the larger society. Virtually all of the leaders in the Sportianity movement are reluctant to take a stand on moral issues within sports. In reviewing the numerous publications circulated by the organizations involved in Sportianity, one thing stands out rather glaringly, namely that there is little in the way of thoughtful critique of the culture of sport or little direct effort being channeled into improving the morality of sports.

There is no noticeable social reform movement on the part of the Sportianity movement. The various organizations and their members have not taken forceful or prominent stands against or been at the forefront against racism, sexism, cheating, violence, the evils of collegiate athletic recruiting, or any of the other well-known unethical practices, excesses, and abuses in the world of sport, with the exception of exhortations about refraining from drugs. Instead, the pervasive theme is "stick with the positive; don't deal with the problems in sports." The impression is "don't stir the waters. Just publicize the good story about the good ole boy who does good things."

One reason for this posture is articulated by Hoffman:

> Sport faith organizations need access to sport and sport personalities, and those in the movement know that this could easily vanish if the sport establishment were alienated by suggestions that Christian athletes apply the ethical tenets of their faith to their sporting experiences. Thus, the partnership assures that the sport industry will continue to provide access to athletes, just as religious organizations assure that such thorny theological standards as captured in the Sermon on the Mount or in the Golden Rule will not be strenuously applied to sport. Ironically, the compact guarantees that sport will remain largely shielded from the effects of the religious message it so effectively promotes. . . . Moreover,

where religion has touched sport, it hasn't been to ennoble it, but to appropriate it in the interest of a "higher fanaticism."[33]

In the final analysis, then, sports morality does not appear to have been improved by the Sportianity movement. Instead, Sportianity seems willing to accept sport as is and seems more devoted to recruiting new members and publicizing the achievements of athletes and coaches who publicly avow their religion than to dealing with sports as a social practice with many of the same problems of the larger society that need attention and resolution.

VALUE ORIENTATIONS OF RELIGION AND SPORT

Value orientations underlying competitive sports in North America may appear only remotely connected with religion, but most values that are central to sports are more or less secularized versions of the core values of Protestantism, which has been a dominant religious belief system throughout American and Canadian history.

The Protestant Ethic and Sports

The classic treatise of the Protestant ethic and its relationship to other spheres of social life is Max Weber's *The Protestant Ethic and the Spirit of Capitalism,* originally published near the beginning of the twentieth century.[34] The essence of Weber's thesis is that there is a parallel relationship between the Calvinist doctrine of Protestantism as a theological belief system and the growth of capitalism as a mode of economic organization. Weber suggested the relationship between Protestantism and capitalism was one of mutual influence; he used the term *elective affinity* (one of his translators used the word *correlation* in place of *elective affinity*).

The relationship exists in this way: For John Calvin, God could foresee and therefore know the future; thus, the future was predestined. In a world whose future was foreordained, the fate of every person was preestablished. Each person was, then, saved or doomed from birth by a kind of divine decree; nothing the individual did could change what God had done. Although each person's fate was sealed, the individual was plagued by "salvation anxiety" and craved some visible sign of his or her fate; and since Calvin taught that those elected by God acted in a godly manner, the elected could exhibit their salvation by glorifying God, especially by their work in this world.

According to Weber, "the only way of living acceptably to God . . . was through the fulfillment of obligations imposed upon the individual by . . . his calling." Thus, the best available sign of being among the chosen was to do one's job, to follow one's profession, to succeed in one's chosen career. According to Weber, "In practice this means that God helps those who help themselves." Work per se was exalted; indeed, it was sacred. The clearest manifestation of being chosen by God was success in one's work. Whoever enjoyed grace could not fail since success at work was visible evidence of election. Thus, successful persons could think of themselves, and be thought of by others, as the righteous persons. The upshot was that this produced an extreme drive toward individual achievement, resulting in what Weber called "ascetic Protestantism," a life of strict discipline and hard work as the best means of glorifying God.[35]

Although the Protestant ethic gave divine sanction to the drive to excel and encouraged success in business, industry, and science, it condemned the material enjoyment of success. The chosen person merely used success to document salvation. Persons who used success for personal gratification and luxury merely showed that they were doomed by God. To avoid the accumulation of vast personal wealth, Calvinism promoted the reinvestment of profits to produce more goods, which created more profits and, in turn, represented more capital for investment ad infinitum, the essence of entrepreneurial capitalism.

Weber's study of the relationship between religious beliefs and capitalism investigated the religious principles that provided a rationale for the ideology of capitalism and for the authority of the capitalist. The spirit of capitalism, according to

Weber, consisted of several principles, each of which was compatible with Protestant principles. Collectively, they constituted a clear, elective affinity (correlation) between Calvinist Protestantism and the spirit of capitalism. Weber made it quite clear that he was not suggesting that one social process was a causal agent for the other. In his final paragraph, he said: "It is . . . not my aim to substitute for a one-sided materialistic an equally one-sided spiritualistic causal interpretation of culture and history."[36]

What does this have to do with sport? It is rather obvious that Weber's notion about the relationship between the Protestant ethic and the spirit of capitalism can be applied to the "spirit" of sport. In a book-length essay titled *The Influence of the Protestant Ethic on Sport and Recreation*, Steven Overman undertook to examine "the forms, values, meanings, and spirit of American sport and recreation within the context of secular Protestant culture." He argues that "American sport reveals the legacy of Protestantism. The Protestant ethic transformed sports into a medium in which individuals proved themselves through hard work and by the applications of scientific training. . . . What I am proposing is that the Protestant ethic has instilled American sport with a spirit, an *ethos*, which provides its distinct character, meaning, and guiding beliefs."[37]

Anyone familiar with contemporary sports and the Protestant ethic cannot overlook the unmistakable link between them (a correspondence also exists between capitalistic ideology and modern sports, but that will not be examined here). The emergence of sport as a pervasive feature of North American life undoubtedly owes its development to various social forces, one of which may be Protestant Christianity, the value orientations of which form the basis of the fundamental doctrine of the North American sport ideology. This ideology suggests that persons involved with sports, especially coaches and athletes, adhere to a particular kind of ideology, the overriding orientation of which is individual achievement through competition. The phrase *ideology of sport* is a generic designation for all ideas espoused by or for those who participate in and exercise authority in sports as they seek to explain and justify their beliefs.

If we place the values inherent in the Protestant ethic and the ideology of sport side by side, it immediately becomes apparent that the two are congruent; that is, they share a significant equivalence. Without attempting to claim a causal link between the two belief systems, it does seem possible to suggest an elective affinity between them. Success, self-discipline, and hard work, the original tenets of the Protestant ethic, are the most highly valued qualities in sport.

Success

The Protestant stress on successful, individual achievement is in keeping with the values of contemporary sport. The characteristics of the good Christian are also those needed by the successful athlete. The social climate of organized sport is competitive, with an overriding sense of wins and losses. The notion that achievement separates the chosen from the doomed is seen in the winning-is-everything ideology in sports. Winners are the good people; personal worth is equated with winning. The loser is obviously not one of God's chosen people; failure in one's occupation stamps the Protestant-ethic believer as doomed to hell.

The Protestant ethic re-created in sport was captured by one scholar: "Christians play their games for fun, but more important than fun is the responsibility to play them well and, of course, to win." Elaborating on this point, he continued:

> Anyone close to the sports scene knows that competition, even between the most amicable opponents, often becomes a rite of unholy unction, a sacrament, in which aggression is vented, old scores settled, number one taken care of, and where the discourteous act looms as the principal liturgical device. Even in contests played in the shadow of church walls—the church league softball or basketball game—tempers can flare and the spiritual graces of compassion and sensitivity can place second to winning one for "good ole First Baptist."[38]

One self-described "Christian athlete" told a researcher studying values in sports that to be successful in sports "you've got to be downright mean sometimes, and . . . you've got to beat your opponent up to do well." The researcher found that "the majority of the Christian athletes he studied did *not* appear to "have any conflict between the values of their Christian faith and the values of their sporting practices."[39]

The importance of winning is legitimized by implying that Christ himself would do whatever it takes to win. As one Major League Baseball player who was a member of Baseball Chapel said, "If Jesus Christ was sliding into second base, he would knock the second baseman into left field to break up a double play."[40]

Religious groups that use athletes to evangelize and persuade potential converts to religion recognize the importance of selecting athletes who are winners. They know quite well that evangelical appeals by chronic losers or bench sitters are not likely to be effective. As one member of an Athletes in Action team put it, "We have to win. That's what the world looks at. The world won't listen to our message if we are losers." This is true. Winning is critical to evangelical work. To the similar values of Protestantism and sports can be added American societal values. Another AIA player noted: "It's important for us to win, not because God wants winners, but because Americans do."[41]

Although the quest, even the obsession, for victory in sport is congruent with the Calvinistic view as it is manifested in the Protestant ethic, the theology of Christianity contains a worldview that places the unmitigated quest for winning in question. To the question What Would Jesus Do? on the baseball field, Frank Deford, a Hall of Fame member of the National Association of Sportscasters and Sportswriters, describes the sports ideal of Hall of Fame Major League Baseball pitcher Christy Mathewson, a practicing "muscular Christian," in this way: "[Y]oung Christian men didn't have to be wimps. They won games, but they won them only in Jesus' image, playing by the rules."[42]

Self-Discipline

The notion that dedication, self-discipline, and sports participation may be an occupational calling is central to the ideology of Sportianity. God is glorified best, so the thinking goes, when athletes give totally of themselves in striving for success and victory. This is manifested in the traditional Christian asceticism that emphasizes sacrifice, control, and self-discipline as relevant means to salvation. Christian athletes frequently describe their self-discipline and commitment in terms of not wanting to disappoint Jesus by giving anything less than a total effort with the talents they have been given by God. The greatest self-discipline challenge for the Christian athlete is to maintain the desire to win without compromising his or her faith, to maintain competitive enthusiasm with just the right amount of spiritual grace, in order to create the requisite competitive disposition without diminishing their Christian witness. The eternal quest of Christian athletes seems to be to attain spiritual control over their competitive attitudes while being careful not to be overly controlled and thus ineffective as a competitor.

Hard Work

Just as the businessperson is responsible to God to develop his or her talents to the fullest, according to the Protestant ethic, so is the athlete equally responsible. If God has granted one athletic abilities, then one is obligated to use those abilities to glorify and honor God; anything less than total dedication to the task is insufficient. A major league pitcher echoed this sentiment, saying that he had a responsibility for the talent he had been given, and that on the days when he didn't give his best, God should be upset with him.

Firmly embedded in the North American sport culture is a belief that hard work, training, and unremitting dedication by athletes and coaches not only will lead to success but are ways of using God-given abilities to glorify God, an important Protestant requirement. Sport culture is replete with slogans touting the necessity for hard work: "Workers are winners." "The harder you work, the luckier you get." "Winning is 99 percent perspiration and 1 percent inspiration." A favorite exhortation of coaches during practices is "Work, work, work!" And the highest praise a coach can give an athlete is to say that she or he "has a good work ethic."

Success can be considered as the justly deserved reward of a person's purposeful, self-denying, God-guided hard work. Giving less than 100 percent is regarded by some Christian athletes as a direct violation of God's law. A player selected for *USA Today*'s high school All-USA team said: "I have been blessed by God with a lot of ability. My motivation [for working hard] is to use tools that God gave me for His glory."[43]

Protestantism and Contemporary Sport

Any belief system that can help provide athletes and coaches with a rationale for their deep commitment to sports provides a means of expressing the essence of their striving, and Protestant theology does just that. In short, it is a belief system to which athletes and coaches can hold an elective affinity. Whether they actually do hold such an elective affinity remains a matter of speculation. Moreover, we hasten to add that Protestantism certainly is not responsible for the creation of the sport culture, but it does provide religious reinforcement for it.

Perhaps it is not coincidental that the belief systems of fundamentalist Protestantism and modern sports are so congruent. The two institutions use similar means to respond to their members' needs. Each tries to enforce and maintain, through a strict code of behavior and ritual, a strict belief system that is typically adopted and internalized by most involved. Each performs cohesive, integrative, and social control functions for its members, giving them meaningful ways to organize their world. Both religion and sport, because of the sacredness nurtured by these systems, resist social change and, in this way, support traditional values and practices.

SPORT USES RELIGION

Religious observances and competitive sports constantly impinge on each other, and religious practices of various kinds are found wherever one finds sports. Religion can be viewed from one point of view as an important means of coping with situations of stress. There are several categories of stress situations. One of these comprises situations in which largely uncontrolled and unpredictable forces may imperil the vital personal and social concerns of an individual or group. Sports competition falls into this category of stress because competition involves a great deal of uncertainty about a typically important outcome—winning and losing a sports event.

Coaches and athletes have great respect for the technical knowledge, skills, tactics, and strategy required for successful sports performance, but they are also aware of their limitations. As a supplement to the practical techniques, sports participants often employ religious practices. Coaches and athletes do not believe that these practices make up for their lack of technical knowledge, failure to acquire necessary skills, or employment of appropriate strategy. However, religious practices help them adjust to stress by providing opportunities for them to dramatize their anxieties, thus reinforcing their self-confidence. Religion invokes a sense of "doing something about it" in uncertain undertakings where practical knowledge and techniques alone cannot guarantee success. One of the most noted twentieth-century anthropologists, Bronislaw Malinowski, concluded from his research that when the outcome of vital social activities is greatly uncertain, magico-religious or other comparable techniques are inevitably used as a means of allaying tension and promoting adjustment.[44]

The Use of Prayer and Divine Intervention

Prayer is perhaps the most frequently employed use of religion by coaches and athletes; prayer for protection in competition, prayer for good performance, and prayer for victory are three examples. Sometimes the act of prayer is observed in gestures, such as a Roman Catholic basketball player crossing himself or herself before shooting a free throw or an athlete pointing an index finger skyward, or a football team praying in the huddle before or after a game. One researcher who studied

Tennessee Titans and New Orleans Saints players gather for a prayer at midfield after their game. (AP Photo/Ann Heisenfelt)

what he called "Born-Again Sport" said, "most born-again athletes use prayer to influence God to help their team win or to help them perform well."[45]

The first historical example of prayer and the direct intervention of gods in sports competition is described by Homer in the *Iliad*. During the funeral games held in honor of Patroclus, who was killed in battle, one of the events was a footrace in which three men competed. Ajax took the lead from the start, followed closely by Odysseus: "Thus Odysseus ran close behind him and trod in his footsteps before the dust could settle in them, and on the head of Ajax fell the breath of the godlike hero running lightly and relentlessly on." As they neared the finish line, Odysseus prayed for divine assistance, and his prayer was answered by Athena, who not only inspired him to make a last-minute dash but caused Ajax to slip and fall in a mass of cow dung, and Odysseus won the race. Ajax received an ox as second prize: "He stood holding the horns of the ox and spitting out dung, and exclaimed: 'Curse it, that goddess tripped me up. She always stands by Odysseus like a mother and helps him.'"[46]

Very little is known about the actual extent to which individual athletes use prayer in conjunction with their participation, but it seems probable that if some athletes are seen praying, others are doing so without outward, observable signs. Coaches often arrange to have religious services on the Sabbath or on game days. At present, almost every professional Major League Baseball and football team—more than fifty of them—hold Sunday chapel services, at home and away, and Sunday services are also held in sports as varied as

NASCAR racing and golf. One of the claims for these religious services and prayers is that it strengthens a group's sense of its own identity, provides unity, and accentuates its "we" feeling.

There are probably other reasons why coaches sanction locker-room prayers. Observers who suspect that locker-room prayers are about coaches' only concession to religion imply that one coach does it because the other coaches are doing it, and "you can't let them get the edge." Others have suggested that it may be only a sweaty-palmed response to the anxieties and uncertainties of competition, a way to seek help in those gut-wrenching moments before a big game. In *The Prince of Tides*, author Pat Conroy relates the events in one high school locker room before a football game. Although the book is a novel and the locker room is therefore fictitious, the situation as Conroy relates it seems very close to the reality many athletes have experienced in real-life locker rooms.

The coach began to speak:

> "Tonight I'm gonna learn and the town's gonna learn who my hitters are. All you've proved so far is that you know how to put on pads and get dates to the sock hop after the game, but until I see you in action, I won't know if you're hitters or not. Real hitters. Now a real hitter is a headhunter who puts his head in the chest of his opponent and ain't happy if his opponent is still breathing after the play. A real hitter doesn't know what fear is except when he sees it in the eyes of a ball carrier he's about to split in half. A real hitter loves pain, loves the screaming and the sweating and the brawling and the hatred of life down in the trenches. He likes to be at the spot where the blood flows and the teeth get kicked out. That's what this sport's all about, men. It's war, pure and simple. Now tonight, you go out there and kick butt all over that field. If something moves, hit it. If something breathes, hit it. . . .
>
> "Now do I have me some hitters?" he screamed, veins throbbing along his temple.
>
> "Yes, sir," we screamed back. . . .
>
> "Do I have me some goddamn headhunters?"
>
> "Yes, sir."
>
> "Am I going to see blood?"
>
> "Yes, sir."
>
> "Am I going to see their guts hanging off your helmets?"
>
> "Yes, sir."
>
> "Am I going to hear their bones breaking all over the field?"
>
> "Yes, sir," we happy hitters cried aloud. "Let us pray," he said.
>
> He led the team in the recitation of the Lord's Prayer.[47]

This seems to epitomize what many coaches have been accused of—treating religion as group bonding that has little, if anything, to do with genuine heartfelt religious faith.

Although there is little empirical work on the use of prayer by athletes and coaches, those who pray in connection with sports are likely to be regular churchgoers with a strong religious orientation. Thus, coaches and athletes who pray at game time probably do it because prayer is something they use in numerous situations of their daily life, not because the sports event elicits such prayers any more than other stressful episodes in daily life.

Many athletes who pray believe that the use of prayer might affect the outcome of the game. So they ask God for a victory. One professional athlete asserted, "The question was posed to us, 'Does [God] control wins and losses?' Yes, He does." Another described the prayer he uses: "I ask for victories: 'God, I want to win so I have an even bigger platform for you.'" A University of Nebraska football player acknowledged that he and his teammates prayed that an opposing placekicker would miss a field goal that, if made, would have defeated Nebraska. After the field goal was missed, the Nebraska player said: "God came through and answered all our prayers on the sidelines and out there on the field."[48]

Many athletes, coaches, and sport managers strongly believe that God intervenes on their behalf. The winner of the Most Valuable Player award at the 2000 Orange Bowl game said: "I asked God to let me have my best game, and I feel like He did that for me." In an interview after beating Tiger Woods to win the 2007 Master's Golf Tournament, Fellowship of Christian Athletes member Zach Johnson said, "I felt like there was certainly another power that was walking with me and guiding me." In 2006, Major League Baseball's Colorado Rockies, from the owners down, revealed they have become an organization guided by Christianity, and they believe God has had a hand in the team's improvement. General Manager Dan O'Dowd asserted, "You look at things that have happened to us this year. You look at some of the moves we made and didn't make. You look at some of the games we're winning. Those aren't just a coincidence. God has definitely had a hand in this."[49]

Perhaps the most public sign that athletes believe that God is aiding their performance is the seemingly ever-present pointed index finger to the sky thanking God. The expression has become commonplace at sports venues, even after run-of-the-mill performances. A few athletes have claimed that they use the sign to pay tribute to a relative or friend. Most admit it is a "thank you" to God.[50]

Some religious leaders, athletes, coaches, and even fans renounce asking God for a victory, claiming it is crass and greedy. Furthermore, for many of them the idea that God intervenes in sports—that God roots for one team, but not the other—is offensive, even absurd and blasphemous. The Rev. Patrick Kelly, a faculty member of Seattle University's Center for the Study of Sport, said: "We don't want to get into this thing where God is on my side helping me to win all the time. God isn't there to help us achieve. He's there in much more significant ways." More generally, Leo Sandon, professor emeritus of religion and American studies at Florida State University, declared: [T]eams or individuals believing they have become champions because they are Christians 'can represent a shallow if not tawdry religiosity.'"[51]

Freedom of religious expression is guaranteed to citizens of both Canada and the United States. But less than 40 percent of the people in these countries regularly attend religious services, in spite of there being a greater diversity of religious groups than in any other industrialized countries. Moreover, millions of Canadians and Americans do not subscribe to any institutionalized religion. Thus, it probably is not surprising that in North America there is growing resentment and opposition to the use of prayers in the locker room before games, in the huddles before and after games, and as public ceremonies before sports events, especially when they are part of public school events. If we assume journalists somewhat have their finger on the pulse of the public, the titles of recent newspaper articles clearly illustrate the collective mind on this issue of sports' use of religion: "For God's Sake, Leave Religion Out of the Game." "Prayer by Athletes Better Left on Sidelines." "Avoid Mix of Prayer and Points." "Athletes' Moralizing Cheapens Religion." Undoubtedly, the most controversial practice is for clergy, athletes, and coaches to use prayer as a part of public school and university sporting events—especially in the United States, where the Constitution requires the separation of religion and state. Controversy over the proper interpretation of church-state relations in public educational institutions has a long history in the United States. On the one side, Christian individuals and organizations have promoted prayer and other religious activities in the schools; on the other side have been individuals and groups who have claimed that the First Amendment to the Constitution specifically prohibits religious practices of any kind under the jurisdiction of the public schools. Since 1962 the U.S. Supreme Court has handed down several rulings on prayer in the schools, but lawsuits continue to arise against schools that practice religious observances of various kinds.

Two of the most recent incidents to gain widespread media coverage, and the most recent Supreme Court ruling, occurred in Texas and Colorado. In the first, organized student-led prayers at the high school in Galveston, Texas, during graduation exercises and football games resulted in a lawsuit filed by a Roman Catholic family and a Mormon family challenging prayers at these school functions (*Santa Fe Independent School District v. Doe*). In the second, in the fall of 2005 a veteran East Brunswick, New Jersey, high school football coach, Marcus Borden, was told he would have to stop leading or taking part in prayers he initiated at pregame meals and before the games. School officials explained that the prayers violated the separation between church and state in public schools.

In the Galveston, Texas, lawsuit, the Supreme Court delivered a strong rejection of prayer in public schools (see Box 8.1, *Thinking about Sport*). A *USA Today* writer noted: "The court provided an unusually direct condemnation of school-sanctioned prayer. 'School sponsorship of a religious message is impermissible because it [tells] members of the audience who are non-adherents that they are outsiders,' Justice Paul Stevens wrote."[52]

Since the Court's ruling on this case, advocates of school pregame prayer who contend the government should not limit prayers at high school events have experimented with a variety of ways to defy the Court's ruling. The defiance has been most pronounced in the southern states, the so-called Bible Belt, where public expressions of religious faith are a part of the daily routine, including school life. In a commentary about the Court's decision in this case, a legal scholar also addressed those who defy the Court's decision, saying, "it is reasonable for concerned citizens to disagree strongly about when student prayer crosses the constitutional line. But, when those who disagree with *Santa Fe* deliberately violate the decision, they are unintentionally undermining respect for all of the laws they want others to uphold."[53]

As for the issue of the New Jersey high school football coach, Coach Borden immediately resigned, saying that coaches across the state lead similar prayers with their teams. He subsequently returned to his job but brought a lawsuit against

---

Box 8.1   *Thinking about Sport* **Pregame Prayer at Public School Sports Events: Constitutional or Unconstitutional?**

The fusing of sport and religion is readily observable at sporting events: the index finger pointed to the sky after a good performance, a team huddling together to pray just before or immediately after a game, religious objects worn around the neck, and so forth are tangible religious symbols that have become a common feature of the sports landscape. Many athletes admit to silently making a brief prayer just before shooting a free throw, stepping into the batters box, while crouching in the starting blocks, etc. These are all acts of individual conscience and do not require anyone's attention or participation. They also meet the First Amendment "freedom of speech" guarantee.

The U.S. Constitution uses the word *religion* only once, stating: "no religious test shall ever be required as a qualification to any office or public trust under the United States" (Article VI, C). The First Amendment to the Constitution states: "Congress shall make no law respecting an establishment of religion, or prohibiting the free exercise thereof." It is clear that the Founders of the Constitution wished to establish a separation of church and state, and once the United States was established, many of them spoke out and wrote adamantly opposing any state-church integration. Indeed, Thomas Jefferson referred to the First Amendment as creating a "wall of separation" between church and state.

But efforts to merge state and religion have been persistent throughout the history of the United States. However, when these efforts have confronted the U.S. judicial system, the courts have overwhelmingly sided with the separation of church and state doctrine.

Individual acts of religious prayer and ritual, such as those mentioned above, have been interpreted by the courts as protected by the "free exercise thereof" phrase in the First Amendment because the state has no role in their practice. On the other hand, when prayers or religious rituals are conducted under the auspices of a federal, state, or municipal governmental entity during a public event, the courts have interpreted these as falling within the "establishment clause of the First Amendment," meaning the state is favoring a religion and is therefore illegal.

From the beginning of public education in the early nineteenth century to the present, some Christian church leaders and their congregations have attempted to use the power of government, through the schools, as an instrument for promoting one favored view of religion—Christianity. Holding official prayers in the classrooms, posting the Ten Commandments in classrooms, distributing Bibles to students, and promoting attendance at specific churches during classes are a few of the techniques used.

With the rise of modern sports organizations during the twentieth century, two pregame rituals gradually became widespread: playing/singing the national anthem and prayers being given by a clergy or a designee. The

continues

the East Brunswick school district, claiming the school district's action violated his First and Fourteenth Amendment rights to free speech, free association, and academic freedom. In the lawsuit, Coach Borden contended that he merely bowed his head and "took a knee" during prayers initiated and led by student-athletes. In July 2006, a U.S. district judge ruled that officials at East Brunswick High School could not prohibit their football coach, Marcus Borden, from participating in his players' voluntary student-led prayers by silently bowing his head and taking a knee as the athletes' prayers were said.

It is important to note that the *Borden v. East Brunswick School District* decision did not give Coach Borden permission to actually initiate and lead pregame prayers. Previous Supreme Court decisions have established that public school officials and employees may not offer, initiate, or lead prayers before sporting events. "The court framed the legal issue" as a test of "whether a reasonable, objective observer would view 'head bowing' or 'taking a knee' as government endorsement of religion. The court found that neither gesture amounts to endorsement, but merely signals respect and solidarity with the team."[54]

Religious services in connection with sporting events are still held at church-sponsored high schools and colleges, as well as at professional sporting events; indeed, to have an important sports event started by a religious invocation is not unusual. Some invocations are brief and to the

---

Box 8.1   Continued

former was a patriotic observance while the latter was clearly a religious ceremony. When a public prayer is conducted at a sporting event under the jurisdiction of a private organization, such as a professional sports event, or a religious organization, the courts have judged them to be legal, since government agencies are not involved.

However, when a pregame prayer is conducted at a sporting event sponsored by a government agency, such as a public high school or college, it clearly raises an issue about violating the "establishment clause" of the First Amendment. In 1999 a Mormon and a Roman Catholic family filed a lawsuit against the Galveston, Texas, Santa Fe Independent School District for permitting "student-selected, student-given" prayers being read over the public address system at football games. Such prayers are a long-standing tradition in Texas, and some other states as well. Nevertheless, the U.S. Court of Appeals for the Fifth Circuit declared the Santa Fe School District practice to be unconstitutional, saying that football games are "hardly the type of event that can be appropriately solemnized with prayer."

Then governor of Texas George W. Bush instructed the Texas attorney general to file an appeal, and thirteen Texas congressmen introduced a resolution in the U.S. House of Representatives to negate the Circuit Court of Appeals decision. Congress passed a nonbinding resolution—which has no legal status in law—that encouraged Christian prayer before public school athletic games. Within two weeks of the congressional resolution, the U.S. Supreme Court announced that it would hear arguments on this case during 2000.

Consistent with several previous court decisions in similar cases, on 19 June 2000, by a vote of six to three, the U.S. Supreme Court declared that the practice of Santa Fe School District school administrators of allowing students to conduct formal prayers before school games was unconstitutional. The Court found that:

- Including prayers before a sports event when school administrators were involved was a state-sponsored religious activity and was therefore unconstitutional.
- Formal prayers unconstitutionally coerced attendees into participating in a religious activity.
- The state may not endorse overtly religious messages, even if the majority of the people favor it.
- A truly initiated prayer by an individual student is protected free speech. For example, a player can spontaneously call for a group prayer huddle. A person in the stands can assemble an informal group prayer.
- An individual, truly voluntary prayer by a student is protected speech, both before, during, and after school.

Source: The text of the Supreme Court's decision in *Santa Fe Independent School District v. Doe* is at http://supct.law.cornell.edu/supct/html/99-62.ZS.html.

point, but others are used by clergy to conduct a religious service or to metaphorically dramatize the relationship between sports and religion.

The Use of Magic

The reader may be surprised, even shocked, that a section on magic is included in this chapter, because many people see no relationship between magical practices and religion. In practice, however, religion and magic, as defined by anthropologists, are closely intertwined. Although magic and religion are alike in assuming the existence of supernatural powers, a significant difference exists between the ends that they seek. Religion is oriented to the otherworldly, toward a supreme supernatural god, and religion typically centers on such overarching issues as salvation and the meaning of life and death; this is not true of magic. The practitioner of magic seeks ends that are in the everyday world of events; magic is oriented toward immediate, practical goals.

There are other ways in which religion and magic differ. Religious worshipers possess an attitude of awe and reverence toward the sacred ends they pursue, but the users of magic are in business for practical and arbitrarily chosen ends. The latter are manipulators of the supernatural for their own private advantage rather than worshipers of it; the attitude of magic users is likely to be utilitarian. In this respect, Bronislaw Malinowski noted that magic has an end in pursuit of which the magical ritual is performed. The religious ritual has no purpose, that is, the ritual is not a means to an end but an end in itself. Malinowski said, "While in the magical act the underlying idea and aim is always clear, straightforward and definite, in religious ceremony there is no purpose directed toward a subsequent event."[55] Furthermore, the content of magic and religion differs. The content of magic has no unified inclusive theory but instead tends to be atomistic, somewhat like a book of recipes. Religion, on the other hand, tends to encompass the whole of life; it often provides a comprehensive theory of both the supernatural and human society.

The Malinowski Thesis

According to Malinowski, magic flourishes in situations of uncertainty and threat; it is most commonly invoked in situations of high anxiety about accomplishing desired ends. The origin of most magical rites can be traced to fears experienced individually or collectively. These rites are associated with human helplessness in the face of danger and unpredictability, which give rise to superstitious beliefs and overt practices to ward off impending danger or failure and to bring good luck. Malinowski reported: "We find magic wherever the elements of chance and accident, and the emotional play between hope and fear have a wide and extensive range. We do not find magic wherever the pursuit is certain, reliable, and well under control of rational methods."[56] In support of this contention, Malinowski compared two forms of fishing among natives of the Trobriand Islands of Melanesia: lagoon and open-sea fishing. "It is most significant that in the lagoon fishing, where man can rely completely upon his knowledge and skill, magic does not exist, while in the open-sea fishing, full of danger and uncertainty, there is extensive magical ritual to secure safety and good results."[57]

Malinowski's thesis about the conditions under which magic appears is applicable to the world of sport. Athletes and coaches are engaged in an activity of uncertain outcome in which they have a great deal of emotional investment. Even dedicated conditioning and practice and the acquisition of high-level skills do not guarantee victory because opponents are often evenly matched and player injury and other dangers are often present. Thus, "getting the breaks" or "lucking out" may be the determining factor in the outcome of a contest. Having a weakly hit baseball fall in for a base hit, a deflected hockey puck go in the net, or a deflected football pass caught by an unintended receiver are examples of luck or "getting the breaks" in sports. Although the cliché "the best team always wins" is part of the folk wisdom of sport, athletes and coaches know that this is not always so and indeed believe that factors leading to a win or a loss are somewhat out of their control.

According to Malinowski's theory, athletes and coaches may use magic to bring them luck and to ensure that they "get the breaks," thus supplying themselves with beliefs that serve to bridge over uncertainty and threat in their pursuit of victories. The magic enables them to carry out their actions with a sense of assurance and confidence and to maintain poise and mental integrity in the face of opponents.

Magic and Its Uses in Sports

It is difficult to assess just how extensive the uses of magic are in sport. Newspaper and magazine stories leave little doubt, however, that magical beliefs and practices play a prominent role in the lives of athletes and coaches. In a book-length treatment of magic in sports, the authors claim that their book, *Locker Room Mojo: True Tales of Superstitions in Sports*, is a "glorious tribute to the magical soul of sports."[58] In their book, they illustrate that athletes and coaches employ almost anything imaginable that might ensure "getting the breaks," and this often involves some form of superstitious behavior. Superstition is a belief that one's fate is in the hands of mysterious external powers, governed by forces over which one has no control. It is a form of magical belief. Sports studies scholars who have scrutinized the superstitions of athletes claim that many athletes turn to superstitions for the same reasons that others turn to religion—they provide a mental confidence, a feeling of assurance, that often makes the difference between success and failure at the highest levels of athletic competition.

There have been a few attempts to study empirically the uses of magic in sport. The findings of those studies can be summarized as follows: Sport superstitions are similar for athletes who compete in teams and for those who compete in individual sports, but team athletes indicate greater use of superstitions related to equipment and its use, to the order of entering the sports arena, and to dressing-room rituals than do individual-sport athletes. Pregame superstitions of basketball players center on warm-up rituals; game superstitions are directed toward free-throw shooting, team cheers, and gum chewing. Endorsement of superstitions increases with involvement in sport; in other words, the higher the competitive level and the greater the involvement in a sport, the greater the prevalence of superstition. The gender of the athlete is less important than the level of involvement. Superstitions are related to the uncertainty and importance of the outcome, as Malinowski indicated.

Applying the Malinowski thesis to baseball, anthropologist George Gmelch, a former professional ball player, published what has now become one of the classic studies of athletes and their uses of magical practices. Gmelch hypothesized that in baseball magical practices would be associated more with hitting and pitching than with fielding; the first two involve a high degree of chance and unpredictability, whereas the average fielding success rate is about 97 percent, reflecting almost complete control over the outcome. From his observations as a participant in professional baseball, Gmelch reported that there was indeed a greater incidence and variety of rituals, taboos, and use of fetishes related to hitting and pitching than in fielding. He concluded:

> In keeping with Malinowski's hypothesis about the relationship between magic and uncertainty, my research shows that baseball players associate magic with hitting and pitching, but not with fielding. Despite the wide assortment of magic—which includes rituals, taboos, and fetishes—associated with both hitting and pitching, I have never observed any directly connected to fielding.[59]

What emerges in these investigations is that athletes use magical practices extensively in their sport experiences. Among the specific forms of magic practiced in sport are ritual, taboo, fetishism, and witchcraft.

Ritual
Rituals are standardized actions directed toward entreating or controlling the supernatural powers in regard to some particular situation, and sports are infused with ritualistic practices. An almost infinite variety of rituals are practiced in sport, because all athletes are free to ritualize any activity

they consider important for successful performance. Whether they are a psychological placebo, a desire to control fate, or merely a way of sustaining a winning method, rituals have been a long-standing staple in sports.

Typically, rituals arise from successful performances. Unable to attribute an exceptional performance to skill alone but hoping to repeat it in future contests, athletes and coaches single out something they did before the performance as being responsible for their success. That "something" might be a certain food they had eaten before the game, a new pair of socks or sneakers they had put on, or a specific sequence of behaviors preceding the contest. Some examples are:

- Michael Jordan wouldn't step on the basketball court without his lucky shorts.
- When Major League Baseball catcher A. J. Pierzynski wakes up, his first thought is "Who am I catching tonight?" If it is a right-handed pitcher, he must get out of bed on the right side.
- Major League Baseball shortstop Nomar Garciaparra steps out of the batter's box after each pitch, kicks the dirt with each toe, adjusts his right batting glove, adjusts his left batting glove, and then touches his helmet before moving back into the batter's box.
- Tiger Woods wears a red shirt on the last day of tournaments he plays.
- Pro tennis player Mary Pierce insists her mother wash the same outfit night after night when she is playing.

In addition to individual rituals, there are a number of team rituals. In basketball the ritual of stacking hands is frequently employed just before the team takes the floor at the beginning of the game and after time-outs. The most universal hockey ritual occurs just before the start of a game when players skate in front of their goal and tap their goalie on the pads for good luck. In a story of the rituals of a girls' high school field hockey team, the reporter revealed that before every game the girls would kneel before the coach; he

Basketball players stacking hands before a game, one of the oldest rituals in basketball. (iStockphoto)

then blessed them with a charitable helping of "Hockey Dust" (which was actually an exclusive blend of ninety-nine-cent sparkle and precious good luck).

Taboo

A taboo is a strong social norm prohibiting certain actions that are punishable by the group or by magical consequences. There are numerous institutional taboos in each sport and, of course, many personal taboos. Athletes and coaches believe breaking a taboo will lead to undesirable outcomes or bad luck. Two of the strongest taboos in baseball prohibit crossing the handles of bats and mentioning that the pitcher has a no-hitter in progress. Crossing bats is believed to bring bad luck and mentioning a no-hitter to the pitcher is believed to break his spell on the batters, ending his chances to complete a no-hit game.

During a winning streak, athletes and coaches in many sports will insist on wearing some or all of the same clothing—uniform, socks, jock, bra, shoes, sweatshirt, warm-up, etc.—that they were wearing when the winning streak started. Washing apparel during a winning streak is one of the most common taboos. Several years ago the entire uniforms of the Purdue University women's rugby team went unwashed, as long as they were winning. The coach explained the taboo this way: "If the luck is in the fabric, why risk washing it out?"[60]

Some athletes develop taboos about not stepping on portions of the playing surface, such as the chalk foul lines (just as children avoid stepping on sidewalk cracks) or about not wearing certain parts of the uniform, such as socks. In addition to his pregame rituals, former Major League Baseball player Wade Boggs also had game taboos: Boggs stepped over the foul line when he sprinted on the field to play third base and stepped on it when he returned to the dugout. He never stood on the mound during a pitchers' conference.

Fetishism

Fetishes are revered objects believed to have "supernatural" power to attain the desired ends for the person who possesses or uses them. Fetishes are standard equipment for coaches and athletes. They include a bewildering assortment of objects: rabbits' feet, pictures of heroes or loved ones, pins, coins, remnants of old equipment, certain numbered uniforms, and so forth. Typically, these objects obtain their power through association with successful performances. For example, if the athlete or coach happens to be wearing or using the object during a victory, the individual attributes the good fortune to the object; it then becomes a fetish embodied with supernatural power. The extent to which some athletes take fetishes seriously is illustrated by this Colorado State University men's basketball player: In December 2003 Michael Morris made two three-pointers in the final seven-tenths of a second in an unexpected comeback victory over Purdue University. Directors at the Basketball Hall of Fame requested the shoes Morris was wearing at the time of his incredible feat so they could place them in a display case in the Hall of Fame. Believing that his shoes had magical power, Morris made the Hall of Fame wait until the end of the season before turning over the shoes. Those shoes had become a fetish to Morris.

Particular items of athletic apparel and equipment commonly are turned into fetishes, and athletes and coaches believe that not wearing that apparel or not using certain equipment will result in poor performance and cause a loss. Almost everyone who has been around sports has a story of an athlete, coach, or team that had apparel or equipment fetishes of some kind and went to bizarre extremes to make sure nothing interfered with the use of those items.

Witchcraft

Magical practices that are intended to bring misfortune on others are known as black magic, witchcraft, or sorcery. In sport, those who employ this form of magic believe that supernatural powers are being harnessed to harm or bring misfortune on opponents. In Africa witchcraft dominates some sports. Medicine men who claim that they can make the ball disappear or that they can cast a spell on opposing players are especially active in soccer. In 2002 in the African country of Cameroon, a soccer coach was banned from coaching for a year when he was charged with dropping a charm believed to contain black magic onto the field during a semifinal match at the African Cup of Nations. It is estimated that about 95 percent of Kenyan soccer teams hire witch doctors to help them win, and matches have been marred by witchcraft-inspired riots.

In North America we laugh when reading about African soccer teams traveling with witch doctors, and we are amused by such practices of witchcraft as players painting their bodies with pig fat to ward off evil spirits, reasoning that sports teams in North America are much too sophisticated to travel with witch doctors or to wear pig fat. Our teams, instead, travel with Catholic priests and Protestant ministers and wear medals around their necks! A number of college and professional sports teams have traveling chaplains who accompany the teams on road trips. We may not recognize that some of the social antics of our athletes and coaches aimed at calling for the intervention of the supernatural on their behalf can be viewed as acts of sorcery.

Actually, witchcraft is not confined to African sports. During an American League baseball playoff game several years ago, a Kansas City player hit a two-run homer to beat the New York Yankees. One of the Kansas City coaches claimed that the victory was the result of his enlisting the help of his godfather, a practitioner of voodoo. The coach revealed that he called his godfather to ask what could be done to ensure that the Royals would win the pennant. Although the godfather was a Yankees fan, he felt obligated to help his godson, and so he told him, "Stick the Yankee line-up card in the freezer," an action that he said would "freeze their bats." Before the game, the Kansas City coach dutifully obtained a copy of the New York lineup, went into a back room in Yankee Stadium and placed the card in a freezer. This is why, the coach said, the Yankees scored only two runs and lost the game.

SUMMARY

In this chapter we have examined the reciprocal relationship between sport and religion. Although sport and religion may appear to have little in common, we have attempted to demonstrate that contemporary sport and contemporary religion are related in a variety of ways. Religions perform several important functions: At the individual level they provide individuals with emotional support; at the interpersonal level they provide a form of human bonding; at the institutional level they serve as a vehicle for social control; and at the societal level they promote social integration. For many centuries Christian church dogma was antithetical to play and sport activities, but over the past century, with the enormous growth of organized sport, churches and religious leaders have welded a link between these two institutions by sponsoring sports events under religious auspices and by proselytizing athletes to religion and then using them as missionaries to convert new members.

Although contemporary religion uses sport for the promotion of its causes, sport uses religion as well. Numerous activities with a religious connotation—ceremonies, rituals, and so forth—are employed in connection with sports contests.

The most common use of religion by athletes, coaches, and fans is prayer. One of the persisting social problems is the use of public prayer ceremonies before sporting events and the practice of some coaches of conducting prayers with their athletes in locker rooms and in sporting venues before a sporting event. Such practices give rise to many personal objections and legal controversies. The practice of magic—through rituals, taboos, fetishism, and witchcraft—is widespread in sport. Such behaviors are most common in sporting situations where there is uncertainty, threat, and high anxiety about accomplishing desired ends.

WEB RESOURCES

www.fca.org
The official site for the Fellowship of Christian Athletes has links to information about huddles, camps, resources, and global FCA.

www.athletesinaction.org
This Athletes in Action site describes the AIA mission and what they do and has links to ministry sites.

www.accesschristian.com
This Access Christian Sport site has reports of various sports ministries, articles about Christian sports topics, and links to mission resources, Christian resources, and devotionals.

www.sportsambassadors.org
This website for People to People Sports Ambassadors has descriptions of history, programs, tournaments, and coaches.

www.baseballchapel.org
The website of the Baseball Chapel has discussions of its mission, vision, and history and the impact of the Baseball Chapel.

www.promisekeepers.org
The website for the Promise Keepers. It mainly features news and articles about Promise Keepers and other Christian sport topics.

www.sportsspectrum.com
Sports Spectrum magazine online. Claims to feature Christians who happen to be some of the world's top athletes.

NOTES

1. Rick Reilly, "Let Us Play," *Sports Illustrated*, 26 April 2004, 172.
2. Emile Durkheim, *The Elementary Forms of Religious Life*, trans. J. W. Swain (New York: Free Press, 1965), 62.
3. Inger Furseth and Pal Repstad, *An Introduction to the Sociology of Religion: Classical and Contemporary Perspectives* (Burlington, Vt.: Ashgate Publishing, 2006); Michele Dillon, ed., *Handbook of the Sociology of Religion* (Cambridge: Cambridge University Press, 2003).
4. Karl Marx, *Selected Writings in Sociology and Social Philosophy*, trans. and ed. Tom B. Bottomore and Maximilien Rubel (New York: McGraw-Hill, 1964), 26–27.
5. Stewart Culin, *Games of the North American Indian* (Washington, D.C.: U.S. Government Printing Office, 1907), 34; see also Joseph Oxendine, *American Indian Sports Heritage* (Champagne, Ill.: Human Kinetics, 1998); Donald M. Fisher, *Lacrosse: A History of the Game* (Baltimore: Johns Hopkins University Press, 2002).
6. Stephen G. Miller, *Ancient Greek Athletics* (New Haven: Yale University Press, 2006); Judith Swaddling, *The Ancient Olympic Games*, 2nd ed. (Austin: University of Texas Press, 1999).
7. Bruce C. Daniels, *Puritans at Play: Leisure and Recreation in Colonial New England* (New York: Palgrave, 2005), 166. See also Robert J. Higgs, *God in the Stadium: Sports and Religion in America* (Lexington: University Press of Kentucky, 1995), 22–35.
8. R. Laurence Moore, *Touchdown Jesus: The Mixing of Sacred and Secular in American History* (Louisville, KY: Westminster John Knox Press, 2003); Nancy L. Struna, *People of Prowess: Sport, Leisure, and Labor in Early Anglo-America* (Urbana: University of Illinois Press, 1996).
9. "Amusements," *New Englander* 9 (1851): 358; see also Steven J. Overman, *The Influence of the Protestant Ethic on Sport and Recreation* (Brookfield, Vt.: Avebury, 1997), 134–157; Tony Ladd and James A. Mathisen, *Muscular Christianity: Evangelical Protestants and the Development of American Sports* (Grand Rapids, Mich.: Baker Books, 1999), 22–68.
10. Ladd and Mathisen, *Muscular Christianity*, 78; see also William J. Baker, *Playing with God: Religion and Modern Sport* (Cambridge, Mass.: Harvard University Press, 2007).
11. Shirl Hoffman, "The Decline of Civility and the Rise of Religion in American Sport," *Quest* 51 (February 1999): 80.
12. Michael Novak, "The Natural Religion," in *Sport and Religion*, ed. Shirl J. Hoffman (Champaign, Ill.: Human Kinetics, 1992), 36, 39.
13. Charles S. Prebish, comp., *Religion and Sport: The Meeting of Sacred and Profane* (Westport, Conn.: Greenwood, 1993), 62, 74.
14. Tom Faulkner, "A Puckish Reflection on Religion in Canada," in *From Season to Season: Sports as American Religion*, ed. Joseph L. Price (Macon, Ga.: Mercer University Press, 2001), 185, 200.
15. *The Speeches of Avery Brundage* (Lausanne, Switzerland: Comité International Olympique, 1968), 80.
16. James A. Vlasich, *A Legend for the Legendary: The Origins of the Baseball Hall of Fame* (Bowling Green, Ohio: Bowling Green State University Popular Press, 1990); Eldon E. Snyder, "Sociology of Nostalgia: Sports Halls of Fame and Museums in America," *Sociology of Sport Journal* 8 (September 1991): 228–238.
17. Higgs, *God in the Stadium*, 21; see also Robert J. Higgs and Michael C. Braswell, *An Unholy Alliance: The Sacred and Modern Sports* (Macon, Ga.: Mercer University Press, 2004).
18. James A. Mathisen, "American Sport as Folk Religion: Examining a Test of Its Strength," in *From Season to Season: Sports as American Religion*, ed. Price, 142; Joseph L. Price, *Rounding the Bases: Baseball and Religion in America* (Macon, Ga.: Mercer University Press, 2006), 175.
19. David L. Moore, "BYU Sports: Mission Accomplished," *USA Today*, 22 October 1986, p. 2C.
20. Jerry Falwell, "Falwell Confidential," 4 May 2000, pp. 1–2, www.falwell.com!confidenJfc000504.htm; Jerry Falwell, "Falwell Confidential," 25 February 2000, pp. 1–2, www.falwell.com!confidenJfc000225.htm; see also Ladd and Mathisen, *Muscular Christianity*, 161–193.
21. David Whitford, *A Payroll to Meet: A Story of Greed, Corruption and Football at SMU* (New York: Macmillan, 1989).
22. Higgs, *God in the Stadium*, 67–88.
23. Official site for the Fellowship of Christian Athletes, www.gospelcom.neUfca/whoisfca; see also Ladd and Mathisen, *Muscular Christianity*, 129–136.
24. Warren St. John, "Sports and Salvation on Faith Night at the Stadium," *New York Times*, 2 June 2006, Sport Pages, p. 1A.
25. Tom Krattenmaker, "Does Proselytizing Cross the Line in Pro Sports?" *USA Today*, 7 November 2005, p. 13A; see also Tom Krattenmaker, "Should God Go to the Ballgame?" *Los Angeles Times*, 18 August 2007, p. 19A.
26. Home page, *Sports Spectrum Magazine*, http://www.sportsspectrum.com/daily/.
27. "About Athletes in Action," *Athletes in Action Online*, www.athletesinaction.org/A1A_mission.htm.
28. Ladd and Mathisen, *Muscular Christianity*, 123–160; see also S. Hubbard, *Faith in Sports: Athletes and*

Their Religion on and off the Field (New York: Doubleday, 1998).

29. Shirl J. Hoffman, "God, Guts, and Glory: Evangelicalism in American Sport" (paper presented at the National Convention of American Alliance for Health, Physical Education, Recreation and Dance, 1982), 15.

30. Quotes by McCartney in Michael Romano, "Keeping the Promise of God," *Rocky Mountain News*, 17 July 1994, pp. 16A, 17A; see also "A World of Change: Promise Keepers Focus on Smaller, More Local Events," *Greeley Tribune*, 25 August 2007, pp. B8, B10.

31. George D. Randels, Jr., and Becky Beal, "What Makes a Man? Religion, Sport and Negotiating Masculine Identity in the Promise Keepers," in *With God on Their Side: Sport in the Service of Religion*, ed. Tara Magdalinski and Timothy J. L. Chandler (New York: Routledge, 2002), 160.

32. Becky Beal, "The Promise Keepers' Use of Sport in Defining 'Christlike' Masculinity," *Journal of Sport and Social Issues* 21, no. 3 (August 1997): 282; see also Randels and Beal, "What Makes a Man?" 160–176.

33. Hoffman, "The Decline of Civility and the Rise of Religion in American Sport," 83.

34. Max Weber, *The Protestant Ethic and the Spirit of Capitalism*, 2nd ed., trans. Talcott Parsons (Los Angeles: Roxbury, 1998). This essay, probably the most famous work on the sociology of religion, has aroused a great deal of controversy among sociologists and historians.

35. Ibid., 80, 115.

36. Ibid., 183.

37. Overman, *The Influence of the Protestant Ethic on Sport and Recreation*, 10, 158, 159.

38. Shirl J. Hoffman, "Evangelicalism and the Revitalization of Religious Ritual in Sport," in Hoffman, *Sport and Religion*, 114.

39. Christopher L. Stevenson, "The Christian-Athlete: An Interactionist-Developmental Analysis," *Sociology of Sport Journal* 8 (1991): 365, 367.

40. Quoted in "No Comment," *Progressive* 55 (July 1991): 11.

41. Carol Flake, "The Spirit of Winning: Sports and the Total Man," in Hoffman, *Sport and Religion*, 166.

42. Frank Deford, *The Old Ball Game* (New York: Atlantic Monthly Press, 2005), 36.

43. Dennis Johnson, "All-USA Team," *USA Today*, 31 December 1997, p. 9C.

44. Bronislaw Malinowski, *Magic, Science, and Religion and Other Essays* (Long Grove, Ill.: Waverland Press, 1992).

45. Brian W. W. Aitken, "The Emergence of Born-Again Sport," in Prebish, *Religion and Sport*, 208.

46. Louise R. Loomis, ed., *The Iliad of Homer*, trans. Samuel Butler (Ann Arbor, Mich.: Borders Classics, 2006), 307.

47. Pat Conroy, *The Prince of Tides* (New York: Bantam Press Trade Paperbacks, 2002), 394–395.

48. Quotes from William Nack, "Does God Care Who Wins the Super Bowl?" *Sports Illustrated*, 26 January 1998, 47, 48; see also Electra Draper, "Faith on the Field," *Denver Post*, pp. 1A, 21A.

49. Quotes from Dave Zirin, "The Rockies Pitch Religion," *The Nation*, 2 June 2006, http://www.thenation.com/doc/20060619/zirin. See also David Plotz, "The God of the Gridiron," *Slate*, 4 February 2000, http://www.slate.com/id/74294; Anne-Marie Dorning, "Meet the God Squad," *ABC News Internet Ventures*, http://abcnews.go.com/print?id=3027407, 1; Bob Nightengale, "Rockies Seek Revival on and off Field," *USA Today*, 31 May 2006, p. 2A.

50. Jorge L. Ortiz, "It Isn't Just for Pop-Ups Anymore," *USA Today*, 14 June 2006, p. 3C.

51. Ibid; Dorning, "Meet the God Squad," 2.

52. Joan Biskupic, "School Prayer Rejected," *USA Today*, 20 June 2000, p. 1A. See also Adam Thompson, "Prayer and Preps," *Denver Post*, 20 June 2000, pp. 1D, 8D.

53. David Schimmel, "Court Outlaws School-Sponsored Student Prayer: An Analysis of *Santa Fe* v. *Doe*," *West's Education Law Reporter* 150, no. 1 (1 March 2001): 13; see also Cathy Lynn Grossman, "Prayers Are Heard at Football Games Despite Ruling," *USA Today*, 28 August 2000, p. 1A; Timothy Roche, "Too Much Like a Prayer?" *Time*, 18 September 2000, 59.

54. *Borden v. East Brunswick School District*, No. 05-5923 (D.N.J. July 25, 2006), http://nsba.org/site/print.asp? TRACKID=&vid=50&CID=468&DID=38981.

55. Malinowski, *Magic, Science, and Religion*, 12–30.

56. Ibid., 116.

57. Ibid., 14.

58. Nick Newton and Bill Minutaglio, *Locker Room Mojo: True Tales of Superstitions in Sports* (Austin, Tex.: Middlefork Press, 1999).

59. George Gmelch, "Baseball Magic," *Human Nature* 1, no. 8 (August 1978): 35; see also George Gmelch, *Inside Pitch: Life in Professional Baseball* (Washington, D.C.: Smithsonian Institute Press, 2001).

60. Newton and Minutaglio, *Locker Room Mojo*, 68.

CHAPTER 9
Sport and Politics

A giant American flag is displayed on the field during the national anthem in commemoration of the victims of 11 September before the game between the Miami Dolphins and the Denver Broncos Sunday, 11 September 2005, in Miami. (AP Photo/Luis M. Alvarez)

Power is a central concept for sociologists because it is present in all social organizations. Sociologists ask: How is power distributed? Who has power and who does not and why? Who benefits by the power arrangements and who does not? How is the distribution of power changed? Max Weber, one of the most important classical sociologists, defined *power* as the ability to get others to do one's will even in the face of opposition. Power can be exercised by force, threat of force, or extraordinary personal qualities ("charisma") of the power holder.[1] Thus, power is present in personal relationships, in groups, in formal organizations, and in nation-states. The term *politics* refers to these power relations. For our purposes, we are interested in how politics is manifested in the world of sports.[2]

The argument of this chapter is that sport and politics are closely intertwined. Several characteristics inherent in sport serve to guarantee this strong relationship.

First, sports participants typically represent and have an allegiance to some social organization (e.g., school, factory, neighborhood, community, region, or nation). Much of the ritual accompanying sporting events (such as slogans, chants, music, wearing of special clothing, and so forth) is aimed at symbolically reaffirming fidelity to the sponsoring organization. Phillip Goodhart and Christopher Chataway argued that there are four kinds of sport: sport as exercise, sport as gambling, sport as spectacle, and representative sport. *Representative sport* is

> a limited conflict with clearly defined rules, in which representatives of towns, regions, or nations are pitted against each other. It is primarily an affair for the spectators: they are drawn to it not so much by the mere spectacle, by the ritual, or by an appreciation of the skills involved, but because they identify themselves with their representatives....
>
> Most people will watch [the Olympic Games] for one reason only: there will be a competitor who, they feel, is representing them. That figure in the striped singlet will be their man—running, jumping, or boxing for their country. For a matter of minutes at least, their own estimation of themselves will be bound up with his performance. He will be the embodiment of their nation's strength or weakness. Victory for him will be victory for them; defeat for him, defeat for them.[3]

This last point requires emphasis. Evidence from the Olympics or from other international competition shows that for many nations and their citizens, victory is an index of that nation's superiority (in its military might, its politico-economic system, and its culture). Clearly, the outcomes of international contests are very often interpreted politically, an argument we will return to later in this chapter.

A second basis for a close relationship between sport and politics is inherent in the process of organization itself. As sport has become increasingly organized, numerous teams, leagues, players' associations, and ruling bodies have been created. These groups acquire certain powers that by their very creation are distributed unequally.[4] Thus, a power struggle can develop between players and owners (e.g., threats of strikes by the players or lockouts by the owners), within an organization (e.g., the NCAA or individual athletic departments moving too slowly on gender equity), between leagues, or between various sanctioning bodies.

The essence of politics is power. As just elaborated, organizations have power over sports, teams, coaches, and athletes. Power and control over sport also occur in less obvious guises. Sport, for example, has been affected mightily by television. Television networks, paying billions for rights, have insisted on changes such as converting golf from match play to medal play and interrupting the continuous sports of basketball, soccer, and hockey with mandatory time-outs. The Disney Corporation owns ABC Sports and ESPN and through these entities has exerted tremendous power over schedules, moving times and dates to accommodate them rather than the fans or the teams involved. Consider also the power exerted over sports by Time Warner, which owns *Sports Illustrated*, and TNT, HBO, and TBS television networks. Behind the scenes, power brokers for television networks have sometimes determined the opponents in football bowl games and invitational basketball tournaments. Other corporations, most notably those selling beer, soda, cars, cable television, and athletic apparel, have enormous power over sport. Some of these corporations actually own teams (e.g., Molson Brewing owns 20 percent of the Montreal Canadiens; Cablevision Systems owns Madison Square Garden, the New York Knicks, and the New York Rangers). Corporations provide the money to television through buying advertising time; they buy scoreboards and other equipment for local teams from professional teams to college and high school teams; they pay millions to become the official soft drink of the NFL or the Olympics or billions for television rights (e.g., NBC paid $3.5 billion for the television rights to the Olympic Games); the shoe companies in particular have coaches under contract (college and even some high school coaches), they run summer camps for prospective college athletes, and they have multimillion-dollar contracts with star athletes in a number of sports.

The linkage between sport and politics is quite obvious when the impact of the government on sports is considered. Several illustrations at the federal level make this point: (1) Legislation has been passed exempting professional sports from antitrust laws; (2) tax laws give special concessions to owners of professional teams (see chapter 10); (3) the blackouts of televised home games have been lifted for professional football under certain circumstances despite the protests of the league commissioner and the owners; (4) Congress decides which sport organization will have the exclusive right to select and train athletes for the Olympic Games; and (5) Congress crafts legislation that exempts college sports and their benefactors from taxes (see Box 9.1, *Thinking about Sport*, for more information on this subject).

Moreover, governments may encourage sport through various forms of funding. As we will see in the next chapter, municipal governments are very generous in subsidizing local teams owned

---

Box 9.1   *Thinking about Sport* Government Decisions Aid Big-Time College Sports

Congress has passed legislation that subsidizes athletic programs through a variety of tax breaks:

- Boosters are allowed to claim 80 percent of the money they spend on the premiums (fees) they pay to obtain season tickets. These are considered (by Congress) to be charitable contributions.
- Corporations underwrite bowl games and pay millions for the right to connect their corporate names to the bowls and to display their names and logos throughout the stadiums. Congress ruled that this is not advertising but philanthropy, thus exempting the bowl committees from taxation on the income money received from the corporations.
- Athletic departments benefit from taxpayer-subsidized loans to construct stadiums and arenas. Much of the $4 billion building boom in college athletics is underwritten with bonds that, because of the college's charitable status, are tax-exempt. This helps the purchasers of the bonds to escape taxes and saves the schools millions of dollars because the bonds pay interest several points below market level.

- College sports are exempt from the Unrelated Business Income Tax, a tax levy on the commercial activities of nonprofit organizations. This means, in effect, that the colleges pay no taxes on the income they receive from individual contributors, booster clubs, television networks, bowl and tournament payouts, corporate gifts, and ticket sales (including the sale of luxury suites).

These subsidies to college sports amount to at least $50 million a year. Congress justifies these subsidies because it has determined that college sport is a vital part of the broader educational mission of universities (for a contrary argument, see chapter 6).

Sources: Data are from a five-part series written by Gilbert M. Gaul and Frank Fitzpatrick for the *Philadelphia Inquirer* (10–24 September 2000), under the overall title "Rise of the Athletic Empires," http://inq.philly.com/contenVinquirer/2000/09/10/ front page/COLLEGE10.htm. See especially "Athletic Empires Depend on Taxpayer Dollars," http://philainq.infi.net/content/ inquirer/2000/09/13/front page/COLLEGE13.htm.

by private entrepreneurs. For the 2002 Winter Olympics in Salt Lake City, the federal government gave the local organizing committee hundreds of millions of dollars for road construction and laying fiber-optic cable—but especially for security, given the heightened fears of terrorist acts following the attacks on the World Trade Center in New York City and the Pentagon just five months earlier. The Utah state government also spent millions on public buildings, road construction, and security related to the Olympics. Salt Lake City and other local governments spent millions more on Olympics-related projects.

Another indication of the close relationship between sport and politics is that sports events and political situations have reciprocal effects. A famous example of a sports event affecting politics was the tour of China in 1971 by the American table tennis contingent. This tour proved to be the prelude to political exchanges between the two nations. Other examples were the wars that erupted between El Salvador and Honduras and between Gabon and the Congo after soccer matches. There are also many examples of political situations that have affected sports. The apartheid policies of South Africa have resulted many times in that nation being barred from sports competitions.

The U.S. boycott of the 1980 Olympics and Russia's boycott of the 1984 Olympics provide examples of another way in which sport and politics are related. They demonstrate clearly that sport is a tool of foreign policy. Sport is used to achieve legitimacy for a political regime, and sport can be used as a prelude to formal relations between countries. Conversely, refusal by one country to compete against another is a way of pressuring that country.

The institutional character of sport is a final source of the strong relationship between sport and politics. The institution of sport, just as other institutions, is conservative; it serves as a preserver and a legitimator of the existing order. The patriotic pageants that accompany sporting events reinforce the political system. Moreover, sport perpetuates many myths, such as that anyone with talent, regardless of race or social station, has an equal chance to succeed.

We have seen that the very nature of sport makes politics endemic to it. The remainder of this chapter will demonstrate this relationship further by examining the various political uses of sport, and the politics of the Olympic Games.

THE POLITICAL USES OF SPORT

Sport as a Propaganda Vehicle

Success in international competition frequently serves as a mechanism by which a society's ruling elite unites its citizens and attempts to impress the citizens of other countries. A classic example of this was Adolf Hitler's use of the 1936 Olympic Games to strengthen his control over the German

America's Jesse Owens, center, salutes during the presentation of his gold medal for the long jump on 11 August 1936, after defeating Nazi Germany's Lutz Long and Japan's Naoto Tajima. Owens was the first athlete to win four gold medals at a single Olympic Games. (AP Photo)

people and to introduce Nazi culture to the entire world. According to Richard D. Mandell in his book *The Nazi Olympics,* the festival planned for these games was a shrewdly propagandistic and brilliantly conceived charade that reinforced and mobilized the hysterical patriotism of the German masses.[5] The success of the German athletes at those Olympics—they won 89 medals, 23 more than U.S. athletes, and more than four times as many as any other country won—was "proof" of German superiority.

Before the breakup of the Eastern bloc countries, the reunification of the two Germanys, and the demise of the Soviet Union, the Communist nations used sport for promoting their common cause. During their heyday, the Communist countries dominated the Olympics, even though they were about 10 percent of the athletes at those events. This, the Communists argued, provided convincing evidence of the superiority of the Communist politico-economic system. Of the remaining Communist nations, perhaps Cuba takes sport the most seriously. Fidel Castro, Cuba's former leader, decreed that sport is a right of the people. No admission is ever charged to a sporting event. The most promising athletes are given the best coaching and training. Cuba devotes 3 percent of its national budget to its sports ministry, which encourages and trains elite athletes. In the Pan-American Games, Cuba tends to win about fifteen times more medals than the United States on a per capita basis, and Cuban premier Fidel Castro has proclaimed to Latin America that this is proof of the superiority of the Cuban people and the Cuban system (see Table 9.1 for an analysis of how the nations ranked in the 2004 Summer Olympics, taking population into account).

The most striking example of success in the modern Olympics before the breakdown of the Communist countries was East Germany. Although it was a nation smaller in population than California (16.6 million compared to 25 million in California at the time), East Germany consistently ranked in the top three nations in total medals and clearly outdistanced the Soviet Union and the United States on a per capita basis. In 1987, East Germany spent about 1 percent of its national budget on its massive sports program. From the age of seven, children were tested, and the most promising athletes were enrolled in sixteen special schools, where they received special training, medical and scientific expertise, and expert coaching in addition to their normal schooling. After their formal education was completed, the star athletes were given special jobs, permanent military deferments, and apartments. Why did East Germany devote so much money, time, and talent to sport? One reason was the competition between East and West Germany. A second reason

Table 9.1 Medal Standings per Country and per Population, Athens Olympics, 2004

Medals per country

1. United States	212
2. Russia	173
3. China	144
4. Australia	99
5. Japan	78
6. France	64
7. South Korea	60
8. United Kingdom	57
9. Cuba	52
10. Ukraine	46

Medals per million people

1. Bahamas	12.739
2. Australia	4.980
3. Cuba	4.604
4. Hungary	3.848
5. Jamaica	3.782
6. Norway	3.502
7. Latvia	3.442
8. New Zealand	3.249
9. Greece	3.091
10. Estonia	2.956
*	
*	
25. Russia	1.194
*	
*	
40. United States	0.727
Average for entire world	0.293

Source: Yahoo! GeoCities, "Population Adjusted Olympic Medal Table," http://www.geocities.com/unclebryan/Polympic.html?200719.

was East Germany's goal of international acceptance as a sovereign state. Another reason was the desire to demonstrate the superiority of the Communist way of life. According to Lynn Rosellini, "For the Communist nations, each victory was proof, as East German party General Secretary Erich Honecker put it, of 'their better socialist system.'"[6] East Germany was not unlike the other Communist countries in using sport for the accomplishment of political goals.

Currently, China is using the Soviet model to develop sports talent and to enhance the stature of the Chinese political and social system worldwide. About six million young athletes are trained at sport schools, with those at the highest levels subsidized by the state. The United States estimated that China spent from $400 million to $500 million to train athletes in the four years leading up to the 2008 Olympic Games.[7]

National efforts to use sport for political purposes are not limited to Communist countries. International sports victories are just as important to nations such as Canada and the United States. Canada has a federal agency, Sport Canada, and similar organizations at the provincial level that work to promote sports excellence in elite athletes. There is a federal Athlete Assistance Program, which gives living and training grants to outstanding athletes. There is a network of national training centers, with professionalized coaching, and a calendar of events. These efforts are done, according to former elite Canadian athlete and now sociology of sport scholar Bruce Kidd, to "enhance Canadian nationalism and [the Canadian state's] legitimacy."[8]

After the 1972 Olympics, when the Americans fared worse than was expected (especially in track and basketball), many editorial writers and politicians advocated plans whereby American athletes would be subsidized and would receive the best coaching and facilities to regain international athletic supremacy. This did not happen, and the cry arose again after the 1976 Olympics. As a result, Congress then appropriated funds for the United States Olympic Committee (USOC) and for the establishment of permanent training sites for the Winter and Summer Games. Also, since 1976 the USOC has gradually loosened the eligibility rules for participation. By 1984 this meant that athletes could be subsidized by corporations (e.g., Nike) and still compete. Most significant, athletes were permitted to retain their "amateur" standing even while receiving huge sums of money for appearances, performances, and endorsements, which means that world-class athletes make hundreds of thousands, some surpassing $1 million, without losing their eligibility. Currently, elite athletes receive money from these sources and, most significant, from the USOC and the sports' national governing bodies, which spent around $225 million from 2004 to 2008 to prepare them for the 2008 Olympic Games.

The U.S. government uses athletes to promote international goodwill and to enhance the American image abroad. The State Department, for example, sponsors tours of athletes to foreign countries for these purposes. In 2007, President Bush appointed Hall of Fame baseball player Cal Ripken, Jr., as a special envoy for the State Department.

Sport as an instrument of national policy is not limited to the industrialized nations of the world. The developing countries use sport even more for this purpose, with almost 90 percent having a cabinet-level post related to sport. The probable reason for such keen interest is that sport provides a relatively cheap political tool to accomplish national objectives of prestige abroad and unity at home.

Sport and Nationalism

Success in international sports competition tends to trigger pride among a nation's citizens. For example, even war-ravaged Iraq, with its ethnic and sectarian divides, was united briefly in 2007 when the national Iraq soccer team, composed of Shiites, Sunnis, and Kurds, won its first-ever Asian Cup. Spontaneous celebrations occurred with people dancing in the streets and waving Iraqi flags.

As mentioned previously, the Olympics and other international games tend to promote an "us versus them" feeling among athletes, coaches, politicians, the press, and fans. The Olympic Games, in this sense, represent a political contest, a symbolic world war in which nations win or lose.

This interpretation is commonly held; that is why citizens of each nation involved unite behind their flag and their athletes.

The integral interrelationship of sport and nationalism is easily seen in the blatantly militaristic pageantry that surrounds sports contests. The playing of the national anthem, the presentation of the colors, the jet aircraft flyovers, and the band forming a flag or a liberty bell are all political acts supportive of the existing political system.

This patriotic pageantry was especially evident at sports events following the terrorist attacks on 11 September 2001. Such a crisis can bring people together, uniting them in a common cause and a common bond of patriotism. Whereas before the terrorist tragedies, sports events began with the traditional singing of the national anthem, after 11 September sports events began with a moment of silent tribute to the fallen, a patriotic display of huge flags and other symbols, cannons firing, presentation of the colors, crowd chants of "U-S-A, U-S-A," and the crowds singing the national anthem with enthusiasm.

> The first Super Bowl after the September attack, on February 3, 2002, in New Orleans, outdid itself in nationalistic fervor. For the first gathering of 131 million U.S. households since September 11th, television and the NFL took the opportunity to celebrate all things American. Fox's three-hour pregame TV program had as its theme "Hope, Heroes, and Homeland," which it advertised in *USA Today* as a "celebration of football and the American spirit." Included in the event was a reenactment of the signing of the Declaration of Independence with famous athletes reciting that document, former presidents reading passages of Abraham Lincoln's speeches, Barry Manilow singing "Let Freedom Ring," and Paul McCartney singing his song "Freedom," with young women dressed as Statues of Liberty, military personnel, firefighters, and police holding flags. . . . At halftime, the NFL presented the band U2, who sang several songs on a stage in front of a huge unfurling scroll listing those whose lives were lost September 11th.[9]

In such ways, sports can have the important political consequence of helping to "glue" the American people back together after a national tragedy.

The irony is that nationalistic displays typically are not generally interpreted as political because they support the status quo. But what would happen if during the Iraq War, a college band would form a peace symbol at halftime? Such a display of antiwar spirit would be seen as blatantly political. But is not a halftime show in support of the government just as political?

Athletes who do not show proper respect for the flag or for the national anthem are subject to stiff penalties. When Tommie Smith and John Carlos raised gloved, clenched fists and bowed their heads during the national anthem at the 1968 Olympics, the USOC stripped them of their medals and banned them from further Olympic competition. Vince Mathews and Wayne Collett received the same penalty for their alleged disrespect to "The Star-Spangled Banner" at the 1972 Olympics. The USOC made such decisions even though they claim the Olympics are nonpolitical events—a claim that could not be further from the truth, as we will see later in this chapter.

Why are patriotic displays commonplace at sports contests but not at most other public events (e.g., plays, lectures, concerts, and movies)? The support for these patriotic rituals is so strong that whenever an occasional administrator decides not to play the national anthem at a sports event, there is, typically, a public outcry. Tom Wicker of the *New York Times* made the following speculation as to why athletic events are so overladen with patriotic themes:

> What is the correlation, if any, between patriotism and people battering one another in the boxing ring or in football games—or for that matter between patriotism and track meets, baseball games and other athletic events that are not so violent?
>
> The explanation probably is that symbols like the flag and the anthem, appropriate as they are to the warlike spirit, are equally appropriate to sports events, with their displays of the instinct to combat and the will to win. Even the so-called "noncontact" sports exalt competition and the pursuit of victory, including the kind of individual heroism and team spirit that are evoked in wartime.[10]

For whatever reason, sport competition and nationalism are closely intertwined. When athletes of one country compete against those of another, national unity is the result for both sides, unless the athletes of one do poorly. Citizens take pride in their representatives' accomplishments, viewing them as collective achievements. This identification with athletes and their cause of winning for the nation's glory tends to unite the citizenry regardless of social class, race, and regional differences (see Box 9.2, *Thinking about Sport,* concerning South Africa). Thus, sport can be used by political leaders whose nations have problems with divisiveness.

Sport as an Opiate of the Masses

We have shown that sport success can unite a nation through pride. This pride in a nation's success, because it transcends the social classes, serves as an "opiate of the masses." It enables the poor to forget partially the harshness of their lives. In 1994, for example, when Haiti was on the verge of a severe crisis, the embattled military ruler, Raoul Cedras, paid for the broadcasting rights to the World Cup soccer matches. The spirits of the Haitians were raised as their adopted team, Brazil, was successful. Rather than massing in the streets to demonstrate against a political regime that oppressed them, the citizenry danced in the streets as their favorite team won. Moreover, as the games were played on the government-owned station, the rulers used halftime to inflame anti-American feelings by showing footage of the U.S. invasion of Panama in 1989, focusing on the bombing of res-

---

Box 9.2 *Thinking about Sport* **Sport Unifies Whites and Blacks in South Africa**

South Africa was barred for a time from the Olympic Games and other international competitions, most notably the World Cup of the favorite sport of whites—rugby. With the fall of apartheid and the election of Nelson Mandela, the sports world accepted South Africa: so much so that it was allowed to host the 1995 World Cup in rugby.

President Mandela used the rugby World Cup as an opportunity to bring change in South Africa. He visited the training camp of South Africa's team—the Springboks. While there he put on a Springbok cap.

This was no casual gesture. The nickname Springbok is controversial in South Africa, strongly associated with the proapartheid white regimes of the past. Then Mandela pointedly told the rugby players, "The whole nation is behind you."

The Springboks (white except for one black player) took that message to heart. The day before their game against Australia the players requested a tour of Robben Island, off Cape Town, where Mandela had been imprisoned for eighteen years. They visited his former cell and afterward vowed to dedicate their efforts in the World Cup to their president.

Before one of the matches Mandela gave a speech before a primarily black audience. He said, "This cap does honor to our boys. I ask you to stand by them tomorrow because they are our kind." To which *Sports Illustrated* remarked:

> Our kind. Not black. Not white. South African. The rugby team became a symbol for the country as a whole. . . .

Given the right time and place, sport is capable of starting such a process in a society. It is only a start, of course. The hard work lies ahead, after the crowds have dispersed and the headlines have ceased. South Africa's racial and economic woes are not behind it. Far from it. But thanks to the common ground supplied by a rugby pitch, those problems appear less imposing than they did only a month ago.

The Springboks won the World Cup, defeating the world's two rugby powers, Australia and New Zealand, in the process. For the first time in South Africa's troubled history, whites and blacks found themselves unified by a sport.

That was 1995. Now fast forward to 2006. Whereas the Springboks had only one black player in 1995, eleven years later they had 6 black or colored players in the starting 15. For the first time in the history of South African cricket, the national team was captained by a nonwhite player in 2006, and 5 of its squad of 13 were black or colored. Clearly, there has been progress, but whites, who are but 9 percent of the population, remain the majority on the field. The point, though, is that the national teams in rugby and cricket are multiracial, and in this country obsessed by sport, that is an important symbol of progress toward racial integration and national unity.

Sources: E. M. Swift, "Bok to the Future," *Sports Illustrated,* 3 July 1995, 32–33; and "On a Sticky Wicket," *The Economist,* 22 July 2006, 46–47.

idential areas. Thus, sport serves as a safety valve for releasing tensions that might otherwise be directed toward disrupting the existing social order.

Sport also acts as an opiate by perpetuating the belief that persons from the lowest classes can be upwardly mobile through success in sports. Chapter 12 will deal with this topic in more detail; meanwhile, it is enough to say that for every major leaguer who came up from poverty, tens of thousands did not. The point, however, is that most Americans believe that sport is a mobility escalator and that it is merely a reflection of the opportunity structure of the society in general. Again, poor youths who might otherwise invest their energies in changing the system work instead on a jump shot. The potential for change is thus impeded by sport.[11]

The Exploitation of Sport by Politicians

Politicians may use athletics and athletes in several ways. First, an athlete can use his or her athletic fame as a springboard to getting elected or appointed to office. Some examples are: Professional basketball players Tom McMillen and Bill Bradley served in Congress; world-class runners Ralph Metcalfe, Bob Mathias, and Jim Ryun were congressmen; professional football players Steve Largent, J. C. Watts, and Jack Kemp were elected to the House of Representatives; and Major League Baseball players Wilmer "Vinegar Bend" Mizell and Heath Shuler served in the House and Jim Bunning in the Senate. Incidentally, the vast majority of ex-athletes who become successful politicians are Republicans. This may be the consequence of athletes being financially successful or it may be that they are conservative because the political system has been good to them.[12]

Of course, these persons may have had the political skills to be successful in political races anyway, but athletic fame undoubtedly helped them. Politicians also find it beneficial to get the approval and active campaign support of sports stars. Athletes, because they are well known and admired, can get votes for either themselves or for candidates whom they support. Sport is so popular in American society that politicians may use examples of sport or sport metaphors to communicate with the public.[13] Moreover, politicians find it useful to identify with teams and to attend sports events. For example, on that special evening in 1995 when Cal Ripken, Jr., broke Lou Gehrig's record of 2,130 consecutive games played, President Clinton attended and was highly visible as he congratulated Ripken publicly and spent time in the television booth during the broadcast. Presidents Ronald Reagan, George H. W. Bush, Bill Clinton, and George W. Bush have thrived on interaction with athletes and sports teams. Routinely, champions from colleges, the professionals, and the Olympics are invited to the White House. The trend is for presidents, governors, members of Congress, mayors, and other political officials to identify more and more with sports and sports heroes.

Politicians capitalize on the popularity of athletes by using them to support the system. In the United States, for example, athletes are often sent overseas to maintain the morale of service personnel. Athletes appear in advertisements that urge the viewer or reader to join the military or Reserve Officers' Training Corps (ROTC), to vote, and to avoid drugs. Athletes are also asked to give patriotic speeches on holidays and other occasions.

Use of athletes for the maintenance of the status quo is common in other countries as well. Athletes may be asked to visit factories and villages to hold demonstrations and make political speeches. These activities spread the philosophy of the rulers, help unify the people, and bolster the morale of the factory and farm workers to increase production.

Sport as a Vehicle of Change in Society

A recurring theme of this book is that sport reflects the dynamics of the larger society. It is not surprising, therefore, that the social and political turmoil of American society in the 1960s had its effect on the sports world.

Sport and sporting events were used by revolutionaries and by reformers to attack racism and American involvement in Vietnam, the two major societal problems. Racism was attacked in a number of ways. Most dramatic was the proposed boycott of the 1968 Olympics by African American athletes. Harry Edwards, an African American sociologist and former athlete, was a leader of this boycott. His rationale for the protest was: "The roots of the revolt of the black athlete spring from the same seed that produced the sit-ins, the freedom rides, and the rebellions in Watts, Detroit, and Newark. The athletic revolt springs from a disgust and dissatisfaction with the racism prevalent in American society—including the sports world."[14]

Another boycott was directed against the New York Athletic Club's annual indoor track meet. The goal of this action was to dramatize and to change the club's policy of excluding Jews, African Americans, and other minorities from membership. African American athletes at schools such as San Jose State and the University of Wyoming participated in a symbolic protest in the late 1960s against Brigham Young, a Mormon-supported university (the Wyoming protestors were removed from the team by the coach). These athletes wore armbands to symbolize their contempt for the racial policies of the Mormon Church, which at that time excluded African American males from the priesthood.

Two examples from the early 1990s show another avenue for sport changing society, this time by the power structure of sport. In 1990 the Professional Golf Association (PGA) made it a policy to no longer hold its championship at country clubs that excluded minorities as members. This forced Shoal Creek Country Club in Birmingham, Alabama, the site of the 1990 championship, to alter its admissions policies. Similarly, many country clubs opened their memberships (although a few refused and, as a result, were ineligible to host a PGA championship). The second example of the power structure using its power to reduce racism was a political decision by the National Football League. The league decided to take the 1993 Super Bowl away from Phoenix because Arizona refused to have an official, statewide holiday to celebrate the birthday of Martin Luther King, Jr. In effect, the league was saying to the citizens of Arizona, "If you want to play the game of bigotry, we'll take our millions of dollars in tourist trade and scores of hours of television time someplace else."[15] This ploy worked, as Arizona accepted the King holiday, followed by the league awarding Phoenix the 1996 Super Bowl.

Another example of a sports organization using its power to bring social change occurred when the NCAA executive committee in 2001 agreed not to schedule championship events in South Carolina until at least 2004 because the Confederate flag is displayed on the statehouse grounds. This boycott of South Carolina began in January 2000 with actions by the National Association for the Advancement of Colored People (NAACP), followed by individual teams canceling games and matches in South Carolina. Several prominent individuals in sport expressed support of the boycott, including Lou Holtz, then head football coach at the University of South Carolina.

The NCAA ruled in 2005 that any school with a nickname or logo considered racially or ethnically "hostile" or "abusive" would be prohibited from using it in postseason events. This meant that mascots would not be allowed to perform at tournament games, and band members and cheerleaders would be barred from using Native Americans as symbols on their uniforms. Thus, the NCAA made a political decision—that it would not permit the use of Native American symbols by athletic teams at their championship events because they often are demeaning caricatures of Native peoples.

At another level, there has been an international campaign against the use of sweatshop labor to produce sporting goods in developing nations. United Students Against Sweatshops organized anti-sweatshop campaigns on hundreds of campuses, mandating that the clothes bearing their collegiate logos be manufactured under fair and ethical conditions. This effort, most notably against Nike's exploitation of Third World workers, has been student-led in the United States. As a consequence of activists pressing Nike and other companies, Nike in 2005 revealed the location of its factories in the Third World and admitted to widespread problems in its Asian factories. Nike has joined the Fair Labor Association. This group, which includes other footwear and clothing makers as well as nongovernmental organizations and universities, conducts independent audits designed to improve working conditions across the industry.[16]

These examples are interesting for three reasons: (1) The power structure of sports has never taken the lead in social causes before (these acts may, therefore, be anomalies or, perhaps, the beginning of a trend); (2) they have political potential, ironically, either way (positively, because the leagues hold the power to "blackmail" recalcitrants into line, or negatively, because of a backlash from the public who resents blatant politics [i.e., anti-status quo politics] from sports organizations); and (3) these examples show once again how sport and politics are intertwined. The worldwide popularity of sport and the importance attached to it by fans and politicians alike make sport an ideal platform for political protest. However, the use of sport for protest, especially from the powerless, although an important means of dramatizing social problems, is generally unsuccessful in causing meaningful change. This is a tribute to the institutional character of sport, with its built-in bias for preserving and legitimizing the status quo.

THE GLOBALIZATION OF SPORT

Our identification with a sports team typically has a geographical base.[17] In this sense, sports are local. We identify with the local high school, college, professional team. So, too, with national teams and athletes competing with their foreign counterparts, which we concentrate on here. Sports competition is clearly *us* versus *them*. But this identification with the local is breaking down. College and professional teams now often have foreign players, some of whom do not speak English well and are unfamiliar with U.S. customs. Some sports, golf and tennis, for example, are already global sports with athletes competing in tournaments worldwide. Women's professional golf in the United States is dominated by South Koreans and Mexicans. The U.S. Open in tennis is routinely won by a Swiss (on the men's side) and either a Belgian or a Russian (on the women's side). (We will return to this global migration of athletes in chapter 13.) There is a spread of U.S. influence around the world as sports events are televised globally and U.S. sports leagues seek global expansion. Transnational corporations use sports and athletes to market their products worldwide.

Globalization, of course, is not limited to sport. Globalization refers to the ever greater connectedness among the world's people. It is a process whereby goods, information, people, money, communication, sport, and various forms of culture such as fashion move across national boundaries. Globalization is not a recent phenomenon. For thousands of years, people have traveled, traded, and migrated across political boundaries exchanging food, artifacts, and knowledge. In sports, the cultural imperialism employed by British colonists, for example, brought their sports (soccer, rugby, cricket) to their colonies, where they flourished. Golf began in Scotland and has become a sport played almost everywhere. The Olympic movement spread around the globe during the twentieth century. While baseball began in the United States, it is now extremely popular in Latin America, the Caribbean countries, Japan, and South Korea. So, too, with basketball, which has spread especially to China, Australia, and Western and Central Europe.

The globalization of sport has political consequences. The process blurs national allegiances. Friendships through sport extend across political boundaries. Transnational corporations exert their power for profit, power that often exceeds that of the nations in which they operate. Local cultures may readily adopt new sports forms from other societies or they may interpret them as cultural imperialism. Nationalism may be exacerbated or diminished by global processes. The use of low-wage labor in poor countries to produce products for consumers in wealthy countries increases the economic divide among nations. Transnational sports organizations may decide to exclude certain nations from participation because of their political actions, as we will see in the next section.

THE POLITICAL OLYMPICS

The motto of the Olympic Games is "Citius, Altius, Fortius" ("Faster, Higher, Stronger"). It implies that athletes should strive for ever better performances. Moreover, the objective of the Olympic movement is "to educate young people through sport in a spirit of better understanding between each other and of friendship, thereby helping to build a better and more peaceful world." However, since the revival of the Olympics in 1896, there has been an erosion of the prominence of athletic accomplishments and the corresponding ascendance of political considerations. This section addresses the political side of the Olympics and offers suggestions for reducing the corrosive effects of politics on the Olympic movement and its ideals.

Political Problems

Politics surrounding the Olympics is manifested in five major ways: (1) excessive nationalism within nations concerning the performance of their athletes in the Olympics; (2) use of the Olympics as a site for political demonstrations and violence by political dissidents in the host country; (3) decisions by ruling bodies to deny participation by certain nations; (4) decisions by nations to boycott the Games for political reasons; and (5) the political organization of the Olympics.

Excessive Nationalism within Nations
Nationalism related to the Olympics that goes beyond its appropriate boundaries is expressed in several ways. Foremost, there is the use of athletics to promote political goals. As we have seen, Hitler turned the 1936 Games in Berlin into a propaganda show to legitimate Nazi Germany. Similarly, nations tend to use their showing in international athletic events as an indicator of the superiority of their politico-economic systems. Some nations are quite blatant in their efforts to demonstrate their superiority, offering large prizes to their athletes who win medals.

A second manifestation of excessive nationalism is that in the zeal to win, some nations may promote the use of performance-enhancing drugs for their athletes. This was clearly true for the East Germans before 1990. Each subsequent Olympic Games results in some athletes being forced to forfeit medals because they have failed drug tests.

A third indication of national chauvinism has to do with the reporting of international events. Members of the media in reporting the Olympics may let their politics distort their analyses. Jay Coakley puts it this way:

> Television companies buy the rights to take the video images they want from the Olympics and combine them with their own narratives to appeal to audiences in their countries. Thus, instead of bringing the world together around a single experience, the coverage presents heavily nationalized and commercialized versions of the Olympic Games.[18]

Use of the Olympics by Political Dissidents in the Host Country
This is a common problem associated with the Olympics. At virtually every recent Olympics there have been political demonstrations, threats, and violence by disaffected groups. The host country has usually responded with extra security and police violence. The 1992 Olympics in Barcelona faced this problem as Basque separatists threatened to use the Olympics as a vehicle for worldwide recognition of their plight. A bomb was exploded at the Atlanta Olympics in 1996 by a domestic terrorist who objected to the legalization of abortion. At the Sydney Olympics in 2000, there were peaceful demonstrations by Aborigines against the discrimination they face in Australia. At the Athens Olympics in 2004, demonstrators against the Iraq War marched on the U.S. embassy, protesting a visit of U.S. Secretary of State Colin Powell.

Use of the Olympics for Political Purposes by Organizations outside the Host Nation
In 1968 Harry Edwards asked African American athletes to boycott the Olympic Games in Mexico City as a way to inform the world of the indignities of second-class treatment suffered by U.S. blacks. The call to boycott failed (although a few athletes did boycott), but for many African American athletes who did participate in the Olympics, their

Demonstrators in front of European Commission headquarters in Brussels wear banners in protest of China's hosting of the 2008 Olympics and against the alleged Chinese abuses of the Tibetan people. (AP Photo/Virginia Mayo)

mood was sullen and resentful. Tommie Smith broke the world record in the 200 meters and his teammate John Carlos took the bronze medal. Following the presentation of medals for that race as the U.S. national anthem was played, Smith and Carlos gave the Black Power salute to dramatize on the world stage the plight of U.S. African Americans.

Four years later at the Munich Olympics a group of Palestinian terrorists stormed the living quarters of the Israeli team, capturing them. Their goal was to negotiate a trade whereby the Israeli athletes would be freed if Israel would release 234 Palestinians held in Israeli jails. German commandos tried to free the captive athletes, but a terrorist unpinned a grenade, killing eleven athletes and five kidnappers.

These are examples of how the Olympics have been used as a stage for political purposes. With the terrorist attacks on the World Trade Center in New York City and the Pentagon in Washington, D.C., on 11 September 2001, the world was on heightened alert for future attacks, whether by planes, bombs, germs, or computer. For example, the Greeks in 2004 spent an unprecedented 1 billion euros for the security of the first post–11 September Summer Games. At those Olympics, Tibetan activists began a four-year campaign to spoil China's hosting of the 2008 Olympics, scuffling with police just before organizers of the 2008 Beijing Games were to receive the Olympic flag at the closing ceremony. At the same time, a protest was staged in Beijing, aiming to focus attention, in their words, on Tibetan political prisoners and stating that the Tibetan people live without human rights under Chinese rule. Preceding the Beijing Olympics, various groups protested against China's alleged complicity with mass killings in Sudan (because the Sudanese sell the Chinese four hundred thousand barrels of oil a day and China owns 40 percent of Sudan's largest oil company), calling those Games the "Genocide Olympics." Other anti-Chinese protests centered on human rights issues such as the working conditions in Chinese factories, political prisoners, and the environment.

Political Decisions by National and International Olympic Committees

The International and National Olympic ruling bodies make a number of decisions based on politics. The choice of Olympic sites is made by the members of the IOC. This decision is crucial to the potential host nations and cities because of the possible economic benefits, the legitimacy of that nation's government, and the potential of being the center of world attention. This site-selection decision historically has been based on either bribery or politics (or both). Let's consider bribery first. Andrew Jennings, an investigative journalist, has cited numerous scandals involving the IOC, including the use of bribery to buy votes for Olympics site selection.[19] His argument was validated by the scandals associated with the awarding of the 2002 Winter Olympics to Salt Lake City. The USOC spent $60,000 on favors for foreign sports officials who, in return, supported Salt Lake City's bid. Another $1.2 million was spent by the Salt Lake City Organizing Committee on scholarships, shopping sprees, cash payments, free housing, jobs, and other gifts to those who would make the decision—IOC members and their family members. Similar bribes were made by the organizers of the Nagano Winter Olympics in 1998, and the Atlanta organizers for the 1996 Summer Games.

During the Cold War the IOC was careful to alternate Olympic sites between countries in the U.S. sphere and Communist nations. In 2001 the IOC selected Beijing for the 2008 Olympics in a highly charged political atmosphere. Opponents argued that China was in violation of human rights. Others argued that giving China the Olympics might promote a greater opening up of the country, promote ties with Taiwan, and ease tensions with the United States and its allies. Friends of China argued that awarding the Games to China would be a sign of that country's emergence as a major power, one befitting its population of 1.2 billion. Although they do not officially vote in these decisions on Olympic sites, some unofficial players have power: corporations that pay as much as many millions of dollars for the designation as an official sponsor. If a number of them threatened to withdraw their support, the IOC would likely give in to their demands. Likewise, when NBC pays the IOC $3.5 billion for the rights to televise the Olympics from 2000 to 2008, it becomes a major player in the decisionmaking.

In addition to site selection, the IOC has made a number of other blatantly political decisions. The following are a few examples from the last sixty years of decisions made for political reasons by Olympics ruling bodies.[20]

- 1936: As a concession to the Nazis, the United States dropped two Jewish sprinters from the 400-meter relay.
- 1948: Israel was excluded from participation after a threat of an Arab boycott.
- 1952: East Germany was denied participation because it was not a "recognized state."
- 1960: The IOC decreed that North and South Korea should compete as one team, using the same flag, emblem, and uniform. Nationalist China was forced to compete under the name of Taiwan.
- 1964: South Africa was banned from the Olympics for its apartheid policies.
- 1968: Tommie Smith and John Carlos of the United States raised a Black Power salute during the American national anthem. The IOC was outraged. It ordered the USOC to disallow the two from further competition in Mexico City. The United States refused but capitulated when the IOC threatened that it would disqualify the entire U.S. track-and-field team. The USOC sent Smith and Carlos home and banned them from Olympic competition for life.
- 1972: The IOC ruled that Rhodesia would be allowed to participate. Many African nations were incensed by this action because of the racist policies of the ruling elite in Rhodesia and threatened a boycott of the Games unless Rhodesia was barred. The IOC bowed to this pressure and rescinded its earlier action.
- 1991: The International Olympic Committee agreed to let South Africa participate in the 1992 Olympics provided that it meet certain conditions regarding the dismantling of apartheid.
- 2000: North and South Korea marched as one nation in the opening ceremonies under a single white flag with a blue depiction of an undivided peninsula, though they competed as separate nations.
- 2008: Research by the Center on Housing Rights and Evictions on Olympic Games from 1988 through 2008 shows that the host nations displaced thousands.[21] (See Box 9.3, *Thinking about Sport,* for examples.)

Political Decisions by Individual Nations Regarding the Olympics

International incidents that have nothing to do with the Olympic Games have sometimes caused

Box 9.3 Thinking about Sport The Olympic Games and the Displacement of People

The Switzerland-based Centre on Housing Rights and Evictions examined each Olympic Games from 1988 to the buildup for the Beijing Games in 2008 and concluded that the host countries, collectively, had displaced more than two million people, mostly minorities such as the homeless and the poor. Consider these examples:

- Policies at the 1988 Olympics in Seoul, South Korea, evicted 720,000 people from their homes to provide space for various venues. To clean up the city for visitors, street vendors were banned, and homeless people and beggars were rounded up and housed in a prison camp.
- The Barcelona Games in 1992 saw Gypsy communities evicted and dispersed. The streets were "cleansed" by dispersing beggars, prostitutes, and street sellers. Between 1986 and 1992, housing prices rose by 240 percent as the Olympic districts were gentrified and public housing demolished.
- In preparation for the 1996 Olympics in Atlanta, large housing projects (mostly housing African Americans) were demolished and replaced with middle-class homes. Around 30,000 families were evicted, and 9,000 homeless people were arrested and locked up until the Games were over.
- Because the 2000 Games in Sydney were built on surplus government land, no one was directly displaced, but the city's gentrification led to housing prices more than doubling from 1996 to 2003 and rents soaring by 40 percent, forcing people to move. In the year before the Olympics, there was a 400 percent increase in tenant evictions.
- In Beijing, a year before the Games were to begin, 1.25 million people had already been displaced and another 250,000 were due to be evicted.

So, while the Olympic Games enhance the prestige of the host city and nation, and many businesses and individuals benefit economically, some bear the burden. Not surprisingly, the costs and burdens are borne by those least able to bear them—the powerless.

Sources: Centre on Housing Rights and Evictions, "Fair Play for Housing Rights: Mega-Events, Olympic Games and Housing Rights," 2007, http://www.cohre.org/store/attachments/COHRE%27s%20Olympics%20Report.pdf; George Monbiot, "Everywhere They Go, the Olympic Games Become an Excuse for Eviction and Displacement," *The Guardian,* 2 July 2007; and Calum MacLeod and Paul Wiseman, "Whatever It Takes, China Aims for Dazzling Games," *USA Today,* 6 August 2007, pp. IC, 2C.

---

nations to withdraw their teams from competition. Some examples are:

- 1952: Taiwan boycotted the Games when Communist China was admitted to the International Olympic Committee.
- 1956: Egypt, Lebanon, and Iraq boycotted the Olympics because of the Anglo-French seizure of the Suez Canal. Spain, Switzerland, and the Netherlands withdrew from the Olympics in protest after the Soviet Union invaded Hungary.
- 1976: Twenty-eight African nations boycotted the Games because New Zealand, whose rugby team had toured South Africa, was allowed to compete.
- 1980: Some fifty-four nations, including the United States, West Germany, Canada, and Japan, boycotted the Games because of the Soviet Union's invasion of Afghanistan.
- 1984: Fourteen nations, most notably the Soviet Union, East Germany, Cuba, Bulgaria, and Poland, boycotted the Games because they were held in the United States.
- 1988: Cuba boycotted the Summer Games because North Korea was not allowed to co-host the Games with South Korea. North Korea joined in the boycott.

The Political Organization of the Olympics

In addition to the corruptions of the Olympic ideals that have been outlined, the very ways that the Games are organized are political. Nations select which athletes will perform (i.e., no athlete can perform without national sponsorship). The IOC provides ceremonies where athletes march behind their country's flag. After each event, the winner's national anthem is played and the flags of the three medal winners are raised at the awards ceremony. The IOC also considers political criteria in the selection of the site of the Olympics and in the choice of judges.

A Proposal for Change

To be fair in this appraisal, the Olympic Games do attempt to promote the idea of oneness with the use of the Olympic hymn and the Olympic flag (five interlaced rings representing "the union of the five continents and the meeting of athletes from all over the world at the Olympic Games in a spirit of fair and frank competition"). However, as Gilbert Cranberg has pointed out, "nationalism not merely intrudes, it dominates." For him, another Olympiad will be another "orgy of flag-waving. Not just literally, but in the way Olympic contests get the patriotic juices flowing."[22]

Is there a way to organize the Olympics to accomplish the aim of neutralizing the crippling political problems that work to negate the Olympic ideals? We offer the following proposals to achieve that aim:

1. *Establish two permanent sites for the Games.* Each permanent site must be neutral, for otherwise the Games will continue to be subject to the influence of power politics. The choices most often mentioned are Greece for the Summer Olympics and Switzerland for the Winter Games. Greece is a natural choice because the ancient Olympian Games were held there every four years for more than one thousand years, ending in 393 C.E. Even better, each of these permanent sites should be in a free zone. A free zone would be land ceded to the International Olympic Committee and therefore land that no nation claims, just as the United Nations is located in a free zone in New York City. Jay Coakley has presented an alternative to permanent sites that has merit.[23] He suggests the use of multiple sites for each Olympic Games. In other words, track and field could be held in one nation, swimming in another, and so on. This would enable poorer nations to be hosts and to benefit economically. It would also enable media spectators to see and appreciate a variety of cultural settings rather than just a narrow focus on one city and nation as is now the case.

2. *Restrict the events to competition among individuals.* All team sports must be eliminated because political considerations are inevitable when teams represent nations. A second reason for eliminating team sports is that they are inherently unfair; the larger the population base of a nation, the more likely that country will be able to field a superior team.

3. *Athletes must represent only themselves.* Athletes, in actuality and symbolically, should not represent a country, nor should any nation-state be represented by uniforms, flags, national anthems, or political leaders. When an athlete is awarded his or her medal for winning an event, only the Olympic hymn should be played. Athletes should also be randomly assigned to housing and eating arrangements at the Games to reduce national identification and to maximize cross-national interaction.

4. *Revise the opening ceremonies so that athletes enter the area with other athletes in their events.* As Jay Coakley has argued, "This would emphasize unity and fellowship rather than the political and economic systems into which the athletes were born through no choice of their own."[24]

5. *Make all athletes (amateur and professional) eligible for competition.* The nation-state should not be involved in the selection process because this encourages nationalistic feelings. To ensure that the best athletes of the world are able to compete, a minimum standard for each event should be set by the governing board. Athletes meeting this standard would have all expenses to meet in regional competition paid by the Olympic Committee. At the regionals another and higher standard of excellence would be set for ath-

letes to qualify for the Olympics. Again, for those athletes qualifying for the Olympics, all expenses for travel and per diem would be paid by the Olympic Committee.

6. *Subsidize the cost of the Olympics from revenues generated from spectators' admissions to the regionals, from admissions to the Games, and from television.* By establishing permanent sites and eliminating team events, the cost of the Olympics would be reduced significantly. Revenues from admissions and television (the IOC receives one-third of television revenues) should cover the costs after the Games are established. During the building of the permanent sites, though, the Olympic Committee may need a subsidy or loan from the United Nations. Television revenues present a particularly thorny problem because the revenue potential is great and this lends itself to threats of overcommercialization, the intrusion of corporations into the decision-making arena, and jingoism by chauvinistic television commentators. To reduce these potential dangers, the events could be televised and reported by a company strictly controlled by the Olympic Committee. The televising of the Olympics would be provided to each country at a cost determined by the existing number of television sets in that country. Each nation would decide how the fee would be paid, but the important point is that no country would have any control over what would be shown or the commentary emanating from the Games.

7. *Establish an Olympic Committee and a secretary-general to prepare for and oversee the Games.* The composition of this committee would be crucial. Currently the members of the IOC are taken from national committees, with an important criterion being the maintenance of a political balance between opposing factions. The concept of a ruling body is essential, but the committee should be reorganized to reduce political considerations. This is a baffling problem because the selection will inevitably involve politics. One possibility would be to incorporate the selection procedures used in the United Nations to select its secretary-general. These procedures have worked, even during the darkest days of the Cold War, toward the selection of a competent, objective, and nonaligned (of neither a pro-Western or a pro-Eastern bloc) arbitrator. In addition to an Olympic secretary-general, a governing board and a permanent staff would have to be established.

Now is a propitious time to depoliticize the Olympics. The tensions and paranoia associated with the Cold War have receded. We have seen cooperative efforts between the two superpowers that have not occurred since World War II. The Eastern bloc is no longer a force. East and West Germany are now Germany. The European Economic Community will break down nationalistic barriers further. Although there are international tensions, wars, and acts of terrorism, could we take this turning point in history and reorganize the Olympics to eliminate as much of the politics from it as possible? The task is challenging but not impossible. The Olympic movement is important. That is why it must be radically altered from its present form if its lofty goals are to be realized.

SUMMARY

Two themes have dominated this chapter: Sport is political in character, and sport, like all institutions, is conservative. This basic conservatism in sport has two important implications for society. First, the athletic programs of the schools, to which most persons are exposed, support and reinforce a view of the world and of society that perpetuates the status quo. In the United States this is accomplished through the promotion of American values and the support of the American politico-economic system.

A second implication, given the institutional character of sport, is that efforts to change sport will rarely come from those who control sport. Moreover, any attack on sport will be defined as an attack on society itself. Thus, change in sport will be slow and congruent with what is happening in society.

WEB RESOURCES

www.The5rings.com
Unofficial source for Olympic Games information, both past and present.

www.olympic.org
Official site of the International Olympic Committee.

www.usoc.org
Official site for the USOC.

www.ajennings.8m.com
The website of Andrew Jennings, an investigative reporter who focuses on scandals associated with the Olympic Games.

www.cohre.org/store/attachments/COHRE%27s%20Olympics%20Report.pdf
This is a report by the Centre on Housing Rights and Evictions that shows how the staging of megaevents, most notably the Olympic Games, creates the forced eviction of thousands of people from their homes, causing severe hardship and misery.

www.aafla.com
The site of the Amateur Athletic Foundation. Go to "Sports Library" for historical and political information about sports.

www.studentsagainstsweatshops.org
The site of the Sweat-Free Campus campaign, which has been successful in achieving better wages and humane working conditions for workers making athletic apparel.

NOTES

1. Max Weber, *Economy and Society,* trans. Guenther Roth and G. Wittick (New York: Bedminster Press, 1968), first published in 1922.

2. Barrie Houlihan, "Politics and Sport," in *Handbook of Sport Studies,* ed. Jay Coakley and Eric Dunning (London: Sage, 2000), 213–227.

3. Phillip Goodhart and Christopher Chataway, *War without Weapons* (London: Allen, 1968).

4. See Ralf Dahrendorf, *Class and Class Conflict in Industrial Society* (Palo Alto, Calif.: Stanford University Press, 1959), and Robert Michels, *Political Parties* (New York: Dover, 1959), first published in 1914.

5. Richard D. Mandell, *The Nazi Olympics* (New York: Macmillan, 1971).

6. Cited in Lynn Rosellini, "The Sports Factories," *U.S. News and World Report,* 17 February 1992, 51.

7. Calum MacLeod, "Chinese Sports Schools Feel an Urgency to Find Gold," *USA Today,* 14 June 2007, pp. 1A, 6A, 8.

8. Bruce Kidd, "How Do We Find Our Own Voices in the 'New World Order'?" *Sociology of Sport Journal* 8 (June 1991): 182. See also Donald Macintosh, Tom Bedecki, and C. E. S. Franks, *Sport and Politics in Canada: Federal Government Involvement since 1981* (Kingston, Ont.: McGill-Queen's University Press, 1987); and Donald Macintosh and Don Whitson, *The Game Planners: Transforming Canada's Sports System* (Kingston, Ont.: McGill-Queen's University Press, 1990).

9. D. Stanley Eitzen, *Fair and Foul: Beyond the Myths and Paradoxes of Sport,* 3rd ed. (Lanham, Md.: Rowman & Littlefield, 2006).

10. Tom Wicker, "Patriotism for the Wrong Ends," *New York Times,* 19 January 1973.

11. For greater depth on the theme of sport as an opiate, see Paul Hoch, *Rip Off the Big Game* (New York: Doubleday, 1972); and Jean-Marie Brohm, *Sport: A Prison of Measured Time,* trans. Ian Fraser (London: Ink Links, 1978).

12. Frank Deford, "Athletes Turning Politicians, Go Republican," National Public Radio, 3 May 2006, www.npr.org/templates/topics/topic.php?topicID=1012.

13. See Sue Curry Jansen and Don Sabo, "The Sport/War Metaphor: Hegemonic Masculinity, the Persian Gulf War, and the New World Order," *Sociology of Sport Journal* 11 (March 1994): 1–17; and Ike Balbus, "Politics as Sports: The Political Ascendancy of the Sports Metaphor in America," *Monthly Review* 26 (March 1975): 26–39.

14. See Jansen and Sabo, "The Sport/War Metaphor: Hegemonic Masculinity, the Persian Gulf War, and the New World Order," 1–17; and Balbus, "Politics as Sports: The Political Ascendancy of the Sports Metaphor in America," 26–39.

15. Teri Thompson, "Ban the Klan," *Westword,* 13 November 1993, p. 28.

16. David Teather, "Nike Acknowledges Massive Labor Exploitation in Its Overseas Sweatshops," *The*

Guardian, 14 April 2005, reprinted at http://www.organicconsumers.org/clothes/nike041504.cfm. See also George H. Sage, "Justice Do It! The Nike Transnational Advocacy Network: Organization, Collective Actions, and Outcomes," *Sociology of Sport Journal* 16 (1999): 206–233; and George H. Sage, "Corporate Globalization and Sporting Goods Manufacturing: The Case of Nike," in *Sport in Contemporary Society: An Anthology,* 7th ed., ed. D. Stanley Eitzen (Boulder, Colo.: Paradigm, 2005), 78–86.

17. Much of this section is from Eitzen, *Fair and Foul,* chap. 11; and D. Stanley Eitzen and Maxine Baca Zinn, eds., *Globalization: The Transformation of Social Worlds,* 2nd ed. (Belmont, Calif.: Wadsworth, 2009), chap. 1.

18. Jay J. Coakley, *Sports in Society: Issues and Controversies,* 9th ed. (New York: McGraw-Hill, 2007), 460.

19. Andrew Jennings, *The New Lord of the Rings* (London: Pocket Books, 1996); Andrew Jennings and Clare Sambrook, *The Great Olympic Swindle: When the World Wanted the Games Back* (New York: Simon & Schuster, 2000).

20. For a sample of the sources dealing with the political aspects of the Olympics, see Mandell, *The Nazi Olympics;* Richard Espy, *The Politics of the Olympic Games* (Berkeley: University of California Press, 1979); Allen Guttmann, *The Games Must Go On: Avery Brundage and the Olympic Movement* (New York: Columbia University Press, 1984); Allen Guttmann, *The Olympics: A History of the Modern Games,* 2nd ed. (Urbana: University of Illinois Press, 2002); Harry Edwards, "Sportpolitics: Los Angeles, 1984—'The Olympic Tradition Continues,'" *Sociology of Sport Journal* 1, no. 2 (1984): 172–183; Robert A. Mechikoff, "The Olympic Games: Sport as International Politics," *Journal of Physical Education, Recreation and Dance* 55 (March 1984): 23–25.

21. Centre on Housing Rights and Evictions, "Fair Play for Housing Rights: Mega-Events, Olympic Games and Housing Rights," Geneva, Switzerland, 2007, http://www.cohre.org/store/attachments/COHRE%27s%20Olympics%20Report.pdf.

22. Gilbert Cranberg, "Excess Nationalism Harms the Olympics," *USA Today,* 23 September 1988, p. 6A.

23. Coakley, *Sports in Society,* 462.

24. Ibid.

CHAPTER 10

Sport and the Economy

Tony Stewart (20) leads a pack of cars down the back straightaway during the NASCAR Sprint Cup Series Food City 500 auto race in Bristol, Tennessee, 16 March 2008. Sport is big business and corporate sponsorships are commonplace. About 70 percent of the Fortune 500 companies are currently involved in NASCAR. (AP Photo/Mark Humphrey)

Chapter 1 characterized three levels of sport: informal sport, organized sport, and corporate sport, the latter referring to levels of sporting activity dominated by factors, economic or political, extrinsic to sport itself. Corporate sport, in which the relatively spontaneous, pristine nature of informal sport has been corrupted, is characteristic of sport in contemporary North America. Money has become the foundation of sport, even at the so-called amateur level. The profit motive shapes the decisions of owners, school administrators, and the corporations that use sport. Lawsuits and strikes have redistributed the wealth and shifted the balance of power in the professional leagues. The money mania has eroded owner and player loyalties. Fans are left with the gnawing sense that they are the victims of the greed of owners and players alike. John Underwood, writing in 1984 when money and sport were connected, but not to the extent they are now, criticized this trend by saying that sport "has been transformed into economic snake oil. From something wonderful, it has been made grotesque by commerce. It has been distorted and polluted by money, and the never-ending quest for more."[1]

Sport is big business. Some recent facts demonstrate this relationship.

- The estimated size of the entire sports industry in 2006 in the United States was $390 billion.[2]
- In the 1960s the prize money for the entire Professional Golf Association tour was about $7 million. In 2007 it was $266 million, with the winner of the FedExCup earning an additional $10 million.
- The National Football League has total revenues of $6 billion a year.
- The Oscar De La Hoya/Floyd Mayweather, Jr., boxing match in 2007 generated $120 million from pay-per-view revenue.
- Tiger Woods is the first $100-million-a-year athlete, making $111,941,827 in 2007 (about $100 million is from endorsements).
- More than $8 billion is bet illegally on the annual Super Bowl. Another $100 million is bet legally in Nevada on this game.
- Sports video games represent a $1 billion industry, accounting for more than 30 percent of all video game sales.

There is no longer any question that corporate sport is a business, although the owners and certainly big-time sport universities would like to perpetuate the myth that it is not. In this chapter we will examine the intimate interrelationship between money and sport and the consequences of this trend.

WHO BENEFITS ECONOMICALLY FROM SPORTS?

Only a small percentage of the people participating in sport activities derive direct economic benefits from them. (The instrumental use of sports, for example businesses using golf, tennis, and so forth as a means of entertaining clients or customers, is another situation.) As we will document more fully in chapter 12, the number of professional athletes in major league competition is extremely small. For instance, the total number of full-time major league players in the four top North American team sports, which are baseball, basketball, football, and hockey, is slightly more than thirty-one hundred annually. Add to this the very few professional golfers who earn their living on the tour and a handful of tennis players, race-car drivers, boxers, and jockeys, and it is apparent that the business of professional sport is based on the exploits of a very small group of talented individuals. For those who have attained major league status, the financial benefits can be substantial, but the well-publicized salaries of a handful of super-stars have given the public a distorted and inflated idea of professional athletes' incomes. These salaries should be balanced against the brief, often tenuous, careers of professional athletes. For instance, the median length of a professional football player's career is 3.4 years, which does not even qualify the typical player for a pension.

Successful professional athletes receive many additional benefits through product endorsements; speeches and other public appearances;

Tiger Woods, after making birdie on the second hole during the final round of the 2007 Masters Tournament at the Augusta National Golf Club in Augusta, Georgia, 8 April 2007. Woods ranked first of the top U.S. athletes in 2007, with an income of $111.9 million. (AP Photo/Elise Amendola)

jobs as actors, entertainers, and sports announcers; opportunities for investments in business ventures as diverse as sports camps, real estate developments, quick-order franchises, motels, and restaurants; and many other advantages. *Sports Illustrated* ranked the top fifty U.S. athletes in income in 2007 from various sources. Tiger Woods led the way with $111.9 million, more than $50 million more than boxer Oscar De La Hoya at $55 million. Half of the Fortunate 50 were NBA players, while only 12 baseball players and 5 football players made the list. There were 3 NASCAR drivers and just 1 woman (Michelle Wie, who ranked twenty-second with an income of $20,235,224).[3] For most whose livelihoods are dependent on athletic abilities, the financial rewards are not nearly so great as they are for the publicized athletes.

- More than twenty-five hundred individuals play minor league baseball, and only 7 percent of them will make it to the major leagues. None of these minor league players is covered by the minimum salary scales of Major League Baseball.
- In professional golf 350 men and 270 women pursue the multimillion-dollar prize money, but only about 200 make a living at it. The rest have trouble making expenses.
- An individual needs over $1 million a year for expenses to be competitive on the auto racing circuit. This money comes from commercial sponsors who give it, typically, to the already successful and their sons (e.g., some sons of famous drivers who began their careers with considerable corporate sponsorship are Michael Andretti, Al Unser, Jr., Dale Earnhardt, Jr., and Kyle Petty). Meanwhile, unknowns, people of color, and women have great difficulty obtaining sponsorships.
- In professional basketball a lucrative sports career awaits the successful athlete but only about 276 players, and approximately 40 rookies, are hired each year. And while the average annual salary of NBA players in 2007 exceeded $5 million, those just one rung below in the developmental league make only $12,000 to $24,000 a season.[4]
- The scholarship athlete in college is paid virtual slave wages for his or her services. Calculated on the basis of the room, books, meals, and tuition allowed by the NCAA, a college athlete's salary does not greatly exceed the federal government's stated poverty level and is about at the federally established minimum hourly pay scale.

Coaches are in a category of professional athletes frequently overlooked in calculating the economic effects of sport in America. About 200,000 coaches are employed in secondary schools, and 22,000 men and 4,200 women are engaged in coaching at the college level.

Umpires and referees constitute another sports occupational category. Baseball umpires are the best paid, with salaries ranging from $104,704 to $324,545. Hockey and basketball also require full-time officials, but the pay is lower. Professional football pays its officials on a part-time, game-by-game basis. Thousands more officiate at the other levels of sport for relatively low fees (e.g., in Class A minor league baseball, umpires receive $11,400 to $14,400 a season). At a lower level still, there are many thousands who officiate high school sports. In Colorado, for example, there were almost five thousand registered officials for thirteen different sports. The per game pay per official in Colorado is $54 for football and $46 to $54 for basketball.[5]

Another occupational category dependent on sport is the specialist in sports medicine. The treatment of sports injuries requires special techniques, and sports medicine clinics are becoming relatively commonplace in metropolitan centers.

A relatively new sports job is that of the player agent. With the advent of free agents and accelerated player salaries, agents for the players are performing an ever greater function in professional sports. They provide a service to the players because they know the tax laws and the market value of the athletes. Their goal is to maximize monetary benefits for the athlete by extracting the most beneficial contract from management. For this service the agent receives a percentage of the agreement (from 5 to 10 percent), which can be a considerable amount in this era of multimillion-dollar contracts. This business is so lucrative (and unregulated) that some agents have taken advantage of their naive clients by, for example, having them sign huge contracts with payments deferred over as many as forty years; the agent takes a percentage of the total up front, while the player receives no interest on the deferred money, which is further devalued by inflation. Agents also sometimes violate NCAA amateur rules by signing college athletes and giving them bonuses.

In addition to those directly involved in producing the sport product, many auxiliary businesses benefit from the sports boom. Hotels, taxis, restaurants, parking, and other business establishments can thereby increase their volume of business. The presence of a major league team generates millions of dollars for a city's economy, and this is why cities are so generous to sports teams (in stadium rentals, concessions revenues, and various tax subsidies). Huge sports spectaculars such as the Kentucky Derby, the Indianapolis 500, the World Series, and the Super Bowl are major tourist attractions bringing an economic bonanza to numerous ancillary businesses (hotels, restaurants, stores, casinos, caterers, florists). The 2006 Super Bowl, for example, poured an estimated $300 million into the Detroit area economy (see Box 10.1, *Thinking about Sport,* for the numbers generated from the 2006 Super Bowl).

The concessions business provides sports spectators with food, drink, and merchandise. A concessionaire is typically given a monopoly by a team management, league, or city; in return the grantor receives a percentage of the proceeds. The five-dollar beers and hot dogs consumed by tens of thousands generate a lot of revenue for every game.

As sports mania has pervaded the country, public pressure to legalize sports betting has intensified, pressure exerted both by the financial distress of many state governments and by bet-eager constituents. As a result the majority of states have legal pari-mutuel wagering on horse racing and greyhound racing, and a few even have legal wagering on jai alai.

Corporations are the greatest beneficiaries from sport, both directly, through the sale of sports-related products, and indirectly, through the use of sports to generate interest in their products. Sport is big business (see Box 10.2, *Thinking about Sport,* on Nike, for a look at the leading sports corporation).

Sport enhances big business. Sports themes and prominent athletes are used in advertisements to sell products. Companies are convinced that through the proper selection of sports and sports personalities, they can reach particular pre-identified consumer categories or strengthen the general visibility of their products.

The commercialization of sport is easily seen in the advertising at the ballparks, stadiums, and arenas of professional, college, and even high school sports. Many of these arenas have corporate names, purchased at significant cost. In 2005 there were sixty-nine professional league North American sports facilities with corporate names with a sponsorship value of more than $4.2 billion.

> **Box 10.1**   *Thinking about Sport* **2006 Super Bowl in Detroit: An Economic Contradiction**
>
> The Super Bowl is much more than a football game. It is business—big business, the magnitude of which is seen in these numbers for the 2006 game in Detroit, Michigan:
>
> - Super Bowl visitors spent about $180 million. The total economic impact was $300 million.
> - The face value of tickets was $600–$700, but many sold for over $2,700. A stadium suite with twenty seats, food, and drink cost $176,475. This was up from $12, the highest-priced ticket for the first Super Bowl, played in 1967.
> - Roughly 140 million viewers watched on television (which is 80 million more than go to church on an average Sunday in the United States). The average cost for a thirty-second TV commercial was $2.5 million.
> - The estimated amount of money bet legally and illegally on the game was $8.1 billion.
> - Eighty percent of those attending the game were executives, managers, sales representatives, or professionals.
> - The amounts received by each member of the winning team and losing team were $73,000 and $38,000, respectively. The winners also receive Super Bowl rings, with a base price of $5,000 each, paid for by the NFL.
>
> The Super Bowl is a celebration of concentrated wealth—wealthy players and very wealthy owners, corporation executives and their affluent clients, lobbyists and legislators, and high rollers of various stripes with money to spend on lavish parties, food, and lodging at very inflated prices. As columnist Sandy Grady described the situation for the 2006 Super Bowl in Detroit:
>
>> Once again an armada of Lear jets delivers platoons of America's corporate tycoons. Streets will be jammed with stretch limos, their bars stocked with $500 bottles of champagne. Hotel suites will be agog with the rich, the celebrated and the lucky. . . . the games our frenzied Mardi Gras. . . . But Surreal Bowl XL is different—a raw symbol of class disparity.
>
> The context for the 2006 Super Bowl with its gala parties and excess was the rust belt city of Detroit. Since 1950 Detroit's population had shrunk from 1.8 million to less than 900,000. Its jobless rate was 6.8 percent (among big cities only New Orleans was higher), and one-third of its residents were below the poverty line (the highest poverty rate in the nation). General Motors and Ford (the game is played at Ford Field), the most prominent employers in the area, each had announced that thirty thousand workers would be terminated and entire plants shut down. Both corporations were losing billions of dollars annually, not keeping up with their Japanese and German competitors. The city had a budget deficit of $78 million and laid off fourteen hundred workers. Again, quoting Sandy Grady: "The orgiastic display of lobbyists, CEOs, advertisers and celebs in luxury boxes is a harsh contrast to Detroit's ravaged industry."
>
> Dave Zirin is appalled by the bacchanalia exhibited at the Detroit Super Bowl and its stark contrast with the abject urban suffering:
>
>> For a city that built a stable "middle class" out of union struggle and the auto plants, this is injury added to insult. But have no fear, NORAD, the North American Aerospace Defense Command, will be flying sorties over Ford Field to protect everyone from terrorist missile attacks. There is no NORAD however on the streets of Detroit to protect people from Operation Enduring Class War otherwise known as the Super Bowl.
>
> *Sources:* Michael McCarthy, "Games an Excuse for Splashy Parties," *USA Today*, 30 January 2007, p. 6C; Sandy Grady, "Detroit's 'Surreal Bowl,'" *USA Today*, 1 February 2006, p. 11A; Judy Keen, "Host's Super Bowl Strategy Includes Comeback Victory," *USA Today*, 30 January 2006, p. 3A; and Dave Zirin, "Super Bowl City on the Brink," *AlterNet*, 3 February 2006, http://www.alternet.org/module/lprintversion/31635.

When the New York Mets begin play in their new stadium in 2009, the field will be called CitiField, costing Citibank $20 million a year for at least twenty years for the naming rights. Even game time is for sale—7-Eleven pays the Chicago White Sox $500,000 a year to start their home games at 7:11 P.M.

Corporations have also paid to have their names associated with various college bowl games (e.g., the Tostitos Fiesta Bowl, the Meineke Car Care Bowl, the Insight.com Bowl, the Galleryfurniture.com Bowl, and the Micropc.com Bowl). Political observer Jim Hightower refers to golf to illustrate corporate ties with sport:

> The professional golf tour has always struck me as the ultimate expression of the corporate presence in sports, not only because the tournaments themselves are unabashedly organized to hype a com-

Box 10.2 Thinking about Sport Nike, the Sports Corporate Behemoth

In 1964 legendary University of Oregon track coach Bill Bowerman and one of his former distance runners, Phil Knight, formed a company called Blue Ribbon Sports to manufacture and sell running shoes. This company later became Nike, Inc., and today it is a huge global corporation with more than five hundred factories and offices located in forty-five countries and sales in fiscal 2007 of $16.326 billion. Nike's products have expanded to all types of athletic shoes, apparel, sports equipment, and accessories.

Nike has signed many of the world's major athletes to focus attention on its products—e.g., Michael Jordan, LeBron James, and Kobe Bryant in basketball; cyclist Lance Armstrong, skateboarder Paul Rodriguez, Jr., and golfer Tiger Woods; tennis players Roger Federer, Rafael Nadal, and Maria Sharapova; motorsport racer Michael Schumacher; and several Chinese athletes in basketball, track, and swimming. In fact, Nike sponsors twenty-two of the twenty-eight Chinese athletic federations. In the 2004 Olympics in Athens, 12 Chinese athletes who won gold medals in the 2004 Olympics were sponsored by Nike.

In the United States Nike provides equipment free to professional, college, and some high school teams. Multimillion-dollar deals have been made with many major collegiate teams to supply equipment and supplements for coaches' salaries. Nike also sponsors U.S. elite track-and-field athletes, allowing them to train without having to work at a job. Nike also sponsors high school tournaments and track meets and over five hundred sports camps in fifteen different sports.

There is a dark side to the Nike story. Most of its products are manufactured in low-wage countries of Asia, where labor is not only cheap but regulations are scarce. There have been charges of exploitation of young women and children working under oppressive conditions for pennies an hour, making goods that sell for a huge profit in the United States. A Nike transnational advocacy network was formed to publicize these labor abuses and to mobilize efforts to pressure Nike (and other sports manufacturing firms) to stop these human rights abuses. Slowly, Nike has responded with some policy changes but has seemed less committed to reform than to damage control and public relations.

Labor relations within the United States has also been a negative for Nike. For example, a class-action race discrimination lawsuit against Nike was filed on behalf of four hundred African American employees of the company's Niketown Chicago store. Although Nike denied the allegations, it reached a $7.6 million settlement.

Nike has also been accused of having an undue influence on college sports. By giving equipment and money worth millions to big-time college programs, Nike has increased the gap between the college "haves" and the "have-nots." There is also a Nike network, which means that when there is a coaching vacancy, a "Nike school" may be limited to selecting a "Nike coach," that is, a coach who has a contractual agreement with Nike. Similarly, Nike's sponsorship of certain prominent high schools, Amateur Athletic Union (AAU) teams, tournaments, and sports camps may have an influence on recruiting for colleges. That is, "Nike high school coaches" or "Nike AAU coaches" may steer their athletes to "Nike colleges."

Sources: CNN, "Nike Opens Flagship Store in Beijing," 8 August 2007, http://money.cnn.com/news/newsfeeds/articles/prnewswire/AQF05303082007-1.htm; Associated Press, "Nike Settles Chicago Race Case for $7.6 Million," 30 July 2007, http://www.msnbc.msn.com/id/20041551; Steve Boggan, "Nike Admits to Mistakes over Child Labor," Common Dreams News Center, 20 October 2001, http://www.commondreams.org/cgi-bin/print.cgi?file=headlines01/1020-01.htm; and George H. Sage, "Corporate Globalization and Sporting Goods Manufacturing: The Case of Nike," in *Sport in Contemporary Society*, 7th ed., ed. D. Stanley Eitzen (Boulder, Colo.: Paradigm, 2005), 362–382.

---

pany ("AT&T Pebble Beach Pro-Am," "Buick Invitational," "Honda Classic," "MasterCard Colonial," "Lincoln-Mercury Kapalua International," "Shell Houston Open," and "Anderson Consulting World Championship of Golf," to name a few), and not only because golfers are walking sandwich boards (with corporate logos adorning their shirts, shoes, hats, wristbands, knickers, golf bags, club covers, golf balls, caddies, and every other salable space), but especially because the PGA's ranking of top players is determined each year not by the scores they make, but how much money they make—Wall Street's true measure of one's worthiness.[6]

The use of sport to promote business interests takes a number of other forms as well, some reciprocal. Corporations sponsor such sports as running, bowling, golf, rodeo, tractor pulls, tennis, and skiing. For example, becoming a "title sponsor" on the PGA tour costs as much as $6 million.

Sponsorship has been especially crucial to the gain in women's professional sports: Virginia

Slims, Carlton, Colgate, L'eggs, Bonnie Bell, Sarah Coventry, Sears, S & H Green Stamps, and Sealy have all underwritten women's golf and tennis tournaments and have thus significantly raised the prize money and the visibility of women's sports.

The major corporations of the United States have been active in the sponsorship of the U.S. Olympic team for the presumed benefits of public relations, advertising, and a generous allotment of tickets. For the rights to televise the Olympics from the 2000 Sydney Games through the 2008 Beijing Games, NBC paid $3.5 billion, which they will make up in the sale of thirty-second advertising spots to various advertisers. Various corporations pay the IOC for the right to be the official soft drink (or whatever) of the Olympics. About half of the budget for the 2002 Winter Games in Salt Lake City came from the sale of corporate sponsorships.

The most blatant use of sport for commercial purposes occurs in automobile racing. Here, drivers and owners of race cars receive a fee for using a corporation's logo on their racing vehicle and on the clothing of the driver. These logos usually represent corporations involved in products for automobiles (e.g., tires, oil, auto parts, mufflers, shock absorbers) but they also include corporations selling chewing tobacco, cigarettes, clothing, soft drinks, and the like. The cost for advertising placed on a racing car depends on its size and location. For example, a corporate logo on the hood costs the corporation $7 million to $12 million, depending on the popularity of the driver of that car; a logo placed on the trunk or back will cost between $350,000 and $1.5 million, whereas on the lower rear quarter panel, the cost varies from $250,000 to $1 million.

A special relationship seems to exist between the beer companies and sport. Beer is largely consumed by men, and men are overrepresented among the spectators at sporting events and among the avid followers of sport. The result is that the beer companies have partially subsidized sport. Some have owned teams: Coors is part owner of the Colorado Rockies, and the stadium is named Coors Stadium; Molson Breweries of Canada owns the Montreal Canadiens. Most sports teams have several sponsors for their local radio and television broadcasts, but a beer company is almost always one of them.

PROFESSIONAL SPORT AS A BUSINESS

Contrary to what some owners would have the public believe, professional sport is big business. This section examines how professional sport is structured to maximize profit. This requires that we examine how sport is profitable, the advantages of monopoly, and the public subsidization of professional teams. We also consider the changes in the owner-player relationship brought about by the players' agitation to increase their power and monetary rewards.

Professional Sport as a Monopoly

The sport industry is not only a monopoly but also an unregulated one. Unlike the broadcasting industry, for example, whose monopolistic practices are regulated by the Federal Communications Commission, the sport industry is left to regulate itself. Each professional league operates as a cartel (competitors joining together as a self-regulating monopoly). This means that the teams make agreements on matters of mutual interest (e.g., rules, schedules, promotions, expansion, and media contracts). Such agreements are illegal in most other businesses because they lead to collusion, price-fixing, and restraint of trade. Economists James Quick and Rodney Fort argue that all of the problems of professional sports teams arise from the monopoly power of the sports leagues.

> Eliminate the monopoly power of leagues and you eliminate the blackmailing of cities to subsidize teams. Eliminate the monopoly power of leagues and you eliminate the sources of revenue that provide the wherewithal for high player salaries. Eliminate the monopoly power of leagues and you eliminate the problem of lack of competitive balance in a league due to disparity in drawing potential among

league teams. Eliminate the monopoly power of leagues and you transfer power from the insiders, owners and players alike, to the outsiders, fans and taxpayers.[7]

The enormous advantages to the league cartel are several. Foremost, each sports franchise is protected from competition. The owner of the Kansas City Royals, for instance, is guaranteed that no other Major League Baseball team will be allowed to locate in his or her territory. There are some metropolitan areas with two Major League Baseball teams, but these exceptions occurred before baseball had agreed to territorial exclusivity. Even in these cases, the teams are in different leagues, ensuring that, for example, a Chicago baseball fan who wants to see American League games can see them only by attending White Sox games (and in the few interleague games).

This protection from competition eliminates price wars. The owners of a franchise can continue to charge the maximum without fear of price cutting by competitors.

The cartel also controls the number of franchises allowed. Each cartel is generally reluctant to add new teams because scarcity permits higher ticket prices, more beneficial media arrangements, and continued territorial purity. In short, the value of each franchise increases by the restriction on the number of teams. When new teams are added, such as the addition of the Denver and Miami franchises in 1993 to baseball's National League, they are selected with economic criteria paramount, especially concerning new television markets (neither the Rocky Mountain time zone nor Florida had a major league team, making them attractive additions to the league).

This monopolistic situation enables a league to negotiate television contracts for the benefit of all members of the cartel. The 1961 Sports Broadcast Act allowed sports leagues to sell their national television rights as a group without being subject to the antitrust laws. As a result, the national networks and cable systems may bid for the right to televise, for example, professional football.

The final advantage of the monopoly is that the players are drastically limited in their choices and bargaining power. In football, players are drafted out of college. If they want to play in the NFL, they must negotiate with the team that drafted them. Their other choice is to play in the much less prestigious Arena League or to play in Canada (but Canadian teams limit the number of Americans allowed per team, and the average pay is about one-third that offered by U.S. teams) or not to play that year. We will return to the owner-player relationship later in this chapter.

Public Subsidization of Professional Team Franchises

The subsidies to franchise owners take two forms—tax breaks and the availability of arenas at very low cost. Let us examine these in turn.

The bleak financial picture typically painted by some owners of professional teams is misleading because it refers only to accounting losses (expenses exceeding income). The tax benefits available to sports promoters have been largely unpublicized. Even in those cases in which owners have not profited directly from their investments, owning a professional team is by no means the liability that publicly stated accounting losses would indicate. In short, for many wealthy individuals, owning a sports franchise has lucrative tax advantages.

Investment in professional franchises enables a wealthy owner to offset the team's gate losses or to minimize taxable profits of the team or of other investments by large depreciation allowances. The purchase of a professional sports franchise includes (1) the legal right to the franchise; (2) player contracts; and (3) assets such as equipment, buildings, cars, and so forth. However, since the most valuable assets of a pro sports team are its players, most of the purchase cost will be attributed to player contracts, which, in turn, can be depreciated in the same way a steel company depreciates the investment costs of a new blast furnace. Similarly, acquisition of a player from another team will enable the new owner to depreciate the player's value over a period of years, usually five. Thus, the player's status as property is readily apparent, for no other business in the United States depreciates the value of human beings as part of the cost of its operation. There is an inconsistency here—the team is allowed to depreciate its players, but players are not permitted to depreciate themselves for tax purposes. This anomaly indicates the bias in the tax code of owners over players and that players are considered as property.

Ownership of professional sports franchises provides this kind of tax shelter even if the team shows accounting losses. That is why it has become an attractive investment for many wealthy persons, who can use losses and player depreciation as a means of offsetting other taxes on individual income.

These factors contribute to a relatively high turnover of professional team ownership. Since a team can depreciate the value of its players over a relatively short period (five years or less), expansion teams or newly franchised teams composed of players purchased from other owners can depreciate, but old leagues and established teams cannot, except with players purchased from previously established clubs. Thus, buying and selling teams is more profitable than retaining them for extended periods of time.

Consider the example of the tax shelter benefits of the NFL franchise in Houston owned by Robert McNair. As reported by economist Andrew Zimbalist:

> Assuming McNair holds the team as a partnership or subchapter S corporation, the IRS will allow him to presume that up to 50 percent of the team's purchase price ($350 million) is attributable to the player contracts he will eventually sign. This amount is generally amortizable over five years, allowing McNair to add $70 million annually to the team's costs before calculating its tax liability. (Of course, McNair will also be allowed to expense players' salaries.) Then McNair can transfer any reported losses from the team to reduce his personal income-tax liability, potentially saving him some $28 million a year for five years.... On top of this, McNair will benefit from the pleasures, perquisites, and power that accrue to the elite owners of NFL teams.[8]

The second type of public subsidy of professional sport is the provision of sports facilities to most franchises at very low cost. Adequate facilities are of great concern to sports promoters because they are essential to the financial success and spectator appeal of professional and big-time amateur sports. Conventional wisdom holds that the presence of major league sports teams enhances a city's prestige and generates considerable economic activity. Regarding the former, image is important, at least to civic boosters, and having a major league team gives the impression of being a first-class city. Concerning the latter, the myth is that the presence of a major league team brings substantial economic growth. This is a myth for at least three reasons. First, subsidizing a team drains government resources (the cost of building and maintaining arenas, providing access roads, and the loss of revenues because of "sweetheart deals" with team owners. Second, the deflection of government money toward a sports team often means that services to the poor will be reduced or dropped altogether. Third, the economic benefits are not spread equally throughout the community. The wealthy benefit (team owners, owners of hotels and restaurants) while the costs are paid disproportionately by the middle and lower classes.[9] As John Underwood, referring to the major subsidy of a stadium, has summarized: "The point that never quite gets made in this process is that no hard evidence exists to support the notion that building stadiums for professional sports franchises is anything close to economic good sense for a community. The opposite is closer to the truth. Every study not subsidized by those with a stake in the matter indicates that taxpayers invariably get left holding the bag, and that the bag brims over with I.O.U.'s."[10]

As the boom in sports in America has increased, so also has the demand for facilities to accommodate the demands of fans for entertainment and of promoters for profits. About 78 percent of the costs for some thirty-seven stadium building projects for the NFL teams from 1970 through 2003 were subsidized by the public.[11] Generally, these subsidies are from revenue bonds that allegedly are to be paid off with the revenue from the project. However, whenever a bond-financed public project cannot pay for itself, the obligation becomes a general public one. Other subsidies are indirect, such as providing light rail to the stadiums or access roads to interstate highways.

These new facilities, most of them publicly financed, are being built at the same time that the human needs for housing, schools, and medical facilities have reached crisis proportions, especially in U.S. cities. Two examples make the point. First, in Pittsburgh the public schools in 1999 had a $30 million shortfall, yet the Pittsburgh Pirates (baseball) and Steelers (football) were given new arenas with the state kicking in $160 million toward the cost. And, second, on the day when the Minnesota Twins were to celebrate the groundbreaking for their $480 million stadium, $350 million of which was to be paid by a county sales tax, a major bridge connecting Minneapolis with St. Paul collapsed. Ironically, that is the estimated cost to rebuild that bridge.

Stadium funding with public money to support wealthy owners has not been without public criticism, although it is significant that bond elections for stadium construction have often succeeded when other proposed expenditures (e.g., for education and for municipal facilities) have been defeated. Numerous critics have scorned the priorities demonstrated and have argued that these facilities represent a direct subsidy to the sports industry by the public, many of whom are not even sports fans and few of whom are able to use or to benefit from the facilities their money supports.

Another subsidy to the owners involves the 50 percent tax deduction for business entertainment expenses. Professional teams rely on corporations to buy blocks of season tickets and to rent expensive skyboxes. A significant feature of the new stadiums is the building of these skyboxes, private suites, and club seats, because the revenues from them are not shared with visiting teams and thus are a huge benefit to the resident owner. So powerful is the urge by municipal officials and local chambers of commerce to have big-league teams in their cities that they will go to extreme lengths to placate present or future owners.

- St. Louis enticed the Rams to leave Los Angeles with a package that included a new $300 million stadium, all proceeds from concessions, parking, club seats and luxury suites, and a $15 million practice facility. To pay for this largesse, Missouri taxpayers pay $24 million a year, St. Louis taxpayers pay another $12.5 million, and visitors to the county pay a 7.25 percent room tax to raise another $6 million annually.
- Art Modell, owner of the Cleveland Browns (which averaged seventy thousand tickets sold per game), moved the team to Baltimore because he was given a $200 million stadium with 108 luxury boxes and 7,500 club seats, $75 million for moving expenses, $50 million for doing the deal, and all revenues from ticket sales, concessions, parking, and stadium advertising. The taxpayers guarantee sellout crowds for ten years. Moreover, when the stadium is used for other events, Modell will collect a 10 percent management fee plus half the profits. Use of the stadium is rent-free for thirty years, although Modell will pay back $24 million in construction costs.
- The taxpayers in six counties surrounding Denver paid $156 million of the $180 million cost to build the Colorado Rockies field. The owners were given the right to name the stadium, which they sold to the Coors Brewing Company for $15 million. The team owners received seat rights, luxury suites, advertising, parking, and concession rights for seventeen years at no cost. They also received all revenues from nonbaseball events for parking, concessions, and rent. And, as stadium managers, the owners receive an annual fee of $2.65 million.

In short, the owners are greatly subsidized to provide teams. To what extent do the communities that pay these subsidies benefit? We argue that the benefits are not widespread for the following reasons:

1. The wealthy benefit disproportionately from the letting of building contracts and through the feeding and housing of persons wishing to see the games. Although more jobs may be created, the profits will

accrue to the capitalists, not to the workers. Team owners (and stockholders) especially will profit from attendance without any investment in the land or construction. They cannot lose financially because the burden is on the taxpayers. This is clearly a case of the wealthy receiving a public subsidy.

2. The prices of individual and season tickets are usually too high for the lower classes. Ironically, bringing a major league team to an area (a primary reason for building a new stadium) usually means that the poor see fewer games than before if the home games are blacked out on television. (This ban on televised home football games is lifted if the game is sold out forty-eight hours before game time.) Moreover, building a new stadium or refurbishing an old one invariably raises ticket prices. John Underwood states:

> The greatest damage done by this new elitism [expensive stadiums with lavish skyboxes] is that even the cheapest seats in almost every big-league facility are now priced out of reach of a large segment of the population. Those who are most critically in need of affordable entertainment, the underclass (and even the lower-middle class), have been effectively shut out.
>
> And this is especially hateful because spectator sport, by its very nature, has been the great escape for the men and women who have worked all day for small pay and traditionally provided the biggest numbers of a sport's core support. As it now stands, they are as good as disenfranchised—a vast number of the taxpaying public who will never set foot inside these stadiums and arenas. That's not just cynical, it's criminal.[12]

3. New stadiums are often built in suburban or downtown locations rather than in residential areas. The old stadiums, typically in rundown neighborhoods, are abandoned upon completion of the new. One consequence is that the poor living near the old stadiums are deprived of incomes previously derived from the games (e.g., jobs as parking attendants, salespersons, janitors, cooks, and so forth). They are also deprived of easy access to the games. Their lack of money and the generally insufficient system of mass transportation make their attendance all the more improbable. When the stadiums are built in downtown locations, they often displace old warehouses and cheap hotels with upscale restaurants, apartments, and boutiques. This gentrification increases rents and other costs, forcing the poor to live elsewhere.

4. Publicly financed arenas are built for those sports that appeal more to the affluent, for example, baseball, football, basketball, and hockey. "Prole" sports, in other words sports for the working classes, tend to occur in privately owned arenas (see chapter 12).

The obvious beneficiaries of subsidized public arenas are the owners of sports teams, plus the owners of hotels, media, commercial modes of transportation, restaurants, construction firms, and property affected by the location of the new arena site. There is a strong relationship between professional team owners and the decision makers at the highest political, corporate, financial, and media levels. These strong ties may explain the commonly found affirmative consensus among the political and economic elite for the building of public sports arenas.[13]

Finally, research shows that public subsidization of sports facilities does not have a positive economic impact on the community. Economist Robert A. Baade concludes, "Using economics as a justification for the subsidy is a political expedient, perhaps necessity, but it is not consonant with the statistical evidence."[14]

Ownership for Profit

For those teams owned by individuals, psychic gratifications are inherent in owning a professional team. Many owners derive great personal satisfaction from knowing athletes personally. In addition, owners are feted by the community as service leaders and achieve a degree of prominence otherwise unattainable in their business ventures.

Apart from the "psychic income" of team ownership, there are very substantial economic motives (see Box 10.3, *Thinking about Sport*, for a discussion of the NASCAR empire). Indeed, for most investors the primary motivation would seem to be a rationally economic one: Sport is a profitable long-range investment. Ownership of a sports franchise also provides celebrity status, social prestige, and publicity that can enhance other facets of an individual's business.

Moreover, the value of sports franchises has consistently increased. Several examples make this point: The Philadelphia Eagles entered the NFL at a cost of $2,500 in 1933. In 1949 the franchise was sold for $250,000. The value of the Eagles franchise in 2006 was estimated by *Forbes* at $1.02 billion.[15] In 1960 Clint Murchison purchased the Dallas Cowboys franchise for $50,000 plus another $550,000 for the players. In 1984 he sold the Cowboys and the Dallas Stadium for $80 million. In

---

Box 10.3 *Thinking about Sport* **The NASCAR Billion-Dollar Empire**

The National Association for Stock Car Auto Racing (NASCAR) is in the same league (in terms of money) as the NFL, the NBA, and Major League Baseball. There is a major difference, however, because NASCAR is a dictatorship controlled by a single family—the children of the founder Bill France, Sr., who died in 1992. NASCAR is a closed culture, unique in professional sports, with its chairman making decisions without negotiating with the drivers or the owners of the cars. There is no debate over how the profits are to be shared or the way NASCAR is to be run. The family controls television money, race dates, the assignment of races to certain tracks, the cars' specifications, and the rules. The France family makes money in two ways: as sole owners of NASCAR and as the major stockholders of International Speedway Corporation, a publicly held company that owns thirteen racetracks and hosts nearly half the races on the Winston Circuit. The exact amount of money earned is not known because NASCAR is privately owned, but this much is known: Two members of the France family are both listed by *Forbes* as among the world's billionaires. The other players in stock car racing put up their own money, in the hope of making money.

- The owners of the racetracks put up the prize money and pay NASCAR a fee (around $1 million, depending on the prestige of the event). Track owners make about 50 percent from the ticket sales. They also sell the venues' naming rights. These tracks are privately owned. They (and NASCAR) are subsidized indirectly by the tax breaks corporations get for their sponsorship and the tax breaks businesses receive for their buying of tickets and luxury suites at the races.
- Race team owners pay 60 to 80 percent of the cost for the cars and expenses (the remainder they hope to make up in winnings from the races).
- The drivers split their winnings evenly with the owner of their race team. The successful drivers earn millions annually.
- Corporate sponsors underwrite the annual budgets for the race teams ($20 million for a top team) in exchange for advertising rights on each car. Corporations also pay NASCAR a fee to be NASCAR's official beer (or whatever). NASCAR lifted its self-imposed ban on displaying liquor logos on its cars in 2005.
- About 70 percent of the Fortune 500 companies are currently involved in NASCAR.
- The value of the leading racing team—Rouch Racing—was estimated by *Forbes* at $218 million in 2006.
- Stock car racing is experiencing a wave of popularity, as evidenced by its first national television deal—a six-year, $2.4 billion pact with Fox, NBC, and TBS that began in 2001. The television money is divided so that NASCAR gets 10 percent, track owners get 65 percent, and race teams get 25 percent. NASCAR has the highest average ticket price in sports ($90) and draws crowds averaging 127,000 per race. Stock car racing is a money machine run as a monopoly by the France family as a kind of benevolent dictatorship.

Sources: Liz Clarke and Thomas Heath, "Driven to Succeed: In the Hands of One Family since 1947, NASCAR Has Grown into a Billion-Dollar Empire," *Washington Post National Weekly Edition*, 16 July 2000, pp. 19–20; Skip Wood, "NASCAR Follows Its Own Road," *USA Today*, 31 July 2001, pp. 1C–2C; and Jack Gage, "Racing for Sponsors," *Forbes*, 5 June 2006, 127–130.

1989 the Cowboys were purchased by Jerry Jones for an unprecedented $140 million. Seventeen years later that franchise had increased in value by $1.03 billion to $1.176 billion. In one of the quickest and most lucrative capital gains deals, Edgar Kaiser purchased the Denver Broncos in 1980 for about $35 million and sold the team four years later for $70 million. The new owner, Patrick Bowlen, saw the value of the Broncos continue to increase from $70 million in 1984 to $975 million in 2006. Similar increases have occurred in the three other major professional team sports, with the increases correlating closely with new stadium and arena construction at taxpayers' expense.

The reasons for the great appreciation in franchise value are, as we have seen, the advantages of monopoly, television revenues, tax breaks, and subsidized arenas. That the structure of professional team sports tends to be lucrative is established, but what about the primary motivations of the owners for their involvement? Are they profit-oriented entrepreneurs or wealthy persons willing to take financial risks to provide a service to their respective communities? This is an important question because its answer should determine whether professional sport is a sport or a business. If it is a business, then special tax concessions, antitrust exemptions, and arena subsidies are inappropriate. If, on the other hand, professional team owners deserve these advantages because they are providing sport as a community service, then their profits should be scaled down and the benefits should accrue to the players and the fans.

Perhaps the best test of the owners' primary motivation involves their policies regarding ticket prices. The test is simple. If the owner is basically civic-minded, then the better the attendance during the season, the lower will be the prices. The data show consistently that the greater the demand for tickets, the higher the prices tend to be.

Consider, for example, the cost for attending the Washington Nationals in their new stadium when it opens in the spring of 2008. Fans in the eighteen hundred most desirable seats will pay at least $150 per game, with the most expensive seat at $400 (the most expensive seat in the old stadium was $140 in 2007). These prices, by the way, do not include prices for the new stadium's sixty-six luxury suites, which start at $150,000 for the season. The new stadium was built with $611 million in public funds. As Thomas Heath observes, "The opening of a new stadium typically gives professional teams an increase in ticket demand and a corresponding opportunity to increase prices to match that demand."[16]

The rationale usually offered to explain ticket price increases is that costs are skyrocketing, especially because of the high salaries of superstars. As a result, fans typically vent their anger on the well-paid athletes rather than on the owners. The anger seems misplaced; apparently the fans do not recognize that greed motivates the owners as well as the players. Profit is, of course, the basic rule of capitalism. Still, the owners should not have it both ways. If they are capitalists, then subsidies are inappropriate. Their monopolies should not be supported by the Congress and the courts. Their tax breaks should be eliminated. If public arenas are provided for professional teams, then the rent should be fair for both the owners of the teams and the citizens of the city.

One thing is clear: Owning a team is profitable, very profitable. In a facetious vein, *Denver Post* sports columnist Woody Paige characterized team owners this way: "Christopher Columbus would have made an appropriate club owner. He didn't know where he was going. He didn't know where he was when he got there. He treated people like slaves. *And he did it with other people's money.*"[17]

THE RELATIONSHIP BETWEEN OWNER AND ATHLETE

Ownership of a professional team has tended to be profitable because the courts have allowed sport exemption from the antitrust laws. In 1922 Supreme Court Justice Oliver Wendell Holmes ruled that baseball was a game that did not involve interstate commerce and was therefore exempt from federal antitrust laws. The special legal status conferred on professional sport by this decision persisted until the mid-1970s. Of special interest has been one consequence of sport monopoly: the right of owners to own and control their players.

The Draft and the Reserve Clause

The 1970s were characterized by a concerted attack by athletes on the employment practices of sport. Unlike employees of other businesses, athletes were not free to sell their services to whomever they pleased. Players' salaries were determined solely by each team's owner. In baseball, before the landmark cases of the mid-1970s, once a player signed a contract with a club, that team had exclusive rights over him, and he was no longer free to negotiate with any other team. In succeeding years, the player had to sell his services solely to the club that owned his contract unless it released, sold, or traded him, or he chose to retire. The reserve clause specified that the owner had the exclusive right to renew the player's contract annually, and thus the player was bound perpetually to negotiate with only one club; he became its property and could be sold to another club without his own consent.

Professional football was more restrictive in one respect and more open (at least on paper) in another. Unlike baseball, football had a draft of college players, and the selected athletes had no choice of the team for which they would play. The player would play for the team that drafted him and at the salary offered or else join a team in the Canadian League (the number of Americans allowed to play in Canada is limited, however, so that option was a real one only for the most sought-after athletes). As in baseball, after signing with a team, the football player was bound to that team. He could, however, play out his option, in other words, play a year at 90 percent of his previous salary without signing a contract, whereupon he would be free to negotiate with another team. This apparent freedom of movement for the players was severely limited, however, by the "Rozelle Rule." This rule allowed the NFL commissioner at that time, Pete Rozelle, to require the team signing any such "free agent" to compensate (with other athletes or with money of equal value) the club the player had left. This rule made signing free agents rarely in a club's interest; therefore, the free agent did not in reality have full economic freedom.

These provisions in football and baseball (and similar ones in basketball and hockey) were clearly one-sided, giving all the power to the owners. Michael I. Sovern, dean of Columbia University's School of Law, described this asymmetrical relationship: "The reserve clause binds the employee without binding the employer. . . . The owner is free to decide whether to continue the relationship: the player is not."[18] As another observer put it: "After the Civil War settled the slavery issue, owning a ball club was the closest one could come to owning a plantation."[19]

Free Agency

The late 1960s was a period in American history when various downtrodden groups (racial minorities, women, gays) became militant in attempts to change existing power arrangements. Within this society-wide framework, athletes, too, began to recognize their common plight and organized to change it. Most fundamentally, professional athletes felt that because the owners had all the power, the players did not receive their true value in the marketplace. The result was that athletes, singly and together in player associations, began to assert themselves against what they considered to be an unfair system.

Several cases were especially instrumental in the modification of the reserve clause in baseball. First, there was Curt Flood, who was traded by the baseball Cardinals to the Philadelphia Phillies but refused to play for them. He did not play the next year (1970) in protest and brought suit against organized baseball, alleging that the reserve system constituted a system of peonage. The United States Supreme Court ruled five to three against Flood but recognized that the system should be changed by congressional action.[20]

In 1974 Jim "Catfish" Hunter of the Oakland Athletics was allowed by an arbitrator to be released from his contract because the owner had failed to make payments on an insurance policy that was part of the contract. The subsequent bidding for

Hunter's services resulted in his signing a multiyear contract with the New York Yankees for $3.5 million. This showed the other athletes very clearly that they were not being paid their true worth and had much to do with increasing their militancy.

Finally, the reserve system in baseball died in December 1975 with the decision by an arbitration panel that two players, Andy Messersmith and Dave McNally, were free agents because they had played out their existing contracts plus an additional year. McNally did not pursue his career because of an injury, but Messersmith signed a three-year, no-cut contract with the Atlanta Braves for about $1 million. This was a huge salary, when you consider that the average salary at the time was $44,676.

These landmark cases led to an agreement between the owners of professional baseball teams and the Players' Association in July 1976. The provisions allowed (1) players without 1976 or 1977 contracts to become free agents and (2) players with six or more years in the major leagues to become free agents without waiting a one-year option period. Most importantly, there would be no compensation for the free agent's former team.

The first test of baseball's free-agent system occurred in November 1976 when the eligible players entered the reentry draft (called by some the "auction of freed slaves"). What happened had several important implications for the future of baseball. First, contrary to many predictions, only 24 out of the pool of some 600 athletes took the free-agent route. This was probably a consequence of the second result: Salaries had been raised to mollify the athletes under contract. Third, again contrary to expectations, the competitive balance of baseball was generally enhanced. Of the twelve teams with winning seasons in 1976, three signed a total of 4 new players. Of the twelve with losing records, seven teams purchased 14 free agents (by the end of 1976, 6 players remained unsigned). Fourth, the owners' profits were now being shared more equitably with the athletes, especially the star athletes. The first 14 free agents signed long-term agreements ranging from three to ten years that totaled $20.5 million in bonuses, salaries, and deferred payments. To put this in perspective, Gene Autry purchased the Angels in 1960 for $2.1 million. In 1976 he paid more than $5 million for three athletes: Joe Rudi, Bobby Grich, and Don Baylor. Baseball was still profitable for owners but less so. The attendance at Major League Baseball games in 1976 was thirty-three million. When this is multiplied by the average cost of tickets ($3.45), the total is $113,850,000, not counting parking and concessions revenues. Moreover, according to Marvin Miller, executive director of the Players' Association, radio and television revenues produce 150 percent of baseball's payroll.[21] While baseball franchise owners continued to make profits, the momentous decisions in baseball clearly restructured the power relationship between owner and athlete. When the effects on other sports are considered, the year 1976 can truly be considered the year of "jock liberation."

The victories for the baseball players were not won easily. The owners fought them at every instance. There were strikes by the players and lockouts by the owners. Most significant, the owners were found guilty by the courts of *collusion,* that is, they conspired not to sign free agents from 1985 to 1987. This was an attempt to stop the salary spiral in baseball by taking away the players' power. The arbitrator, George Nicolau, in his opinion found that "there was no vestige of a free market [during these years]. It was replaced by a patent pattern of deliberate contravention of baseball's collective bargaining agreement." As a result, the owners had to pay $280 million in damages to the players adversely affected by the owners' collusion. In 2000 a federal appeals court commented on this collusion in a case involving ex-player Steve Garvey. The court wrote in a unanimous opinion, "The owners' mendacity in the 1980s collusive effort to depress the ballplayers' income was in many ways as damaging to baseball as the Black Sox scandal of 1919 [referring to the Chicago White Sox throwing the World Series against Cincinnati]. The scope of the owners' deceit and fabrications in their 1980s effort to cheat their employees out of their rightful wages was wholly unprecedented, as was the financial injury suffered by the players."[22] (See Box 10.4, *Thinking about Sport,* for a summary of how the power has shifted in Major League Baseball.)

> **Box 10.4** *Thinking about Sport* **The Business of Baseball: Shifting Power and Increased Salaries**
>
> 1879—Reserve rules instituted.
> 1922—The Supreme Court decided that baseball was not a trade in interstate commerce and therefore not subject to federal antitrust laws.
> 1953—A minor league player, George Toolson, wanted to change teams but was denied. The Supreme Court agreed with the owners that the players were bound to a club for life, citing the 1922 decision.
> 1966—Marvin Miller was elected executive director of the Players' Association. At this time the average player salary was $19,000, and the minimum for a major league player was $6,000 (a rise of only $1,000 since 1947).
> 1968—Players agreed not to sign 1969 contracts until a benefits plan (pensions and health insurance) agreement could be reached. This was the first mass holdout in baseball history. The minimum salary was increased to $10,000.
> 1970—The Players' Association negotiated a grievance and arbitration procedure with the owners.
> 1970—Curt Flood refused to leave the St. Louis Cardinals for Philadelphia.
> 1972—The Supreme Court ruled five to three against Flood.
> 1972—The first strike in the history of professional sports, lasting 13 days—4 in the preseason and 9 during the season—occurred. As a result the owners added $500,000 to the health care insurance and agreed to a cost-of-living increase in retirement benefits. The average salary was $22,000, and the minimum salary was $13,500.
> 1974—Jim "Catfish" Hunter became a free agent. As a result he left his $100,000 salary with Oakland for $750,000 with the Yankees.
> 1975—Andy Messersmith and Dave McNally became free agents.
> 1976—Free agency rights were created in the contracts of baseball. The average salary at this time was $51,500.
> 1979—The average salary was $113,558.
> 1980—A new pension agreement increased all benefits. The owners' contribution to the pension plan was one-third of the national television and radio package.
> 1981—A strike occurred for fifty days because the owners demanded restricted free agency (compensation for the loss of a free agent), which would have lost what the players had won in 1976. The players lost $34 million (an average of $52,000 each) in the strike, but they won by retaining free agency. The average salary at this time was $186,000.
> 1985—The average salary was $371,000.
> 1989—The average salary was $489,000.
> 1990—The average salary was $597,000, with the minimum salary at $100,000. The combined salaries for major leaguers was $388 million, and the owners' combined revenues were $1.5 billion (players thus received 26 percent of the revenues they generated).
> 1992—The average salary was $1 million.
> 1994–1995—A 232-day shutdown of Major League Baseball with no World Series in 1994. After a delay of the 1995 season and still no labor agreement, attendance for the season was down around 18 percent and television audiences were off by 11 percent.
> 1998—Congress passed the Curt Flood Act, a compromise that amended the special exemptions from antitrust for major league players, but excluded minor league players and baseball owners in dealing with communities over franchise location.
> 2001—The owners voted to eliminate two teams.
> 2001—The average player salary was $2.29 million.
> 2006—The average player salary was $2.699 million.
>
> *Sources:* Marvin Miller, *A Whole Different Ball Game: The Sport and Business of Baseball* (New York: Birch Lane Press, 1991), and Major League Baseball Players' Association, Associated Press release, 21 December 2006.

Baseball reached an impasse in 1994. The owners and the players could not reach a collective bargaining agreement, resulting in a strike that ended the season prematurely and canceled the World Series. Over the winter the issues were not resolved, resulting in the 1995 season not beginning as scheduled. The parties agreed to play a shortened 1995 season without a collective bargaining agreement. At issue was a salary cap for each team (as used in the NFL and NBA). A salary cap, of course, limits the potential income of the athletes and, therefore, controls salary escalation. The owners argued that a salary cap is needed so that the small-market teams such as Milwaukee,

Pittsburgh, and Kansas City can compete with the large-market teams that have greater revenues (attendance, local TV and radio, advertising). The players argued that the salary cap makes the players pay for this balance, rather than the owners who should develop ways to divert money from the large-market teams to the small-market teams (revenue sharing by participating equally in all broadcasting revenues—the Yankees receive about $60 million from local radio and television, while other clubs may receive only $5 million; a 50/50 split in ticket sales instead of the 60/40 split that is now the norm, etc.).

Professional football did not have as far to go as baseball did because players were already allowed to play out their option. The obstacle, as we noted earlier, was the Rozelle Rule, which was voided after two court cases. The first occurred when quarterback Joe Kapp signed a nonstandard contract with the New England Patriots and it was voided by Commissioner Rozelle. Kapp gave up his career and sued the league. A district court judge ruled in Kapp's favor in 1974, saying that the standard player contract violated federal antitrust laws and that the Rozelle Rule was illegal.

Since the Kapp case involved an individual player rather than the entire NFL system and was subject to a prolonged appeal process, the NFL Players' Association brought suit to change the system for all players in December 1975 (*Mackey v. NFL*). A federal court judge decided that the Rozelle Rule was illegal. He directed the NFL and its twenty-six teams to cease enforcing the rule. The result was that in May 1976 twenty-four new free agents began searching for the best offers: Larry Csonka signed for more than $1 million covering four seasons; John Riggins, who as a New York Jet played his option year for $67,500, put his price at $1.5 million for five years, payable at $100,000 a year until 1990.

Another significant case occurred in 1976. In a suit brought by former Washington Redskin Jim ("Yazoo") Smith, the college draft was struck down also because it violated antitrust law. In response to the court cases, fear of additional litigation, and owner-player strife, the owners and the National Football League Players' Association came to terms on a collective bargaining agreement in 1977. This contract was significant to the players because it recognized the union, voided arbitrary hair and dress codes, set minimum salaries, and awarded the union $13.65 million for damages arising in the *Mackey* case. In return, the union accepted the college draft and killed free agency. That is, they permitted the Rozelle Rule to continue, although in modified form. Under this arrangement, when a team signs a player entering his third year for $280,000 or more, it owes his old team two first-draft picks; for $230,000 to $280,000, a first and second pick; for $180,000 to $230,000, a first and a third; and so on. The net effect of this rule is that NFL teams almost never sign free agents, thus depressing the potential salaries of the better players. The net effect, according to one critic, is that the union "traded free agency and the abolished draft—unprecedented, monumental breakthroughs for the players—for nothing much more than a healthy union treasury."[23]

In 1982 the NFL Players' Association conducted a fifty-seven-day strike that cost the owners $210 million in lost revenues. The eventual settlement allowed the modified Rozelle Rule to continue but gave considerable overall monetary benefits to the players ($1.6 billion over five years, designating 46 percent of the NFL owners' gross to the players). In 1987 the union again went on strike—missing forty-two games—demanding free agency and $18 million for the pension fund. The strike failed as the owners hired replacement players, the networks televised the games, and public opinion sided with the owners. The strike cost the players $79 million in lost salaries and the owners $42 million in fewer ticket sales and $60 million in rebates to the television networks. Although the players lost this battle, the war was not over. A groundbreaking 1993 agreement instituted a salary cap and unrestricted free agency (eliminating the Rozelle Rule). Then in 2001 the owners and the players' union agreed to a three-year extension of the collective bargaining agreement that would ensure labor peace until 2007, which has been extended further. Under this agreement players receive 63 percent of the NFL's designated gross revenue and have a rich benefits package.

This revenue sharing is especially lucrative given the $17.6 billion television package over eight years.

Historically, negotiations within professional basketball, unlike those in football and baseball, have been characterized by considerable cooperation between owners and athletes. Agreements have also been much more progressive. This spirit of cooperation on the part of the owners, however, has been prompted by clear messages of the court decisions in the other sports: Owners may no longer treat their players as highly paid slaves. The most significant provisions of the 1976 NBA settlement were:

1. The option clause was to be eliminated from nonrookie player contracts, beginning with those that expired with the 1976 season. In other words, a veteran was no longer bound to a team for one year after his or her contract ran out.
2. In 1980 the owner of a player whose contract had expired would have the right of first refusal if that player was offered a contract by another team. By equaling the best offer, the owner could keep the player; otherwise, the player would be free to join the new team.

In 1983 the NBA owners and players agreed to revenue sharing and the first salary cap in professional sports. The purpose of this provision was to allow poor teams to compete for star players and to slow the acceleration in player salaries.

Some teams, however, were permitted to surpass the cap through a "grandfather" clause for salaries already exceeding the limit, and all teams were permitted to spend any amount to retain their own free agents. The salary cap agreement granted the players 53 percent of the total league revenues. As a result, the average player salary increased from $240,000 in 1983 to $510,000 in 1987 to $990,000 in 1991 and $1,870,000 in 1994.

In 1995, after the NBA Players' Association negotiated a deal with the league, a number of high-profile athletes (e.g., Michael Jordan, Patrick Ewing) led an attempt by the players to decertify the union. The union members voted against this effort, followed by the owners' ratification of the collective bargaining agreement. This new plan will allow a dramatic increase in the salary cap and will take the average player salary to nearly $3 million by the conclusion of the contract, decrease the amount of rookie contracts, and guarantee all first-round choices three-year deals, after which they will become free agents.

Salaries

The legal decisions favoring the athletes had one major impact, which was that salaries increased dramatically (see Table 10.1). As a result, the gap between the salary of the average professional athlete and that of the average worker has increased even more dramatically.

In Major League Baseball, for example, in 1950 the average baseball player earned $13,300 a year, a little more than four times the median family income. By 2007, the average baseball player was earning $2.92 million, about fifty-three times as much as the median family income. These higher average salaries reflect the very high salaries paid to superstars and do not reflect the salaries for most players. In baseball, for example, the New York Yankees had a total player payroll of $189.6 million in 2007. The average player salary was $6.5 million, because eleven players exceeded $10 million in salary. A better measure is the use of the median salary (the midpoint, with half

Table 10.1 Average Salaries in Major Professional Leagues for Selected Years (in dollars)

Year	National Basketball Association	Major League Baseball	National Football League	National Hockey League
1968	20,000	19,000	21,000	20,000
1976	110,000	51,500	63,200	90,000
1984	246,000	325,900	162,000	130,000
1991	990,000	850,000	355,000	370,000
1994	1,870,000	1,186,000	737,000	463,000
2001	3,170,000	2,290,000	1,169,000	1,430,000
2007	5,200,000	2,920,000	1,400,000	1,600,000

above and half below), which in 2007 was $1.5 million for the Yankees (thirteen players were below $1 million).

Athletes of superstar status in individual sports sometimes receive even higher incomes than those in team sports. The most popular heavyweight boxers can make as much as $20 million for a single fight. The elite tennis players make more than $5 million annually. A few golfers approach $10 million a year in winnings, as do a few auto racers and jockeys.

These huge incomes, which are supplemented by endorsements and personal appearances (see Box 10.5, *Thinking about Sport*, for the phenomenal amount that Tiger Woods generates), raise two important questions: (1) Are athletes paid too much? and (2) how do such enormous salaries for athletes affect the fans?

To the fans, their once-noble athletic heroes are now businesspeople. Athletes demand huge salaries to perform in games. They threaten not to play. They no longer seem to have loyalty to their team or city. Roger Angell observed that fans do not appear to object so much to the large salaries of the superstars as to the across-the-board affluence of athletes.

> Large payments to athletes are not enjoyed or approved of by us, the fans, if the payment is made broadly, to all the athletes engaged in a particular trade at the big-league level—all basketball players,

---

Box 10.5 *Thinking about Sport* **Tiger Woods: On His Way to Becoming the First Billion-Dollar Athlete**

Tiger Woods was born in 1975 to a mother who is a native of Thailand and an African American father. Under his father's tutelage, Tiger took up golf as a toddler and by age 15 was the youngest Junior Amateur Champion in golf history. At 18 he became the youngest person, and the first member of a racial minority, to win the U.S. Amateur Championship. By age 20 he had won that tournament three consecutive times, the first person in history to do so, and he was also *Sports Illustrated*'s Sportsman of the Year. At age 21 and in his first full year as a professional, he was the leading money winner on the PGA Tour, winner of the prestigious Masters (the youngest person, and the first of African or Asian descent, to win that championship), PGA Player of the Year, and Associated Press Male Athlete of the Year. In 2000 he became the fifth player in history and the youngest ever to complete a career Grand Slam (Masters, U.S. Open, British Open, and PGA Championship). By the end of 2007, at age 31, he had won 61 PGA Tour events (including thirteen majors); he was the all-time career money leader, surpassing $77 million (and a $10 million retirement annuity); and he had been Player of the Year nine of the last eleven years. And, perhaps most astounding, he has won 28.4 percent (61 out of 215) of his professional starts on the PGA tour.

Tiger's popularity has translated into a huge growth in sales of golf equipment, golf lessons, and the number of rounds of golf played. Most significantly, it has meant ultimately billions of dollars to the PGA Tour in increased television revenues and a dramatic rise in the prize money for the various tournaments. Whenever Woods is a contender, TV ratings go up 113 percent, with the audience of young males (ages eighteen to twenty-four) tripling. As a consequences of this, Tiger Woods has more power than any other player in the sport's history.

When Tiger Woods turned professional in 1996, he signed a five-year, $40 million contract with Nike, an amount unprecedented for a rookie in any sport. In 2000 Nike upped the contract to $100 million for five years, the largest contract in sports marketing history, which was later upped again. In addition, Woods had endorsement deals with Buick, American Express, EA Sports, Upper Deck, Accenture, Tag Heuer, and Gillette, totaling about $100 million endorsement income annually. Moreover, he receives appearance fees overseas for as much as $3 million each. In 2007 his estimated total income was $111,941,827 (or $308,333 a day). Tiger's endorsement and appearance income increases an average of 13 percent a year. At that pace he will surpass $1 billion in total career earnings by 2010 or before—the first athlete to do so.

Sources: Jonah Freedman, "The Fortunate 50," *Sports Illustrated,* 4 June 2007, http://sportsillustrated.cnn.com/more/specials/fortunate50/2007/index.html; All Headline News, "Tiger Woods Signs New Nike Endorsement Contract," 12 December 2006, http://www.allheadlinenews.comm/articles/7005832939; and Darren Rovell, "Amex Slices Woods: Is Tiger Worth Price of Endorsement?" *SportsBiz,* 7 August 2007, http://www.cnbc.com/id/20161363.

all hockey players, and so on. "The players have gotten too greedy," "They're all paid too much"—these are current grandstand convictions, which I also hear from other people, in and out of the sports world. As I pick up this complaint, however, it seems to apply more to a well-paid journeyman than to the superstar.... It would be extremely interesting to measure this, if we could. What it means, I think, is that high pay for athletes is resented if they are seen as employees. And when these employees behave like contemporary workmen, trying to extract the most money and the most favorable working conditions and retirement benefits from a typically reluctant and unsympathetic employer, and forming a union to press their demands—which is what the baseball and football and basketball players have all done in recent years—then they are resented even more deeply, almost to the point of hatred. This is an extraordinary turn of events in a labor-conscious, success-oriented society like ours.[24]

Ironically, the fans have tended to take the side of the team owners in many salary disputes, strikes, and other disruptions, even though the owners over the years have had the monopoly, have taken economic advantage of their athletes, and have had the temerity to move franchises to more lucrative communities.

One irony is that fans resent the high salaries of athletes but take in stride the huge salaries of other entertainers. In 2007, for example, an entertainer—Oprah Winfrey—had an annual compensation of $260 million, more than two and a half times that of the highest-paid athlete—Tiger Woods, who was the only athlete among the top fifteen in celebrity income.[25] For some reason the huge monies collected by these and other entertainers are accepted by the public, but the lesser monies received by athletes tend to foster resentment.

In addition to the entertainment analogy, several other arguments justify the amounts paid to superstars for playing games. The first is that their salaries are paid on the basis of scarcity. If there are 242 professional basketball players in a nation of some 300 million people, that makes the athlete less than one in a million, and he or she should be paid accordingly. The second argument is that a sports career is so brief that players should be paid extra (out of the 242 players in the NBA, only 30 or so are thirty years of age or older). Third, the owners are only paying the athletes what they are worth, because the superstars bring out the fans. Finally, related to the last point, salaries have escalated but so too have owners' revenues from television, ticket sales, royalties from the sale of merchandise, and the like. In 2007, the NFL received $2.2 billion from television contracts, the NBA $500 million, Major League Baseball $479 million, and the National Hockey League some $160 million.

A Radical Question: Are Owners Necessary?

Owners receive anywhere from 50 to 75 percent of the profits from professional teams. What have they provided to receive such generous compensation? They did buy the teams from other owners, but what else? The stadiums and arenas, except on rare occasions, have been provided by taxpayers. So, too, are the practice facilities. Why don't the municipalities own these teams? They could hire competent general managers to sign players, make schedules, hire coaches and support staff, and work with others for television and radio contracts. David Meggyesy, a former professional football player and now employed by the NFL Players' Association, has argued the following:

> You know, people say, "Oh, those jocks are making all that money," but what about the owners? It's a relative thing. Remember, the players are everything in this game. They are both the hired hands and the machinery, both the coal and the coal miners, however you want to say it. In every meeting I have, I tell my guys, "You are the game. You are the people the fans come to see, not the owners sipping their scotch in their luxury boxes."[26]

The Green Bay Packers professional football team is the only major team owned by the people. As such, it provides a model for what could be.

> Some 1,900 of the locals, including truckers, barkeeps, merchants, and bus drivers, own a piece of the Pack, organized back in 1923 as a community-

owned, nonprofit company. The stockholders draw no profit, and the locally elected board of directors that operates the team is unpaid, but all concerned draw great pleasure from knowing that the Packers are theirs. . . .

Get this: No ticket costs more than $28, no parking space is more than $7, there is free parking within four blocks of the stadium. . . . Charities run the stadium's concessions. . . . Off-duty police provide stadium security, and are paid overtime by the team.

Green Bay fans and citizens never have to worry that some pirate of an owner is going to hijack the Pack and haul their team to Los Angeles or any other big-city market, because Green Bay is their team. It stands as a shining model of how fans in other cities could get control of their teams and stop corporate rip-offs.[27]

AMATEUR SPORT AS A BUSINESS

The trend toward greater bureaucratization, commercialization, and institutionalism—the trend toward corporate sport—is not restricted to professional athletics; it is also true of much of organized amateur athletics. Analysis of the sports industry must therefore deal with these two categories of sports participation, although in reality they are often virtually indistinguishable.

The amateur concept was a product of the late eighteenth-century leisure class, whose ideal of the patrician sportsman was part of their pursuit of conspicuous leisure. Consequently, to be a pure amateur required independent wealth, because the true amateur derived no income from his sports participation. Explicit in the amateur ideal is the belief that one's athletic endeavor must be unrelated to one's work or livelihood and that sport itself is somehow sullied, tarnished, or demeaned if one is paid for performing it.[28]

In most cases the distinction between professional and amateur sport is artificial. This has been recognized in tennis, which has laid aside the archaic idea that amateurs and professionals cannot compete against each other. Also, the Olympics, through their various international sport organizations, have eliminated the notion of

professional in many sports (e.g., track and field, skiing, basketball, tennis). In other sports, though, the distinction is still made and, usually, applied inconsistently.

The most frequent means of subsidizing amateur athletes is through scholarships to colleges and universities. Ignoring for the moment the long-range value of a college degree, the typical U.S. athletic scholarship (a legal maximum of room, books, board, tuition, and fees, as specified by the NCAA) has an annual value of twenty thousand dollars at a state-supported school with low tuition and fifty thousand dollars at a private school with high tuition. These sums do not include the widespread illicit payments frequently discovered through NCAA investigations. College scholarships do not constitute incomes comparable to professional contracts; nevertheless, college athletes are being compensated financially for their athletic exploits. Most athletes in highly competitive sports are subsidized in some way, and thus the distinction between amateur and professional sport is primarily one of degree.

The decisions made by various ruling bodies as to who is amateur and who is not result in considerable hypocrisy. As former basketball great Bill Russell put it:

> The hypocrisy of amateur sports is offensive to anybody who cares. To me, being an amateur is like being a virgin. It is an old idea that has some innocence and charm, celebrated mostly by people to whom it doesn't apply. It doesn't look as good on old people as on young ones. It is impossible to keep partially, though many try to do so. It is associated with deception and pretense. And even if you love the idea, you still can't help being suspicious when you see the pious members of the U.S. Chastity Committee charging the public money to peep at their soiled virgins.[29]

The Economics of Collegiate Sport

The business dimension of amateur sport is most fully developed in the athletic programs of United States colleges and universities. The intercollegiate sports system, initially student-organized and student-run, came under the control of school administrators early in the twentieth century. It has since become a major business proposition, generating, as noted in chapter 6, as much as $100 million budgets, millions for bowl appearances, and lucrative television contracts.

Operating a big-time collegiate athletic program is a business proposition, which means that financial losses are unacceptable. There have been different responses to the financial crisis in intercollegiate sports. The NCAA has responded by permitting first-year students to compete in varsity athletics, by reducing the maximum number of scholarships that each school may annually award, and by eliminating the fifteen-dollar "laundry" money previously allowed athletes each month. Some schools have reduced their commitment to intercollegiate athletics, either by de-emphasizing the level of competition in their athletic programs or by dropping support of specific (typically nonrevenue) sports, such as golf, tennis, swimming, wrestling, soccer, rugby, and lacrosse.

However, in many instances the sports dropped by a university administration as financially prohibitive are being reinstituted as student-initiated and student-run affairs without any real institutional assistance, thus moving them back to their original level: organized sport.

Financial losses have most frequently prompted the individual athletic programs to redouble their efforts to remain competitive and thus to approach fiscal solvency. One response is to fire the incumbent coach and replace him or her with another who promises to reverse the institution's athletic fortunes, the agreement to coach frequently having been obtained by the university's commitment of greater financial outlays to support the new and invigorated program. The most far-reaching consequences of these escalating costs are that they further intensify the pressures to recruit athletes legally and illegally.

The lure of money affects even teams below the big-time level. A common practice is for lesser teams to schedule big-time teams just for a guaranteed fee. Both schools benefit from such an arrangement. The small school makes relatively big money, and the big-time school adds to its winning record and pockets most of the gate receipts.

The extensive financial involvement of American colleges and universities in athletics makes it difficult to distinguish their operation from noncollegiate professional enterprises. In fact, the average game attendance of many universities in football and basketball exceeds that of professional teams. As mentioned earlier, the salaries paid college athletes raise the question of how they are to be distinguished from professionals. In other words, the money an admitted professional receives is merely greater than that paid the typical college player (although the professional player is not confronted with the necessity of diverting energies to studies, to the hassle of remaining academically eligible; the professional is free to devote himself or herself solely to developing athletic skills).

Not surprisingly, collusive practices similar to those employed by professional promoters have infiltrated college athletics because the professional-amateur distinction is difficult to make realistically. As with professional athletes, a free market does not exist for college athletes; they are subject to severe restrictions by the NCAA, the major governing body of college athletics, which functions as a cartel. NCAA regulations regarding recruiting, scholarships, and eligibility are collusive, and like the reserve clause in professional sports, their effect is to prevent one team from raiding another for players. Although colleges have not yet fully rationalized procedures to the point of instituting a draft of eligible high school and community college players, fierce competition exists. The national and conference letters of intent require a player to declare his or her intention of enrolling in and competing for a specific school, which "has the effect of insulating a given university-firm from competition for inputs by other university-firms in its conference."[30]

The effect of such practices is, of course, advantageous for competing schools; it enables them to restrict their feverish recruiting of high school talent to a few months of the year. NCAA rules also preclude "tampering" with players who have already committed their services: A school cannot recruit a player already at another school unless the player is willing to be penalized by being declared ineligible for a year. This rule against transfers has an effect similar to the option clause in professional sports. Only if the player is willing to forgo competing for a year can the student transfer his or her services to another school's team. (The practice does not apply to the coaches of intercollegiate teams, only to the players.)

Other NCAA regulations also seriously limit the freedom of college athletes. First, players may not compete for more than four years in a single sport, nor may they compete in intercollegiate athletics after they have received the baccalaureate degree. This rule has led to the somewhat common situation of players having the requisite number of credits to fulfill the institution's graduation requirements but refusing to accept their degrees until after completing their intercollegiate athletic eligibility. Graduate students in English universities are allowed to compete in British collegiate sports, but graduate students in the United States are prohibited from doing so. Moreover, the NCAA stipulates that an athlete cannot compete more than five years after initially entering college, except in the case of interruption of college career for military or missionary service. The student who drops out of school for any other reason and returns several years later may not participate in intercollegiate athletics.

As James Koch concluded, the effect of these NCAA regulations is to permit American colleges to operate their athletic programs in a monopolistic manner by regulating and limiting the freedom of potential athletes. They establish a ceiling on players' salaries, regulate the length and criteria for participation, and limit player mobility.[31]

Despite the pervasive commercialization of college sport, it still retains (or attempts to retain) an aura of wholesomeness. We must, though, recognize the professional aspect of the big-time college athletic system. Especially in football and men's basketball, and to a lesser but increasing extent in baseball and hockey, intercollegiate sports serve as the minor league farm systems for major league professional team sports and as sources of free publicity for future pro stars.

Collegiate sports participation has historically been the prelude to professional competition in basketball and football, whereas this has been infrequently (although increasingly) the case in baseball and hockey. Although the minor league system of Major League Baseball has diminished considerably from its heyday immediately after World War II, it is still much more extensive than that of any other major professional team sport. The primary difference between the baseball and hockey minor leagues and those of the other pro sports is that there is little mobility among the latter. Whereas for a baseball or hockey professional not to have served at least a minimal apprenticeship in the minor leagues is highly atypical, for a professional basketball or football player to have done so is highly atypical.

Awareness of the professionalism of collegiate sports and their function as minor leagues, or training grounds, for future major leaguers has led to the suggestion that the professionalism of collegiate athletics be explicitly recognized. This would be accomplished by having a college athlete's letter of intent be considered a legal contract with the school in the same way that a professional athlete's contract is owned by his or her team. Major league owners desiring the services of such an athlete would have to purchase the contract, thereby reimbursing that school for the cost of player development and training and simultaneously improving the financial position of the school team supplying the pro team with its raw material.

Recognizing this natural source of player development, professional basketball and football teams have entered into informal agreements with colleges and universities. The pro teams promise that they will not tamper or try to negotiate with undergraduate players until they have completed four years of athletic eligibility. Thus, a player like Wilt Chamberlain, who competed for only three of four years at Kansas University, was unable to play in the NBA during the fourth year because he was not yet deemed eligible for the draft. The effect of these arrangements within the professional leagues is clearly collusive, and was legally declared so soon after the fledgling American Basketball Association challenged the rule by signing undergraduate players to contracts in their sophomore and junior years. The National Basketball Association once refused to permit this practice unless the player was deemed a hardship case, in which instance, because of his or her family's alleged dire economic condition, he must receive more substantial wages than his university can provide. The NBA now permits anyone to declare his candidacy for the professional draft, although high school graduates must wait at least one year after graduating before entering the draft.

Professional football, reluctantly, has followed the lead of basketball. College players may declare themselves eligible for the draft prior to their senior year. The NCAA has vigorously opposed players leaving early for professional careers. They have allowed this only because their attempts to prohibit this would not stand up in court.

SUMMARY

We have shown the economic side of sport in this chapter. The message is clear: In professional and in big-time collegiate sport, the dollar is king. Sport is used by big business in a multimillion-dollar effort to sell products. Owners squeeze as much money as they can from fans and taxpayers. Players' demands for money seem incapable of satiation. The result is the ultimate corruption of sport as a meaningful, joyous activity in itself into corporate sport. Let us review briefly the various components that demonstrate the businesslike atmosphere of sport.

1. Sport has sold out to the demands of television. In return for large contracts, the leagues and the NCAA allow the television networks to dictate schedules, time-outs, and the like.
2. The principle of supply and demand operates in setting admission charges for athletic events. If sport were truly a game rather than a business, the most successful teams would charge the lowest ticket prices, but this is not the case.
3. The owners of professional teams are in a constant search of better markets and higher profits. The possibility that a franchise will move increases the probability that municipalities will provide facilities or other inducements at taxpayers' expense to entice teams to their city or to encourage them to remain there.
4. Athletes seemingly put self-interest ahead of team play and loyalty to their fans. Players demand very high salaries and other monetary inducements (bonuses, retirement benefits, insurance policies, interest-free loans, and so forth). The frequent result is pugnacious negotiations between owners and athletes.
5. A struggle exists between athletes (through union-like organizations) and entrepreneurs for the power to regulate sports and to apportion profits. This is manifested in court battles, player strikes, owner lockouts, and press agency by both sides to sway public opinion.

In sum, instead of being an escape from the workaday world of moneymaking, strikes, strife, and legal complexities, sport has become similar to the world of work. As such, it reveals, in microcosm, the values of the larger society. As Roger Angell said of baseball (and the same is true of all corporate sport): "Professional sports now form a noisy and substantial, if irrelevant and distracting, part of the world, and it seems as if baseball games taken entirely—off the field as well as on it, in the courts and in the front offices as well as down on the diamonds—may now tell us more about ourselves than they ever did before."[32]

WEB RESOURCES

www.askmen.com/sports/business
This website for a men's magazine often includes essays on the business aspects of sports, including the Olympics, and the accounting practices of professional teams.

www.fieldofschemes.com
This site provides information critical of public subsidies for building stadiums and arenas for private profit.

www.forbes.com
Forbes magazine from time to time provides data on wealthy Americans (including owners of professional teams) and financial information on professional teams.

www.heartland.org/studies/sports/sports-studies.htm
The Heartland Institute investigates and reports how the public subsidizes the building of stadiums for teams owned by wealthy entrepreneurs.

NOTES

1. John Underwood, *Spoiled Sport* (Boston: Little, Brown, 1984), 4–5.
2. Plunkett Research, "Sports Industry Overview," http://www.plunkettresearc.com/Sports/Sports Statistics/tabid/273/Default.aspx.
3. Jonah Freedman, "The Fortunate 50," *Sports Illustrated*, 4 June 2007, http://sportsillustrated.cnn.com/more/specials/fortunat50/2007/index.html.
4. Tom Goldman, "Almost-NBA players Take Home Paltry Salaries," National Public Radio, 7 February 2007, http://www.npr.org/templates/story/story.php?storyID=7239948.
5. Hap Fry, "Under Pressure, They Make the Call," *Fort Collins Coloradoan*, 8 August 2007, http://www.coloradoan.com/apps/pbcs.d11/article?AID=/20070808/NEW501/708080321/1002.
6. Jim Hightower, *There's Nothing in the Middle of the Road but Yellow Stripes and Armadillos* (New York: HarperCollins, 1997), 11.
7. James Quirk and Rodney Fort, *Hard Ball: The Abuse of Power in Pro Team Sports* (Princeton: Princeton University Press, 1999), 9.
8. See Andrew Zimbalist, "The NFL's New Math," *The Bottom Line: Observations and Arguments on the Sports Business* (Philadelphia: Temple University Press, 2006), 29–30; Kevin J. Delaney and Rick Eckstein, *Public Dollars, Private Stadiums: The Battle over Building Sports Stadiums* (New Brunswick, N.J.: Rutgers University Press, 2003); J. G. Long, "Full Court: The Real Cost of Public Funding for Major League Sports Facilities," *Journal of Sports Economics* 6, no. 2 (2005): 119–143; Mark S. Rosentraub, *Major League Lo$ers: The Real Cost of Sports and Who's Paying for It* (New York: Basic Books, 1997); and George H. Sage, "Stealing Home: Political, Economic, and Media Power and a Publicly Funded Baseball Stadium in Denver," *Journal of Sport and Social Issues* 17 (August 1993): 110–124.
9. Zimbalist, "The NFL's New Math," 130–170.
10. John Underwood, "From Baseball and Apple Pie to Greed and Sky Boxes," *New York Times*, 31 October 1993, p. 115; see also Jay Weiner, *Stadium Games* (Minneapolis: University of Minnesota Press, 2000); Joanna Cagan and Neil deMause, *Field of Schemes* (Monroe, Maine: Common Courage Press, 1998); Roger G. Noll and Andrew Zimbalist, eds., *Sports, Jobs and Taxes* (Washington, D.C.: Brookings Institution, 1997); David Barringer, "The New Urban Gamble," *American Prospect* 34 (September/October 1997): 28–34; and D. Stanley Eitzen, "Public Teams, Private Profits," *Dollars and Sense*, March/April 2000, 21–23, 43.
11. Jeffrey G. Owen and William J. Polley, "Cities and Professional Sports Teams," *International Journal of Sport Finance* 2 (2007): 71.
12. Underwood, "From Baseball and Apple Pie to Greed and Sky Boxes," 22.
13. Sage, "Stealing Home." For a similar analysis in Canada, see Richard S. Gruneau, "Elites, Class and Corporate Power in Canadian Sport," in *Sport, Culture and Society*, 2nd ed., ed. John W. Loy, Jr., Gerald S. Kenyon, and Barry D. McPherson (Philadelphia: Lea K. Febiger, 1981), 348–731.
14. Robert A. Baade, "Stadium Subsidies Make Little Economic Sense for Cities," *Journal of Urban Affairs* 18, no. 1 (1996): 37. See also Rosentraub, *Major League Lo$ers*, 129–178.
15. The following NFL team values are found in "NFL Team Valuations," *Forbes*, 18 September 2006, 114.
16. Thomas Heath, "That's Not Peanuts," *Washington Post National Weekly Edition*, 18 June 2007, p. 56.
17. Woody Paige, "For Owners in a League of Their Own," *Denver Post*, 20 January 1993, sec. C, p. 1.
18. Michael I. Sovern, quoted in Leonard Koppett, "Don't Blame It All on the Free Agents," *Sporting News*, 2 July 1977, pp. 4, 16.
19. Alex Ben Block, "So, You Want to Own a Ball Club," *Forbes*, 1 April 1977, 37.
20. Sandy Grady, "The Man Who Changed the Game," *USA Today*, 3 April 2007, p. 15A. For extensive discussions of the legal cases, see John C. Weistart and Cym H. Lowell, *The Law of Sports* (Indianapolis: Bobbs-Merrill, 1979), 477–776; Robert C. Berry and Glenn M. Wong, *Law and Business of the Sports Industries: Professional Sports Leagues*, vol. 1 (Dover, Mass.: Auburn House, 1986); Edward R. Garvey, "From Chattel to Employee: The Athlete's Quest for Freedom and Dignity," *Annals* 445 (September 1979): 91–101; U.S. Congress,

House, *Rights of Professional Athletes* (Washington, D.C.: U.S. Government Printing Office, 1975), serial 59; Marvin Miller, *A Whole Different Ball Game: The Sport and Business of Baseball* (New York: Birch Lane Press, 1991); and Paul C. Weiler, *Leveling the Playing Field: How the Law Can Make Sports Better for the Fans* (Cambridge, Mass.: Harvard University Press, 2000).

21. Marvin Miller, quoted in Red Smith, "When Prices Go Up, Up, Up," *New York Times*, 28 November 1976, p. 35.

22. Quoted in "Court Says '80s Collusion as Bad as Scandal in '19," *Arizona Republic*, 15 February 2000, p. 6C.

23. Mike Trope, *Necessary Roughness* (Chicago: Contemporary Books, 1987), 169–170.

24. Roger Angell, "In the Counting House," *New Yorker*, 10 May 1976, 109–110.

25. "Celebrity 100," *Forbes*, 2 July 2007.

26. Matthew Goodman, "David Meggyesy Interview," *Z. Magazine*, 3 September 1990, 88–89.

27. Hightower, *There's Nothing in the Middle of the Road*, 22–23. See also Joanna Cagan and Neil deMause, "Buy the Bums Out," *In These Times*, 9 December 1996, 15–17.

28. D. Stanley Eitzen, "The Sociology of Amateur Sport: An Overview," *International Review for the Sociology of Sport* 24, no. 2 (1989): 95–104.

29. Bill Russell and Taylor Branch, "Money and Sports," *Professional Sports Journal* 1 (February 1980): 26.

30. James V. Koch, "The Economics of 'Big-Time' Intercollegiate Athletics," *Social Science Quarterly* 52 (September 1971): 253.

31. Ibid.

32. Angell, "In the Counting House," 107.

Chapter 11

Sport and the Mass Media

A symbiotic relationship exists between sport and the mass media; each is a commercial industry whose success has been greatly influenced by the other. (Big Stock Photo)

Social institutions that appear to be independent of one another frequently are found, on closer examination, to be very interdependent. Such is the case of sport and the mass media, even though the former is concerned with physical action, skill in a highly problematic task, and the outcome of a competitive event, while the latter communicates information and entertains. Both commercial sports and the printed and electronic media are preeminently commercial industries that constitute two of the most successful businesses in North America. Thus, the goal (and logic) of both is mainly economic profit. As one mass communication scholar noted:

> The mediation of sport cannot be missed on the contemporary cultural horizon. A daily newspaper without a sports section is an anomaly. Local news broadcasts feature sports far more prominently than they do coverage of local politics. Traditional television networks lose even more of their foothold on the market when they lose contractual rights to broadcast a popular sport. Cable and satellite networks build their ever more elaborate plans for global expansion on the ability of sport-related products to penetrate new markets and cross national borders with ease.[1]

SOCIAL ROLES OF THE MASS MEDIA

The term *mass media* refers to all of the technically organized means of communication that reach large numbers of diverse people quickly and efficiently. These systems of communication can be grouped into two major categories: printed media (newspapers, magazines, and books) and electronic media (radio, television, movies, and the Internet).

Prominent and Subtle Roles of the Media

One of the prominent roles of the mass media is the communication of information. Culture depends upon communication; indeed, culture cannot exist without an effective system of transmitting and disseminating information. In small primitive societies information is transmitted by direct one-to-one, face-to-face contact, but this form of information transmission is efficient only in a society of limited size, sparse population, and minimal social differentiation. Modern societies require complex networks of printed and electronic media to keep people informed about other people and events. Information binds people to their neighbors, cities, states, and other nations and the world.

Another prominent role of the mass media is to provide entertainment for people in all walks of life. Newspapers carry special features and the comics. Magazines and books offer stories of adventure, humor, and mystery. Radio and television provide a wide variety of entertainment, from music to sporting events. The Internet, the newest form of mass communication, offers everything that the other media offer, but it offers such a stunning variety of everything that it is impossible to try to enumerate its entertainment forms.

In performing these two roles (communication and entertainment), the mass media fulfills at least two subtle roles: social integration and social change. To the extent that a social institution, such as the media, promotes shared values and norms and secures a common consensus among citizens, it may be said to contribute to social integration. Shared information and entertainment contribute to the socialization of citizens in a particular culture and thus serve to integrate persons in that culture. It may be seen, then, that the mass media is a powerful ideological institution because the messages and images that it creates help shape and mold the national and international cultural atmosphere.

In spite of accusations about there being a "liberal media," the reality is that a strongly conservative ideology is conveyed in the North American mass media; indeed, critics of this social role of the media contend that it tends to promote and sustain the unequal distribution of power and wealth, as well as legitimizing existing unequal social relations related to class, gender, and race.

Although the media play an important role in the promotion of the status quo, they nevertheless promote social change as well. They present information about cutting-edge research, new social practices and values, and critiques of contemporary attitudes and behaviors; thus they also support social change. The mere reporting of new ideas and events stimulates reinterpretations of the world and promotes changes in many spheres of life.[2]

THE SYMBIOSIS OF MASS MEDIA AND SPORT

The four roles of the media—information, entertainment, social integration, and social change—are sustained in their association with sports. First, the media supply information about sports—for example, game results and statistics about individual players and teams. Second, they provide exciting entertainment. Reading about, listening to, or watching sporting events allows individuals opportunities to escape temporarily the burdens and frustrations that bind them to reality. Media sport has the perfect combination for entertainment, including controlled violence, excitement, and lots of audio and visual power.

Social integration, one of the media's subtle roles, is often played out through conversations about sport. One can ask almost any stranger about sports or well-known sporting events and the stranger will likely know the relevant information because he or she has read about it, heard about it, or seen it in the media; consequently, the conversation can be sustained and sometimes transformed into a more enduring social relationship. Media sport, then, provides a communal focus whereby large segments of the population can share common norms, rituals, ceremonies, and values.

Finally, the media have played a role in the creation of some sports, the popularity of others, and rule changes of others (more about this later in the chapter). The media have played a significant role in social change as it relates to sports.

Linkages between the Mass Media and Sport

Little did the inventors of our technical means of communication realize how their inventions would become associated with sport. Johannes Gutenberg invented movable type in the mid-fifteenth century. As his invention was refined during the following centuries, the ability of the printing press to produce reading material quickly and cheaply increased and made possible the growth of the publishing industry. Wireless telegraphy, invented at the end of the nineteenth century, served as the technological foundation for radio and television.

Newspapers

In the mid-nineteenth century American newspapers began periodic coverage of sports events, but it was not until the 1890s that the first sports section became a regular feature of a newspaper. In 1895, William Randolph Hearst, publisher of the *New York Journal*, developed the first modern sports section.

Over the past hundred years the symbiosis between the newspaper and sport has become so well established that in many of North America's most popular newspapers, sports coverage constitutes almost 50 percent of the space devoted to local, national, and international stories, and the sports pages have about five times as many readers as any other section of the newspaper. So the newspaper sports section has not been curtailed by the growth of either radio or television; instead, radio and television have strengthened rather than replaced the sports section of newspapers.[3]

Magazines

Even before the newspaper sports section, magazines and books chronicled the activities of athletes and teams. In the years between the American Revolution and the 1830s, there arose a widespread interest in journals of all kinds, and magazines cropped up everywhere to exploit the popular interest in horse racing, hunting, fishing, and athletic sports. The momentum of sports literature accelerated in the 1830s, and the first prominent sports journal in the United States, *Spirit of the Times*, began publication in 1831. This journal featured horse racing in particular but also reported on other sports and indirectly helped to establish what was to become "the national pastime"—baseball. Another popular nineteenth-century sports magazine, *The Sporting News,* began publication in 1886 and continues to be one of the most successful sport magazines.

Magazines specializing in sports have been standard fare in the publishing business for the past one hundred years, with almost every sport having its own publication. Indeed, one indication that a new sport is rising in popularity is the appearance of a magazine describing its techniques and strategies, profiling its best players, and advertising equipment and accessories for playing or watching the sport. *Sports Illustrated,* founded in 1954, is currently the best-selling sports magazine and is read by more than twenty-five million adults each week.

In the spring of 1993, media conglomerate Time Warner Inc. launched a Canadian version of *Sports Illustrated* titled *Sports Illustrated Canada* (*SI Canada*), with the goal of publishing a weekly sports magazine specifically targeted to the Canadian market. Although *SI Canada* did publish more articles with specific Canadian content than the American version, its content did not differ greatly from articles appearing in the American *Sports Illustrated* issues. Consequently, production of *SI Canada* ceased in December 1995, a little less than three years after it began.

Books

The first massive book wave in the United States began in the two decades before the Civil War as dime novels began to appear in large quantities. Numerous books on field sports, horse racing, boxing, and the increasingly popular team sports poured from the publishing houses throughout the late nineteenth century, but the youth literature contributed most significantly to arousing interest in sports among the youngsters of this era. Undoubtedly the most prolific of the youth literature authors was Burt L. Standish (whose real name was Gilbert Patten), who in 1896 began turning out a story every week about a fictitious schoolboy athlete, Frank Merriwell. In the early 1900s the Merriwell stories sold about 135,000 copies weekly. Youth athletic stories also streamed from the pens of many other authors.

Serious novelists tended not to focus on sport to any extent, although some of the most powerful passages in Ernest Hemingway's novels dealt with blood sports (e.g., bullfighting). A trend has now developed toward serious writing about sport, and North American novelists have increasingly employed sports themes in their works. Inspired by the use of sports-related themes and characters in the works of esteemed writers such as Ernest Hemingway, John Updike, Roger Angell, Philip Roth, William Faulkner, and others, a coalition of university professors and friends founded the Sport Literature Association in the early 1980s; it publishes *Aethlon: The Journal of Sport Literature,* which issues works about sport literature, including original fiction and poetry.

Perhaps the greatest impact of sport on the literary field has been made by former athletes and sports journalists. The United States and Canada have been virtually deluged with books by professional athletes (most of these are actually ghostwritten) who describe their experiences in sports. A number of former athletes have written "kiss-and-tell" books either mocking or criticizing their sports experiences. Sports journalists have also shared in the publishing windfall; several have written what might be called exposé, or muckraking, types of books. Most bookstores have an entire section of sports books.

Radio

While sports sections of newspapers, sport magazines, and books about sports continue to have significant linkages to sport, the electronic media—radio, motion pictures, television, and the Internet—have made dramatic inroads into the traditional information and entertainment functions of the printed media. Only a few years separated the invention of wireless broadcasting and the advent of radio sportscasts. The first permanent commercial radio station, KDKA in Pittsburgh, went on the air in 1920. Less than a year later, in July 1921, the first heavyweight championship-boxing bout was broadcast. From the mid-1920s to the early 1950s, radio reigned supreme in broadcasting sports news and live sports events.

Radio's popularity as a medium for sport information and entertainment declined with the beginning of network television in the 1950s.

Nevertheless, there are some 11,000 radio stations in North America that broadcast more than 700,000 hours of sport annually. Sports call-in shows, interviews with sports celebrities, as well as play-by-play game reporting have sustained the role of radio in sports, and the twenty-four-hour-per-day, all-sports radio stations appear to have created excitement in this industry. There are now more than 435 all-sports radio stations in the United States and 7 in Canada, devoted almost solely to discussion, debate, and analysis of athletes and teams by both hosts and callers.[4]

Motion Pictures

Thomas Edison's rudimentary motion-picture camera, the kinetoscope, which he patented in 1891, marked the birth of the movie industry. Movies quickly became a favorite popular culture phenomenon. As popular as the movies were, though, sports stories were relatively rare before 1970, although *Knute Rockne All-American*, the story of the legendary Notre Dame coach, and *The Pride of the Yankees*, the story of the famous New York Yankee first baseman Lou Gehrig, among a few others, had gained some popularity. In recent decades several sports films have received critical acclaim; *Rocky* and *Chariots of Fire* were awarded Oscars for best picture.

In 2007, ESPN ranked what it considered the top 20 sports movies of all time. The top 12 were:

1. *Bull Durham* (1988)
2. *Rocky* (1976)
3. *Raging Bull* (1980)
4. *Hoosiers* (1986)
5. *Slap Shot* (1977)
6. *The Natural* (1984)
7. *Field of Dreams* (1989)
8. *Caddyshack* (1980)
9. *The Hustler* (1961)
10. *The Longest Yard* (2005)
11. *North Dallas Forty* (1979)
12. *Jerry Maguire* (1996)

Of course, these ESPN selections are arbitrary.[5] Increasingly, sports films are transcending mere entertainment and attempting to explore broader social issues of power, race, masculinity, and gender relations.

Television

Currently the predominant mass media presenter of sport is television. The technology to produce telecasts was developed during the 1930s, but World War II delayed the large-scale growth of commercial television for nearly a decade. When television began to grow, however, its rate of growth was staggering. In 1950 less than 10 percent of households had television; in 2006, 98 percent of North American homes had at least one set, 38 percent had two sets, and 40 percent had three or more sets.

The average television viewer received only 4 or 5 channels in 1970, 3 of which were broadcast networks; the average viewer in 2006 received around 65 channels (broadcast and cable), and some received more than 100. There are currently about 11,000 cable TV systems offering more than 150 channels of programming. To watch this plethora of TV choices, North Americans own more than 240 million television sets, representing more than one-third of the world's total. According to Nielsen Media Research, on average, North American *households* watch more than eight hours of television a day, and the average *individual* watches four and one-half hours a day.[6]

TELEVISION: THE MONSTER OF THE SPORTS WORLD

Television has come to have a dominating grasp on sport, but the influence has been reciprocal; television programming is greatly influenced by sport as well. Sport made a union with television while the tube was still in its infancy. The first televised sports event was a college baseball game between Columbia and Princeton in 1939. The announcer was located in the stands with the spectators; there was only one camera, and its range was so limited that it could not show the batter and the pitcher at the same time. Other technical difficulties made it almost impossible for viewers to know what was happening during the game. In describing the TV coverage, the *New York Times* reported: "The players were best described by observers as appearing like white flies running across the screen.... When the ball flashed across the grass, it appeared as a comet-like white pinpoint ... the commentator saved the day, otherwise there would be no way to follow the play or tell where the ball went except to see the players run in its direction."[7]

Despite the many problems encountered by the infant television industry, it grew enormously in a short time, and television is now by far the most popular and most time-consuming leisure activity in the United States.

Increasing TV Sports Coverage

The most dramatic programming trend in television has been the enormous increase in sports coverage. Spectators consume sport to a far greater extent through television than through personal attendance at events. Table 11.1 displays the variety of sports television that now exists.

In the United States, more than 2,500 hours of televised sport are programmed per year by the major commercial networks. Cable TV networks, such as ESPN and ESPN2, which reach over 80 percent of American homes with cable TV, broadcast more than 9,000 hours of live sports each year. Regional sports cable networks and direct satellite broadcasts are growing rapidly, and they broadcast countless thousands of hours of sport each year. The trend that is perhaps the most remarkable is the sport organizations that are becoming their own media companies—such as the NFL (NFL Network) and NBA (NBATV) and the Big Ten Network—and thus bypassing the traditional TV and cable networks.

The Super Bowl has dominated network TV ratings during the past two decades, ranking as the top TV program nine years of the past twenty years. Super Bowl telecasts usually attract 40 to 45 percent of the households watching TV. In recent years, over 200 countries and territories have had TV coverage of the Super Bowl.

But the Super Bowl is not the only mega-TV sport. An estimated six billion people worldwide tuned in to at least some of the televised coverage of the 2004 Athens Summer Olympic Games. In the years when the World Cup is played, the monthlong tournament draws a total worldwide audience of up to forty billion viewers.

One feature of TV sports that seems destined to become more prominent is pay-per-view (PPV), a variant of cable in which the subscriber agrees to pay a specific fee, in advance, so that the signal for a specific event will be beamed to the subscriber's set. Nonsubscribers do not receive that programming. Television analysts claim that PPV will become a major factor by 2015. PPV championship boxing matches have been on the forefront of this trend, but in the fall of 1995, DIRECTV began offering, via the Digital Satellite System (DSS), up to fourteen NFL football games every Sunday on its *NFL Sunday Ticket*. This service is a form of PPV. Some television executives believe that within ten years all of the top sports events, including the Super Bowl, Gray Cup, World Cup, Stanley Cup, Kentucky Derby, Indianapolis 500, Olympics, college bowl games, and the like, will be available only via PPV.

Economic Aspects of Televised Sports

Accompanying the enormous expansion in sports programming has been the incredible economic

Table 11.1 The Expanding Sports Television Menu

Original major networks	ABC—*Wide World of Sports* (1961) NBC—Olympic Games (1980) CBS—Sunday afternoon football
New major networks	FOX—FOX Sports, formed in 1994
Regional sports networks	Team-owned channels, YES Network, Altitude Sports, regional cable networks, Comcast Sports Net Chicago, FOX Sports Net Pittsburgh
Cable sports networks	ESPN, Versus (previous name OLN)
Superstations that broadcast sports	TBS, WGN
Single sports channels	NFL Network, Golf Channel, NBATV, Tennis Channel
Satellite TV	NFL Sunday Ticket (by DirectTV), subscriptions give viewers access to NFL games

impact of televised sport. Money is the fuel propelling the TV sports machine, and sport and television are mutual beneficiaries in one of the most lucrative business associations. In return for the rights to telecast sports events, professional and collegiate sports receive free publicity as well as broadcast rights fees. At the same time, television companies profit from the use of their products (the telecasts) by sport consumers.

The system works this way: Television networks pay money for the rights to broadcast a professional (or college) league's (e.g., NFL) games. The networks hope to get that money back, plus a profit, by selling advertising time to corporations, like General Motors, for the games. Administrators of the sports leagues take the money received from the television network and distribute it according to the sports leagues' policies. In essence, then, the television industry is basically a broker, bringing together the sellers (sports leagues), the buyers (advertisers), and consumers (fans). The relationship between media and sport is one of planned, calculated business rationality.

The extent to which the fees for telecasting rights have escalated can be seen in Table 11.2.

Table 11.2 Television Network Rights Fees for Olympic Games (in dollars)

Summer Olympic Games	Television Rights Costs
1960	394,000
1972	7,500,000
1984	225,000,000
1996	456,000,000
2008	894,000,000
2012	1,180,000,000

Winter Olympic Games	Television Rights Costs
1960	50,000
1972	15,500,000
1984	243,000,000
1996	545,000,000
2006	614,000,000
2010	820,000,000
2014	not determined

The economics of television are changing because of these escalating rights fees, and the reign of the television networks as the exclusive carrier of the Olympics ended after the 1988 Summer Games in Seoul. Cable television has gotten a larger and larger piece of the Olympic pie. Satellite is also making its mark in the industry.

Professional sports are able to operate the way they do primarily through the television contracts they have been able to negotiate. Realizing the popularity of broadcast sports, the sports industry has successfully negotiated large contracts with media organizations for the rights to broadcast events. This in turn helps make commercial sports profitable. Following are a few examples of recent contracts:

- The rights to televise National Football League games from 2006 to 2011 were sold to several networks for $3.735 billion; about 65 percent of all NFL team revenues comes from the sale of television rights.
- The national TV and radio rights to Major League Baseball were sold to Fox and Turner for $3 billion over seven years (2006–2013); MLB shares 24 percent of its revenues with its thirty teams. About half the teams can pay their entire annual player payrolls just from their national broadcast revenues.
- The NBA has a six-year TV contract (2002 to 2008) with the Walt Disney Co. and AOL Time Warner for $4.6 billion, a huge increase over the previous TV rights contract.
- In the fall of 1999, CBS signed an eleven-year TV broadcast rights contract (2003–2014) with the NCAA for $6.2 billion for the Division I men's basketball tournament; this was a 252 percent increase over the previous contract.
- NBC paid $793 million in broadcast rights fees for the 2004 Summer Olympics in Athens, and $894 million for the 2008 Summer Olympics in Beijing.

It can be seen that the networks, the superstations, the cable sports stations, and local TV stations have bankrolled commercialized team sports with a veritable bonanza of dollars. Contracts like these have made the commercial sports industry very profitable, resulting in expanded franchises, higher salaries, and all-around plush lifestyles for many in the industry.

One might ask, why is television so eager to spend such lavish sums for the rights to telecast sporting events? It's simple. Corporations spend lavishly on advertising during sports events in order to create a demand for their products. Broadcast sporting events are immensely popular and attract large audiences; many people are interested in the beauty and drama of sports events, and find them more exciting and suspenseful than most other broadcast programming. Audiences who hear and see the broadcast commercials become consumers of the products, bringing profits to the advertisers. So sports are a natural setting for corporate advertising.

The escalating rates of advertising time can be seen from the following examples of Super Bowl rates for a thirty-second commercial.

Table 11.3 Super Bowl Rates for a Thirty-Second Commercial (in dollars)

Year	Advertising Rate
1970	75,000
1985	500,000
1996	1,200,000
2002	1,900,000
2005	2,300,000
2006	2,500,000
2007	2,600,000
2008	2,700,000

TELEVISION'S INFLUENCE ON SPORT

Each medium has made an impact on sport in its own way. Newspapers of the late nineteenth century and early twentieth century contributed to the rise of professional and collegiate sports by creating an interest in these activities. Magazines and books helped create and sustain the hero worship of the athlete in succeeding generations. Radio brought live sports action into the home for the first time. It was television, though, that had the most profound impact. Several interpreters of the impact of television on sport have argued that TV has produced more revolutionary and irrevocable changes in sport than anything since such modern sport began in the mid-nineteenth century.

Increases in Sport Revenue

Before the advent of television, professional sport was only a skeleton of what it has become, and the professional franchises that did exist were struggling financially. There were only sixteen Major League Baseball teams in the 1950s, and no new teams had come into the leagues in more than fifty years; now there are thirty teams. This expansion, and baseball's prosperity, have been due to television. Similar patterns can be seen in professional football, basketball, and hockey. All of these sports entered the 1950s as struggling enterprises with fewer than ten franchises each, and neither the owners nor the players were making much money. These sports now have more than twenty-five franchises each, and all have expansion plans. Television contributes a substantial portion of every league's revenues. Professional golf, tennis, soccer, and other professional sports either did not exist or were inconsequential prior to the infusion of large sums of television money.

The extent to which professional sport has become dependent upon television revenue is captured in remarks frequently made by sports executives, such as "There is no way we could survive without television" or "If sports lost television revenues, we'd all be out of business." Indeed, so many pro sports organizations have built their budgets around TV income that if television ever did withdraw its money, the entire pro sports structure in its present form would collapse.[8]

Professional sports owners have not been the only beneficiaries of this windfall. Television money has increased the social mobility of athletes as well. Pro athletes' salaries have tripled or even quadrupled; television money has made it possible for them to command their enormous salaries.

The extent to which sport has been influenced by its increasing economic dependence on television was brought into focus by the late sportswriter Leonard Shecter, who was an early interpreter of TV's impact on sports: "Television buys sports. Television supports sports. It moves it with its money and supports sports in a style to which they have become accustomed and then, like a bought lady, sports become so used to luxurious living they cannot extricate themselves. So, slowly, at first, but inevitably, television tells sports what to do. It is sports and it runs them the way it does most other things, more flamboyantly than honestly."[9]

Shecter was an accurate prophet. His observation that "television buys sports" is not rhetorical chatter. It is literally true, as a number of professional sports teams are owned wholly or partly by media companies. For example, in 2007 four Major League Baseball teams were owned by media corporations: the Atlanta Braves by Liberty Media, the Chicago Cubs by Tribune Company, the Seattle Mariners by Nintendo, and the Toronto Blue Jays by Rogers Communications. Rupert Murdoch, the media mogul with arguably the largest global media empire, once called sports the "cornerstone of our worldwide efforts." A *Forbes* magazine writer claimed that "when News Corp. and the Walt Disney Co. owned the Los Angeles Dodgers and Anaheim Angels, respectively, they were willing to take operating losses in order to use the teams as promotional vehicles for their television networks."[10]

Indirect Business Linkages between Media and Sport

Beyond the direct financial association between the mass media and sport, there are several indirect financial linkages between them. Commercial sport receives an enormous amount of free publicity via the media. Media coverage of sports itself tends to promote sports—the leagues, teams, athletes, and coaches—but typical sports coverage is blatant boosterism designed to hype interest in the athletes and teams. Newspaper sport sections are basically advertising sections for commercial sports. Radio and television segments dealing with sports news are essentially advertising for commercial sports. Indeed, many sports news announcers act like cheerleaders for the local professional sports teams, often referring to them as "our team." No other privately owned, profit-making industry—which is what the commercial sport industry is—receives as much free publicity for its product. Of course, the reciprocal business aspects of this are quite clear: The more interest generated in commercial sports, the greater the profits for the mass media.[11]

Table 11.4 Media Corporations That Have Had Ownership in Professional Sports between 1997 and 2007

Corporations	Teams
Walt Disney	NHL's Mighty Ducks, MLB's Anaheim Angels
Time Warner/Liberty Media	MLB's Atlanta Braves, NBA's Atlanta Hawks
Rogers Communications	MLB's Toronto Blue Jays
Comcast/Spectacor	NBA's Philadelphia 76ers, NHL's Philadelphia Flyers
Tribune Company	MLB's Chicago Cubs
Madison Square Garden LP	NBA's New York Knicks, NHL's New York Rangers
Paul Allen Group	NBA's Portland Trail Blazers
Ackerley Group	NBA's Seattle Supersonics
Murdoch's News Corp	MLB's Los Angeles Dodgers
Anschutz Entertainment	MLS's Colorado Rapids, Los Angeles Kings, New York–New Jersey MetroStars
Nintendo	Seattle Mariners

Popularity Shifts

Television's dominating role is demonstrated most clearly in the changing popularity of the various sports. Telecasts have greatly increased the popularity of some sports and decreased interest in others. Football and baseball with their series of crises, tennis with its evolving drama, basketball with its fast action, and boxing with its violence in a confined space are ideal sports for television. Natural breaks in the action permit viewers to contemplate the next moves; more importantly, they provide the opportunity for periodic commercial breaks without seriously disturbing the flow of the sporting event. Other sports, such as soccer, have been less successful because they lack predictable crises, natural breaks, or action in a manageable space.

If television viewing is the criterion of national pastime status, football has replaced baseball as America's national pastime. It has also eroded the TV popularity of ice hockey in Canada. There is little doubt that football is ideally suited for television, with its fast, violent action confined to a rather restricted area, its periods of inaction between plays, and its rigidly controlled time orientation.

Professional Sports Franchise Locations and the Media

Not only has television influenced the popularity and the fortunes of entire sports, it has more selectively come to play a direct role in decisions about the number and locations of professional franchises. The promise of lucrative television contracts explains why the number of professional football, basketball, baseball, and hockey franchises has more than doubled in the past three decades. Moreover, as the NFL, NBA, MLB, and NHL have awarded new franchises, the size of the potential television market in a region has been a major consideration.

Prior to television, professional sports franchises were considered to be permanent fixtures in a city, but the practice of jumping from city to city has become common. There have been seven moves of NFL teams since 1983 (two in 1997 alone—Cleveland Browns to Baltimore, where they became the Ravens, and Houston Oilers to Tennessee, where they became the Titans) and more than a dozen city changes for NBA teams, the most recent being the Vancouver Grizzlies, who moved to Memphis in 2001, and the Hornets, formerly of Charlotte, who moved to New Orleans in 2002. A major factor for moving in almost every case has been the promise of additional television revenues. Given the economic structure of professional sports, it is not surprising that professional leagues and their franchise owners gravitate toward television money.[12]

Although television revenues have been responsible for the health and expansion of some professional sports enterprises, the lack of network television contracts has been responsible for the demise of others. In the early 1980s the United States Football League failed to secure network sponsorship and folded. Professional track died for similar reasons, and professional volleyball and several women's professional sports have had an off-and-on existence for lack of television contracts. On the other hand, the NFL European League (NFLEL) was created by the NFL in 1991 primarily to provide American football to European audiences to capitalize on the popularity of televised American football. In 2006 the NFLEL rebranded itself as NFL Europa. Then in the summer of 2007, it was shut down by the NFL, mostly for media reasons. Mark Waller, senior vice president of NFL International, explained: "The time is right to re-focus the NFL's strategy on initiatives with global impact, including worldwide media coverage of our sport and the staging of live regular-season NFL games."[13]

Intercollegiate Sport

At the same time that television was enhancing the expansion and financial status of the openly professional sports, it was also furthering the professionalization of a self-proclaimed amateur sport enterprise, intercollegiate sport, which has actually been a professional enterprise for many years. When collegiate football became one of the most popular viewer events on early TV, the NCAA, the controlling organization of intercollegiate athletics, quickly stepped in to regulate television coverage of collegiate football games. Under that system of regulation, the NCAA always limited the number of football games that could be televised each week and the number of times a particular team could appear on television each season. Nevertheless, a few of the football "powers" were seen rather frequently, while most collegiate football teams never appeared on television. Teams that were televised received large payments per appearance, so the television package increased the gap between the "haves" and the "have-nots" in college football.[14]

A challenge of the NCAA's right to negotiate TV contracts on behalf of all of its member institutions was settled by a U.S. Supreme Court decision in which the Court invalidated the NCAA's exclusive college football TV contract. The effect was to free individual colleges and conferences to negotiate their own television contracts with the networks, cable companies, and local stations.[15] College football broadcasts on national cable and syndication channels have skyrocketed since that decision.

In a book with the lengthy title *The Fifty-Year Seduction: How Television Manipulated College Football, from the Birth of the Modern NCAA to the Creation of the BCS*, the author explains that the "book is about how television helped shape the modern sport [of college football] and . . . about how the medium became the common denominator in the game's rise as a big business." In summary, he declares: "Over the last half-century, televised college football has manufactured money, greed, dependence, and envy; altered the recruiting process, eventually forcing the colleges to compete with the irresistible force of National Football League riches; . . . fomented the realignment of conferences; and seized control of the postseason bowl games, including the formation of the lucrative and controversial Bowl Championship Series."[16]

The Supreme Court decision regarding college football did not affect the NCAA's control over its men's basketball tournament. The growth of the NCAA men's basketball tournament provides a vivid demonstration of television's influence on collegiate sports. The more teams in the NCAA basketball tournament, the greater the television revenue, and the greater the amount of money paid to the NCAA. Therefore, the NCAA continued to increase the number of teams participating in the tournament until it became a 64-team tournament.

In 1990 CBS signed a 7-year $1 billion (yes, billion) contract with the NCAA for the rights to televise the men's basketball tournament. In December 1994 that contract was replaced with a new 7-year *$1.725 billion* deal. In 2001 the NCAA negotiated a new *$6.2 billion* 11-year television rights fee with CBS to televise the Division I men's basketball tournament from 2003 to 2014. In mid-2001, the NCAA signed an 11-year, $200 million television rights contract with ESPN, giving the network broadcasting control of the women's basketball tournament and twenty other national championships.[17]

What is the financial impact of these television contracts on intercollegiate sports? The majority of universities with big-time intercollegiate sports programs run a deficit in their annual budgets; the deficits would be larger were it not for television money, and for those who do not run a deficit it is largely because of the television money they receive. Television money is the financial foundation for the administrative agency of college sports—the NCAA. The men's basketball TV contract provides around 80 percent of the NCAA's total revenue!

With a view toward receiving television money and public exposure, universities throughout the country throw enormous human and financial resources into their football and basketball programs while they have been dropping other sports from their offerings. Some universities have dropped as many as six sports in the past decade. Universities have frequently blamed the abolishment of sports on Title IX, which requires gender equity in the expenditures of resources. But in most cases the dropping of sports has been precipitated by the desire to pour more money into foot-

An NCAA women's basketball game, 23 March 2008, in Norfolk, Virginia. North Carolina won 85–50. (AP Photo/Haraz N. Ghanbari)

ball and men's basketball in the hopes of attracting more media money to the athletic program.[18]

High School Sport

The television industry has reached down to tap a different source of revenue: high school sports. In the fall of 1989, SportsChannel America, a cable network, signed a multiyear agreement with the National Federation of State High School Associations, the administrative organization for high school sports. At the time the negotiations were under way, an executive for SportsChannel said: "We think high school sports are going to be the TV sport of the 90s." Although this prediction was a little too optimistic, televised high school sports, especially football and basketball, have become a regular feature of local television stations throughout the United States and Canada during the first decade of the twenty-first century.

Television coverage of state championships and tournaments has become an annual event in many states. Several state high school activity associations have begun coverage of regular season games. This trend is exactly what many educators feared. Can pressures for national high school championships be far behind if television becomes the financial support for high school sports? The answer is "no." In fact, there have been several proposals in recent years for national championship in high school sports. Educational leaders fear that if that happens, educational priorities will be sacrificed in the interests of keeping the television industry happy.

Television has even become a factor in recruitment of high school athletes. Many athletes are choosing to attend a university because of the TV coverage that university gets. The football games of some universities are carried on national TV much more frequently than others. In the case of big-time collegiate basketball, some athletes are selecting eastern universities because the viewing audiences of the games are much larger than in midwestern or western states due to the time the games are played. The athletes in football and basketball believe that greater television exposure helps their chances of being drafted by the pros.

Modifying Sports to Accommodate TV

To enhance spectator appeal and to accommodate programming needs, the television industry has increasingly manipulated the structure and the processes of televised sports. Because TV networks charge corporations advertising fees based on the anticipated number of viewers—the more viewers, the larger the advertising fee—the networks want the sports events to which they have bought broadcast rights to attract huge audiences. In their pursuit of viewers, media networks have been able to persuade pro sport leagues and franchise owners (who want larger rights fees) to modify rules and schedules in the hopes of attracting larger numbers of viewers. Because broadcasting rights fees are based on anticipated audience size, pro sport owners and leagues have been willing to make these changes to the game. Thus, to enhance viewer appeal and accommodate programming needs, both the media sports industry and the commercial sports industry have manipulated the structures and processes of sport. Here are some examples:

- In NFL football, rule changes (such as moving the sideline hash marks and the kickoff spot, reducing defensive backs' contact with receivers, and liberalizing offensive holding) have been adopted to open up the games and make them more attractive to television viewers. Other modifications have been introduced to permit more commercials—time-outs are called at the discretion of television officials, and the automatic two-minute warning near game's end is used as a TV time-out.
- To enhance spectator and viewer interest, NBA basketball led in the adoption of the shot clock, the slam dunk, and the three-point shot. The NBA has acceded to a more physical, rougher style of play because television decision makers believe that fans prefer this style and are more likely to watch games of this kind.
- In televised golf, match play (where the golfers compete hole by hole, and the golfer who wins the most holes is the winner) has largely been replaced by medal play (the golfer with the lowest score over the entire course wins). The skins game—another variation of professional golf, where large sums of money ride on the outcome of each hole—has become a popular form of televised professional golf. These new forms of golf competition are more compatible with television coverage.
- In professional tennis, to accommodate television scheduling, tennis executives established the tiebreaker system for sets tied at six games all; tiebreakers tend to play out quickly, making it easier to complete matches within a designated time period.
- Major League Baseball introduced the designated hitter and lowered the strike zone, and there is strong suspicion that the baseball itself has been modified to make it livelier. All of these changes have been motivated by an interest in increasing what spectators like to

see: more extra-base hits and home runs. Time-honored afternoon World Series and All-Star games were switched to evenings to serve the interests of television.

- The sudden-death tiebreaking rule in football, ice hockey, and soccer, and the extended playoff system in all of the pro sports leagues, are additional examples of modifying rules to increase TV viewer interest, and make the sporting events more profitable for both TV networks and professional sports.
- For recent Winter and Summer Olympic Games, the International Olympic Committee agreed to reschedule championship events so they take place during America's prime time, to accommodate television networks. However, much of the Olympic Games TV coverage is broadcast after the events are completed, but frequently the events are presented to television viewers without informing them of this fact, leading them to believe they are seeing events live.

There are other ways television has modified sports that could be mentioned, but it suffices to say that most of the changes identified here, and others, are tied directly to television's interest in enhancing the action for television viewers and keeping them in their chairs to watch the commercials. This is, after all, the means by which the television industry makes its profits. As the television industry's investment in sports continues to grow, so does TV's resolution to get the most for its investment by orchestrating the sporting events for maximum viewer appeal.

Television's Own Sports

As we have noted, sports have been an important part of television programming since the early years of network TV. Because sports are so popular with television viewers, television executives sought ways to broadcast other events involving sport-like characteristics—such as competition requiring physical strength, endurance, agility, tenacity, speed, and skill. This resulted in TV networks creating made-for-television sports events.

Made-for-television sports began with outstanding elite athletes competing in physically competitive events contrived by TV executives. The idea of the program was promoted as a way to find out who the "best" athletes were and which sports had the "best" athletes. Winners of these events were awarded titles like "world's best athlete." The point was to exploit the celebrity status of athletes, whose status as celebrities had been constructed by the media, in order to attract viewers to the contrived sports program—and to the commercials shown on the program. Actually, though, the TV networks' motive was economic.

Made-for-television sports events had names like "Challenge of the Sexes," which pitted top male athletes against top female athletes, with the males handicapped to heighten the uncertainty of the outcome; "Battle of the Network Stars" pitted celebrities from the three major networks against one another in epic tugs-of-war, relay races, and other contrived competitions. Competitions of this sort were often called "trash sports."

Most of the original made-for-television sports events have disappeared from sports programming. But with the popularity of almost any kind of competitive event, and with the all-sports TV channels needing to fill numerous hours of programming time, various made-for-television and alternative sporting events now appear. Some of these are legitimate sports, but few have a large number of participating athletes or a large spectator following. However, when they are telecast, nearly all aspects of the events are aimed at making the events appealing to viewers, and thus to corporate advertisers and sponsors.

ESPN's X Games (originally called eXtreme Games) fits in this genre of TV sports. Some of the X Games activities, such as skateboarding, in-line skating, freestyle biking, and snowboarding, were originally popular among teenagers who were looking for alternatives to the traditional individual and team sports. In 1995 ESPN created the X Games as a made-for-TV alternative multisports festival. The X Games appeal to a very large, young, TV-watching audience because many of them are involved in these action activities. ESPN's marketing director said the network aims to "reach anybody between

12 and 24 who is interested" in alternative sports. Currently, these games are divided into two seasons: The Winter X Games, held in January or February, and X Games, usually held in August. Because the X Games were created by and are owned by ESPN, the network does not have to pay broadcast rights fees to air them. Thus, the network keeps all revenue from advertisers. Reruns and qualifying events fill many hours on the ESPN broadcast schedule. Advertising revenues pour in to ESPN from all of these.[19]

There is widespread criticism of the XGames among alternative sports enthusiasts, claiming that ESPN's X Games have turned informal, alternative physical activities into mainstream sports with the codification of rules, equipment, categories of participants, and so forth. There is also the complaint that these annual events are fundamentally an advertising medium, targeting specific age, gender, and racial groups. Indeed, the X Games seem to illustrate social analyst Harry Braverman's claim that capitalism—in this case in the form of television networks—is so enterprising that it will find a way to turn everything into a marketable commodity.

In the spring of 2001, the WWE and NBC cocreated a made-for-television football league called the XFL. With teams nicknamed the Enforcers, the Hitmen, and the Maniacs, the World Wrestling Federation (WWF) and NBC hyped a violent, trash-talking, sexualized form of football for the XFL. It was promoted as a pro wrestling style of football and was clearly designed to attract TV fans to watch outrageous behavior on and off the field. Hopes were high for favorable TV ratings. XFL games started with TV ratings well above expectations, but interest declined drastically, and the league was cancelled after the first season.

One of the newest contributions to the merging of sports to create a fanatical TV audience is called Ultimate Fighting, which is a combat sport combining the striking techniques of boxing and kickboxing with floor techniques of jujitsu and wrestling. The action takes place in an octagon cage. As with the X Games, many of the young men attracted to combat sports disliked the mainstream combat sports and experimented with alternatives, one of which became Ultimate Fighting. It quickly became popular with the eighteen to thirty-four male demographic.

Once TV executives saw how popular it was becoming, TV contracts followed. By 2007 Spike TV's UFC programs often had higher television ratings than the NBA and baseball playoff games in the eighteen to thirty-four age audience. UFC events had bigger pay-per-view numbers than any pro wrestling event or boxing events. In 2006 UFC's pay-per-view revenues were almost $223 million, compared with $177 million for boxing on HBO and $200 million for World Wrestling Entertainment.[20]

Televised Sport as a Mediated Event

Television has not only revised the way sport is played and the way it is watched, it has redefined the meaning of sport in many ways. Contemporary sport has become part of media culture, meaning that its form and content have been altered to suit the interests of the media. A common assumption among the public is that a broadcast sport event is an objective mirror of the reality of the contest, and that TV's framing, camera angles, use of scan and zoom, and sportscaster commentary are neutral conduits for presenting "the facts" of the event. In reality, however, a broadcast game is an entertainment spectacle sold in the marketplace, a tool for attracting and keeping listeners and viewers so the media can broadcast the commercials they have sold to advertisers.

Superficially, sportscasters simply keep listeners and viewers apprised of essential information as the contest unfolds. But they do much more: They mediate the event and thus create the listeners' and viewers' experiences of the event through their intervention. Because of sportscasters' mediation, a sporting event becomes a collage of happenings—and thus "reality" is socially constructed by the sportscasters, who decide what to reveal to listeners and viewers and how. What they reveal and what they conceal become, in effect, the "event," and the way listeners and viewers experience it becomes their reference point for its very existence—but it is a mediated version of reality.

In a televised sports event, cameras, camera angles, producers' choices of focus, and sportscasters' interpretations—all of which are the invisible apparatus of a televised presentation—stand between the viewers and the event. Viewers do not see the entire event; instead, they see only those parts that are sifted and filtered through the broadcasting process. This is very different from attending the event itself. Spectators in a stadium or arena perceive the event as is (at least, what can be seen and heard of it from the seats). But broadcast listeners and viewers experience an event that is socially constructed by a team of broadcast professional gatekeepers and dramatic embellishers.

The public has many options as to what to listen to and watch, so a variety of techniques are used to attract listeners and viewers. Some of the most important decisions media executives must make are about selection—decisions about which sports events to broadcast and which sports events not to broadcast, decisions to accentuate certain aspects of the sporting event for listeners and viewers and not others. Thus, televised sports are the result of a carefully crafted selection process that takes into account listener and viewer interests, attitudes, and beliefs about sports.

Two examples of broadcast selection can illustrate the selection and exclusion in media sports coverage. First, coverage of male sporting events dominates broadcast sports and helps reinforce cultural attitudes about gender specificity in sport and gender appropriateness of sports. Second, team sports have dominated sports broadcasts. Indeed, male team sports are TV's "authorized sports"; in many ways the media have advanced the popularity of male team sports at the expense of other forms of sport. Thus, social values are conveyed through particular choices made by the media's selective coverage.[21]

The selection process is at work within a particular sporting event. Production executives foreground particular aspects of the event for the viewers. In baseball, home runs are highlighted over "routine" singles; in football the quarterback gets the focus, rather than any of the ten other positions; in multiple events, such as track and field, some events get more attention than others; for example, in track and field the sprints get more coverage than most other events.

Beyond mere selecting, viewers are provided with descriptions of what has been selected through narrative themes and interpretations of preferred meaning about the action or the event itself. Televised sporting events do not merely consist of pictures, they also involve commentary on the pictures—a commentary that shapes what viewers are seeing and believing.

This selective highlighting is not "natural." It is based on media assumptions about what is good television and what keeps viewers watching. These decisions are socially constructed. They involve preferences about what to reveal to the viewers. Televised sport involves an active process of representation; what viewers see, then, is not the actual event, but a mediated event, in other words, a media event.

Once particular sports events are chosen for broadcasting, the next task is to "hook" listeners and viewers to the broadcasts. This begins with pregame programs that are mostly a contrived mix of interviews, network promos, and hoopla (e.g., theme building). The main purpose of these programs is to frame and contextualize the game by artificially building dramatic tension and solidifying allegiances, thus convincing listeners and viewers to stay tuned to the event, while preparing them for how they should hear, see, and understand it. The rhetoric concentrates listeners' and viewers' attention on the overall importance of this particular contest, individual athletes' (and coaches') personalities, "matchups," statistics, records, and team styles of play.

To enhance the excitement and suspense of a sports event, sportscasters sometimes alter the broadcast of an event to portray something quite different from what actually happened during the event. For example, in the women's team gymnastic competition during the Olympic Games, one of the American gymnasts injured an ankle in a landing during the vault competition. In spite of the obvious pain, the gymnast ran down the runway and completed her second vault. A courageous act, but at the time of her second vault there was no way of determining how her score would affect the overall outcome of the competition. However, in the delayed telecast of the meet, NBC revised the sequence of the competition and selected her performance as the last for the vaulters and thus the culminating factor in the overall competition. Television viewers were led to believe not only that the televised event was live, but also that the competition took place in exactly that sequence.[22]

The selecting, screening, and filtering of sports events that are carried out by television through images and verbal commentary result in the presentation of a whole new game, a game created from an entertainment perspective, because in essence entertainment is what televised sport is all about. In consequence, the basis for interest in sport has changed from an appreciation of the beauty, style, skill, and technical accomplishments of the performers to a primary concern for titillating excitement and productive action, usually meaning scoring and winning.

The overarching value in media sport is winning. Broadcast sports tend to be single-minded odes to winning, so much so that almost any action in the pursuit of victory is considered justified; indeed, athletes often are lionized for illegal play. Sportscasters frequently admiringly declare that an athlete will do "whatever it takes to win." No sacrifice is too great in the interest of winning; athletes who surmount injury, endure pain, and continue to play are valorized. During one NFL football game, the camera zoomed in on the heavily taped right arm of a defensive lineman. One of the sportscasters then explained that the player had incurred a compound fracture of one of his fingers—meaning the bone was sticking out of the skin. The player had gone to the bench, shoved the bone back in, taped up the finger, and returned to the game. The sportscaster then said, in a thoroughly admiring manner: "It just goes to show how badly these guys want to win." Another example: During an NFL game, one of the sportscasters applauded a quarterback by saying, "Here's a guy that probably had to take a painkiller shot in his lower back so he could play tonight." Because the definitions, values, and practices of media sport commentary are privileged, they become the "commonsense" constructions about sport that grow out of the production of broadcast sport.

The intrinsic, process-oriented participation motive to engage in sport has been redefined by media sport, as it has increasingly become the national definer of meaning in sport and how to "do" sport. Media sport valorizes the obsession with victory above all else. Television executives, camera personnel, sportscasters, and even the vast majority of viewers are not attuned to the aesthetic nuances of a well-executed play; instead the overriding ethos is a win by whatever means it takes. Indeed, the mantra expressed over and over by sportscasters is "Whatever it takes."

THE IMPACT OF SPORT ON THE MASS MEDIA

Increased Sport in the Media

The relationship between the mass media and sport is one of financial interdependence. As noted in an earlier section of this chapter, the sports section helps sell newspapers; indeed, a close observer will have noticed that sports are becoming more prominent every year in the papers. In many, sports occupy a special, separate section—a development of recent years. Print media managers like to say they publish what the public wants, and it's obvious that newspaper editors believe that the public wants vast amounts of sports news and that sports information will sell more and more papers.

Sport has also invaded other sections of newspapers. Not too many years ago a sports story or photo on the front page of papers like the *New York Times* would have been unheard of. Now it is a regular occurrence. *USA Today,* the self-proclaimed "Nation's Newspaper," regularly features stories about sports in its "News" section and often has a special section about sports leagues (e.g., NFL) and about major sporting events (e.g., the Masters, the Indy 500). Editorial cartoonists routinely use sport themes to illustrate political, economic, and social issues.

The last half of the twentieth century began with televised sports in its infancy. Over the next fifty years, there were many peaks and valleys, as TV networks competed against each other for sports events, struggled with advertisers for revenue, and sought viewers for televised sports events. But during all those years TV viewers were becoming increasingly addicted to watching sports of all kinds on TV. Even the prime-time evening slots were invaded by Monday Night Football, All-Star games, the World Series, and the Super Bowl. As we have seen, the enormous popularity of all kinds of sports programs led television to create its own sports. Sports also led to the creation of entire television networks, such as ESPN.[23] But ESPN has moved well beyond televising sports events. Table 11.5 illustrates how ESPN communicates with its fans through numerous distribution channels.

In the first decade of the twenty-first century, network television sells advertisers $1 billion worth of time for sports programs, which greatly contributes to the $30 to $50 million profit that the networks report each year.

Sport's Privileged Treatment by the Media

The mass media are fiercely independent (or claim to be), and reporters staunchly defend their right to freedom of the press. Sport, however, is one arena in which the media's reporting of events is blatantly manipulated. Stories are withheld or distorted, and sports news is edited to ensure a favorable image of the home team. Millions of dollars in free publicity are generously contributed to sports. Indeed, with respect to professional sports, no other privately owned, profit-making business receives as much free publicity for its product. Newspapers carry daily accounts of the activities of local pro teams, and television newscasters keep viewers informed in the same way. The media exposure is enough in itself to promote pro sports, but typically the stories are reported in a blatantly booster fashion, clearly designed to hype local interest in the teams.

Of course, the motives of the media are quite clear: The media ethos is rooted in profit maximization, and it is driven by the competition to be number one to reap the power and prestige that accompanies this. The more interest generated in local sports, the more people will buy local newspapers, listen to radio, and watch local television to follow the teams. The result is greater profits for the local mass media.

Sports Consumers and the Mass Media

The home has become the major site of leisure in postindustrial society. The main force for this has been the mass production of cheap home entertainment systems in the form of radio, television, audio and video equipment, and the computer. Exact figures on the amount of time people spend with the mass media are not readily available, but the best estimates for both the United States and Canada indicate that newspaper reading accounts for about two and one-half hours per person per week and television viewing for some sixty hours per household per week.

Televised sports have produced a dramatic shift in the mode of the fans' consumption of sport. In the pretelevision era the only way a fan could see a sports event was to attend, usually paying admission to do so. Television has, of course, changed that. Indeed, television has become the most important source of sports spectating for the sports consumer, and television provides this at a very low cost to the fan (even assuming the price of the television set and the advertising costs that are passed on to the public). The opportunity to see sports events on television at low cost has also had the effect of creating fans among parts of the population that have traditionally had little interest in sport, especially women and the elderly.

Table 11.5	ESPN's Pipelines of Sports Media
Television	ESPN, ESPN2, ESPNNEWS, ESPN Classic, ESPNDeportes, ESPNU
Radio	ESPN Radio
Magazine	*ESPN the Magazine*
Mobile Phone	ESPN Mobile
Restaurant	ESPN Zone

Surveys of adults in the United States conducted by various opinion research agencies have consistently found that professional football and baseball were the most favorite sports to watch. Next most popular were college football, college basketball, and pro basketball. All other sports were viewed by less than 10 percent of those polled. Viewing televised sports tended to increase in proportion to the viewer's education level.

But people in all walks of life find enjoyment in watching televised sports events. The specific factors that contribute to viewers' enjoyment are not well understood at present, but research into this topic has led to some tentative answers. Mass-communications researchers have found that viewers' enjoyment is related to broadcast commentary, the presence of a crowd, the skill displayed by the athletes, and the viewers' disposition toward the players and the teams in competition. The enjoyment of televised sports closely corresponds to the perception of roughness, enthusiasm, and even violence, and the perceptions of all of these aspects of play are strongly influenced by the commentary of the telecasters. The larger the crowd and the more enthusiastic its responses to play on the field, the more television viewers enjoy a game. Seeing teams battle down to the wire enhances suspense and increases the viewers' enjoyment. Finally, the highest level of fan enjoyment results when a well-liked team defeats an intensely disliked team.[24]

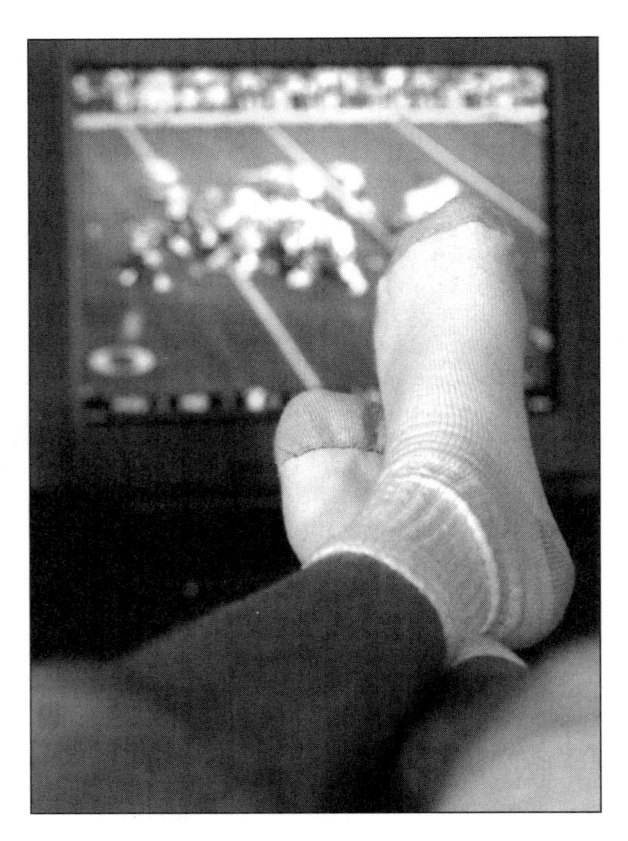

The Internet: The Newest Form of Mass Communications for Sports

The current cutting edge in communications for sports consumers is the Internet. It is a quantum leap beyond previous forms of communication because it makes possible the inexpensive transmission of messages and images throughout the world in seconds. By 2007, more than 80 percent of the U.S. population had access to the Internet from their homes. The Internet had its origins in U.S. Defense Department research done in the late 1960s, but by the mid-1990s it was almost entirely funded by private communications conglomerates, some of them originally founded as Internet firms or as print media or broadcast corporations. The implications for the Internet as a source of sports information of all kinds for sports consumers are seemingly limitless. It has the potential to someday surpass all other forms of mass communication as a source of sport information and entertainment. Literally millions of websites currently provide sports information to consumers. In September 2007, a website search at www.google.com using keywords *sports AND Web sites* produced a list of 50,820,000 websites. One sports analysis reports: "In the short history of the Internet, sports sites consistently rank among the leaders in terms of traffic and commercial activity."[25] The most-visited sports websites in February 2005 are shown in Table 11.6.

Surveys of adults in the United States conducted by various opinion research agencies have consistently found that professional football and baseball were the most favorite sports to watch. (iStockphoto)

Table 11.6 The Most-Visited Sports Websites in February 2005 (in millions)

ESPN	11.5
FoxSports.com	9.2
Yahoo! Sports	8.4
SI.com	7.3
AOL	7.1
NFL Internet Network	6.3
MLB.com	4.3
CollegeSports.com	4.0
NASCAR.com	4.0
NBA Internet Network	3.5

Source: The Sports Business Market Research Yearbook (Loganville, Ga.: Richard K. Miller and Associates, 2006).

Because of the popularity of many sporting events, full-motion video of sports events became inevitable. Most sports organizations currently place restrictions on websites' coverage to protect their lucrative TV rights contracts. But once the technology was developed to make the Internet respect geographical borders, sports organizations began offering its TV rights holders the option to show sports events video on their websites. Online live sports coverage hit the big time in 2007 when TBS, for mlb.com, produced live online coverage of first-round MLB playoff games and the National League Championship series. Even bigger, NBC will show more than two thousand hours of free live Internet video coverage of the 2008 Beijing Summer Olympics. In addition, NBC will show three thousand hours of free online Beijing Olympic highlights and replays.[26]

Video games. Video games are one of the by-products of the integration of television, the internet, and computer technologies, which were introduced commercially in the early 1970s. The video game industry, like other by-products of these technologies, has had a rapid and sustained growth and is now a $10 billion industry that rivals the motion picture industry as the most profitable entertainment medium in the world.

A sports game, *Tennis for Two* (1958), was one of the first video games. Over the past fifty years, virtually every sport played in the world has had its own video game. Like the auto industry, the sports video game industry brings out a new version annually to prime the pump for profits. The processing power of the new generation of video game equipment—Microsoft's X box 360, Sony Computer's PlayStation 3, and Nintendo's Wii—has brought the real world—like real-time weather conditions—into game play.

As with other forms of entertainment, especially television, sociological questions have arisen about the effects of video game playing on the habits, behaviors, and social development of players. For example, how does playing sports video games affect the play habits of children and youth who play these games? Do the games influence attitudes and behaviors toward values, such as sportsmanship, nonviolence, and morality? Does prolonged sports video game playing affect physical fitness, weight management, and social interaction with peers of participants? There is little research at this time that provides answers to these questions and many others as well, but undoubtedly this will be a rich area for psychological and sociological scholarship in the coming years.[27]

Reproduction of Hegemonic Masculinity in Media Sport

Linkages between sport and masculinity are longstanding. The British slogan "The Battle of Waterloo was won on the fields of Eton" suggests that participation in sport formed the manly qualities of a military leader. Parents urge their sons to play sports because "sports make men out of boys." Ideals of masculinity are constructed through competitive sport.

Communications scholars who have analyzed how male athletes and the male body are portrayed in the media make clear that media sport is a prominent site for sustaining and displaying traditional Western cultural ideals of masculinity. Verbal and visual media representations of the male athletic body are interpreted as a key source in cultivating, legitimating, and reinforcing the dominant definitions of masculinity as well as general masculine dominance. Although this is accomplished to some extent in all media sports, the sports that are especially physically violent—such as rugby,

American football, ice hockey, and boxing—present the most frequent and most vivid examples of hegemonic masculinity. In their influential book *Hockey Night in Canada,* Richard Gruneau and David Whitson argue that ice "hockey has come to occupy the place it holds in Canadian culture in part because it provides a public platform for celebrating a very traditional masculine ideal."[28]

Communications researcher Nick Trujillo, in a study of how traditional images of masculinity are reproduced in NFL football telecasts, found compelling evidence that three images of the male body—as instrument, weapon, and object of gaze—were regularly reproduced in those telecasts. He noted:

> Football is a kind of work, organized in accordance with military images, that requires the body to be used as an instrument of sanctioned aggression and violence. Television transforms these weapon-like bodies into objects of fascination and the aggressive and violent acts they perform into graceful gestures that can be appreciated aesthetically, even erotically. . . . American football reproduces hegemonic masculinity by demonstrating that the male body is most powerful when it is used for work and violence, and when it performs in a homosocial (but heterosexual) environment.[29]

Trujillo concluded that hegemonic masculinity propagated in media sport has serious consequences for both women and men—marginalizing, subordinating, and symbolically annihilating women; it also marginalizes nontraditional images of masculinity for men, especially nonwhite and nonheterosexual images.

Michael Messner and his colleagues made a textual analysis of televised sports programs and their accompanying commercial advertisements.[30] See Box 11.1, *Thinking about Sport.*

Media Sport and Gender Inequities

Females were marginalized in the world of organized sport until the 1970s because sport was considered an exclusively male domain. Thus, there was little in the way of female sports for the mass media to cover, so sportswomen were rarely seen in either print or broadcast media. When they were, their achievements were denigrated; the women were framed in terms of women's traditional private roles, such as girlfriends, wives, or mothers; they were objectified in ways similar to softcore pornography; and their sports records were often compared with men's to deliberately belittle women's achievements.

Box 11.1   *Thinking about Sport* The Televised Sports Manhood Formula

Three sociologists analyzed a range of televised sporting events that had been identified as programs most often watched by boys. Their analysis revealed that sports programming presents boys with a narrow portrait of masculinity, which codifies a consistent and coherent message about what it means to be a man. They call this message the Televised Sports Manhood Formula, and explain it this way:

> What is a Real Man? A Real Man is strong, tough, aggressive, and above all, a winner in what is still a Man's World. To be a winner he has to do what needs to be done. He must be willing to compromise his own long-term health by showing guts in the face of danger, by fighting other men when necessary, and by "playing hurt" when he's injured. He must avoid being soft; he must be the aggressor, both on the "battle fields" of sports and in his consumption choices. Whether he is playing sports or making choices about which snack food or auto products to purchase, his aggressiveness will net him the ultimate prize: the adoring attention of conventionally beautiful women. He will know if and when he has arrived as a Real Man when the Voices of Authority—White *Males—say* he is a Real Man. But even when he has finally managed to win the big one, has the good car, the right beer, and is surrounded by beautiful women, he will be reminded by these very same Voices of Authority just how fragile this Real Manhood really is: After all, he has to come out and prove himself all over again tomorrow. You're only as good as your last game (or your last purchase).

Source: Michael A. Messner, Michele Dunbar, and Darnell Hunt, "The Televised Sports Manhood Formula," *Journal of Sport and Social Issues* 24, no. 4 (November 2000): 380–394.

By the first decade of the twenty-first century, considerable progress has been made in how media sport represent females, but women's sports have not achieved parity with men's sports in any of the media forms. Studies of the contents of newspapers and magazines in the United States and Canada, as well as several other countries, have consistently found that stories and photos of women's sports constituted a minority of the coverage; stories and photos of men's sports dominated the print media. Although the percentage of feature articles about females in sports roles has increased in recent years, many articles still reveal a conventional and restricted view of female sport participation, typically framing female athletes in terms of sexual appeal, homosexuality, and sports achievements that do not measure up to those of males. To illustrate, several of the major findings of a 2005 report on gender in televised sports follow:

- Women's sports were underreported in the six weeks of early evening and late night television sports news on three network affiliates sampled in the study.
- Men's sports received 91.4 percent of the airtime, women's sports 6.3 percent, and gender-neutral topics 2.4 percent. These numbers indicate a decline in the coverage of women's sports since 1999.
- On ESPN's nationally televised program *SportsCenter* and on the Fox *Southern California Sports Report*, the proportion of stories and airtime devoted to women's sports was even lower than on the local Los Angeles sports news shows. Whereas on the Los Angeles news, men's sports reports outnumbered women's sports stories by a 9:1 ratio, Fox's male-to-female ratio was 15:1, and *SportsCenter*'s ratio was a whopping 20:1.

All of the *SportsCenter* programs, all of the Fox programs, and 96.2 percent of the network affiliate sports news shows in the sample began with a men's sports topic as the lead story. There were many broadcasts in the sample that contained no coverage of women's sports whatsoever. Well over half (58 percent) of the network affiliate news shows included no women's sports stories, and 48 percent of the Fox and ESPN highlights shows included no women's sports stories. Meanwhile, 100 percent of the 279 news and highlights broadcasts in the sample included coverage of men's sports.[31]

One of the most promising trends toward increasing women's sports coverage is the emergence of magazines and websites devoted exclusively (or almost exclusively) to women's sport and fitness. *Women's Sports and Fitness* is highly acclaimed for its variety of articles. LadySports Online (www.ladysports.com), Women's Sports Wire (www.womenssportwire.com), and Women's Sports Network (www.wspn.net) are three examples of websites devoted exclusively to women's sports. These print and Internet outlets provide comprehensive coverage of women's sport activities, focusing on individual female athletes, women's teams, and women's sport organizations; they also examine issues and problems in women's sports.

Until 1996, no women's professional team sport league had ever secured a major national TV network contract. No doubt there were several reasons for this, but certainly a major one was that advertisers were not convinced that women would watch women's sport. Advertisers buy sports programming to reach a targeted audience, so they did not buy women's sports events. This pattern was broken in the fall of 1996 when the new American Basketball League (ABL) secured a national cable network contract; in 1997 when the Women's National Basketball Association (WNBA) began play, a national network television contract was in place. The ABL went out of business, but the WNBA network coverage remained in place, and several WNBA teams negotiated local TV contracts with regional sports networks. In 2007, a major breakthrough came along for the WNBA when the organization reached an eight-year, multimillion-dollar TV deal that for the first time will pay broadcast rights to the WNBA. Furthermore, network radio and TV contracts for other women's sports organizations are gradually increasing.

In the past thirty years there has been a significant social transformation in opportunities for females to engage in sports of every kind at every level. Accompanying this trend, significant strides have been made to include women in media sport, but their accomplishments will be unfulfilled until sportswriters and broadcasters accord them the respect and coverage their achievements in sports deserve. Ironically, as women strive for parity with men in media sport, they are being co-opted by the forces of commercialism in subtle ways that make them just another commodity to be sold to media sports audiences.[32]

Media Sport and Racial and Ethnic Inequities

In chapters 2 and 13 we discuss the historical and contemporary struggles of racial and ethic minority North Americans for involvement in sport; here we focus rather specifically on ethnic and racial issues in media sport.

Racism against black people has been present in all Western countries, but arguably the worst historical record of discrimination against blacks is found in colonial America and the United States. African Americans were largely segregated from commercial sports in the United States until about forty years ago. Over the past four decades most barriers to African American participation in organized sports have been swept away. Consequently, African American male athletes have played an increasingly prominent role in American sports; indeed, they dominate some of them, in terms of percentage of players at the elite levels.

The recent history of outstanding African American and minority male athletes playing on the same teams with, and competing against, white male athletes has made it essential for the media to recognize and report their performances and achievements. Still, several studies over the past 20 years have documented under-representation of African American and minority male athlete coverage by both print and electronic media. African American sportswomen have suffered more from the lack of coverage in media sport than African American males. One example will suffice to illustrate this point: There was a 30-year gap between the first and second *Sports Illustrated* cover featuring an African American female; over a 35-year period, African American female athletes appeared on only 5 of 1,835 covers of *Sports Illustrated*.

Wherever African American, Native American, Asian American, and Latino American athletes have had a presence in American sport, subtle racial stereotyping has been present in all the media forms. The most blatant examples are the frequent attributions of black athletes' achievements to their "natural" abilities to run fast and jump high and their "instincts" to react fast; at the same time, white athletes' achievements are typically attributed to their "intelligence" and superior "thinking ability." Historical stereotypes of black athletes are coded into characterizations of this kind.[33]

Male African American athletes have also been stereotyped in media sport commentaries as innately violent, thuggish, sexually uncontrolled, selfish, and arrogant. The social transgressions of high-profile black athletes and media accounts of professional black athletes as out-of-wedlock fathers and as drug addicts often are highlighted in print and broadcast news. For example, on 10 April 2007, the front page of the sports section of *USA Today* was virtually filled with what looked like police mugshots of 41 NFL football players. Accompanying the photos was a statement saying that "since 2006 more than 50 arrests have been made of NFL football players." Of the 41 photos, all but 2 were African Americans. The title of the article was "NFL Confronts Discipline Issue." Assuming the article that accompanied the photos is true, it was a legitimate news story, but the impression that set of photos made was unmistakable. Clearly, it reinforced stereotypical prejudiced representations of African American males, even though the percentage of black athletes involved in such actions is small. *USA Today* editors knew very well how the set of photos would be interpreted by millions with racist beliefs.[34]

The U.S. government's reservation system has been a major structural barrier to sport opportunities for Native American youth. Typically, the sports facilities at reservation schools are inadequate for Native Americans to develop sports skills and experience sports competition against a variety of skilled athletes. The media have always emphasized and portrayed stereotypical representations of the few Native American athletes who have achieved elite-level status. Nicknames like "the Chief," "Redskin," and "Wahoo" appear in media stories on Native American athletes. Native Americans' images as team mascots are approvingly portrayed in the media as TV cameras pan the spectators in areas and stadiums when fans do the tomahawk chop and show close-up camera shots of costumed "Indians" dancing around venues after touchdowns and three-point baskets.[35]

Asian American and Latino American athletes have been either neglected in the media or, when covered, given stereotyped representations and nicknames. In light of the limited personal contact between most whites and people of color in North America, media portrayals, rather than personal experiences, become the primary source of information that shapes whites' perceptions of other groups. Unfortunately, the depictions in media sports help institutionalize the social and information gap between people of color and whites.

SPORTS JOURNALISM AND THE MASS MEDIA

Sports journalism, including sportscasting, is a peculiar occupation. On the one hand, a certain amount of prestige and power is associated with the occupation. Sports journalists' names are seen and heard by the public daily, they control access to the sports information that the public wants, and their stories and commentaries can influence the destinies of franchises and athletes. On the other hand, in *Sports Journalism: Context and Issues,* the author (a sportswriter) claims: "In the hierarchy of professional journalism, [sports journalism] has been traditionally viewed disparagingly as the 'toy department,' a bastion of easy living, sloppy journalism and 'soft' news." Another sportswriter remarked: "Sports writing is categorized alongside beer-tasting and aphrodisiac-evaluation. People say 'More of a hobby than a job, isn't it.'"[36]

Ostensibly, sports journalists are expected to report information about the results of sports events; to provide inside information on particular players, teams, and sports organizations; and to give opinions that help the public interpret sports news. While accuracy and objectivity in reporting are valued norms in journalism, the image of the sports journalist is one of obsequious appeasement. More than one critic of sportswriters has observed that their work all too often reflects jock worship, press-agentry, and awe rather than solid, in-depth reporting.[37]

Several practices of sports journalists contribute to their disparagement as objective reporters. Some sportswriters, through their columns and reports about the local teams, convey the impression that they are extensions of the teams; these are frequently called "housemen" or "housewomen" because their stories often read like public relations on behalf of the local team or teams. In return the local teams are expected to treat these reporters favorably in obtaining access to coaches and players and obtaining exclusive stories about the team or teams. This practice has declined because of the criticism within the journalism occupation itself, but it is easy to see how such an approach can create a cozy interdependence between journalists and sports teams.

A second practice that contributes to the low status of sport journalism is the TV sports news reporters, who share time with anchors reporting on local, national, and international events and with weather forecasters are relegated to a very few minutes that are filled mostly with reporting scores and hyping upcoming events. In cities where pro teams reside, or big-time collegiate sports (or both) are nearby, the TV sports reporters are frequently outright cheerleaders for these local teams, referring to them as "our team." In some cases they virtually become public relations agents for them.

In general, there is not anyplace in the sports news broadcasts for investigative journalism. The major reason for the lack of a commitment to pursuing serious news issues is that when media corporations, such as CBS and NBC, are sponsoring sports events and generating profits, critical reporting can create conflicts and problems. Media corporations have major business relationships with sports organizations that are worth billions of dollars and are renewable, so journalists working for, say, CBS Sports cannot readily critique the morals of the sports organizations that CBS does business with.[38]

In other words, because of the cozy business relations between the television industry and sports, television news does not operate in a serious journalistic manner; its concern is more with promoting the teams and leagues in which it has invested than with operating in a serious journalistic manner.

Sportscasters: Narrators of Mediated Sport

Because radio and TV sportscasters "tutor" listeners and viewers in what they should hear, see, and believe about the sports events being broadcast, they are extremely important in such broadcasts. Consequently, they are carefully selected for their ability to command credibility, because they play a big role in attracting and holding listeners' and viewers' attention. The usual selections are former professional and elite amateur athletes and coaches with high name recognition. As sporting celebrities and "certified experts," these former athletes and coaches have immediate recognition and credibility with the listeners and viewers, and audiences of sporting event broadcasts will accept their interpretations and opinions as objective and true.

Employing former athletes and coaches to describe the technical skills, strategy, and tactics used during a broadcast sports event may seem reasonable enough, but it is important to realize that they also act to articulate moral values and to comment prescriptively on social relationships. Former sport stars are uniquely qualified for this task because they are survivors—even models—of the competitive sport meritocracy. Largely their attitudes and values are congruent with commercialized sports perspectives because they are fully integrated into the dominant values and beliefs of that system.

Preventing viewer boredom is one of the main concerns of broadcast producers, so one basic job of sportscasters is to keep listeners and viewers tuned in to the broadcast. To do this, they provide a commentary that heightens the drama of the event, using methods like these:

- Constructing themes, such as "these teams hate each other" or "this is a grudge game." The message in both cases: The audience can expect a hard-fought contest with lots of fierce action.
- Highlighting "matchups" between players on opposite teams. This sets up a kind of one-on-one competition on which the audience can focus. Similarly, elaborate discussions of "keys to winning" are calculated to get viewers absorbed in the contest.
- Framing the game as an extremely crucial game for both teams (even if they are both hopelessly out of championship contention); heightening the significance of the game enhances audience interest (or so it is believed).
- Other sportscaster techniques include personal interest stories, recitation of statistics and records, anticipation of what to expect, dramatic embellishments of the action, and second-guessing.

All of these narratives are designed to keep audiences tuned in to the broadcast.

Another important job of sportscasters is selling the sport organizations, league, and network for which they are broadcasting. Game commentary is frequently commercial hype for those organizations. For example, sportscasters tend to effusively praise the athletes, teams, and leagues throughout the broadcasts. Another favorite "sales" practice of sportscasters is creating attention-attracting monikers to develop team name recognition and get fans to identify with teams or athletes; for instance, the Dallas Cowboys of the NFL have become known as "America's Team" through sportscaster commentary.[39]

Sportscasters who broadcast live events on radio or television typically have no background in journalism, and indeed the journalism profession has disavowed any connection with their work. They are usually selected by radio and television executives for their ability to narrate sports events as much as for their knowledge of the game. Many are former athletes and coaches who are articulate in explaining the intricacies of the game or are charismatic. They must satisfy not only the media corporation that employs them but also the league commissioners and team owners whose games are being broadcast. The latter routinely screen the announcers and instruct the media executives as to how the announcers can improve their performances, letting it be known that all comments should cast the league, teams, and players in a favorable light. Consequently, objective reporting takes a backseat to the creation and maintenance of a favorable image of both sport and the media. A sportswriter for the *New York Times* once noted that "televised sports is not journalism; it is entertainment, shaped to keep people in front of the beer advertisements as long as possible." And other media analysts have suggested that a more appropriate portrayal of sportscasters would be sport public relations agents, whose main function is to elevate the banal.

Several analyses of professional football telecasts have revealed that a sizable portion of the audio narration of the coverage is devoted to dramatic embellishments of the event. In other words, sportscasters serve not only to fill in the lack of viewer knowledge about the sport but also to add histrionics to the human drama of athletic events.

In studies of the impact of commentary on audience perception and appreciation, researchers have exposed subjects to two segments of prerecorded, televised games that have been pretested for perception of roughness. Viewers were exposed to one of two presentation modes: with or without sportscasters' commentary. The results showed that the viewers' perceptions of the play were dramatically influenced by the nature of the accompanying commentary. Thus, through the commentary by sportscasters, viewers can be influenced to "see" fierce competition and roughness where it really does not exist. The researchers concluded that viewers seem to become "caught up" in the commentary and the sportscasters' interpretation of the game, and they allow themselves to be persuaded by the narration of "drama" in the event. There is, then, overwhelming evidence that sports telecasts can be presented and manipulated to create different levels of enjoyment for viewers.[40]

Broadcast audiences are largely unaware that sportscasters, in addition to describing the action, are actually providing a constant commercial for the sport on which they are reporting. Much of their commentary is pure promotion for the league and sport organization that is independent of the corporate product commercials for which commercial breaks occur periodically during an event.

It is one thing for television networks to employ up to three sportscasters to cover a game; it is quite another to believe that these persons are giving viewers an accurate or inside view of the game. They are, in fact, doing just the opposite. They report actions where they do not exist; they protect owners, coaches, and athletes from serious scrutiny; and they constantly hype the sport and its participants. All of these actions are predicated on obtaining high ratings for the network. Of course, the bottom line is that both professional sport and television are big businesses, each dependent upon the fiscal health of the other. By reporting an exciting game, the sportscasters promote both sport and television.

The rise of celebrity sportscasters can be directly attributed to television. Through their own interpretations, they translate games into mass entertainment while at the same time influencing viewers' perceptions of the action. As a group, sport announcers generally have shared low marks for their banal patter and pompous second-guessing. As faithful employees of television and sports, sportscasters promote sport; rarely do they go beyond the superficial or the obvious.

Wrapping Up

What a person sees and reads about sports via the mass media has been deliberately filtered to show the best side of sports. Although a certain amount of criticism may be reported, sports journalists in the main are supportive of the system. Very few report anything that might cause discomfort. By omission and commission, complicity and docility, the media reports seldom stray from the promotion of sport. Despite an occasional exposé, and for all the talk about muckraking, sports journalists have very little to say about the seamier aspects of sports.

The reason for sports journalists' cooperation with the sports establishment may be more fundamental than selling newspapers or obtaining high radio and TV ratings. Those few sports journalists who do not report sport in the traditional way often incur the outrage of committed sports fans. They are often targets of hate letters and ugly phone calls in the middle of the night. In one way, this is understandable because it is almost heretical to attack sport. To attack sport is to impugn the North American value system. To challenge the sanctity of sport is to criticize what for many people is their main anchor for understanding how the real world works.

Minority Sport Journalists and Broadcasters

Sportswriting and broadcasting have been largely white male professions in the United States and Canada, closely mirroring the hierarchical racial division of labor so evident in the broader mass communications occupational structure. Examples are: In 2007, according to the American Society of Newspaper Editors, minorities, who constitute about 32 percent of the American population, account for just 13.62 percent of newspaper journalists; only 16 percent of full-time journalists working on their newspapers' websites were minorities; 392 newspapers had no minorities on their full-time staff. A recent survey of the diversity of over fifty-one hundred Associated Press (AP) staff by sport studies scholar Richard Lapchick and his colleagues at the University of Central Florida found that white men and women comprised 88 percent of the total staffs of all AP newspapers; African Americans were only 6.2 percent, Latinos 3.6 percent, and Asians 1.3 percent of the total.

These are dismal findings for minority opportunities in the newspaper industry.[41]

The Radio-Television News Directors Association (RTNDA) reports annually on minorities in that industry. The general pattern has been a slow, but gradual, increase of minorities working in radio and television, but the percentage of minorities on television news staffs is still less than 25 percent, while the minority workforce in radio remains below 12 percent. The percentage of minority TV news directors is less than 15 percent; in radio, minority news directors comprise less than 6 percent. Of course, diversity is not just about numbers; it is about making journalism and broadcasting better. Diverse staffs lead to better journalism and broadcasting.

Many fans have formed the impression that African Americans represent a substantial portion of sports journalism because, while watching televised sports, fans see African American former professional athletes and coaches in the broadcast booths of professional and intercollegiate sports events. The reality is something quite different. According to *The 2006 Racial and Gender Report Card of the Associated Press Sports Editors* (APSE), 94.7 percent of APSE members were white; African Americans held less than 2 percent of APSE sports editor positions and about 5 percent of assistant sports editor positions.[42] (See Table 11.7.) These are bleak figures when one considers the fact that in the world of sports, a disproportionate number of athletes in basketball, football, and baseball are African Americans.

Many barriers have fallen by the wayside, as ethnic minorities and blacks have gained increasing respect for their sports reporting and broadcasting skills, but one fact is clear: There are still very few minority sportswriters and sportscasters in this profession. The percentages of those working in sports journalism and broadcasting are a poor reflection of the proportion of black and minority athletes playing sports in North America. The subordination of minorities in media sports continues, and each new breakthrough requires concerted struggle against the persistent white-dominated division of labor in media sport.

Table 11.7 The 2006 Racial and Gender Report Card of the Associated Press Sports Editors

Sports Editors	Number	Percentage
White	303	94.69
African Americans	5	1.56
Latino	9	2.81
Asian	0	0
Other	3	0.94
Women	16	5.00

Assistant Sports Editors

White	446	86.94
African American	27	5.26
Latino	28	5.46
Asian	8	1.56
Other	4	0.78
Women	65	12.67

Source: Richard Lapchick, Jenny Brenden, and Brian Wright, *The 2006 Racial and Gender Report Card of the Associated Press Sports Editors* (Orlando: DeVos Sports Business Management Program, University of Central Florida, 2006).

Women Sport Journalists and Broadcasters

Women who have wished to have careers in journalism and broadcasting have had an arduous struggle. Media organizations currently do not provide a level playing field for women. Women make up more than 50 percent of the adult population, but Lapchick and his colleagues found that women at AP newspapers make up merely 12 percent of total staffs of AP member newspapers. Among AP columnists, only 6 percent were women; of the 2,128 reporters in the AP survey, 9 were females. Not a pretty picture for the principle of gender equity in media organizations. Conditions are better in radio and television broadcasting. A recent report by the RTNDA found that the percentage of women in radio news was near 25 percent, while the percentage of women radio news directors was about 20 percent.[43]

Traditional views of sport as a male domain have helped perpetuate the dominance of male sports coverage by the mass media and of men employed to write and broadcast sports. Because sport has traditionally been viewed as a male preserve, the message to any female who might have been interested in a career in sports journalism was clear: Women do not understand sports, so they certainly would not know how to report them. Despite the indignities and the discrimination that female sportswriters and sportscasters have experienced, and the relatively few women in the field, gains have been made. Women now hold important positions in both print and broadcast media sports in the United States and Canada. Women sports journalists have acquired access to press boxes, locker rooms, and other facilities important to their work. New breakthroughs occur each year, as women continue their struggle for equality in sports journalism. For example, in June 2007, TV viewers got something unprecedented—Wendy Venturini, a woman sports TV reporter, called a top-flight NASCAR race on TV. A few sportscasters, such as Robin Roberts, have moved into prestigious network positions.

Notwithstanding the increased number of women in sports journalism and broadcasting, Lapchick's Associated Press report conveys a sobering account of just how far women in sports media have come. At a time when 86 percent of the AP sports editor positions are held by white males and only 5 percent by women, it is clear that there are substantial barriers to gender equity for women in sports journalism. The women in these positions do not receive equal pay for equal work; the highest-paid men in these positions receive up to five times the salary of the highest-paid women. So in an era when their presence in journalism and broadcasting is growing, women are still a small minority in the sports broadcasting business.[44]

SUMMARY

A symbiotic relationship exists between sport and the mass media; each is a commercial industry whose success has been greatly influenced by the other. The print media contributed to the rise of sport during the nineteenth century. At the same time, the interest in sports information assisted in the growth of newspapers, magazines, and books. The electronic media—radio and television—have been instrumental in the promotion of big-time intercollegiate sports and professional sports. Indeed, without these media, collegiate and professional sports could not function as they presently do.

The dominating role that the mass media play in the economic aspects of sport has a number of effects. Televised sport has produced a dramatic shift in the mode of fans' consumption of sport; the popularity of several sports has been greatly influenced by television; and television has furthered the professionalization of amateur sport enterprises, such as intercollegiate athletics and the Olympic Games. Television has also manipulated the structure, meaning, and process of sports.

Figures on the amount of time people spend with the mass media are scarce, but studies estimate that television viewing accounts for some eight hours per household per day. Televised sports programs are some of the most popular on TV. The three major commercial networks no longer are the main sports events providers. Beginning with ESPN as the first all-sports all-the-time network and continuing with regional sports networks, single sport networks, satellite networks, and so on, countless hours of live sports are a significant feature of contemporary entertainment and news. Internet sports have become a huge player in the mediated sports industry, and some media analysts contend that its potential is overwhelming.

Many barriers have fallen by the wayside in Western countries, as ethnic minorities and blacks have gained increasing respect for their sports reporting and broadcasting skills, but one fact is clear: There are still very few minority sportswriters and sportscasters in this profession. The percentages of those working in sports journalism and broadcasting are a poor reflection of the proportion of black and minority athletes playing sports in any country. The subordination of minorities in media sport continues, and each new breakthrough requires concerted struggle against the persistent, white-dominated division of labor in media sport.

Media sport is a site where verbal and visual representations of the male athletic body are interpreted as a key source in cultivating, legitimating, and reinforcing the dominant definitions of masculinity as well as general masculine dominance. The sports that are especially physically violent—such as rugby, American football, ice hockey, and boxing—present the most frequent and most vivid images of hegemonic masculinity.

With the rise of media coverage, sports journalists have grown in number, but they have a rather low status among other journalists. The sports department of a newspaper, a radio, or a television newsroom is commonly referred to as the "toy department."

One reason for news reporters' low regard for sports journalists (especially sportscasters) is that they are not actually professionally trained reporters; they are, instead, employees of professional teams or of television networks, and their jobs are basically promotional. They do not merely report the events; instead, they manage the accounts of the events to make them more interesting, more dramatic, and more important than they really are. Their role, rather than to provide information, is to translate games into mass entertainment aimed at high ratings. In doing so, they promote the media and the sports in which they are employed.

Discrimination, both gender and racial, has been present in the ways in which the mass media report sports and in the hiring practices of media corporations. There are, however, encouraging signs that conditions are improving for women and minorities.

WEB RESOURCES

www.usa.com/sports
This website is the home of the sports section of *USA Today*. It has the daily sports stories and an archives link from which the user can secure copies of previous *USA Today* sports articles.

www.sportsillustrated.com
This is the website for *Sports Illustrated,* which has the largest circulation of any sports magazine. This site reports on a variety of sports news items

and has links to a variety of news sources and specific sports.

www.cnnsi.com/movies
This is a CNN/*Sports Illustrated* website that reviews the top movies and provides a gallery of great moments in sports movies.

www.awsmonline.org
The official website of the Association for Women in Sports Media. This is an organization of women who work in the sports media and of women and men who support them in their work. It has online features and news.

www.real-sports.com
This website is titled the Worldwide Sporting Authority, Online Sporting Magazine and Sports Authority. And it arguably lives up to its name.

NOTES

1. Lawrence A. Wenner, *MediaSport* (New York: Routledge, 1998), xiii; see also David Rowe, *Sport, Culture and the Media: The Unholy Trinity*, 2nd ed. (Maidenhead, Berkshire, UK: Open University Press, 2004).

2. Paul Kivel, *You Call This a Democracy?* (New York: The Apex Press, 2004), 125–127, 135–136; see also Shirley Biagi, *Media/Impact: An Introduction to Mass Media*, 8th ed. (Belmont, Calif.: Wadsworth Publishing, 2006).

3. Phil Andrews, *Sports Journalism: A Practical Introduction* (Thousand Oaks, Calif.: Sage Publications, 2005); see also Mark D. Lowes, *Inside the Sports Pages: Work Routines, Professional Ideologies, and the Manufacture of Sports News* (Toronto: University of Toronto Press, 1999).

4. John Mark Dempsey, ed., *Sports-Talk Radio in America: Its Context and Culture* (Binghamton, N.Y.: Haworth Half-Court Press, 2006); see also David Nylund, *Beer, Babes, and Balls: Masculinity and Sports Talk Radio* (Albany: State University of New York Press, 2007); John W. Owens, "The Coverage of Sport on Radio," in *Handbook of Sports and Media*, ed. Arthur A. Raney and Jennings Bryant (Hillsdale, N.J.: Lawrence Erlbaum, 2006), 117–129.

5. ESPN.com Page 2, *Top 20 Sports Movies of All Time*, http://espn.go.com/page2/movies/s/top20/fullllist.html.

6. Geoff Colvin, "TV Is Dying? Long Live TV!" *Fortune*, 5 February 2007, 43.

7. "First Television of Baseball Scene," *New York Times*, 18 May 1939, p. 29.

8. Jerry Gorman and Kirk Calhoun, *The Name of the Game: The Business of Sports* (New York: Wiley, 2004); Rodney D. Fort, *Sports Economics*, 2nd ed. (Upper Saddle River, N.J.: Prentice Hall, 2006).

9. Leonard Shecter, *The Jocks* (New York: Paperback Library, 1970), 79.

10. Matt Woolsey, "Can Corporate Ownership Save Baseball?" *Forbes.com*, 17 February 2007, http://www.forbes.com/2007/02/16/baseball-team-ownership-biz-cx.

11. Lowes, *Inside the Sports Pages;* see also Rowe, *Sport, Culture and the Media*, 117–141.

12. *The 2006 Sports Business Research Yearbook* (Loganville, Ga.: Richard K. Miller & Associates), 76.

13. "NFL Europa Closes," *NFL.com*, 3 August 2007, http://www.nfl.com/news/story?id=09000d5d801308ec&template=without-video&confirm=true.

14. John S. Watterson, *College Football: History, Spectacle, Controversy* (Baltimore: Johns Hopkins University Press, 2000).

15. Andrew Zimbalist, *Unpaid Professionals: Commercialism and Conflict in Big-Time College Sports* (Princeton: Princeton University Press, 1999), 90–124.

16. Keith Dunnavant, *The Fifty-Year Seduction: How Television Manipulated College Football, from the Birth of the Modern NCAA to the Creation of the BCS* (New York: St. Martin's Press, 2004), xvi.

17. Steve Wieberg, "Players Want a Cut of $6 Billion TV Contract," *USA Today*, 30 March–1 April 2001, pp. 1A–2A.

18. John R. Thelin, *Games Colleges Play: Scandal and Reform in Intercollegiate Athletics* (Baltimore: Johns Hopkins University Press, 2004); see also James J. Duderstadt, *Intercollegiate Athletics and the American University: A President's Perspective* (Ann Arbor: University of Michigan Press, 2003).

19. Peter Yoon, "X Games Take a Turn for the Better," *Los Angeles Times*, 7 August 2006, p. D11; Matt Higgins, "ESPN Is Going Where the Action Is," *New York Times*, 3 August 2006, p. D7; Michael Hiestand, "X Games Still Tries to Be Hip, Gain Viewers," *USA Today*, 1 August 2007, p. 2C.

20. L. John Wertheim, "The New Main Event," *Sports Illustrated*, 28 May 2007, 52–60.

21. Garry Whannel, *Media Sport Stars: Masculinities and Moralities* (New York: Routledge, 2001); Michael A.

Messner, Michele Dunbar, and Darnell Hunt, "The Televised Sports Manhood Formula," in *Sport in Contemporary Society: An Anthology*, 7th ed., ed. D. Stanley Eitzen, (Boulder, Colo.: Paradigm Publishers, 2005), 98–111.

22. Kerri Strug, *Landing on My Feet: A Diary of Dreams* (Riverside, N.J.: Andrews McMeel Publishers, 1998); see also David B. Sullivan, "Broadcast Television and the Game of Packaging Sports," in Raney and Bryant, *Handbook of Sports and Media*, 131–145.

23. Michael Freeman, *ESPN: The Uncensored History*, reprint ed. (Lanham, Md.: Taylor Trade Publishing, 2002); see also Museum of Broadcast Communications, *Sports and Television*, http://www.museum.tv/archives/etv/S/htmlS/sportsandte/sportsandte.htm.

24. Arthur A. Raney, "Why We Watch and Enjoy Mediated Sports," in Raney and Bryant, *Handbook of Sports and Media*, 313–329.

25. Phil Schaaf, *Sports, Inc: 100 Years of Sports Business* (Amherst, N.Y.: Prometheus Books, 2003), 27.

26. Michael Hiestand, "NBC Wired about Expanding Olympic Coverage to Cable, Online Outlets," *USA Today*, 8 August 2007, p. 8C; Michael Hiestand, "Streaming Video Mainstream," *USA Today*, 6 August 2007, p. 6C.

27. ESPN, "Simulating Sports: The Video Game Craze," *Outside the Lines*, 16 May 2002; see also Katherine E. and Craig A. Anderson, "A Theoretical Model of the Effects and Consequences of Playing Video Games," in *Playing Video Games: Motives, Responses, and Consequences*, ed. Peter Vorderer and Jennings Bryant (Mahwah, N.J.: Lawrence Erlbaum, 2006), 363–378.

28. Richard Gruneau and David Whitson, *Hockey Night in Canada* (Toronto: Garamond Press, 1993), 190; see also Messner, Dunbar, and Hunt, "The Televised Sports Manhood Formula," 98–111.

29. Nick Trujillo, "Machines, Missiles, and Men: Images of the Male Body on ABC's Monday Night Football," *Sociology of Sport Journal* 12, no. 4 (1995): 419; see also Don Sabo and Sue E. Jansen, "Prometheus Unbound: Constructions of Masculinity in the Sports Media," in Wenner, *MediaSport*, 202–217.

30. Messner, Dunbar, and Hunt, "The Televised Sports Manhood Formula," 98–111.

31. Margaret Carlisle Duncan and Michael A. Messner, *Gender in Televised Sports: News and Highlights Shows, 1989–2004* (Los Angeles: Amateur Athletic Foundation of Los Angeles, 2005), 4.

32. Pamela J. Creedon and Judith Cramer, eds., *Women in Mass Communication* (Thousand Oaks, Calif.: Sage Publications, 2007).

33. Dana D. Brooks and Ronald C. Althouse, eds., *Diversity and Social Justice in College Sports: Sport Management and the Student Athlete* (Morgantown, W.V.: Fitness Information Technology, 2007), sec. 4, "Media, Media Images, and Stereotyping."

34. Jarrett Bell, "NFL Confronts Discipline Issue," *USA Today*, 10 April 2007, pp. 1C–2C; see also Richard Lapchick, *Smashing Barriers: Race and Sport in the New Millennium* (New York: Madison Books, 2001), 265–280.

35. C. Richard King, *Native Americans in Sports* (Armonk, N.Y.: Sharpe Reference, 2003); John Bloom, *To Show What an Indian Can Do: Sports at Native American Boarding Schools*, new ed. (Minneapolis: University of Minnesota Press, 2005).

36. These two quotes are from Raymond Boyle, *Sports Journalism: Context and Issues* (Thousand Oaks, Calif.: Sage Publications, 2006), 1; see also Andrew Baker, *Where Am I and Who's Winning? Travelling the World of Sport* (London: Yellow Jersey Press, 2004), ix.

37. Bradley Schultz, *Sports Media: Reporting, Producing, and Planning*, 2nd ed. (New York: Focal Press, 2005).

38. Boyle, *Sports Journalism: Context and Issues*.

39. Rowe, *Sport, Culture and the Media: The Unholy Trinity*, 117–202.

40. Raney, "Why We Watch and Enjoy Mediated Sports," 313–329; see also Arthur A. Raney and Anthony J. Depalma, "The Effect of Viewing Varying Levels and Contexts of Violent Sports Programming on Enjoyment, Mood, and Perceived Violence," *Mass Communication and Society* 9, no. 3 (2006): 321–338.

41. "Diversity Slips in U.S. Newsrooms," ASNE, http://www.asne.org/index.cfm?ID=6506; Richard Lapchick, Jenny Brenden, and Brian Wright, *The 2006 Racial and Gender Report Card of the Associated Press Sports Editors* (Orlando: DeVos Sport Business Management Program, University of Central Florida, 2006).

42. Lapchick, Brenden, and Wright, *The 2006 Racial and Gender Report Card*; see also Doris R. Corbett and Aaron B. Stills, "African Americans and the Media, Roles, and Opportunities to Be Broadcasters, Journalists, Reporters, and Announcers," in *Diversity and Social Justice in College Sports: Sport Management and the Student Athlete*, ed. Brooks and Althouse.

43. Noreen Welle, "Minorities Gain on Local Television News Staffs," 5 July 2006, http://aaja.org/news/releases/2006_07_07_02; see also Lapchick, Brenden, and Wright, *The 2006 Racial and Gender Report Card*.

44. Ibid.

Chapter 12

Sport, Social Stratification, and Social Mobility

Sport is generally assumed to be an egalitarian institution that promotes interaction across social class and racial lines. Sport, however, like the larger society, is highly stratified, and like all institutions, sport accommodates and reinforces the existing structure of social inequality. Many activities, such as sailing, are too expensive for the less well-to-do. (iStockphoto)

Sport is generally assumed to be an egalitarian and a meritocratic institution. Sport is accepted as egalitarian because it promotes interaction across social class and racial lines and because interest in sport transcends class and social boundaries. Sport is believed to be meritocratic because within it persons who have talent, regardless of social background, can be upwardly mobile. A speech by former president Ronald Reagan at the NCAA Honors Banquet in 1990 illustrates these commonly held beliefs: "When men and women compete on the athletics field socioeconomic status disappears. Black or white, Christian or Jew, rich or poor . . . all that matters is that you're out there on the field giving your all. [It's the same way in the stands, where] corporate presidents sit next to janitors . . . and they high-five each other when their team scores . . . which makes me wonder if it [status] should matter at all."[1] The goal of this chapter is to show that these widely held assumptions are myths.

The empirical examination of the sports world demonstrates that sport, like the larger society, is highly stratified. Like all institutions, sport accommodates and reinforces the existing structure of social inequality. There are exceptions, as we will note, but as exceptions they prove the rule.

MAJOR CONCEPTS

This chapter is about social inequality and its consequences for sport. As background, we begin with a brief discussion of the major concepts dealing with social inequality and the dimensions of inequality as found in the United States.[2]

People differ in age, physical attributes, skills, and what they do for a living. The process of categorizing people by age, height, occupation, or some other personal attribute is called *social differentiation*. When these attributes are ranked hierarchically (that is, seen as superior or inferior), we have *social stratification*. This implies that social inequality is structured (socially patterned)—inequalities are socially recognized and given importance by being incorporated into the beliefs, attitudes, and values of the members of society. Sociologist Harold Kerbo summarizes what is meant by social stratification:

> *Social stratification* means that inequality has been hardened or *institutionalized,* and there is a system of social relationships that determines who gets what, and why. When we say *institutionalized* we mean that a system of layered hierarchy has been established. People have come to expect that individuals and groups with certain positions will be able to demand more influence and respect and accumulate a greater share of goods and services. Such inequality may or may not be accepted equally by a majority in the society, but it is recognized as the way things are.[3]

When a number of people occupy the same relative economic rank in the stratification system, they form a *social class*. People are socially located in a class position on the basis of income, occupation, and education, either alone or in combination. One's placement in the class hierarchy determines access to the rewards and resources of society, such as wealth, power, and privilege. And, crucially, differential access to these societal resources and rewards produces different life experiences and different life chances. *Life chances* are the chances one has throughout one's life cycle to live and experience the good things in life. This means that the affluent and their children will have a good education, good medical care, comfortable homes, safe neighborhoods, expert services of all kinds, and the best in leisure activities. The converse, of course, is that the poor and the near-poor will have inadequate health care, shelter, and diets. Their lives will be more miserable, and they will die sooner.

In addition to class, race and gender are also structured systems of inequality that organize society as a whole and create varied environments for individuals and families through their unequal distribution of social opportunities. These structures of inequality array the resources and advantages (life chances) of society in patterned ways. These hierarchies are also structured systems of exploitation and discrimination in which the affluent dominate the poor, men dominate women, and whites dominate people of color.[4]

DIMENSIONS OF INEQUALITY

People in the United States rank differently from one another on a number of socioeconomic dimensions: wealth, income, education, and occupation. Wealth and income, the bases of social class, are concentrated among individuals and families.

The following facts illustrate the range on each of these dimensions:

- In 2006 the four hundred richest Americans had a total net worth of $1.25 trillion. At the other extreme, 37 million Americans were living below the poverty line.[5]
- The top 1 percent of wealth holders controlled 33.4 percent of total net worth in 2004, while the bottom 50 percent accounted for just 2.5 percent of the wealth.[6]
- The share of the national income of the richest 20 percent of households was 50.1 percent in 2005, while the bottom 20 percent received only 3.4 percent of the nation's income.[7]
- In 2003, some 2.7 percent of the population age twenty-five and older had a doctorate or professional degree; about 6.6 percent had an eighth-grade education or less.[8]
- Occupational prestige is correlated with income level, but the gender of the worker makes a tremendous difference: Women make about three-fourths, on average, of what men earn. Women also find it more difficult than men to reach the highest levels of management (to move above the "glass ceiling").
- Forty-seven million Americans do not have health insurance.

These facts make clear that the United States is not a classless society. There are wide disparities in economic resources and what those resources can purchase. The remainder of this chapter deals with two issues involving inequality and sport: (1) the influence of stratification on sports participation and spectatorship and (2) the possibility that sport can help individuals move up (increase their upward social mobility) in the stratification hierarchy.

SOCIAL CLASS AND SPORT

North Americans enjoy playing and watching sports. Is what they do or prefer to do related to their socioeconomic status or not? Looking first at participation, the evidence from empirical studies provides consistent support for the generalization that the higher the socioeconomic status of the individual, the more likely that individual will be to participate actively in leisure activities.

Adult Participation Preferences for Sports by Socioeconomic Status

The evidence is clear that high-income, high-education, and high-status occupational groups have the highest rates of active sport participation and attendance at sports events.[9] Consider first the data in Table 12.1, which show a consistent and strong pattern for the relationship between social class and involvement in sports. That is, the greater a person's level of educational attainment

Table 12.1 Attendance at Sports Events and Participation in Sports by Education and Income, 2002 (in percent)

Variable	Attendance at Sports Events	Participation in Sports
Education (highest level attained)		
Grade school	9.4	6.9
Some high school	17.4	17.2
High school graduate	28.3	22.6
Some college	39.9	35.2
College graduate	51.0	45.2
Graduate school	48.3	43.6
Income ($)		
Less than 10,000	16.5	15.0
10,000 to 19,999	20.1	18.5
20,000 to 29,999	23.0	21.4
30,000 to 39,999	30.0	26.6
40,000 to 49,999	34.8	29.3
50,000 to 74,999	44.8	36.0
75,000 or more	53.3	48.0

Source: U.S. Census Bureau, *Statistical Abstract of the United States: 2007,* 126th ed. (Washington, D.C., 2007), table 1222.

and income, the more likely a person is to attend a sports event and to participate in sports.

Similarly, Table 12.2 shows that for all types of individual and team sports activities, the higher the income, the greater the rate of participation. There are several bases for this relationship. The most obvious is that many activities (e.g., sailing, skiing, and golf) are too expensive for the less well-to-do. The affluent also have access to private clubs and resorts where golf, tennis, skiing, boating, and swimming are available. Communities rarely provide inexpensive access to these activities, other than tennis and swimming.

An interesting speculation as to why the affluent are disposed toward certain sports was presented by Thorstein Veblen in 1899. He argued that the affluent engaged in leisure activities in order to impress upon observers that they can afford expensive and wasteful activities. In other words, sport is used by these persons as a form of *conspicuous consumption,* to prove that they can spend great amounts of time away from work.[10]

This rationale explains why the upper class have held amateur sport as an ideal and why Olympic competition was traditionally limited to the more well-to-do. Another explanation for the greater likelihood of the affluent to engage in sports is that their occupations, unlike the jobs of the lower classes, provide them with more flexible schedules. This allows them more freedom to go to the gym, club, or golf course at various times.

The affluent and educated are more prone than lower socioeconomic groups to engage in health and physical fitness activities such as running, Pilates, aerobics, and bicycling. An interesting difference between white-collar and blue-collar workers involves participation in workplace-centered fitness programs. Many corporations provide sports equipment and facilities for their workers and encourage them to participate. The typical reaction is enthusiastic support from the salaried professionals and relative nonsupport from the hourly workers.[11] There are several reasons for this. First, the lower the social status, the less likely

Table 12.2 Participation in Selected Sports Activities by Household Income, 2004 (in percent)

Activity	Under $25,000	$25,000–$74,999	$75,000 and above
Team Sports			
Football	1.7	3.1	3.4
Basketball	7.4	10.7	13.7
Baseball	4.4	5.8	8.2
Volleyball	2.3	4.7	4.8
Soccer	2.4	4.8	8.0
Softball	4.0	4.5	6.2
Individual sports/leisure			
Aerobic exercising	6.8	11.3	15.4
Exercising with equipment	10.1	19.7	29.3
Exercise walking	29.4	32.6	35.9
Running/jogging	5.8	9.6	12.5
Martial arts	1.4	1.7	2.4
Golf	3.6	8.2	16.6
Tennis	2.2	2.8	6.6
Skiing (alpine)	.5	2.2	2.9
Waterskiing	.5	1.9	1.8
Sailing	.5	0.8	1.8
Swimming	17.5	20.4	27.0
Weight lifting	4.7	10.6	13.8

Source: U.S. Bureau of the Census, *Statistical Abstract of the United States: 2007,* 126th ed. (Washington, D.C., 2007). Percentages calculated from data in Table 1233.

the individual will be to exercise regularly, to participate in wellness programs, to maintain a proper weight, and to stop smoking. Second, the activities provided (e.g., running, swimming, and racquetball) are of more interest to higher-status workers. Third, blue-collar workers may mistrust such programs because they suspect that management provides exercise programs because they serve the interests of management, not the workers. Finally, many blue-collar workers may resent the money spent on exercise equipment and the like because it does not address their real needs (e.g., the monotony of repetitive work, the exposure to toxic chemicals or other dangers, and the negative effects of shift work). "Health promotion offers a luxury but fails to provide a necessity: relief from the physical harshness of much blue-collar work."[12] In other words, when blue-collar workers are encouraged to become more self-reliant and to take charge of their health, they see this as "blaming the victim" because it refocuses the need for change from the job environment to the individual.

At the lowest end of the stratification hierarchy—the working poor or the unemployed poor—participation in organized team sports is practically nonexistent. Their access to organized sports is severely limited by their lack of resources and the unavailability of teams, equipment, or facilities.

Youth Sport Participation by Socioeconomic Status

There are several tendencies concerning sports participation by the children of the poor. First, they are more likely than the children of the affluent to engage in sports. This is a social arena where they can be somebody, where they can achieve the respect they otherwise do not get.[13] Second, they are more likely than their wealthier counterparts to participate in physical/contact sports (wrestling, boxing, football). Evidence from the United States, Canada, and Germany confirms the generalization that athletes from lower social origins are much more likely to compete in contact sports. Related to that inclination is the tendency of such persons to gravitate to sports that emphasize physical strength (e.g., weight lifting or arm wrestling) and physical toughness (e.g., boxing or wrestling).

A third tendency for children of the poor is to engage in sports that require little equipment or that are publicly funded, such as community youth programs and schools. Basketball, both the playground variety and school teams, is the sport at which urban children of the poor tend to excel. Prowess in basketball begins for these youngsters not in organized leagues or teams, but as individuals joining with individuals to challenge another

Poor children tend to engage in sports that require little equipment or that are funded by the community and schools. (Shutter Point/Ahmed Roberson)

loosely organized group of individuals. Pete Axthelm sensitively characterized it in this way:

> Basketball is the city game. Its battlegrounds are strips of asphalt between tattered wire fences or crumbling buildings; its rhythms grow from the uneven thump of a ball against hard surfaces. It demands no open spaces or lush backyards or elaborate equipment. It doesn't even require specified numbers of players; a one-on-one confrontation in a playground can be as memorable as a full-scale organized game.
>
> Basketball is the game for young athletes without cars or allowances—the game whose drama and action are intensified by its confined spaces and chaotic surroundings....
>
> The game is simple, an act of one man challenging another, twisting, feinting, then perhaps breaking free to leap upward, directing a ball toward a target, a metal hoop ten feet above the ground. But its simple motions swirl into intricate patterns, its variations become almost endless, its brief soaring moments merge into a fascinating dance. To the uninitiated, the patterns may seem fleeting, elusive, even confusing; but on a city playground, a classic play is frozen in the minds of those who see it—a moment of order and achievement in a turbulent, frustrating existence. And a one-on-one challenge takes on wider meaning, defining identity and manhood in an urban society that breeds invisibility.[14]

The fiscal crisis at all levels of government (federal, state, and local) has a negative impact on sports programs for the children of the poor. Municipal governments often cannot fund recreational programs at an appropriate level. City schools are especially hard hit as their funds, which come mostly from property taxes, diminish and federal and state assistance programs are reduced or eliminated.

The children of the affluent, on the other hand, either go to private schools or attend public schools in wealthier districts. Wealthy districts provide more sports opportunities, more coaches, and better facilities and equipment than do the poorer districts. When sports in the more affluent areas are threatened by cuts, the shortfall can usually be saved by "participation fees," which increases the gap between sports participation possibilities for the children of the poor and the nonpoor.

For youngsters growing up in a country club milieu, interest in the sports provided there is natural, and they tend to develop the skills, enhanced by coaches at the clubs, important to the successful performance of these individual sports. Children of the poor, on the other hand, do not have access to golf courses, tennis courts, and swimming pools. Nor do they receive coaching in these individual sports. The only individual sports in which they tend to receive coaching outside of schools are track and field (through community track clubs) and boxing because gyms are located in the poorest and racially segregated urban areas.[15]

Spectator Preferences for Sports by Socioeconomic Status

The mass media have been instrumental in generating an interest in professional football, basketball, baseball, and hockey that transcends social class. Although lacking precise data, we may reasonably assume that since over 98 percent of all U.S. homes have at least one television set, those tuning in to the Super Bowl or the World Series will not be disproportionately from one social class.

There are two kinds of spectators—those who attend in person and those who watch or listen on television or radio.[16] Examining first the attendance at a live sporting event, the data show a consistently strong relationship between sports attendance and social class (see Table 12.1). Foremost, the higher the income, the educational attainment, or both, the more likely the individual will attend. This is not surprising, given the relatively high cost for travel, tickets, parking, and concessions. The average ticket for a National Football League game in 2005, for example, cost $58.95. When the Washington Nationals open their new stadium in the spring of 2008, the tickets will cost as much as $400 per game. As noted in the previous chapter, this is ironic because the stadium was built with $611 million in public funds, yet only the affluent can afford to attend.[17]

Statistics on sports watching on television reveal these patterns: (1) The affluent are much more likely than the poor to watch golf and tennis; (2) the college-educated are more likely to watch college sports than those who did not attend college; and (3) high school graduates or those who have less education are overrepresented among those watching auto racing, demolition derbies, tractor pulls, bowling, and professional wrestling.

An excellent indicator of what type of audience watches a sporting event on television is the sponsor who has purchased advertising for them. Advertisers for golf events include corporations such as IBM, Xerox, Prudential, and United Airlines; professional wrestling is typically sponsored by used-car dealers, beer distributors, and country-music record companies. Clearly, advertisers have researched sports audiences and have discerned that for some sports activities, the audiences are disproportionately from certain social classes.

While simple logic suggests why college graduates appreciate college sports, there is no ready explanation for why the working classes gravitate toward "prole" sports, a name derived from Karl Marx's term for the working class, *proletariat*.

Prole Sports

Why are blue-collar workers especially attracted to particular kinds of sport activities—such as boxing, strongest man competitions, demolition derbies, NASCAR, kickboxing, and drag racing? The economic demographics for drag racing enthusiasts, for example, are that 38 percent have incomes between $30,000 and $39,999; 21 percent

Drag race at the Winter Nationals in Pomona, California, 2007. The various forms of automobile and motorcycle racing appeal especially to the working class. (Shutter Point/William Baer)

are in the $40,000 to $49,999 income bracket; and only 12 percent have incomes of $50,000 or more.[18] On the surface, it would appear that these sports have several common attributes: speed, machines, daring, physical strength, and violence. Let us examine such activities more closely to see why these and other characteristics make them so appealing to this socioeconomic category. However, the possible reasons are speculative because no systematic research has yet been undertaken to assess the actual motivations of blue-collar fans.

The various forms of automobile and motorcycle racing appeal to working-class members for several reasons. First, the artifacts (the machines, the necessary tools, and the equipment) are part of lower-class experience. Blue-collar workers easily identify with these sports because they have access to the machines and the skills to drive them. A second reason is that these vehicles and their drivers represent speed, excitement, and daring to persons whose work is often dull and repetitive. Another possible symbolic reason is that automobiles and motorcycles are symbols of liberation to the working-class person who otherwise feels trapped by his or her situation. The image is one of human and machine united in rebellion against a hostile environment. Two sociologists, Thomas Martin and Kenneth Berry, have suggested that motocross racing is especially attractive to working-class persons because it offers them a chance to prove their worth in aggressive, competitive situations. Such opportunities are not found in their work situations, so they seek them elsewhere.[19]

Pseudosports

Professional wrestling, which we have characterized as a *pseudosport* because its competition is contrived, depends in very large measure on the interest and attendance of blue-collar workers and their families. These types of shows have several common characteristics that may offer some clues as to why the lower classes are especially attracted to them. First, they emphasize strength, power, and violence rather than agility, strategy, and finesse. Second, the actors are easy to identify with. Some emphasize their ethnic or racial background; some are fat; some are muscular; some are heroes (often wrapped in patriotic symbols); and some are villains (often representing the nation's enemies). Female athletes are featured, unlike other sports, allowing lower-class women someone with whom they can identify. There is a strong propensity for spectators to become physically and emotionally involved in the events because of the drama ("good" vs. "evil"). They shout encouragement to their heroes, boo the villains, and occasionally throw things when they get upset with the officiating or with the outcome of the event. The intensity of their feelings is also occasionally manifested in arguments or fights among themselves. The crowd behavior at these events is exactly the opposite of behavior found at country club events such as golf or tennis. Unlike the passivity of spectators at those sports, the fans at wrestling matches are intensely involved.

Symbolically, wrestling matches are morality plays. As sociologist Gregory Stone put it: "There is always the 'hero' who attempts to defeat the 'villain' within the moral framework of the rules of the game. It is a case of law versus outlaw, cops and robbers, the 'good guys' versus the 'bad guys.'"[20] The fans tend to identify with the virtuous hero. When justice prevails and the hero triumphs, the fans' belief in law and order is reinforced. When the villain wins, the victory is attributed to foul play; when the rematch occurs, justice will finally reign. If it does not, then an alternate view of the world is reinforced. In this view, which Arthur Shostak posited as a major working-class belief, the world operates so that some persons take advantage of others and get away with it.[21]

In summary, the prole sports and pseudosports have several characteristics in common that make them especially attractive to the working classes:

1. The necessary equipment (such as automobiles or muscles) and skills (driving, mechanical aptitude, or self-defense) are part of working-class life.
2. The sports emphasize physical prowess and manhood (machismo).
3. They are exciting and therefore serve as an emotional outlet and an antidote to other-

wise routine lives. Some focus on the danger of high speed and powerful machines. Others stress violence to machines or human beings. Still others contrive events to excite the crowds (e.g., wrestling events such as tag teams, Texas Death Matches, and the Battle Royales). And recently the sport of mixed martial arts (Ultimate Fighting Championship) has emerged, where the combatants hit, kick, and pummel each other with few if any limitations. The goal is to defeat the opponent without the normal rules of combat.
4. There is strong identification with heroes who are like the spectators in ethnicity, language, or behavior.
5. The sports are not school related.
6. With few exceptions, working-class spectator sports, as opposed to working-class participation sports, are individual, rather than team-oriented.

Segregation in Sports by Social Class

We have noted that the different social strata have some unique preferences in sport. Although they enjoy some sports in common (especially the mass media presentations of professional football, basketball, and baseball), the self-selection process in sports tends to segregate by social class. Let us look beyond this process to ascertain whether there are any other barriers that separate the social classes.

At the participatory level, some barriers serve to segregate the social classes. In sports such as swimming, golf, and tennis, the affluent compete in private clubs or at facilities limited to residents in an exclusive neighborhood or condominium complex (at some of these, access is controlled by fences, walls, and even armed guards). The middle classes and lower classes may participate in these sports only at public facilities. In a given city, then, a dual system of competition often exists—tournaments or competitions for the wealthy and a separate set of events for the general public. The quality of play at these two levels varies, with the wealthy usually rated better because of their access to better facilities, equipment, and private tutors. This difference in skill also serves to segregate affluent from less affluent players.

Spectators, too, are often segregated by social class at general-interest sporting events. This is accomplished in several ways. First, ticket prices often exclude the poor, especially when season tickets are considered. The common practice of different prices according to seating location also tends to segregate persons by socioeconomic status (contrary to the image suggested by former president Reagan of the corporate executive sitting next to a janitor at a game). The affluent rarely sit in the relatively low-cost bleacher seats, and the poor rarely purchase reserved seats or box seats and do not have access to seats in the skyboxes.

The ultimate in differentially priced seating locations, and thus segregation by social class, is the purchase of exclusive luxury suites (also called "skyboxes"). These rooms are typically outfitted with expensive furniture, a bar, and other luxuries. They are purchased by individuals or corporations for very high prices, as noted in chapter 10. For example, the prices for the luxury suites of the Washington Nationals start at $150,000 a season.

This ostentatious display of wealth is an example of *conspicuous consumption,* the purchase and display of expensive items to flaunt one's high status. This phenomenon is found among the wealthy, the near-wealthy, and those who fake wealth. Although all sports offer this opportunity, conspicuous consumption is most commonly found at the premier events, for example, at the Super Bowl, the World Series, the Indianapolis 500, the Kentucky Derby, and heavyweight boxing championship matches. Many status-conscious persons use these highly visible events to impress others. They buy the expensive seats, wear costly jewelry and furs, and are driven in limousines to the arena.

At the other end of the stratification hierarchy, the poor and near-poor cannot afford to attend sports. The high costs likely keep the poorest away from the sports arenas except as workers (vendors, janitors, parking attendants). Even if the poor could afford seats for regular events, they are priced out completely from premier events. Since these games are sold out (with corporate sponsors holding huge blocks of seats), scalpers sell the precious few remaining seats at premium prices.[22] To repeat John Underwood's observation in chapter 10, the high cost of going to sports events has prevented the poor and the working poor from attending them.[23]

SOCIAL MOBILITY AND SPORT

Typically, North Americans believe that the United States and Canada have "open" class systems—that positions of high pay and prestige are open to those with the requisite talents and aptitudes, regardless of their social origin. The world of sport has done more than its share to give substance to this belief as poor boys (not girls) from rural and urban areas, whether white or black, have skyrocketed to fame and fortune through success in sports. This section investigates the extent to which social mobility actually operates in the sports world. Let us first examine the arguments and evidence supporting this belief.

Sport as a Mobility Escalator

The most obvious examples of sports participation facilitating upward social mobility are persons from low socioeconomic backgrounds who become wealthy and famous because of their athletic ability. This happens in almost all sports except those largely restricted to the upper class, such as polo, yachting, and, to a great extent, golf and tennis. Most typically, it occurs in boxing, in which the athletes are recruited almost exclusively from the lower socioeconomic levels, and some will earn many millions of dollars during their careers.

Successful athletes in some sports (football and basketball in particular) must attend both high school and college. In this way, sports participation has the effect of encouraging or (in some cases) forcing persons to attain more education than they might otherwise achieve. This, in turn, increases their opportunities for success outside the sports world.

At the high school level, athletic participation appears to have consequences. Research shows consistently that, compared to their nonathlete peers, athletes as a category have better grades, more positive attitudes toward school, and more interest in continuing their education after high school.[24] There are three confounding problems with the findings in this research. First, researchers have found it difficult to determine whether sports participation makes the difference or whether there are qualities that successful athletes have that also give them an edge in school, such as willingness to work hard and follow orders as well as a strong goal-orientation. There is a powerful selection factor at work here as young people choose to participate or not. Similarly, coaches might weed out certain types of problematic individuals. Second, perhaps the differences are effects of family background and social class. And third, there is a problem with comparing athletes with nonathletes on grades, delinquency, and the like if athletes must maintain a minimum grade point average to remain athletes. Similarly, students can also lose their athlete status if they get in serious trouble in school or in the community. Removing problem people from the athlete category "loads the dice" in favor of finding positive results comparing athletes with nonathletes.

For all of these reasons we should be wary of research comparing athletes with nonathletes. That said, the research shows that there are positive consequences for participation in high school sports. Sports success translates into high status in the school, which has positive benefits for self-concept and for identifying positively with the school. Athletes are less likely than nonathletes to drop out of school.[25] And athletes who believe that they will get a scholarship to college will be motivated to prepare for post–high school education.

College athletes who come from a family of low social status will almost automatically surpass their parents because of their superior educational attainments. (This comparison of children's status with that of their parents measures *intergenerational mobility*.) This has been confirmed by

John Loy's study of 1,020 athletes who had competed at UCLA for four years.[26] The data from this study suggest several interesting relationships. First, although the job prestige of former college athletes is fairly stable regardless of the sport played, the occupational prestige of fathers varies a good deal. Apparently, a college education (remember, these athletes had played at least four years) makes the attainment of upper-middle-class jobs possible, regardless of the student's social origin. Second, sons surpassed their fathers in occupational prestige regardless of the sport. Thus, these data indicate the increased social mobility achieved by college athletes when they are compared with their fathers.

This seemingly great mobility by college athletes compared to their fathers may be spurious, however. First, the comparison guarantees that the sons will have exceeded the fathers. Not all of the fathers have graduated from college, but the sample is composed of sons who have. Second, a gap between fathers and sons will always exist because of the general trend to upgrade educational levels. The best method to determine whether athletes have more potential for social mobility, therefore, is to compare them with nonathletes.

We have seen that success in sports enhances the possibility of attending college. This, in turn, increases the probability of attaining a high-status job, as the Loy study and several other studies have demonstrated. Let's examine four representative studies.

In an important study, Allen L. Sack and Robert Thiel compared football players with nonathletes who had graduated from Notre Dame between 1946 and 1965.[27] They found that (1) although the football players had come from poorer backgrounds, they had achieved equivalent incomes with the nonathletes; (2) nonathletes were more likely to have higher-status jobs and to have obtained advanced degrees; and (3) first-string players had much higher incomes than nonstarters and were overrepresented among top-ranking executives in their companies. This study provided strong evidence that athletic participation in college plus graduation does enhance upward social mobility.

Clifford Adelman compared the mobility of college athletes with that of nonathletes at a number of colleges and universities.[28] This research followed a group of 1972 high school seniors through 1986, looking at a subsample of those males who played football and basketball in college and those males who did not. He found that the athletes (1) were more likely to be home owners, (2) were less likely to be unemployed, and (3) had earnings 10 percent above the average for the nonfootball and nonbasketball group. We should be cautious in generalizing from these data, however, because the study did not differentiate athletes who participated in big-time football and basketball programs from those at smaller colleges.

Another study compared male athletes and nonathletes who entered college in 1970 and surveyed them in 1980, six years after their expected graduation.[29] The researchers found that former athletes working in business, military, or manual labor occupations were better off financially than former nonathletes. The exception was that former athletes who had become high school teachers lagged behind nonathletes in income.

As a final example, a study of 1992 high school seniors compared the educational and labor market outcomes for athletes and nonathletes eight years after scheduled high school graduation.[30] The findings were that high school athletes, compared to nonathletes, were more likely to (1) have attended college and earned a bachelor's degree, (2) be employed full-time, and (3) be earning a higher income.

These representative studies lead to the tentative conclusion that male athletes are upwardly mobile. There are at least three possible reasons for this. First, athletic participation may lead to various forms of "occupational sponsorship." The male college athlete is a popular hero; therefore, a greater likelihood exists that he will date and marry a woman who comes from a higher socioeconomic background than if he were a nonathlete. If this occurs, then the chances are that the college athlete's father-in-law will provide him with benefits in the business world much greater than those available to the average nonathlete. Another form of sponsorship may come from well-placed alumni who offer former athletes positions in their businesses after graduation. This may be done to help the firm's public relations, or it may be part of a payoff in the recruiting wars that some alumni are willing to underwrite.

A second reason why athletes may fare better is that the selection process for many jobs requires the applicant to be "well-rounded," that is, to have had a number of successful experiences outside the classroom. An extreme example of this is in the selection of Rhodes Scholars, which requires, in addition to superior grades, participation in extracurricular activities and demonstrated athletic ability.

Finally, there is the possibility that participation in highly competitive sports situations will lead to the development of attitudes and behavior patterns highly valued in the larger occupational world. If attributes such as leadership, human relations skills, teamwork, good work habits, and a well-developed competitive drive are acquired in sports, they may ensure that athletes will succeed in other endeavors. (See chapter 5.) Considerable debate surrounds the issue of whether sports build character or whether only certain kinds of personalities survive the sport experience. There may be a self-fulfilling prophecy at work here, however: If employers assume that athletes possess these valued character traits, they will make their hiring and advancement decisions accordingly, giving athletes the advantage.

Demythologizing the Social Mobility-through-Sport Hypothesis

The belief that sport is a mobility escalator is built on a succession of myths. These *myths* are: (1) Sport provides a free college education. (2) Sport leads to a college degree. (3) A professional sports career is possible. (4) Sport is a way out of poverty, especially for racial minorities. (5) Because of Title IX, women now have many opportunities for upward mobility through sport. (6) A professional sports career provides security for life.

Myth: Sport Provides a Free Education

One assumption of the "social mobility through sports participation" position is that involvement in high school sport leads to college scholarships, which is especially helpful to poor youth who could not afford college otherwise. The problem with this assumption is that few high school athletes receive full ride scholarships. Consider the following facts:

- Item: In 2003 there were 5.75 million students in the NCAA Division I, II, or III institutions. Of these, about 132,758 (2.3 percent) had some form of athletic scholarship. Most of these, however, were on partial scholarships. Only 17,561 of the athletes (4.7 percent) had full scholarships providing room, food, tuition, and books.[31]
- Item: According to the National Federation of State High School Associations, only 1 percent of the seven million high school students in the United States will receive Division I scholarships.
- Item: While women comprise about 57 percent of all college students, they make up only 43 percent of intercollegiate athletes and receive only about 38 percent of the athletic scholarship money.[32]
- Item: If you are a male athlete in a so-called minor sport (swimming, tennis, golf, gymnastics, cross-country, wrestling), the chances of a full-ride scholarship are virtually nil. The best hope is a partial scholarship, if that, since these sports are underfunded and in danger of being eliminated at many schools.

Myth: Participation in Sports Leads to a College Degree

A problem with the assumption that sports participation leads to a college degree is that only about half of college athletes receive college degrees (see chapter 6). This is especially true for those athletes who believe that they will become professional athletes. Football, basketball, and, increasingly, baseball players play college ball for at least a while before turning to the professional level. This practice of using college sport as preparation for a professional career should have the benefit of encouraging athletes to graduate, which would help their careers after sports. Data show, however, that relatively few professional athletes do graduate from college (for example, only one-fifth of those in the NBA and one-third in the NFL have college degrees; the rate is even lower for professional baseball, where 86 percent have not graduated, and in hockey, where 92 percent of NHL players have not graduated).

There are a number of barriers to graduation for athletes. One obvious problem is the inordinate demand on their time and energy for practice, meetings, travel, and other sport-related activities. Many athletes, because of these pressures, are counseled to take easy courses that maintain eligibility but that may not meet graduation requirements. The result is either to delay graduation or to make graduation an unrealistic goal.

Another barrier to graduation for many college athletes is that they are recruited for athletic prowess rather than for academic ability. About 12 percent of recruited athletes in Division I schools failed to meet the regular admission standards of their universities. Athletes from the ghetto who have attended inferior high schools, for example, are generally not prepared for the intellectual demands of college. As noted in chapter 6, after six years, only about 4 out of 10 black football players and 3 out of 10 black basketball players in big-time programs graduate. Put another way, *whereas about one-half of white players do not graduate, two-thirds of black players do not graduate.*

A third barrier to graduation for college athletes is themselves, as they do not take advantage of their scholarships to work toward graduation. This is the case for those who perceive their college experience only as preparation for their professional careers in sport. Study for them is necessary only to maintain their eligibility. Such a view is unrealistic for all but the superstars, as we will see shortly. It is also shortsighted because even a successful professional athletic career is limited to a few years, and not many professional athletes are able to translate their success in the pros to success in their postathletic careers. Such a problem is especially true for blacks, who often face employment discrimination in the wider society.

Myth: A Professional Sports Career Is Probable

A survey by the Center for the Study of Sport in Society found that two-thirds of African American athletes between the ages of thirteen and eighteen believed that they could earn a living playing professional sports (more than double the proportion of young white males who held such beliefs). Moreover, African American parents were four times more likely than white parents to believe that their children were destined for careers as professional athletes.[33]

If these young athletes do play as professionals, the economic rewards are excellent, as shown in the previous chapter. The dream of financial success through a professional sports career is just, however, a dream for all but an infinitesimal number.[34] A career in professional sport is nearly impossible to attain because of the fierce competition for so few openings. Sociologist Wilbert Leonard has calculated that the odds that an American male between the ages of fifteen and thirty-nine will be a professional athlete in the four major team sports are about 20,000 to 1.[35]

Not only are the odds long of making it to the professional level, if one is good enough and lucky enough to make it, the career will be short, averaging three to seven years in team sports and three to twelve years in individual sports.[36]

Myth: Sport Is a Way Out of Poverty, Especially for Racial Minorities

Sport appears to be a major way for African Americans to escape the ghetto. The major professional sports are dominated numerically by blacks. Though only 12 percent of the population, African Americans constitute around 80 percent of the players in professional basketball and about two-thirds of the players in professional football. Moreover, blacks lead the list of the highest moneymakers in sport (salaries, commercial sponsorships). These facts, while true, are illusory. Consider the following:

- Blacks are rarely found in certain sports (automobile racing, tennis, golf, bowling, hockey).

- Blacks are rarely found in positions of authority in sport (head coaches, athletic directors, general managers, owners).
- Only a very small percentage of African Americans make it to the professional level as athletes. Of the 40,000 young blacks who play high school basketball, only 35 will make the NBA and 7 will be starters. In sum, using the words of Harry Edwards as he referred to the slim chances for young black athletes: "Statistically, you have a better chance of getting hit by a meteorite in the next 10 years than getting work as an athlete, and the chances for African American women are much less than for men."[37]

The myth is so pervasive. That is why many boys spend many hours per day developing their speed, strength, or "moves" to the virtual exclusion of those abilities that have a greater likelihood of paying off in upward mobility—mathematical reasoning and communication skills. Although this is true for many lower-class boys, it is especially damaging for blacks whose heroes are almost exclusively in music or in sports. As Jack Scott asked: "Gifted black athletes will usually make out all right, but what happens to the thousands of young unathletic black children whose only heroes are sports stars? How many brilliant doctors, lawyers, teachers, poets, and artists have been lost because intelligent but uncoordinated black youths had been led to believe by a racist society that their only chance for getting ahead was to develop a thirty foot jump shot or to run the hundred [yards] in 9.3?"[38]

This futile pursuit of sports stardom is of serious consequence to the black community, according to Harry Edwards. Blacks, spending their energies and talents on athletic skills, are not pursuing occupations that would help them meet their political and material needs. Thus, because of belief in the sports myth, they remain dependent on whites and white institutions.[39]

Despite the low odds of making it as a professional athlete, many young black males see sport as their only hope to escape from a life of crime, poverty, and despair. They latch on to the dream of athletic success partly because they have few opportunities for middle-class success. They spend many hours per day developing their speed, strength, jumping height, or "moves," to the virtual exclusion of abilities that have a greater likelihood of paying off in upward mobility, such as reading comprehension, mathematical reasoning, communication skills, and computer literacy. Sociologist Jay Coakley puts it this way:

> My best guess is that fewer than 6,000 African Americans, or about 1 in 6,600, are making a good living as professional athletes. Data from the U.S. Department of Labor indicates that, in 2004, 18,640 African American men and women were classified as athletes, coaches, umpires, and related workers. In that same year, 50,630 African Americans were physicians and surgeons, 44,840 were lawyers, and 69,388 were college and university teachers. Therefore, there were thirty-six times more African Americans working in these prestigious professions than African Americans working in all of sports. Furthermore, physicians, lawyers, and college teachers have greater lifetime earnings than most athletes whose playing careers, on average, last less than five years.[40]

This futile pursuit of sports stardom has serious consequences for individual African Americans as well as for the African American community. Foremost, they spend their time learning skills that are worthless in the job market. Thus, their belief in the "sports as a way up" myth causes them to remain dependent on whites and white institutions. Salim Muwakkil, an African American political analyst, argues:

> If African Americans are to exploit the socioeconomic options opened by varied civil rights struggles more fully, blacks must reduce the disproportionate allure of sports in their communities. Black leadership must contextualize athletic success by promoting other avenues to social status, intensifying the struggle for access to those avenues and better educating youth about those potholes on the road to the stadium.[41]

John Hoberman also challenges the assumption that sport has progressive consequences.[42] The success of African Americans in the highly visible sports gives white America a false sense of black progress and interracial harmony. But the social progress of African Americans in general has little relationship to the apparent integration that they have achieved on the country's playing fields:

> The illusory sense of racial harmony on countless playing fields across America masks the true depth of the racial conflict that survives in one and the same society. In this sense, the material gains of a Michael Jordan or a Tiger Woods impede the process of social change. For every black Superstar, there are thousands of blacks behind bars.[43]

Hoberman also contends that the numerical superiority of African Americans in sport, coupled with their disproportionate underrepresentation in other professions, reinforces the racist ideology that African Americans are physically superior to whites but are inferior to them intellectually. In short, sport harms African Americans by serving up imagery and metaphors that reinforce racism and the racial divisions that continue to plague U.S. society.

All of this is not meant to suggest that talented African Americans should not seek a career in professional sport. Professional sport is a legitimate career with the potential for exceptional monetary rewards. What is harmful, to reiterate, is that the odds of success are so slim—rendering extraordinary, sustained effort futile and misguided for the vast majority. If this effort were directed at areas having better odds of success, then upward mobility would occur for many more. The late African American tennis star Arthur Ashe argued that "we have been on the same roads—sports and entertainment—too long. We need to pull over, fill up at the library and speed away to Congress, and the Supreme Court, the unions, and the business world."[44]

Myth: Women Now Have Sport as a Vehicle for Upward Mobility Because of New Opportunities

Since the passage of Title IX in 1972 (see chapter 14), sports participation by women in high school and college has increased dramatically. In 1973, for example, while fifty thousand men received some form of college scholarship for their athletic abilities, women received only fifty. Now women receive about 45 percent of the money allotted to athletic scholarship (still less than half, but a considerable improvement). This has allowed many women to attend college who otherwise could not have afforded it. That is positive because of the indirect educational benefits accruing from athletic ability. Upward mobility from sport is another matter for women. Women have fewer opportunities than men in professional team sports. The opportunities are few and the rewards minimal in beach volleyball (where, by the way, the uniforms are skimpy bikinis), soccer, and professional basketball. The salaries for professional women basketball players, for example, fall far behind those of men. In 2007, women with four or more years of experience in the WNBA received $49,134, and the maximum salary was $93,000 (with few endorsement opportunities). Compare this with the average player salary of more than $5 million in the NBA, with the highest paid, Shaquille O'Neal, making $20 million in salary and another $15 million in endorsements.

A few women in individual professional sports do well financially—Serena and Venus Williams in tennis, Michelle Wie in golf, Danica Patrick in automobile racing, and a relative handful of others. But the opportunities for American women are few in tennis and golf, where women from other countries have tended to dominate. And in automobile racing, the sport is almost exclusively male (owners, drivers, pit crews). Women in sports are rare.

Women have more opportunities as professionals in individual sports such as tennis, golf, ice skating, bowling, pool, and track. Ironically, the sports with the greatest monetary rewards for women are those of the middle and upper classes. These sports are expensive, and they require considerable individual coaching as well as access to private facilities. In short, sport offers poor women only very limited opportunities for upward mobility. Speaking of African Americans in this regard, Harry Edwards has observed, "We must also consider that to the extent that sport provides an escape route from the ghetto at all, it does so only for black males . . . and the escape of a few black men does not mean that an equal number of black women will go with them as their wives or girlfriends; consequently there is no guarantee that even a few black women will benefit from the success achieved by black male professional athletes."[45]

Opportunities in sport apart from the athlete role (trainers, scouts, referees, sports journalists, and coaches) are more limited for women than for men. Ironically, with the passage of Title IX, which increased the participation rates of women in schools so dramatically, there has been a decline in the number and proportion of women as coaches and athletic administrators. In 2007, for example, women coached only 43 percent of women's collegiate teams and held less than 8 percent of athletic director positions.[46]

Myth: A Professional Sports Career Provides Lifelong Security

Even when a professional sport career is attained, the probabilities of fame and fortune are limited. The average length of a career in professional sport is short. This leaves, on average, about forty additional years before retirement. The pay may be relatively high, but the employment does not last very long. Even those few athletes with careers exceeding ten years face the reality that by their middle thirties they are no longer employable as athletes.

Ex–professional athletes leave sport, on average, when they are in their late twenties or early thirties, at a time when their nonathlete peers have begun to establish themselves in occupations leading toward retirement in forty years or so. What are the ex–professional athletes to do with their remaining productive years?

Exiting a sports career can be relatively smooth or it can be difficult. Some athletes plan ahead, preparing themselves for other careers in sport (coaching, scouting, reporting, administering) or for a nonsport occupation. Others do not prepare themselves for this abrupt change. They may not have a college degree. They often do not spend their off-seasons apprenticing in nonsport jobs. Exiting the athlete role is difficult for many because they *lose* (1) what they have focused on for most of their lives, (2) the primary source of their personal identity, (3) their physical prowess, (4) adulation bordering on worship from others, (5) the money and perquisites fame, (6) the camaraderie with teammates, (7) the intense "highs" of competition, and (8) status (most ex-athletes are downwardly mobile upon retirement from sport). A study by the NFL Players Association found that emotional difficulties, divorce, and financial strain were common problems for retired professional football players.[47]

For most, the real world is a step down. Big-time pro athletes are pampered like royalty. They fly first class while hired hands pay the bills and tote the luggage. High-powered executives and heads of state fawn over them. "You begin to feel like Louis XIV," says Wilbert McClure, a two-time Golden Gloves boxing champion who is now a psychologist and counselor to basketball players. Step off the pedestal and everything changes. McClure likens it to "being dipped into hell."[48]

There is some potential for a sports-related career after one's playing days are over: coaching, managing, scouting, sportscasting, public relations, and administration are all possibilities for the former athlete, but the opportunities are severely limited, especially if the athlete is a minority group member (see chapter 13) or a woman.

SUMMARY

Two themes dominate this chapter. The first theme is that sport, like the larger society, is stratified. Socioeconomic status is related to the types of sports one participates in and watches. The lower one's status, the more one is inclined toward contact sports and such pseudosports as professional wrestling. The socioeconomic strata are segregated in sport not only by preferences but also by such barriers as entrance requirements and prohibitive costs.

The second theme is that sports participation has limited potential as a social mobility escalator. There is evidence that being a successful athlete enhances self-confidence and the probability of attending college. Thus, social mobility is accomplished through sport indirectly because of the increased employment potential from educational attainment. Social mobility through sport is limited, however, if one is provided an inferior education, as is often the case. It is also limited by failure to graduate and the very low number of positions in professional sport. It is limited, even almost nonexistent, for women. Even for those who attain major league status, the probabilities of fame and fortune are small because of the relatively short careers and injuries.

The myth that sport is a mobility escalator is especially dangerous for minority youth. Ghetto youngsters who devote their lives to the pursuit of athletic stardom are, except for the fortunate few, doomed to failure in sport and in the real world, where sports skills are essentially irrelevant to occupational placement and advancement.

Another negative consequence is more subtle but is very important. Sport contributes to the ideology that legitimizes social inequalities and promotes the myth that all it takes to succeed is extraordinary effort. George Sage makes this point forcefully:

> The overall effect of the few athletes who do become professional athletes reproduces the belief system among the general public that the American social class system is more open to social mobility than it really is. Because the few rags-to-riches athletes are made so visible, the social mobility theme is maintained. This reflects the opportunity structure of society in general—the success of a few reproduces the belief in social mobility among the many.[49]

WEB RESOURCES

www.forbes.com
Forbes magazine provides lists each year on the richest entertainers (including athletes), richest Americans, and richest people worldwide.

www.ssc.wisc.edu/irp
For information on poverty in the United States, see this website for the University of Wisconsin's Institute for Research on Poverty.

www.inequality.org
This website provides general information on various dimensions of inequality in the United States.

www.bus.ucf.edu/sport
This website is for the center for the Institute for Diversity and Ethics in Sport, University of Central Florida. Annually it produces a *Race and Gender Report Card* that provides the most recent data on the placement of racial/ethnic minorities and women in various sports occupations (coach, administrator, sports information director, etc.).

http://www.teammarketing.com/
This website provides the Fan Cost Index for all teams in the MLB, NBA, NFL, and NHL.

NOTES

1. Ronald Reagan quoted in "Athletics a Great Equalizer, Reagan Tells NCAA," *NCAA News*, 10 January 1990, p. 1.

2. This section is taken from D. Stanley Eitzen and Maxine Baca Zinn, *In Conflict and Order: Understanding Society*, 11th ed. (Boston: Allyn & Bacon, 2007), 229–236, 253–276. For a discussion on the sociological theories of inequality and their relevance to sport, see John Sugden and Alan Thomlinson, "Theorizing Sport, Social Class and Status," in *Handbook of Sport Studies*, ed. Jay Coakley and Eric Dunning (London: Sage, 2000), 309–321.

3. Harold Kerbo, *Social Stratification and Inequality* (New York: McGraw-Hill, 1983), 11.

4. Joe R. Feagin and Clairece Booher Feagin, *Social Problems*, 5th ed. (Upper Saddle River, N.J.: Prentice Hall, 1997), 26–27.

5. "400 Richest People in America," *Forbes*, 9 October 2006.

6. Federal Reserve data, reported in Teresa Tritch, "The Rise of the Super-Rich," *New York Times*, 19 July 2006, http://select.nytimes.com/2006/07/19/opinion/19talkingpoints.html?pagewanted=print.

7. Bernard Sanders, "Whiter American Democracy," *Los Angeles Times*, 16 January 2004, p. B1.

8. U.S. Census Bureau data reported in *The Chronicle of Higher Education*, 27 August 2004.

9. Jay Coakley, *Sports in Society*, 9th ed. (New York: McGraw-Hill), 329–331.

10. Thorstein Veblen, *Theory of the Leisure Class* (New York: Macmillan, 1899).

11. Kerry Pechter, "Corporate Fitness and Blue-Collar Fears," *Across the Board* 23 (October 1986): 14–21.

12. Ibid., 17.

13. Michael A. Messner, *Power at Play* (Boston: Beacon Press, 1992).

14. Pete Axthelm, *The City Game: Basketball in New York* (New York: Harper and Row, 1970), ix–x.

15. L. J. D. Wacquant, "The Social Logic of Boxing in Black Chicago: Toward a Sociology of Pugilism," *Sociology of Sport Journal* 9 (September 1992): 221–254.

16. For a scholarly historical analysis of sports spectators, see Allen Guttmann, *Sports Spectators* (New York: Columbia University Press, 1986).

17. Thomas Heath, "That's Not Peanuts," *Washington Post National Weekly Edition*, 18 June 2007, p. 36.

18. Candyce March Racing, "Sponsorship Inquiries," n.d., http://Candycemarsh.com/taw/sponsorship.htm.

19. Thomas W. Martin and Kenneth J. Berry, "Competitive Sport in Post-Industrial Society: The Case of the Motocross Racer," *Journal of Popular Culture* 8 (Summer 1974): 107–120.

20. Gregory P. Stone, "American Sports: Play and Display," in *Sport: Readings from a Sociological Perspective*, ed. Eric Dunning (Toronto: University of Toronto Press, 1972), 59.

21. Arthur B. Shostak, *Blue Collar Life* (New York: Random House, 1969), 202.

22. D. Stanley Eitzen, "Classism in Sport: The Powerless Bear the Burden," *Journal of Sport and Social Issues* 20 (February 1996): 113–116.

23. John Underwood, "From Baseball and Apple Pie, to Greed and Sky Boxes," *New York Times*, 31 October 1993, sec. A, p. 22.

24. See, for example, C. Roger Rees and Andrew W. Miracle, "Sport and Education," in Coakley and Dunning, *Handbook of Sport Studies*, 277–290. See also James P. McHale, Penelope G. Vendon, Loren Bush, Derek Richer, David Shaw, and Brienne Smith, "Patterns of Personal and Social Adjustment among Sport-Involved and Noninvolved Urban Middle-School Children," *Sociology of Sport Journal* 22, no. 2 (2005): 119–136.

25. R. B. McNeal, Jr., "Extracurricular Activities and High School Dropouts," *Sociology of Education* 64 (1995): 62–81.

26. John W. Loy, Jr., "The Study of Sport and Social Mobility," *International Review of Sport Sociology* 7 (1972): 5–23.

27. Allen L. Sack and Robert Thiel, "College Football and Social Mobility: A Case Study of Notre Dame Football Players," *Sociology of Education* 52 (January 1979): 60–66.

28. Douglas Lederman, "Students Who Competed in College Sports Fare Better in Job Market Than Those Who Didn't, Report Says," *Chronicle of Higher Education*, 26 September 1990, sec. A, 47–48.

29. Daniel J. Henderson, Alexandre Olbrecht, and Solomon W. Polachek, "Do Former Athletes Earn More at Work?" *Journal of Human Resources* (Summer 2006): 558–577.

30. Devon Carlson and Leslie Scott, "What Is the Status of High School Athletes Eight Years after Their Senior Year?" (NCES 2005-303, National Center for Education Statistics, "Statistics in Brief," September 2005).

31. Coakley, *Sports in Society*, 308.

32. Women's Sports Foundation, "Pay Inequity in Athletics" (New York: Women's Sports Foundation, 2007).

33. Cited in John Cimons, "Improbable Dreams: African Americans Are a Dominant Presence in Professional Sports—Do Blacks Suffer as a Result?" *U.S. News and World Report*, 24 March 1997, 46–52.

34. Much of the remainder of the chapter is dependent on D. Stanley Eitzen, *Fair and Foul: Beyond the Myths and Paradoxes of Sport*, 3rd ed. (Lanham, Md.: Rowman & Littlefield, 2006), chap. 9.

35. W. M. Leonard II, "The Odds of Transiting from One Level of Sports Participation to Another," *Sociology of Sport Journal* 13, no. 3 (1996): 288–299.

36. Coakley, *Sports in Society*, 300.

37. Harry Edwards, quoted in Bob Oates, "The Great American Tease: Sport as a Way Out of the Ghetto," *New York Times*, 8 June 1979, p. 32. See also Harry Edwards, "Crisis of Black Athletes on the Eve of the 21st Century," *Society* 37 (March/April 2000): 9–13.

38. Jack Scott, *The Athletic Revolution* (New York: Free Press, 1971), 178–179.

39. Harry Edwards, "The Black Athletes: 20th Century Gladiators for White Americans," *Psychology Today*, November 1973, 43–52.

40. Coakley, *Sports in Society*, 348.

41. Salim Muwakkil, "Which Team Are You On?" *In These Times*, 3 May 1998, p. 16.

42. John Hoberman, *Darwin's Athletes: How Sport Has Damaged Black America and Preserved the Myth of Race* (Boston: Houghton Mifflin, 1997); and John Hoberman, "The Price of 'Black Dominance,'" *Society* 37 (March/April 2000): 49–56.

43. Jim Nadell, review of Hoberman's *Darwin's Athletes*, *Z Magazine*, December 1997, 54.

44. Arthur Ashe, "Send Your Children to the Libraries," *New York Times*, 6 February 1977, p. 2S.

45. Edwards, "The Black Athletes," 47.

46. Women's Sports Foundation, "Pay Inequity in Athletics."

47. JoAnne Tremaine Drahota and D. Stanley Eitzen, "The Role Exit of Professional Athletes," *Sociology of Sport Journal* 15 (September 1998): 263–278; JoAnne Tremaine Drahota, "The Role Exit of Professional Athletes" (Ph.D. dissertation, Colorado State University, 1996); and Michael A. Messner, *Power at Play*.

48. Reported in a five-part series by Brian Hewitt in the *Chicago Sun-Times,* 19–22 September 1993.

49. George H. Sage, *Power and Ideology in American Sport*, 2nd ed. (Champaign, Ill.: Human Kinetics, 1998), 53.

CHAPTER 13

Racial-Ethnic Minorities and Sport

Marty Cutler and Jack Johnson in the ring, ca. 1914. In 1908 Johnson became the first African American world heavyweight champion. (Library of Congress)

Racial minorities in the United States continue to face systematic and pervasive discrimination against them. Although most Americans agree with this sociological fact, they also tend to believe that sport is an oasis free of racial problems and tensions. After all, the argument goes, sports are competitive; fans, coaches, and players want to win; clearly, the color of the players involved is not a factor, only their performance. A further argument is that the proportion of African Americans in the major team sports, which far exceeds their proportion in the U.S. population, indicates an absence of racism. The facts, however, lead to a very different conclusion. Rather than being free from racism, sport as a microcosm of the larger society reflects the same racial problems as society.

The objective of this chapter is to document the facts showing that discrimination based on race and ethnicity is prevalent in sport. We hope to alert the reader to this continuing societal problem and to bury the belief that sport is a meritocracy in which skin color is disregarded.

RACIAL-ETHNIC MINORITIES: SOME DEFINITIONS

Race is a social category regarded as distinct because the members supposedly share some genetically transmitted traits.[1] The races, however, are socially constructed categories. People have arbitrarily placed others into racial categories based on their physical attributes (most notably skin color)—but these differences are really minor attributes and can vary greatly within each category. Moreover, the categories used to divide people into races are not fixed; they vary from society to society. Historically, in the United States the laws defining who is black, for example, have varied from state to state. Tennessee law once defined as black anyone who had at least one great-grandparent who was black. Other southern states defined as black any person who had black ancestry (the "one drop of black blood" rule). By either of these laws Tiger Woods would be black, because he is one-fourth African American, one-fourth Thai, one-fourth Chinese, one-eighth Native American, and one-eighth white European. In Brazil he would be considered white; in the U.S. media he is described as black.

Social scientists reject race as a valid way to define human groups. The accepted view in the scientific community is that races are a social invention. They do not exist biologically. Scientific examination of the human genome finds no genetic differences between the so-called races. Fossil and deoxyribonucleic acid (DNA) evidence shows that humans are all one race, evolved in the last one hundred thousand years from the same small number of tribes that migrated out of Africa and colonized the world.[2] Although there is no such thing as biological race, races are real insofar as they are *socially defined*. In other words, races are real because people believe they are real. Worldwide, and certainly within the United States, race divides people between "us" and "them."

Ethnicity, unlike race, refers to the cultural heritage of a group rather than biology. An ethnic group is a category of people who share a common culture (language or dialect, religion, customs, and history). Examples of ethnic groups in the United States are Italian Americans, Arab Americans, Greek Americans, Irish Americans, and Mexican Americans.

In the United States, race and ethnicity both serve to mark groups as different and typically as "others." Groups labeled "races" by the larger society are bounded together by their common social and economic conditions. As a result, they develop distinctive cultural (ethnic) characteristics. Thus, we often refer to them as *racial-ethnic groups* (or racially defined ethnic groups). The term "racial-ethnic group" refers to groups that are socially subordinated and culturally distinct in society. It is meant to include (1) the systematic discrimination of socially constructed racial groups and (2) their distinctive cultural arrangements. The categories *African American, Latino, Asian American,* and *Native American* have been constructed as both racially and culturally distinct.

Different racial and ethnic groups are unequal in power, resources, and prestige. Why are some groups dominant and others subordinate? The basic reason is power—power derived from technology, weapons, property, or economic resources.

Those holding superior power in a society—the *majority group*—establish a system of inequality by dominating less powerful groups. A *minority group* is any distinct group in society that shares common group characteristics and is forced to occupy low status in society because of discrimination. A group may be a minority on some characteristics such as race, ethnicity, sexual preference, disability, or age. Crucially, the distinction between a majority and a minority is not numerical superiority but power—with the minority having less power, and therefore low status, relative to other groups in society.

The key to understanding the problems arising in sport concerning minorities is that the problems have structural foundations. This framework challenges misperceptions about race and race relations. Many people believe that discrimination has disappeared and that minorities are no longer disadvantaged. But they are:

- The median family income for black families was only 61 percent of median white family income in 2006. The ratio for Latinos was 72 percent.[3]
- The poverty rate in 2006 for whites was 8.2 percent, Latinos 20.6 percent, and blacks 24.2 percent.[4]
- In 2006, 10.8 percent of whites were not covered by health insurance, and neither were 20.5 percent of blacks and 34.1 percent of Latinos.[5] The gap between whites and nonwhites in health insurance coverage is increasing.
- With each step up the ladder of academic achievement, the gap in lifetime income between blacks and whites increases. "Over a work life, black high school graduates earn $300,000 less, black college graduates earn $500,000 less, and blacks with advanced degrees earn $600,000 less than comparably educated whites."[6]
- At every level of educational achievement blacks and Latinos have higher rates of unemployment than whites.[7]
- In 2003, there were 3,590 black men and women in prison for every 100,000 black residents in the United States, and there were 1,315 Latino prisoners for every 100,000 Latino residents. In sharp contrast, only 503 whites per 100,000 were in prison.[8]

These differences by race/ethnicity are not the fault of racial minorities. Instead, the problems lie in social institutions—the common way things are done, such as the way schools are financed by local taxes, using class-based testing to place children in tracks, bank lending practices, "racial profiling" by the police, bias in the criminal justice system, the eligibility requirements for jobs, the informal requirements for job promotion, and the seemingly fair practice of "last hired, first fired"—all of which prevent racial and ethnic "others" from achieving economic and social parity with the dominant whites. This pattern of negative treatment and oppression by society's institutions is called *institutional racism*. This form of discrimination can occur without prejudice or malice toward minorities. Anderson and Taylor put it this way:

> Consider this: Even if every White person in the country lost all of his or her prejudices, and even if he or she stopped engaging in individual acts of discrimination, institutional racism would still persist for some time. Over the years, it has become so much a part of U.S. institutions (hence, the term institutional racism) that discrimination can occur even when no single person is causing it. Existing at the level of social structure rather than at the level of individual attitude or behavior, it is "external" to the individual personality.[9]

This chapter focuses on institutional racism in the institution of sport. The chapter is divided into several parts: (1) sports participation by the various racial-ethnic groups, (2) explanations for the dominance of blacks in many sports, and (3) discrimination against minority group members in sport. Although the discussion refers to a variety of minorities, a disproportionate amount focuses on African Americans because they are the most prominent racial minority in U.S. sport. Also, the discussion will describe minorities in broad brushstrokes, concealing the diversity within each group. As background for the discussion see Figure 13.1, which provides the population data by race/

ethnicity for 1990 and 2000 and projected for 2025 and 2050. Note that (1) in 2000, Latinos surpassed blacks as the largest racial-ethnic category; (2) Latinos will be about one-fourth of the U.S. population in 2050; and (3) minorities will be about one-half of the U.S. population in 2050. These trends have important implications for sports participation and the popularity of particular sports.

SPORTS PARTICIPATION AMONG RACIAL-ETHNIC MINORITIES

Until about 1950, U.S. racial-ethnic minorities typically were excluded from sport. Since then they continue to be excluded in some sports and are underrepresented in leadership positions.

The History of African American Involvement in U.S. Sport

Despite systematic and pervasive discrimination against African Americans throughout their history in North America, they have played a continuing and significant role in the rise and development of modern sport. The history of black involvement in sport can be divided roughly into four stages: (1) exclusion before the Civil War, (2) breakthroughs following the Emancipation Proclamation, (3) racial segregation between the two world wars, and (4) racial integration after World War II. This last period is especially interesting and significant from a sociological standpoint, and we will focus on it during this chapter.

Africans were brought to North America as slaves throughout the colonial period and into the first half of the nineteenth century. They were concentrated in the southern states because of the plantation system. Plantation owners often used black slaves to stage boxing matches, and they used them as jockeys in horse races. Occasionally in boxing, when a slave boxer won an important bout and won his owner a lot of money, he might be set free. Tom Molineaux, a black slave, was a beneficiary of such an arrangement. In the early nineteenth century, after gaining his freedom, he had quite a reputation in boxing circles in the northern states and in England.

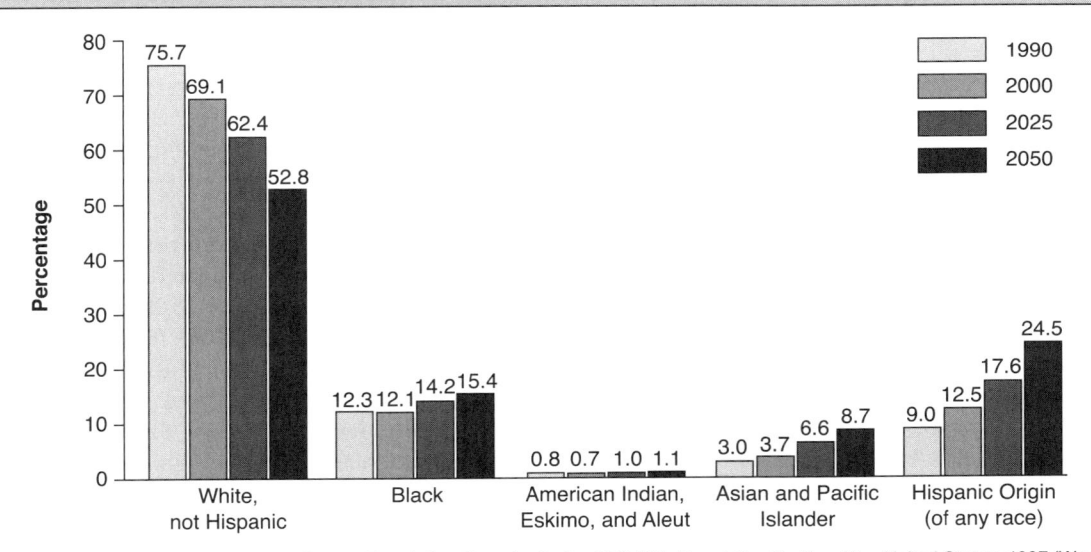

Figure 13.1 Percentage of Population by Race and Hispanic Origin, 1900, 2000, 2025, 2050 (Middle-Series Projection)

Group	1990	2000	2025	2050
White, not Hispanic	75.7	69.1	62.4	52.8
Black	12.3	12.1	14.2	15.4
American Indian, Eskimo, and Aleut	0.8	0.7	1.0	1.1
Asian and Pacific Islander	3.0	3.7	6.6	8.7
Hispanic Origin (of any race)	9.0	12.5	17.6	24.5

Source: U.S. Bureau of the Census, Current Population Reports, Series P23-194, *Population Profile of the United States: 1997* (Washington, D.C.: U.S. Government Printing Office), p. 9; accessed online at www.census.gov/population/www/cen2000.

After the Civil War, African Americans made contributions to the rise of spectator sport as boxers, jockeys, and team players, but they were clearly exceptions. Society and sport remained racially segregated by custom and in some places by law (e.g., Jim Crow laws in the South). Between the first Kentucky Derby in 1875 and about 1910, black jockeys dominated the sport of horse racing. Of the fifteen jockeys in the first Kentucky Derby, fourteen were African Americans, including the winner. By the first decade of the twentieth century, however, horse owners and trainers had succumbed to the segregationist doctrine and no longer employed black jockeys. Blacks did remain in much lower-status positions around racing, exercising the horses, grooming the horses, and cleaning out their stalls.

When blacks were barred from professional baseball, football, and basketball in the late nineteenth and early twentieth centuries, they formed all-black teams and leagues.[10] The Harlem Globetrotters and the famous players of the black baseball leagues such as Satchel Paige and Josh Gibson emerged from this segregated situation. When Jackie Robinson broke the color barrier, first in 1946 in the minor leagues (the first black in the International League in fifty-seven years) and then in 1947 in the majors, he received much verbal and physical abuse from players and fans who resented a black playing on an equal level with whites. The great major league player Rogers Hornsby uttered the common attitude of the time: "They've been getting along all right playing together and they should stay where they belong in their league."[11]

Although some champions would not fight them, African Americans made early gains in boxing and increased their numbers over the years, even when they were excluded from other professional sports. Perhaps boxing was the exception because it has typically recruited from the most oppressed urban groups. In 1908 Jack Johnson became the world heavyweight champion, the first African American to win this title. Throughout the twentieth century blacks have steadily increased their numbers in boxing. Though blacks were allowed by the boxing establishment to participate continuously during the early 1900s, they were still the objects of discrimination. White boxers tended to receive more money than blacks. The white promoters, because of the great-white-hope myth, liked to match whites against blacks in the ring, and blacks often consented to lose just to obtain a match.[12] The observers of black boxers often referred to them in racist terms. Consider, for example, the following from Paul Gallico, a noted sportswriter, writing of the great black boxer Joe Louis: "Louis, the magnificent animal. . . . He eats. He sleeps. He fights. . . . Is he all instinct, all animal? Or have a hundred million years left a fold upon his brain? I see in this colored man something so cold, so hard, so cruel that I wonder as to his bravery. Courage in the animal is desperation. Courage in the human is something incalculable and divine."[13]

Sportswriters referred to blacks in other sports in racist terms as well. Consider, for example, the prediction of Jimmy Powers, sports editor of the *New York Daily News:* "[Jackie] Robinson will not make the grade in major league baseball. He is a thousand-to-one shot at best. The Negro players simply don't have the brains or skills."[14]

African Americans were absent, with a few exceptions, from intercollegiate sports for the first half of this century. A few Ivy League and other eastern schools had black athletes at an early time, but they were exceptions. For the most part, though, prior to World War II African Americans played at all-black colleges in black leagues. Although the system was segregated, it did provide many blacks with the opportunity to engage in organized sport.

Paralleling the situation in professional sports, college sports remained segregated, except for isolated instances, until after World War II. In 1948, for example, only 10 percent of college basketball teams had one or more blacks on their rosters. The last major conference to integrate was the Southeastern Conference (SEC). The University of Tennessee broke the barrier by signing a defensive back in 1966, and Vanderbilt signed a black basketball player in that same year. By 1975, black athletes were common in the SEC and in all the other conferences. The transition from a segregated program to an integrated one is perhaps best illustrated by the University of Alabama: In 1968 there were no blacks on any of its teams, but its 1975 basketball team had an all-black starting lineup.

As more and more schools searched for talented blacks to bolster their athletic programs, black schools lost their monopoly on black athletic talent. The best black athletes found it advantageous to play at predominantly white schools because of greater visibility, especially on television. This visibility meant, for the best athletes, a better chance to become a professional athlete. The result of this trend was a depleted athletic program at black schools, forcing some to drop their athletic programs and some previously black leagues to disband.

Another consequence of black athletes attending white schools has been their increased exploitation by their schools. Many of them have been kept eligible, as shown in chapter 6, where some schools still graduate none or only a small proportion of their athletes. Harry Edwards has called this "a case of the farmer caring for his turkeys—right up until Thanksgiving Day. Then it's back to the ghetto, without an education, without a prayer."[15]

Since World War II, blacks have made tremendous strides in professional team sports (except for hockey). From 1940 to 2006 the percentages of blacks in professional football went from zero to 66 percent, in professional basketball from zero to 75 percent, and in baseball from zero to 8 percent (with another 29 percent Latino in baseball). (See Box 13.1, *Thinking about Sport*.) There are now black head coaches in professional football, basketball, and baseball. Blacks now officiate games; they are now part of the media reporting the games in newspapers, magazines, and television. Discrimination remains, however, as we will document in the final part of this chapter. Moreover, African American girls face dual barriers: racism and sexism.

Latino Involvement in U.S. Sport

We use the term *Latino* to include men and women whose heritage is traced to Spanish-speaking countries (we use *Latino* even though this usage is sexist because the term is "masculine"; women Latinos are Latinas). This is an inclusive category that shares the Spanish language and Catholicism, but the category is actually quite heterogeneous. For example, among Latinos there are Mexicans, Puerto Ricans, Dominicans, Nicaraguans, Venezuelans, and Cubans, each group with its own cultural heritage. But even within these subdivisions, there are often crucial differences. For instance, Cubans who left Cuba for the United States when Batista ruled Cuba are quite different in social class, occupations, and political behaviors from those who left Cuba later, fleeing Castro.

Latinos in American sport are found most notably in baseball, soccer, and boxing. Latinos are also prominent as fans of these sports. Let's begin with baseball. Latinos have been in the major leagues since 1902, with at least forty-five Latinos, mostly Cubans, playing before Jackie Robinson's breakthrough for blacks in 1947. Darker-skinned Latinos whose African ancestry was evident—such as the legendary player Josh Gibson—were barred from the big leagues.

Once Robinson entered the game, all things racial in baseball were overtaken by his story. But the historians have never given Robinson credit for opening the doors of opportunity for the best players Latin America had to offer—men who were black as well as Latino.[16]

Latinos in U.S. Major League Baseball today constitute 29 percent of all the players (up from 13 percent in 1987), exceeding the 8 percent of African Americans. If the minor leagues are included, Latinos account for 43 percent of all players in organized U.S. baseball. Many of the Latinos playing Major League Baseball are foreign-born. Almost 3 out of 10 major league players are Latin American, with the Dominican Republic leading the way with roughly 1 out of 7 of all players (Venezuela has half as many players, followed in order by Puerto Rico, Mexico, Cuba, Colombia, and Nicaragua). Many of these Latinos were born outside the United States and were discovered by major league scouts as teenagers; they faced language barriers, social isolation, and culture shock when they moved into the Anglo world of U.S.

> **Box 13.1** *Thinking about Sport* **An Anomaly: The Declining Proportion of Blacks in Baseball**
>
> Baseball was rigidly segregated before World War II. Talented African Americans were limited to playing in the Negro Leagues. But in 1947, Branch Rickey, owner of the Brooklyn Dodgers, integrated the major leagues when he played Jackie Robinson against the vehement opposition of his fellow owners. Beginning with Robinson's playing excellence, blacks soon achieved prominence in baseball and ultimately were accepted by white players and fans.
>
> By 1975, 27.5 percent of all the players were black. Since then, the numbers—in sharp contrast to what has happened in professional basketball and football—have dwindled at a stunning rate. According to Lapchick, in 2006 blacks were only 8.4 percent of major league rosters and only 3 percent of players on NCAA Division I baseball teams.
>
> Moreover, it is estimated that African American turnout at major league games is only 8 percent of total attendance. That is below what one might expect, considering that African Americans are about 13 percent of the population and constitute almost half of the population of central cities where more than a third of major league teams are located. For example, only 4.5 percent of blacks attend games of the Chicago White Sox, in a city with an African American population of 37 percent (Hyman 2006). The high cost might be a factor, but the cost for Major League Baseball is considerably less than to attend professional basketball, where blacks attend in much greater numbers.
>
> Something is going on to suppress the number of black players. It is *not* discrimination against players of color, as was the case until Jackie Robinson's breakthrough. In 2005, 40.5 percent of the players in Major League Baseball were people of color. What has occurred, of course, is the major influx into baseball of Latino players, who have replaced blacks as the dominating force in baseball. Teams are devoting much more in resources to find and recruit Latino players because those from Latin American countries are much cheaper to sign. Also, baseball teams have established baseball academies in Latin America to locate talent and hone baseball skills. They have not established similar academies in the inner city where blacks are located.
>
> A possible reason for the decline of blacks in Major League Baseball is that the inner cities do not have the space for baseball fields, a luxury found in abundance in the white suburbs. While this does not explain the large proportion of blacks playing football, it does explain the black interest in basketball. Clearly basketball is more accessible than baseball to urban youth.
>
> Football and especially basketball are more appealing to black youth. When baseball was becoming integrated, there were great black players for black youth to emulate, such as Jackie Robinson, John Roseboro, Bob Gibson, Willie Mays, and Hank Aaron. Two of the greatest contemporary black players—Barry Bonds and Ken Griffey, Jr.—are sons of players from that earlier era. Young black athletes today are looking elsewhere for sports to follow. About the time black participation began to decline, basketball players became the sports idols of youth—most notably Michael Jordan.
>
> According to Harris, young African Americans began abandoning baseball in large numbers in the 1980s exactly when flashier black athletes were rising to megastardom in football and basketball. Michael Jordan, with his high-flying dunks and widely popular line of shoes, especially epitomized the intoxicating blend of money, talent, power, and fame that kids wanted to copy.
>
> Finally, the route to athletic stardom is longer for baseball than for either football or basketball. For aspiring baseball players there are two routes to the major leagues. One is to play in college. But baseball is a minor sport in most schools, so there are fewer scholarships (many are partial) than available for football and basketball players. The other route is to play in the minor leagues for several years. In either case, the rewards are few. In football and basketball, in contrast, there are full scholarships. For the truly gifted, they can become superstars in the professional ranks at age twenty or so, an extremely rare feat in baseball.
>
> So, it appears that discrimination does not explain the relative paucity of African Americans in Major League Baseball. While there are some structural barriers to black participation, young black athletes seem to be choosing basketball and football over baseball.
>
> *Sources:* Gerald Early, "Where Have We Gone, Mr. Robinson?" *Time,* 12 April 2007, 48–49; Vahe Gregorian, "Baseball's Blackout," *Wichita Eagle,* 2 July 2006, p. 9D; James Harris, "Baseball? That Ain't Hood," *Truthdig,* 3 January 2006, http://www.truthdig.com/report/print/20060104_baseball/; Mark Hyman, "The Racial Gap in the Grandstands," *Business Week,* 2 October 2006, 78–79; Sandy Grady, "Baseball's Black Exodus," *USA Today,* 4 April 2006, p. 15A; and Richard Lapchick, *The 2006 Racial and Gender Report Card: Major League Baseball* (Orlando: DeVos Management Program, University of Central Florida, 2006).

baseball. Although most come to the United States through normal immigration patterns, the players from Cuba have arrived by defecting (they left Cuba illegally, but they were welcomed in the United States because they provide evidence of the "evils" of the Castro regime).

There are two reasons for the overrepresentation of foreign-born Latinos in Major League Baseball. First, baseball is an extremely popular sport in many Latin American countries, where young boys play year-round developing their skills. Many of the poor youth believe that the way out of the barrio is either to play baseball in the United States or to join the drug trade. They are motivated by the success of previous Latino players such as Sammy Sosa, who grew up in poverty and shined shoes to later become a huge star in the major leagues. In 2007 Latinos such as Alex Rodriguez, Manny Ramirez, and Carlos Delgado were among the highest-paid athletes in Major League Baseball. The second reason for the expanding Latino presence in baseball is that Major League Baseball teams have found a lot of raw but talented athletes whom they can sign much cheaper than U.S.-born athletes. All thirty major league teams scout talent in Latin America (referred to by owners as "the Republic of Baseball"), and a number of teams have elaborate multimillion-dollar baseball academies.[17]

There is a dark side to the mining of baseball talent in the Caribbean and Central and South America. The baseball teams sign these players for

Boston Red Sox Manny Ramirez follows through on a three-run home run against the New York Yankees, 22 May 2007 at Yankee Stadium in New York. In 2007, Latinos such as Ramirez, Alex Rodriguez, and Carlos Delgado were among the highest-paid athletes in Major League Baseball. (AP Photo/Julie Jacobson)

much less than they would pay a U.S.-born player. Joe Kehoskie, an American sports agent, says:

> Traditionally in the Latin market, I would say players sign for about 5 to 10 cents on the dollar compared to their U.S. counterparts. [Moreover] a lot of times kids just quit school at 10, 11, 12, and play baseball full-time. It's great, it's great for the kids that make it because they become superstars and get millions of dollars in the big leagues. But for ninety-eight kids out of 100, it results in a kid that is 18, 19, with no education.[18]

Approximately 90 to 95 percent of Latino players who sign contracts never reach the major leagues. The vast majority never get a chance to play in the United States at any level. The ones who make it to the United States but fail to make a team tend to stay in the country as undocumented immigrants, working for low wages rather than returning home as "failures." "These castoffs represent the underside of the Sammy Sosa story, the rule rather than the exception in the high-stakes recruitment of ball players from Latin America and the Caribbean."[19]

There are two major sports in Latin America—baseball and soccer. Major League Soccer teams include a number of foreign players, most from Latin America. Unlike other professional team sports, in soccer the players sign a contract with the league, which then assigns players to a franchise. Not surprisingly, the Latino players are assigned to franchises in cities with large Latino populations. As a result, 80 percent of the fans in heavily Latino Los Angeles are Latinos. The games are televised on Univision, the nation's largest Spanish-language television company. With the Latino population expected to triple to around one hundred million by 2050, the popularity of Major League Soccer should grow just as rapidly. See Box 13.2, *Thinking about Sport,* which describes the ethnic differences between the two professional soccer (futbol) teams in Los Angeles.

Almost all boxers come from the lowest social classes. Poor racial minorities with little hope for upward mobility other than through sport are likely candidates to become boxers. Thus African Americans and Latinos are heavily overrepresented among boxers and spectators of boxing. A few boxers (e.g., Oscar DeLaHoya) do extraordinarily well financially. Most, however, do not. Many are exploited by unscrupulous promoters. For example, promising U.S. boxers need to build a history of wins to become known and command higher purses. Many promoters bring overmatched boxers from Mexico (the most important supplier of boxing opponents to the United States) to lose to their boxers. The unknown Mexican boxers are paid $100 for each three-minute round. This is more than they can make in Mexico as boxers or laborers, so they risk injury for the money and the hope of making it.[20]

Domestically, young male Latinos tend to participate in soccer, football, and wrestling. This has consequences in areas where the population is shifting from predominantly Anglo to Latino. For example, the 2007 population in Seward County, Kansas, was 51 percent Latino (up from 42 percent in 2000). The largest school district in that county is 67 percent Latino. As a result, "the high school soccer team is as popular as—sometimes more than—its football team."[21]

High school–age Latinas are underrepresented in sports. Nationally, about 36 percent of Latina sophomores played interscholastic sports, compared to 42 percent of non-Latinas.[22] Many Latinas in the United States are first- or second-generation immigrants, bringing with them the traditional cultural expectations that girls are to do household tasks (tasks their brothers are not expected to do). Those Latinas that do participate in interscholastic sports (most commonly third-generation) participate mainly in soccer, track, and softball.

Asian American Involvement in U.S. Sport

A few Asians have become stars on the U.S. sports scene: figure skaters Kristi Yamaguchi and Michelle Kwan, speed skater Apolo Ohno, basketball player Yao Ming, Major League Baseball players Ichiro Suzuki and Daisuke Matsuzaka, and golfer Tiger Woods (whose mother is Thai). More recently, Asians have been making the greatest

Box 13.2 *Thinking about Sport* In L.A., It's Soccer vs. Futbol

Renowned metrosexual megastar David Beckham is earning some street cred. When the $250-million man first arrived in Los Angeles last month, he seemed too famous and too fragile to deign to take the pitch at Carson's Home Depot Center.

But that was then; this is now. On Wednesday, he suffered a knee injury when he didn't flinch from a rough collision. The week before, in the "super *clasico*" matchup between Los Angeles' two teams—Beckham's Galaxy and Chivas USA—the Englishman stoically played all 90 minutes despite having played an international match against Germany the day before—in London! What's more, "Becks" even got involved in a melee; well, sort of. Shortly before halftime, he stared down Chivas midfielder Jesse Marsch after being fouled violently, though he allowed his teammates to do the actual shoving.

The fact that soccer has become a must-have ticket in town—Beckham's unveiling in July had the feel of a Hollywood premiere—must be disconcerting to California nativists, who distrust all things foreign and who had been feeling pretty good about themselves of late in the aftermath of the stalled immigration reform. Now that über-foreign sport, the only true form of global popular culture not driven by the U.S., is taking a big step toward becoming mainstream, indeed glamorous. What's next, California going metric?

But the arrival of Beckham to the Galaxy, along with the team's budding rivalry with Chivas, actually serves to make the sport less foreign to L.A. fans by accentuating the Galaxy's Anglo appeal. Beckham's ostensible mission is to raise the profile of American soccer, but a corollary aim of those who brought him here may well be to "de-ethnicize" the sport in this town. The Galaxy have positioned themselves as the non-Latino team in town, whose game days are reassuringly "mainstream."

This wasn't always the case. The Galaxy's early days, when the crowd was less dominated by soccer moms and kids, were a heavily Latino affair. The Galaxy imported some of Mexico's most fabled veterans to pack the stands—players such as Jorge Campos, Carlow Hermosillo and Luis Hernandez, who were far bigger draws for Mexican immigrants (if not for Tom Cruise) than Beckham will ever be.

But the Galaxy's Latino flavor began to change when Mexico's storied Chivas de Guadalajara club founded its own Chivas USA franchise in Los Angeles a couple of years ago. This was the equivalent of the Dodgers opening a franchise in Mexico.

Chivas marketed itself as the Mexican squad in town, with the opening-season slogan "*Adios Soccer, El Futbol Esta Aqui*" (Goodbye, Soccer, Futbol Is Here). Mexican team owner Jorge Vergara memorably told *The Times*: "It's the Latinos versus the gringos, and we're going to win."

Chivas' home games have a far more foreign feel to them than the Galaxy's games. Spanish is the preferred language, and plenty of fans wear jerseys that blend the red-and-white stripes of Chivas with the solid green of Mexico's national team. (In Mexico, the Chivas franchise is considered almost a proxy for the national team because of its refusal to field foreign players.) The raucous fan section is called "Legion 1908," just like its counterpart in Guadalajara; the name commemorates the year the Mexican team won its first amateur title.

It may be no accident that the Galaxy's roster of 26 players has fewer than five Latino players, compared with about a dozen who play for Chivas.

The teams, of course, dispute that they are engaged in ethnic typecasting. Thursday's edition of *La Opinion* even featured a front-page interview with Beckham in which he professed his love of Mexican food, especially—way to go way out on a limb!—chicken burritos. Chivas officials, for their part, have been less jingoistic in their marketing since their first season. But the ethnic overlay to Los Angeles' soccer rivalry remains indisputable, if not as vitriolic, as the Catalan-Castilian divide between FC Barcelona and Espanyol in Barcelona or the Protestant-Catholic divide between Rangers and Celtics in Glasgow.

Put it this way: You can be sure that when the national teams of Mexico and the U.S. face off, far more Chivas fans than Galaxy fans are rooting for Mexico.

So each of America's competing soccer cultures—suburban Anglos and urban Latinos—has a team in Los Angeles, giving Major League Soccer some much-needed edge.

Big-time soccer has had its share of false starts in this country—Pele's stint with the Cosmos in the 1970s, the 1994 World Cup—but there is something fitting about the world's entertainment capital establishing itself on the map of the world's top sport.

Source: Andrés Martinez, "In L.A., It's Soccer *vs.* Futbol," *Los Angeles Times*, 1 September 2007. Online at http://www.latimes.com/news/opinion/la-oe-martinez1sep01,0,4152143,print.story?coll=la-opinion-center.

inroads in women's golf. For example, for the 2007 season, 10 of the top 25 women professional golfers were Asian, most typically of Korean heritage. In 1998 Se Ri Pak was the only South Korean on the Ladies Professional Golf Association (LPGA) tour. By 2001 there were 10 South Koreans on the tour. In 2007 there were 45, and from 2005 to mid-2007 South Koreans won 20 times, including three majors.[23]

All of the sports mentioned here are individual sports. This relationship is strengthened when other individual sports are added where Asian Americans excel, such as diving, gymnastics, and the various martial arts (karate, tae kwon do, and judo, sports with Asian origins).

A recent trend is for athletes born in Japan, where baseball is popular, to make it in U.S. Major League Baseball. For example, Daisuke Matsuzaka (his American nickname is "Dice-K") was a superstar in Japan. His rights, owned by the Seibu Lions, were sold at auction to the Boston Red Sox for $51 million. He then signed a six-year, $52 million contract, beginning in 2007. He follows the Japanese superstar Ichiro Suzuki of the Seattle Mariners, who in 2001 won both the American League's "Rookie of the Year" and "Most Valuable Player" awards. His location on the West Coast, where there is a significant Asian population (including nearby Vancouver, British Columbia, where the population is 25 percent Asian), has been important because it has changed the racial-ethnic composition of spectators at Mariners games (at home and away) and even affected the media (there are Japanese-language broadcasts of Mariners games in Japan).

When considering sports participation of Asian Americans at the high school level, there are differences depending on two diversity dimensions. First, there is immigration history—that is, the length of time that the immigrant group has been in this country. Generally, Chinese, Filipino, and Japanese families have been in the United States for many generations and therefore have been assimilated into the culture of the United States. This is in sharp contrast to many South Asian immigrants (Thai, Vietnamese, Cambodian), who are typically first- or second-generation and are tugged in different directions by their culture of origin and the new culture in which they are immersed. A second dimension is the social class of recent immigrants. Some migrants were successful in their country and arrived with resources and skills that give them advantages over other migrants. Others were peasants destined, at least initially, to work at demeaning and low-paying jobs. Clearly, the greater the economic resources of the family, the greater the likelihood that children will receive sports lessons, attend sports camps, and purchase the requisite equipment. The poorer the family, the greater the probability that children will have to forgo sports participation and instead work to support the family.[24]

Native American Involvement in U.S. Sport

There were about four million Native Americans and Native Alaskans in 2005 (1.4 percent of the U.S. population). The tribes located in North America were and are heterogeneous, with major differences in physical characteristics, language, and social organization. When Europeans arrived in North America, there were as many as seven million indigenous people, but disease, warfare, and in some cases genocide reduced the Native American population to less than 250,000 by 1890. In the first half of the nineteenth century the U.S. government forced Indians to leave their homelands and move to areas with marginal land and other resources. The government also developed a reservation system that subordinated Native Americans. By the end of the twentieth century, Native Americans, although better off than they were in the early 1900s, ranked at the bottom on most indicators of well-being (life expectancy, per capita income, employment, and education).

A few Native Americans have been recognized nationally for their sports prowess. Most notably, a century ago Jim Thorpe was an Olympic hero and a football and baseball star. Then in the 1964 Olympics, the relatively unknown Billy Mills won the 10,000 meters. More recently, Notah Begay III, a Navajo, has played on the professional golf tour. But only six Native Americans have ever played in the National Basketball Association. And in 2005 only 0.4 percent of athletic scholarship students in

Mohamed Gamoudi (615) of Tunisia tries to squeeze his arm ahead of U.S. Marine Lt. Billy Mills as Mills pulls off a stunning upset in winning the 10,000-meter Olympic race in Tokyo, 14 October 1964. Mills, a Native American, set an Olympic record of 28:24.4 and is the only American ever to win the event. (AP Photo)

Table 13.1 Scholarship Athletes in Division I by Race/Ethnicity and Gender, 2005 (in percent)

Race/Ethnicity	Male	Female	U.S. Population
White	62.2	70.5	67.1
African American	24.8	5.4	12.5
Latino	3.7	3.3	14.0
Native American/Alaskan	0.4	0.4	1.4
Asian	1.7	2.2	3.8
Resident aliens	4.1	4.9	—
Other	3.1	3.3	—

Source: Adapted from Richard E. Lapchick, *2005 Racial and Gender Report Card* (Orlando: Institute for Diversity and Ethics in Sport, University of Central Florida, 20 December 2006), 69.

Division I were Native Americans (see Table 13.1). There are athletically talented Native American high school athletes, as evidenced by many state basketball championships and cross-country and track titles, but many choose not to attend college or if they do, many return home rather than play at the college level. Some of the reasons for this are the racism they experience away from home (see Box 13.3, *Thinking about Sport*), their lack of economic resources, and not fitting into another social world. Most important:

> There's ... an inherent tension between white and Indian culture: One values the individual above all else; the other, the tribe. To go away to college means largely to forgo what is good about reservation life: the land, the hunting and fishing, the ceremony, the ties to family, community and history. It means forgoing, at least temporarily, much of what you have learned is the very essence of Indian life.[25]

As Billy Mills says, "If you go too far into society, there's a fear of losing your Indian-ness. There's a spiritual factor that comes into play. To become part of white society you give up half your soul."[26]

The Effects of Globalization on Ethnic Diversity in U.S. Sport Participation

Political boundaries across the globe are becoming increasingly blurred by the ease of communication and transportation and the easing of trade restrictions among nations. One consequence of this trend toward globalization is the movement of athletes from nation to nation. Some of these migration patterns are seasonal, as athletes move from one climate area to another. North American skiers, for example, might train in the Southern Hemisphere in places such as South America or New Zealand during its winter (and the Northern Hemisphere's summer). Many world-class runners come to Colorado, locating in Boulder or Alamosa, so that they can train at high altitude. U.S. universities are eager to give scholarships to foreign-born athletes who can help their programs. This is true for both men and women athletes, most notably in sports such as track and field, basketball, soccer, and volleyball.

> **Box 13.3** ***Thinking about Sport* The Negative Images of Native Americans in Certain Sport Names, Logos, and Mascots**
>
> Sports teams use symbols (team names, logos, colors, and mascots) to evoke strong emotions of solidarity among the team members and their followers. Most teams use symbols of aggression and ferocity for their athletic teams (birds such as hawks, animals such as tigers, human categories such as pirates, and even the otherworldly such as devils).
>
> There is a potential dark side to the use of these symbols. The names, mascots, and logos selected for some teams might be derogatory to some group. Such symbols might dismiss, demean, and trivialize marginalized groups such as African Americans, Native Americans, and women. These symbols then serve to maintain the dominance of the majority and the subordination of groups categorized as "others." That may not be the intent of those using negative symbols, but the symbols diminish these "others" nonetheless and help maintain the racial and gender inequities found in the larger society.
>
> Native Americans are the racial-ethnic group most commonly demeaned by team names. Many professional teams have Native American names—for instance, the Atlanta Braves, Cleveland Indians, Washington Redskins, Kansas City Chiefs, Golden State Warriors, and Chicago Blackhawks. There are high schools, colleges, and universities known as Redmen, Seminoles, Hurons, Choctaws, Utes, Fighting Illini, Fighting Sioux, and Savages.
>
> Defenders of such use of Native American names for sports teams argue that their use is a tribute to the indigenous people. In such uses, the argument goes, Native Americans are portrayed as brave, resourceful, and strong. Native American names were chosen for sports teams precisely because they represent these positive traits. Other defenders claim that the use of Native American names and mascots is no different from the use of names and mascots that represent other ethnic groups, such as the Irish or the Vikings, and that people from those heritages accept the use of their names.
>
> But many Native Americans do object to their symbols being used by athletic teams. Names such as Indians, Braves, Warriors, and Chiefs are not manifestly offensive, but some names, logos, and mascots project a violent caricature of Native Americans (as scalpers, savages, and so on).
>
> Teams that use Native American names commonly employ the tomahawk chop, war paint, and mascots who dress as Native Americans and perform replicas of ceremonial dances, which trivializes the meaning of Native American rituals.
>
> Clyde Bellecourt, national director of the American Indian Movement (AIM), summarizes the complaints:
>
> > If you look up the word "redskin" in both the Webster's and Random House dictionaries, you'll find the word is defined as being offensive. Can you imagine if they called the Washington Jews and the team mascot was a rabbi leading them in [the song] *Hava Nagila,* fans in the stands wearing yarmulkes and waving sponge torahs? The word Indian isn't offensive. Brave isn't offensive, but it's the behavior that accompanies all of this that's offensive. The rubber tomahawks. The chicken-feather headdresses. People wearing war paint and making these ridiculous war whoops with a tomahawk in one hand and a beer in the other. All of these things have significant meaning for us. And the psychological impact it has, especially on our youth, is devastating.
>
> After many protests, many high school and college teams have dropped their racially insulting Native American nicknames (e.g., Stanford, Syracuse, Dartmouth, Marquette, St. John's, Siena, Miami of Ohio, and Dickinson State), but no professional sports team has taken a similar step.
>
> *continues*

Some foreign-born athletes become U.S. citizens and compete for U.S. national teams in the Olympics and in the World Cup. Professional sports, with the exception of football, are becoming increasingly stocked with foreign-born athletes. In baseball, about 30 percent of major leaguers are foreign-born, as are almost half of minor league players. In the National Hockey League, U.S.-based teams are dominated by Canadians and players from nations such as Sweden, Finland, the Czech Republic, Hungary, and the various countries that once were part of the Soviet Union. Similarly, the National Basketball Association has players from many other countries, including Germany, the Czech Republic, Russia, Australia, and Serbia. As we have already seen, Major League Baseball has had an enormous influx of players from the Dominican Republic, Cuba, Venezuela, Colombia, Japan, and Korea. And approximately 25 percent of Major League Soccer's players were born outside the United States. Professional golf and tennis are truly global sports. The top five men golfers on the U.S. tour in 2007 included two Americans, a South African, a South Korean, and one Fijian. For women, the top five included two Americans, a South Korean, a Mexican, and a Swede.

These athletes are a form of "global migrant workers."[27] Many come to the United States for an

> **Box 13.3 Continued**
>
> A number of prestigious organizations have publicly opposed the negative use of Native American symbols, including the National Congress of American Indians, the National Education Association, the U.S. Commission on Civil Rights, the American Sociological Association, and the North American Society for the Sociology of Sport. Most significantly, the NCAA ruled in 2005 that it will not conduct championships on the campuses of member institutions where the use of nicknames and mascots representing American Indians is considered hostile and abusive. Several institutions with Native American symbols have appealed this decision. To date, Illinois, North Dakota, and Indiana of Pennsylvania have lost their appeals. As a consequence, the University of Illinois announced that Chief Illiniwek will no longer perform at athletic events on the Urbana-Champaign campus, and the university is now eligible to host postseason NCAA championship events.
>
> *Sources*: D. Stanley Eitzen, *Fair and Foul: Beyond the Myths and Paradoxes of Sport*, 3rd ed. (Lanham, Md.: Rowman & Littlefield, 2006), 37–40; Bob Kravitz, "Aim of Native Americans' Protest Is True," *Rocky Mountain News,* 21 January 1992, p. 39; Barbara Munson, "Not for Sport: A Native American Activist Calls for an End to 'Indian' Team Mascots," *Teaching Tolerance,* no. 15 (Spring 1999): 40–43; Ellen J. Staurowsky, "The Cleveland 'Indians': A Case Study in American Indian Cultural Dispossession," *Sociology of Sport Journal* 17, no. 4 (2000): 307–330; Richard Lapchick, "Mascots Are a Matter of Respect," *ESPN.com,* 2005, http://sports.espn.go.com/espn/print?id=2142041&type=story; Salim Muwakkil, "Accepting the Slurs," *In These Times,* 24 October 2005, 14; Steve Wieberg, "Bolder NCAA Faces Up to New Challenges," *USA Today,* 22 February 2006, p. 3C; Laurel R. Davis, "The Problems with Native American Mascots," in *Sport in Contemporary Society,* ed. D. Stanley Eitzen (Boulder, Colo.: Paradigm, 2005), 115–120; D. Stanley Eitzen and Maxine Baca Zinn, "The Dark Side of Sports Symbols," *USA Today: The Magazine of the American Scene* 129, January 2001, 48–51; Carol Spindel, *Dancing at Halftime: Sports and the Controversy over American Indian Mascots* (New York: New York University Press, 2000); and C. Richard King and C. F. Springwood, eds., *Team Spirits: The Native American Mascots Controversy* (Lincoln: Bison Books and the University of Nebraska Press, 2001).

education and the opportunities for economic rewards. Both are possible, but so, too, are the sorts of exploitation experienced by foreign-born boxers and baseball players. At a personal level, many of these "migrant workers" find it difficult to adjust to living in a new society, with its language barriers, cultural differences, social isolation, and various forms of racial and ethnic bigotry. Some teams expect their foreign-born athletes to adjust on their own; others provide support to help them learn English and understand the norms and values of their new cultural setting.

BLACK DOMINANCE IN SPORT

Since World War II, the number of African Americans in major team sports has increased dramatically. The watershed year in professional sports (when the proportion of blacks approximated their proportion in the national population) was, for baseball, 1957; for basketball, 1958; and for football, 1960. Since then, however, the rate, except for baseball, has virtually exploded, compared to whites and other races and ethnic groups. By 2005, as already noted, although African Americans only constituted 12.5 percent of the general population, they were 73 percent of all professional basketball players, 58 percent of all NCAA Division I basketball players, 66 percent of all professional football players, and 9 percent of Major League Baseball players.[28]

There are three possible explanations (genetic, cultural, and social) for this disproportionate presence of blacks in American team sports. We examine the genetic hypothesis first.

Race-Linked Physical Differences

A common explanation for the overrepresentation of African Americans in certain sports is that they are naturally better athletes than whites and that their predominance in sports is therefore attributable to innate physical supremacy. There are some problems with this biological determinism argument. First, there is the issue of who is black. Racial categories in any society, but particularly in the United States, where amalgamation of Africans, Caucasians, and Native Americans continues, are ill-defined, and of course, socially defined. The point is that racial categories are not fixed, unambiguous, and dichotomous. Because blacks, like whites, exhibit a wide range of physical builds and other physiological features, sampling becomes a problem. Does the scientist compare randomly selected whites with randomly selected blacks? More logically, to answer the question of athletic superiority, does the researcher compare a random selection of superior white athletes with superior black athletes? Unfortunately, the latter has not been the case. The key is that blacks are not a homogeneous physical category. In fact, the recent Human Genome study found that, genetically speaking, there are greater ranges of differences within races than between races.

The word "black" provides little information about anyone or any group. Of the 100,000 genes that determine human makeup, only one to six regulate skin color, so we should assume almost nothing about anyone based on skin color alone. West Africans and East Africans are both black, but in many physical ways they are *more unlike each other* than they are *different from most whites*. When it comes to assumptions about Africans, we should make just one: That the peoples of Africa, short and tall, thick and thin, fast and slow, white and black, represent the fullest and most spectacular variations of humankind to be found anywhere.[29]

Another problem in comparing races on some behavioral pattern is the impossibility of eliminating social variables (social, cultural, and political factors) from consideration. Why, for example, do blacks from Kenya tend to excel in distance running while blacks from Nigeria do not? Is this major difference explained by differences in diet, cultural emphasis, geography, or what? Whatever the explanation, it is not racial difference. A Stanford biologist, Robert Sapolsky, argues that although genes are important, they do not work independently of the environment. Genes are influenced by environmental factors that trigger chemical changes. He concludes that biology alone cannot explain human differences.[30] Hence, perhaps the issue is not nature versus nurture, but how nature interacts with nurture.

The biological determinist explanation for black athletic superiority also has racist implications.[31] First, the assumption that biological differences exist by race (i.e., blacks are "physically superior" and whites are "mentally superior") reinforces stereotypes of blacks as "naturally" suited for physical activities and, by implication, not suited for activities requiring discipline, intelligence, and judgment. Second, such beliefs reinforce an ideology that seeks to explain and justify the political status quo where blacks are second to whites in power, authority, and resources. Third, this explanation implies that black athletes do not have to work hard to be successful in sport and that white athletes achieve success due to hard work and intelligence.

The problems with existing empirical studies on racial differences lead us to conclude that they are meaningless on the one hand, that is, they make assumptions that obscure the realities of race as a social rather than biological category, and dangerous, that is, racist, on the other. Moreover, whatever differences found to exist among the races are explained not by genetic advantages of one social category over another but by cultural and social reasons.

Race-Linked Cultural Differences

The Kalenjin tribe of the Great Rift Valley, in Kenya, represents two thousand of the earth's population of more than six billion, yet they win 40 percent of the top international distance-running honors.[32] With all of their physical advantages for endurance sports, why are Kenyans missing from such endurance events as the Tour de France bicycle competition and other endurance bicycle races, which are dominated by whites? Similarly, if blacks are so good at jumping, as evidenced by their basketball prowess, why don't they dominate the high jump and the pole vault in track? If blacks are superior in physical strength, why don't they excel in the shot put, discus, and weight-lifting events? Why do Russians dominate chess? Why in the music world are there so many superstar Italian tenors?[33] The answer to each of these questions is that categories of people with a similar culture place a greater emphasis on some activities while ignoring others.

African Americans may be overrepresented in sport because of the uniqueness of the black subculture in the United States. James Green argued that black subculture places a positive emphasis on the importance of physical (and verbal) skill and dexterity. Athletic prowess in men is highly valued by both black women and black men. The athletically superior male is comparable to the successful hustler or rap singer; he is something of a folk hero. He achieves a level of status and recognition among his peers, whether he is a publicly applauded sports hero or not.[34] There is ample evidence of just such adulation accorded black basketball players, regardless of age, in the urban playgrounds of the United States.

Cultural differences probably do account for the differences in sport performance between black Africans and black Americans. Here, where physical differences are more or less controlled (although black Americans are more racially mixed), there are great variances. At elite-level track events, for instance, black Africans excel in distance running but not in the sprints and jumping events. Black Americans, on the other hand, have dominated the sprints, hurdles, and the long and triple jumps but have had negligible success in the distance events. Clearly, something other than the physiology of race must explain this variance. Cultural differences, along with differences in history and geography, account for much of the sharp contrast.

Unique forms of dance, music, art, and humor have emerged from the black subculture. Perhaps that subculture also accounts for the interest and ability of black Americans in basketball where moves, speed, and aggression predominate. The interest of other groups in particular sports is easily explained that way. For example, Japanese Americans, who constitute less than 0.3 percent of the total population, make up over 20 percent of the top AAU judo competitors.[35] Although black culture might similarly contribute to black excellence in athletics, especially in certain sports, there is little systematic empirical evidence at present to substantiate the claim.

Social Structure Constraints

The most plausible reasons for black dominance in some sports are found in the structural constraints on blacks in American society. These constraints can be divided into two types: (1) occupational structure and (2) sports opportunity structure.

African Americans may perceive sport to be one of the few means by which they can succeed in the highly competitive American society because their opportunities for upward mobility in American society are limited. A young black male's primary role models are much more likely to be athletic heroes than are a young white male's models. The determination and motivation devoted by the black adolescent to the pursuit of an athletic career may, therefore, be more intense than those of the white adolescent, whose career options are greater. As Harry Edwards argued:

> Black society, as does the dominant white society, teaches its members to strive for that which is defined as the most desirable among potentially achievable goals—*among potentially achievable goals*. Since the onset of integrated, highly rewarding sports opportunities and the impact of television in communicating to all the ostensible influence . . . glamour, affluence, and so forth, of the successful black athlete, the talents of Afro-American males (and females, again, to a lesser extent) are disproportionately concentrated toward achievement in this one area. In high-prestige occupational positions outside of the sports realm, black role models are an all but insignificant few. These are not readily visible, and they seldom have contact or communications with the masses of blacks. . . . Thus, given the competition among athletic organizations for top-flight athletes, it is to be expected that a high proportion of the extremely gifted black individuals would be in sports. Whites, on the other hand, because they have visible alternative role models and greater potential access to alternative high-prestige positions, distribute their talents over a broader range of endeavors. Thus, the concentration of highly gifted whites in sports is proportionately less than the number of blacks. Under such circumstances, black athletes dominate sports in terms of excellence of performance, where both groups participate in numbers.[36]

Occupational limitations for African Americans do not explain why they tend to gravitate toward some sports, such as boxing, basketball, football, and track, and why they are underrepresented in others, such as swimming, golf, skiing, tennis, and polo. John C. Phillips argued that the reason blacks tend to participate in certain sports lies in what he called the "sports opportunity structure."[37] Blacks tend to excel in those sports in which facilities, coaching, and competition are available to them: in the schools and community recreation programs. Blacks are rarely found in those sports that require the facilities, coaching, and competition usually provided only in private clubs. There are few excellent black golfers, for example, and they had to overcome the disadvantages of being self-taught and limited to playing at municipal courses. Few blacks are competitive skiers for the obvious reasons that most blacks live far from snow and mountains and that skiing is very expensive.

Structural reasons clarify why blacks outperform whites in certain sports. Basketball provides an excellent example because the style of black basketball players differs so significantly from that of white players. The former tend to be more aggressive, better jumpers and rebounders, better at playing close to the basket, better at performing individual moves, and more flamboyant. Whites, on the other hand, tend to be better outside shooters and free throwers, more disciplined, and better grounded in the fundamentals. Donald Carlston has provided a plausible structural explanation for these differences.[38] Most black college and professional players learned the game under substantially different conditions than white players. The inner-city basketball courts frequented by blacks are generally crowded with large numbers competing for valuable playing time on the limited facilities. The norms that prevail under these conditions shape the skills and behaviors of the inner-city players in predictable ways. The games are intensely competitive, with winning teams staying on the court to meet the next challengers. Players must learn to dribble, pass, and shoot in close quarters against a tight person-to-person defense. Players in these circumstances learn to fake and to alter shots in midair. Players are expected to score without much help from teammates. They accept contact as routine. The spectators often present at inner-city games encourage flair and flamboyance.

Most white college and professional players, in contrast, developed their basketball talents in rural, small-town, and suburban communities. Basketball in these settings is characterized by player scarcity rather than a crowding of teams and players on the courts. For those who maintain a year-round interest in basketball, play is limited to many hours of solitary practice in one's own driveway and to occasional pick up games. The noncity player develops playing skills largely free from intense competition, honing excellent shooting skills but not the moves necessary to defeat an aggressive defender one-on-one. The paucity of players leads to rules that encourage the participation of marginal players, make use of skills developed in solo practice, and keep the pace relatively slow. Thus, whites develop pure shooting skills and the ability to score when wide open. In sum, Carlston's analysis suggests that the differences in play between whites and blacks are not found in racial differences but in the structural conditions under which they develop their basketball skills.

Another structural basis for racial differences in participation is that African Americans have been denied membership in private clubs (thus, they are denied access to the best facilities and coaching in sports such as swimming, golf, and tennis) for economic and social reasons. The economic barrier to membership is the result of the discriminatory practices (in types of jobs, salaries, and chances for promotion) that deny most blacks affluence. The social barriers have occurred because of the discriminatory practices of many private clubs that exclude various racial and ethnic groups. Sports in private organizations have been particularly resistant to racial integration. As Jay J. Coakley has noted: "Golf, tennis, swimming, and other sports [that are] often learned and played in private clubs where social interaction is personal and often involves relationships between males and females have been slow to welcome racial and ethnic diversity. As the degree of social closeness increases in any setting, including sports, people are more likely to enforce various forms of exclusion."[39]

There is, however, another type of discrimination implied in the sports opportunity structure: The powerful in some sports have denied access to blacks, even to blacks with the requisite skills and financial support. Certain golf tournaments (the Masters, for instance) have been reluctant to admit blacks. Lee Elder became the first black to play the Masters in 1975. Just as golf until recently allowed black caddies but not black golfers, horse racing in the twentieth century until recently has allowed blacks as exercise boys but not as jockeys. Automobile racing is another sport in which blacks have had great difficulty in participating. The Indianapolis 500 waited until 1991 for its first black driver. The explanation for this delay in having a black driver surely lies not in the limitations of blacks in driving fast and with inferior skills but in the reluctance of corporate sponsors to give financial support to black drivers.

RACIAL DISCRIMINATION IN SPORT

Sport is not free of racial discrimination. However, the dominant presence of African Americans in the three major team sports appears to belie the existence of racism in sport. Moreover, the prominence and huge salaries of minority superstars such as Tiger Woods, Alex Rodriguez, and Shaquille O'Neal have led many Americans, black and white, to infer that collegiate and professional athletics have provided an avenue of upward mobility for racial-ethnic minorities unavailable elsewhere.

Many commentators—social scientists, journalists, and the athletes themselves—have argued, however, that black visibility in collegiate and professional sports has merely served to mask the racism that pervades the entire sport establishment. According to these critics, the existence of racism in collegiate and professional sports is especially insidious because the promoters of and commentators on athletics have made sport sacred by projecting its image as the single institution that is relatively immune from racism.

This section focuses on two aspects of the athletic world that have been alleged to be racially biased: the assignment of playing positions and the rewards and authority structures. The analysis is limited to the major professional team sports (baseball, basketball, and football) in which minorities are found most prominently. In addition to describing and explaining the current situations, we assess whether any substantial changes have occurred or can be anticipated in the future.

Stacking

One of the best-documented forms of discrimination in both college and professional ranks is popularly known as *stacking*. The term refers to situations in which minority group members are disproportionately found in specific team positions and underrepresented in others. In Major League Baseball in 2005, for example, when African Americans were 9 percent of the major league players, they were underrepresented with 3 percent of the pitchers and overrepresented among outfielders with 26 percent.

Examination of the stacking phenomenon was first undertaken by John W. Loy, Jr., and Joseph F. McElvogue, who argued that racial segregation in sports is a function of centrality, that is, spatial location in a team sports unit.[40] To explain positional racial segregation in sport, they combined organizational principles advanced by Hubert M. Blalock and Oscar Grusky. Blalock argued that (1) the lower the degree of purely social interaction on the job, the lower will be the degree of (racial) discrimination, and (2) to the extent that performance level is relatively independent of skill in interpersonal relations, the degree of (racial) discrimination is lower.[41] Grusky's notions about the formal structure of organizations are similar: "All else being equal, the more central one's spatial location: (1) the greater the likelihood dependent or coordinative tasks will be performed and (2) the greater the rate of interaction with the occupants of other positions. Also, the performance of dependent tasks is positively related to frequency of interactions."[42]

Combining these propositions, Loy and McElvogue hypothesized that "racial segregation in professional team sports is positively related to centrality."[43] Their analysis of football (in which the central positions are quarterback, center, offensive guard, and linebacker) and baseball (in which the central positions are catcher, pitcher, shortstop, second base, and third base) demonstrated that the central positions were indeed overwhelmingly held by whites and that blacks were overrepresented in the peripheral (noncentral) positions. Empirical research has found this relationship consistently (the one exception is basketball, where stacking has broken down with the increased proportion of blacks) in racially mixed team sports. For example:

- In women's intercollegiate volleyball, blacks are overrepresented at the hitter position and whites at setter (the central position) and bumper.[44]
- In Canadian hockey, French Canadians are overrepresented at goalie (the central position), and English Canadians are disproportionately represented in defensive positions.[45]
- In British soccer, black West Indians and black Africans are overrepresented in the wide forward positions, and whites are overrepresented at goal and midfielder (both central positions).[46]
- In Australian rugby, whites are overrepresented in the central team positions, and Aborigines are found disproportionately in the wide positions.[47]

The situation for professional football and baseball is found in Table 13.2. Examination of this table reveals that (1) stacking continues thirty-five years after the Loy and McElvogue research; (2) looking at football, blacks are found more commonly on defense (where the requisite requirement is "reacting" to the offense) than on offense (which is control-oriented); and (3) whites are found disproportionately at the thinking, leadership, and most central positions, while blacks are found at those peripheral positions requiring physical attributes (speed, quickness, strength).

Football and baseball have stacking, but basketball, which once did, is no longer characterized by racial segregation by position (both in college and in the pros). This change appears to be related to the proportion of a minority in a sport. When college and professional basketball were dominated numerically by whites, stacking occurred (with whites disproportionately at the point guard and blacks overrepresented at the strong forward position). This trend is no longer the case in college men's basketball, where blacks are now a majority. In professional basketball, where more than 73 percent of the players are black, stacking has ceased to exist. These patterns substantiate the hypothesis of Rosabeth Moss Kanter that the greater the numerical proportion of a minority in a social organization, the more likely genuine integration will occur.[48]

Explanations for Stacking

Several explanations have been advanced to account for the stacking phenomenon. The Loy and McElvogue interpretation rested primarily on a position's spatial location in a team unit. However, Edwards argued that the actual spatial location of

Table 13.2 Positional Breakdown by Race/Ethnicity, 2005 (in percent)

National Football League[a]	White	Black	Other
Offensive positions			
Quarterback	82	16	1
Running back	9	89	2
Wide receiver	9	91	—
Tight end	57	40	3
Offensive tackle	44	55	1
Offensive guard	54	39	7
Center	69	24	7
Defensive positions			
Cornerback	5	95	—
Safety	14	83	6
Linebacker	26	71	3
Defensive end	24	75	1
Defensive tackle	69	24	7

Major League Baseball[b]	White	Black	Latino	Asian
Pitcher	69	3	26	3
Catcher	62	1	36	1
Infielder	48	11	39	2
Outfielder	48	26	22	3

Source: Richard E. Lapchick, *2005 Racial and Gender Report Card* (Orlando: Institute for Diversity and Ethics in Sport, University of Central Florida, 20 December 2006).

a. Sixty-seven percent of all players in the NFL in 2005 were black, 32 percent of all players were white, and 1 percent of all players were either Pacific Islander, Latino, or Asian American.

b. Sixty percent of Major League Baseball players in 2005 were white, 9 percent were African American, 29 percent were Latino, and 3 percent were Asian.

a playing position is an incidental factor; according to him, the crucial variable involved in positional segregation is the degree of outcome control or leadership responsibility found in each position. For example, quarterbacks have greater team authority and ability to affect the outcome of the game than players who occupy noncentral positions. Thus, it is the leadership and the degree of responsibility for the game's outcome built into the position that account for the paucity of blacks in central positions.

Edwards's explanation is consonant with the stereotype hypothesis advanced by Jonathan J. Brower (specifically for football, but it applies to other sports as well):

> The combined function of centrality in terms of responsibility and interaction provides a frame for exclusion of blacks and constitutes a definition of the situation for coaches and management. People in the world of professional football believe that various football positions require specific types of physically—and intellectually—endowed athletes. When these beliefs are combined with the stereotypes of blacks and whites, blacks are excluded from certain positions. Normal organizational processes when interlaced with racist conceptions of the world spell out an important consequence, namely, the racial basis of the division of labor in professional football.[49]

This view, then, posits that it is the racial stereotypes of blacks' abilities that lead to the belief that they are more ideally suited to those positions labeled "noncentral." For example, Brower compared the requirements for the central and noncentral positions in football and found that the former require leadership, thinking ability, highly refined techniques, stability under pressure, and responsibility for the outcome of the game. Noncentral positions, on the other hand, require athletes with speed, aggressiveness, "good hands," and "instinct."[50] Evidence for the racial-stereotype explanation for stacking was found in the paucity of blacks at the most important positions of outcome control in football: quarterback, kicker, and placekick holder. It is inconceivable to us that blacks lack the ability to play these positions at the professional level. Placekick holders (mostly whites) must, for example, have good hands, an important quality for pass receivers (who are mostly blacks). Nine out of ten of the pass receivers were black, but not one was selected as a placekick holder. Kicking requires a strong leg and the development of accuracy. Are blacks unable to develop strong legs or to master the necessary technique? The conclusion seems inescapable: Blacks are relegated to noncentral positions that require speed, strength, and quick reactions and are precluded from occupying leadership positions (such as the quarterback and the center, who calls out the blocking assignments) because subtle but widely held stereotypes of black intellectual and leadership abilities still persist in the sports world.

Another explanation for stacking was advanced by Barry D. McPherson, who argued that black youths may segregate themselves into specific sport roles because they wish to emulate black stars.[51] Contrary to the belief that stacking can be attributed to discriminatory acts by members of the majority group, his interpretation holds that the playing roles to which black youths aspire are those in which blacks have previously attained high levels of achievement. The first positions to be occupied by blacks in professional football were in the offensive and defensive backfield and in the defensive line; therefore, subsequent imitation of their techniques by black youths has resulted in blacks being overrepresented in these positions. This explanation may be relevant in explaining the high proportion of Latino baseball players in the positions of second base, third base, and shortstop (see Table 13.2).

McPherson produced no empirical support for his explanation, so D. Stanley Eitzen and David C. Sanford sought to determine whether black athletes changed from central to noncentral positions more frequently than whites as they moved from high school to college to professional competition.[52] Their data from a sample of 387 professional football players indicated that there had been a statistically significant shift by blacks from central positions to noncentral ones. Blacks in high school and in college occupying central positions held primarily by whites in professional football casts doubt on McPherson's socialization model. Athletic role models or heroes will most likely have greater attraction for younger individuals in high school and in college than for older athletes in professional sports. Furthermore, professional players were found distributed at all positions during their high school playing days. The socialization model also assumes a high degree of irrationality on the part of the players. It assumes that as they become older and enter more keenly into competitive playing conditions, they will more likely seek positions because of their earlier identification with black stars rather than make rational assessments maximizing their ultimate athletic skills.

It is possible, however, that socialization variables do contribute to the racial stacking patterns in baseball and football, but in a negative sense. That is, given discrimination in the allocation of playing positions (or at least the belief in its existence), young black males may consciously avoid those positions for which opportunities are (or are believed to be) low (e.g., catcher, pitcher, quarterback) and will select instead those positions where they are most likely to succeed (e.g., outfielder, running or defensive back).

The Consequences of Stacking

The effects of stacking are far-reaching. First, the stacking of whites in "thinking/leadership" positions and blacks in "physical" positions reinforces negative stereotypes about blacks and the ideology of white supremacy. Second, athletes in those positions requiring speed, quickness, and agility have shorter careers than those in highly skilled positions requiring technique and thinking. The shortened careers for blacks that result mean lower lifetime earnings and more limited benefits from the players' pension fund, which provides support based on longevity. Also, as we will see shortly, playing at noncentral positions reduces significantly the chances of a career as a coach or manager.

Rewards and Authority

Racial minorities also do not have the same opportunities as whites when their playing careers are finished. This is reflected in media positions, where blacks and Latinos are rarely found in radio and television sportscasting, even rarer as play-by-play announcers, and infrequently as sportswriters.

Officiating is another area that is disproportionately white. In 2005, in the NBA, for example, where 73 percent of the players were African American, 64 percent of the referee positions were held by whites. Similar disparities are found in the NFL and Major League Baseball. Each of these leagues hires a disproportionate number of whites as game officials, but it is important to note that the percentages indicate that professional basketball is the most progressive of the professional leagues on the various forms of discrimination.

Although the percentage of minority players in each of the three most prominent American professional sports greatly exceeds their percentage of the total population, ample evidence indicates that few opportunities are available to them in managerial and entrepreneurial roles. For example, in 2005, some 37 percent of the head coaches in the NBA were racial minorities (all African American). In the NFL, 6 percent of the head coaches were racial minorities (all African American). In Major League Baseball, 23 percent of the managers were people of color (four African Americans and three Latinos). There were no racial minorities in head coaching positions in the NHL, and Major League Soccer had three Latino head coaches (25 percent of the total). (See Table 13.3 for the race/ethnicity breakdown for owners, head coaches, and assistants in professional sports.) In the women's professional basketball league (the WNBA), there were 2 African American head coaches (11 percent of the total) and 17 black assistant coaches (53 percent).[53]

Leadership in college sports is also predominantly a white male domain. Richard Lapchick, summarizing the data from his 2006 study of diversity in Division IA schools, states: "The study shows that the vast majority of the most powerful people in college sport are still white. In Division IA, this includes 94.1 percent of the presidents, 89.1 percent of the athletics directors, 94.1 percent of the faculty athletics reps and 100 percent of the conference commissioners."[54]

The specifics from that study of the 119 Division IA schools include the following:[55]

- Of the university presidents in these 119 Division IA schools, 4 were African American

Table 13.3 Players, Ownership, and Coaching Positions in Professional Sports by Race/Ethnicity, 2005 (in percent)

League	White	Black	Latino	Asian
National Football League				
Players	31.5	65.5	0.1	2.0
Ownership	100	0	0	0
Head coaches	81	19	0	0
Asst. coaches	66	32	1	0
National Basketball Association				
Players	22	73	0.1	2
Ownership	98	2	0	0
Head coaches	63	37	0	0
Asst. coaches	62	38	0	0
Major League Baseball				
Players	60	8.5	28.7	2.5
Ownership	97	0	3	0
Managers	77	13	10	0
Coaches	71	15	14	0

Source: Richard E. Lapchick, *2005 Racial and Gender Report Card* (Orlando: Institute for Diversity and Ethics in Sport, University of Central Florida, 20 December 2006).

men, 3 were Latino men, and 15 were white women. In other words, 94.1 percent were white and 81.5 percent were white men.
- Of the 119 athletics directors, 10 (8.4 percent) were African American men, 3 (2.5 percent) were Latino men, and 5 (4.2 percent) were white women. In short, 89.1 percent of the athletics directors were white and 84.9 percent were white men.
- Head football coaches in the 2005 season were 2.5 percent African American and 0.8 percent Latino. Ten percent of the offensive and defensive coordinators were African American, 0.8 percent were Latino, and 1.2 percent were Asian. Thus, some 88 percent of the coordinators (most important assistant coaches) were white.
- Contrast these disparities with the racial/ethnic breakdown of players on the Division I football teams in the 2005 season: 49.7 percent were African Americans, 1.8 percent were Latinos, 2.2 percent were Asians, and 46.7 percent were white.

Black women who aspire to coaching and management positions are victims of double jeopardy—their race and their gender. The barriers are especially difficult because black women have had so few opportunities to participate in high-quality programs and because few persons in the position to hire are willing to take what they consider to be high risks. Some further examples from Division I college athletics are:[56]

- There are no African American women serving as conference commissioners, and only 0.5 percent of the Division I athletic directors were African American women. In all of the women's sports programs combined, only 3 percent of the head coaches were African American women. Some 6.9 percent of the assistant coaches in all women's sports were African American women.
- In Division I women's sports programs, African American women held 9.3 percent of the head coaching positions in basketball and 6.0 percent were head coaches of cross-country/track.

The paucity of minorities in positions of leadership (coaches and administrators) in professional and college sports could be the result of two forms of discrimination. Overt discrimination occurs when owners ignore competent blacks because of their prejudices or because they fear the negative reaction of fans to blacks in leadership positions. The other form of discrimination is more subtle. Blacks are not considered for coaching positions because they did not, during their playing days, play at high interactive positions requiring leadership and decisionmaking. We know that major league managers, for example, tend to have played as catchers or infielders. Blacks, because of stacking, have tended to be in the outfield and therefore do not possess the requisite infield experience that traditionally has provided access to the position of manager. The situation is similar in football. Research has shown that the majority of coaches attended major universities playing at the central positions of quarterback, offensive center, guard, or linebacker. Blacks are underrepresented at these positions and are thus almost automatically excluded from head coaching responsibilities. And the same pattern has been found for basketball, in which two-thirds of professional and college head coaches played at guard (the most central position). Once again, since black athletes in the past were underrepresented at guard, they are less likely than whites to be selected as coaches when vacancies occur.

Following the scandalous remarks in 1987 by Al Campanis, a Los Angeles Dodgers executive, on national television that "blacks lacked the necessities to be leaders," a number of sports leaders vowed that the hiring of black executives and coaches was a top priority. Moreover, the National Football League adopted the Rooney Rule in 2002 (named after the owner of the Pittsburgh Steelers, Dan Rooney), which mandated that any team with a head coach opening must interview at least one minority for the job unless it was promoting one of its own assistants. That rule has made a difference: Whereas the league had only 2 black head coaches in 2002, by 2007 there were 6, and 2 of them coached the competing teams in the 2007 Super Bowl. College football remains behind the NFL in hiring black head coaches. In 2007 only 7 of the 119 head coaches in Division IA were minorities, compared to 6 of the 32 in the NFL. While there has been some progress in other sports, vacancies still tend to be filled by whites. Professional basketball is the most progressive in hiring blacks in leadership positions, but even there the powerful positions remain predominantly white.

SUMMARY

Minorities' participation in sports continues to increase. This has led many observers to conclude incorrectly that sports participation is free of racial discrimination. As our analysis has demonstrated, stacking in football and baseball, while occurring less than twenty-five years ago, remains pronounced. Blacks are disproportionately found in those positions requiring physical rather than cognitive or leadership abilities. Moreover, the data indicate that although the patterns have been substantially altered in collegiate and professional basketball, black athletes in the two other major team sports have been and continue to be found disproportionately in starting roles and relatively absent from substitute roles.

Nearly as dramatic is the dearth of minorities in administrative, managerial, and officiating roles. Although athletes of color have made significant advances in the past quarter-century, they have not gained comparable access to decision-making positions. With the exception of professional basketball, the corporate and decision-making structure of professional sports is about as white as it was before Jackie Robinson entered Major League Baseball in 1947. The distribution of minorities in the sports world is therefore not unlike that in the larger society. Minorities are admitted to lower-level occupations but virtually excluded from positions of authority and power.

Despite some indications of change, discrimination against minority athletes continues in American team sports. Sport is not a meritocratic realm where race and ethnicity are ignored. Equality of opportunity is not the rule if race is a variable. Even where there have been significant positive changes, discrimination continues.

WEB RESOURCES

www.nativeweb.org
General websites on race information about Native Americans.

www.bus.ucf.edu/sport
This website is for the Center for the Institute for Diversity and Ethics in Sport, University of Central Florida. This site provides the annual *Racial and Gender Report Card* with current data on race and gender in sport.

www.hispaniconline.corn/sports&/index.html
This online magazine has a section on Latinos and sport.

www.eric-web.tc.columbia.edu//abstracts/ed312356.html
This website focuses on the effects of school sports participation on the social, educational, and career mobility of minority students.

www.sscnet.kucla.edu/csrc
Resources on Latinos from the University of California–Los Angeles (UCLA) Chicano Studies Research Center.

www.lainet.com/-joejones
The African American home page.

www.mit.edu:S001/afs/athena/mit.edu/user/i/r/irie/www/aar.html
Asian American resources.

fas-www.Harvard.edu/-mideast
The website for Harvard's Center for Middle Eastern Studies.

NOTES

1. This section on definitions is dependent on D. Stanley Eitzen and Maxine Baca Zinn, *In Conflict and Order: Understanding Society*, 12th ed. (Boston: Allyn & Bacon, forthcoming), chap. 11; and Margaret L. Andersen and Howard F. Taylor, *Sociology: Understanding a Diverse Society* (Belmont, Calif.: Wadsworth, 2000), chap. 11.

2. American Sociological Association, *The Importance of Collecting Data and Doing Research on Race* (Washington, D.C.: American Sociological Association, 2003). See also Carol Mukhopadhyay and Rosemary C. Henz, "How Real Is Race? Using Anthropology to Make Sense of Human Diversity," *Phi Delta Kappan* (May 2003): 669–678.

3. Carmen DeNavas-Walt, Bernadette D. Proctor, and Jessica Smith, "Income, Poverty, and Health Insurance Coverage in the United States: 2006," *Current Population Reports*, P60-233 (August 2007).

4. Ibid.
5. Ibid.
6. Dedrick Muhammad, "The Black/White Divide," *Inequality.Org*, 12 June 2007, http://www.demos.org/inequality/article.cfm?blogid=253418EE-3FF4-6C82-577DD9DOF/.

7. Jonathan Teller-Elsberg, Nancy Folbre, and James Heinz, with the Center for Popular Economics, *Field Guide to the U.S. Economy* (New York: The New Press, 2006), 62.

8. Ibid., 67.
9. Andersen and Taylor, *Sociology*, 290.
10. See John Holway, *Black Diamonds: Life in the Negro Leagues from the Men Who Lived It* (Westport, Conn.: Meckler, 1989); and Charles K. Ross, *Outside the Lines: African Americans and the Integration of the National Football League* (New York: New York University Press, 1999).

11. Rogers Hornsby, quoted in Ocania Chalk, *Pioneers of Black Sport* (New York: Dodd, Mead, 1975), 78. See also Jules Tygiel, *Baseball's Great Experiment: Jackie Robinson and His Legacy* (New York: Oxford University Press, 1983).

12. Robert H. Boyle, *Sports: Mirror of American Life* (Boston: Little, Brown, 1963), 103.

13. Paul Gallico, quoted in Jay J. Coakley, *Sports in Society*, 4th ed. (St. Louis: Times Mirror/Mosby, 1990), 204.

14. Jimmy Powers, quoted in Phillip M. Hoose, *Necessities: Racial Barriers in American Sports* (New York: Random House, 1989), xviii.

15. Harry Edwards, quoted in John Underwood, "On the Playground," *Life*, Spring 1988, 104.

16. Marcos Breton, "Latinos and Baseball," *ColorLines*, Spring 2000, 16. See also Marco Breton and Jose Luis Villegas, *Home Is Everything: The Latino Baseball Story: From the Barrio to the Major Leagues* (El Paso, Tex.: Cinco Puntos Press, 2003); Rob Ruck, *The Tropic of Baseball: Baseball in the Dominican Republic* (Lincoln: University of Nebraska Press, 1999); and Alan M. Klein, *Growing the Game: The Globalization of Major League Baseball* (New Haven, Conn.: Yale University Press, 2006).

17. Dave Zirin, "Say It Ain't So, Big Leagues," *The Nation*, 14 November 2005, 22–24.

18. Cited in ibid., 22.
19. Breton, "Latinos and Baseball," 15.
20. Alan Zarembo, "Taking a Real Beating," *Newsweek*, 6 December 1999, 70–73.

21. Brent D. Wisdom, "Hispanic Influx Gives Liberal a New Face," *Wichita Eagle*, 2 September 2007, p. 4A.

22. Reported in MaryJo Sylvester, "Hispanic Girls in Sports Held Back by Tradition," *USA Today*, 29 March 2005, pp. 1A–2A.

23. Steve DiMeglio, "Fire within Trailblazer Park Successfully Rekindled," *USA Today*, 7 June 2007, p. 9C.

24. For a discussion of Asian American girls and sports participation, see Sandra L. Hanson, "Hidden Dragons: Asian American Women and Sports," *Journal of Sport and Social Issues* 29 (August 2005): 259–265. For the dilemmas faced by recent Asian immigrants, see Mark Grey, "Playing Sports and Social Acceptance: The Experiences of Immigrant and Refugee Students in Garden City, Kansas," in *Inside Sports*, ed. Jay Coakley and Peter Donnelly (London: Routledge, 1999), 28–36.

25. Frank Clancy, "Warriors," *USA Weekend*, 12 February 1999, p. 4. See also Kevin Simpson, "Sporting Dreams Die on the 'Rez,'" in *Sport in Contemporary Society*, 7th ed., ed. D. Stanley Eitzen (New York: Worth, 2005), 259–265; Larry Colton, *Counting Coup: A True*

Story of Basketball and Honor on the Little Big Horn (New York: Warner Books, 2000); and Greg Boeck, "The Native American Barrier: Group Culture and Individualism," *USA Today*, 22 February 2007, pp. 1C–2C.

26. Quoted in Simpson, "Sporting Dreams Die on the 'Rez,'" 265.

27. Jay Coakley, *Sports in Society*, 9th ed. (St. Louis: McGraw-Hill, 2007), 466–468.

28. Richard E. Lapchick, *2005 Racial and Gender Report Card* (Orlando: Institute for Diversity and Ethics in Sport, University of Central Florida, 2006).

29. Amby Burfoot, "White Men Can't Run," *Runner's World*, August 1992, 94.

30. Robert Sapolsky, "It's Not All in the Genes," *Newsweek*, 10 April 2000, 68. For an argument that gives more primacy to genetics, see Jon Entine, *Taboo: Why Black Athletes Dominate Sports and Why We're Afraid to Talk About It* (New York: Public Affairs, 2000).

31. Laurel R. Davis, "The Articulation of Difference: White Preoccupation with the Question of Racially Linked Genetic Differences among Athletes," *Sociology of Sport Journal* 7 (June 1990): 179–187.

32. Anne Marie Owens, "Genes Give Black Runners Edge: Findings," *National Post Online*, 27 November 2000, www.nationalpost.corn/search/story.html?f=stories/s0001127/384654.html.

33. Rob Beamish, Queen's University, e-mail to nasserv@listserve.bc.edu, 8 October 2001.

34. James Green, personal communication to Norman R. Yetman and D. Stanley Eitzen.

35. John C. Phillips, *Sociology of Sport* (Boston: Allyn & Bacon, 1993), 173.

36. Harry Edwards, *Sociology of Sport* (Homewood, Ill.: Dorsey, 1973), 201–202; see also Terry Bledsoe, "Black Dominance of Sports: Strictly from Hunger," *Progressive* 37 (June 1973): 16–19; Phillips, *Sociology of Sport*, 173–179.

37. Phillips, *Sociology of Sport*, 173–179.

38. Donal E. Carlston, "An Environmental Explanation for Race Differences in Basketball Performance," *Journal of Sport and Social Issues* 7 (Summer/Autumn 1983): 30–51.

39. Jay J. Coakley, *Sports in Society: Issues and Controversies*, 9th ed. (New York: McGraw-Hill, 2007), 310.

40. John W. Loy, Jr., and Joseph F. McElvogue, "Racial Segregation in American Sport," *International Review of Sport Sociology* 5 (1970): 5–24.

41. Hubert M. Blalock, Jr., "Occupational Discrimination: Some Theoretical Propositions," *Social Problems* 9 (Winter 1962): 246.

42. Oscar Grusky, "The Effects of Formal Structure on Managerial Recruitment: A Study of Baseball Organization," *Sociometry* 26 (September 1963): 345–353.

43. Loy and McElvogue, "Racial Segregation in American Sport."

44. D. Stanley Eitzen and David Furst, "Racial Bias in Women's Intercollegiate Sports," *Journal of Sport and Social Issues* 13 (Spring 1989): 46–51.

45. Mare Lavoie, "Stacking, Performance Differentials, and Salary Discrimination in Professional Ice Hockey," *Sociology of Sport Journal* 6 (March 1989): 17–35.

46. Joe A. Maguire, "Race and Position Assignment in English Soccer," *Sociology of Sport Journal* 5 (September 1988): 257–269; and Merrill Melnick, "Racial Segregation by Playing Position in the English Football League," *Journal of Sport and Social Issues* 12 (Fall 1988): 122–130.

47. Christopher Hallinan, "Aborigines and Positional Segregation in the Australian Rugby League," *International Review for the Sociology of Sport* 26, no. 2 (1991): 69–81.

48. Rosabeth Moss Kanter, "Some Effects of Proportions on Group Life: Skewed Sex Ratios and Responses to Token Women," *American Journal of Sociology* 82 (March 1977): 965–990.

49. Jonathan J. Brower, "The Racial Basis of the Division of Labor among Players in the National Football League as a Function of Stereotypes" (paper presented at the annual meeting of the Pacific Sociological Association, Portland, Ore., 1972), 27. This argument is also advanced by R. Williams and Y. Youssef, "Division of Labor in College Football along Racial Lines," *International Journal of Sports Psychology* 6 (1975): 3–13.

50. Brower, "The Racial Basis of the Division of Labor among Players," 3–27.

51. Barry D. McPherson, "The Segregation by Playing Position Hypothesis in Sport: An Alternative Hypothesis," *Social Science Quarterly* 55 (March 1975): 960–966.

52. D. Stanley Eitzen and David C. Sanford, "The Segregation of Blacks by Playing Position in Football: Accident or Design?" *Social Science Quarterly* 55 (March 1975): 948–959.

53. Lapchick, *2005 Racial and Gender Report Card*.

54. Quoted in "Decisions from the Top: Diversity among Campus, Conference Leaders at Division I-A Institutions" (Orlando: Institute for Diversity and Ethics in Sport, University of Central Florida, 25 January 2006).

55. Ibid.

56. Ibid. The percentages for other women of color are even lower than for African American women.

Chapter 14

Gender in North American Sport
Continuity and Change

The flood of girls into team sports is one of the major sports trends of the past decade. (Shutter Point/Charles Barner)

One may question the need for a separate chapter dealing with gender and sport, particularly because we have included gender topics and issues in chapters throughout this book. We believe that in spite of the tremendous social change that has taken place over the past twenty-five years, sport still promotes and preserves traditional gender differences in many ways. As a consequence, a focused and in-depth consideration needs to be given to gender in a way that has not been possible in the other chapters. In this chapter, the primary focus will be on injustices and inequities females have faced in sports. We realize, however, that gender problems in sports do not involve just females, so we also discuss gender issues related to males in this chapter.

American and Canadian societies pride themselves in their concern for the fullest development of each person's human potential, but they have historically been quite insensitive to the social injustices and inequality toward females. A most fundamental feature of both societies is the pervasiveness of male privilege. Male/female disparities in wealth, power, and prestige are ubiquitous social phenomena. Men are privileged throughout the occupational structure; they experience greater material rewards, a higher level of deference and esteem, and a more dominant position in the control of both their personal lives and their social activities.[1]

That is only one of the issues that require attention. Another involves the processes of the social construction of gender relations and understanding how meanings about masculinity and femininity serve to promote and sustain gender inequities and injustices, thus creating problems for both men and women. One of the North American cultural practices that is most influential in the construction of meanings about masculinity and femininity is sport. Historically, it has been a significant cultural practice in constructing and reproducing gender relations.

THE HERITAGE OF GENDER INEQUALITY IN SPORT

During one's childhood, adolescence, and early adulthood, there is a tendency to believe that current social conditions have always existed. There is typically a lack of understanding that current social conditions are historically rooted and have emerged out of quite different conditions in the past. This is certainly the case with gender relations and sport. Young people today see girls playing a variety of youth sports, they see girls on high school teams winning state championships, women in intercollegiate athletics capturing NCAA national championships, and professional women athletes earning incomes of more than a million dollars a year. Little do they realize that such opportunities and achievements were unheard of only forty years ago. Here is a tip for college-age readers of this book: Ask your grandmothers to tell you what conditions for females in sport were like when they were growing up. We think you will be amazed at what you will hear.

In order to develop an understanding about contemporary gender relations, it is helpful to place social relations between the sexes in historical perspective. For the past three thousand years Western cultural ideology has been firmly grounded in patriarchy, which is a set of personal, social, and economic relations that enable men to have power over women and the services they provide. Patriarchal ideology defines females as inferior to and dependent on men, and their primary gender-role prescriptions are seen as child-bearers, child-rearers, homemakers, and sex objects.

The traditions of Western civilization have been perpetuated in North America with respect to the status of women. When the framers of the U.S. Declaration of Independence wrote that "all men are created equal" (excluding black and Native American men, of course), that is literally what they meant, and it was not until 144 years later (1920) that women were even considered worthy of the right to vote.

Thus, cultural definitions of female role expectations are embedded in the traditions of Western civilization that are foundational to North American society. The overemphasis on protecting women and girls from the experiences of achievement and success and the underemphasis on developing physical skills fit the historical socialization pattern of preparing women for their adult role as passive helpmates of men, standing on the sidelines of history, cheering men on to their achievements and successes.

As modern sport developed in the latter nineteenth century, it served as one of the most powerful cultural forces for reinforcing the ideology of male superiority and dominance. Organized sport created symbols, rituals, and values that preserved patriarchy and women's subordinate status in society. By celebrating the achievements of males through their sporting achievements and marginalizing females into the roles of spectators and cheerleaders, sport reproduced the male claim to privileged status. The overriding societal attitude with respect to sport was that it was for males and not for females.[2]

The combined role of woman and athlete was virtually unthinkable in North America in the nineteenth century. Women who wished to participate in competitive sports and remain "feminine" faced almost certain social isolation and censure. By choosing the physically active life, a woman was repudiating traditional female gender-role expectations. It might seem, therefore, that females would have little role to play in the burgeoning expansion of sport. Notwithstanding the cultural obstacles women had to overcome, their increasing presence and persistent involvement in sport in the late nineteenth and early twentieth centuries actually made a significant contribution to the rise of modern sport.

The latter nineteenth century brought many social changes, and industrialization brought more wealth and leisure to more North Americans. Middle- and upper-class women experienced more freedom than they had ever known. Their interests expanded to activities outside the home, and as organized sport grew, women were often some of the most ardent participants. Croquet, roller-skating, ice-skating, bowling, archery, lawn tennis, golf, and bicycling were a few of the sports that captured the interest and enthusiasm of women during the latter part of the nineteenth century.[3]

One important trend in sport in the latter nineteenth century took place at women's colleges. Several of the best-known women's colleges began including sports as part of their physical education programs. Boating, skating, bowling, horseback riding, swimming, tennis, and golf were all popular on campuses, and they were respectable because participants were protected from public view while they played. When basketball was developed as a sport in the 1890s, it quickly became popular at women's colleges. The English game of field hockey was introduced into the United States in the early twentieth century, and it too became immediately popular in the eastern women's colleges.

Throughout the twentieth century, females faced a continuing struggle for equality and justice in sports. It is obvious from the following statement made by two *Sports Illustrated* writers in 1973 that females still encountered oppression and inequality in the world of sport: "There may be worse (more socially serious) forms of prejudice in the United States, but there is no sharper example of discrimination today than that which operates against girls and women who take part in competitive sports, wish to take part, or might wish to if society did not scorn such endeavors."[4]

This statement makes it quite clear that the sport culture was pretty much the exclusive domain of males. Men typically engaged more often in sports and manifested greater interest in sporting achievements. Sports heroes and superstars were mostly males, and male dominance was notable in the administrative and leadership branches of sports, where men clearly overshadowed women in power and numbers. Female athletes did not suit the ideal of femininity, and those who persisted in sport suffered for it. These same *Sports Illustrated* writers characterized the prevailing view in the 1970s: "Sports may be good for people, but they are considered a lot gooder for male people than for female people."[5]

During the last three decades of the twentieth century, women intensified their struggle for gender equality, and North America witnessed a social revolution—a women's liberation movement. As one dimension of this movement, women responded to inequalities in organized sport by demanding their rightful place as equals. They were no longer content to be the cheerleaders and the pom-pom girls, urging on male athletes to glory, prestige, and power. Their targets for change varied from the kinds of legal and extralegal restrictions that prevented females from having equal access to sport opportunities to attempts to elevate the social and political consciousness of women as a group. Coming under special attack were stereotypes of the ways males and females were supposed to behave. One writer summarized the progress that had been made by the early 1990s in this way:

> As a result of Title IX as well as the fitness movement of the eighties, more women and girls play sports, including highly competitive sports, than ever before.... They are getting pleasure out of sheer physical competence.... Women athletes now have female stars to model themselves after, and those stars are gaining more fame and fortune than would have been thought possible twenty years ago. Sports participation has given millions of women new self-confidence and has taken them to where they never were before—onto what used to be male turf.[6]

Sport opportunities for girls and women have increased tremendously—mainly because of court decisions and federal laws. However, prejudices are not altered by courts and legislation, and culturally conditioned responses to gender ideology are ubiquitous and resistant to sudden changes. Therefore, laws may force compliance in equality of opportunity for females in the world of sport, but inequities in sport continue, albeit in more subtle and insidious forms, as has been the case with racism.

SOCIAL SOURCES OF GENDER INEQUALITY IN SPORT

The ultimate basis of gender inequality in North American sport is embedded in the sociocultural milieu of society and in the traditions of Western societies that are foundational to the United States and Canada. The historical foundations of the North American gender system and how it has specified behaviors, activities, and values of the sexes were described previously. We showed how the gender system has operated as a mechanism of inequality by ranking women as inferior and unable and by conferring privilege and status to males. In addition to the historical sociocultural influences, more specific socialization agents and agencies tend to reproduce the gender system with each new generation. We now turn to an examination of some of these influences, emphasizing the role of several social institutions in gender socialization.

Parental Child-Rearing Practices and Gender Construction

Sex is a biological characteristic while gender refers to an ongoing cultural process that socially constructs differences between men and women. Each culture *constructs and teaches its young* the social role expectations for males and females, about what is considered masculine and what is considered feminine. Thus, humans are immersed in a complex network of sex and gender norms throughout life. Almost everything is gendered, and all societies have attitudes, values, beliefs, and expectations based on sex.[7]

The teaching of gender-role ideology comes from a range of social sources, including peers, teachers, ministers, mass media, and so forth, but the earliest and most persistent instruction takes place in the family. Parents are major contributors to the shaping of gender-role ideology by acting differently toward sons and daughters as early as their first exposure to them and throughout the remaining years of their rearing. From infancy there are both marked and subtle differences in the way parents speak to sons and daughters, the way children are dressed, the toys they are given, and the activities in which they are encouraged and permitted to engage. A certain amount of aggression is not only permitted but is encouraged in boys; much less is tolerated in girls. Techniques of control tend to differ also: Praise and withdrawal of love are used more often with girls, physical punishment relatively more often with boys.

Children rapidly learn the difference in parental expectations concerning gender-appropriate behavior. The traditional parental message has been that desirable qualities for males are aggressiveness, independence, and individual achievement striving and that desirable qualities for females are passivity, affiliation, nurturance, and dependence. Studies of the childhood experiences of female and male athletes have found that in a variety of ways, parents, especially fathers, encouraged the sport involvement of their sons more than that of their daughters.[8]

The School and Gender Construction

The school serves to reinforce and extend the gender-role stereotyping that begins in the home. Teachers are in close contact with students throughout the day, day after day, year after year; therefore they are the major influence on children and youth. Teachers mold the traditional gender-role differences both directly and indirectly.

An indirect means by which the school reinforces traditional gender roles is through its own authority structure. While some 82 percent of all elementary school teachers are women, over 44 percent of the elementary school principals are men, and about 76 percent of secondary school principals are men, even though some 59 percent of the teachers at this educational level are women. Less than 25 percent of all superintendents are women. Thus, schoolchildren learn the differential status of men and women simply by attending school.

Another mechanism of gender-role reinforcement is sex-segregated, or at least single-sex-dominated, classes. Classes that teach cooking, sewing, and other homemaking skills are considered to be primarily for girls, classes in woodworking or shop primarily for boys. In high school, certain subjects such as math and science are often viewed as male subjects, and English and fine arts are regarded as female subjects.

Some textbooks, one of the basic sources of learning in schools, perpetuate gender-role ideology. The kind of history they purvey and the kinds of suggestions they present for adult occupational choices and leisure-time pursuits suggest a negative image of women as unimportant and unable. In studies of the treatment of gender roles in textbooks, investigators have found that women tend to be marginalized in the world of politics, science, and sports, and their future presented as consisting primarily of glamour and service.[9]

Much of every school day is lived outside the classrooms in hallways, on the playgrounds, and going to and from school. It is during these times that a great deal of interaction takes place between same-sex classmates and between opposite-sex classmates. Much of this time is spent in conversations, informal fun and games, and just plain "horsing around." These interactions between boys and girls turn out to be what some researchers call "power play." By that they mean that through these school-related ritualized interactions gender is socially constructed.[10]

A lot has changed in high school sports in the past twenty years, and we will discuss those changes in more detail later in this chapter. In spite of the greater opportunities for females in interschool sports, these programs are still testimony to the importance of boys and the secondary status of girls. Thus, extracurricular activities, like school athletics, play an important role in the production and reproduction of gender differences. Having said that, this gender differentiation in school sports is not nearly as conspicuous as it once was.

The Mass Media and Gender Construction

As we emphasized in chapter 11 on sport and the mass media, social contexts and descriptions of women in the mass media—including newspapers, magazines, radio, television, and motion pictures—generally reinforce the gender-role stereotypes. However, a sea change has taken place in media coverage of women's sports in the past decade. Prior to that, the media did little to promote an attitude of respect for female athletes and their achievements in sports. Coverage of women in sport tended to reinforce the stereotypes firmly embedded in the cultural heritage regarding women. Women's sports now have a prominent place in all of the media, although coverage does not match the total volume and detail of the coverage of men's sports. Stories about female athletes, when they do appear in the media, often center on a discussion of figures and fashions, something that never happens with stories about male athletes. Still, girls and women, as well as boys and men, are able to read about and see the achievements of female athletes in a variety of sports. Media coverage of female athletes and their teams inspires girls and women to become involved in sport and, for a few, to aspire to the top levels of sport.

Despite this significant transformation in media treatment of women in sport, there are still major differences in women's and men's sports coverage. Male sports still dominate sports sections in newspapers, and the content of the vast majority of sport magazines focuses on males. In the leading sports magazine, *Sports Illustrated*, 60 to 80 percent of the articles in each issue are about male athletes and teams. Between 1997 and 2004 only 29 out of 416 *Sports Illustrated* covers were devoted to women. Even worse, of the 52 issues of *Sports Illustrated* in 2006, not a single cover featured a female, except the annual swimsuit issue, which is entirely devoted to women wearing the skimpiest of swimsuits and positioned in soft-porn poses.

Motion pictures are also a powerful influence in keeping women in their place. Movie producers have tended to project two identities for women, that as a sex object or as a wife/mother figure, but seldom as a physically active athlete. There have been numerous movies about male athletes, but very few about female athletes.

Television, because of its omnipresence, plays a powerful role in depicting gender relations. Studies extending over twenty years convincingly show the unequal treatment of women's sports on TV. Even television commercials where sports figures are used to endorse or advertise products overwhelmingly feature male sports figures.[11]

Gender stereotyping and sexist commentary have become less frequent by TV sportscasters. However, commentary during a women's sports event will still occasionally focus on the physical attractiveness of the performers, their fashionable attire, their grooming, or their "cute" personality characteristics; commentary on such subjects is rarely part of a men's event. See the "Media Sport and Gender Inequities" section in chapter 11 for a more detailed account of this topic.

Nicknames, Mascots, and Heroines

One of the vestiges of the past that is gradually disappearing is the trivialization of female sports teams through the nicknames and mascots that are used for high school girls' and college women's teams. Although the nicknames and mascots are chosen by the institutions, it is through the mass media that they are largely communicated to the public. Tigerettes, Rambelles, Teddy Bears, and other "cutesy" mascot names may seem harmless but they have the effect of defining female athletes and females' athletic programs as frivolous, insignificant, even trivial.[12]

An individual or group of individuals whose behavior in a particular role provides a standard or model by which other persons can determine appropriate attitudes and actions is said to be a role model. Through media accounts of their achievements, athletes become widely known to the public and become celebrities. Media portrayals of these sport celebrities tend to link their personal lives with their sports achievements; if a socially positive character is created, they become role models or heroes and heroines, especially to children and adolescents.

Historically, there have been few feminine counterparts to sport superstars Michael Jordan, Wayne Gretsky, Emmitt Smith, Pete Sampras, and Cal Ripken, Jr. Boys are bombarded with daily accounts of high school, college, and professional athletes, but until the past decade girls rarely read, heard, or saw reports about the feats of outstanding female athletes. However, the remarkable achievements of female professional, collegiate, and elite amateur athletes in recent years have provided a foundation for role modeling by young female athletes. Women athletes such as Serena and Venus Williams, Annika Sorenstam, Lisa Leslie, and Mia Hamm have achieved celebrity status comparable to that of many male athletes, and many women's teams—such as America's World Cup women's soccer team and the women's basketball teams at the University of Connecticut and

American tennis player Serena Williams and her sister Venus, right, in action during a match at the Bangalore Open 2008 women's tennis tournament in Bangalore, India. (AP Photo/Aijaz Rahi)

University of Tennessee—are world-renowned. Thus, "name" female athletes do exist in several sports, and girls of the present generation now have sport heroines to admire.

FEMALES SURMOUNT SOCIAL BARRIERS TO PARTICIPATION IN SPORT

Gender inequality directed against females, like prejudice and discrimination of any kind, is insidious and denigrating. For females, it has taken many forms: the perpetuation of myths about the biological and psychological weaknesses of females, unequal opportunity for participation in many activities, and unequal access to the authority and power structure. Each of these forms of gender inequality has been used to discourage women and girls from participating in sports and to deny them equal access to the rewards that sport has to offer.

Negative Myths

A variety of folklore, myths, and slogans traditionally prevalent in North American society supported sport as an exclusively masculine activity and served as barriers to female participation in sport until recently.

Myth: Athletic Participation Masculinizes Females

One of the oldest and most persistent notions about female participation in sport, and a main deterrent, was the idea that vigorous physical activity tended to "masculinize" the physique and behavior of girls and women. For years, women of physical competence were stigmatized as "masculine" by claims that women who engaged in physical activities were not "feminine." This was like a doomsday weapon to discourage female interest and involvement in sport.

From the beginning of modern sport, sport was a male preserve, and images of ideal masculinity for males were culturally constructed through sports. The cultural script was that males validated their masculinity through athletic endeavors. Females had no place there; it could only make them masculine, as it does males. The founder of the modern Olympic Games and an influential leader in sport, Pierre de Coubertin, opposed what he called the "indecency, ugliness and impropriety of women in . . . sports [because] women engaging in strenuous activities were destroying their feminine charm and leading to the downfall and degradation of . . . sport."[13] At another time, de Coubertin drove home the same point: "Would . . . sports practiced by women constitute an edifying sight before crowds assembled for an Olympiad? Such is not [the International Olympic Committee's] idea of the Olympic

Games in which we have tried . . . to achieve the solemn and periodic exaltation of male athleticism with internationalism as a base, loyalty as a means, art for its setting, and female applause as its reward."[14]

The impression that physical activity produces masculine body types is undoubtedly due to the fact that some females who become serious athletes do indeed develop muscular and movement characteristics appropriate for performing the skills of a sport. Such muscle development and movement patterns have nothing to do with maleness or femaleness but are merely the most efficient use of the body to accomplish movement tasks. Nevertheless, the threat of masculinization was sufficiently terrifying to discourage many females from becoming physically active, and those who did become athletes often lived with the fear of becoming "masculine."

Even into the twenty-first century, many female athletes attempt to maintain a "ladylike" appearance in deference to the ideology that sport masculinizes females. They often compensate for the perceived threat to their femininity by wearing feminine artifacts with their athletic attire. By wearing ruffles, pastel colors, or lacy designs and styles they seem to be saying, "Even though I'm a highly skilled athlete, I'm still feminine." See Box 14.1, *Thinking about Sport*, for a discussion of this issue.

There is, of course, no evidence to support the notion that vigorous physical activity alters the basic biological constitution of a female, making her more "male." This is not to suggest that no physical or psychological differences exist between female athletes and female nonathletes. Prolonged physical training in a sport alters the female physique, physiological support systems, and psychosocial characteristics just as it does in the male. Indeed, athletes as a group seem to have somewhat special physical and psychological characteristics, but these personal characteristics may have existed before the individual became involved in sport. Actually, these traits may have attracted them to sport in the first place. Sociologist Nancy Theberge studied the sources of pleasure and satisfaction in women ice hockey players and

Action at the 2006 Women's Rugby World Cup final at Commonwealth Stadium in Edmonton, Alberta, Canada. (AP Photo/CP, Ian Jackson)

found that many of them were attracted to ice hockey because of the physicality involved in playing it. One of the players told Theberge, "I like the fight for the puck; it's who's going to fight for the puck. . . . That's where the competitiveness comes in, that's where my aggressiveness comes from: this [the puck] is mine and I'm not giving it to you kind of thing. . . . I like a physical game."[15]

There is another social sanction used against active females that is closely linked to the "sport masculinizes females" argument, and that is a charge about female athletes and their sexuality. Two interrelated arguments fuel the supposed connections between sports and lesbianism. One is that there is a profusion of women athletes who are lesbians. The second is that sports participation converts females to lesbianism. Although there is no scientific evidence for the perpetuation of this myth, it has had the effect of producing homophobic (meaning dislike and intolerance of homosexuals) claims about rampant lesbianism among female athletes. Given the widespread homophobic public attitudes that prevail in North American societies, this charge has had ominous consequences for females who might wish to become involved in sports and for those

> **Box 14.1** *Thinking about Sport* **Anyone for Rugby?! Challenging Discourses of Feminine Bodies in American Culture**
>
> Women's participation in rugby both challenges and reinforces dominant discourses of sport and sporting bodies. It presents a cultural site, where the shape and size of the female sporting body often contradict dominant ideas of feminine bodies in American culture.
>
> ### TACKLING NORMATIVE FEMININITY
>
> Rugby provided the women in this study with the opportunity to participate in an aggressive, physically demanding collision sport. For many of them it was the first time they had participated in an organized collision sport. Several of the women had tried to or had considered playing high school football because of the tackling and physicality required in football. But many of these women described actively searching for an outlet for their physicality.
>
> Many women in the study discussed how their participation in rugby had changed how they thought and felt about their bodies and their performance. Andrea, who is one of the smaller players on the Missouri team, addressed rugby's impact on the way she feels about her body:
>
>> Definitely I want to be stronger. Since I started playing rugby and lifting weights I want big shoulders. There is some gene in me that says you're not going to have big shoulders because I've been trying for a long time and I haven't gotten them yet. But I want to be stronger and fitter. I don't want to be, you know I used to want to be thin, everybody wants to be skinny, now I don't want to be that, I want to look, I want to be muscular. I want to look like I have muscles. I want to be able to see definition in my arms or my legs. I want that. I don't care if I have a six-pack but I want muscle there. If you can't see it I at least want it to be there anyway. I just want to be strong.
>
> Natalie revealed that playing rugby had changed the poor relationship she had with her body. She wanted to look like a muscular, professional, female athlete instead of an emaciated supermodel. This suggests that Natalie had become aware that idealizing a supermodel body was problematic and that desiring an ultra-thin body was not healthy. Her involvement in rugby significantly changed how she felt about her body.
>
> ### RESISTING DOMINANT FEMALE BODY IDEALS
>
> While women's rugby bodies are normalized into the disciplinary, docile sporting bodies that they quite unquestionably celebrate, they also enjoy the disciplinary process because it disrupts the disciplinary gaze supervising the construction of ideal female bodies. Many of these women recognized that by playing rugby they were challenging images of the ideal female body and using their bodies in ways that disturb the boundaries of what is appropriate for women. Shelby very effectively described the pleasure some of the women took in resisting these boundaries:
>
>> I mean that's body on body, women pushing, determination, everything that's ever been told that they can't ever do, they are doing right then. I mean everything, I mean you're not supposed to be tough, you're not supposed to get dirty, you're not supposed to bleed, you're not supposed to whatever, you know don't perspire, what is that? You don't sweat, you glisten, my ass, you know you've got women over there with their ears taped down, and their hair flopping out of their ponytails. I'm sure not everybody thinks about it when they are out there playing but like everything we've been told we can't do, it's like you know what, fuck you, I'm doing it, and it's like, I'm going to kick mud in your face, and I'm going to breathe and I'm going to be dirty and I'm going to love it, and it is the best, to have your body hurt like that, to push it all the way past the end, I mean beyond the end.
>
> This research contributes to answering the call for the recognition of the importance of the body and physicality in women's sport. . . . The women in this study actively work to construct athletic and powerful bodies that challenged ideals of normative feminine bodies, and they displayed a critical awareness of how their bodies challenge these ideals.
>
> *Source:* Laura Frances Chase, "(Un)Disciplined Bodies: A Foucauldian Analysis of Women's Rugby," *Sociology of Sport Journal* 23 (2006): 229–247.

who are involved in sports. It has certainly had a profoundly stigmatizing effect on them.

The claims about sport's presumed "masculinizing" and "lesbianizing" of females have been vigorously attacked by a broad spectrum of scholars and scientists who have exposed the ideological foundations of these arguments. They have emphasized that definitions of feminine and masculine behavior are culturally constructed—that they are not natural, biological characteristics at all. Moreover, they emphasize that sexual orientation is irrelevant with regard to sport participation, and there are heterosexual as well as homosexual males and females in sport just as there are in every other sector of social life.

Martina Navratilova, one of the greatest tennis players of all time, was the first well-known female athlete to openly acknowledge she was a lesbian. Since then, a number of other top women athletes have done likewise. In the fall of 2005, WNBA star Sheryl Swoopes publicly announced that she was gay. In a *Sports Illustrated* interview with Swoopes, she was asked whether the public's reaction was what she expected. Swoopes replied that the support she had gotten had been phenomenal and that on the first five road trips after her announcement there were standing ovations when she was introduced, and not just from gay women or gay men. Sheryl and other women athletes maintain that contemporary women are no longer willing to have traditional definitions of masculine/feminine and sexuality imposed on them, especially when such definitions prevent females from experiencing highly valued social activities.[16]

It is now quite clear that the presumptions that women become masculinized and their sexual orientation is influenced by sports participation have served as social weapons to reinforce cultural traditions of male privilege and female subordination, but they are now being widely rejected. Indeed, some women have completely repudiated the traditional definitions that identify muscles with masculinity and homosexuality, and such sports as bodybuilding and weight lifting are growing rapidly among sportswomen. Like male bodybuilders, women bodybuilders are judged on the symmetry and proportions of their physiques, on their muscularity and definition, and on their posing routines, and women weight lifters are judged by how much weight they can lift, just like men. Furthermore, their sexuality is no more important than is men's.[17]

Of course there are females in sports who are lesbians, just as there are lesbians in every other walk of life. They suffer many of the social troubles that all lesbians live with. In her book *Strong Women, Deep Closets: Lesbians and Homophobia in Sports*, Pat Griffin details some of them: the sense of isolation, feelings of loneliness, fear of being outed, and, if they do come out, prejudice and discrimination among friends and family. In spite of pervasive homophobia within sport and the wider society, gay females in increasing numbers are deciding to come out and live their sexual orientation openly and with pride in the honesty of their decision.[18]

Gender-role reconceptualization is taking several forms, but in all its variations a prominent place is reserved for the active woman. In the evolving trends in sports and gender roles, girls and women are struggling for identity, and sport has become a significant medium through which females realize meaning in their lives. Sport is one way in which feminist cultural politics are being employed as a form of "organized opposition to the domination of men in sport and through the freeing and empowering of the bodies of women from diverse backgrounds."[19]

It may be seen, then, that contemporary women refuse to be locked into outmoded role prescriptions and baseless assertions, especially those that limit their physical potential.

Myth: Sports Participation Is Harmful to the Health of Females

From the beginnings of modern sport forms in the mid-nineteenth century, women were cautioned about participation in sport. It was widely claimed that sport was harmful to female health. Principally concerned with physical injury to the reproductive organs and the breasts and with possible effects on the menstrual cycle, pregnancy, and the psychological well-being of females, the literature of the past one hundred years is laden with such opinions. Early in the twentieth century, a noted physical educator and actually a promoter of women's physical education discouraged women from engaging in competitive sports because of "the peculiar constitution of [a female's] nervous system and the greater emotional disturbances to which she is subjected."[20]

Women themselves reinforced the view that female health was harmed by competitive sports. In 1928 the chairperson of the Executive Committee of the Women's Division of the National Amateur Athletic Federation voiced her opposition to women's Olympic participation: "Girls are not suited for the same athletic programs as boys. The difference between them cannot be ignored. . . . Under prolonged intense physical strain a girl goes to pieces nervously."[21] Placing the focus of health dangers exclusively on females had an ideological foundation grounded in the preservation of male privilege. Its purpose was the maintenance and continuation of gender differentiation, with exclusive male access to a socially esteemed activity—sport.

Biomedical and psychological research over the past twenty-five years clearly shows that intensive sports training and competition, especially at the elite levels of sport, do have a number of health risks for both men and women. The increased participation of females in high levels of sport competition, combined with the growth of the sport sciences, has helped to clarify some specific potential health risks for female athletes. Some of them are amenorrhea (cessation of menstrual function without menopause) and related effects (osteoporosis, stress fractures), delayed menarche, high frequency of knee injuries, and relationship of reduced body fat to eating disorders. These health risks increase as the intensity, duration, and frequency of the training and competition increase.[22] There are individual and sex-specific physiological and psychological differences and responses to sport participation, but that is no reason not to provide equal access and opportunity for sporting experiences to females. Furthermore, for the vast majority of females the physiological, psychological, and social benefits gained through physical activity and sports competition are pretty much the same as they are for males.

Myth: Women Are Not Interested in, or Very Good at, Sports

Male domination of sport culture was so complete until the past two decades that females could be denied opportunities in sport by asserting that women were not really interested in or very good at sports. Those who made this point typically referred to the paucity of women in sports, and claimed that the best performances of those who did participate in sport were inferior to men's performances. Thus, women's sports have been subject to a cultural grand jury not applied to men's sports. Such arguments, like all cultural norm explanations of social regularities, tended to ignore social structure.

Women in the past chose to pursue certain roles and not others not just because that was the cultural norm, but because males and females were related to each other in a relatively stable social structure of power and differential status. This was a structure in which males appropriated the roles they preferred because they had the power to do so and could thus promote more status for themselves. Women's roles were residual, and the norm merely sustained the existing structure of power and status. Females were simply socialized out of sport by a variety of powerful social agents and agencies; was it any wonder they took little interest in sport? Without interest and encouragement, few indeed did play or play very well.

Female achievements in sport during the 1990s and the first decade of the twenty-first century are too numerous and too remarkable to list. In ultradistance running, swimming, and cycling, as well as equestrian events, dogsled racing, and horse and auto racing, women and men now compete together, even at the highest levels of competition. Women win their share of those events, too. World and Olympic records once set by male athletes in swimming, distance running, cycling, and other sports as well have been broken by female athletes. Clearly, the argument that females are not interested in sports and that they do not play them well enough to be taken seriously has been put to rest for even the most hardened skeptics of women's potential.[23]

Attitudes toward Female Athletes

Attitudes involve what people think and how they feel about and behave toward other people or objects. They are socially learned rather than innate, and they are enduring but changeable.

Attitudes toward female athletes and active women have changed rapidly. Enlightened persons have come to recognize that negative attitudes toward female athletic participation of any kind are incongruent with the realities of female potential. Moreover, many now realize that attitudes that sort sports into "appropriate" and "inappropriate" for females are embedded in a cultural ideology of gender inequality and injustice.

There is a high level of acceptance and support for female sports participants among general segments of the population. Moreover, female athletes themselves are increasingly reporting very positive self-images in general; a concept of femininity exists that combines fitness, strength, and health through physical activities with a firm belief that this in no way diminishes their potential or capability to fulfill whatever other roles they wish to pursue.

THE OPPORTUNITY AND REWARD STRUCTURE FOR FEMALES IN SPORT

Denial of equal access to various opportunities and unequal rewards for achievements are the two most ubiquitous injustices that females have historically experienced in relation to sport. Although the opportunity and reward structures for female sports participants have greatly improved (more females are involved in sports and receiving more rewards for their achievements than ever before), there are still numerous ways in which girls and women are deprived of equal opportunity and receive inferior rewards. In this section we will describe some of the torment females have suffered, and continue to suffer, as well as some of the changes that have opened up opportunities for women to experience the access and rewards of sports participation at all levels.

From Boys-Only Youth Sports to Opportunities for Both Sexes

As we noted in chapter 4, youth sports programs introduce most children to the experience of organized sports. The Little League, Babe Ruth, and Connie Mack baseball leagues are three of the most popular baseball programs. Pop Warner football, Junior Hockey, and Biddie basketball initiate youngsters to tackling, blocking, ice-skating, and jump shooting. Age-group programs in swimming, track and field, and gymnastics are only a few of the more than twenty-five youth sports programs that involve millions of youth annually.

Until the mid-1970s, Little League baseball had an all-male policy that prevented girls from playing on its teams as part of its federal charter. This policy was challenged by several girls or their representatives, and it was reluctantly rescinded by Little League officers. Public opinion as well as the laws rapidly turned against those who wished to perpetuate the traditional gender differentiation in physical activities. A 2007 national survey of organized youth sports participation sponsored by the Sporting Goods Manufacturers Association (SGMA) found that some twelve million girls ages six to seventeen—48 percent of all girls in that age range—were members of an organized team. The flood of girls into team sports is one of the major sports trends of the past decade.[24] To a large extent this was because the young parents of these children were the first generation of parents since the women's movement began. They were the first generation to renounce the traditional cultural edicts of strict gender differentiation in social life. They tend to have a more favorable attitude toward gender equity, including equity in sport.

Toward Gender Equity in High School Sports

In 2007, 41 percent of participants in high school sport in the United States were females. Girls' high school sports have become so popular that they rival boys' high school sports for attention in many communities. Indeed, in some communities the girls' teams have a larger following of fans because of their winning records. These conditions for girls' high school sport are quite recent. Prior to the mid-1970s, discrimination in sports opportunities for females in high schools was at a scandalous level. The national governing body of high school sports, the National Federation of State High School Associations (NFHS), actually listed nine states that prohibited interschool sports for girls. Little more than twenty years ago, a high school with ten or twelve teams for boys might have no teams, or only a few teams, for girls. Boys' sports seasons might run three months with 15 or 20 scheduled contests; the season for a girls' sport typically extended a mere three to four weeks, with 2 or 3 contests.

However, when the Educational Amendments Act of 1972 was passed, Title IX, a key provision, required schools that receive federal funds to provide equal opportunities for males and females. Title IX will be described in more detail in the next section. Title IX constituted a considerable weapon against sex discrimination in the American public school and collegiate sports programs, because some 16,000 public school districts and more than 2,600 colleges and universities benefit from federal funds.

In Canada nothing comparable to Title IX has existed, but sex equality issues have been dealt with in several ways. The Canadian Charter of Rights and Freedoms Constitution Act of 1982 provides legal and constitutional rights of gender equity. The Fitness and Amateur Sports Women's Program was established in 1980, and it provides government programs, training, and policy standards for females. The Canadian Association for the Advancement of Women and Sport (CAAWS) was formed in 1981 "to advance the position of women by defining, promoting, and supporting a feminist perspective on sport and to improve the status of women in sport."[25] The publication *Women in Sport: A Sport Canada Policy* in 1986 defined a national policy for women in sport. It established goals of equality of opportunity for women in sport and called for specific action-based programs to achieve the goals.

In the United States Title IX proved to be the beginning of a sports revolution for girls and women. Within the next ten years, the number of female high school athletes in the United States jumped from 294,000 to just under 2 million. Table 14.1 illustrates the staggering increases that have occurred in girls' high school athletic participation. In the past thirty years the number of girls participating in high school athletic programs

Table 14.1 High School Sports Participation Survey Totals

Year	Boy Participants	Girl Participants
1972	3,770,621	817,073
1975–1976	4,109,125	1,645,039
1989–1990	3,398,192	1,858,659
2000–2001	3,921,069	2,784,154
2006–2007	4,321,103	3,021,807

Source: The National Federation of State High School Associations, "Participation in High School Athletic Programs, 1972–2007," 2007, http://www.infoplease.com/ipa/A0779930.html.

throughout the nation has increased by more than 900 percent. As we noted above, by 2007 about 41 percent of all high school sport participants were female, and the number of sports available to them was more than twice the number available in 1980.[26]

In spite of a federal law requiring schools to treat the sexes equally, the transition from a predominantly male athletic program to a two-sex program did not occur without controversy and litigation. Title IX was silent or vague on some issues; therefore, high school girls had to challenge the discrimination in their school sports programs through legal and legislative action. A number of lawsuits were brought by girls against school districts or state high school athletic regulatory bodies. In general, the cases fell into two categories: (1) A girl desired to participate on the boys' team when a girls' team was not provided at her school, or (2) a girl wished to be on the boys' team even though her school provided a girls' team. In the first type of case, the courts generally ruled in favor of the girl, though some of these suits required appeals. In the second type of case, the girl was usually not successful because the court reasoned that equal opportunity had not been denied her.

Although many positive strides have been made, issues about participation still persist. Each fall a few girls go out for high school football teams. Some states have ruled that they may not become members of the team. Others have ruled that if they can make the team, they may remain.

High school wrestling illustrates the trend that has been taking place with regard to girls' participation. When high school girls first came out for wrestling, they found various legal and policy barriers. They also found less formal objections. In the case of one girl who was a member of a high school wrestling team in Arizona, a fundamentalist religious group protested, saying it was immoral for a boy to wrestle a girl. One coach protested because a girl did not weigh in with the rest of the boys, stripped of all clothing. One of her opponents refused to wrestle her because of "strong moral convictions." Despite such barriers and objections, more than five thousand girls now participate on high school wrestling teams across the country annually.

A development that has shown increasing strength involves requests by boys to be allowed to participate on girls' high school teams. In almost every case, the boys have wanted to take part on the girls' team because the school did not have a boys' team in that sport. Volleyball, soccer, gymnastics, field hockey, and swimming have been the sports that have most commonly drawn requests.

In several instances the boys have won the right to play on the girls' team. During the fall of 2001, seven of the twenty-one girls' field hockey teams in western Massachusetts had at least one boy on their rosters. Boys were starters on Division I state field hockey championship teams for two of the previous three seasons. Massachusetts has an equal rights amendment in its constitution, and the state's superior court has ruled that the amendment applies to sports. Because the state's high schools do not provide field hockey teams for boys, boys are eligible to join girls' field hockey teams. According to the NFHS participation survey, more than seven hundred boys were playing high school field hockey in 2006.[27] However, throughout the nation, it is clear that boys will not wish to play on girls' teams in large numbers, but the situation does illustrate the unintended consequences of efforts to address gender equity against one sex.

Toward Gender Equity in Intercollegiate Sports

To comprehend the issues, controversies, and current status of intercollegiate sports for women, one must have some detailed understanding of Title IX of the Educational Amendments Act of 1972, because the struggles of intercollegiate sports for women have been intricately bound to Title IX for the past thirty-five years. So before we address the issues of gender equity in intercollegiate sport, we describe the legislative and legal incidents surrounding Title IX.

Title IX and Subsequent Legislative and Legal Incidents

Title IX specifies: "No person in the United States shall, on the basis of sex, be excluded from participation in, be denied the benefits of, or be subjected to discrimination under any education program or activity receiving Federal financial assistance." Although the clear intent of this legislation seems to provide equal educational opportunities to females and males where federal funds are being used, Title IX has not brought about the goal of gender equality. A variety of legal challenges to it have been mounted by various groups, including the federal government, the NCAA, and individual universities, many of which still resist, or at least resent, complying with the intent of the legislation.

A devastating setback for advocates of a broad interpretation of Title IX came in 1984 when the U.S. Supreme Court ruled in *Grove City College v. Bell* that the Title IX language applied only to a specific program or department that received federal funds. This decision negated the original intent of the law: that an educational institution receiving federal funds must provide equal opportunity in all of its programs and activities. In effect, the Court's decision said that women could be denied equality in sports. Indeed, that is what happened; within a year of *Grove City*, the Office for Civil Rights (OCR) in the U.S. Department of Education (DOE) suspended sixty-four investigations, more than half involving college athletics. At that point one lawyer said, "The discrimination is so apparent, so blatant. Without the support and nourishment of the law, we see how fragile the support to maintain women's athletics really is."[28]

Immediately after the *Grove City* decision, various women's groups began to lobby Congress to pass legislation restoring the weakened civil rights. After four years, both houses of Congress overrode President Reagan's veto, and the Civil Rights Restoration Act became law. The act is designed to ensure that federal funds are not used to subsidize discrimination based on sex, race, age, or physical disability. One of its implications was the restoration of the original broad interpretation of Title IX.

In the meantime, the OCR in 1979 issued what became known as the "three-part test" policy. That policy provided that a university sponsoring an athletic program must provide equal athletic opportunities for members of both sexes. Among other factors, the regulation required that an institution must effectively accommodate the athletic interests and abilities of students of both sexes to the extent necessary to provide equal athletic opportunity. The OCR indicated that it would apply the three-part test to assess whether an institution is providing nondiscriminatory participation opportunities for individuals of both sexes. An institution only had to meet one of the three parts of the test:

1. *Substantial Proportionality:* Are participation opportunities substantially proportionate to enrollment?
   - This part is satisfied when participation opportunities for men and women are substantially proportionate to their respective undergraduate enrollments.
   - Thus, if 51 percent of the students are female, at least 46 percent and no more than 56 percent of the student-athletes should be female. A few percentage points' deviation from perfect equality is allowed.
2. *History and Continuing Practice:* Is there a history and continuing practice of program expansion for the underrepresented sex?
   - This part is satisfied when an institution demonstrates a continuing history of improving gender equity in its sports program.
3. *Effectively Accommodating Interests and Abilities:* Is the institution fully and effectively accommodating the interests and abilities of the underrepresented sex?
   - This part is satisfied when an institution is meeting the abilities and interests of its female (or male) students even when there are disproportionately fewer female (or male) student-athletes.
   - Here, if there are disproportionately fewer female (or male) student-athletes, the institution must prove that the women (or men) do not have enough ability or interest to provide additional sports opportunities, or that new teams would not be able to compete against other teams.[29]

Although the three-part test for compliance with Title IX has been in place for more than twenty-five years, resistance to full compliance and the achievement of gender equity in college sport persists into the twenty-first century. Resistance to gender equity in intercollegiate athletics has been met by complaints filed with the DOE's Office for Civil Rights and by legal action through the courts. More than a thousand complaints have been filed with the OCR involving sports. Dozens of lawsuits have been filed on behalf of gender equity in college sports, and in most cases the party or parties claiming discrimination have won.

To give readers a "feeling" for what has taken place, we present two examples. During the mid-1990s, Brown University lost a sex discrimination suit brought by women athletes seeking reinstatement of women's gymnastics and volleyball teams that Brown had dropped from varsity status to cut athletic costs. After nearly five years of litigation, including an appeal by Brown to the U.S. Supreme Court (which was denied), the federal courts ruled in favor of the female athletes, basing their ruling on Brown's failure to satisfy any part of the Office for Civil Rights' three-part test for compliance with Title IX. In 1998 a federal court approved a settlement that Brown had reached, agreeing to maintain women's athletics participation within 3.5 percent of women's enrollment at the university and to increase spending on four women's sports.[30]

In a different challenge to Title IX, in 2002 the National Wrestling Coaches Association (NWCA) and several other wrestling organizations brought a lawsuit against the DOE claiming that the DOE's interpretation of Title IX and its policies had a discriminatory impact on male athletes, especially in wrestling programs. The DOE asked for a dismissal of the lawsuit on the grounds that the alleged injuries to the wrestling programs could not be traced to Title IX. A federal appeals court upheld the dismissal of the suit, saying that the wrestling organizations failed to show how Title IX directly caused a reduction in men's sports. The wrestling organizations appealed to the U.S. Supreme Court; in 2005 the Supreme Court rejected without comment the appeal of the suit by the wrestling organizations.[31]

The basic argument of the wrestling organizations—that Title IX was reducing participation opportunities for male athletes by eliminating men's athletic teams or limiting the number of participants on the teams—turned out to be false. From 1988 to 2005 NCAA institutions actually had a net gain of seventy sports for men. From 1981 to 2005, annual male sports participation increased by 146,962 athletes.

About the time of the Supreme Court's decision on the wrestling organization's lawsuit, the OCR issued a clarification to the three-part test allowing educational institutions to use Internet e-mail-based interest surveys alone to determine if they were meeting the athletic interests and abilities of girls and women in their institutions. Moreover, the clarification stated that student nonresponse to the e-mail surveys would be interpreted as a lack of interest by the underrepresented gender. Many athletic administrators, Title IX compliance officers, and coaches were highly critical, and since spokespersons at the DOE have said that this clarification is simply guidance that institutions can choose to use the survey or not—it's their choice—few institutions have chosen to use it.[32]

The NCAA makes periodic gender equity reports. The most recent report at the time this chapter was written found:

- Females comprise 57 percent of the college student population, but only 43 percent of NCAA participants were women.
- Male college athletes receive 55 percent of college athletic scholarship dollars; female college athletes receive 45 percent.
- 68 percent of the total basketball recruiting expenses went to men, 32 percent to women.
- NCAA colleges spend 33 percent of student-athlete recruitment money on females, 67 percent on male student-athletes.

It is clear from the report that, although women have been making gains toward gender equity in intercollegiate athletics, progress is being made much too slowly and there are still inequities that need to be abolished.

Governance and Control Issues

Prior to the passage of Title IX, only about 15 percent of college athletes were women. In colleges with a female enrollment nearly equal to male enrollment, women's intercollegiate athletic budgets accounted for only 2 percent of the total budget. Females needed bake sales, bazaar nights, and Christmas tree sales to finance their athletic programs, while male programs in the same institutions provided new and expensive uniforms and equipment, disbursed generous per diem travel expenses, and never requested the male athletes to help raise money or to spend any of their own. Facilities for female college programs were most often second-rate. The newer and larger gyms routinely went to the men; the older gyms were routinely given to the women.

Conditions in college sport improved for women in the 1970s with the founding of the Association for Intercollegiate Athletics for Women (AIAW), a counterpart to the NCAA. By 1981 the AIAW had more than 950 members. Thirty-nine championships were contested in 1980–1981 under AIAW's aegis.

The NCAA, a bastion of male dominance in collegiate athletics, fought the development of women's intercollegiate athletics with every resource at its command, including litigation against applying Title IX in collegiate athletics. In 1980, however, in a surprising and controversial move, the NCAA voted to begin sponsoring women's championships. This was an action clearly designed to destroy the AIAW and to integrate women into the NCAA. The AIAW filed an antitrust suit against the NCAA, claiming that its action was a "conspiracy to restrain trade and commerce in the governance, program, and promotion of women's athletics." Beset by loss of income and loss of members (35 percent of its members switched to the NCAA in the 1981–1982 school year), the AIAW ceased to offer programs and services in mid-1982.

Since then, governance of women's sport in colleges has been male-dominated. Leadership opportunities for women have lagged far behind those for men. Even well into the first decade of the twenty-first century, the executive director position, the highest position in the NCAA, has never been occupied by a woman; only 25 percent of the vice president/chief of staff positions have been women, and within the chief aide/director level only 24 percent have been women. Each NCAA institution has a faculty athletics representative (FAR) to the NCAA. FARs represent their university on issues regarding athletics. Women from Division I universities held only 23 percent of these posts; there were 28 percent from Division II and 32 percent from Division III institutions.[33]

During the past two decades, concern has arisen that an elite, professionalized approach similar to that of the men's athletic programs was emerging. It has now become clear that despite some protests by women's coaches and athletic directors, many of them have actually embraced the NCAA commercial model of college sports and see the NCAA as providing the best avenue for getting on with the "business" of women's collegiate athletics. Indeed, this is exactly the direction that most major university athletic programs have taken. At the University of Tennessee, average attendance at women's basketball games is more than 14,500; at the University of Connecticut it is more than 10,000. Several other universities report an average basketball attendance of more than 8,000. Other women's sports, especially volleyball, soccer, and softball, have experienced escalating spectator appeal.

With the professionalization of women's intercollegiate athletics, involving money, prestige, and popularity, has come falling graduation rates and violations of NCAA rules similar to the kind prevalent in men's programs. In the fall of 2007, fourteen women's sports teams were on probation. Several others have received reprimands for NCAA rules violations—and not just in one or two sports. The teams involved include basketball, tennis, track and field, volleyball, and swimming.

Some sportswomen are distressed about what has happened to women's collegiate sports. They see women's programs being absorbed into male-dominated sporting structures and losing their chance to advance a different ethic and form for intercollegiate sport. It appears such a structure is already well advanced, and there is no discernible sign that women's athletic leaders have any plan for creating a different model of college sports.

Gender Equity and Men's Intercollegiate Sports

Not all gender equity complaints and lawsuits have come on behalf of women. University officials, principally presidents and athletic directors, have refused to rein in the extravagant expenditures of football and men's basketball; therefore athletic budgets have been under pressure as women's sports teams have been added to meet gender equity provisions of Title IX. Consequently, universities throughout the country have dropped some men's "minor" sports (e.g., swimming, gymnastics, golf, wrestling, etc.).

In a previous section of this chapter we described the lawsuit that the NWCA and several other wrestling organizations brought against the DOE. But the cuts in men's sports have led to wide-ranging claims that compliance with Title IX will be the death knell of men's intercollegiate sports and that women's sports leaders are just greedy and out to abolish men's sports. The NWCA charged that Title IX has been hijacked, diverted from its original purpose of eliminating gender-based discrimination, and fashioned into a handy weapon to enforce a de facto quota system. The assistant secretary of civil rights responsible for dealing with Title IX cases has been accused of being a bureaucrat who is notorious for her indifference to the imminent extinction of male sports programs. In a book titled *Tilting the Playing Field:*

Schools, Sports, Sex and Title IX, author Jessica Gavora attacks the way Title IX is being interpreted, arguing that Title IX was not designed to require that a high school or college sports program reflect the male-female ratio of its student body because males are more interested in sports than are females. Thus, for Gavora, males should have more sport opportunities than females, but according to Gavora, institutions are dropping male sports to add female sports just to meet Title IX standards.[34] While NCAA institutions have certainly dropped many sports teams over the past twenty years, research by the NCAA shows quite clearly that male athletes have not lost *opportunities* as a result of Title IX.

- From 1988–1989 to 2003–2004, NCAA universities added 2,346 sports for men while dropping 2,276 men's sports, for a net gain of 70 men's sports teams.
- From 1981–1982 to 2004–2005, NCAA male sports participation increased 32 percent.

Furthermore, it appears that NCAA Division I universities have dropped men's sports teams in order to divert more resources into men's football and basketball teams rather than to meet Title IX requirements, as they often claim. But from 1988–1989 to 2004–2005, NCAA Division I-A universities had a net loss of 239 men's teams, whereas Division II universities had a net gain of 44 men's teams and Division III universities had a net gain of 265 men's teams.[35]

Over the same period cited above, many more women's sports teams than men's sports programs were added—as would be expected, given the undeveloped condition of women's intercollegiate sports opportunities prior to Title IX. However, increases in women's sports programs have not been accompanied by downsizing men's programs, except for Division I-A universities with the largest athletic budgets.

The controversy over the effects of Title IX on men's intercollegiate athletics continues to be perhaps the most contentious issue in intercollegiate sports. In the summer of 2007, the College Sports Council (CSC), an advocacy group for men's sports, filed a petition asking the Department of Education for additional clarification of Title IX because the CSC believes the first test of the three-part test—proportionality—that the DOE uses for compliance with Title IX has led to fewer athletics opportunities for men in college and that the same thing could happen to boys in high schools. While there is no disputing that hundreds of men's teams have been abolished throughout the nation in the past twenty years, there is also no disputing that 57 percent of NCAA student-athletes are men and only 43 percent are women—in colleges and universities where 57 percent of the students are women.

Most of those who defend the progress toward gender equity in women's intercollegiate sports do not advocate eliminating men's sports teams to achieve that end. They contend that universities and their athletic departments make decisions to drop men's sports or reduce the squad sizes for a number of reasons, not always just to increase the number of women's teams. So to blame Title IX for universities' decisions to drop some men's sports is misleading and untrue. Moreover, they argue that universities have other options to achieve gender equity. For example, they argue that men's sports are eliminated largely due to fiscal mismanagement: Schools spend enormous sums of money for revenue-generating, but overwhelmingly non-profit-making, football and basketball programs. Indeed, fewer than 10 percent of intercollegiate football and basketball teams generate a profit; most are by far the biggest financial drain on athletic department budgets, when revenue and expenditures are both considered. Several sport studies scholars have questioned why Division I-A football teams need ten assistant coaches, why football and basketball coaches must be paid more than $2 million annually, and why Division I-A football teams need eighty-five scholarship players when NFL teams have only fifty-man rosters. They argue that ways and means could be found to reduce spending in areas such as these and divert the savings into preserving men's sports teams.[36]

For their part, most male administrators, coaches, and athletes agree with the spirit behind

Title IX. For them, it is the strict gender-based quota they object to. In *The Game of Life,* a book about college sports and educational values, the authors say, "Although one can empathize with the male athletes and coaches who feel that their sports programs now face restrictions, and who in some cases see gender equity as the cause of those restrictions, the major financial discrepancies between spending on men's and women's sports tell their own story."[37] The good news is that recent trends in intercollegiate sports show that the gap between men's and women's intercollegiate sports—in terms of participation, teams, operating expenses, and so forth—is narrowing, without the elimination of men's teams, and that is the intent of Title IX—to end gender-based discrimination.

MEN RULE IN THE COACHING AND ADMINISTRATION OF WOMEN'S SPORTS

First, it is important to recognize that men dominate the professional/occupational structure in North American society. Overwhelmingly, they hold the most prestigious positions, occupy the powerful leadership roles, and command the highest salaries. So throughout the professional/occupational structure there are differentiated opportunities and rewards for men and women, and careers in sports follow the same patterns found elsewhere.[38]

High School and College Women's Coaching and Administration

Title IX does not apply to coaches and administrators, so gender equity is not required with respect to the employment or salaries of high school and college women coaches and administrators. One ironic consequence is that as opportunities for female athletes opened up and high school and college sports programs expanded, positions in coaching and athletic administration formerly held by women were sought and filled by men. In high school, for example, at the time Title IX became law in 1972, 80 to 90 percent of high school girls' sports were coached by women; within fifteen years, just 35 to 42 percent were coached by women.

This trend slowly reversed itself until an increasing percentage of girls' high school sports are being coached by women. In a very few high schools, women are coaching boys' teams. In the 2007–2008 school year there were several dozen women among the more than sixty thousand or so coaches of boys' high school sports teams across the United States.

Administrative positions in high school sports have remained overwhelmingly held by men. High school athletics directors (sometimes called athletic coordinators) are typically men, with a woman as the assistant, when there is such a position. As of 2007, only 3 of the 51 directors of state high school associations were women; there were only 3 women who served on the NFHS's 12-member Board of Directors.

The coaching pattern that has just been described for high school girls' teams has been duplicated at the collegiate level. In the early 1970s almost all coaches of women's intercollegiate teams were women, but the situation changed rapidly and by 1990 only 48 percent of coaches of women's intercollegiate teams at four-year institutions were women (see Figure 14.1).

By 2006 the percentage had declined to 40 at NCAA Division I institutions (34 percent Division II; 43 percent Division III). Even more disturbing, the percentage of African American women head coaches of women's Division I basketball teams was 9 percent, which starkly contrasts with the 44 percent of student-athletes playing women's basketball who were African American. Assistant coaching positions are often seen as a stepping-stone to the position of head coach. There is a marginally higher percentage of college women assistant coaches than head coaches—about 53 percent across the three divisions of the NCAA—hardly an impressive figure when one considers that females have been involved in high-level college sports for more than 35 years.[39]

It is still an open question as to the long-term trend in hiring practices, but every year there are more women who are experienced and successful

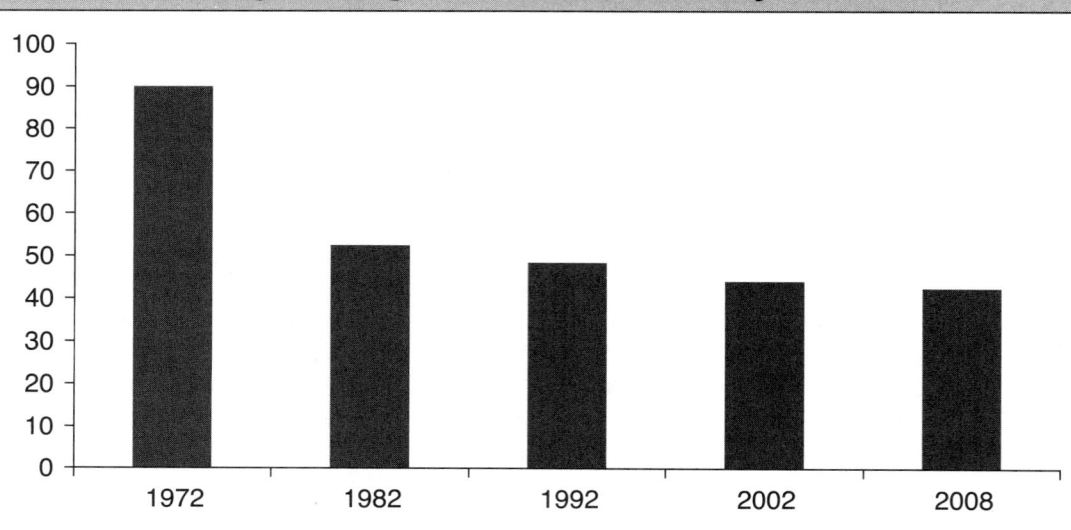

Figure 14.1 Percentage of College Women's Teams Coached by Women

Year	Percentage
1972	90
1982	52
1992	48
2002	43
2008	42

Source: R. Vivian Acosta and Linda Carpenter, "Women in Intercollegiate Sport: A Longitudinal Study—Thirty-One Year Update, 1977–2008." (Carpenter/Acosta, P.O. Box 42, West Brookfield, Mass., 2008).

coaches, and it will be increasingly difficult for higher education officials to hire men for positions that women are as qualified for (or better qualified for) as male applicants. Indeed, there are some women coaching men's teams, but they are less than 3 percent. However, there is a growing belief that in the not-too-distant future one of the highly successful women basketball coaches will be hired to coach a men's college basketball team.

Another issue for women college coaches involves payment for services rendered. In a 1992 NCAA survey, the average salary for men coaches was almost twice as much as that of women coaches. That shocking finding caused universities throughout the country to reassess their salary structures because gender equity can never be achieved as long as there are such wide differences in salary for men and women doing essentially the same tasks. Nevertheless, even near the end of the first decade of the twenty-first century, Division I head coaches of women's basketball teams earned only about 47 percent of the salaries of head coaches of men's teams. There is a wide range of salaries for both men and women basketball coaches, but at the upper extremes several Division I men's basketball coaches have annual salaries exceeding $2 million; the annual salaries of the two eminent coaches of women's basketball teams at Tennessee and Connecticut—Pat Summitt and Geno Auriemma—are about $1 million less.

Those defending the difference in salaries for men and women coaches contend that many men's programs generate more money than women's programs, so differential salaries are justified. That argument is countered with claims that because women's programs receive far less for their operating budgets, women are not given equal opportunity to promote and market their programs, factors that are essential to generate equal revenue in return.

Female athletic administrators have lost out too during the past thirty years. Women's intercollegiate athletic programs in the mid-1970s were administered almost exclusively by women with the title of athletic director. Then, as women's programs grew, many colleges combined their men's and women's athletic departments into one. Most such mergers followed a pattern: After the merger, there emerged a male athletic director and several assistant directors, one of whom was often a woman in charge of women's athletics or the less visible sports.

According to two researchers who have been conducting a longitudinal study of colleges and universities for thirty-five years, in 1972 more than 90 percent of women's intercollegiate programs were headed by a female administrator; in 2008 only 21.3 percent were headed by a female. For 11.6 percent of all intercollegiate programs, no female is involved in the administrative structure. Thus, the practice of institutions to hire men as athletic administrators is continuing into the twenty-first century.

There are signs that the trends may be reversing. In 1995 only four women in the United States headed athletic departments at Division I universities; in 2008 there were six (8.4 percent) in Division I, 18.9 percent in Division II, and 33.7 percent in Division III. Their demonstrated competence and accomplishments show quite convincingly that in this career, just as in many others that have opened up to women, they are quite capable of performing just as well as men. Nevertheless, it seems likely that men will hold the vast majority of these key athletic positions for the foreseeable future.

Leadership opportunities for women in other types of collegiate governance have been negligible. In 2007, three of the sixteen NCAA Executive Committee members were women, and women had 35 percent of all administrative jobs within all divisions of the NCAA, at a time when 43 percent of the student-athletes were women.

Canadian high schools and colleges have experienced a similar pattern of declining percentages of female coaches and athletic administrators. Moreover, the percentage of women coaches decreases in proportion to men as the level of competition increases. However, that has begun to turn around in the past few years.

OWNERSHIP, MANAGEMENT, AND COACHING IN PROFESSIONAL SPORTS

The pattern of men owning, managing, and coaching women's sport teams prevails at the professional level, just as it does at the other levels of sport. The WNBA has perhaps the highest profile of all women's professional sports. The league operates under the auspices of the NBA—although five of the WNBA franchises are independently owned—and is the beneficiary of the NBA's marketing and promotional resources. The players are some of the most recognizable and popular athletes—women or men. Still, the ownership, management, and coaching are overwhelmingly male. During the 2007 season, nine of the total thirteen head WNBA coaches were men, and that pattern has prevailed since the league began.[40] WNBA players seem to have mixed feelings about being coached by men. In one survey of WNBA players, 64 percent indicated they didn't have a preference.

Beyond ownership and coaching, men have a commanding presence from top to bottom in most women's professional sports, and women's involvement in professional men's sports is extremely rare. As we pointed out in chapter 11, newswomen are greatly underrepresented as sportswriters. Despite the addition of a few women sports reporters to the staffs of television networks and a few newspapers, there are still relatively few women in the field. Women are also underrepresented as sports officials, judges, commissioners, athletic trainers, racehorse trainers, and most other sports-related occupations.

There have been six women umpires in professional baseball history, and none has ever reached the major leagues. Pam Postema came the closest, spending 13 years in the minor leagues, including 7 in Triple-A. She almost broke into the majors—calling 2 years of spring training games at her peak—but she was dropped in 1989, and Major League Baseball still awaits its first woman umpire.

In 1997 the NBA gave two women, Dee Kantner and Violet Palmer, officiating assignments in the league, but as of the 2007–2008 season, Palmer remained the sole woman among the NBA's fifty-nine-member officiating staff and the lone female official at the top level in any of the four major professional sports.

In the fall of 2007 Sarah Thomas became the first woman to officiate a game involving NCAA

NBA referee Violet Palmer explains a call to Houston Rockets' Tracy McGrady (1) during a game in Cleveland, Ohio. (AP Photo/Mark Duncan)

Division I-A football teams. She worked as a line judge in a game between Memphis University and Jacksonville State.

Fortunately, many barriers to women's involvement in sport careers are falling, and it is becoming more difficult each year to keep women from fulfilling their sport career goals.

Coaching and Administration in U.S. Olympic Organizations

The U.S. Olympic organizations continue to be bastions of male dominance. There are hundreds of coaches with U.S. Olympic teams, and the fluid movement into and out of those positions makes it difficult to determine the percentage of men and women with any accuracy. One generalization is possible, however: The overwhelming majority of coaches are men. Men coach all of the men's U.S. Olympic teams, and men coach many of the women's teams as well. Where the head coach of a women's team is a woman, there are often men holding positions as assistants, or special position, coaches.

Positions with the USOC are predominantly male, too. In 2007 only 29 percent of the USOC management staff were women and 27 percent of the Board of Directors were female. Of the 115 active members of the IOC, only 15 are women, and there is only 1 woman on the 15-member IOC Executive Board.

Why Have Men Been Hired to Coach and Administer Women's Sports?

Considerable speculation has centered on why girls' and women's sports coaching and administration have become dominated by men. Some have suggested that higher salaries are attracting men into coaching and administration careers; others have suggested that men have greater access to the hiring system through an "old boys" network, and others contend that when men and women apply for sports jobs, men are perceived to be better qualified because sport has traditionally been a male domain.

On the other hand, there are those who maintain that the changing social and occupational conditions for women in the past twenty years have enabled women to have a much greater menu from which to choose a career. They argue that women who have the drive, determination, self-confidence, and intelligence to make good coaches and sports administrators also now have the option to become physicians, lawyers, and business leaders. These positions often pay better than coaching or administering sports programs, especially when women's salaries for coaching and sports administration lag behind men's in those positions.

Gender and Careers at the Top Levels of Sport

As one might expect, opportunities for women to engage in sports at the highest levels have been severely restricted historically, and differential rewards have been the norm. However, progress has been made toward expanding opportunities for females in top levels of sport during the past two decades. The most popular professional sports for women have traditionally been individual sports, especially golf and tennis, because they have traditionally been "socially approved" sports for women, particularly by the affluent social classes.

Professional women's team sports have been less successful in their struggle for acceptance. Some examples are listed below. As you read the list below, use the sociological perspective we introduced in chapter 1 to try to understand why some professional women's sports efforts to form stable women's professional sport organizations have succeeded while others failed.

- *Tennis:* Currently, there are some 200 women on the Sony Ericsson Woman's Tennis Tour. The top five to ten women on the pro tennis circuit typically win about one-half as much prize money as the men. However, men's and women's championship prize monies are the same at the U.S. Open, French Open, and Australian tennis tournaments and almost the same at Wimbledon.
- *Golf:* With more than 260 players on the LPGA tour, the top five money leaders earn only about 25 percent of what the top five men's PGA tour money leaders win.
- *Baseball:* As far back as World War II, there was a women's professional baseball—yes, baseball—league. It remained a viable league until 1954. Several efforts have been made to establish professional baseball for women, but all have been short-lived.
- *Softball:* The Women's Professional Softball League was formed in the mid-1970s but was disbanded after four years. As in baseball, several unsuccessful attempts have been made to establish a stable women's professional softball league. In 1997 the Women's Pro Softball League (WPSL) was formed, but it folded in 2001. In 2004 the WPSL was revived under the name National Pro Fastpitch (NPF) and was still operating in 2007, featuring six teams.
- *Volleyball:* Women's professional volleyball has had a number of leagues and several formats during the past twenty-five years. Some of the leagues were mixed gender, some have been indoor, and some have been outdoor. But there has been very little stability in any of them. The Association of Volleyball Professionals (AVP) Crocs beach volleyball tour is the nation's most prominent professional volleyball tour. It features more than 150 of the top beach volleyball players in the world.
- *Basketball:* Between the mid-1970s and mid-1990s several attempts were made to make a go of women's professional basketball in the United States. All of those efforts ultimately failed. Then in the mid-1990s, two professional leagues began play: the ABL and the WNBA. The former lasted a little less than three years before going out of business. Meanwhile, the WNBA has flourished, having grown to a thirteen-team league by 2007. In spite of its seeming success, its financial viability is heavily dependent upon the financial backing, marketing, and promotions of the NBA. The structure of WNBA players' salaries is paltry compared to NBA salaries.
- *Soccer:* When American women won the Women's World Cup in 1999, interest in women's soccer skyrocketed. Women's soccer organizations immediately began talking about forming a women's professional soccer league. But the reality of having to raise a minimum of $30 to $50 million to get even a modest league off the ground stalled the formation of a league. It was not until the spring of 2001 that the Women's United Soccer Association (WUSA) launched its inaugural season of play. Averaging 8,104 admissions per game, the WUSA exceeded expectations at the gate, but within a year it failed. In the fall of 2007, plans were announced to launch a new professional women's soccer league in 2009 with the name Women's Professional Soccer (WPS).
- *Football:* There have been several unsuccessful efforts to develop a viable women's football league. The most recent attempt, the Women's Professional Football League (WPFL), "kicked off" in the fall of 2000 with fourteen teams; fifteen teams competed in the league during the 2006 season. Money problems forced the earlier leagues to fold, and the newest league seems saddled with the same problems. None of the athletes earn enough money to make a living, so it is more

of a "semi-pro" than full-blown professional operation. Within the past few years the United Football League, the Independent Women's Football League, and the National Women's Football Association have all attempted to form stable organizations, with little success.

- *Foreign Professional Sports:* Opportunities to play on foreign teams in Europe and Asia have opened up for women in several team sports, and more than three hundred North American female athletes currently participate in foreign leagues. Top players can earn very good salaries.
- *Other Professional Sports:* Professional opportunities in sports are continuing to diversify for women. Professional ice-skating has provided a chance for a few skaters to make very high salaries, and more than a hundred women are doing well as jockeys in thoroughbred horse racing. A few female track and field athletes, distance runners, triathletes, and race car drivers are making six-figure salaries.

The reality is that except for a few hundred female professional athletes, very few women make a living in pro sports (see Table 14.2), and with the current social and economic conditions for female professional athletes, the day is far away when more than a handful of women can make sports a full-time job.[41]

Table 14.2 2007 Professional Athlete Average Salaries (in dollars)

Event	Men	Women
U.S. Open (golf)	1,225,000	560,000
British Open	1,338,480	300,000
PGA/LPGA Championship	1,224,000	300,000
Professional basketball[a]	5,000,000	50,000
Baseball/softball[b]	2,900,000	3,750
NYC marathon	130,000	130,000
Boston marathon	100,000	100,000

Source: Data from "Coming a Longish Way, Baby," *Sports Illustrated,* 5 March 2007, 24.

a. NBA, WNBA
b. MLB and NPF

Female Olympic Athletes

Gender inequality has prevailed in the Olympic Games since the modern Games began in 1896. The quotes by the founder of the modern Olympics in an earlier section of this chapter make quite clear his belief that females did not belong. While female events have gradually been added to the Olympics over the years, there are still vast gender inequities. For example, in the 1992 Barcelona Summer Olympics there were 159 events open to men and only 86 open to women. Females comprised 28.5 percent of the total participants in those Games. The situation was not much better at the 1994 Winter Games at Lillehammer, Norway. That year, 1,302 men and only 542 women competed. See Figure 14.2 for an illustration of the participation pattern in Winter Olympic Games.

By the 2004 Athens Summer Olympic Games there were over 120 women's events and more than 170 men's events (about a dozen were mixed). So not only were there more women's events than ever before, but the gap between the number of men's events and the number of women's events narrowed to an all-time low. At those Games, 41 percent of the total participants were women and 59 percent were men; thus, men still outnumbered women as Olympic athletes.

But the percentage of women has been increasing in every Olympiad for the past fifty years. There are, of course, wide variations in the percentage of women representing each country at every Olympic Games. For the Athens Summer Olympics, more than twenty countries sent no women; about half of the all-male Olympic teams represented Islamic regimes. On the other hand, at the 1996 Atlanta Olympics, Canada and China had more women than men on their teams. At the 2000 Sydney Olympics, of the 309 Canadian athletes, 158 were female and 151 were male.

New opportunities are opening up for women in the Olympics. Women's ice hockey was added for the 1994 Winter Games in Lillehammer, and women's softball and soccer were part of the 1996 Summer Games in Atlanta. In 2000 and 2004, sev-

Figure 14.2 Number of Athletes Competing in Winter Olympic Games

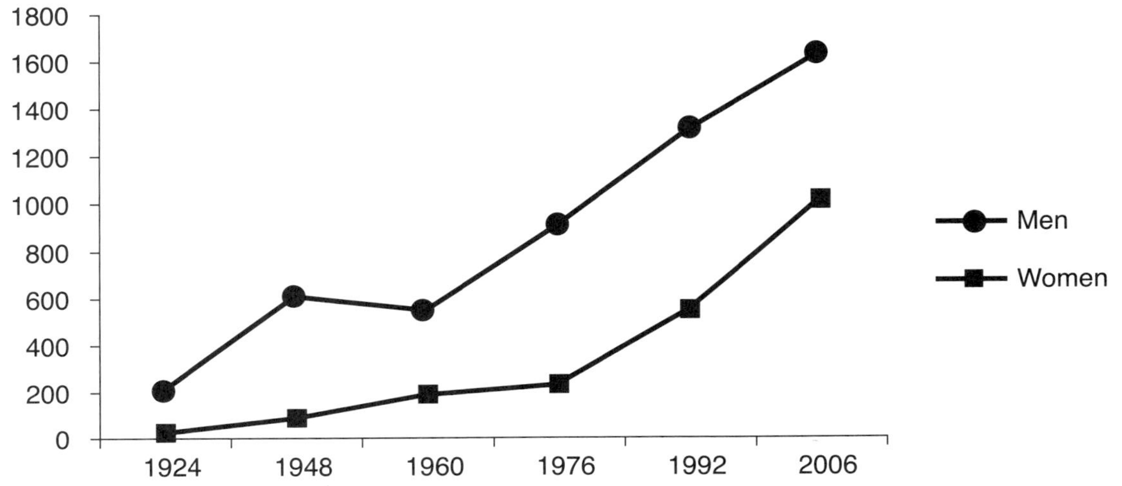

Source: Zurn, L., D. Lopiano, and M. Snyder (2006). *Women in the 2006 Olympic and Paralympic Winter Games: An Analysis of Participation, Leadership, and Media Coverage.* (East Meadow, NY: Women's Sports Foundation.)

Table 14.3 Male and Female U.S. Athletes' Participation at Summer Olympic Games

Olympic Year	Total on U.S. Team	Number of U.S. Female Athletes	Female Athletes as a Percentage of All U.S. Athletes
2004	537	257	47.9
2000	602	264	45.2
1996	672	277	42.2
1992	619	203	35.1
1988	609	227	36.9
1984	584	209	35.0
1980	466	NA	NA
1976	425	128	30.1
1972	428	90	21.0

Source: Women's Sports Foundation and U.S. Olympic Committee, 2005.

eral new sports and more than twenty new events for women were added to the Summer Olympic Games. New women's sports events have been added to recent Winter Olympic Games.

The U.S. Olympic Committee and its many sport federations provide various kinds of subsidies to U.S. Olympic athletes—from training expenses to grants of money. Some members of U.S. women's teams, as well as female athletes in individual sports, have been paid more than $50,000 annually while they were preparing for the next Olympic Games. This practice was first adopted for male U.S. Olympians, but widespread objections to male-only subsidies resulted in opening them up to women.

SPORT AND GENDER IDENTITY FOR MALES

Although this chapter has primarily focused on inequities females have faced in the sports world, gender issues are not just about inequality, injustice, and sexuality involving females. Attention has been focused on these issues in this chapter, while in other chapters in the book we have examined gender issues related to males as part of other topics of the sports world. However, in this section we do wish to discuss the role of sports in the social construction of masculinity and its consequences for males. Traditional gender role prescriptions have perpetuated problems for males as well as for females.

At the same time that various social barriers discouraged females from sport involvement to preserve their feminine identity, males have been socialized into attitudes, values, and behaviors in which sport plays a dominant role in actually shaping their masculine identities. Sport has been the cultural activity that makes it seem natural to equate masculinity with competition, physicality, aggressiveness, movement skills, and physical achievements. Two of the best-known slogans that reinforce this are "Sports makes men out of boys" and "Sport builds character."

The competitive structures of the sports world socialize young boys into the exciting world of physical skills, tactics, and strategy in the pursuit of victory, but they also introduce them into the structured world of autocratic leadership, hierarchical organization, and bureaucratic relations. That is how the institution of sport is organized at every level. Teams are commanded by strong, forceful male coaches, whose word is taken as incontestable. Sports rules and coaches' orders are understood to be followed without question. Athletes are expected to sacrifice their individual interests, skills, and goals for the benefit of the team. Personal relations are structured around competition against teammates for positions on the team as well as, of course, competition against opponents. While friendships and feelings of connection often develop among teammates, these are not deliberately structured in sport organizations. Instead, what develops from an interpersonal connectedness standpoint is a conditional self-worth, meaning masculine identity and personal value are dependent upon one's individual achievements.[42]

Along with other attitudes and values boys acquire through their sport experiences, they also learn about masculine sexuality. One of the most profound things they learn about masculine sexuality through the sport culture is that to be homosexual, or even be suspected of it, is detestable. Males who have been uninterested in sport or unwilling to allow dominant gender definitions of masculinity force them into sport or into "appropriate" masculine attitudes, values, and behaviors have often faced gender bigotry from both males and females. They have been the butt of jokes about their "effeminacy," and they have been labeled "fags," "queers," and "fairies." Many times they have been physically abused in various ways.

Thus, gender inequality and injustice have been directed at males who for one reason or another do not conform to dominant cultural definitions of masculinity. In a collection of personal stories by gay athletes, one athlete remarked: "Starting with Little League or Pop Warner [football], there's this concept that to be a man is to be an athlete, to be an athlete is to be strong, and to be strong you have to have a certain attitude" about sexuality: Athletes are not gay.[43] Although there is growing evidence that gay athletes have competed, and continue to compete, at all levels of sport, mostly closeted, the sports world has remained steadfastly homophobic. In 1995, when Olympic diving champion Greg Louganis revealed he was gay, a flood of testimonials came from other gay athletes in other sports, illustrating that sport is no different from other sectors of life, notwithstanding the stigma about homosexuality in sport culture.[44]

Only a handful of male professional athletes have come out, and all of them were retired when they made their sexuality public. In 1975 former NFL player David Kopay became the first athlete from the four major professional team sports to reveal his homosexuality. Since then, former players from all of the four major pro team sports have come out. The most recent announcement came in early 2007 on ESPN's *Outside the Lines* by former NBA player John Amaechi. Amaechi has followed up the announcement with a memoir titled *Man in the Middle*.[45]

All of these former professional athletes have received homophobic remarks from former teammates. A former Seattle Seahawks teammate of Esera Tuaolo, who came out after he retired from the NFL, said that Tuaolo was wise to have concealed his homosexuality while he was an active player because Seahawks players would have beaten him up so badly in practices that he would never have been able to play a game on Sunday. NBA superstar LeBron James, reacting to Amaechi's announcement, said an openly gay person could not survive in the NBA. James continued: "With teammates you have to be trustworthy, and if you're gay and you're not admitting that you are then you are not trustworthy."[46]

In March 2005 NBC and USA Network commissioned a national poll on the issue of homosexuality in sports. Although the results suggest that homophobia is not as pronounced as usually believed, there is still considerable conflict and ambiguity toward gays. For example, 86 percent of the respondents believed that it is okay for male athletes to participate in sports, even if they are openly gay. But nearly 25 percent responded that having an openly gay player would hurt the entire team. Sixty-eight percent believed that it would hurt an athlete's career to be openly gay. Sixty-two percent agree that the reason there is so little coverage of gays in sports is that America is not ready to accept gay athletes. In spite of the seeming contradictions and ambiguity, 79 percent of the respondents to the poll believed that Americans are more accepting of gays in sports today than they were twenty years ago.[47]

One year later, in 2006, *Sports Illustrated* conducted a survey of professional athletes playing in the four major team sports: NBA, MLB, NHL, and NFL. One question was asked of the athletes: "Would you welcome an openly gay teammate?" The results are shown in Table 14.4.

We would guess that most readers would be surprised at these results, because in all of the sports a substantial majority said they would welcome an openly gay teammate. Skeptical interpreters of these results would probably argue that what the athletes say and how they would actually behave toward a gay teammate would likely be quite different, with many who answered "yes" to the question actually being less welcoming. Optimistic interpreters would likely say that the sport culture has changed and is not as homophobic as often believed. We would like to believe that the optimistic interpreters are closer to an accurate understanding of current attitudes toward homosexuality than the skeptics.[48]

Beyond sport there has been a flourishing gay and lesbian social movement for the past quarter century. Fundamentally, members of the movement have the same goals as the women's movement—to be treated equally in all sectors of social life. This movement has had considerable success over the past decade. Local communities, individual states, and even the federal government have enacted laws and statutes giving gays and lesbians the same rights and protections as other citizens. Massachusetts now allows same-sex marriages, and other states permit domestic partnership or civil unions.

A 2006 *New York Times* poll showed that nearly three-fifths of Americans favor some form of legal recognition for gay couples.[49] While the broader issue of gay and lesbian rights has been a source of some controversy, there is increasing support for giving them the same legal rights as other citizens enjoy. Homophobia has not disappeared, but a growing sense of social humanitarianism has weakened it.

One of the outcomes of the gay/lesbian liberation movement has been the founding of sport organizations by and for gays and lesbians. Gay sports clubs are now found in most major cities of North America; also, a wide variety of gay sports, fitness, and recreational organizations—camping groups, bicycling tours, skiing, hiking, canoeing, and so forth—are popular in urban areas. Gay-governed organizations have developed in a variety of sports; they include the International Gay and Lesbian Aquatics Association, the Gay and Lesbian Hockey Association, and the International Gay Bowling

Table 14.4 Responses to 2006 *Sports Illustrated* Survey Question: "Would You Welcome an Openly Gay Teammate?" (in percent)

Responses	MLB	NBA	NFL	NHL
Yes	61.5	59.6	56.9	79.9
No	34.8	38.6	39.6	18.0
Don't Know	3.7	1.8	3.5	2.1

Source: "SI Players Poll," *Sports Illustrated*, 6 March 2006, 32.

Association. The most prestigious gay sport organization, and event, is the Federation of Gay Games, which governs the Gay Games. The first Gay Games were founded by a former Olympic decathlete, Tom Waddell, and held in 1982 in San Francisco. The Gay Games are held every four years as a celebration of the international gay community. Athletes and teams compete in a variety of sports, and many of the routines and ceremonies are patterned after the International Olympic Games.

Sports commentator Bob Costas, in an assessment of the book *Jocks: True Stories of America's Gay Male Athletes*, made an eloquent statement that brings an insightful note to the topic of gays and lesbians in sport. Costas was referring to the stories of gay male athletes in that book, but his comment is relevant to the broader topic of gay and lesbian athletes. He said that the book "challenges the perceptions and stereotypes still held by millions of Americans. Whether they know it or not, whether they like it or not, a new day is coming, moving us closer to the day when people are regarded primarily as individuals rather than as members of groups."[50]

SUMMARY

In this chapter we have examined the social bases for the gender inequality and injustice that have traditionally confronted females in sport, the consequences of the processes, and the developments in this topic. Gender inequality and injustice against females in sport have taken many forms. First, a number of myths about the biological and psychological effects on women of competitive sports effectively discouraged their participation. Second, unequal opportunity for participation in sports existed for a long time. Finally, women had unequal access to the authority and power structure of sport. Patriarchal ideology has been employed to socialize females out of sports and to deny them equal access to its rewards.

Legislation and court decisions have made it more difficult for discrimination to be imposed on women and girls in sports. Greater opportunities are now available for those who wish to compete.

Making discrimination illegal does not eliminate it, however, as previous experiences with civil rights legislation so clearly illustrate. Socially conditioned attitudes are slow to change. In some individual cases, they cannot be changed. Stereotypes are persistent and feed on the examples that confirm them. Nevertheless, attitudes and behaviors have changed in remarkably significant ways in response to challenges and demands as well as to federal legislation.

Gender inequality and injustice involve males as well as females. Traditional masculine identity is closely bound with sport culture, and males who do not conform to the social prescriptions face a variety of negative social sanctions.

WEB RESOURCES

www.womenssportsfoundation.org
The website of the Women's Sports Foundation. This is arguably the leading women's sport organization. It is very active in promoting and advancing the cause of women in sport.

www.education.umn.edu/tuckercenter
Directed by sport sociologist Mary Jo Kane, the Tucker Center for Research on Girls and Women in Sport is dedicated to exploring how sport, recreation, and physical activity affect the lives of girls and women. This center, the first of its kind in the United States, is interdisciplinary and is leading a pioneering effort in significant research, education, community outreach, and public service.

www.caaws.ca
The website of the Canadian Association for the Advancement of Women and Sport and Physical Activity. CAAWS works to encourage girls and women to get out of the bleachers, off the sidelines, and onto the fields and rinks, into the pools, locker rooms, and boardrooms, of Canada. It has good links to other websites.

www.feminist.org
The website of the Feminist Majority Foundation, an organization dedicated to women's equality, re-

productive health, and nonviolence. It utilizes research and action to empower women economically, socially, and politically. Many of the actions and activities of this organization involve women in sport.

www.womensportswire.com
Women's Sports Wire. This site advertises itself as the number one resource for women's sports news and information. It has lots of useful links.

www.cbs.sportsline.com/u/women
This CBS Sports Line website has news, announcements, and general reporting on women's sports and links to many other sites.

NOTES

1. Maxine Baca Zinn, Pierrette Hondagneu-Sotelo, and Michael A. Messner, eds., *Gender through the Prism of Difference*, 3rd ed. (New York: Oxford University Press, 2005); Julie McMullin, *Understanding Social Inequality: Intersections of Class, Age, Gender, Ethnicity, and Race in Canada* (New York: Oxford University Press, 2004); Laura Kramer, *The Sociology of Gender: A Brief Introduction* (New York: Roxbury Publishing, 2004).

2. Jean O'Reilly and Susan K. Cahn, eds., *Women and Sports in the United States: A Documentary Reader* (Boston: Northeastern University Press, 2007), pt. 1; see also M. Ann Hall, *The Girl and the Game: A History of Women's Sport in Canada* (Peterborough, Ont.: Broadview Press, 2002); Lynn Couturier and Stevie Chepko, "Separate World, Separate Lives, Separate Sporting Models," in *Women in Sport Issues and Controversies*, 2nd ed., ed. Greta L. Cohen (Oxon Hill, Md.: AAHPERD Publications, 2001), 57–78.

3. Couturier and Chepko, "Separate World, Separate Lives, Separate Sporting Models"; Patricia Vertinsky, "Women, Sport, and Exercise in the 19th Century," in *Women and Sport: Interdisciplinary Perspectives*, ed. D. Margaret Costa and Sharon R. Guthrie (Champaign, Ill.: Human Kinetics Publishers, 1994), 63–82.

4. Bil Gilbert and Nancy Williamson, "Sport Is Unfair to Women," *Sports Illustrated*, 28 May 1973, 90; see also Stevie Chepko and Lynn Couturier, "From Intersection to Collision: Women's Sports from 1920–1980," in *Women in Sport Issues and Controversies*, ed. Cohen, 79–109.

5. Ibid., 88.

6. Mariah Burton Nelson, *Are We Winning Yet? How Women Are Changing Sports and Sports Are Changing Women* (New York: Random House, 1991), 4.

7. Zinn, Hondagneu-Sotelo, and Messner, *Gender through the Prism of Difference*; see also Linda L. Lindsey, *Gender Roles: A Sociological Perspective*, 4th ed. (Upper Saddle River, N.J.: Prentice Hall, 2004).

8. Sohaila Shakib and Michele D. Dunbar, "How High School Athletes Talk about Maternal and Paternal Sporting Experiences," *International Review for the Sociology of Sport* 39, no. 3 (2004): 275–300; see also Susan Witt, "Parental Influence on Children's Socialization to Gender Roles," *Adolescence* 32, no. 126 (1997): 253–259.

9. Linda Brannon, *Gender: Psychological Perspectives*, 5th ed. (Boston: Allyn & Bacon, 2007); see also David Sadker, "Gender Equity: Still Knocking at the Classroom Door," *Educational Leadership* 56, no. 7 (April 1999): 22–26.

10. Patricia A. Adler and Peter Adler, *Peer Power: Preadolescent Culture and Identity* (New Brunswick, N.J.: Rutgers University Press, 1998).

11. Margaret Carlisle Duncan, "Gender Warriors in Sport: Women and the Mass Media," in *Handbook of Sports and Media*, ed. Arthur A. Raney and Jennings Bryant (Mahwah, N.J.: Lawrence Erlbaum, 2006), 231–252.

12. D. Stanley Eitzen and Maxine Baca Zinn, "The De-athleticization of Women: The Naming and Gender Marking of Collegiate Sport Teams," in *Sport in Contemporary Society: An Anthology*, 7th ed., ed. D. Stanley Eitzen (Boulder, Colo.: Paradigm Publishers, 2005), 129–138; see also D. Stanley Eitzen, *Fair and Foul: Beyond the Myths and Paradoxes of Sport*, 2nd ed. (New York: Rowman & Littlefield, 2003), 33–337.

13. Pierre de Coubertin, quoted in Sheila Mitchell, "Women's Participation in the Olympic Games, 1900–1926," *Journal of Sport History* 4 (Summer 1977): 211.

14. Pierre de Coubertin, quoted in Ellen Gerber, Jan Felshin, and Waneen Wyrick, *The American Woman in Sport* (Reading, Mass.: Addison-Wesley, 1974), 137–138.

15. Nancy Theberge, *Higher Goals: Women's Ice Hockey and the Politics of Gender* (Albany: State University of New York Press, 2000), 113; see also Lisa Taggart, *Women Who Win: Female Athletes on Being the Best* (Emeryville, Calif.: Seal Press, 2007).

16. Scorecard, "Q&A," *Sports Illustrated*, 26 June 2006, 25; see also Hark Harris, "Women, Gays, and Basketball," *Z Magazine*, January 2006, 49–50; Jayne Caudwell, ed., *Sport, Sexualities and Queer/Theory* (New York: Routledge, 2006).

17. Kristin Kaye, *Iron Maidens: The Celebration of the Most Awesome Female Muscle in the World* (New York: Thunder's Mouth Press, 2005); see also Lori Incledon, *Strength Training for Women* (Champaign, Ill.: Human Kinetics, 2004); Maria R. Lowe, *Women of Steel: Female Bodybuilders and the Struggle for Self-Definition* (New York: New York University Press, 1998); Leslie Heywood, *Bodymakers: A Cultural Anatomy of Women's Body Building* (New Brunswick, N.J.: Rutgers University Press, 1998); Shirley Castelnuovo and Sharon R. Guthrie, *Feminism and the Female Body: Liberating the Amazon Within* (Boulder, Colo.: Lynne Rienner, 1998), 49–65.

18. Pat Griffin, *Strong Women, Deep Closets: Lesbians and Homophobia in Sport* (Champaign, Ill.: Human Kinetics, 1998); see also Vikki Krane, "We Can Be Athletic and Feminine, but Do We Want To? Challenging Hegemonic Femininity in Women's Sport," *Quest* 53, no. 1 (February 2001): 115–133; Jennifer Hargreaves, *Heroines of Sport: The Politics of Difference and Identity* (New York: Routledge, 2000), 129–173.

19. Hargreaves, *Heroines of Sport*, 232.

20. Dudley A. Sargent, "Are Athletics Making Girls Masculine?" *Ladies Home Journal* 29, 1912, 72. For a good discussion of how the same ideas were being promulgated in Canada, see Helen Lenskyj, "Common Sense and Physiology: North American Medical Views on Women and Sport, 1890–1930," *Canadian Journal of History of Sport* 21 (May 1990): 49–64.

21. Ethel Perrin, "A Crisis in Girls Athletics," *Sportsmanship* 1 (December 1928): 10–12.

22. For a superb comprehensive report on the biomedical and psychological aspects of women in sport, see Barbara L. Drinkwater, ed., *Women in Sport*, vol. 8 of *The Encyclopedia of Sports Medicine* (London: Blackwell Science, 2000).

23. Taggart, *Women Who Win*.

24. Sporting Goods Manufacturers Association, *2007 Sports and Fitness Report* (Washington, D.C.: Sporting Goods Manufacturers Association, 2007).

25. Quoted in Hall, *The Girl and the Game*, 173; also see pp. 163–187 for a detailed description of the struggle for gender equity in sport in Canada during the 1970s and 1980s.

26. National Federation of State High School Associations, "2007 Athletics Participation Totals," 2007, http://www.nfhs.org/custom/participation_figures/default.aspx/.

27. Ibid.

28. Quoted in Debbie Becker, "Title IX Has Lost Its Clout on Campuses," *USA Today*, 16 September 1986, p. 2C; for in-depth accounts of Title IX, see Welch Suggs, *A Place on the Team: The Triumph and Tragedy of Title IX* (Princeton: Princeton University Press, 2005); Linda Jean Carpenter and R. Vivian Acosta, *Title IX* (Champaign, Ill.: Human Kinetics, 2005); Karen Blumenthal, *Let Me Play: The Story of Title IX* (New York: Atheneum Books, 2005); Rita J. Simon, ed., *Sporting Equality: Title IX Thirty Years Later* (New Brunswick, N.J.: Transaction Books, 2005).

29. U.S. Department of Education, Office for Civil Rights, the Assistant Secretary, "Clarification of Intercollegiate Athletics Policy Guidance: The Three-Part Test," 16 January 1996, www.ed.gov/offices/OCR!docs/clarific.html; for a more detailed discussion of the three-part test, see Suggs, *A Place on the Team*, 232–239.

30. Karla Hayworth, "Colleges, Sporting Groups, and Lawmakers Back Brown U.'s Appeal in Title IX Case," *Chronicle of Higher Education*, 4 April 1997, A35; see also Jim Naughton, "Judge Approves Settlement of Brown U.'s Title IX Case," *Chronicle of Higher Education*, 3 July 1998.

31. Adam Epstein, "Stand or Fall: Wrestlers Continue to Grapple with Defeat," *Journal of Physical Education, Recreation, and Dance* 75, no. 9 (November/December 2004): 7–8; Update, "Council Might Sue Schools over Title IX," *USA Today*, 7 June 2005, p. 13C.

32. U.S. Department of Education, *Title IX: Additional Clarification of Intercollegiate Athletics Policy: Three-part Test—Part Three* (Washington, D.C.: U.S. Department of Education, 1996), 17 March 2005; Erik Brady, "Title IX," *USA Today*, 17 May 2005, p. 10C; Erik Brady, "Ex-members of Title IX Panel Urge Schools Not to Use Surveys," *USA Today*, 18 October 2005, p. 9C.

33. Richard Lapchick, *The 2005 Racial and Gender Report Card: College Sports* (Orlando: University of Central Florida, 2006).

34. Jessica Gavora, *Tilting the Playing Field: School, Sports, Sex and Title IX* (San Francisco: Encounter Books, 2002); see also Jodi Upton, "Title IX Tussle: Which Numbers Are Correct?" *USA Today*, 13 July 2007, p. 14C.

35. Cited from Women's Sports Foundation, "2007 Statistics—Gender Equity in High School and College Athletics: Most Recent Participation and Budget Statistics," http://womenssportsfoundation.org/cgi-bin/iowa/issues/article.html?record=1017.

36. Upton, "Title IX Tussle: Which Numbers Are Correct?"

37. James L. Shulman and William G. Bowen, *The Game of Life: College Sports and Educational Values* (Princeton: Princeton University Press, 2001), 124.

38. D. Stanley Eitzen and Maxine Baca Zinn, *In Conflict and Order: Understanding Society*, 10th ed. (Boston: Allyn & Bacon, 2004), 345–352.

39. Lapchick, *The 2005 Racial and Gender Report Card*; see also Ken Fowler, "WOMEN IN SPORT; No Sense of Entitlement for Women; Thirty-five Years after Title IX, the Number of Females Coaching Teams Continues to Decline," *Los Angeles Times* 2 December 2007, p. D1; Sara Gogol, *Hard Fought Victories: Women Coaches Making a Difference* (Terre Haute, Ind.: Wish Publishing, 2002).

40. Mike Terry, "Men Dominate WNBA Coaching Ranks," *Los Angeles Times*, 2 August 2006, p. D8; see also Jill Lieber Steeg, "New Owners Stake Claim in Overhauling WNBA," *USA Today*, 12 June 2007, p. 9C.

41. Diane Pucin, "What, No Leagues of Their Own?" *Los Angeles Times*, 2 August 2006, pp. D1–D8; Oscar Dixon, "More Players Profit from Testing Waters," *USA Today*, 21 August 2007, p. 10C.

42. Varda Burstyn, *The Rites of Men: Manhood, Politics, and the Culture of Sport* (Toronto: University of Toronto Press, 1999); see also Caudwell, *Sport, Sexualities and Queer/Theory*.

43. Quoted in Dan Woog, *Jocks: True Stories of America's Gay Male Athletes* (Los Angeles: Alyson Books, 1998), 43–44.

44. Greg Louganis, *Breaking the Surface* (New York: Random House, 1995).

45. John Amaechi, *Man in the Middle* (New York: ESPN Books, 2007); see also Esera Tuaolo and John Rosengren, *Alone in the Trenches: My Life as a Gay Man in the NFL* (Naperville, Ill.: Sourcebooks, 2006).

46. L. John Wertheim, "Gays in Sports: A Poll," *Sports Illustrated*, 18 April 2005, 64–65; quoted from Gene Farris, "Amaechi Takes Bold Step," *USA Today*, 8 February 2007, p. 11C.

47. Wertheim, "Gays in Sports: A Poll."

48. "SI Players Poll," *Sports Illustrated*, 6 March 2006, 32.

49. Cited in "Law and Civil Rights," CBS News/New York Times Poll, 27–31 October 2006, polling report, http://www.pollingreport.com/civil.htm.

50. Quoted on back cover of Woog, *Jocks*.

Chapter 15

Contemporary Trends and the Future of Sport in North America

In the past decade the number of North Americans participating in outdoor ecosport activities has grown dramatically. (iStockphoto)

"We live in a changing society" is an often-heard cliché. It is voguish to depict contemporary social life as dynamic and progressive, the pace of living as fast, growth and change as the only constants, and an accelerating rate of change as likely to inflict "future shock" on many of us. These ideas are buttressed by an apparent obsession with the future. Business leaders look for predictions about population trends and shifts in consumer preferences; young adults seek information about trends in occupations in hopes that the career for which they prepare will be a gateway to opportunity rather than a dead-end street; and even video games have a definite futuristic orientation, as much of the simulated action takes place in outer space. Several of the most popular books of the past few years have been futuristic: *The Extreme Future: The Top Trends That Will Reshape the World for the Next 5, 10, and 20 Years; Future Net: The Essential Guide to Internet and Technology Megatrends; The Culture of the New Capitalism;* and *Microtrends.*[1]

Meanwhile groups of social forecasters, societal scientists who are actively involved in forecasting societal activity, have also been busy with futuristic studies under the auspices of private foundations and government agencies. Some of the most well known are the International Institute of Forecasters, the Trends Research Institute, and the National Research Council of Canada Study of 2010. The World Future Society is a thriving organization of twenty-five thousand members in more than eighty countries who are interested in how social and technological developments are shaping the future. Finally, the publication of at least five periodicals on futurism (e.g., *The Futurist*) indicates that people like to read speculation about what this twenty-first century is going to be like.

Notwithstanding the cliché, change in North America is a ubiquitous fact. Today's social and physical environments are vastly different from those of only a generation ago, to say nothing of those of three or four generations ago. The changes over the past three decades have been in direction as well as in rate, and the total amount of change has been so vast and thorough that it can only be conceptualized as a social and cultural revolution. Therefore, we conclude this volume with a chapter that examines the trends and the future of sport in North America, for as we have frequently argued, sport reflects society, and as the society changes, sport will also undoubtedly undergo transformation.

DEMOGRAPHIC TRENDS IN NORTH AMERICA

One of the divisions of sociological study is called demography; it focuses on population size, characteristics, trends of groups, neighborhoods, communities, patterns of migration, and analyses of change. In describing the assumptions of the sociological perspective in chapter 1, we noted that humans are naturally social beings who are greatly affected by their social and natural environments, but they are also capable of changing those social and natural formations within their lives. We have emphasized at various places in this volume that changes in population characteristics have played an important role in the rise of modern sport forms, the popularity and demise of some sports, and who plays and does not play sports. We now turn to trends in North American population and the potential impact they may have on sport. Trends in population growth, composition, and location are sociologically significant because they impact the social lives of people, including their lives as participants and consumers of sports.

One of the most significant trends in North America is the changing nature of its population—total numbers, composition, and location. Futurists are much concerned about population trends. Although improved birth control measures and a vague social commitment to zero population growth have partially controlled the numbers of newborns, a continued increase has occurred as the "baby boom" generation reached adulthood and began producing families of its own. Indeed, during the 1990s, the U.S. population grew by 32.7 million, an increase of 10 percent. Estimates are that the population of the United States will increase from 302 million in 2007 to around 325 million by 2020. Canadian population, presently

33 million, is expected to increase to 35 million by 2020.[2] Thus, the populations of both the United States and Canada will continue to grow in the next generation. In all likelihood, sports will continue expanding as well.

Population Composition

During most of the twentieth century North America had a young population because the birthrate remained high for an increasing number of people of childbearing age. This condition is now changing rapidly because the long-term trends for birthrates and death rates are expected to decline. Thus, the proportion of young people will diminish, and the proportion of older people will increase, markedly affecting population composition. The average age in the United States will rise dramatically, from 37 in 2007 to about 40 in 2040. The U.S. Bureau of the Census projects that the over-65 population will more than double between 2007 and 2050, when one in five Americans will be over 65 years old. (See Figure 15.1.) The trend is similar for Canada. Even more dramatic will be the average life expectancy, which will climb from the current 77.1 to an estimated 82.6 years by 2050. Persons aged 65 and older currently make up 12 percent of Canada's population; that will rise to between 20 and 25 percent in 2025. Not only will there be many more older persons, but they will be healthier and more active than ever before.[3]

Both the United States and Canada have long been havens for immigrants, but the nationalities of those who have come to these two countries have changed with the political and economic winds. Political oppression or economic hardship was the incentive for millions of people to migrate, legally or illegally. Due to both immigration and high birthrates, the Hispanic population in the United States grew from 14.6 million in 1980 to 32 million in 2000, over 100 percent in 20 years. At the anticipated rate of growth, Hispanics will be the largest ethnic minority by 2010, surpassing African Americans. Even more remarkable, while the United States as a whole grew 19.8 percent, growth in the Asian American population from 1980 to 2000 was 200 percent, mostly due to immi-

Figure 15.1   Projections of U.S. Seniors 65 and Older

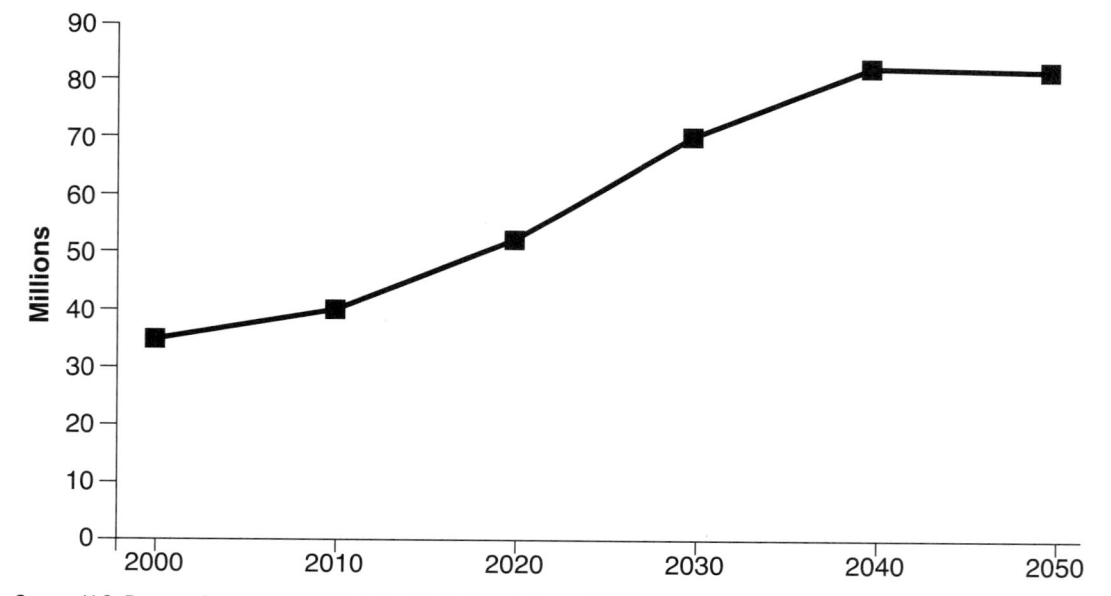

Source: U.S. Bureau of the Census, *Population Projections* (released 2004).

gration. It is projected that the U.S. population will continue to become more diverse in the coming decades, and half of the U.S. population will likely be minorities by 2050.

In an effort to preserve its essentially loyal British character, Canada severely curtailed immigration from countries outside Europe right up until the reforms of the Trudeau administration in the 1960s. Consequently, prior to the 1960s, 80 percent of all immigrants came from Europe. In the past two decades, 70 percent of immigrants to Canada have been Asian or "nontraditional" (mostly Africans and Latin Americans). This rapidly changing ethnic and racial complexion in North America will alter everything in society, from politics and education to industry, values, and sports and leisure activities.

Location of Population

North Americans continue to gravitate toward large metropolitan areas, with about 82 percent of Americans living in central cities and their surrounding suburbs, and the majority of Canadians living within one hundred miles of the U.S.-Canadian border are urbanites. Over the next quarter century Americans will probably continue to congregate in megacities, or megalopolises, that futurists have labeled "Boswash," "Chippits," and "Sansan." Boswash will extend between Boston and Washington, D.C.; Chicago; and Pittsburgh will be the centers for Chippitts; and Sansan will stretch from San Francisco to San Diego. These megalopolises appear likely to contain about one-half of the total U.S. population, including the majority of the most technologically and scientifically advanced, prosperous, intellectual, and creative elements.

In the United States the migration from the Northeast and Midwest into states in the South and West has been the most pronounced demographic shift in the past two decades. The surge of newcomers helped the population of the South jump by 25 percent and of the West by 30 percent between 1980 and 2000; indeed, the Sun Belt has absorbed virtually all the U.S. population growth since 1975, and the trend is expected to continue.

The West and South are projected to be the fastest-growing regions in the United States, and the two regions combined are projected to account for 82 percent of the sixty-eight million persons added to the nation's population between the mid-1990s and 2020. In Canada, population in the Atlantic provinces is slipping significantly, and the big gains have been in Alberta and British Columbia. Ontario and Quebec have substantially more than half the country's population, and they will still have a majority in the year 2010, but the winds from the west are rising.[4]

Population Trends and Sport

The giant metropolitan areas, stretching out over hundreds of miles and engulfing many small communities as well as large cities, may very well require the reorganization of professional sports organizations on some feature other than a city name. Indeed, professional sport managements are already preparing for a future in which state and regional considerations will take precedence over city loyalties. The names of professional team sport franchises demonstrate that the leagues and owners are aware of the outmoded practice of single-city affiliation. Several of the franchises have adopted state or regionalistic team names:

> Major League Baseball
> > Minnesota Twins
> > Texas Rangers
> > Florida Marlins
> > Colorado Rockies
> > Arizona Diamondbacks
>
> National Football League
> > New England Patriots
> > Arizona Cardinals
> > Minnesota Vikings
> > Carolina Panthers
> > Tennessee Titans
>
> National Basketball Association
> > Golden State Warriors
> > New Jersey Nets
> > Indiana Pacers
> > Minnesota Timberwolves
> > Utah Jazz

National Hockey League
  New Jersey Devils
  Florida Panthers
  Colorado Avalanche
  Carolina Hurricanes
  Minnesota Wild

Professional sport has been one of the most financially successful and growing industries during the past twenty years, riding the crest of a huge population of young people. Consumer-spectator interest appears to have no limit. New franchises spring up all over North America to be greeted by sellout crowds. Expansion continued throughout the 1990s. Major League Baseball expanded by two teams in 1993 (Colorado Rockies, Florida Marlins) and another two teams in 1998 (Arizona Diamondbacks, Tampa Bay Devil Rays); the National Hockey League added nine new franchises between 1991 and 2000; and the NFL and NBA expanded by two teams in 1995 (NFL: Carolina Panthers, Jacksonville Jaguars; NBA: Toronto Raptors, Vancouver Grizzlies), with the NFL adding two more franchises since then (Houston Texans, Cleveland Browns).

The World Cup held in the United States in 1994 served as a strong stimulus to the growing popularity of soccer. Furthermore, the increase in immigrant populations from Mexico, Central and South America, and Asian countries, where soccer is extremely popular, helped create a subculture of support for the creation of the ten-team Major League Soccer league in 1996. Although still not as popular as the traditional professional sports leagues, professional soccer is gradually acquiring a devoted following of fans.

As we noted in chapter 14, Title IX and the expansion of high school and college sports for females, in conjunction with trends in population characteristics, created opportunities for women's professional sports to grow. Perhaps the most notable example of this was the launching of two women's professional basketball leagues in the mid-1990s, the American Basketball League and the WNBA. Although only the WNBA remains, it shows signs of becoming a permanent part of professional sports.

Professional men's and women's golf and tennis have extended their tour seasons, and both tennis and golf now have seniors' tours. In addition, a number of other professional sports (such as NASCAR, cycling, distance running, and lacrosse) are gaining a following in live attendance and television coverage. The future trajectory seems quite clear: Professional sports will become another global industry in the next two decades. They are already well on the way, with team franchises, tournaments, and championship events held around the globe.

Over the past two decades a wide variety of sports have acquired professional status—including cycling, triathlon, racquetball, distance running, beach volleyball, and lacrosse—and with the changing interests of the younger generations, some will challenge the more established sports for fans. Within twenty years the total number of professional sports could double. We will have more to say about some of these sports in later sections of this chapter.

A growing population, especially an older population, forms an infrastructure for the continued financial success of professional sports. However, ticket prices have skyrocketed at a rate four to five times the rise in the cost of living, and at a time when real income has increased very little. Figures compiled by various sources have begun to show that, for the average fan, these prices will take their toll on live attendance over the next decade. Actually, low- and average-income fans have already been priced out of attending. A survey conducted by the NHL revealed that the household income of fans attending its games averaged in the top 15 percent of North American family incomes.

A larger proportion of the population is now forty years old and older, a fact that is manifested in sport in a number of ways. Some of the biggest sports stories of the past few years have been about older athletes: Randy Johnson continuing to pitch in Major League Baseball well into his forties, Cal Ripken breaking Lou Gehrig's consecutive-games record, and golf pro Annika Sorenstam captivating the hearts of North American sports fans by continuing to play excellent golf way past her prime years. The senior tours of the Professional Golfers Association and the Professional Tennis Association illustrate quite well that older athletes can perform at high levels, and that sports fans will pay to see them compete in their sport.

There is little doubt that people are remaining physically active later in their lives, and more and more sports programs are being created to allow the aging population to participate. Recent surveys have found that about 48 percent of seniors between the ages of 55 and 74 participate in exercise programs and 15 percent of the same age group report playing a sport. Women over 65 grew up and passed through their early adulthood at a time when women had few opportunities to be involved in sport activities, but many senior women have now embraced the physically active life they see girls and younger women enjoying. Many senior women are as involved in physical activities as their male counterparts.[5]

The Masters Sports Tournaments and Senior Olympics have become major forces in organizing competitive sports for senior men and women. These are only the most visible programs. Retirement communities are typically built to encourage the sport interests of their citizens. Many community recreation departments have expanded their programs to include senior leagues in several sports; indeed, in some communities these leagues are the fastest growing. In all likelihood, participant sports will be a major growth industry wherever large groups of older persons settle.

The changing racial and ethnic composition of the North American population has provided greater opportunity for minority groups in sports. It is one of the most salient trends at the present and will, if futurists' predictions are correct, continue in the coming years. One of the main reasons to expect that minorities will secure increasing access and opportunities is, as we described previously, that their percentage of the population is increasing dramatically. There is no question that organized sports, from youth programs to the professional level, have made great strides toward equalizing opportunities in the past decade, but the goal has not yet been achieved. In chapters 13 and 14 we demonstrated that overt discrimination against African Americans and females, such as denying them access to sports, has been gradually eliminated, but that inequalities and injustices continue in subtler forms. Even these are giving way, as more and more racial, ethnic, and gender diversity is achieved in positions of prestige, power, and leadership within sport.

In general, minorities are underrepresented in many of the most popular high school, college, and professional sports, but each year new inroads are made into more and more sports. Minorities are taking their rightful place among teammates, and they hold coaching and management positions in a number of sports programs. The future for racial, ethnic, and gender diversity in North American sports appears to be quite promising.

DOMINATING FORCES IN OUR LIVES: WORK, TECHNOLOGY, AND SPORTING ACTIVITIES

For the vast majority of adults, involvement in sport is related to their work. Whether they are participating in sport themselves or watching others perform, the extent to which they can do either depends upon the nonwork time (so-called free time) available to them. In brief, the less time they must work, the more free time they have available for sporting activities; thus, trends in the work life of people will be instrumental in trends that take place in sport.

Industrialization and technology changed not only the way that goods are produced but also the conditions under which they are produced. At first, factories brought workers into sweatshops to toil, literally, from sunrise to sunset. Later, as steel and other large industries grew, workers were attracted to the plants by the prospect of steady work and a livable wage. Hours were long, but until the emergence of labor unions, workers could do little about that if they wished to remain employed. However, in the early twentieth century, a gradual reduction in the average workweek began for nonagricultural workers, from about sixty-five hours to just under forty hours. The trend toward a shorter workweek, which started in the early twentieth century, began to reverse itself in the past two decades (more on that below). Accompanying and supporting working trends over the past century have been remarkable technological innovations, and technology is increasingly dominating the economy. The previous state of the art in production and services is being quickly replaced by new high-tech developments. Large transnational corporations have come to dominate economies around the world. Indeed, economically they exceed the size of many nation-states. Combined, these forces form the most salient feature of North American life, and their effects are manifested in the contours of labor and leisure.[6]

An Information/Service North American Society

The ways in which the economy is being transformed and the occupational system reworked by new technology confirm that North Americans have entered an "information-based" society, or an information-producing service economy, rather than a goods-producing manufacturing economy.

Futurists predict that computers and other technological innovations will change the nature of work and the balance between jobs and personal lives. In the next ten years, four out of five people will be doing jobs differently from the way they have been done in the last thirty years. Computer networking will be one reason for this trend. We will, in essence, become a computer-connected society, as computer networking enables work to be done anywhere, at any time, at any distance from the office or factory.

Robotics and computer-integrated manufacturing are creating entirely new industries, employing millions of people in jobs that did not exist a decade ago. The use of robots has been growing rapidly in the past decade. The Robotics Industries Association reported that sales of factory robots increased 48 percent from 2004 to 2006, and it has been predicted that applications will skyrocket between 2007 and 2020.[7]

Careers in information services are well under way. Some 65 percent of North American workers are currently in information industries. Indeed, more people are involved in information and communication occupations than in mining, agriculture, manufacturing, and personal services combined; by the year 2020, over three-fourths of the workforce will be information workers.

Technological developments that have brought about, on an ever-increasing scale, giant organizations have spawned a depersonalization of social relationships and the eclipse of personalized community. In 2000, in a widely read and publicly discussed book titled *Bowling Alone: The Collapse and Revival of American Community,* the author, Robert Putnam, amassed impressive data on the decline of social capital and civic engagement in the past few decades. According to Putnam, Americans have lost much of the social glue—he calls it "social capital"—that once held our society together, that we have become a nation of strangers to one another, lacking mutual social bonds. More recently several other social analysts have taken up the same theme.[8]

Although most North Americans would not wish to give up many of the products of technological creations—television, central heating, air conditioning, automobiles, and so forth—there are, nevertheless, many people who find that the technocratic-bureaucratic society is dehumanizing. There has been a growing hostility to many forms of technological innovation and transnational corporate organization, and a wide range of spontaneous, activist, and democratic actions in an effort to recapture some sense of control over daily lives.[9]

The Information/Service Workplace and Sporting Activities

One promise made by industry and technology, at least covertly if not overtly, has been that modernization and technological advances will ultimately free the ties that bind workers to their jobs. Accompanying this promise has been the prediction that there will be a "great flowering of leisure-time" activities for the common person. Despite the promises about the diminishing workweek, the flowering of leisure time has not yet materialized, and some people question whether it will occur in the near future.

To a great extent, the prediction of a "leisure society" was based on a misperception of the amount of leisure time that would be made available by technological advances. The work-nonwork cycle created by modernizing the workplace has been altered over the past century, so that there now appears to be more time away from work. But recent studies have found that the annual hours worked by American workers exceed by one week to ten weeks the annual hours of workers in other industrialized countries. In addition, average commuting time for American workers is twenty-six minutes. The consequence of longer commutes is that workers are spending as much as an additional working week traveling to and from work every year (see Table 15.1). In studies carried out at the Families and Work Institute in New York, 44 percent of the respondents said they were overworked often or very often, and many wished they could reduce their work hours. In *Overwork in America: When the Way We Work Becomes Too Much*, researchers reported that one-third of the U.S. workforce can be viewed as being chronically overworked.[10]

The male "breadwinner" household is now the exception. Some 68 percent of households are now two-income households, and the proportion is expected to increase to 80 percent by 2020. Although this markedly increases the hours worked per week in households, the increased income has expanded the market for consumer goods and services and leisure activities.

Four-Day and Flextime Workweeks and Free Time

Many private and public organizations have experimented with four-day and flextime workweek schedules. The number of firms using flexible work hours has more than doubled in the past twenty years. These flexible arrangements take different forms, such as satellite work centers, customized work schedules, staggered shifts, and telecommuting with personal computers to the place of work. A 2005 Society for Human Resource Management study found fewer companies offering flextime than in 2002. But most business and economic analysts do not expect that to become a trend. Their projections suggest that by 2020 over half the workforce could be on some form of flextime.

These work schemes have been hailed as important steps toward creating a leisure society. However, in all four-day and flextime schemes tried so far the workweek remains near forty hours, so this trend has little to do with a reduction in working time; it is merely a rescheduling of the workload. It fails to even touch upon the more important issue of the desirability of a reduction in the overall length of the workweek.

Although the hours of the workweek remain about the same under the various nontraditional plans, several potential benefits accrue with respect to leisure time. The extra-long weekends make travel and other extended leisure activities possible, and commuting time may be reduced, some of which might be used for leisure activities. On the other hand, the extra time afforded by the four-day workweek may be a mixed blessing. For example, many people use the time working at a second job because continuing inflation tends to require more money to maintain the current living standard. Increases in free time, then, are often used primarily as an opportunity to perform extra work of some kind. It appears that the emergence of a true leisure society will require a respiritualization of our society and the rise of a fundamentally different valuation of work and leisure.

Table 15.1 Average Annual Hours of Work, Nonagricultural Industries

	1969	2004	Change 1969–2004
All participants	1,786	1,950	+164
Men	2,054	2,080	+ 26
Women	1,406	1,795	+389

Source: Extrapolated from U.S. Department of Labor, *Labor Force Statistics from the Current Population Survey, 2007* (Bureau of Labor Statistics, 2007).

Ignoring for the moment that the greater amount of free time that technology was supposed to have provided has not materialized, how then can we account for participation rates in leisure activities and expenditure on leisure pursuits being at an all-time high? Leisure accounts for about one in every eight dollars spent by North American consumers. Explanations for the leisure pursuits of North Americans tend to converge on the idea that people are just cramming more activities into each twenty-four hours. The commonly heard "24/7" isn't just an expression; it's a cultural earthquake that is changing the way people live. The main argument is that the nation's business day is now twenty-four hours long because many businesses stay open all night, and cell phones, iPods, and iPhones enable business communication and transactions to be conducted "24/7."

The traditional schedule of being awake during the day and asleep at night has become obsolete; millions of people are awake at any given time throughout the twenty-four-hour day. Those who are awake do not just shop at supermarkets and department stores. They engage in around-the-clock leisure activities, including sports. Many golf ranges, batting cages, tennis courts, swimming pools, and so forth are now open around the clock. Televised sports can be found on cable and satellite at every hour of the day. Sports consumers have many choices "24/7" to meet their sporting interests.

The tendency to do several things simultaneously and many things in a short period of time—including using the ever-present digital devices—has been called "time deepening." It has also been called "the more, the more"—meaning that under the pressure of expanding interests and motivations, the more people do, the more they wish to do, and vice versa. The consequence is that many people suffer from "leisure-time stress." Despite feeling "free" during their free time, many people worry about leisure and hurry from one activity to another, leaving little time to stop and think. Moreover, obsessive consumer attitudes about leisure time do not allow personal initiative and doing one's own thing.

A FUTURE SOCIETY AND SPORT

The twenty-first-century society is expected to become increasingly more of a "learning society." In part, this will be a function of the "information explosion"; thus, information (its acquisition and use) will become extremely important. A major problem will be the adequate supply of educated persons with professional and technical competence; therefore futurists expect education, especially college and graduate education, to be acquired by a much greater proportion of the population than at present.[11]

What are the implications for sport for a highly educated population? Two opposing predictions have been proposed. The first suggests that there will be a trend away from violent forms of sport with a greater emphasis upon "cerebral" sports; the other suggests that violent sports will increase.

Cerebral Sports of the Future

Some futurists propose that as we become more cerebral, our choices will trend away from such violent sports as football, hockey, boxing, and auto racing. In addition, greater attention may be paid to the technical competence of the performers rather than just the outcome of the contest.

Perhaps one indication that intellectual or cerebral activities are gaining in popularity is that the latest forms of indoor recreation for young people are "smart" board games and computer and video games in which the players are expected to outwit or to outthink each other, or, in the case of the latter, beat the game program. PlayStation 3, Nintendo Wii, and XBox games pose daunting intellectual challenges requiring detailed strategy, role-playing, and simulations. There are thousands of video games available, and according to the Entertainment Software Association, 50 percent of all Americans play video games. The average game player is thirty-three years old. The best of the computer-driven games are called "simulations" because of their capability to re-create the strategic requirements and sensuous experiences of the real sports. Entertainment Arts' Madden Football, FIFA Soccer, and MVP Baseball are among the most popular in the market. About one-fourth of the products sold by computer game companies are simulated sports games. Players of simulation games say that your muscles tighten, your pulse quickens, and you feel you're actually in the game. Even more realistic simulation sports games will be developed in the future. The goal in this industry is true-to-life experience.

Fantasy sport leagues have emerged as an extremely popular form of "intellectual" sport, especially among young men—but women are becoming attracted as well. Football is the most popular of the growing fantasy sports games; it is estimated that there are more than fifteen million fantasy football players. This form of sport involvement enables a "player" to get involved in selecting a team of athletes from a league, such as the NFL, to compete in a fantasy league. After each of the games played by the "real" players, the members of the fantasy league compile the statistics for each of the athletes the members of the fantasy league players have drafted. Those statistics determine how each of the fantasy league "players" have "performed." The first generation of fantasy sports involved face-to-face interaction between participants, usually friends. Belonging to a fantasy sports club was a particularly satisfying social experience because members were able to engage in a social activity in which everyone in the group had an interest—professional sports. All of this involved accumulating an extensive knowledge about athletes, teams, and strategy in "real" leagues, creatively thinking about their use, and outsmarting the others in the fantasy league. So participating was intensely cerebral for each member.

With the growth and popularity of the Internet, the popularity of Internet sports fantasy leagues—where all interactions take place online—has skyrocketed during the past decade. A search on Google.com for "Internet sports fantasy leagues" turned up 2,570,000 websites. Subscribers to an Internet sports fantasy league pay a fee to become a member, or "team owner." An estimated $1.44 *billion* is paid annually in league entry fees.

The Web's ability to deliver immediate sports statistics takes interaction in the fantasy league to a completely new level, increasing the enjoyment of fantasy games by providing a more exciting experience for participants. Subscribing to a sports fantasy league is the closest thing you can find to owning your own team franchise and becoming the team's manager and president all in one. You make all the decisions. You are supplied with everything you need to build a team in the best manner possible. Armed with all these resources, you are free to create the team of your dreams. To be a winner, you have to be astute because all the other owners are equally determined to win.[12] Winners of Internet-based fantasy sport leagues typically win prize money. The 2006 Sports Fantasy Leagues 500 Racing Challenge gave away six thousand dollars in guaranteed weekly prize money.

Many of the technosports and ecosports, both to be discussed in a later section of this chapter, can also be considered cerebral sports.

Violent Sports of the Future

Violence continues as a prominent part of both our real world and our sports world. High homicide rates plague our cities and even small towns; indeed, it is dangerous to be on the streets in some urban areas after dark. Some of the most popular television programs and movies feature gratuitous violence, and the high-tech violence of TV and movies may foretell future violent societies.

Given the broad societal violence, the possibility of continued or even increased violence in sports certainly exists. As we noted in chapter 7, there are those who believe that sport provides a cathartic discharge of aggressive urges, and, therefore, violence done under the auspices of sports keeps the cap on social violence. Still others propose that the meaning of sport may be in the "quest for excitement in an unexciting society," and vigorous and violent sport may serve to restore tension and excitement.[13]

The popularity of football, hockey, boxing, professional wrestling, ultimate fighting, and auto racing validates the public interest in violent sports. The public image of these sports projected through radio and television commercials promotes the idea of violence. For example, the National Hockey League has consistently marketed its games through television commercials as violent, almost promising fans that they can expect to see lots of fighting. For many years, the opening commercial for Monday Night Football showed a helmet of each of the competing teams for that night; the helmets turned to face each other and smashed together, with fragments of each flying away. The message of the imagery was clear: The viewer could expect to see some violent collisions.

World Wrestling Entertainment debuted on the USA Network in 1983, and it has maintained a fanatical following into the first decade of the twenty-first century. The staged violence of the World Wrestling Federation, its interlacing narratives, its music, pyrotechnic stagecraft, and good-versus-evil plots are timeless theater, and some forecasters of future sports believe that it will be a powerful influence in the sports world of the future.

In the previous section of this chapter we described the widespread popularity of computer-driven games, especially sport simulation games. These are extreme caricatures of professional baseball and basketball where gratuitous violence and questionable morality are rampant. One of these, MLB SlugFest—advertised as "the most aggressive arcade-style baseball games EVER"—takes Major League Baseball to the extreme, with hard tags, home plate collisions, breaking up double plays with spikes high, pitchers throwing at batters, and fights breaking out after nearly every play.

From their beginning, video games and computer-driven games have overwhelmingly had violent themes—warfare, enemies from outer space, urban crime, etc. It seems that games such as MLB SlugFest have merely transferred the violence from nonsport settings to a sport setting. Computer-based games have embedded themselves into American culture. The role of violence in future computer-based games will depend on consumer demand and, possibly, legislation regulating them.

Technology and Future Sport

The world of sports has made tremendous use of technology, and much in current sport is the product of technological innovation. The type of sport that emerges from technological advances has sometimes been called technosport.

Technosport and the Future

Technology has always altered the way sports are played and observed. Scientific advances in materials have revolutionized sporting goods and equipment and transformed training and coaching methods. The high-tech synthetic materials now used in athletes' apparel and equipment have been major contributors to the improvement of athletes' performances in almost every sport. Technological innovations are transforming many sports—from NASCAR (aerodynamic cars) to the NFL (helmet radio)—modifying strategy, playing styles, and even game rules.[14]

As for training, conditioning, and coaching, to a great extent the emergence of superior athletic performance is a consequence of a pool of specialized experts who are knowledgeable about the newest biotechnologies. These are sport scientists—biomechanists, exercise physiologists, biochemists, nutritionists, and orthopedists—whose expertise is being widely used by trainers and coaches. One of the areas in which sports scientists have been involved is attempting to select potentially superior athletes more deliberately and rationally. In recent years, biochemical, biomechanical, and behavioral sciences have been used with young children in an effort to sort out the potential future champions from the average athlete.

We may expect that scientific selection of future athletes during their early childhood on the basis of their physical and psychological attributes will become commonplace in the future. Once potential athletes have been identified, they will receive special training in preparation for their ultimate careers in sport. There are already programs of this type under way in North America in the form of elite sports academies and youth clubs, and the successes in Olympic Games of some of the athletes from these programs are publicly attributed to the early selection procedures.[15]

Many of the record-breaking feats of the past few years can be attributed to advanced training techniques and better equipment and facilities, but a growing trend among athletes and their coaches is to resort to various chemical substances in order to enhance sports performance, as we noted in chapter 7. As performance standards increase in every sport, substance abuse will probably escalate. It is likely that new biotechnology will enable biochemists to perfect substances that will increase athletes' chances of winning and will be undetectable in the fluids of the body. In spite of increased sophistication in drug-testing procedures, some new drugs are undetectable before or after competition. Futurists expect that the development of new substances might enable a runner, for example, to shave seven- or eight-tenths of a second off his or her 100-meter dash or a javelin thrower to gain an extra seven or eight feet on his or her throw.

At perhaps the most futuristic extreme, sport technologists might turn to "genetic engineering." Indeed, the World Anti-Doping Agency (WADA) has already asked scientists to help find ways to prevent gene therapy from becoming the newest means of doping. But eventually, preventing athletes from gaining access to gene therapy may become impossible.[16] Technosport will be evident in the playing arenas of the future. The domed stadiums built during the past twenty years are miniature prototypes of the giant arenas on the drawing boards. Specialists in stadium design believe that in the future most stadiums and ballparks will be built with fully retractable roofs. The entire natural grass field of the recently completed stadium of the Phoenix Cardinals NFL team is retractable. The grass field remains outside the stadium in the sun until game day, getting the maximum amount of sunshine and nourishment. While the field is outside the stadium, this provides unrestricted access to the stadium floor for events and staging of various kinds.

Future edifices will be equipped with many spectacular accouterments, including push-button vending machines and individual video screens mounted on each seat. As the new millennium began, New York's Madison Square Garden outfitted four sections of club seating and all luxury suites with interactive seats. Through a complex system of computers and touch-screen monitors, those seating areas can access live, isolated camera angles, multiperspective replays with slow motion, sports highlights and statistics, and stored video and outside network feeds. Undoubtedly, entire venues will be wired like this in the future, with additional features. Seats will be equipped with earphones so that spectators can listen to press-box scouts giving advice to the bench, conversations at the pitching mounds, quarterbacks' calls in the huddle, and even locker-room pep talks.

Architects and developers of future sports venues see them as more than purveyors of sporting events. They believe that in the synergistic bliss of the globalized economy, stadiums and arenas will simply turn into malls and food courts. The live sporting events themselves will become, at best, a point-of-purchase display. Although at first one might find this statement merely cynical, a close study of the business establishments within current sports venues clearly shows that they have moved beyond being just food and drink outlets and have indeed begun to become social settings like shopping malls.

Computers will be the central objects because future society will be an information-based society. Computers will be a staple for technosport, just as they will be for technoindustry. Coaches and athletes will be able to receive instant information about their own teams and their opponents. Coaches at all levels have used computers for several years for the selection of athletes and as an aid in scouting opponents, and such computer use will proliferate. In football, college and professional teams often use computers to print out tables about opponents' tendencies and to help coaches and athletes make decisions during the game. This trend will undoubtedly accelerate during the next decade, perhaps to the point where each play in football will be called on the basis of printouts, and baseball coaches will use computers to call each pitch and each infield shift.

The fascination with enhanced sports performances and the obsession with winning has meant that technological innovations have been eagerly sought and employed in sports. However, thoughtful people within and outside the sports world are raising important social questions such as: Just because science and technology makes it possible for athletes and teams to set new speed, distance, and weight records, should they? Are the higher risks to the life and limbs of athletes' worth using whatever is scientifically and technologically possible?[17]

Many times people simply accept the idea that if it can be done, it should be done; the question of whether something should be done is seldom asked. There are compelling social and psychological reasons why that question, and others like it, will be increasingly asked, and with good reason. For example, there is no doubt that one of the consequences of employing the latest technological innovations is that various injuries and illnesses are increasing for athletes. Their incidence and seriousness are rising in many sports at the elite levels.[18]

Scientific and technical terminology, when used in sport, often conceives of athletes as objects, little different from inanimate machines. Indeed, the terms "human machine" and "mortal engine" have been favorite metaphors for athletes' bodies among sport technicians. However, the human-as-machine notion has inherent dangers. Humans are not machines, and acting as if they are can be a source of major problems. After all, when a machine ceases to function properly, or quits working altogether, it can be discarded or scrapped. Humans are their body, and they have only one body, and it must last a lifetime; if it is damaged or parts of it destroyed, the quality of life is irreparably damaged.

There is another dimension to questioning the unqualified acceptance of scientific and technical developments in the interest of enhanced performances and sporting victories. The scientific-technical ethos gives priority to the product—the outcome; but the aspect of sport that has always been its prevailing essence is its process—its fun, its spontaneity, its creativeness, its expressiveness. Scientizing and technocizing sport subvert what have always been sport's most endearing features.[19]

It is likely that over the next twenty years a major debate will center on the social-ethical questions that have been raised here about the scientific-technical directions of sport. The dominant view that prevails in the sports world is not guaranteed. Resistance, opposition, even rejection of that dominant view have already begun, and will probably continue in some form for the foreseeable future.

A Counterpoint to Technosports: Ecosports

At the same time that technosports trends are altering sports at an incredible pace, another trend is moving forward with an extraordinary momentum of its own. For lack of a better name for it, many of its participants refer to it as "ecosports." Ecosports involves natural play and unstructured games; many of them are done out-of-doors, without boundaries, and with few or no codified rules. Ecosports also include a variety of what have been called "nontraditional" or "alternative" physical activities. Some of the various forms of ecosports tend to emphasize cooperation rather than competition, the struggle rather than the triumph; the main point of many of them is to play, to enjoy, and to exist.

Ecosports and the Future

Early twenty-first-century society confronts us with a congested urban lifestyle. Houses are jammed tightly against each other, apartments are stacked story on story, offices and factories are made up of steel and concrete, and our jobs are forcing us to work among multitudes of our fellow human beings. Thus, many North Americans yearn for the out-of-doors, to be away from the crush of people. The mountains, oceans, lakes, rivers, and sky all beckon.

Many North Americans yearn for the out-of-doors, to be away from the crush of people. Backcountry skiing is among a new category of sports, "adventure sports." (iStockphoto)

The outdoor form of the ecosport movement is well under way, manifested in activities such as hiking, rock climbing, kayaking, scuba diving, canoeing, sailing, waterskiing, skydiving, snowboarding, and so forth. Attendance at national parks, recreational facilities, and local parks has skyrocketed. In the past decade the number of North Americans participating in outdoor ecosport activities has grown dramatically: Cross-country skiers increased from a few thousand in 1980 to more than 3 million in 2007. There are an estimated 30 million runners, including a group of more than 8 million "hard-core" runners (they prefer *not* to be called joggers) who run at least 120 days a year. The number of hikers has more than doubled in the past ten years to about 38 million. At the national parks, backpacking increased by more than 100 percent between 1985 and 2007. The number of mountaineers has been doubling about every five years. The trend is clear: The public mindset is moving in favor of outdoor physical activities as an alternative to traditional organized sports.

There are even new categories of ecosports. One of these is called "action sports" by the sporting goods industry. In-line skating, with twenty-nine million skaters, is one of the largest contributors to the explosive growth in action sports in North America. Other rapidly growing sports in this category are skateboarding, snowboarding, windsurfing, BMX, triathlon, kayaking, and downhill mountain biking.

Another new category of sports is called "adventure sports." Although it is rather new as a distinct category, there is already an astonishing variety of these sports, including adventure racing (biking, running, climbing, hiking, and canoeing over courses of 80 miles or more), long-distance cycling (the Race Across America race is 2,983 miles), and extreme trail hiking—the Pacific Crest Trail is 2,655 miles long, the Continental Divide Trail is 2,600 miles long, the Appalachian Trail is 2,168 miles long. The Primal Quest Adventure Race and others like it are five- to ten-day competitions of trekking, mountain biking, and whitewater rafting.[20]

Some of the action sports and adventure sports overlap into a rather ill-defined category called "extreme sports." We discussed extreme sports in chapter 11 in connection with the X Games competitions, broadcast on ESPN. For many people, what ESPN covers in its telecasts of extreme sports competitions defines extreme sports. But for those who participate in the plethora of nontraditional sports, there is a much broader variety of sports that are considered "extreme." Perhaps the most extreme of these is BASE (an acronym for building, antenna, span [bridge], and earth [cliffs] jumping). Between 1985 and 2005, more than fifty participants were killed in this extreme sport. BASE is an example of a new approach to sports that coincides with a larger sensation-seeking cultural shift toward collecting experiences. Experiences are a large status symbol for people of all ages. They feel satisfaction in saying, "I jumped off this . . ." or "I climbed that. . . ."

Nontraditional or "alternative" indoor ecosports include several of the Oriental martial arts, such as aikido, karate, judo, and tae kwon do, as well as various forms of yoga. Most do not require elaborate equipment and organization; also competition is not important to their mastery (indeed, in aikido, competition is forbidden). Skilled movements in these activities are frequently like dances, and the performers achieve a transcendent beauty in the whirling, throwing, kicking, and jumping common to these activities.

Most ecosports do not attract the publicity of the technosports, and most of them certainly do not attract masses of spectators. For many participants in ecosports, the essence is participation, so the fanfare and hoopla associated with technosport are not missed. That is precisely what is attractive about these sports for many of the participants.

Will the ecosport momentum carry through the first decades of the twenty-first century? Many social dynamics influence the popularity of sports, but most forecasters of sport in the twenty-first century agree that this form of sport will increase in popularity.

Some view these forms of sport as a reaction not only against the technocorporate form of organization characteristic of North American social institutions but also against the organized and corporate levels of sport described in chapter 1, where the outcome supersedes the process. This certainly may be why many of the participants of these sports took them up and popularized them, but ecosports are increasingly being seized on by commercial interests as new markets for products and services.

The commercial sport industry seeks to organize sports activities on strict market principles—the pursuit of profits, rather than the satisfaction of personal and social needs. The play elements of the activities are squeezed out as corporate profit motives increase. Social analyst Harry Braverman eloquently described this trend toward the commercialization of all sporting activities. He says, "So enterprising is [capitalism] that even where the effort is made by one or another section of the population to find a way to nurture sports . . . through personal activity . . . these activities are rapidly incorporated into the market so far as is possible."[21]

There is compelling evidence that this phenomenon is occurring in ecosports. Jogging and running began as a way to increase health and fitness, but within a few years a massive commercial "running industry" had emerged with multinational firms selling high-tech running shoes and a variety of other apparel and accessories. "Fun runs" were largely replaced with 10-K and marathon races, then triathlons, and finally "Ironman" competitions with corporate sponsors and prize money winners. On Ironmanlive.com there is a sidebar titled "The Anatomy of an Ironman Product," followed by this statement:

> The process of identifying, developing, manufacturing and selling an Ironman-Triathlon-branded product can be just as challenging as the long and obstacle-ridden path an athlete follows to become an Ironman. Just like every elite triathlete who crosses an Ironman finish line anywhere, these products can only bear the Ironman label if they can meet the Ironman standards. Simply put, Ironman-licensed products must deliver the benefits implied by the Ironman label.[22]

This makes clear that Ironman sports is a brand name that is for sale.

Aerobic exercise began as a movement to improve cardiovascular conditioning in people who were in poor physical condition. Before long, several related commercial industries appeared: aerobic centers, aerobic shoes, and aerobic apparel. Local, state, and national championships are now part of the aerobics industry, all sponsored by commercial firms that market and sell their products and services to aerobics participants. But they also use aerobics practitioners as models to sell a wide variety of products and services that consumers associate with the lean, hard-body look of the models.

In chapter 11 we described how nontraditional, youth-oriented sports had been captured by ESPN and turned into the X Games TV programming, which is an advertising bonanza for corporations selling products to a teenage following.

Consequently, X Games have gone from anti-establishment to mainstream and commercial—becoming extremely organized, with special training camps and elite coaches. Famed X Games skateboarder Tony Hawk, whose name is on dozens of products, was voted "coolest big-time athlete," ahead of megasport superstars such as Michael Jordan, Tiger Woods, and Serena Williams, in a poll conducted by a marketing firm.[23] Similar trends can be seen with all of the action and adventure sports. Unfortunately for those who seek physical activities that are not dominated by codified rules, professional event organizers, and corporate sponsorships, or hyped by paid endorsers, the tendencies of the past suggest the trends of the future will be in the direction of commercial takeover rather than blissful carefree independence.

TRENDS IN THE ECONOMY AND FUTURE SPORTS

The North American economic systems are complex mixtures of capitalism and socialism, and the free trade agreements between the United States, Canada, and Mexico tend to integrate the individual economies. Throughout the world during the twentieth century there was steady movement away from laissez-faire (virtually unregulated) capitalism and toward managerial capitalism, with the adoption of many socialistic features, which has caused some observers to predict that capitalism will die in North America. This view is not shared by most futurists, however. Capitalism has proved extremely adaptable, and despite the growth in social entitlement programs and the growth in government over the past twenty years, there has been no fundamental challenge to the capitalist economy in North America.

Given the enormous influence of the corporate rich and the tendency for most North Americans to accept the present economic structure as proper, capitalism will undoubtedly remain a pillar of society in the United States and Canada.

The future economy, barring nuclear holocaust, unforeseen energy problems, or other catastrophic events, will probably continue to go through its cycles of prosperity and recession. The terrorist attacks on 11 September 2001 were a severe shock to the social climate and economic systems of North America. Everyone has heard "The world will never be the same" repeated over and over. But in spite of these events, and the security measures that we all live with in their aftermath, our lives do go on. According to economic forecasters, North America will face increasing international economic competition and will be challenged to find better ways to accommodate the emerging global economy rather than trying to dominate international economic competitors.[24]

The Future of Professional Sports

The professional sports industry in North America has grown at an unprecedented rate in the past twenty years. It is now a sprawling, multibillion-dollar-a-year industry that is clearly big business, and in which winning and losing count far less than making a profit. Professional sport franchise owners once generally had a deep emotional commitment to the sport and believed that the administration and financial operations were merely necessary adjuncts to owning a team.

Current owners are increasingly corporate conglomerates of one kind or another, and they think primarily of maximizing profit through rational business procedures. Providing sports entertainment for loyal hometown fans is only a secondary consideration. The most visible example of this is found in the numerous threats by ownership to move franchises if demands for new stadiums, better lease deals, and so forth are not met. They are not idle threats, as can be seen in the number of franchise moves.[25]

As we indicated in an earlier section in this chapter, the trend appears to be toward an expansion of professional sports in the foreseeable future. However, most sports forecasters predict that there will be little expansion in the four major North American team sports (MLB, NFL, NHL, NBA) in the next twenty years. Instead, expansion will take place in other sports, such as soccer, lacrosse, auto racing, and women's basketball. One way professional sports might expand is by becoming more international. The four major North American team sports are played worldwide, and with air travel speeds increasing, there seems little reason not to expand into other continents. Soccer is already a sport played worldwide, and it seems imminent that North American soccer teams will be incorporated into European and/or Asian soccer leagues.

Fan support depends on adequate disposable income. Within the past decade, serious economic downturns have occurred in North America. Should a prolonged economic downturn occur, people will have less disposable income, and this could adversely affect professional sports. Moreover, as noted earlier, if ticket prices outstrip cost of living, professional sports may price themselves out of the market.

The Future of Televised Sports

Television Coverage
Before television rescued the professional sports industry, professional sports owners were beset with decreasing attendance and the prospect of failure. The importance of television and radio markets has been a prominent factor in the growth and expansion of all professional sports. Professional sport and television enjoy a reciprocal relationship. Both pro sport and television executives realize that if any of the professional sports lost television revenues, their industry would be devastated. Therefore, for professional sports to maintain their entertainment status and continue to expand, they will have to depend on the benevolence of television. As long as the television networks consider pro sports a moneymaker, pro sports will prosper.

In the future, sports leagues and teams will develop pipelines directly targeted at their fans. In an article titled "The Future of Sports Media," the authors claim that sports properties will become "their own media companies, interacting directly with their consumers without the filter of traditional media." For example, despite the NFL's television rights monopoly, the NFL "has been building its own television channel, the NFL Network . . . which broadcast eight regular season games in the 2006 season . . . and builds the legends of the league with its popular NFL Films content . . . along with the National Basketball Association's NBATV, the Baseball network, and other team-only channels . . . [it] is redefining sports television and transforming the once-reliable sports rights infrastructure." In summary, the authors say, "The only certainty about the sports media marketplace is that it is adapting, and for stakeholders, this means constant monitoring of change and a commitment to innovation."[26]

Television Technology and Sports Viewing
Mediated sports spectating at first meant people sitting in their living rooms listening to accounts of the events on their radios. Today many people sit in their home entertainment centers and watch sports events on their huge high-definition TV screens. But that will change too. Anticipated technological advances with computer enhancement in the next decade or two will enable TV viewers to interact with the coverage and the game and to customize the content of the broadcast sports coverage they receive. Viewers will have control over what aspects of events they will watch. They will be able to direct camera angles and request regular and slow-motion replays of viewer-defined action. They will be able to call up certain cameras to focus on a single player, coach, or part of the field or court, and they will be able to ask for statistics and personal background on the players and coaches. Sports TV networks will also proliferate. The prospect of the thousand-channel universe has excited many sports fans. It seems likely that all of the most popular sports will have their own networks, so viewers will be able to watch their favorite sport 24/7.

As we noted in chapter 11, PPV television is going to become a major factor in the next decade. There appears to be little doubt that within ten years sports fans will have to pay for many events they now see on free TV or basic cable. Some forecasters predict that as costs to attend sports events escalate and as television increasingly makes viewing of all important sports events available at low cost, attendance at sports facilities will dwindle.

Regardless of the trends in viewing options and interactivity, high-definition television gives sports viewers a much sharper view of the action than was once possible. Those who have high-definition equipment confirm that the images are so incredibly clear and lifelike that regular TV pictures look blurred and out of focus.

Internet Technology and Sports Viewing

We discussed the Internet in a previous section in connection with cerebral sports. But it is pertinent to mention it here as well. The Internet is one of the most sophisticated and useful outcomes of innovations in modern technology. Those who work on the cutting edge of this technology claim that we are still in the early stages of achieving what the future holds for the Internet. Within a short time the complete integration of Internet technology, computer technology, telecommunications, and the World Wide Web will make it possible for users to use computers, the Internet, and television interchangeably. They will not only have incredible choices of sporting events at their command but will also have virtually unlimited control over what they will watch and how they will view the events. (See Box 15.1, *Thinking about Sport*.)

MLB has developed an Internet infrastructure for streaming live video of its games throughout the season. MLB.com Mosaic offers online real-time simultaneous viewing of six games, and for a

---

Box 15.1 *Thinking about Sport* **Mediated Sports and Fans of the Future**

The rise of professional and intercollegiate sports in the latter half of the nineteenth century gave rise to sports fandom and one of the prime reasons for groups to gather to be entertained. Moreover, people formed alliances toward specific teams for various reasons. On-site spectatorship was a way to know about the game—who won and who lost—but also to witness the performances of the players and coaches.

But on-site spectatorship had its limitations; only those with the location, time, and means to actually view the game knew what happened in the contest. The print media—newspapers and magazines—quickly realized there was a market for pregame information as well as postgame information about sports events. A mediated—meaning acting or brought about through an intervening agency—sports industry was born. Print media was the only mediated sport until the 1920s, when radio broadcasts of sports events brought families, drinking friends, and workers together to listen to sports events.

With the technological innovations of the 1940s and 1950s, television quickly became a dominating force around which families and bar buddies gathered to watch televised sports events. For fifty years television was the preferred way for social groupings to participate in mediated sports.

The explosive development of the World Wide Web in the last decade of the twentieth century became an ideal mediated sports medium and useful resource for dedicated sports fans. Media scholar Michael Real asserts: "Its accessibility, interactivity, speed, and multimedia content are triggering a fundamental change in the delivery of mediated sports, a change for which no one can yet predict the outcome."

Social scientists are concerned with what effect a computer-based Internet-connected lifestyle will have on social relations. Although television tended to turn social life indoors and socially isolate entertainment, it did bring families together to watch the programs, especially sports, and sports bars became a popular social site for watching sports events. As ownership of computers, cell phones, iPhones, and iPods becomes universal and as free live online coverage of sports events becomes mainstream, mediated sports may become an individual, rather than a social, activity.

The way some futurists see it, with everyone in a home owning a computer, and with so many live online sports to view, each member of the family will retreat to his or her corner of the house to view preferred sports events. In addition, cell phones, iPhones, iPods, and future handheld instruments will contribute to individual, independent, nonsocial viewing of mediated sports. One sports media analyst who claims that the next great frontier for mediated sports is probably in your pocket right now believes that it will provide a personal rather than a social form of spectating.

Source: Michael Real, "Sports Online: The Newest Player in Media Sport," in *Handbook of Sports and Media*, ed. Arthur A. Raney and Jennings Bryant (Mahwah, N.J.: Lawrence Erlbaum Associates, 2006), 171.

subscription fee, fans can watch almost all MLB games throughout the season on their computer. This is a model for the ways that other professional sport leagues and teams in the future will emulate sports broadcasting on the Internet while making a profit in the process. And it is only a matter of time before it becomes a part of college and high school sports.

Video Technology and Sports Video Games

Another form of mediated sports "participation" is video games. Video games, which provide simulations of various kinds, are extremely popular with a broad spectrum of age groups, but especially with teenagers. Sports games, in particular, are plentiful. Some of the most popular are exhilarating simulations of professional and college football and basketball games, but racing games are also popular, as are extreme sports videos.

With the increase in technological sophistication over the past decade, the best sport video games feature outstanding graphics and put players squarely in the middle of the action. In football video games, players have play-calling options that mirror actual coaches' playbooks, making for a seamlessly realistic experience. Incredibly photorealistic graphics make the virtual sports games mesmerizing.

Sony, Microsoft, and Nintendo, the major makers of video game systems, are working diligently to make the audio and video of these games more and more realistic, and the control equipment more precise. Given the growth of all forms of mediated sports over the past decade, there is every reason to expect that the introduction of remarkable new video game systems will be an annual event in the foreseeable future.

A number of futurists have expressed concern that TV, Internet, and video technology will become so exciting, so mesmerizing, that it will have an isolating effect. They fear that masses of sports fans may choose to remain in the comfort of their homes with their TV sets, computers, and video game systems rather than actually attending sports events. A number of social scientists have been warning that the privatization of leisure, through the retreat into the home for entertainment, has the danger of bringing about a collapse of a civic ethic within society, the sense of belonging to a society.

Intercollegiate Athletics and the Future

As we have noted at several places in this volume, professional sport is not limited to privately owned sport franchises. Big-time collegiate sports constitute a professional industry in every sense of the word. They are every bit as dependent on economic considerations as other professional sports, and one can confidently predict that as television goes, with respect to buying rights to broadcast intercollegiate sports events, so will go the big-time collegiate programs.

Even with the bonanza of television money, intercollegiate athletic programs have had increasing financial problems. The major problem is money—or the lack of it. Growth in attendance has slowed as competition, from both professional sports and other attractions, has increased. Meanwhile, increased costs have taken a brutal toll on the athletic budgets of many colleges. Adding additional games to the traditional ten-game football schedule, permitting first-year students to play on varsity teams, expanding play-off schedules in basketball and bowl games in football, limiting the size of coaching staffs, and de-emphasizing or dropping so-called nonrevenue sports are all economic measures that have been adopted to add revenue or to reduce expenses in intercollegiate athletics.

All is still not well on the campuses. For example, many state-supported universities receive substantial support for collegiate athletics from tax funds, and public opposition to this is growing. Legislatures are weighing the athletic appropriations against, for example, faculty salaries and state aid for disadvantaged students. Other educational considerations include more spending for community colleges and expansion of vocational education. Needs are also being considered in other fields, such as mental health, welfare, law enforcement, and the general administration of government.

What does the future hold for intercollegiate athletics? Finally, slowly, gradually, and reluctantly, major universities with big-time football and basketball programs are moving toward paying college athletes a salary for their hard work on behalf of the university. The charade that universities have advanced—that college sports are amateur athletics and therefore the athletes must not accept financial remuneration for playing—has become so ludicrous that even leaders in the NCAA have begun to acknowledge that athletes should be given some form of direct payment. As we described in chapter 6, football and basketball coaches at major universities are making annual salaries of more than $2 million; major university budgets range from $40 to $90+ million. Assistant coaches, athletic trainers, sports information directors, even equipment managers receive livable incomes. Only the athletes are without a salary. Prognosticators for intercollegiate sports expect that within the next five to ten years the NCAA and its member universities will develop a system for direct payment to student-athletes at major universities. It is a disservice to intercollegiate athletes to remain committed to an outdated code of amateurism for economic controls.[27]

The Game of Life: College Sports and Educational Values, a book highly critical of the practice of colleges admitting a large number of academically unqualified athletes and possibly diminishing the academic environment of their campuses, prompted a number of small liberal arts colleges in the northeastern states to change their admission policies. Beginning in 2002, these colleges admitted fewer applicants "for whom prowess in athletics is the difference between being admitted and being rejected by the college considering them." The new policy has stimulated supportive talk throughout higher education. It is too soon to know whether this recent action will create a new trend in higher education, but the widespread dissatisfaction with admitting academically unqualified athletes suggests that the new directions taken by a few small colleges might gain support and emulation.[28]

Sports club programs are growing on college campuses. These are student-oriented sports teams coached by older students or interested persons with a love for the sport (they typically receive no pay) and are funded by the participants or by small sums from the institution's student activity funds. Some higher education administrators have even predicted that over the next twenty years most of the athletic teams on a college campus will be of the sports club type, with the university having only one or two sports of the high-visibility, commercial type.

Secondary School Sports and the Future

Over the past two decades high school sports have been faced with two major challenges: bringing the sports programs into compliance with Title IX and coping with the increasing costs of conducting the expanding sports programs. In the latter case, in 2006 the NFHS reported that for the seventeenth consecutive year the number of student participants in high school athletics increased. But the increasing reluctance of taxpayers to support education and the hesitancy of many state legislatures to raise taxes combined to force many school systems to consider reducing extracurricular activities, including sports programs. Even though the cost of a high school athletic program is only 1 to 3 percent of a high school's overall budget, the general public seems increasingly indifferent to supporting these programs.[29]

If financial difficulties continue to plague secondary schools, modifications in the funding of the programs will probably occur. Indeed, one trend of the past decade is the "pay-for-play" plans that require athletes to assume some of the costs of equipment and other expenses associated with their participation. This trend is likely to grow, as it has been successful in many communities. Other means may be tried in the next decade to salvage high school sports programs. More active booster clubs, corporate sponsorship, and television contracts have all been tried, but further development is likely. As an alternative to high school athletics, some communities may consider phasing sports out of the schools entirely and having the municipal recreation departments administer sports programs for all age groups.

TRENDS IN SOCIAL VALUES AND FUTURE SPORT

In chapter 3 we identified the dominant values in Canadian and American societies. These mainstream values include an entire constellation of beliefs involving the importance of personal effort and accomplishment in defining one's status and worth, both economic and social, and one's relation to social institutions. These values, like other aspects of North American life, have been undergoing significant change; indeed, some social scientists claim we are on the verge of a cultural crisis that will ultimately revolutionize our values and institutions. The roots of this crisis reside in a strong disillusionment with traditional values.

The Quest for Democracy and Equality

During the past twenty years a continuing debate has taken place in North America, as well as in countries throughout the world, over the issue of democracy and equality. We have witnessed the downfall of autocratic governments on every continent. Leaders of almost every political revolution or of countries with substantial chronic social unrest have vowed to provide greater democracy and equality; indeed, there is said to be a worldwide yearning for a "democratic revolution." This is a theme with great appeal to people throughout North America who have been disadvantaged by their ascribed statuses and are demanding to be considered full members of society.[30]

North Americans have actually been in the forefront of those seeking a democracy and equality revolution, and futurists expect that there will continue to be demands for more autonomy, more democracy, and greater participation in places of work and in government. All of these demands add up to a quest for more control over one's life and for the reduction of economic, political, and social inequalities that now restrict people from improving their quality of life.

The essence of the quest for social change is related to new ideas about humanity and methods of interpersonal relations. A more optimistic, democratic, humanistic conception of human nature is emerging. These new values have already had an impact on such social institutions as education, politics, and religion, and they are making their presence felt in the business world.

There is no longer only one acceptable lifestyle; nor is there one set of social values. Because of this, we find many changes in economic and political organization and a variety of sports activities and leisure patterns. The result has been a shift in consciousness, a shift in personal goals and priorities and in the ways of perceiving and ordering the world outside the individual. According to scholars who track social change and trends, more North Americans are beginning to resist the frantic pace of the business world and feeling the urge to return life to a time of greater simplicity and ease. People are turning to relaxing hobbies like gardening and fishing, and some are seeking balance through job sharing or telecommuting. Many younger citizens are protesting traditional rules, policies, and social practices through various social movements.[31]

Several years ago, economic historian and Nobel laureate Robert Fogel demonstrated through his research that eras of great affluence, such as the 1990s, typically are followed by what he refers to as "Great Awakenings," and we may be due for one in the next decade.[32] As a consequence, futurists expect the next twenty years to be characterized by more humane, expressive, and creative approaches to life. Futurists predict that many young people will discover satisfaction in the opportunity to become involved with activities that test their talents, give them more responsibility for their behavior, and let them stretch their minds and bodies.

Trends in Sports Values

Social practices are based on traditional norms and values and are therefore vulnerable to the effects of value changes among significant segments of the society. Many traditional values have come under attack in the past decade, and since sport is a social practice, it too has been challenged by emerging values.

Democracy and Equality in Sport

Traditional athletic priorities and practices have begun to be challenged by a new set of standards premised on the notion that democratic processes have relevance in sport as well as other sectors of life. Consequently, athletes are demanding changes in sports at all levels; they are especially pressing for greater participation in the decisions that affect their athletic lives and for a greater responsiveness on the part of coaches and athletic administrators. They have also pressed for more autonomy, for the freedom to be what they want to be and to choose how they will live.

Although some athletes have called for a change toward greater freedom and personal responsibility within the structure and functioning of sport, they have been a minority, and it is unlikely that athletes will be in the vanguard of social change in the future. The world of sports generates a fundamental acceptance of the established norms and values. Even if athletes as a group do not catalyze much change, they are nevertheless members of their own youth culture, a culture that is pressing for change. The old athletes tended to confront authorities infrequently; current professional and collegiate athletes are more likely to challenge the management establishment. This attitude is demonstrated by the strikes in pro baseball, hockey, and football. In the past decade, collegiate and Olympic athletes have demanded, and have won, representation on important decision-making committees of the NCAA and the U.S. and Canadian Olympic committees. Directions in sport, then, suggest increased egalitarianism, democracy, and humanism, but these are trends that will occur only gradually and only as they become a part of society.

Opportunity and Equality for Special Groups in Sport

Historical inequalities and injustices for females and racial-ethnic minorities were described in chapters 13 and 14. As part of each chapter, we also highlighted the remarkable changes that have taken place in the sports world in the past generation that have given greater access and opportunity to African Americans, women, and ethnic minorities in sport. Other groups as well have experienced historical discrimination in sport, but here too conditions are changing for the better and will likely continue to do so.

People with Disabilities and Sport. One of those groups is people with disabilities, who make up about 20 percent of the population. People with disabilities historically have been subject to systematic prejudice and injustice, and only in the past few decades have national laws and enlightened public attitudes reversed the practices that treated people with disabilities as outcasts.

One of the oldest and most effective organizations supporting and promoting sports for people with disabilities is the nonprofit National Sports Center for the Disabled (NSCD), which began in 1970 with children with amputations from Children's Hospital in Denver, Colorado. Presently, participants come to the NSCD from all fifty states and from countries all over the world. They can choose among twenty different winter and summer sports, from skiing and snowshoeing to river rafting and rock climbing. More than seventeen thousand lessons were provided in 2006 alone. The NSCD Competition Program is the largest of its kind in North America. The program has been very successful at attracting and training some of the best ski racers with disabilities and placing them on the U.S. Disabled Ski Team.[33]

Another national organization serving the needs of the disabled is Disabled Sports USA (DS/USA), which was founded in 1967 by disabled Vietnam veterans. It was then called the National Amputee Skiers Association. After going through a series of names, it settled on its present name. Its website states that it

> offers nationwide sports rehabilitation programs to anyone with a permanent disability. Activities include winter skiing, water sports, summer and winter competitions, fitness and special sports events.

Participants include those with visual impairments, amputations, spinal cord injury, dwarfism, multiple sclerosis, head injury, cerebral palsy, and other neuromuscular and orthopedic conditions. As a member of the United States Olympic Committee, DS/USA sanctions and conducts competitions and training camps to prepare and select athletes to represent the United States at the Summer and Winter Paralympic Games.[34]

As one of the many horrible legacies of the Iraq War, more than 720 (as of November 2007) young American men and women are now amputees. Sports are helping some of them recover and reclaim a somewhat normal life. Several special sports events have been established to help military amputees in the rehabilitation and return to healthy, active lives.[35]

The Paralympic Games are the Olympic equivalent competitions for individuals with disabilities and are recognized by the International Olympic Committee. In 1960, in parallel with the Summer Olympic Games in Rome, a Games for wheelchair users was organized. Four hundred athletes from twenty-three countries competed, and these Games are considered the first Paralympic Games. The 2004 Athens Paralympics had some 4,000 disabled athletes competing for 525 gold medals in nineteen sports. The most recent Winter Paralympics were held in 2006 in Turin, Italy, with 486 athletes representing thirty-nine countries.[36]

Our discussion has focused on the dramatic changes that have occurred in the past two decades for disabled athletes. It is clear that athletes with disabilities now have access and opportunities not only to participate in sport, but also to become elite athletes competing for gold medals and large sums of money. The future for disabled athletes looks very encouraging because widespread support is now in place for opportunities to increase.

Another world-renowned program for people with special needs is the Special Olympics—an international program of year-round sports training

Canadian Kimberly Joines skis her way to a bronze medal in the women's sitting Super-G race at the Turin 2006 Paralympic Winter Games in Sestriere, Italy. (AP Photo/Claudio Scaccini)

and athletic competition for developmentally disabled children and adults. Special Olympics began in 1968 when Eunice Kennedy Shriver organized the First International Special Olympics Games at Soldier Field in Chicago. Since then, millions of developmentally disabled children and adults have participated in Special Olympics. The mission is to provide year-round sports training and athletic competition in a variety of Olympic-type sports for developmentally disabled individuals, thereby giving them opportunities to develop physical fitness, experience joy, and participate in a sharing of skills and friendship with their families and other Special Olympics athletes.

In the United States, there are Special Olympics chapters in all fifty states, the District of Columbia, Guam, the Virgin Islands, and American Samoa. About 25,000 communities in the United States have Special Olympics programs. In addition, there are accredited Special Olympics programs in nearly 150 countries. There has been sustaining public support for the Special Olympics and other programs for individuals with developmental disabilities.[37] There seems little doubt that these programs will continue to grow in the coming years and provide sporting opportunities to a broader spectrum of individuals with disabilities.

Senior Populations and Sport. In an earlier section of this chapter, we noted that the over-65 population will more than double between 2010 and 2050, when one in five North Americans will be over 65 years old. The trend toward a greater proportion of the population being over 50 years of age has been under way for some time now, and older adults are remaining physically active. The organizations they choose to join to continue to play sports vary from local community recreation programs to the National Senior Games Association (NSGA). The NSGA is a nonprofit organization dedicated to motivating senior men and women to lead a healthy lifestyle through the senior games movement. The organization governs the Summer National Senior Games (Senior Olympics) and the Winter National Senior Games. About 250,000 senior athletes participate in these senior games competitions each year.

Participating athletes must be fifty years old or older and must qualify in an NSGA-sanctioned state senior game in order to compete. The Senior Olympics has grown to be one of the largest multisports athletic competitions in the world. Participation in the Summer National Senior Games has grown rapidly. In 2007, twelve thousand athletes participated in this event.

The Winter National Senior Games provide an opportunity for a new and different population of senior athletes to compete in a national sports event. The first-ever biennial Winter National Senior Games were held in 2000, in Lake Placid, New York.[38] Demographic trends that point to increasing life expectancy and a growing population of seniors who are healthy and active clearly indicate that sports of all kinds will grow in popularity and in participation among seniors. Indeed, sport planners claim that new sport organizations for seniors are where the action will be in the coming years.

Gays and Lesbians in Sport. Another group that has faced pervasive injustice is homosexuals. Historically, there has been little toleration for homosexuality in North America. Despite substantially improved attitudes over the past decade, gays and lesbians still suffer various forms of social stigma and injustice. As we noted in chapter 14, sport has been a bastion of homophobia; indeed, sport has been a cultural practice where homophobic attitudes have actually been socially constructed and reproduced.

As with other sectors of society, attitudes and values about human sexuality are gradually changing, and there is a greater acceptance of individuality in sexual orientation. In sport, as well, gays and lesbians have been "coming out," acknowledging their homosexuality. While there is still a deep division in attitudes toward homosexuality among North Americans, the taboo about homosexuality that once prevailed in sport is beginning to diminish.

Gay and lesbian athletes compete at all levels of sport, from novice to Olympic champions. In addition to competing with and against heterosexual athletes in sports at all age and proficiency levels, many gays and lesbians participate in privately sponsored and community-sponsored leagues and events. In her book about lesbians in sport, Pat Griffin explains that the "largely rural Northampton-Amherst, Massachusetts area . . . has supported 14 to 16 lesbian softball teams in an independent league for 20 years."[39] She also describes several other sports events for lesbians and gays that are regularly held in different regions of North America.

To provide a special sporting event for homosexual athletes and improve public attitudes about homosexuality, leaders of the homosexual community organized the first Gay Games in 1982 (name changed to Federation of Gay Games in 1989), which are patterned after the Olympic Games and held every four years. The number of participants in the Federation of Gay Games has grown phenomenally—from twelve hundred in the first Games to more than twelve thousand from seventy countries in the 2006 Games. The number of spectators has grown from a few thousand to more than a million. The Federation of Gay Games believes the growth potential for the future of these Games looks excellent.

Gays and lesbians are also dedicated and loyal sports fans, and their attendance and support for some sports events and leagues are well known. One of the notable aspects of the new open visibility of gays and lesbians as sports fans is that they are beginning to be viewed as a "niche market" by commercial interests. The San Francisco Giants are often credited with being the first professional team to market to gay fans. Beginning in 1994 the team designated one game per season as a fundraiser for acquired immunodeficiency syndrome (AIDS) research. The Giants say technically the game is not a "gay game day," but it does draw twice as many fans as a "normal" day game, and it is obvious that gay fans make that difference.

It is obvious that the WNBA understands that lesbians have been its fan base since the league started. The league needs the money, so their marketing efforts are targeting lesbians. Some WNBA teams claim they have always sought the support of lesbian fans. Several promotions directors for WNBA teams say they have been doing it from day one and that members of the lesbian community are indicating their support.

The kinds of value changes that are taking place in North America and the adoption of new values in sport point clearly to a future where stereotyped and marginalized groups—people with disabilities, seniors, gays, lesbians, and others—are going to have more opportunities to play an integral role in sports of the future.

New Emphasis on Participation and Cooperation

Traditional youth and high school sports programs were practically built on a foundation in which a few athletes played on a few "varsity" teams, while the vast majority of people became "substitutes" or spectators. A new, active, participative orientation is gaining adherents. One visible trend in youth sports programs is the structuring of play to foster participation, cooperation, and sportsmanship. For example, rules decreeing that every child who registers should be assigned to a team and that every child on a team should play in every game are becoming more common. Some leagues feature no-win games, that is, no points are awarded for a win or loss and no records are kept of league standings or of leading scorers. Those who conduct such programs report that the youngsters appear to have a lot more fun than under the traditional format.

Earlier in this chapter we discussed various forms of alternative sports—action, adventure, extreme—that are rapidly gaining adherents and are flourishing. There seems to be little doubt that sports of these kinds will be the wave of the future. It is also reasonable to expect that new sports will be created. The traditional sports model has been shattered by the alternative sports, and there is now an atmosphere of creative experimentation with new sport forms. One manifestation of that is what is called junkyard sports. These offer an alternative to the traditional sports model because they stress personal involvement, active participation in rules and decisions, creativity, and most of all are inclusive so all share the fun.[40]

New Forms of Intramural Sports

The intramural sports program has been the place where more student-athletes participate than anyplace else on a college campus. It is likely that this will continue as student enrollments get larger and larger. College students are increasingly rejecting the traditional offerings of campus intramural programs and demanding more innovative programs with greater potential to satisfy their immediate and long-term needs. As a consequence, intramural programs have had to devise new and different activities that de-emphasize championships, eliminate trophies, sponsor sports clubs, include equal sports opportunities for women, and provide greater use of facilities for open recreation.

Several colleges have experimented with the abolishment of all extrinsic rewards; no point systems or awards of any kind are employed. The importance of victory is de-emphasized by doing away with championships and limiting protests to on-the-spot, right-or-wrong, final decisions by activity supervisors. Any combination of undergraduate and graduate students and faculty is allowed to form teams. Women participate on teams that compete in the men's division. Here too the social climate is favorable for continuing to create new forms of sports practices. So the trend toward change and innovation to meet student interests will probably endure.

A Troubling Trend: Sports Incivility

Our emphasis throughout this chapter has been on the future and how changes in demography, social relationships, and technology will likely bring about a future of sport forms that will provide greater access, variety, opportunity, and inclusion to participants and fans. The trends that we have identified and discussed point to a generally optimistic future for sport and those involved in sport. However, one current trend is, in our view, detrimental to the advancement and enrichment of sport and everyone associated with it. We are going to identify that trend and suggest why we think it is counterproductive to enriching both the sport and the larger culture. We hope our discussion will stimulate thinking about ways to solve this problem.

Research and everyday experience tell us all that there is a growing social incivility in North American culture. Behavioral and social scientists have been studying this trend for the past decade, and the literature on this issue is enormous. The evidence is clear that civility is increasingly disappearing from our society. In its place is a disrespect, indifference, and uncaring attitude toward other people and toward social institutions and practices. Whether it's on the job or in the marketplace or on the highway, the I-don't-care-about-other-people attitude appears to be worsening.

Multiple factors have contributed to this trend. Some social analysts point to rural-to-urban demographic changes, others to the contingent nature and lack of security in the workplace, others to the individualistic nature of our value system, and still others to the decline of social capital in community life. Although no consensus has formed around the cause, there is uniform agreement that the general mood of incivility is pervasive.

Throughout this text we have emphasized the close connections between the larger North American culture and sporting practices. The issue of growing incivility applies to trends in sport. The weakening social bonds of mutual respect, courtesy, and compassion have carried over into sports. Incidents like the following are becoming more commonplace:

- Vulgarities from fans directed at athletes and coaches during games
- Projectiles, such as beer bottles, batteries, and snowballs, thrown at athletes from the stands
- Fans fighting in the stands
- Fires being set by fans in stadiums
- Player violence and illegal actions that intentionally injure opponents
- Athletes (at all levels now) talking trash, belittling, and seeking to intimidate opponents
- Athletes preening, taunting, and spitting in the faces of opponents
- Street rioting and looting of businesses in cities after the winning or losing of a championship game

As with the decline in civility in society in general, social analysts point to a variety of potential precipitating factors for the growing incivility in sports. There is the obvious explanation that attitudes and behaviors found in the larger society will be manifested in sport. Fan behavior is often explained as an alienation formed by the huge salaries of professional athletes at the same time as free agency has led to a widespread player movement for even better salaries. This has been accompanied by a perceived athlete arrogance toward fans. Simultaneously, owners are perceived as gouging fans with higher and higher ticket prices and threats of moving to another city, unless fans, and other local taxpayers, build the millionaire owner a new arena or stadium. Some analysts see fans believing that the purchase of a ticket or the support of a team allows them to become rowdy, coarse, and lawbreaking. There are even cases where team management encourages fan misbehavior.

While there are additional explanations that we could cite for the spreading uncivil, rude, and unsportsmanlike behaviors of sports fans, athletes, and coaches, we think it is important to say that these practices are unfortunate and inappropriate, and they show disrespect for the sports themselves, for the athletes and coaches, and for one's fellow human beings. The future is not something out there waiting to happen. Sports are practices that are socially constructed within the culture in which they exist, and any adequate account of them must be grounded in an understanding that they can be changed and shaped by the people who are involved with them. For those who would like to contribute to reversing the trend we have been discussing in this section, perhaps a suggestion from well-known social theorist Antonio Gramsci can be an inspiration. He said that those who struggle on behalf of a more humane and benevolent social life should "have a pessimism of the intelligence" (understand how bad things are; it's a way of arming oneself) and an "optimism of the will" (keep fighting back).[41] Sports play an important role in many lives; it is too significant to have it despoiled by a future dominated by rude, disrespectful, and uncivil behaviors.

SUMMARY

This is an era of rapid change in North America, and sport, like other social institutions, is undergoing changes in form and content–changes related to those of the larger society. We have identified a number of the more salient social changes and speculated about how current and future trends may affect sport.

Trends in population suggest that the rapid expansion of professional sports is continuing and that pro franchises are organizing along regional rather than single-city lines. As the average age of the population increases, men and women are going to continue to stay active longer, even in high-level competitive sport. The proportion of minorities in the population is increasing rapidly, and the different cultural traditions of minority groups will influence the trends and patterns of sport involvement. Women, minorities, the oppressed and stereotypical groups have gained greater opportunities in the world of sport, and the egalitarian trend suggests that sport opportunities will increase in the years ahead for all persons.

Industrialization and technology reduced the average workweek until two decades ago, but other conditions have arisen to increase work time and nullify the actual leisure time of adults. The leisure time available in the future may be used in sports of either a more "cerebral" nature or a more violent nature; moreover, technological developments will probably result in new and more techno sport forms, and human reactions against technology will result in many more ecosports.

Professional and big-time intercollegiate sports have become successful business enterprises, mainly because of television involvement. Their future rests heavily upon the directions dictated by television.

Changes in value orientations over the past decade have emphasized equality and pluralism, and the world of sport has experienced protest and even violent revolt as athletes have rebelled against traditional authoritarian leadership. There is a troubling trend in sports that needs serious attention and reform—rude, disrespectful, uncivil behavior.

WEB RESOURCES

www.dol.gov
The U.S. Department of Labor web page. Excellent for the reports on future work—trends and challenges in the twenty-first century.

www.census.gov/compendia/statab
The website for *Statistical Abstract of the United States: 2007* and earlier editions, as well as summary items.

www.statcan.ca
The home page of Statistics Canada. It contains projections for a variety of topics for 2006, 2011, 2016, 2021, and 2026.

www.extremesports.com
The home page for extreme sports, with numerous links to specific sports and future competitive extreme sporting events.

www.dsusa.org
This is the home page for Disabled Sports USA. The site features much information, especially up-to-date information on events and programs.

www.specialolympics.org
This is the home page for the Special Olympics. It has separate pages for each event, tips for coaches and athletes, and a good list of links to other sites.

www.sportinsociety.org
The Center for the Study of Sport in Society at Northeastern University is the world's leading social justice organization that uses sport to create social change.

NOTES

1. James Canton, *The Extreme Future: The Top Trends That Will Reshape the World for the Next 5, 10, and 20 Years* (New York: Dutton, 2006); Jim Ensor, *Future Net: The Essential Guide to Internet and Technology Megatrends* (Victoria, B.C.: Trafford Publishing, 2006); Richard Sennett, *The Culture of the New Capitalism* (New Haven, Conn.: Yale University Press, 2007); Mark Penn and E. Kinney Zalesne, *Microtrends: The Small Forces behind Tomorrow's Big Changes* (New York: Twelve, 2007).

2. U.S. Bureau of the Census, *Statistical Abstract of the United States: 2007*, 126th ed. (Washington, D.C.: U.S. Government Printing Office, 2007), 7–8; "Population Projections for Canada, Provinces and Territories 2005–2031," *Statistics Canada* (Ottawa, Ont.: Statistics Canada, 2005).

3. U.S. Bureau of the Census, *Statistical Abstract of the United States: 2007*; "Population Projections for Canada, Provinces, and Territories 2000–2026," *Statistics Canada* (Ottawa, Ont.: Statistics Canada).

4. "Population and Dwelling Count Highlight Tables, 2006 Census," *Statistics Canada*; U.S. Bureau of the Census, *Statistical Abstracts of the United States: 2007*.

5. U.S. Bureau of the Census, *Statistical Abstract of the United States: 2007*, 763; Ruth E. Heidrich, *Senior Fitness: The Diet and Exercise Program for Maximum Health and Longevity* (New York: Lantern Books, 2005).

6. Joseph E. Stiglitz, *Globalization and Its Discontents* (New York: Norton, 2003); Jurgen Osterhammel, Niels P. Peterson, and Dona Geyer, *Globalization: A Short History* (Princeton: Princeton University Press, 2005).

7. Susan Sweeney, *101 Internet Businesses You Can Start from Home: How to Choose and Build Your Own Successful e-Business*, 2nd ed. (Gulf Breeze, Fla.: Maximum Press, 2006); Scott C. Fox, *Internet Riches: The Simple Money-making Secrets of Online Millionaires* (New York: AMACOM/American Management Association, 2006), audio CD; Arnold Brown, "The Robotic Economy," *The Futurist*, July–August 2006, 50–55.

8. Robert D. Putnam, *Bowling Alone: The Collapse and Revival of American Community* (New York: Simon & Schuster, 2000); see also Manfred Steger, Scott McLean, and David Schultz, eds., *Social Capital: Critical Perspectives on Community and "Bowling Alone"* (New York: New York University Press, 2002); George Ritzer, *Enchanting a Disenchanted World: Revolutionizing the Means of Consumption*, 2nd ed. (Thousand Oaks, Calif.: Pine Forge Press, 2004).

9. George Ritzer, *The McDonaldization of Society*, rev. New Century Edition (Thousand Oaks, Calif.: Pine Forge Press, 2004).

10. Ellen Galinsky, James T. Bond, Stacy S. Kim, Lois Backon, Erin Brownfield, and Kelly Sakai, *Overwork in America: When the Way We Work Becomes Too Much* (New York: Families and Work Institute, 2005); Lawrence Mishel, Jared Bernstein, and Sylvia Allegretto, *The State of Working America, 2006–2007* (Ithaca, N.Y.: ILR Press, 2006), chap. 8; Harriet B. Presser, *Working in a 24/7*

Economy: Challenges for American Families (New York: Russell Sage Foundation, 2005).

11. Roger Von Holzen, "The Emergence of a Learning Society," *The Futurist*, January–February 2005, 24–25; Lynn A. Karoly, *The 21st Century at Work: Forces Shaping the Future Workforce and Workplace in the United States* (Santa Monica, Calif.: Rand Corporation, 2004).

12. Dave Merrill and Mike Snider, "The X's and O's of Fantasy Football," *USA Today*, 6 September 2006, p. 10C; Richard G. Lomax, "Fantasy Sports: History, Game Types, and Research," in *Handbook of Sports Media*, ed. Arthur A. Raney and Jennings Bryant (Mahwah, N.J.: Lawrence Erlbaum, 2006), 383–392.

13. Norbert Elias and Eric Dunning, *The Quest for Excitement: Sport and Leisure in the Civilizing Process* (Cambridge, Mass.: Blackwell, 1993).

14. Linda Bruce, *Sports Technology: How Does It Work?* (North Mankato, Minn.: Smart Apple Media, 2006).

15. One example: Elite Sports Analysis, a world leader in the field of performance analysis consultancy, http://www.elitesportsanalysis.com/whoweare.htm.

16. Andy Miah, *Genetically Modified Athletes: Biomedical Ethics, Gene Doping and Sport* (New York: Routledge, 2004); Angela J. Schneide, *Gene Doping in Sports: The Science and Ethics of Genetically Modified Athletes* (Boston: Elsevier Academic Press, 2006).

17. Claudio Tamburrini and Torbjörn Tännsjö, eds., *Genetic Technology and Sport: Ethical Questions* (New York: Routledge, 2005).

18. Sigmund Loland, Berit Skirstad, and Ivan Waddington, eds., *Pain and Injury in Sport* (New York: Routledge, 2005).

19. George H. Sage, *Power and Ideology in American Sport: A Critical Perspective*, 2nd ed. (Champaign, Ill: Human Kinetics, 1998), 149–157; see also Adrian Walsh and Richard Giulianotti, *Ethics, Money and Sport: This Sporting Mammon* (New York: Routledge, 2006); Pirkko Markula-Denison and Richard Pringle, *Foucault, Sport and Exercise: Power, Knowledge and Transforming the Self* (New York: Routledge, 2006).

20. Steve Shipside, *Adventure Sports: 52 Brilliant Ideas* (Oxford, UK: Infinite Ideas Limited, 2006); Robert E. Rinehart and Synthia Sydnor, *To the Extreme: Alternative Sports, Inside and Out* (Albany: SUNY Press, 2003).

21. Harry Braverman, *Labor and Monopoly Capital* (New York: Monthly Review Press, 1974), 279.

22. Ironmanlive.com, Sponsors and Licensees, http://www.ironmanlive.com/corporate/licensees/sandl.

23. Belinda Wheaton, ed., *Understanding Lifestyle Sport: Consumption, Identity and Difference* (New York: Routledge, 2004); Sal Ruibal, "X Games Upstarts Now Embrace the Olympics," *USA Today*, 26 January 2006, pp. 1A–2A.

24. Robert O'Brien and Marc Williams, *Global Political Economy: Evolution and Dynamics*, 2nd ed. (New York: Palgrave Macmillan, 2007); Frederic L. Pryor, *The Future of U.S. Capitalism* (Cambridge: Cambridge University Press, 2002).

25. Gene A. Budig, *The Inside Pitch . . . and More: Baseball's Business and the Public Trust* (Morgantown: West Virginia University, 2004); Kevin J. Delaney and Rick Eckstein, *The Battle Over Building Sports Stadiums* (New Brunswick, N.J.: Rutgers University Press, 2003).

26. Irving Rein, Philip Kotler, and Ben Shields, "The Future of Sports Media," *The Futurist*, January–February 2007, 42–43.

27. Steve Wieberg, "Prize Money Plan Proposed," *USA Today*, 20 July 2007, p. 14C; see also James J. Duderstadt, *Intercollegiate Athletics and the American University: A President's Perspective* (Ann Arbor: University of Michigan Press, 2003).

28. James L. Shulman and William G. Bowen, *The Game of Life: College Sports and Educational Values* (Princeton: Princeton University Press, 2001); see also Welch Suggs, "Colleges in New England Cut Back on Admitting Athletes," *Chronicle of Higher Education*, 11 January 2002, A48.

29. National Federation of State High School Associations, *2005–2006 High School Athletics Participation Survey* (Indianapolis: National Federation of State High School Associations, 2006), http://www.nfhs.org/core/contentmanager/uploads/2005_06NFHSparticipationsurvey.pdf.

30. Marc D. Weiner, ed., *The Future of American Democratic Politics: Principles and Practices* (New Brunswick, N.J.: Rutgers University Press, 2003); Noam Chomsky, *Government in the Future* (New York: Seven Stories Press, 2005).

31. W. Van De Donk, ed., *Cyberprotest: New Media, Citizens and Social Movements* (New York: Routledge, 2004); Diane Perrons, *Globalization and Social Change: People and Places in the New Economy* (New York: Routledge, 2004).

32. Robert W. Fogel, *The Fourth Great Awakening and the Future of Egalitarianism* (Chicago: University of Chicago Press, 2000).

33. For a thorough description of the programs of the NSCD, go to its website at http://www.nscd.org/.

34. For a complete description of the programs of the DS/USA, go to its website at http://www.dsusa.org.

35. Frank Greve, "Recruiters Struggle to Find an Army," *The Seattle Times*, 12 November 2007, p. 2, http://seattletimes.nwsource.com/html/nationworld/2004008540_recruit12.html; S. L. Price, "Run to Daylight," *Sports Illustrated*, 12 December 2005, 113–120.

36. For more information about the Paralympics, see http://www.paralympic.org/.

37. For more information about the Special Olympics, see http://www.specialolympics.org.

38. For more information about the National Senior Games Association, see http://nsga.com.

39. Pat Griffin, *Strong Women, Deep Closets: Lesbians and Homophobia in Sport* (Champaign, Ill.: Human Kinetics, 1998), 188.

40. Terry Orlick, *Cooperative Games and Sports: Joyful Activities for Everyone* (Champaign, Ill.: Human Kinetics, 2006; Josette Luvmour and Sambhava Luvmour, *Everyone Wins: Cooperative Games and Activities* (Stony Creek, Conn.: New Society Publishers, 2007); Bernie DeKoven, *Junkyard Sports* (Champaign, Ill.: Human Kinetics, 2004).

41. Quintin Hoare and Geoffrey Nowell Smith, eds., *Selection from the Prison Notebooks of Antonio Gramsci* (New York: International Publishers, 1971), 175; see also Janet Kornblum, "Rudeness, Threats, Make the Web a Cruel World," *USA Today*, 31 July 2007, pp. 1A–2A.

Index

Aaron, Hank, 141, 296
AAU. *See* Amateur Athletic Union
Academic benefits, of interscholastic sport, 95–96
Action sports, 359
Administration, 124–125, 333–335, 336. *See also* Leadership
Adult intrusion, in youth sports, 75–80
Adult-sponsored youth sports, 69–71
Adventure sports, 359
Africa, 191
African Americans, 29–30, 123–124, 134, 135, 195, 204, 206–207, 291, 292, 293–295, 296, 303; and social mobility through sport, 283–285. *See also* Blacks
Agents, player, 217
Aggression, 160; definition of, 130–131; theories of, 132–134. *See also* Violence
Aggressive societies, 56
Agriculture, 24
AIA. *See* Athletes in Action
AIAW. *See* Association for Intercollegiate Athletics for Women
Airplane races, 42
Air travel, 41–42
Alcohol, 151–152, 153
Alternative sports, 83–84, 370
Amaechi, John, 340

Amateur Athletic Union (AAU), 77
Amateurism, 116–117, 117–119
Amateur Softball Association, 38
American College Test (ACT), 121, 124
American Council on Education, 105
American Sport Education Program (ASEP), 84
Ancient world, 135–136, 168–169
Andretti, Michael, 216
Angell, Roger, 243
Animal Locomotion (Muybridge), 35
Antitrust legislation, and baseball, 38–39
ASEP. *See* American Sport Education Program
Asian Americans, 291, 298, 300
Association for Intercollegiate Athletics for Women (AIAW), 330–331
Athletes, men; in the future, 356–357, 358; and gender identity, 339–342; and owners, 226–234; as politicians, 203; vs. nonathletes, and social mobility, 280–282; white and black, difference between, 306
Athletes, women; attitudes toward, 325–326; and eating disorders, 156; and health, 324–325; and masculine body types, 321–324; myths about, 321–325; and

social mobility through sport, 285–286. *See also* Gender inequality
Athletes in Action (AIA), 175, 176, 181
Athletes' rights, and intercollegiate sport, 119–120, 125–126
Athletic scholarships, 117, 234, 282, 283, 285, 296, 300–301
Athletic superiority, of blacks, 304–307
Auriemma, Geno, 334
Automobile racing, 41, 220. *See also* National Association for Stock Car Auto Racing
Autry, Gene, 228

Ball, James, 37
Ball Four, 141
Baseball, origins of, 38–39, 40
Baseball Chapel, 175
Basketball, origins of, 39, 40
Batista, 295
Battling Barnett, 43
Baylor, Don, 228
Beckham, David, 2, 299
Beecher, Catharine, 31
Beer companies, 220
Begay, Notah, III, 300
Behavior, and values, 48
Bell, Alexander Graham, 34
Beneficiaries, from sport, 215–220
Bertuzzi, Todd, 79, 138

377

Big business, 2, 215, 217; intercollegiate sport as, 112–117, 234; professional sport as, 220–226. *See also* Commercialization; Corporate sport; Corporations; Endorsements; Materialism; Sponsorship
Bill of rights, for youth sports, 84–85
Bissinger, H. G., 143
Blacks, dominance of, in sports, 303–307. *See also* African Americans
Bonds, Barry, 130, 141, 296
Borden, Marcus, 185, 186–187
Borden v. East Brunswick School District, 187
Borderline violence, 138–139. *See also* Violence
Bowlen, Patrick, 226
Boxing, 43, 137. *See also* Prole sports
Boycotts, 198, 204, 206–207, 208–209
Bradley, Bill, 203
Brown, Sheldon, 137
Brown University, 329
Budget shortfalls, in interscholastic sport, 101, 102
Buffett, Warren, 48–49
Bush, George H. W., 203
Bush, George W., 187, 200, 203

CAAWS. *See* Canadian Association for the Advancement of Women and Sport
CADP. *See* Canadian Anti-Doping Program
Calvin, John, 179
Campanis, Al, 312
Campos, Jorge, 299
Canada, 22, 27, 48, 91
Canadian Anti-Doping Program (CADP), 150
Canadian Association for the Advancement of Women and Sport (CAAWS), 327
Canadian Centre for Ethics in Sport (CCES), 150

Canadian Charter of Rights and Freedoms Constitution Act, 327
Canadian Council on Children and Youth, 86
Canadian Policy Against Doping in Sport (CPADS), 150
Canadian Strategy for Ethical Conduct in Sport, 150
Capitalism, 179–182, 361
Career, in professional sports, 283–284, 286, 310–312
Carlos, John, 201, 207
Carruth, Rae, 142
Castro, Fidel, 199, 295
Catharsis, 131–132, 132–133, 146, 160
Catherwood, Ethel, 37
Catholic Youth Organization (CYO), 170, 173–174
CCES. *See* Canadian Centre for Ethics in Sport
Cedras, Raoul, 202
Centrality, 307–308
Cerebral sports, of the future, 354–355, 372
Chamberlain, Wilt, 236
Character building, 73–75, 96–97
Charter of Rights and Freedoms, for youth sports, 85
Cheating, 50, 54, 72–73, 98–100
Cheerleaders, 99
Childhood; indoor, 82–83; obesity in, 82
Child-rearing practices, and gender inequality, 318–319
Christian church, 169
Church colleges/universities, 174–175
Civil liberties, 100
Civil Rights Restoration Act, 329
Clemens, Roger, 350
Clinton, Bill, 203
Club teams, in youth sports, 76
Clustering, 121
Coaches; African Americans as, 195; as beneficiaries from sport, 216; and cheating, 99, 100; and conformity, 58; conservative, 58; and gender discrimination, 311; and gender inequality, 333–335, 335–336; in intercollegiate sport, 113–114; in interscholastic sport, 99, 100–101, 105; and racial discrimination, 310–311; salaries of, 113–114. *See also* Salaries; shoe-sponsored, in youth sports, 77; as sport socializing agents, 67; and violence, 140; and winning, 53, 54, 100–101; and youth sports, 63–64, 73, 75–80, 84, 85. *See also* Leadership
College degrees, 282–283
College Sports Council (CSC), 332
Collett, Glenna, 37
Collett, Wayne, 201
Colonists, 23, 135, 169–170
Columbus, Christopher, 22
Commercialization, 217–220, 262. *See also* Big business
Committee on Sports Medicine and Fitness (CSMF), 81
Communication, 26–27, 34–35, 42–43
Communication skills, 284
Community, 64, 80, 91, 94–95
Competition, 14, 16, 50, 340; negative consequences of, 54–56; and social Darwinism, 36–37; in society, 49–50; in sport, 53–56; and sportsmanship, 72–73; in youth sports, 81–82
Computer games, 354–355, 356. *See also* Video games
Computers, 43, 357–358, 363
Confederation of Canadian Provinces, 27
Conflict, and power relationships, 15
Conflict theory, 11–12. *See also* Sociological theories
Conspicuous consumption, 274
Continual striving, 50–51
Cook, Myrtle, 37
Cooperative games, 84
Cooperative societies, 56
Corbett, James J., 31
Corporate sport, 17, 215; and alternative youth sports, 83–84; and ecosports, 360–361;

interscholastic sport as, 102–104, 107–108. *See also* Big business
Corporations, 196–197; as beneficiaries from sport, 217–220; and exercise programs, 274–275. *See also* Big business
Costas, Bob, 342
Court/field storming, 147
CPADS. *See* Canadian Policy Against Doping in Sport
Critical theories, 12. *See also* Sociological theories
CSC. *See* College Sports Council
CSMF. *See* Committee on Sports Medicine and Fitness
Csonka, Larry, 230
Cult of manliness, 31–32
Culture, and athletic superiority, of blacks, 304–305
Curt Flood Act, 229
CYO. *See* Catholic Youth Organization

Darwin, Charles, 36
Davis, George, 105–107
De Coubertin, Pierre, 56, 172, 321–322
Deferred gratification, 51
De La Hoya, Oscar, 215, 216, 298
Delgado, Carlos, 297
Democracy, 9–10, 366, 367
Demographic trends, 347–351, 372
Dempsey, Jack, 37
Deviance, 15–16, 74
Disabled Sports USA (DS/USA), 367–368
Discrimination. *See* Gender discrimination; Racial discrimination
Diversity, and values, 48
Divine intervention, 184–185
Donaghy, Tim, 130, 158–159
Donovan, Billy, 113
Draft, 227, 236–237
Drug abuse. *See* Substance abuse
Drug testing programs, 154, 155
DS/USA. *See* Disabled Sports USA
Durkheim, Emile, 166–167

Earnhardt, Dale, Jr., 216

Eating disorders, 130, 155–156, 161
Economy, 215–237; and beneficiaries from sport, 215–220; and future sport, 361–366; and intercollegiate sport, 234–237; and owners, 224–226, 226–234, 233–234; and television, 245–247, 268
Ecosports, 355, 358–361
Edison, Thomas, 35, 244
Education, 292; disruption in, in youth sports, 80–81; and intercollegiate sport, 43–44, 116, 121–124, 125; and interscholastic sport, 92, 97–98, 104–105, 107–108; in twentieth century, 38
Educational Amendments Act, 327, 328. *See also* Title IX
Education inequality, 273–274. *See also* Inequality
Educators, and youth sports, 61
Edwards, Harry, 204, 206
Elder, Lee, 307
Elitism, 101, 103–104, 105, 106–107, 224
Emerson, Ralph Waldo, 31
Endorsements, 58, 215, 232, 285. *See also* Big business
England, 91
Environmental crisis, and competition, 50
Equality, 366, 367, 372. *See also* Inequality
Ethnicity, 291. *See also* Racial-ethnic minorities
Ethnic minorities, 134, 204. *See also* Racial–ethnic minorities
Evangelizing, 176–177
Evans, Tony, 177
Ewing, Patrick, 231
Exercise programs, and corporations, 274–275
Extreme sports, 83, 359–360

Facilities, sports, 222–223, 274–275, 357. *See also* Stadiums
Failure, in interscholastic sport, 97
Fair Labor Association, 204–205
Fair Play Codes, 86
Falwell, Jerry, 174

Families, as sport socializing agents, 65
Fans; in the future, 362, 363; and salaries, 232–233; and violence, 130, 139–140, 140–141, 145–148, 160. *See also* Spectators
Fantasy sport leagues, 355
Faulkner, William, 243
FCA. *See* Fellowship of Christian Athletes
Federal Communications Commission, 220
Federation of Gay Games, 342, 370
Fellowship of Christian Athletes (FCA), 175
Femininity, 316, 317
Feminist theory, 12–13. *See also* Sociological theories
Feminization, 31, 177–178
Fetishism, 191
Field, Cyrus, 34
Fitness and Amateur Sports Women's Program, 327
Flood, Curt, 227, 229
Flow Model, 71
Fogel, Robert, 366
Foley, Jeremy, 113
Football, origins of, 39, 40
Ford, Henry, 41
Franchises, 221–222, 225–226, 249
Free agency, 227–231
Free time. *See* Leisure time
Freud, Sigmund, 131, 132, 133
Friday Night Lights (Bissinger), 143
Frustration-aggression theory, 131–132, 132–133, 134, 160
Fulton, Robert, 25
Functionalism, 10, 11–12. *See also* Sociological theories
Future sport, 354–361; and the economy, 361–366; and technology, 356–358; and television, 362–363; and values, 366–372
Futurism, 347. *See also* Future sport

Gambling, 23, 29, 130, 156–160, 161, 217
Garciaparra, Nomar, 190
Garvey, Steve, 228

INDEX

Gates, Bill, 48–49
Gay and Lesbian Hockey Association, 341
Gay Games, 342, 370
Gay/lesbian liberation movement, 341–342
Gays, 369–370. *See also* Sexual orientation
Gehrig, Lou, 203, 244, 350
Gender discrimination, 311. *See also* Gender inequality
Gender identity, and male athletes, 339–342
Gender inequality, 115, 316–342; in coaching and administration, of women's sports, 333–336; and cult of manliness, 31–32; heritage of, 316–318; in media sport, 260–262, 268; in Olympic Games, 338–339; and opportunity and reward structure, 326–333; social sources of, 318–321; and sport participation, barriers to, 321–326; in sports journalism, 267; in women's team sports, 336–338. *See also* Inequality; Athletes, women
Gender roles, 92, 98, 99, 316–317
Genes, and athletic superiority, of blacks, 303–304
Genetic engineering, 357
Gibson, Bob, 296
Gibson, Josh, 294, 295
Girls, in youth sports programs, 63, 64
Globalization, 205, 301–303
Gmelch, George, 189
Goodyear, Charles, 35
Graduation rates, 121–122, 125, 282–283
Gramsci, Antonio, 372
Gretsky, Wayne, 320
Grich, Bobby, 228
Griffey, Ken, Jr., 296
Groups, characteristics of, 3
Grove City College v. Bell, 328
Gutenberg, Johannes, 242

Hamm, Mia, 320
Harlem Globetrotters, 294
Harper, William Rainey, 32
Hawk, Tony, 361
Hazing, 144–145
Health, and athletes, women, 324–325
Health insurance, 292
Hearst, William Randolph, 34, 242
Hegemony theory, 12. *See also* Sociological theories
Hemingway, Ernest, 243
Hermosillo, Carlow, 299
Hernandez, Luis, 299
Heroines, 320–321
Hingis, Martina, 141
Hitler, Adolf, 198–199, 206
Hockey Ministries International, 175
Holmes, Oliver Wendell, 31, 226
Holtz, Lou, 204
Homophobia, 340–342, 369
Homosexuality, 340–342, 369–370. *See also* Sexual orientation
Hornsby, Roger, 294
Horse racing, 23, 25, 29, 30, 33–34, 40
Horton, Tim, 172
Hughes, Thomas, 35
Human agency, 6
Hunter, Jim "Catfish," 227–228, 229

Ice hockey, origins of, 39, 40
IMG. *See* International Management Group
Immigrants, 22, 27, 30–31, 298, 299, 300, 348–349, 350
Incivility, 73, 146, 371–372. *See also* Sportsmanship
Income inequality, 273–274, 292. *See also* Inequality
Industrialization, 351–352, 372
Industrial revolution, 24, 27
Inequality, 273–274, 292. *See also* Equality; Gender inequality
The Influence of the Protestant Ethic on Sport and Recreation (Overman), 180
Informal sport, 16, 17
Information services, 352–353
Injuries, 81, 137–138, 138–139, 147, 358

Instinct theory, 131–132, 132–133, 134, 160
Institute for Diversity and Ethics in Sport, 79
Institute for International Sport, 73
Institutional racism, 292. *See also* Racial discrimination; Racism
Institutions, 8–10, 198
Intellectual sport, 354–355
Interactionist theory, 13. *See also* Sociological theories
Intercollegiate Athletic Association, 112
Intercollegiate sport, 32, 112–126, 294–295, 301, 307; as big business, 112–117, 234; and the economy, 234–237; and education, 43–44, 121–124; in the future, 364–365, 372; gender inequality in, 328–333, 333–335; reform of, 124–126; and social mobility, 280–281, 281–282; and television, 249–251; and Title IX, 328–330, 331–333. *See also* National Collegiate Athletic Association
Intergenerational mobility, 280
Internal Revenue Service, 118
International Bar Association's Sports Law Committee, 140
International Gay and Lesbian Aquatics Association, 341
International Gay Bowling Association, 341–342
International Institute of Forecasters, 347
International Management Group (IMG), 77
International Olympic Committee (IOC), 17, 207–208, 368
Internet, 157, 258–259, 363–364
Internet sports fantasy leagues, 355
Interscholastic sport, 91–108, 298, 300, 301; consequences of, 92–97; in the future, 365–366; gender inequality in, 326–328, 333–335; problems in, 97–104; reform of, 104–107; and social mobility, 280, 281–282; status

of, 91–92; and television, 251–252
Intramural sports, in the future, 371
IOC. *See* International Olympic Committee
Iraq War, 368

James, William, 133
Jeter, Derrick, 77
Jockeys, African Americans as, 29, 30, 294
Jogging/running, 40. *See also* Participant sports
Johnson, Jack, 294
Johnson, Randy, 350
Jones, Bobby, 37
Jones, Jerry, 226
Jordan, Michael, 190, 231, 296, 320, 361

Kaiser, Edgar, 226
Kantner, Dee, 335
Kapp, Joe, 230
Kemp, Jack, 203
Kerr, John, 131
Kerrigan, Nancy, 141
King, Martin Luther, Jr., 204
Kohlsaat, H. H., 41
Kopay, David, 340
Kreager, Derek A., 143
Kwan, Michelle, 298

Labor unions, 38, 134
Language, in locker room, 143
Largent, Steve, 203
Latinos, 291, 295, 296, 297–298, 299
Leadership, 310–312, 331. *See also* Administration; Coaches; Management; Officials; Owners
LeBron, James, 341
Legal/legislative action, and gender inequality, 327. *See also* U.S. Supreme Court
Leisure time, 52, 351–352, 352–353, 353–354, 372
Lesbians, 322–324, 341–342, 369–370. *See also* Sexual orientation
Leslie, Lisa, 320

Lewis, Oliver, 30
Life chances, 272
Lorenz, Konrad, 131, 132, 133
Louis, Joe, 294

Machen, Bernie, 113
Mackey v. NFL, 230
Made-for-television sports events, 253–254. *See also* Media sport
Magazines, 26, 34, 43, 242–243, 320
Magic, 188–192
Majority group, 292
Male bonding, and violence, 142–143
Male dominance, 15, 143, 177–178, 317
Male privilege, 316
Male superiority, 317
Malinowski, Bronislaw, 188–189
Malinowski thesis, 188–189
Management, 310–311, 335–336. *See also* Leadership
Mandela, Nelson, 202
Manliness. *See* Cult of manliness
Marconi, Marchese Guglielmo, 42
Marsch, Jesse, 299
Marx, Karl, 168, 277
Mascots, and gender inequality, 320
Masculine body types, and athletes, women, 321–324
Masculinity, 259–260, 268, 316, 340
Mass media, 2, 32, 52, 103, 241–268; and alternative youth sports, 83–84; and gender inequality, 319–320; impact of, on sport, 256–263; social roles of, 241–242; and sport, linkage between, 242–244, 248, 267–268. *See also* Media sport; as sport socializing agent, 67–68
Masters Sports Tournaments, 351
Materialism, 14, 51, 57–58. *See also* Big business
Mathematical reasoning, 284
Mathews, Vince, 201
Mathewson, Christy, 181
Mathias, Rob, 203
Matsuzaka, Daisuke, 298, 300

Mays, Willie, 296
Mayweather, Floyd, 215
McCartney, Bill, 177, 178
McMillen, Tom, 203
McNair, Robert, 222
McNally, Dave, 228, 229
Media sport, 242–244, 248, 254–256, 267–268; in the future, 362, 363, 364; gender inequality in, 260–262, 268; masculinity in, 259–260, 268; racial-ethnic minorities in, 262–263, 268. *See also* Mass media
Merriwell, Frank, 35
Messersmith, Andy, 228, 229
Metcalfe, Ralph, 203
Meyer, Urban, 113
Miller, Marvin, 229
Mills, Billy, 300, 301
Mills, C. Wright, 5
Minority group, 292
Missionary work, 176
Mixed martial arts (MMA), 139
Mizell, Wilmer, 203
MMA. *See* Mixed martial arts
Mobility escalator, 280–286, 286–287
Modell, Art, 223
Modern sport; beginnings of, 27–37; framework for, 24–27; maturing of, 37–40
Molineaux, Tom, 293
Money, 57–58, 112–116, 117–118, 215, 216. *See also* Salaries
Monopoly, 220–221
Moody, Helen Willis, 37
Moore, Steve, 79, 138
Moral development, in youth sports, 74
Moral equivalence, 56
Moral reasoning, in youth sports, 74
Morenz, Howie, 37
Morris, Michael 191
Morse, Samuel F. B., 26
Motion pictures, 35, 43, 172–173, 244, 320
Motor Sports Ministries, 175
Murchison, Clint, 225
Murdoch, Rupert, 248

Murphy, Isaac, 30
Muscular Christianity Movement, 31
Muybridge, Eadweard, 35
Myths; about athletes, women, 321–325; about social mobility through sport, 282–286

NAACP. *See* National Association for the Advancement of Colored People
NAIA. *See* National Association of Intercollegiate Athletics
Naismith, James, 39
NASCAR. *See* National Association for Stock Car Auto Racing
National Alliance for Youth Sports, 73, 79, 80
National Amputee Skiers Association, 367
National Association for Stock Car Auto Racing (NASCAR), 138, 225. *See also* Prole sports
National Association for the Advancement of Colored People (NAACP), 204
National Association of Anorexia Nervosa and Associated Disorders, 155
National Association of Intercollegiate Athletics (NAIA), 112
National Baseball Congress, 38
National Basketball Association, 39
National Coaching Certification Program (NCCP), 84
National Coalition Against Violent Athletes (NCAVA), 143–144
National Collegiate Athletic Association (NCAA), 11, 15, 17, 112, 117–120, 123–124, 126, 156, 176, 204, 234, 235–236, 237; and faculty athletics representatives, 331; and gambling, 157–158, 161; and gender inequality, 330–331; and graduation rates, 121–122, 125; and hazing, 144–145; and interscholastic sport, 103, 105; and money, 112–113, 114; and substance abuse, 149–150; and television, 249–250
National Council of Youth Sports, 61
National Federation of State High School Associations, 103, 251
National Football League (NFL), 39
National Hockey League (NHL), 39
National Industrial Basketball League, 38
Nationalism, 200–202, 206, 210–211
National Research Council of Canada Study, 347
National Senior Games Association (NSGA), 369
National Sports Center for the Disabled (NSCD), 367
National Sportsmanship Day, 73
National Task Force on Children's Play, 86
National Wrestling Coaches Association (NWCA), 330, 331
National Youth Sport Coaches Association (NYSCA), 84
Native Americans, 22, 134, 135, 157, 204, 291, 300–301, 302, 303
Navratilova, Martina, 324
NCAA. *See* National Collegiate Athletic Association
NCAVA. *See* National Coalition Against Violent Athletes
NCCP. *See* National Coaching Certification Program
Newspapers, 242, 256, 257; and gender inequality, 320; and interscholastic sport, 103; in nineteenth century, 26–27, 34; and sport, and religion, 185; in twentieth century, 42–43
NFL. *See* National Football League
NHL. *See* National Hockey League
Nicknames, and gender inequality, 320
Nicolau, George, 228
Nike, 204–205, 219
Norms, 8
NSCD. *See* National Sports Center for the Disabled
NSGA. *See* National Senior Games Association
Nutritional supplements, 151
NWCA. *See* National Wrestling Coaches Association
NYSCA. *See* National Youth Sport Coaches Association
NYSCA Code of Ethics, 84, 85

Obesity, 82, 98
Occupational structure, 305–306
Occupation inequality, 273–274. *See also* Inequality
OCR. *See* Office for Civil Rights
Office for Civil Rights (OCR), 328–330
Officials, 195, 310. *See also* Leadership
Ohno, Apolo, 298
Oldfield, Barney, 41
Olympic committees, 207–208, 211
Olympic Games, 198–200, 204, 205, 206–211, 220, 274, 321–322, 368; coaching and administration in, 336; gender inequality in, 338–339
O'Neal, Shaquille, 285, 307
Opiate of the masses, 202–203
Organization, in adult- vs. peer-organized youth sports, 69–70
Organizations, 196, 204, 206–207; and cult of manliness, 31; power relationships in, 15; religious, 175–179
Organized sport, 16–17
Orientations, youth, toward sport, 72
Overman, Steven, 180
Owners, 197; and athletes, 226–234; and the economy, 224–226, 226–234; and gender inequality, 335–336; and violence, 140. *See also* Leaders

Paige, Satchel, 294
Palmer, Violet, 335
PAO. *See* Pro Athletes Outreach
Paralympic Games, 368
Parents, 61, 62, 63–64, 65–66, 73, 75–80, 79, 85–86

Parents Association for Youth Sports (PAYS), 80
Participant sports, 40, 95–97, 273–279, 286–287, 370
Patriarchy, 316
Patrick, Danica, 285
Patriotic pageantry, 201
Patten, Gilbert (pseud. Burt L. Standish), 35, 243
PAYS. *See* Parents Association for Youth Sports
PCA. *See* Positive Coaching Alliance
Pedophiles, in youth sports, 80
Peer play, 69–71
Peers, as sport socializing agents, 67
Pele, 299
People with disabilities, 367–369
Performance enhancement drugs, 54, 357. *See also* Substance abuse
Personal growth, in youth sports, 83
Personal-social attributes, in youth sports, 71–75
Petty, Kyle, 216
Physical abuse, in youth sports, 80
Physical activity; as characteristic of sport, 16; of colonists, 23
Physical Activity and Sport Act, 150
Physical fitness activity, 274–275
Pierce, Mary, 190
Pierzynski, A. J., 190
Pitino, Rick, 113
Plantation system, 120
Plessy v. Ferguson, 30
Political dissidents, 206
Politicians, athletes as, 203
Politics, 196–211; and globalization, 205; and Olympic Games, 206–211; and sport, relationship between, 196–198; as user of sport, 198–205
Popularity shifts, 249
Population, 347–348, 348–351, 372; composition, 348–349; location of, 349; in nineteenth century, 27, 28; of racial-ethnic minorities, 292–293; senior, 369; trends, 349–351; in twentieth century, 37

Positive Coaching Alliance (PCA), 79
Postema, Pam, 335
Poverty, 292; and social mobility through sport, 283–285
Powell, Colin, 206
Power, 196–197, 291–292
Power play, 319
Power relationships; and conflict, 15; in organizations, 15
Prayer, 182–184, 185–188
Pre-Columbian societies, 168
Prep schools, fraudulent, 103
Printing press, 26–27
Pro Athletes Outreach (PAO), 175
Process, in adult- vs. peer-organized youth sports, 70
Professional athletes; as beneficiaries from sport, 215–216; number of, 215
Professional sport; as big business, 220–226; in the future, 361–362, 372
Project 2010, 62
Prole sports, 277–278, 278–279
Promise Keepers, 177–178
Propaganda, 198–200
Proposition 48, 121
Protestant ethic, 179–182
The Protestant Ethic and the Spirit of Capitalism (Weber), 179–180
Protestantism, 169–170
Pseudosports, 17, 278–279
Psychosocial problems, in youth sports, 75–82
Puritanism, 23, 31, 169–170

Race, 291, 303–304
Racial discrimination, 306–307, 307–312, 367; and retirement, from sports, 310–312; and stacking, 307–310. *See also* Racism
Racial-ethnic groups, 291
Racial-ethnic minorities, 134, 204, 291–312; in media sport, 262–263, 268; and racial discrimination, 306–307, 307–312, 367; and social mobility through sport,

283–285; in sports journalism, 266–267, 268
Racial segregation, 30, 293, 294, 307–308, 309. *See also* Racism
Racism, 14–15, 203–204, 284; in mass media, 262–263. *See also* Racial discrimination
Radio, 42, 243–244
Railroad, 26, 32–33, 34, 41
Ramirez, Manny, 297
Reagan, Ronald, 203, 272, 329
Reciprocity, 198
Recreational drugs, 151. *See also* Substance abuse
Recreation programs, 38
Recruitment, 104, 283
Referees, 216–217
Reformation, 169
Religion, 23, 31, 164–192; and capitalism, 179–182; and organizations, 175–179; personal and social role of, 167–168; and society, 166–168; and sport, relationship between, 168–171; sport as, 171–173; sport as user of, 182–192; as user of sport, 173–175; and value orientations, 179–182
Representative sport, 196
Reserve clause, 227
Retirement, from sports, 286, 310–312
Revenue, and television, 247–248
Revenue sharing, 230–231
Riggins, John, 230
Ripken, Cal, Jr., 200, 203, 320, 350
Ritual, 189–190
Robinson, Jackie, 30, 294, 295, 296, 312
Rockne, Knute, 37, 172
Rodriguez, Alex, 57, 297, 307
Role models, 98, 309–310
Romanowski, Bill, 82
Rooney, Dan, 312
Rooney Rule, 312
Rose, Pete, 82, 158
Roseboro, John, 296
Rosenfeld, Bobbie, 37
Roth, Philip, 243
Rozelle, Pete, 227

Rozelle Rule, 227, 230
Rubber, vulcanization of, 35
Rudi, Joe, 228
Rules, as characteristic of sport, 16
Running/jogging, 40. *See also* Participant sports
Ruth, Babe, 37, 141
Ryun, Jim, 203

Saban, Nick, 114
Salaries, 57–58, 215, 216–217, 227, 228, 229–231, 231–233; and gender inequality, 334; in intercollegiate sport, 113–114; of Latino athletes, 298; for women, 285. *See also* Money
Sampras, Pete, 320
Santa Fe Independent School District v. Doe, 185
Scandals, and winning, 54
Schecter, Leonard, 248
Scholastic Assessment Test (SAT), 121, 124
School; and gender inequality, 319; and interscholastic sport, 91, 93–94; prayer in, 185–187; as sport socializing agency, 67
Segregation, by social class, 279–280. *See also* Racial segregation
Seles, Monica, 141
Self-actualization, in youth sports, 83
Self-discipline, 181
Self-image, in youth sports, 75
Senior Olympics, 351, 369
Senior population, 369
September 11, 2001, terrorist attack, 201, 207, 361
Se Ri Pak, 300
Sexual abuse, 79, 80, 142
Sexual orientation, 322–324. *See also* Gays; Homosexuality; Lesbians
Shriver, Eunice Kennedy, 369
Shula, Mike, 114
Shuler, Heath, 203
Siblings, as sport socializing agents, 66–67
Slavery, 293–294
Smith, Emmitt, 320

Smith, Jim "Yazoo," 230
Smith, John L., 114
Smith, Tommie, 201, 207
Social capital, 352
Social change, 203–205, 241–242, 347, 366
Social class, 28–29, 77, 272, 273–280, 317
Social construction of reality, 13
Social Darwinism, 36–37
Social determinism, 4–5
Social differentiation, 272
Social humanitarianism, 341
Social implications, in adult- vs. peer-organized youth sports, 71
Social inequality, 272, 273. *See also* Inequality
Social integration, 241
Socialization, 48, 64–71, 132, 143, 160
Social mobility, 280–286, 286–287
Social organization, 3
Social philosophy, 36–37
Social problems. *See* Eating disorders; Gambling; Substance abuse; Violence
Social reform movement, 31
Social stratification, 272, 273, 275, 279–280, 286
Social structure, and athletic superiority, of blacks, 305–307
Society, sport as microcosm of, 14–16
Socioeconomic status, and participation, in sport, 273–279, 286
Sociological analysis, 6–10
Sociological imagination, 5
Sociological perspective, 3–5, 6
Sociological theories, 10–14
Sociology, 3–14, 36–37
Sorenstam, Annika, 77, 320
South Africa, 202
Spalding, Albert G., 35–36
Spatial location, and stacking, 308–309
Specialization, in interscholastic sport, 101–102
Special Olympics, 368–369
Spectators, 2; and ecosports, 360; and social class, 279–280; and

socioeconomic status, 276–279. *See also* Fans
Spencer, Herbert, 36
The Spirit of the Times, 27
Sponsorship, 61–62, 69–71, 77, 153, 217–220. *See also* Big business
Sport; characteristics of, 16; levels of, 16–17; as microcosm of society, 14–16
Sport culture, and violence, 142–143
Sport Dispute Resolution Centre of Canada, 150
Sportianity movement, 178–179
Sports academies, 62, 76–77, 78
Sports Ambassadors, 175
Sports camps, in youth sports, 76
Sports clubs, 28, 91
Sports consumers, 257–258
Sport-shoe sponsors, 77, 103
Sports Illustrated, 43, 146, 176, 320
Sports journalism, 26–27, 34, 263–267, 268
Sports mania, 2, 52–53
Sportsmanship, 72–73, 100, 370
Sports medicine, 217
Sport socializing agents, 65–68
Sports opportunity structure, 305, 306–307
Sports performance training centers, 77
Sports Spectrum, 176
Stacking, 307–310
Stadiums, 102–103, 223, 224. *See also* Facilities, sports
Stagg, Amos Alonzo, 32
Standish, Burt L. *See* Patten, Gilbert
Stanford, Leland, 35
Student involvement, in interscholastic sport, 105–106
Students with disabilities, 101
Subsidization, 211, 221–224, 234
Substance abuse, 54, 100, 130, 143, 148–155, 160–161, 357; reasons for, 152–153; reducing and preventing, 154–155; scope of, 149–150
Success, 48–49, 53–56, 180–181

Women's team sports, gender inequality in, 336–338
Woods, Tiger, 2, 58, 77, 141, 184, 190, 215, 216, 232, 233, 291, 298, 307, 361
Work, 351–354, 372; and flextime, 353–354; and four-day workweek, 353–354, 372; and information services, 352–353
Workweek, four-day, 353–354, 372
World Anti-Doping Agency (WADA), 357
World Future Society, 347
World Wrestling Entertainment (WWE), 137, 139
Wrestling, 23, 327–328
Wright brothers, 41
Wrigley, Phillip K., 43
WWE. *See* World Wrestling Entertainment

X Games, 61, 83–84, 360–361

Yamaguchi, Kristi, 298
Yao Ming, 298
YMCA. *See* Young Men's Christian Association
Young Griffo, 43
Young Men's Christian Association (YMCA), 173–174
Young Women's Christian Association (YWCA), 173–174
Youth sports, 53–54, 61–86; alternatives to, 82–86; gender inequality in, 326; and personal-social attributes, 71–75; psychosocial problems of, 75–82; and socialization, 64–71; and socioeconomic status, 275–276
Youth sports programs, 61–64
YWCA. *See* Young Women's Christian Association

Zaharias, Babe Didrikson, 172

Sullivan, John L., 31, 34
Summitt, Pat, 113, 334
Sumner, William Graham, 36–37
Super Bowl, 218
Superstition, 189
Suzuki, Ichiro, 298
Sweatshops, 204–205
Swoopes, Sheryl, 324

Taboo, 190–191
Taxes, 221–222, 223
Technological revolution, 24, 25–27
Technology, 351–354, 372; and communication, 26–27, 34–35, 42–43; and future sport, 356–358; in nineteenth century, 25–27, 32–26; and television, 362–363; and transportation, 25–26, 32–34, 40–42; in twentieth century, 40–43
Technosports, 355, 356–358
Television, 42, 196, 244–256, 246, 276, 277; and future sport, 362–363; and gender inequality, 320; influence of, on sport, 244–245, 247–258, 268; and interscholastic sport, 103; and sport, structure and process of, 252–253; as sport socializing agent, 67–68; and sport violence, 139; and technology, 362–363; violence, 135
Tennessee Secondary School Athletic Association (TSSAA), 100
Terrorism, 201, 207, 361
Textbooks, and gender inequality, 319
Thomas, Sarah, 335–336
Thorpe, Jim, 172, 300
Tilden, Bill, 37
Title IX, 11, 92, 98, 115, 250, 285, 286, 318, 365; challenges to, 328–330; and intercollegiate sport, 328–330, 331–333; and interscholastic sport, 327; and three-part test policy, 329–330
Tobacco, 152, 153
Tomjanovich, Rudy, 138
Toolson, George, 229

Transportation, 25–26, 32–34, 40–42
Trends Research Institute, 347
TSSAA. *See* Tennessee Secondary School Athletic Association
Tuaolo, Esera, 340–341
Turnverein (gymnastic clubs), 30

UAW. *See* United Automobile Workers
UFC. *See* Ultimate Fighting Championship
Ultimate Fighting Championship (UFC), 137, 139
Umpires, 216–217
United Automobile Workers (UAW), 38
United States Olympic Committee (USOC), 15, 336
United Students Against Sweatshops, 204
Unser, Al, Jr., 216
Updike, John, 243
Urbanization, 24, 27–28
USA Today, 2, 67–68
U.S. Congress, 15
U.S. Constitution, 154
U.S. Declaration of Independence, 9, 134, 316
U.S. Department of Defense, 258
U.S. Department of Education, 328–330, 332
U.S. Department of Health and Human Services, 149
U.S. Department of State, 200
U.S. Disabled Ski Team, 367
U.S. military, 134
USOC. *See* United States Olympic Committee
U.S. Olympic Committee (USOC), 339
U.S. Soccer Federation, 62
U.S. Supreme Court, 30, 38, 100, 154, 185–187, 227; and Title IX, 328–330

Values, 8, 48–58; and future sport, 366–372; and religion, 179–182
Verbal abuse, in youth sports, 80
Vick, Michael, 130, 159

Video games, 139, 354–355, 356, 364
Violence, 130–148, 160; against athletes, 140–141; in athletes' private lives, 141–145, 160; borderline, 138–139; definition of, 130–131; and fans, 130, 139–140, 140–141, 145–148, 160; fostering and supporting, 139–141; heritage of, 134–135; pressure to use, 140, 160; in sport, legitimate use of, 135–139, 160; theories of, 131–132, 160; in youth sports, 79, 80. *See also* Aggression
Violent sports, of the future, 355–356

WADA. *See* World Anti-Doping Agency
Waddell, Tom, 342
Walton, Samuel, 49
Watts, J. C., 203
Wealth inequality, 273–274. *See also* Inequality
Weber, Max, 179–180, 196
Wie, Michelle, 216, 285
Williams, Serena, 50, 76, 285, 320, 361
Williams, Venus, 50, 76, 77, 285, 320
Winfrey, Oprah, 49, 233
Winning, 49, 53–56; in intercollegiate sport, 115–116; in interscholastic sport, 100–101; in youth sports, 53–54, 81–82
Winter National Senior Games, 369
Witchcraft, 191–192
Women; and sports, interest in, 325; violence against, 143–144. *See also* Athletes, women
Women in Sport: A Sport Canada Policy, 327
Women's colleges, 317
Women's liberation movement, 317–318
Women's organizations, 178
Women's sports, coaching and administration of, 333–336